Dictionary OF Baptists IN America

EDITOR: BILL J. LEONARD

INTERVARSITY PRESS
DOWNERS GROVE, ILLINOIS 60515

InterVarsity Press® is the book-publishing division of InterVarsity Christian Fellowship®, a student movement active on campus at hundreds of universities, colleges and schools of nursing in the United States of America, and a member movement of the International Fellowship of Evangelical Students. For information about local and regional activities, write Public Relations Dept., InterVarsity Christian Fellowship, 6400 Schroeder Rd., P.O. Box 7895, Madison, WI 53707-7895.

ISBN 0-8308-1447-7

Printed in the United States of America ∞

Library of Congress Cataloging-in-Publication Data

Dictionary of Baptists in America/editor, Bill J. Leonard.
    p.   cm.
    Includes bibliograpical references.
    ISBN 0-8308-1447-7
    1. Baptists—United States—Dictionaries.   I. Leonard, Bill.
  BX6211.D53   1994
  286'.0973—dc20   94-31573
                          CIP

18	17	16	15	14	13	12	11	10	9	8	7	6	5	4	3	2	1
09	08	07	06	05	04	03	02	01	00	99	98	97	96	95	94		

In memory of
John Franklin Loftis, Ph.D.
1951-1993
historian, teacher, friend

CONTENTS

PREFACE

The idea for the *Dictionary of Baptists in America* began with the publication of the *Dictionary of Christianity in America,* issued by InterVarsity Press in 1990. The success of that reference work led to the decision to produce another dictionary, this one focused on a specific religious tradition centering in the people called Baptists. The choice of the Baptists was a natural one, since they represent the largest Protestant communion in the United States. Likewise, Baptists represent America's largest religious organization for both Anglo-Saxon and African-American Protestants. Baptist doctrines also extend across the theological spectrum from Arminian to Calvinist, Free Will to Predestinarian. Baptists are indeed a theologically, denominationally, racially and economically diverse people.

While there are numerous books that survey Baptist history and doctrine, and one multivolume encyclopedia (*The Encyclopedia of Southern Baptists,* 4 volumes), up to now there had been no one-volume reference tool for students of the Baptist tradition. The *Dictionary of Baptists in America* is such a resource. The book is designed for use by Baptists and non-Baptists, clergy and laity, educational institutions and parish churches. Bibliographic references at the end of each article point the reader to larger and more specialized sources. While some articles focus on Baptist groups in other parts of North America, particularly Canada, the primary concentration is on the Baptist tradition within the United States.

The primary approach is historical. Most of the contributors are specialists in historical studies. Articles were submitted by persons who are related to a variety of Baptist subgroups and institutions. Every effort was made to maintain objectivity while respecting the autonomy and integrity of each individual contributor. While most of the entries were written specifically for this volume, some were taken from the *Dictionary of Christianity in America.* Articles survey histories, beliefs and practices of specific movements and individuals within the Baptist tradition. Institutions—benevolent, educational, missionary and denominational—are included. Biographical sketches of important leaders and representatives of specific Baptist subgroups are also incorporated into the volume. These are, of course, representative, since no work could adequately encompass information concerning all the individuals who have contributed to the identity and development of every Baptist denomination, agency or institution. Most of the biographical entries involve individuals, now deceased, who made varying contributions to Baptist history. Only a few contemporary leaders have been included. Constraints of space dictated specific length of articles and editorial decisions as to what might or might not be included. Inevitably, some readers may wish for other or longer entries.

Baptists, like most American denominational traditions, are in a time of transition. This volume represents one effort to identify the nature of the Baptist heritage in its unity and diversity within the American experience.

I am particularly grateful to persons who contributed essays to the *Dictionary*. They are a diverse group of scholars who took seriously their tasks and provided outstanding assistance in this project. Daniel G. Reid of IVP offered valuable editorial advice and thoughtful friendship throughout the entire endeavor. I am in his debt. Numerous persons aided in the preparation of the manuscript. Carmon Keith in the Office Services Division at the Southern Baptist Theological Seminary helped begin this project. Iris Christopher, secretary in the department of religion and philosophy at Samford University, did outstanding work in collecting articles and preparing the manuscript. Her successor, Thelma Heywood, helped complete the project. I am grateful to each of them.

This volume is dedicated to the memory of Dr. John F. Loftis, a contributor to the *Dictionary*. Dr. Loftis and his daughter Jessica died in an automobile accident on October 30, 1993. With them and all Christ's church, we look for that "city which hath foundations, whose builder and maker is God."

Bill J. Leonard

HOW TO USE THIS DICTIONARY

Abbreviations

A list of abbreviations used in this dictionary will be found on pages xiii-xiv.

Authorship of Articles

The authors of articles are indicated by their initials and last name at the foot of each article. A full list of contributors will be found on pages xv-xviii, in alphabetical order by last name.

Bibliographies

A bibliography has been appended to many of the articles. In the case of biographical articles, bibliographies usually list secondary sources, while important primary sources are listed in the body of the article. Many biographical articles also contain references to articles in important biographical dictionaries and other reference works, which are noted by their standard abbreviations. All bibliographic items are listed in alphabetical order by the author's last name or, in the case of standard reference works, by the abbreviation of that work.

Cross-References

Subjects will frequently be found covered in both comprehensive articles and brief, focused treatments. A system of cross-references has been utilized to alert readers to other relevant articles within the *Dictionary*.

1. One-line entries direct the reader to the title of the article where the topic is treated:
   American Baptist Convention. *See* AMERICAN BAPTIST CHURCHES IN THE USA

2. An asterisk after a word or phrase indicates that further relevant information will be found in an article approximating that title. Readers should note the following:
   a. The *form* of the word asterisked will not always be precisely the same as that of the title of the article to which the asterisk refers. For example, "call*" directs the reader to the article on **Call to the Ministry, Baptist Views of** and "converted*" to **Conversion, Baptist Views of.**
   b. The asterisk sometimes applies to two or three words rather than to the word immediately preceding the asterisk; examples include "Conservative Baptist Association*" and "Social Gospel.*"

3. References such as "(*see* Southern Baptist Convention)" have been used within the body of articles.

4. Cross-references have been appended to the end of many articles: "*See also* GRAVES, JAMES ROBINSON; LANDMARKISM."

Introductory Essay

This dictionary includes an introductory essay entitled "The Baptists: A People, a History and an Identity." It is intended to provide a synoptic overview and interpretive perspective on Baptists in America, a subject the *Dictionary* has otherwise parsed into alphabetical segments. Since the essay also utilizes asterisks as cross-references, it can serve as a launching point for those who wish to use the *Dictionary* as something more than a quick reference.

ABBREVIATIONS

Books and Journals

A-AE	*African-American Encyclopedia,* ed. M. W. Williams, 6 vols.
AAP	*Annals of the American Pulpit,* ed. W. B. Sprague, 9 vols.
AB	*The American Baptist*
ABQ	*American Baptist Quarterly*
BB	*Baptist Bibliography*
BE	*Baptist Encyclopedia,* ed. W. Cathcart
BHH	*Baptist History and Heritage*
BP	*Baptist Peacemaker*
CH	*Church History*
Chron	*The Chronicle* (1938-1958)
CSR	*Christian Scholars Review*
CTM	*Concordia Theological Monthly*
DAB	*Dictionary of American Biography*
DARB	*Dictionary of American Religious Biography*
DCA	*Dictionary of Christianity in America*
DCB	*Dictionary of Canadian Biography*
EAR	*The Encyclopedia of American Religion,* J. G. Melton
EARE	*Encyclopedia of the American Religious Experience,* ed. C. H. Lippy and P. W. Williams, 3 vols.
EBA	*Encyclopedia of Black America,* ed. W. A. Low et al.
ERS	*Encyclopedia of Religion in the South,* ed. S. S. Hill
ESB	*Encyclopedia of Southern Baptists,* ed. C. J. Allen et al., 4 vols.
FM	*Faith and Mission*
Foun	*Foundations: A Baptist Journal of History and Theology*
IRM	*International Review of Mission*
JCS	*Journal of Church and State*
JNH	*Journal of Negro History*
JRT	*Journal of Religious Thought*
Kat	*Katallagete*
NAW	*Notable American Women: 1607-1950,* 3 vols. (1971)
NBV	*National Baptist Voice*
NCAB	*National Cyclopedia of American Biography,* 55 vols. (1892-1974); Current Series, A-L (1930-1972)
NEQ	*The New England Quarterly*
NHB	*Negro History Bulletin*
NJ	*National Journal*

PRS	*Perspectives in Religious Studies*
QR	*Quarterly Review*
RE	*Review and Expositor*
RRR	*Review of Religious Research*
SBCMJ	*Southern Baptist Church Music Journal*
SHERK	*The New Schaff-Herzog Encyclopedia of Religious Knowledge,* ed. S. M. Jackson
Soj	*Sojourners*
SouthEx	*Southern Exposure*
SwJT	*Southwestern Journal of Theology*
TE	*Theological Educator*
WE	*Watchman-Examiner*

General Abbreviations

b.	born
c.	*circa,* about, approximately
d.	died
fl.	*floruit,* flourished
vol(s).	volume(s)
?	date uncertain
*	subject included in the *Dictionary of Baptists in America*

LIST OF CONTRIBUTORS

Allen, Catherine B., M.B.A., Emory University. President, Women's Department of the Baptist World Alliance.

Allen, W. Loyd, Ph.D., Southern Baptist Theological Seminary. Chair, Department of Religion, Mississippi College.

Anders, Sarah Frances, Ph.D., Florida State University. Senior professor of sociology, Louisiana College, Pineville, Louisiana.

Autry, Renee Smith. Senior religion major, Samford University, Birmingham, Alabama.

Beck, Rosalie, Ph.D., Baylor University. Assistant professor, Baylor University, Waco, Texas.

Bell, Marty G., Ph.D., Vanderbilt University. Assistant professor of religion, Belmont College, Nashville, Tennessee.

Bendroth, Margaret L., Ph.D., Johns Hopkins University. Adjunct professor, Andover Newton Theological School, Newton Centre, Massachusetts.

Blevins, Carolyn, M.A., Southern Baptist Theological Seminary. Associate professor of religion, Carson-Newman College, Jefferson City, Tennessee.

Brackney, William H., Ph.D., Temple University. Principal and professor of historical theology, McMaster Divinity College, Hamilton, Ontario.

Bruce, Marcus C., M.Div., Yale University Divinity School. Instructor, Philosophy/Religion Department, Bates College, Lewiston, Maine.

Carlson, Gordon William, Ph.D., University of Minnesota. Associate professor of history and political science, Bethel College, St. Paul, Minnesota.

Chancey, Andrew S., M.A., University of Georgia. Ph.D. candidate, University of Florida.

Clayton, Glen, Ph.D., Southern Baptist Theological Seminary. Librarian and adjunct professor of religion, Furman University, Greenville, South Carolina.

Clouse, Robert G., Ph.D., University of Iowa. Professor of history, Indiana State University, Terre Haute, Indiana.

Clutter, R. T., Th.D., Dallas Theological Seminary. Professor of church history and theology, Grace Theological Seminary, Winona Lake, Indiana.

Craig, John M., Ph.D., College of William and Mary. Assistant professor, Department of History, Slippery Rock University, Slippery Rock, Pennsylvania.

Deweese, Charles W., Ph.D., Southern Baptist Theological Seminary. Associate director, Southern Baptist Historical Commission, Nashville, Tennessee.

Dorgan, Howard, Ph.D., Louisiana State University. Professor of communication arts, Appalachian State University, Boone, North Carolina.

Dunnavant, Anthony L., Ph.D., Vanderbilt University. Associate professor of church history, Lexington Theological Seminary, Lexington, Kentucky.

Ellis, Walter E., Ph.D., University of Pittsburgh. Senior minister, Fairview Baptist Church, Vancouver, Canada.

Erickson, Millard, Ph.D., Northwestern University. Senior professor of theology, Southwestern Baptist Theological Seminary, Fort Worth, Texas.

Estep, William R., Th.D. Southwestern Baptist Theological Seminary. Senior professor of church history, Southwestern Baptist Theological Seminary, Fort Worth, Texas.

Ewert, David, Ph.D., McGill University. Professor emeritus, Mennonite Brethren Bible College, Winnipeg, Manitoba.

Floding, Matthew D., M.A., Wheaton College. Chaplain of the College, Northwestern College, Orange City, Iowa.

Gardner, Robert G., Ph.D., Duke University. Emeritus professor of religion, Shorter College, Rome, Georgia.

George, Timothy F., Th.D., Harvard University. Dean, Beeson Divinity School, Samford University, Birmingham, Alabama.

Glass, James M., M.Div., Southwestern Baptist Theological Seminary. Pastor, Chapel Hill Baptist Church, Millry, Alabama.

Gravely, William B., Ph.D., Duke University. Professor of religious studies, University of Denver, Denver, Colorado.

Greer, John T. Professor of humanities, Ouachita Baptist University, Arkadelphia, Arkansas.

Grenz, Stanley J., D.Theol., University of Munich. Professor of theology and ethics, Carey/Regent College, Vancouver, British Columbia, Canada.

Hähnlen, Lee W., M.A., Western Kentucky University; D.Theol. candidate, University of South Africa. Assistant professor of church history and theology, Liberty University, Lynchburg, Virginia.

Halbrooks, G. Thomas, Ph.D., Emory University. Dean and professor of church history, Baptist Theological Seminary, Richmond, Virginia.

Hardesty, Nancy A., Ph.D., University of Chicago. Independent scholar, writer and book copyeditor. Visiting assistant professor of philosophy and religion, Clemson University, Clemson, South Carolina.

Hart, D. G., Ph.D., Johns Hopkins University. Director, Montgomery Memorial Library, Westminster Theological Seminary, Philadelphia, Pennsylvania.

Hesselgrave, David J., Ph.D., University of Minnesota. Professor of missions, School of World Missions and Evangelism, Trinity Evangelical Divinity School, Deerfield, Illinois.

Hinson, E. Glenn, Ph.D., Southern Baptist Theological Seminary; D.Phil., Oxford University. Professor of spirituality and the history of the early church, Baptist Theological Seminary, Richmond, Virginia.

Horton, Wade A. Ph.D., Southern Baptist Theological Seminary. Instructor, University of Louisville, Louisville, Kentucky.

Howe, Claude L., Jr., Th.D., New Orleans Baptist Theological Seminary. Chairman, Theological and Historical Studies Division, New Orleans Baptist Theological Seminary, New Orleans, Louisiana.

James, Robison B., Ph.D., Duke University. Professor of religion, University of Richmond, Richmond, Virginia.

Johnson, James E., Ph.D., Syracuse University. Professor of history, Bethel College, St. Paul, Minnesota.

Joiner, Earl E., Ph.D. Southern Baptist Theological Seminary. Professor of religion, Stetson University, DeLand, Florida.

Leonard, Bill J., Ph.D., Boston University. Chair and professor of religion, Department of Religion and Philosophy, Samford University, Birmingham, Alabama.

Leslie, Benjamin C., D.Theol., University of Zurich. Assistant professor of systematic theology and Christian ethics, North American Baptist Theological Seminary, Sioux Falls, South Dakota.

Lewis, Donald M., D.Phil., Oxford University. Associate professor of church history, Regent College, Vancouver, British Columbia.

Linder, Robert D., Ph.D., University of Iowa. Professor of history, Kansas State University, Manhattan, Kansas.

Loftis, John F., Ph.D., Southern Baptist Theological Seminary.

Until his untimely death in 1993, director of the Alabama Baptist Historical Commission, Birmingham, Alabama. Deceased.

McBeth, H. Leon, Ph.D., Southwestern Baptist Theological Seminary. Professor of church history, Southwestern Baptist Theological Seminary, Fort Worth, Texas.

McClellan, Albert. B.D., Southwestern Baptist Theological Seminary. Retired associate executive director, Southern Baptist Convention Executive Committee.

McElrath, Hugh T., Ph.D., Eastman School of Music. Senior professor of church music, Southern Baptist Theological Seminary, Louisville, Kentucky.

McKibbens, Thomas R., Ph.D., Southern Baptist Theological Seminary. Pastor, First Baptist Church, Newton Centre, Massachusetts.

Macleod, Donald, Ph.D., University of Toronto. Francis L. Patton Professor of Preaching and Worship, Princeton Theological Seminary, Princeton, New Jersey.

Magnuson, Norris A., Ph.D., University of Minnesota. Professor of church history and Resource Center director, Bethel Theological Seminary, St. Paul, Minnesota.

Manis, Andrew M., Ph.D., Southern Baptist Theological Seminary. Associate professor of religion, Averett College, Danville, Virginia.

Maring, Norman H., Ph.D., University of Maryland. Emeritus professor of church history, Eastern Baptist Theological Seminary, Philadelphia, Pennsylvania.

Martin, Sandy D., Ph.D., Union Theological Seminary, New York. Associate professor of religion, University of Georgia, Athens, Georgia.

Marty, Martin E., Ph.D., University of Chicago. Fairfax M. Cone Distinguished Service Professor of the History of Modern Christianity, University of Chicago, Chicago, Illinois.

Mathisen, Robert R., D.A., Illinois State University. Professor of history and political science, Grace

College, Winona Lake, Indiana.

Miller, Glen T., Ph.D., Union Theological Seminary, New York. Professor of church history, Bangor Theological Seminary, Bangor, Maine.

Moody, Barry M., Ph.D., Queen's University, Kingston, Ontario. Associate professor of history, Acadia University, Wolfville, Nova Scotia, Canada.

Nash, Robert, Ph.D., Southern Baptist Theological Seminary. Chair and assistant professor of religion, Department of Religion, Judson College, Marion, Alabama.

Nettles, Thomas J., Ph.D., Southwestern Baptist Theological Seminary. Professor of church history, Trinity Evangelical Divinity School, Deerfield, Illinois.

Nordbeck, Elizabeth C., Ph.D., University of Chicago. Dean and professor of church history, Andover Newton Theological School, Newton Centre, Massachusetts.

O'Brien, William R., Ph.D., Southwestern Baptist Theological Seminary. Director, Global Missions Center, Beeson Divinity School, Samford University, Birmingham, Alabama.

Parker, F. Calvin, Th.D., Southwestern Baptist Theological Seminary. Emeritus professor, Seinan Gakuin Theological Seminary, Fukuoka, Japan.

Patterson, James A., Ph.D., Princeton Theological Seminary. Associate professor of church history, Mid-America Baptist Theological Seminary, Memphis, Tennessee.

Patterson, W. Morgan, Ph.D., New Orleans Baptist Theological Seminary. President emeritus, Georgetown College, Georgetown, Kentucky.

Peake, Thomas R., Ph.D., University of North Carolina at Chapel Hill. Professor of history, chairman of Social Science Division, King College, Bristol, Tennessee.

Perko, Francis Michael, S.J., Ph.D., Stanford University. Associate professor of education and history, Loyola University of Chicago.

Petersen, Rodney L., Ph.D., Princeton Theological Seminary. Adjunct professor, Departments of Human Resource Development, Management and International Affairs, Webster University, Geneva, Switzerland.

Pipkin, H. Wayne, Ph.D., Hartford Theological Seminary. Pastor, American Church, Moscow, Russia.

Pitzer, Donald E., Ph.D., Ohio State University. Professor of history and director of Center for Communal Studies, University of Southern Indiana, Evansville, Indiana.

Pleasants, Phyllis Rodgerson, Ph.D., Southern Baptist Theological Seminary. Assistant professor of church history, Northern Baptist Theological Seminary, Lombard, Illinois.

Pratt, Andrew L., Ph.D., Southern Baptist Theological Seminary. Campus minister and adjunct instructor of religion, Southeast Missouri State University, Cape Girardeau, Missouri.

Ratliff, F. William, Ph.D., Southern Baptist Theological Seminary. Professor of theology and philosophy, Midwestern Baptist Theological Seminary, Kansas City, Missouri.

Reid, Daniel G., Ph.D., Fuller Theological Seminary. Reference book editor, InterVarsity Press, Downers Grove, Illinois.

Rennie, Ian S., Ph.D., University of Toronto. Vice president and academic dean, Ontario Theological Seminary, Willowdale, Ontario, Canada.

Robert, Dana L., Ph.D., Yale University. Assistant professor of international mission, Boston University School of Theology, Boston, Massachusetts.

Rogers, William B., Jr., Ed.D., Southwestern Baptist Theological Seminary. Professor of Christian education, Southern Baptist Theological Seminary, Louisville, Kentucky.

Rommen, E., D.Theol., University of Munich. Associate professor of mission, Trinity Evangelical Divinity School, Deerfield, Illinois.

Russell, C. Allyn, Ph.D., Boston University. Emeritus professor of religion, Boston University, Boston, Massachusetts.

Sawyer, Mary R., Ph.D., Duke University. Assistant professor of religious studies, Iowa State University, Ames, Iowa.

Scales, T. Laine Ph.D., University of Kentucky. Assistant professor of social work, Palm Beach Atlantic College, West Palm Beach, Florida.

Sehested, Kenneth, M.Div., Southern Baptist Theological Seminary. Director, Baptist Peace Fellowship of North America, Memphis, Tennessee.

Shelley, Bruce L., Ph.D., University of Iowa. Professor of church history, Denver Seminary, Denver, Colorado.

Shull, L. Craig, Ph.D., Southern Baptist Theological Seminary. Pastor, General Baptist Convention.

Shurden, Walter B., Th.D., New Orleans Baptist Theological Seminary. Professor and chair of the Department of Christianity, Mercer University, Macon, Georgia.

Smith, Karen E., D.Phil., Oxford University. Lecturer in Baptist history, South Wales Baptist College, University of Wales, Cardiff, Wales.

Spivey, James T., D.Phil., Oxford University. Assistant professor of church history, Southwestern Baptist Theological Seminary, Fort Worth, Texas.

Stackhouse, John G., Jr., Ph.D., University of Chicago. Associate professor of religion, University of Manitoba, Winnipeg, Manitoba, Canada.

Still, Sherra L., M.S.W., Southern Baptist Theological Seminary. Homemaker, Lexington, Kentucky.

Stowe, David M., Th.D., Pacific School of Religion. Executive vice president emeritus, United Church Board for World Ministries.

Taylor, Thomas T., Ph.D., University of Illinois, Champaign-Urbana. Assistant professor of history, Department of History, Wittenberg University, Springfield, Ohio.

Teague, Fred A., Ed.D., University of

Oklahoma. Dean of graduate studies, Southwest Baptist University, Bolivar, Missouri.

Toulouse, Mark G., Ph.D., University of Chicago Divinity School. Associate professor of church history, Brite Divinity School, Texas Christian University, Fort Worth, Texas.

Towns, Elmer L., D.Min., Fuller Theological Seminary. Dean, School of Religion, and vice president, Liberty University, Lynchburg, Virginia.

Tucker, Ruth A., Ph.D., Northern Illinois University. Visiting professor, Trinity Evangelical Divinity School, Deerfield, Illinois.

Tyson, John R., Ph.D., Graduate School, Drew University. Associate professor of theology, Houghton College, Houghton, New York.

Wacker, Grant, Ph.D., Harvard University. Professor of church history, Duke University Divinity School, Durham, North Carolina.

Walker, J. Brent, J.D., Stetson University. General counsel and associate director, Baptist Joint Committee on Public Affairs, Washington, D.C.

Weaver, C. Douglas, Ph.D., Southern Baptist Theological Seminary. Associate professor of religion, Brewton-Parker College, Mt. Vernon, Georgia.

Weber, Timothy P., Ph.D., University of Chicago. David T. Porter Professor of Church History, Southern Baptist Theological Seminary, Louisville, Kentucky.

White, Charles E., Ph.D., Boston University. Associate professor of Christian thought and history, Spring Arbor College, Spring Arbor, Michigan.

Whiteman, Curtis W., Ph.D., St. Louis University. Associate professor of historical theology, Westmont College, Santa Barbara, California.

Whitlock, David, Ph.D., Southern Baptist Theological Seminary. Pastor, Livingston First Baptist Church, Livingston, Alabama.

Williams, Lawrence H., Ph.D., University of Iowa. Associate professor of Africana studies and history, Luther College, Decorah, Iowa.

Wills, David W., Ph.D., Harvard University. Professor of religion, Amherst College, Amherst, Massachusetts.

Wilson, Everett A., Ph.D., Stanford University. Academic dean and professor of history, Bethany Bible College, Scotts Valley, California.

Wilt, Paul C., Ph.D., American University. Professor of history, Westmont College, Santa Barbara, California.

Wimmer, John R., Ph.D., Divinity School, University of Chicago. Pastor, Trinity United Methodist Church, Lafayette, Indiana.

Woodbridge, John D., Doctorat de Troisiéme Cycle. Université de Toulouse, Toulouse, France. Professor of church history, Trinity Evangelical Divinity School, Deerfield, Illinois.

Yarbrough, Slayden, Ph.D., Baylor University. Professor of religion, Oklahoma Baptist University, Shawnee, Oklahoma.

Zeman, Jarold K., D.Theol., University of Zurich. Professor of church history, Acadia Divinity College, Acadia University, Wolfville, Nova Scotia, Canada.

Zwier, Robert, Ph.D., University of Wisconsin at Madison. Vice president for academic affairs, Northwestern College, Orange City, Iowa.

Introduction

The Baptists:
A People, a History and an Identity

*I*n 1813 Methodist circuit rider Peter Cartwright wrote of religion along the Cumberland
River:

> We preached in new settlements, and the Lord poured out his Spirit, and we had many
> convictions and many conversions. It was the order of the day, (though I am sorry to say
> it), that we were constantly followed by a certain set of proselyting Baptist preachers.
> These new and wicked settlements were seldom visited by these Baptist preachers until
> the Methodist preachers entered them; then, when a revival was gotten up, or the work
> of God revived, these Baptist preachers came rushing in, and they generally sung their
> sermons; and when they struck the *long roll,* or their sing-song mode of preaching, in
> substance it was "water!" "water!" "you must follow your blessed Lord down to the water!"
> . . . Indeed, they made so much ado about baptism by immersion, that the uninformed
> would suppose that heaven was an island, and there was no way to get there but by *diving*
> or *swimming.*[1]

Cartwright was correct, at least where Baptist identity is concerned. The people called Baptists
have made "much ado" about many things—conversion and baptism, election and free will,
liberation and slavery, individualism and institutionalism. With claims of over thirty million
members, Baptists represent the largest Protestant religious tradition in the United States.
While the Southern Baptist Convention* with its membership of some sixteen million is the
largest single Baptist denomination, there are over eighty groups in the United States that
claim the appellation "Baptist" in some form or another. Demographics suggest that Baptists
represent the majority religious group in most counties in the South and Southwest.[2]

In their response to each other as well as to the broader culture, Baptists may be described,
in historian Walter Shurden's words, as "not a silent people."[3] They are at once outspoken
critics and defenders of culture and religion in the United States. Baptists were among the
earliest advocates of radical religious freedom. Some were outspoken abolitionists, while
others used the Bible to defend human slavery. Many participated in the civil rights move-

[1]

ment, while others staunchly opposed it. Baptists are a diverse and complex people.

Today their numbers are divided across various racial and ethnic lines, with largest numbers in the Anglo-Saxon and African-American communities and growing influence among Hispanics, Asians and other minority groups. They reflect a wide diversity of economic, educational, political and theological backgrounds.

Baptist Origins

Debate and controversy have characterized Baptist identity from the beginning. Indeed, a major source of disagreement among Baptists involves theories of origin. Baptists do not always agree on the nature of their beginnings. The three most popular theories include Baptist successionism, Anabaptist* kinship and English Separatist origins.

Baptist successionism. One popular theory of Baptist origins involves successionism, the idea that Baptist churches exist in an unbroken succession from Jesus' own baptism by John the Baptist in the River Jordan. This theory, sometimes known as Baptist Landmarkism,* suggests that Baptists alone possess the true marks of the church, a tradition kept alive through a series of New Testament churches from the first century to the present. Some successionists attempt to trace a direct lineage through a variety of dissenting groups in Christian history, churches that were "Baptist in everything but name." These include such early sectarian movements as the Montanists, Novatians, Donatists, Paulicians, Waldensians, Albigenses (Cathari), Lollards, Hussites, Anabaptists* and Baptists.* Other advocates of this view are less specific, insisting that there were numerous groups that reflected Baptist concern for the authority of Scripture, faith and baptism,* local church autonomy, priesthood of the laity,* antiestablishmentarianism, and the centrality of Jesus Christ for both the church and the individual—all "landmarks" of Baptist faith.

Successionist views were particularly strong among Baptists in the nineteenth and early twentieth centuries as they sought to relate to, even compete with, other denominations in the pluralistic environment of the American republic. If certain groups could point to a specific historical founder—John Wesley, John Calvin* or Martin Luther—Baptists could claim descent directly from Jesus himself, through none other than John the Baptist. As one frontier Baptist preacher is said to have remarked: "Well, they didn't call him John the Presbyterian, now did they?" Successionism provided an easy and very popular explanation for Baptist origins, one that might be used conveniently in debates with other denominations.

Successionist ideas were built on faulty historical analysis, however, since prior to the seventeenth century, distinct Baptist churches, even by other names, are impossible to document. The theory was a convenient method of promoting Baptist claims to doctrinal integrity and historic continuity with the New Testament church.

Anabaptist kinship. A second theory of Baptist origins involves the idea that Baptists are, directly or indirectly, the heirs of the Anabaptist wing of the sixteenth-century Radical Reformation. These Anabaptist groups include the Swiss Brethren, the Hutterites and the Mennonites. Numerous scholars suggest that Anabaptist concerns for such issues as a believers' church, baptism following a profession of personal faith in Christ, the ministry of the laity, religious liberty* and other issues were certain influences on the earliest Baptists. Yet early Baptists generally did not agree with Anabaptists on various doctrines, including pacifism and nonresistance, oath-taking, holding public office and certain beliefs regarding the Incarnation of Christ (such as that Christ did not receive his physical body from the Virgin Mary). Some believe that the Anabaptist influence can be traced tangibly and directly, while others insist that the ties reflect a more indirect spiritual kinship. Direct lineage is difficult to establish on historical grounds, but scholarly investigation and debate continue.

English Separatist tradition. Perhaps the most widely held theory of Baptist beginnings involves the seventeenth-century congregation that began in Amsterdam and the impact upon it of English Separatist Puritanism. The Puritan Separatists were those persons who came to believe that the Church of England was a false church and that true Christians should separate themselves from it. Influenced by the writings of Robert Browne, John Robinson and others, these Anglicans separated themselves from the church of their birth, a decision that often resulted in imprisonment, execution or exile. One such congregation of Separatists left England for America in 1620, arriving at Plymouth, Massachusetts Colony, and were known as the Pilgrims. Another group, under the leadership of Separatists John Smyth* and Thomas Helwys,* moved to Holland, where in 1609 they repudiated their earlier Anglican baptism and received baptism by affusion (pouring) on the basis of their confession of faith in Christ. They had become convinced that Separatism included not only the nature of church government but also a recognition that the New Testament church knew only the baptism of adult believers. Baptism was not a sign of the covenant given to infants, but a sign of cleansing given only to those who had repented of their sins, placed their faith in Christ and experienced God's grace. Thus the first clearly discernible Baptist church came directly from a group of English Separatists who accepted and articulated what came to be known as Baptist beliefs. In terms of influence and direct historical continuity, Baptist origins seem most closely related to seventeenth-century English Separatism.

Baptist Beliefs: Across the Theological Spectrum

What are the distinctive beliefs of the people called Baptists? They span the theological spectrum from Calvinist* to Arminian,* from liberal* to conservative to fundamentalist.* The original congregation at Amsterdam was General Baptist* in its theological orientation. Arminianism, with its emphasis on free will, general atonement and human participation in the salvific process, characterized their understanding of faith.

By the 1630s in England, another group known as Particular Baptists* was beginning to take shape. Calvinist in belief, they affirmed such doctrines as total depravity, limited atonement, unconditional election, perseverance of the saints and the total work of God alone in bringing sinners to salvation.

Today Baptist groups mirror that diversity of doctrine. Free Will Baptists* affirm an Arminian theology, while Primitive* and Old Regular* Baptists promote a strongly Calvinistic doctrine. Other Baptist groups and individuals fall somewhere in between, emphasizing elements of Calvinism and Arminianism to varying degrees.

In terms of common beliefs and doctrines, historians have often spoken of certain Baptist distinctives. These include the following:

1. The authority of Scripture. Baptists accept the Reformation principle of *sola scriptura*. Scripture alone is the foundation for Christian faith and order.

2. A regenerate church membership. Membership in the church is predicated on personal faith in Jesus Christ as Savior and Lord. All members of the congregation are to declare faith in Christ.

3. Immersion baptism* and the Lord's Supper* as ordinances* of the church. Baptism is administered only to those who claim personal salvation or regeneration. Its normative form is immersion of the entire body into water. Baptism is a symbol of cleansing and entrance into Christ's body, the church. The Lord's Supper* is celebrated by baptized believers as a sign of God's continuing presence, as a memorial of Christ's death on the cross and as a means of uniting Christians to Christ and to each other. Some Baptists also observe footwashing* as an ordinance symbolizing the servanthood of Christians to one another.

4. The autonomy of the local congregation. The authority for church government comes from Christ through the congregation. Each congregation is autonomous in its decision-making and its direction for mission and ministry. Denominational or associational alignments are derived from decisions of local churches.

5. The priesthood of all believers. Baptists generally affirm this Reformation doctrine in their belief that each individual may come to God directly without the intercession of priest or religious tribunal. The doctrine has also influenced the Baptist emphasis on "every believer a minister."

6. Religious liberty. From the beginning Baptists held tenaciously to the idea that God alone, not state or church, was supreme judge of conscience. Early Baptists called not simply for religious toleration but for radical religious freedom in which the state could judge neither the heretic nor the atheist.

Many of these beliefs are not distinctive of Baptists alone but are affirmed by various Protestant traditions. Thus, another way to examine so-called distinctives is to see them less as individual, free-standing dogmas than as interrelated ideals, each of which exists in a distinct tension or balance with others.

The authority of Scripture and the liberty of conscience. From the beginning of their movement, Baptists affirmed the centrality of Scripture as the primary authority for the individual and the church. They were concerned that their teachings be drawn only from Scripture, with particular authority given to the New Testament. Baptists often refer to themselves as "people of the Book," bound by the Word of God as revealed in the written Word, Holy Scripture, and the living Word, Jesus Christ. Teaching and preaching begin with the biblical text and the inspiration of the Holy Spirit. At the same time Baptists often speak of the liberty of conscience, sometimes known as soul liberty, in matters of interpretation and inspiration. In its most basic sense, that idea rests in the radical notion that the individual can be trusted in matters of interpretation and belief.

Such a belief was born of Baptist confrontation with both governmental and ecclesial establishments. Baptists asserted that God alone is judge of conscience, that the state cannot judge the heretic or the atheist, and that each individual is responsible to God alone for the religious decisions he or she does or does not make. Scripture, therefore, is a living Word, not a dead letter, and the believing individual is responsible to read and interpret Scripture according to the dictates of conscience. Such a belief did not mean that Baptist individuals were free to believe anything they wished and still remain Baptists, but under the guidance of the Spirit, within the nurturing environment of the congregation, soul liberty was to be cultivated. Biblical authority kept soul liberty from becoming antinomianism. Soul liberty kept biblical authority from becoming corpse literalism. Maintaining that balance remains difficult for Baptist groups and individuals, a source of controversy and continuing debate.

Local autonomy and associational cooperation. Local autonomy shaped a radical congregationalism in most Baptist groups, leading them to mistrust "hierarchial alliances" that might undermine the local church. Yet even the earliest Baptists sought local or regional associational fellowship and cooperation with other congregations for encouragement and community. Later Baptists, specifically in America, often went on to establish national associations with denominational organizations for missions, education, publication and evangelism. Some, however, still eschew any but the broadest affiliations beyond the local level.

Ideally, authority grew from the congregation to broader participation with other Baptist groups. Again, the difficulty of maintaining such a balance created occasion for numerous schisms over the relationship between the local church and the denomination or association, regional or national.

Ministry: laity and clergy. Baptists have often emphasized the priesthood of the laity and the ministry of all believers. They stress the role of the individual in the interpretation of Scripture and the leadership of the church. Early Baptists often administered the laying on of hands* to all the newly baptized as a sign of their calling* as ministers of the gospel. Yet Baptists were never Quakers in their understanding of the ministry. They also laid hands on those who were set aside for specific ministerial function within the body of Christ. In one sense all were ministers; in another sense pastoral/ministerial leadership was invested in a particular group. Ideally this should lead to a community of ministry and cooperation, each person fulfilling a specific calling for the good of the body. Often it has also produced conflict and schism as churches struggle with the boundaries of each type of ministry.

Regenerate members: dramatic event and nurturing process. Baptists agree that all church members must be regenerate believers in Jesus Christ. Often their words suggest that faith in Christ must involve a dramatic event of conversion when the sinner is confronted by a profound spiritual and moral crisis, responds to grace and enters into salvation. Yet Baptists are also nurturers who begin leading their children to faith almost as soon as they enter the world. Most who grew up in the church testify to a gentle nurturing experience in which grace came less in dramatic event than in gradual process. These two approaches should complement each other, offering different routes to the same faith. Sometimes, however, they create tensions over the nature of salvation itself and who may receive it, as well as when and how salvation is secured. Nonetheless, Baptists have long been concerned with bringing persons to faith.

[5]

Religious liberty and loyalty to the state. Seventeenth-century Baptists in England and America were radicals when it came to the doctrine of religious liberty. They endured imprisonment and even death because they believed that the state could not assume the role of God in judging the heart and soul of the individual. In the United States, Baptists were among the strongest supporters of a constitutional amendment protecting religious liberty. At the same time they were loyal citizens of the state, some of the strongest supporters of the patriot cause in the Revolutionary War. These ideas have led to great tension, sometimes forcing Baptists to exercise religious dissent at odds with certain policies of the state. The tension continues.

Baptist Beginnings in America: The Colonial Experience

These beliefs were evident as Baptists entered the American experience. The story of Baptists in the colonies begins with Roger Williams* and the legacy he established in Rhode Island. Williams arrived in Massachusetts in 1631 and almost immediately encountered controversy with the Puritan religious establishment. Among other things, Williams suggested that the Native Americans, not the English monarch, were the real owners of the American land and should be justly compensated for it. He challenged the idea that New England or any other government could be considered a Christian commonwealth. Likewise, he denounced the attempt to punish persons whose religious beliefs did not conform to the Puritan way. God alone, Williams said, was judge of conscience for the heretic and atheist alike. The Puritan leaders decided that Williams had to go, and they exiled him into the "howling wilderness" of the New England winter of 1636.

The Narragansett Indians saved Williams, and in 1636 he bought land from them to found Providence Plantation. It was there in 1639 that Williams was baptized by Ezekiel Holliman,* a former member of the Puritan church at Salem. Williams then baptized Holliman and ten other persons who formed a church, generally believed to be the First Baptist Church, Providence, Rhode Island.* Ever the dissenter, Williams only remained a Baptist for a few months; thereupon he declared himself to be a Seeker, waiting on a new revelation from God. The Baptists remained, and another congregation was formed in Newport under the leadership of John Clarke* (some claim it as the first Baptist church in America). Both Calvinist and Arminian views were evident among the members of these early churches. Through the influence of Williams, Clarke and others, the Rhode Island colony offered complete religious liberty to all its citizens.

Other Baptist groups were formed elsewhere in New England, and during the 1640s and 1650s in Massachusetts Colony numerous persons were tried for refusing to baptize infants. In 1651 Baptist Obadiah Holmes* was imprisoned and whipped for preaching against infant baptism, and Henry Dunster,* president of Harvard College, was dismissed for refusing to have a child baptized. The First Baptist Church of Boston was founded in 1665, not without severe persecution from the colonial government.

The religious tolerance evident in the Middle Colonies—Pennsylvania, New Jersey, Maryland—offered Baptists a more favorable environment. Under the leadership of Elias Keach* and others, the first Baptist association in America was founded by five congregations, including the Old Pennepack Church and the First Baptist Church of Philadelphia,* founded in 1698. This association of churches produced the first Baptist confession of faith, the Philadelphia Confession of 1742, a Calvinist document which included articles on the laying on of hands at baptism and the singing of hymns* other than psalms in worship. A later document, the New Hampshire Confession of Faith,* which was a more modified Calvinist document written in 1833, also became a popular confession of faith among Baptists in the United States.

In the South the earliest Baptist presence came by the 1690s with the founding of the First Baptist Church, Charleston, South Carolina.* These Baptists were also Calvinist in theological orientation and represented what is known as the Regular Baptist tradition. They sang the Psalms and promoted ministerial education and orderly worship. Their ministers, educated and erudite, were among what are sometimes called the "gentlemen theologians" of the South. By the 1750s another group of Baptists had come into the South, founding the Sandy Creek church under the leadership of Shubal Stearns* and Daniel Marshall.* This church became the mother congregation for over forty churches in the region. It reflected a more revivalistic form of Baptist life, with preachers influenced by and often converted during the First Great Awakening.* They preached spontaneous, lively sermons, sang spirited hymns and called on persons to be converted to escape the wrath of a righteous God. They often seemed to modify their Calvinism a bit, promoting the general atonement and the possibility of salvation for all who would repent and believe.

Baptists and the Struggle for Religious Liberty

Colonial Baptists were outspoken advocates of religious liberty and the Revolutionary cause. In New England the venerable pastor Isaac Backus* was sent to the Continental Congress as an agent of the Warren Association of New England Baptists and an advocate of religious liberty. In Virginia, Baptists frequently found themselves tangling with the Anglican establishment over questions of religious liberty. Baptist preachers were often jailed, beaten or mobbed when they tried to preach, and were charged with disturbing the peace or refusing to secure preaching licenses from the state. John Leland* of Culpepper County, Virginia, was an outspoken leader in the cause of religious liberty. He helped Thomas Jefferson secure passage of the Bill for Religious Liberty in Virginia in 1785. Leland's efforts were significant in the securing of a Bill of Rights to the Constitution of the new nation.

Issues of church and state have received continued attention from Baptists throughout American history. During the twentieth century the Baptist Joint Committee on Public Affairs* became a lobbying agency for representing numerous Baptist groups and concerns in Washington, D.C.

The Frontier and the Second Great Awakening

With the end of the Revolution and the ratification of the new Constitution, Baptists, like other American religious groups, faced new challenges of organization and identity. They were also called upon to respond to a new dimension of American life: the westward frontier, a geographic region that became a cultural mindset. In many respects Baptists were more organizationally prepared for the new American situation than the more establishment denominations. They had a polity that allowed for easy adaptation to diverse situations. Churches could be organized through the consent of a group of Baptist believers without waiting for permission from bishop, diocese or synod. Baptist polity and autonomy fit well with the democratic, individualistic spirit of the times. Baptist ministry was also adapted to a frontier culture through persons known as "farmer-preachers." These individuals, often self-educated, were citizens of the community who supported themselves on the land and on Sundays exercised pulpit gifts in Baptist congregations. Congregations might license* them as a way of trying them out and monitoring their gifts. Later, ordination* would be given, usually after they received a specific call to a particular congregation.

Although the Presbyterians started them, camp meetings were fertile soil for Baptist preachers and converts. Baptists were present at the great camp meeting at Cane Ridge, Kentucky, in 1801, and numerous churches were founded out of that and other revival meetings. The names of Kentucky churches founded during the early nineteenth century illustrate the rural, frontier nature of those communities of faith: Corn Creek, Buffalo Lick, Forks of Elkhorn and Defeated Creek. These churches helped to teach and train new generations of church members, many converted in the camp meetings and protracted revivals of the period. Baptisms were celebrated outdoors in creeks and rivers, each a dramatic scene with congregation on the banks urging the candidates on, drying them off and welcoming them home. So significant was Baptist growth in the awakening and on the frontier that by the mid-nineteenth century Baptists were second in numbers only to the Methodists.

Denominationalizing Impulses: The Triennial Convention

By the early nineteenth century, Baptists, like other American religious groups, had turned their attention to collective efforts at benevolence and missionary activity. Zeal born of the Awakening was channeled into a variety of new endeavors for missions, evangelism and education. In 1810 the Congregationalists founded the American Board of Commissioners for Foreign Missions, an organization that began to send out missionaries to other countries, among them Luther Rice* and Adoniram* and Ann Hasseltine Judson.* On their journey to India for missionary service, these three persons accepted Baptist views, concluding on arrival in India that they could not in good conscience receive funds from the Congregationalists. Rice returned to America to seek funding. One result of his efforts was the founding of the General Missionary Convention of the Baptist Denomination in the United States for Foreign Missions, better known as the Triennial Convention* because of its meeting at three-year intervals. The convention was the first national organization of Baptists in America. Its sole purpose was to fund endeavors for the sending out of Baptist missionaries overseas.

The founding of this and other such agencies was not without significant controversy among Baptists. The antimission movement* was a concerted attempt by staunchly Calvinist Baptists to dissuade churches from participating in any activity that might interfere with the sovereign work of God in saving the elect. Many also objected to the forming of a mission

[8]

society, since such an organization could not be found in the pages of the New Testament. The antimission movement was a bitter conflict among Baptists. One of its most articulate spokespersons was Daniel Parker,* a leader of the Two-Seed-in-the-Spirit Predestinarian Baptists.* He insisted that missionary boards were human creations that had no base in Scripture. Alexander Campbell,* the Baptist turned Restorationist, was another of the popular opponents of missionary and denominational organizations. Many Baptists agreed with Parker and Campbell.

Such opposition, as well as the basic Baptist mistrust of organizational hierarchy, influenced Baptists to reject centralization of functions and to establish separate, autonomous societies charged with implementing specific ministries and missions—home and foreign missions, Sunday-school publications, tract publications—without any direct connections. These societies could receive membership of individuals, churches or associations. Such membership was based on the contribution of money to the specific cause. Churches and individuals could thus cooperate while retaining a high degree of autonomy from national bureaucracies.

Old Landmarkism: The Challenge of the Church

For many nineteenth-century Baptists, the rise of national societies raised questions about the nature of the church and the relationship of congregations to other Baptist and non-Baptist entities. One movement that addressed these questions, creating further controversy among Baptists, was a movement known as Old Landmarkism.* As noted earlier, Landmarkism was one expression of Baptist succession, the effort to trace Baptists in an unbroken line to the New Testament church. Emerging as a movement during the 1850s, Landmarkism offered Baptists a systematic means of understanding their "history," competing with other denominations and defining the nature of the Christian church in Baptist terms. Originating primarily in the South, Landmarkism was shaped by three articulate spokesmen, James R. Graves* and A. C. Dayton* of Tennessee and J. M. Pendleton* of Kentucky.

The Landmarkists' initial concern was whether "pedobaptist" ministers (those who had not received baptism by immersion) should be asked to participate in worship in Baptist churches. They concluded that such participation would not be possible since nonimmersed persons lacked the proper New Testament credentials for ministry. Pedobaptist congregations, therefore, could only be considered "societies," not true churches of Christ since they did not possess the marks of genuine Christianity. Baptist churches alone were the true churches, for they alone could trace their lineage directly to the New Testament and Jesus' own immersion by John. Since the local congregation was the only form of the church, Landmarkists rejected the authority of all denominational organizations beyond the local church. And because Baptist churches alone were the true churches, Landmarkists rejected infant baptism and immersion performed outside Baptist churches, which they termed "alien immersion."* They also insisted that the Lord's Supper could be given only to members of the specific congregation where it was observed, a practice known as "close" or "closed Communion." Landmarkism had a significant impact on many Baptist groups, especially the Southern Baptist Convention,* the Baptist Missionary Association* and the Independent Baptists.*

Baptists' Great Schism: The Slavery Issue

No single issue served to divide and shape the identity of many nineteenth-century Baptists, black and white, more than the South's Peculiar Institution, slavery. Baptists began evangelization efforts among slaves by the late eighteenth century. African-Americans were participants, often preachers, at the frontier camp meetings and received as members of white-majority churches. By the 1780s Baptists, even in certain segments of the South, had organized antislavery societies, one of the most famous of which was known as the Baptized Licking Locust Society, Friends of Humanity, a Kentucky-based organization. These organizations looked primarily to future, not immediate, manumission of slaves. Yet as the issue became more divisive nationwide, Baptist bodies sought to remain neutral, claiming that the matter was political and social, not religious. Leaders knew that any official response would split Baptist societies.

As Northern abolitionism confronted Southern tradition, it became increasingly evident that this volatile issue could not be ignored. In a test case the Georgia Baptist Convention submitted the name of James E. Reeves (some sources say Reeve), a known slaveholder, for appointment by the board of the Home Mission Society.* The board voted seven to five to refuse appointment. Southerners declared that the society had violated its purported neutrality on the slavery issue. They met at First Baptist Church, Augusta, Georgia,* in May 1845 to form a new organization, the Southern Baptist Convention.*

From the beginning this Baptist group was more connectional, linking all boards in a centralized denominational network in order to fulfill a specific missionary imperative. The division created two Baptist denominations in the United States, North and South. In contrast to the Southern Baptists, those in the North continued to relate to specific societies for missions, education and benevolence and did not establish a formal denomination, the Northern Baptist Convention, until 1907. That group became the American Baptist Convention in 1950 and the American Baptist Churches in the USA* in 1972.

African-American Baptists

African-American Baptist organizations took shape in the aftermath of the Civil War and Emancipation. In slavery time in the South, African-Americans were the focus of evangelization efforts on the part of many white Baptist individuals and congregations. African-Americans were frequent participants in frontier revivals and camp meetings, and African-American converts became members of white churches. There they were relegated during worship services to slave galleries or other special areas in the church building. As church members, however, they could bring disciplinary charges against recalcitrant masters guilty of abusive treatment of slaves. By the eighteenth century there were African-American Baptist churches in the South. The Silver Bluff Church in Aiken County, South Carolina, formed sometime between 1773 and 1775, traditionally has been considered the first African-American Baptist congregation. Other recent studies suggest the possibility of an even earlier congregation in the South. It is clear, therefore, that there were such gatherings of black Baptists, some with whites and a smaller number composed only of African-Americans. By the early 1800s there were black congregations in the North, among them New York's Abyssinian Baptist Church, founded in 1809.

Following the Civil War and the Emancipation Proclamation, African-American Baptist churches and denominational organizations took shape. The National Baptist* Convention was established in 1895 through the merger of three regional African-American groups, the Baptist Missionary Convention (1880), the American National Baptist Convention (1886) and the National Baptist Education Convention (1893). During the twentieth century disputes over denominational administration and outlook led to divisions that created three black Baptist groups: the National Baptist Convention, Incorporated,* the National Baptist Convention, Unincorporated* and the National Progressive Baptist Convention.* Numerous African-American churches have become dually aligned* with other Baptist bodies, especially the American Baptist Churches in the USA and the Southern Baptist Convention.

Throughout the twentieth century many African-American Baptist churches and pastors addressed the racial* situation in the United States, providing significant leadership for the civil rights movement of the 1950s and 1960s. In 1955 African-American Protestant churches, Baptists included, led in establishing the Montgomery bus boycott, the success of which marked the beginning of the end of segregated facilities in Alabama and ultimately in the entire South. The Reverend Martin Luther King Jr.* rose to leadership in the civil rights movement from the pulpit of the Dexter Avenue Baptist Church, Montgomery, Alabama. King, the Reverend Ralph David Abernathy* and innumerable other African-American Baptist ministers joined in the broader movement across the South and throughout the nation. Not all African-American Baptists agreed with their methods of direct confrontation with whites, however. The Reverend Joseph Jackson,* longtime president of the National Baptist Convention, Incorporated,* was a frequent critic of King and his methods.

Baptist Denominations: Across the Spectrum

National, Southern and American Baptist groups are but a few of the more than eighty Baptist subdenominations in the United States. Indeed, it is impossible to generalize about Baptist beliefs, actions and structures, since they span such a broad spectrum. A few representative bodies serve as illustrations. Southern and central Appalachia, the region south from Virginia to Georgia, east to portions of Kentucky and Tennessee, is fertile soil for Baptist subgroups. These include the highly Calvinistic Primitive Baptists and the Two-Seed-in-the-Spirit-Predestinarian Baptists as well as the highly Arminian Free Will and General Baptists. Old Regular Baptists,* Union Baptists* and Regular Baptists* also occupy the region. Most of these groups are small in number but distinctive in preaching and practice, many mirroring the earlier nineteenth-century forms of frontier Baptist life. They practice immersion baptism outdoors in creeks and rivers, observing the Lord's Supper often in conjunction with the washing of feet. Their preachers are often unpaid or bivocational, given to spontaneous preaching with a cadence sometimes known as the "holy whine." The churches maintain strong associational fellowship with each other.

Various ethnic groups came to the United States, bringing their Baptist traditions with them.

[11]

Baptist groups were evident among Russian, French, Romanian and French immigrants. Swedish* and German* Baptists showed particular strength in the United States. In 1914 Swedish Baptists founded Bethel Theological Seminary* in St. Paul, Minnesota. German Baptists, sometimes known as the North American Baptist Conference,* also founded schools, among them North American Baptist Seminary* in Sioux Falls, South Dakota. More recently the Baptist movement has thrived among Hispanic Americans, particularly in the Southwest. Asian Baptists have also flourished, especially among Chinese, Korean and Vietnamese immigrants.

In Canada, Baptists reflect a diversity evident in doctrine and demographics. Early Baptist organizations were formed in the Atlantic Provinces in such areas as Nova Scotia and New Brunswick; less significant growth occurred in the Central Provinces of Ontario and Quebec; significant growth occurred in the West—Manitoba, British Columbia and elsewhere. Baptist groups thus are spread throughout the vast Canadian region. By the 1940s many Canadian Baptists* had joined in the Baptist Federation of Canada.*

Fundamentalism divided the Canadian churches during the 1920s. T. T. Shields* and other Canadian fundamentalists attacked liberalism in the churches and in such Baptist educational institutions as McMaster University.* Canadian Baptists also include Free Will Baptists, Primitive Baptists and various churches affiliated with the Southern Baptist Convention. In the United States, Old Landmarkism and fundamentalism likewise produced or shaped a variety of Baptist subgroups. These include the strongly Landmark bodies such as the American Baptist Association,* the Baptist Missionary Association* and the Baptist Missionary Association of America. These groups affirm Landmark and fundamentalist principles. Eschewing mission boards or societies, they encourage each local church to fund specific missionaries through direct contributions. Specifically fundamentalist groups are often known as Independent Baptists since they repudiate formal denominational alignments. They prefer to join together in "fellowships" that claim no organizational connections.

Many of these organizations began out of the so-called liberal-fundamentalist confrontations that began in the late nineteenth and early twentieth centuries. These groups include the General Association of Regular Baptist Churches,* the Baptist Bible Fellowship* and the Conservative Baptist Association of America.* Controversies over fundamentalism and liberalism continue to shape segments of the Baptist communion in the United States. Divisions over fundamentalism struck the Northern Baptist Convention (later American Baptist Churches in the USA) in the 1920s and 1950s. Harry Emerson Fosdick* and W. B. Riley* were among the most prominent Baptist spokespersons for liberalism and fundamentalism, respectively. The Southern Baptist Convention experienced significant division, specifically related to the question of biblical inerrancy,* in the 1980s and 1990s.

The multitude and diversity of Baptist subdenominations and the controversies that often (but not always) spawned them led many to suggest that Baptists are a people "who multiply by dividing."

Baptists: Twentieth-Century Issues

Fundamentalism and liberalism were not the only issues confronting Baptists in the twentieth century. By the late nineteenth century Baptists in the North were offering various responses to the realities of industrialization and urbanization. During this era Baptists, like other American Christians, divided over the implications of the Gospel of Wealth and the Social Gospel.* Walter Rauschenbusch,* the so-called father of the Social Gospel, was a German Baptist pastor and professor at Rochester Theological Seminary.* He described the Social Gospel as "humanity organized according to the will of God." Another Baptist pastor, Russell Conwell,* addressed the issue of wealth and poverty from a different perspective as expressed in his famous sermon "Acres of Diamonds." Conwell saw wealth as a blessing from God, poverty a curse from God. Social Gospel proponents denounced Conwell and those like him for their failure to fulfil the prophetic calling of Christianity and challenge the economic order of the day. Baptist opponents of Social Christianity suggested that the movement promoted political and economic agendas not appropriate to the church's evangelical task.

While there were Baptists of Social Gospel sentiment in the South, most Southern Baptists hesitated to promote Social Christianity except in regard to issues of personal morality such as prostitution, gambling, card-playing, alcohol, cigarette-smoking—issues that did have decidedly communal implications. Debates developed regarding the meaning of the Social Gospel and its relationship to conversion,* racial divisions and personal evangelism.

During the twentieth century, with its two world wars and innumerable "police actions," Baptists also confronted questions relative to peacemaking.* This issue met with various responses from Baptist organizations and individuals, some of whom affirmed nonviolence and pacifism, others of whom upheld the duty of citizens to support their country in military service, even to the sacrifice of their lives. The Baptist Peace Fellowship of North America* is one organization that seeks to address these issues for Baptists and the broader community.

As noted earlier, African-American Baptists were at the forefront of the civil rights movement of the twentieth century. It should also be noted that other Baptists, specifically Anglo-Saxons, exercised various responses to the movement, from indifference to militant opposition. In the South many white churches divided over racial issues, notably over whether to admit African-Americans to membership.

Baptists and Education

Baptists have both promoted and strongly disagreed over issues related to education and educational institutions. In one sense Baptists have emphasized the importance of education, establishing institutions of higher learning throughout the country. In another sense they have been suspicious of education, sometimes fearing that schooling—at least the wrong kind—would undermine individual faith and church doctrine. Perhaps the most divisive question has involved the meaning of a Christian or Baptist educational institution and its responsibility to its constituents. Debate over this issue began with the founding in 1821 of Columbian College,* the first Baptist educational institution, and debate continued on the way to the twenty-first century. Institutions such as Brown University,* the University of Chicago,* Franklin College,* Furman University,* Baylor University* and Samford University* (to mention only a few) demonstrate the Baptist concern for education since the early days of the American republic. Theological schools such as Andover Newton Theological School,* Union Theological Seminary (New York),* Southwestern Baptist Theological Seminary,* Conservative Baptist Theological Seminary* and Mid-America Baptist Seminary* reflect the doctrinal and ecclesial similarities and differences within the Baptist family.

Baptists: Identity in the Twenty-first Century

Baptists face the twenty-first century with the same challenges that confront most other religious groups in the United States and Canada. They encounter a populace in which religious nonaffiliation increases annually. Even among the religiously affiliated, fewer religious Americans think of their primary religious commitment in terms of a denominational identity. Denominational loyalties are increasingly less significant, and denominational mechanisms are fragmenting, or at least changing rapidly. Responses vary. Some congregations continue to function according to traditional denominational-ecclesiastical practices and procedures. Others already minimize their "Baptistness" in order to reach a broader constituency. Many are uncertain which way to turn and how to adapt to changing times and cultural realities. Whatever the response, it is clear that a significant ecclesiastical transition is under way.

Through it all, individuals, congregations, denominations and other Baptist institutions are asking what it means to be Baptist and whether such an identity has meaning for a new century. Many wonder how to pass on a tradition or identity to a new generation and what exactly that identity should involve. Given these realities, perhaps there is no better time to produce a reference book such as this. At its best, this dictionary offers resources for identifying where Baptists have been and how they shaped and were shaped by Holy Scripture, history and the world around them. It may also contribute to a renewed sense of identity on the way to the future.

In another two centuries, perhaps Baptists will continue to make "much ado" (as Peter Cartwright said) about such things as baptism by immersion. If they do not, at least they can hope they know what they have lost and why.

BIBLIOGRAPHY

S. E. Ahlstrom, *A Religious History of the American People* (1972); N. T. Ammerman, *Baptist Battles* (1990); R. A. Baker, *The Southern Baptist Convention and Its People, 1845-1972* (1974); W. W. Barnes, *The Southern Baptist Convention, 1845-1953* (1954); W. H. Brackney, *The Baptists* (1988); W. H. Brackney, ed., *American Baptist Quarterly,* June 1985; J. M. Dawson, *Baptists and the American Republic* (1956); D. Dockery, *Southern Baptists and American Evangelicals* (1994); H. Dorgan, *Giving Glory to God in Appalachia: Worship Practices of Six Baptist Subdenominations* (1987); J. L. Eighmy, *Churches in Cultural Captivity,* rev. ed. (1988); L. Fitts, *A History of Black Baptists* (1985); R. G. Gardner, *Baptists of Early America: A Statistical History* (1983); J. L. Garrett Jr., E. G. Hinson and J. E. Tull, *Are Southern Baptists "Evangelicals"?* (1983); D. J. Garrow, *Bearing the Cross: Martin Luther King Jr. and the Southern Christian Leadership Conference* (1986); E. S. Gaustad, *Baptist Piety: The Last Will and Testimony of Obadiah Holmes,* rev. ed. (1994); C. C. Goen, *Broken Churches, Broken Nation* (1985); B. J. Leonard, *God's Last and Only Hope: The Fragmentation of the Southern Baptist Convention* (1990); W. L. Lumpkin, *Baptist Confessions of Faith* (1959); W. G. McLoughlin, *Soul Liberty: The Baptists' Struggle in New England, 1630-1833* (1991); N. H. Maring and W. S. Hudson, *A Baptist Manual of Polity and Practice,* rev. ed. (1992); M. E. Marty, *Pilgrims in Their Own Land* (1986); T. J. Nettles, *By His Grace and for His Glory: A Historical, Theological and Practical Study of the Doctrines of Grace in Baptist Life* (1986); M. A. Noll, *A History of Christianity in the United States and Canada* (1992); J. L. Peacock and R. W. Tyson Jr., *Pilgrims of Paradox: Calvinism and Experience Among the Primitive Baptists of the Blue Ridge* (1989); E. L. Queen II, *In the South the Baptists Are the Center of Gravity* (1991); W. B. Shurden, *Associationalism Among Baptists in America, 1707-1814* (1980); J. T. Titon, *Powerhouse for God: Speech, Chant and Song in an Appalachian Baptist Church* (1988); J. M. Washington, *Frustrated Fellowship: The Black Baptist Quest for Social Power* (1986).

B. J. Leonard

Notes

[1]Peter Cartwright, *The Autobiography of Peter Cartwright* (New York: Phillips and Hunt, 1856), pp. 133-34.

[2]Frank S. Mead and Samuel S. Hill, *Handbook of Denominations in the United States,* 9th ed.(Nashville: Abingdon, 1990), pp. 34-58; and Edwin S. Gaustad, *Historical Atlas of Religion in America,* rev. ed. (New York: Harper & Row, 1976).

[3]Walter B. Shurden, *Not a Silent People* (Nashville: Broadman, 1972).

A

Aberhart, William ("Bible Bill") (1878-1943). Radio pioneer and premier of Alberta. Born in Ontario and trained as a schoolteacher, Aberhart first emerged into prominence as a Baptist Bible teacher in Calgary, Alberta. His weekly classes on dispensationalism filled the downtown Grand Theatre and were broadcast to a radio audience that was estimated at 350,000. When the Depression came, Aberhart shifted his attention to the economic and political needs of the province and founded the Social Credit Party on the ideas of Englishman C. H. Douglas. With Aberhart devoting much time in his weekly broadcasts to politics, the party won two provincial elections (1935 and 1940). Aberhart died in office, having introduced reforms in the areas of education and farm relief. His increasingly unorthodox theology, egocentricity, sectarianism and, especially, involvement in politics had eventually alienated him from large numbers of evangelicals. But the Social Credit Party remained in power in Alberta until 1971.

BIBLIOGRAPHY. W. Aberhart, *The Douglas System of Economics* (1933); J. A. Boudreau, *Alberta, Aberhart and Social Credit* (1975); D. R. Elliott and I. Miller, *Bible Bill: A Biography of William Aberhart* (1987).

J. G. Stackhouse

Abernathy, Ralph David (1926-1990). African-American civil rights leader and Baptist pastor. Born in Linden, Alabama, on March 11, 1926, the grandson of a former slave, Abernathy was reared on a nearly self-sufficient farm. He announced his call to the Baptist ministry at the Hopewell Baptist Church in Linden in 1948 and later graduated from Alabama State College (B.S., 1950) and Atlanta University (M.A., 1951).

In 1950 Abernathy became pastor of Eastern Star Baptist Church in Demopolis, Alabama, and sociology instructor and dean of men at Alabama State College. Later that year he became pastor of the historic First Baptist Church in Montgomery, where the Baptist Foreign Mission Convention* had been founded in 1880. Along with Martin Luther King Jr.* he helped to start the Montgomery bus boycott in 1955 and the Southern Christian Leadership Conference* (SCLC) in 1957. In 1961 Abernathy moved to Atlanta, the headquarters of the SCLC, and assumed the pastorate of West Hunter Street Baptist Church, where he served from 1961 to 1983.

When King was assassinated in 1968, Abernathy, his closest friend and associate, assumed the presidency of SCLC and the leadership of the Poor People's Campaign. In 1977 he resigned as president of SCLC to run for political office. After years of silence, in 1989 Abernathy authored a controversial book, *And the Walls Came Tumbling Down* (1989), in which he accused King of plagiarism and sexual indiscretion. He died on April 17, 1990, in Atlanta.

BIBLIOGRAPHY. R. D. Abernathy, *And the Walls Came Tumbling Down* (1989); *EBA;* C. D. Lowery and J. R. Marszalek, eds., *Encyclopedia of African-American Civil Rights* (1992).

L. H. Williams

Abolition Movement, Baptist. Postrevolutionary Baptists like David Barrow, John Leland* and Robert Carter provided precedents for later abolitionism. In 1785 the Baptist General Committee of Virginia pronounced slavery "contrary to the word of God." Two years later the Ketockton Association called for gradual emancipation, but protests led the association "to take no further steps in the business." Antislavery Baptists in Kentucky formed the Friends of Humanity and opposed the introduction of slavery into border states. But by the 1830s proslavery influence and Baptist caution about involvement with civil matters had driven most antislavery voices away from the·South. In 1831 William Lloyd Garrison* became an increasingly heterodox Baptist voice among abolitionists, but eventually Baptists and other "Christian abolitionists" parted company with the Garrisonians.

The Baptist movement developed through four phases. During the Inception phase (1831-1840) the abolitionists attempted to win the Triennial Convention* to their views via correspondence and resolutions. The Schism phase (1840-1845) saw abolitionists disrupt denominational balance by increasingly refusing fellowship with slaveholders, refusing support for mission boards and forming many antislavery organizations and "come-outer" sects. In the 1830s black Baptist associations (Providence and Union in Ohio, Wood River in Illinois) included antislavery activities, while Elon Galusha* and Cyrus Grosvenor led white Baptist agitation. In April 1840, whites formed the American Baptist Anti-Slavery Convention,* while in August of the same year blacks formed the American Baptist Missionary Convention.* Others, led by Leonard A. Grimes of Boston, formed the American and Foreign Baptist Missionary Society (later renamed the American Baptist Free Mission Society). Conflict between these groups and proslavery forces culminated in the schismatic formation of the Southern Baptist Convention* in 1845. During the Purgative phase (1845-1865) abolitionists continued agitating to purge slaveholders from churches in border states, helping to move the churches closer to their principles by the end of the Civil War. In the Reconstruction phase (1865-1870) Baptists shifted their concern to the plight of the freedpersons.

BIBLIOGRAPHY. J. Brewer, *Holy Warriors: The Abolitionists and American Slavery* (1976); T. R. Cheatham, "The Rhetorical Structure of the Abolitionist Movement Within the Baptist Church, 1833-1845" (Ph.D. dissertation, Purdue University, 1969); H. L. McBeth, *The Baptist Heritage* (1987); J. R. McKivigan, *The War Against Proslavery Religion* (1984); J. Washington, *Frustrated Fellowship* (1986).   A. M. Manis

Adams, Theodore Floyd (1898-1980). Pastor, educator and leader in the Baptist World Alliance.* Born in Palmyra, New York, the son of a Baptist minister, Adams graduated from Denison University* (B.A., 1921) and Colgate Rochester Divinity School* (B.D., 1924). Ordained in 1924, he served as pastor of the Cleveland Heights Baptist Church in Cleveland, Ohio (1924-1927), and the Ashland Avenue Baptist Church in Toledo, Ohio (1927-1936), before accepting the pastorate

of the historic First Baptist Church of Richmond, Virginia, where he remained as pastor (1936-1968) and pastor emeritus (1968-1980) until his death. For a decade (1968-1978) he taught preaching at Southeastern Seminary.

Adams's balanced ministry at Richmond stressed missions,* pastoral care and social concern. He conducted a daily radio program for twenty-six years and became involved in television locally and nationally. An active trustee of Virginia Union University (from 1941) and the University of Richmond* (from 1942) for almost four decades, he encouraged the founding of Richmond Memorial Hospital (1957) and chaired its board. Adams received ten honorary doctorates and many awards. He served the Baptist World Alliance on its executive committee (1934-1980), as vice president (1947-1950) and as president (1955-1960). He published four books, including *Baptists Around the World* (1967).

BIBLIOGRAPHY. J. W. Carlton, *The World in His Heart: The Life and Legacy of Theodore F. Adams* (1985).   C. L. Howe

Adelphia College. Swedish Baptist* educational institution. Begun as a high school in Seattle in the fall of 1905 under the leadership of scholar-educator Emanuel Schmidt, Adelphia's long-range plans included a four-year college course, a school of theology, and commercial and music departments, the latter two of which were implemented. A preparatory department was added in 1906-1907 for students who had not completed grade school. The five students who enrolled in 1905 increased to thirteen for the fall of 1906 and to twenty-seven during the 1906-1907 school year; in subsequent years enrollment generally ranged between about fifty and ninety. Highlights included the building of Adelphia (1906) and Schmidt (1910) Halls, the first graduates (1909) and the granting of permanent accreditation by the University of Washington (1911-1912). However, despite good enrollment, a qualified faculty and an attractive campus, Adelphia succumbed to financial problems brought about by World War I and by the loss of several supporters, and it ceased operations after the 1917-1918 school year.

BIBLIOGRAPHY. E. Schmidt, "Adelphia College: An Historical Sketch and Annual Reports" (manuscript, n.d.); A. M. Swedberg, "A Short History of Adelphia College" (manuscript, n.d.).

N. A. Magnuson

African Baptist Assembly. Indigenous African Baptist organization. The African Baptist Assembly (ABA) was established by Daniel S. Malekebu, a medical missionary who headed the Providence Industrial Mission (PIM) in Chiradzulu, Nyasaland (present-day Malawi), and was sponsored by the National Baptist Convention, U.S.A. (NBC). Malekebu, a Zulu, had been converted in 1902 under the leadership of John Chilembwe, who had founded the PIM in 1901. In 1915 Chilembwe led an unsuccessful revolt against British colonial authorities. He was executed, and the PIM burned to the ground.

In 1926 the authorities allowed the PIM to reopen under Malekebu's leadership. Malekebu had been trained in the United States in an NBC school, Selma University, and at Meharry Medical College. In 1945 Malekebu founded the ABA, which was patterned after the NBC, and a constitution was adopted. The ABA brought various tribes together as one group, created a sense of Christian fellowship and developed a major degree of self-determinism. Consisting of 20,000 members by 1972, the ABA became one of the strongest Christian organizations in Africa. In 1974, under the leadership of L. C. Muocha, the African Baptist Assembly of Malawi was accepted as a member of the Baptist World Alliance.* By 1982 the ABA consisted of 474 churches with over 40,000 members.

Malekebu died on October 8, 1978, in Blantyre, Malawi, at nearly ninety-two years of age. A few months earlier, three ministers of the ABA had brought suit against the NBC, claiming ownership of the PIM, 492 churches and two farms. But the NBC produced a deed dating to 1902 and proof that Malekebu was a retired employee. On October 12, 1978, the high court ruled in favor of the NBC.

BIBLIOGRAPHY. W. J. Harvey, *Bridges of Faith Across the Seas: The Story of the Foreign Mission Board National Baptist Convention, U.S.A., Inc.* (1989); G. Shepperson and T. Price, *Independent Africa* (1958).

L. H. Williams

African Baptist Congress. Indigenous African Baptist organization. The African Baptist Congress (ABC) was established by Daniel S. Malekebu, a medical missionary who headed the Providence Industrial Mission (PIM) in Chiradzulu, Nyasaland (present-day Malawi), and was sponsored by the National Baptist Convention, U.S.A. (NBC; *see*

National Baptists). Malekebu, a Zulu, had been converted in 1902 under the leadership of John Chilembwe, who founded the PIM in 1901. In 1915 Chilembwe led a revolt against British colonial authorities, but the uprising was aborted. Chilembwe was executed, and the PIM burned to the ground.

In 1926 the authorities allowed the PIM to reopen under Malekebu's leadership. Malekebu had been trained in the United States in an all-black Baptist school, Selma University, and at Meharry Medical College. A 1949 NBC report mentioned a group of more than 300,000 African Baptists in Nyasaland, the Rhodesias, Portuguese East Africa and the Union of South Africa (the latter alone claimed 5,000 members). In 1952 Malekebu founded the ABC, which was patterned after the NBC, consisting of 1,000 churches with 300,000 members. A 1971 NBC report listed 200,000 members, and 450 churches in Malawi alone.

Malekebu died on October 8, 1978, in Blantyre, Malawi. According to Davis Lee Saunders, a retired Southern Baptist missionary, Malekebu's attempt to develop an all-African Baptist Congress had been at best tenuous. But at present there is a small group of indigenous African Baptists that meets annually for an evangelistic conference lasting for several days.

BIBLIOGRAPHY. C. C. Adams and M. A. Talley, *Negro Baptists and Foreign Missions* (1949); E. A. Freeman, *The Epoch of Negro Baptists and the Foreign Mission Board* (1953); D. L. Saunders, "A History of Baptists in East and Central Africa" (Th.D. dissertation, Southern Baptist Theological Seminary, 1973); G. Shepperson and T. Price, *Independent Africa* (1958).

L. H. Williams

African United Baptist Association. Canadian Black Baptist Convention. In 1854 Richard Preston called a meeting of twelve local black Baptist churches in the province of Nova Scotia; this meeting led to the founding of the African United Baptist Association (AUBA). Like Preston, the majority of AUBA's members were refugees from slavery in the United States. As early as the 1830s, Nova Scotian blacks had developed a great degree of community solidarity, usually with a Baptist church at the center. A provincial association was a logical step in developing their religious, social and educational life. In a sense, they organized "American-based Baptist [mutual] aid societies and . . . racially self-conscious associations," part of a trend that had begun earlier among blacks in the United States.

Nova Scotia also had a sizable black Baptist population. By 1897 the AUBA could claim twenty-two churches and 2,440 members. By 1911, 90 percent of Nova Scotia's blacks were Baptists, and by the 1950s the organization's name had been changed to the Colored Baptists of Nova Scotia. By 1961 well over 10 percent of the province's Baptists were blacks, and presently the association claims a membership of over 10,000.

BIBLIOGRAPHY. P. Oliver, *Brief History of the Colored Baptists of Nova Scotia, 1782-1953* (1953); J. W. St. G. Walker, "The Establishment of a Free Black Community in Nova Scotia, 1783-1840," in *The African Diaspora,* ed. M. L. Kilson and R. I. Rotberg (1976); R. W. Winks, *The Black in Canada: A History* (1971).

L. H. Williams

Alien Immersion. A term still used by many Baptists in the South to refer to baptism* by immersion administered by non-Baptists. Although the term was used before the rise of the Landmark movement* in the mid-nineteenth century, it came to prominence through the exclusivistic ecclesiastical theories of J. R. Graves,* J. M. Pendleton* and A. C. Dayton.*

Landmarkers stressed baptism more than any other issue in their ecclesiology.* Graves and others insisted that since only Baptist churches and ministers are valid, only baptism administered in the context of a local Baptist church is valid. Landmark leaders were particularly troubled because some Baptist churches were accepting members who had been immersed only by pedobaptists or Campbellites.

BIBLIOGRAPHY. *BHH* 10, no. 1 (1975); J. E. Barnhart, "Alien Immersion," *ERS* (1984); J. R. Graves, *Old Landmarkism: What Is It?* (1880).

M. G. Bell

Alliance of Baptists. An organization founded by disaffected Southern Baptists* in 1986 to advocate their understanding of Baptist principles.

In response to the fundamentalist takeover of the Southern Baptist Convention beginning in 1979 (*see* Fundamentalism), opponents, known as "moderates," had organized politically to regain control. After several unsuccessful attempts, a group of moderates sought to devise an alter-

native strategy. After preliminary meetings, on December 2, 1986, in Charlotte, North Carolina, twenty-three persons officially organized the Southern Baptist Alliance (SBA) and adopted the following statement of purpose: "The Southern Baptist Alliance is an alliance of individuals and churches dedicated to the preservation of historic Baptist principles, freedoms and traditions and the continuance of our ministry and mission within the Southern Baptist Convention." The SBA dropped the last phrase, "within the Southern Baptist Convention," in 1991 and changed the name to The Alliance of Baptists in 1992.

The group adopted a covenant* setting forth its principles at its next meeting, February 2-3, 1987, and on February 12, in simultaneous news conferences in Atlanta, Charlotte and Raleigh, publicly announced the formation of the Southern Baptist Alliance with Henry Crouch of Charlotte as its first president. The organization was governed by a board of directors and met annually in convocations, the first being in May 1987 in Raleigh, North Carolina.

By 1988, 2,106 individual members and forty member churches added up to a membership of 23,256, and Alan Neely of Wake Forest, North Carolina, was named interim executive director. On January 1, 1989, Stan Hastey of Washington, D.C., became permanent executive director. The same year the SBA launched the Baptist Theological Seminary at Richmond,* and membership climbed to a total of 43,611. The group promulgated its principles, published two books, *Being Baptist Means Freedom* and *The New Has Come,* supported various mission and ministry causes, sought to be inclusive in all its work and entered into dialogue with other Baptists. Support grew steadily; in 1991 the SBA reached a total membership of 71,989 with receipts of $387,191.

Following the founding of the Cooperative Baptist Fellowship* in 1990-1991, however, both membership and financial support began to wane. The two organizations were engaged in dialogue, and many thought the two should merge, with SBA becoming a part of the Cooperative Baptist Fellowship. By the end of 1992 the future of the Alliance was uncertain.

BIBLIOGRAPHY. A. Neely, "The Alliance of Baptists: Remembering Our History" (paper presented at Mercer University, Macon, Georgia, October 8, 1992).

G. T. Halbrooks

Alline, Henry (1748-1784). Evangelist and leader in the First Great Awakening* in Nova Scotia. Born in Rhode Island, he moved to Nova Scotia in 1760. In 1775 he underwent an intense personal conversion that was to form the basis of his preaching. He was a charismatic figure, and his preaching during the American Revolution advanced a revival in Nova Scotia. His sermons were emotional, poetic and characterized by an anti-Calvinism (see Calvinism) that stressed perseverance, free grace and asceticism. He appealed particularly to Yankee expatriates, insisting that the religious outburst in Nova Scotia at the time of the war in New England was proof that God had blessed his adopted land. He published two books, but they did not have the same level of influence as his preaching. His hymns and songs were highly influential. A small edition of twenty-two songs was issued during his lifetime, and a larger compilation of nearly 500 compositions was published after his death and went through several editions. After his death, his New Light message was largely eclipsed by more traditional Calvinism.

BIBLIOGRAPHY. J. Beverley and B. Moody, *The Life and Journal of the Rev. Mr. Henry Alline* (1982); J. M. Bumsted, *Henry Alline: 1748-1784* (1971); G. A. Rawlyk, *Ravished by the Spirit* (1984); G. A. Rawlyk, ed., *New Light Letters and Songs* (1983); G. A. Rawlyk, ed., *The Sermons of Henry Alline* (1986).

H. W. Pipkin

American Baptist Anti-Slavery Convention. Early convention opposing slavery. Emancipationist calls from William Lloyd Garrison* (1831), British Baptists (1833 and 1838) and the New Hampshire Baptist Anti-Slavery Society (1838) led 110 Baptists from thirteen states to form the first national antislavery organization of Baptists. The first annual session was held April 28-30, 1840, at the McDougal Street Baptist Church in New York City, after 700 Baptists requested antislavery action in the denomination. The new convention elected Elon Galusha* as president and Cyrus P. Grosvenor as vice president and sent antislavery addresses to Baptists in both the North and the South. To Northerners they argued the obligation of Baptists to support immediate emancipation and the withdrawal of fellowship from Baptists who did not reject the "evil of slavery." They called upon Southerners to confess "the sin of slaveholding" and warned that if they remained deaf to calls for justice, "we cannot and we dare not recognize you as consistent brethren in Christ." Southerners reacted to such "officious intermeddling" with the warning that "we cannot cooperate with those who stigmatize and excommunicate us."

Other annual sessions followed in 1841 (Boston and New York City), 1842 (Boston) and 1843 (Boston). The convention's strategy focused on separatism. Charles W. Denison served as a special agent traveling among fellow Baptists organizing local denominational antislavery societies. In 1842 a committee was founded to collect and distribute funds for missionary activities from church members no longer willing to cooperate with slaveholders in the regular societies. Mutual threats of nonsupport from both abolitionists and Southern "hot-heads" eventually culminated in denominational schism in 1845.

BIBLIOGRAPHY. T. R. Cheatham, "The Rhetorical Structure of the Abolitionist Movement Within the Baptist Church, 1833-1845" (Ph.D. dissertation, Purdue University, 1969); C. C. Goen, *Broken Churches, Broken Nation* (1985); J. R. McKivigan, *The War Against Proslavery Religion* (1984).

A. M. Manis

American Baptist Association. Landmark* Baptist organization. The formation of the American Baptist Association in Arkansas in 1905 was the culmination of the struggle of Landmarkism in the Southern Baptist Convention* (SBC). In the 1850s Landmarkism, under the leadership of J. R. Graves,* advocated an ecclesiology that emphasized the local church. Its tenets included that Baptist churches are the only true churches; the true church is a local, visible institution; the churches and the kingdom of God are coterminous; valid ordination* derives from a Baptist church; only valid ministers can administer the Lord's Supper* and baptism;* Baptist churches have an unbroken historical succession back to the New Testament; missionary work is to be done by local churches rather than convention boards.

In 1899 Landmarkers formed their first state organization, the East Texas Baptist Convention, later known as the Baptist Missionary Association* (BMA). With Samuel A. Hayden as its most prominent leader, the BMA was outspoken against the SBC and its method of carrying out missionary work through a convention rather than through local churches.

In 1902 Arkansas's "anticonvention" forces rallied against the state convention and formed the General Association of Arkansas Baptists in 1902. Under the dynamic leadership of Ben M. Bogard,* an attempt was made in 1905 to convert the SBC to Landmark views regarding mission methods. Although the attempt failed, Bogard's movement absorbed smaller Landmark bodies, including the BMA of Texas, and was renamed the American Baptist Association in 1924. With headquarters in Texarkana, Arkansas, the ABA operates several schools, a seminary in Little Rock and a publishing house. In the late 1980s there were over 1,700 affiliated churches and an inclusive membership of approximately 250,000.

BIBLIOGRAPHY. E. G. Hinson, *A History of Baptists in Arkansas* (1979); H. L. McBeth, *The Baptist Heritage: Four Centuries of Baptist Witness* (1987).　　　　　　　　　　　　C. D. Weaver

American Baptist Bill of Rights. During the rise of totalitarian regimes in Europe in the 1930s, various Baptist groups became concerned about religious liberty.* The issue was heightened amid the planning for the 1934 meetings of the Baptist World Alliance* in Berlin, Germany.

In 1939 representatives of the Northern Baptist Convention,* the Southern Baptist Convention* and the National Baptist Convention (*see* National Baptists) created and jointly issued the "American Baptist Bill of Rights." It was intended to be a manifesto to the world of the basic rights of every person to religious liberty.

Seizing upon historic Baptist statements, the document called for "full religious liberty" for Protestants, Catholics, Jews and everyone else. Separation of church and state, voluntariness in religion and individual spirituality were hallmarks of the statement. Opposition to a diplomatic mission at the Vatican came as a response to the announced position of the Franklin D. Roosevelt administration to establish closer ties.

The "Bill of Rights" was a significant precursor to the work of what became the Baptist Joint Committee on Public Affairs* (1973).

BIBLIOGRAPHY. *American Baptist Bill of Rights* (Philadelphia: Joint Committee on Publications, 1940); W. H. Brackney, ed., *Baptist Life and Thought, 1600-1980: A Sourcebook* (1983).
　　　　　　　　　　　　W. H. Brackney

American Baptist Churches in the USA. Major Baptist denomination formerly known as the American Baptist Convention (1950-1972) and the Northern Baptist Convention (1907-1950). On May 17, 1907, delegates from local churches, Baptist state conventions and city mission societies of the Northern United States, leaders of the American Baptist Foreign and Home Mission Societies* and the American Baptist Publication Society* met at Calvary Baptist Church in Washington, D.C., to organize formally the Northern Baptist Convention. Charles Evans Hughes, governor of New York, was elected the first president of a loosely federated body of churches and benevolent organizations dedicated to "better and more coherent action as a purely advisory body."

From the establishment of the first Baptist congregation in America at Providence, Rhode Island, about 1638, Baptists had cherished the local governance of their churches. Even with the creation of the first regional association of churches in New England in 1670 (General* Six Principle* Baptists) and Philadelphia in 1707 (Philadelphia Baptist Association*), each local congregation was said to have complete power and authority from Jesus Christ. Gradually, in the second half of the eighteenth century, Baptists had grown in numbers and sought to cooperate in evangelism, missions* and educational enterprises. Permanent organizations beyond local churches evolved slowly. In general, associations gathered as confessional bodies for fellowship and mutual support and to review and debate matters of concern.

Beginning in 1802, modeled on English Baptist and American Congregationalist bodies, Baptists in New England organized a series of benevolent societies to advance the denominational interests. Until 1845, when the Southern Baptist Convention* was formed, these societies represented congregations in the South and West as well. An organizational principle of voluntary individual membership (*see* Voluntarism) with independent charters dominated Baptist life in the Northern states throughout the nineteenth century. This was in marked contrast to the more centralized convention model that Baptists in the Southern states created in 1845.

The driving impulse of Baptists in the North from 1814 was foreign missions. The first national body was organized that year as the General Baptist Missionary Convention, which soon grew to include a college, a seminary and domestic mission endeavors. In 1824 the Baptist General Tract Society was organized (later the American Baptist

Publication Society* and Sunday School Society), and in 1832 the American Baptist Home Mission Society* started in New York City. Women's missionary societies were chartered in the 1870s, and separate conferences for ethnically and racially diverse peoples emerged, beginning in 1851, for German, Swedish, Danish-Norwegian, Italian and Hispanic Americans. Sometimes overlapping in programs, often competing in stewardship drives, the Baptist society model in the North was focused sharply on the local churches, which jealously guarded their autonomy. After financial exigency threatened around 1900, interagency agreements and planning meetings eventually led to the creation of a unified Northern Baptist Convention (NBC) in 1905.

After organization, the leaders of the NBC took some bold steps in ecumenism* and centralization. In 1911 the convention became a charter member of the Federal Council of Churches of Christ* and the International Faith and Order Movement. The same year a merger was effected with the Free Will Baptist* General Conference. Structurally, Northern Baptists created boards for ministerial pensions and education and commissions for stewardship, missions and social service. Controversy ensued over these rapid advances, and by 1920 the convention delegates found themselves embroiled in self-destructive debates between the modernists and fundamentalists (see Fundamentalism). Clusters of churches in the Northeast, Ohio Valley and Oregon left the convention and organized new theologically conservative associations that prevented binding legislative action beyond the local congregations. The main body of Northern Baptists in 1922 assumed a mediating position, affirming the New Testament as the "all-sufficient ground of faith and practice."

In the era of World War II, Northern Baptists looked for a new theme and a revival of denominational life. Following a review commission report, delegates to the 1950 annual meeting of the convention voted to change their name to American Baptist Convention (ABC) and to create an Office of the General Secretary. An open invitation was given to other Baptist bodies to unite with the ABC and achieve a national Baptist body. While many congregations in the black Baptist traditions achieved a dual alignment status and the convention negotiated an associated relationship with the Church of the Brethren, no organic union took place. Instead, American Baptists have participated in more collegial efforts, such as the Baptist World Alliance* and the Baptist Jubilee Advance* in 1964. In 1972 a second major revision of American Baptist denominational structures was adopted, and a new, more connectional polity resulted in the American Baptist Churches in the USA (ABC-USA). A greater share of authority was given to the regional bodies and local churches, with policy matters being ratified by a more democratic General Board, composed of clergy and laity. The older national societies became program boards of the convention, with interlocking directorates and common annual meetings. A series of "covenants of relationships" unite the interests, tasks and resources of sixty distinct regional, national and general organizations.

As of 1988, the ABC-USA claimed 5,805 churches and 1,568,778 members in all fifty states. About 800 congregations were dually aligned with one or more of the black Baptist or mainline Protestant groups. Of the 7,678 ordained clergy that the ABC recognized, 434 were women in ministry. Theologically, American Baptists are broadly evangelical,* with churches and pastors representing conservative, neo-orthodox and liberal* traditions.

Denominational interests are coordinated at the national offices in Valley Forge, Pennsylvania, and at thirty-seven regional, state and city locations across the United States. Churches in a region or state generally meet annually in conventions, while elected convention delegates, representatives to the general board and program administrators hold a biennial meeting in various cities throughout the United States and Puerto Rico. There are fifteen colleges or universities, six theological schools and 122 homes, children's centers and hospitals affiliated with the denomination. The official periodical, The American Baptist, is said to be the oldest Christian magazine continuously in print in North America.

See also AMERICAN BAPTIST FOREIGN MISSION SOCIETY; AMERICAN BAPTIST HOME MISSION SOCIETY; AMERICAN BAPTIST SEMINARY OF THE WEST; JUDSON PRESS; NORTHERN BAPTIST THEOLOGICAL SEMINARY.

BIBLIOGRAPHY. W. C. Bitting, ed., A Manual of the Northern Baptist Convention (1918); W. H. Brackney, The Baptists (1988); W. H. Brackney, ed., Baptist Life and Thought, 1600-1980: A Sourcebook (1983); R. G. Torbet, History of the Baptists (1963); Yearbook of the American Baptist Convention, 1920-1987.

W. H. Brackney

American Baptist Convention. *See* AMERICAN BAPTIST CHURCHES IN THE USA.

American Baptist Education Society. A society of Northern Baptists (*see* American Baptist Churches in the USA) charged with varying dimensions of education for the denomination. The antecedent of the society was the American Baptist Education Commission, founded in 1868. The society was organized in 1888 and continued its active operation until about 1903.

The "Policy of the American Baptist Education Society" was adopted by the executive board of the society on May 17, 1889. The first annual meeting of the society was held in Chicago that same year. Among the responsibilities of the society were attention to educational architecture, establishing relations with already existing local education societies and encouraging those states without them to form them, encouraging university education, and fostering a college in each state and also secondary-level academies. In general the society was charged with arousing the greatest possible local interest in institutions of learning. The society was to make inquiry into the conditions and needs of Baptist education and to advocate the best ways of meeting those needs. The society was influential in the founding of the University of Chicago,* receiving a grant of $100,000 by John D. Rockefeller for that purpose. It became a society of the Northern Baptist Convention after 1912. The membership was composed of all persons who were continuous members of the society and all accredited delegates to each annual meeting of the Northern Baptist Convention. It was thereafter administered by a board of managers.

BIBLIOGRAPHY. *Minutes of the American Baptist Education Society*, 1889ff.

H. W. Pipkin

American Baptist Foreign Mission Society. The name given to the foreign mission enterprise of American Baptists between 1826 and 1846, and again from 1910 to the present.

With the founding of the General Missionary Convention of the Baptist Denomination in the United States of America for Foreign Missions, popularly known as the Triennial Convention,* Baptists laid the groundwork for a system of national voluntary societies. In 1817 that body's mandate was expanded to include "other worthy objects of the Redeemer's kingdom," which really meant domestic missions and a college. Financial difficulties ensued, however, in the early 1820s, and a retrenchment plan put forward by Francis Wayland* and others was approved in 1826. The General Missionary Convention became a voluntary society, based on the New England model, and the offices of the American Baptist Foreign Mission Society (ABFMS) were moved from Washington, D.C., to Boston.

The society in its antebellum phase conducted its work by a board of managers of twenty-nine persons plus salaried agents from time to time. Its mission fields included Burma, Liberia, India, Siam, Europe, China and Native Americans. At its peak, a total of ninety-eight missionary personnel and ninety-five native assistants were employed.

Once the division over the slavery issue was resolved and the Southern Baptist Foreign Mission Board was organized, the society reconstituted itself as the American Baptist Missionary Union.* Because foreign missions was the unifying heritage of the Baptists of the North, the concept of a society was found to be inadequate.

In 1910, however, after reorganization of its executive staff, and partly to recover its heritage as the oldest Baptist mission agency in the United States, the Missionary Union reverted to its original name, American Baptist Foreign Mission Society.

In the early twentieth century, discussions of a merger with the Women's American Baptist Foreign Mission Society began, and finally in 1954 the two bodies were integrated. As American Baptists in the 1960s again became disenchanted with the society model of organization, further reorganization took place, and the Study Commission on Denominational Structures recommended the creation of new "program divisions." Although ABFMS remained the corporate title, in 1973 the work of the society was transferred to the Board of International Ministries of the American Baptist Churches in the USA.

See also MISSIONS, BAPTIST VIEWS OF.

BIBLIOGRAPHY. R. G. Torbet, *Venture of Faith: The Story of the American Baptist Foreign Mission Society and the Women's American Baptist Foreign Mission Society, 1814-1954* (1955); H. C. Vedder, *A Short History of Baptist Missions* (1927).   W. H. Brackney

American Baptist Home Mission Society. The American Baptist Home Mission Society (ABHMS) is an outgrowth of Baptist foreign mission work and the national voluntary society movement (see Voluntarism).

The society's roots lie in the Massachusetts Baptist Missionary Society and its support for missions in the Mississippi Valley. John Mason Peck* and James Welch, among others, were inadequately supported by the General Missionary Convention and the Massachusetts Society at the close of the 1820s. Moreover, other agencies, notably the American Home Missionary Society (Congregationalist), were moving into the West, to the concern of Baptists. In 1832, Peck solicited Eastern assistance and urged action. At an adjourned session of the national Triennial Convention* at New York in 1832, the American Baptist Home Mission Society was formed.

The slavery issue badly divided the society's work in the 1840s, and ultimately Southern Baptists withdrew to form their own board. Work with Native American tribes was the most seriously interrupted. After the resolution of the slavery issue, however, the managers of the society turned to missions among Native Americans, new church development in the Far West and immigrant missions with the Chinese, Germans, Danish-Norwegians, Swedish and inner-city groups. Following quickly on emancipation, the society launched a regionwide effort in the Southern states to educate freedmen, starting over twenty schools, colleges and academies. Often the ABHMS work ran into difficulty with Southern Baptist* interests; in 1898 a comity agreement was reached, which defined the territory of the South, the West and the Caribbean for each group.

In the post-World War II era, the society responded to much change. Competition for constituency resources led to integration of the Woman's American Baptist Home Mission Society* and the ABHMS in 1955. Under the influence of Jitsuo Morikawa, new understandings of evangelism led to a witness to corporate America and new ventures in campus ministry. The Latin American fields were transferred to the Foreign Mission Society in 1971, and with denominational reorganization in 1972-1973, the society transferred its work to the Board of National Ministries, ABCUSA.*

See also MASSACHUSETTS BAPTIST MISSIONARY MAGAZINE; MISSIONS, BAPTIST VIEWS OF.

BIBLIOGRAPHY. G. P. Beers, Ministry to Turbulent America: A History of the American Baptist Home Mission Society Covering Its Fifth Quarter Cen-

tury, 1932-1957 (1957); C. L. White, A Century of Faith (1932).

W. H. Brackney

American Baptist Men. A men's society affiliated with the American Baptist Churches in the USA.* First called National Council of Northern Baptist Men, it arose from a fundraising drive for the denomination in 1917. A permanent organization was created in 1922. Its main emphasis at first was strengthening denominational finances, but it aimed to become a grassroots organization with broader purpose. Leadership is provided by volunteers, but an executive director plays an important role.

The objectives of the organization are to help men into a vital relationship with Jesus Christ, to broaden understanding of the mission of the denomination and to motivate men to practice their ministry at home, at work, in the community and in church life. Fellowship and evangelism are major interests, but members of American Baptist Men have undertaken many projects, such as helping to acquire the American Baptist Assembly at Green Lake, Wisconsin, supporting the Laymen's Hour, moving ABC headquarters to Valley Forge, Pennsylvania, and developing a database to match volunteer skills with mission needs.

N. H. Maring

American Baptist Missionary Convention. The American Baptist Missionary Convention (ABMC) was the first convention of black Baptists in the United States. It was a direct link in African-American Baptist development between the Providence, Ohio, Baptist Association (1834) and the National Baptist Convention (1895; see National Baptists). Organized in August 1840 of congregations mainly in Eastern cities, the convention drew together antebellum black Baptists to address successively antislavery, Reconstruction and black leadership concerns.

Disenchantment with the white conventions on foreign missions and their inability to take an unequivocal stand against slavery led black leaders like Jeremiah Asher* and Sampson White to call for an all-black, antislavery body to handle missions and later chaplaincy during the Civil War. Essentially built on the voluntary society model, the convention encouraged cooperation with the major northern Baptist benevolent societies. At its peak of influence in 1865, the ABMC included about fifty churches and a dozen related organizations. It was to give opportunity to a generation of black leaders who would emerge as national figures in the black church after the Civil War.

During Reconstruction, overtures were made from the predominantly white societies to the several black conventions and organizations to merge efforts. Leaders of the American Baptist Missionary Convention, however, favored an all-black organization and voted to negotiate with the other principal black body, the Northwestern and Southern Baptist Convention.* This merger took place congenially in late 1866 with the formation of the Consolidated American Baptist Missionary Convention.

BIBLIOGRAPHY. J. R. McKivigan, *The War Against Proslavery Religion: Abolitionism and the Northern Churches, 1830-1865* (1984); J. M. Washington, *Frustrated Fellowship: The Black Baptist Quest for Social Power* (1986).

W. H. Brackney

American Baptist Missionary Union. The American Baptist Missionary Union (ABMU) was the successor to the American Baptist Foreign Mission Society* following the reorganization of 1846. As much as any other body, the union helped to regather northern Baptists with a moral resolve in mission. By the 1860s the union was the principal component of the anniversary or annual meetings which gave form to Baptist denominationalism in the Northern states. Among the accomplishments of the union were the adoption in 1874 of the Livingstone Interior Mission in Africa, which became a primary mission field for American Baptists. The outstanding figure of the late nineteenth century was Adoniram Judson Gordon,* a Boston pastor who was elected president of the union in 1871 and served for twenty-three years. Also noteworthy was the application of the Social Gospel* under John Clough* to the Telugu work in India and a church-related educational system for China.

BIBLIOGRAPHY. E. F. Merriam, *The American Baptist Missionary Union and Its Missions* (1897); R. G. Torbet, *Venture of Faith: The Story of the American Baptist Foreign Mission Society and the Women's American Baptist Foreign Mission Society, 1814-1954* (1955).

W. H. Brackney

American Baptist Publication Society. Among the various efforts in the Baptist network of voluntary societies (see Voluntarism) was the publication of literature. Although some Baptists were willing to support the American Tract Society and the American Sunday School Union, the majority of leaders preferred a separate Baptist organization, mainly because of the issue of believer's baptism.*

In 1824 Luther Rice,* Noah Davis and George Wood began the Baptist General Tract Society in Washington, D.C. This was intended to be an important link in Rice's vision for a national Baptist denominational presence in the capital. By the 1830s, however, several associations and leading pastors wanted to expand its ministry.

In 1839 the Hudson River Association proposed that a Baptist Sunday-school union be formed. This led to a reorganization of the Tract Society as the American Baptist Publication and Sunday School Society in 1841. Although the society's first priority was Sunday schools, the words "and Sunday School Society" were dropped from the name in 1845 (see American Baptist Publication Society). The new national society operated from Philadelphia, where it constructed extensive facilities. In 1856 the board of managers purchased the extensive library of the New England Sabbath School Union, making it the largest voluntary organization of its kind in the era.

The society pioneered a system of "colporteurs," derived from a French practice of traveling booksellers. These agents were often local pastors or part-time missionaries who distributed the society's material across the country and in Europe and started Sunday schools and churches. The Publication Society became, therefore, a missionary agency in its own right.

An epoch of significant expansion began in the 1840s with the appointment of John Mason Peck* as corresponding secretary and J. Newton Brown* as book editor. Peck slashed the administrative budget and dramatically increased the number of missionary colporteurs. Brown increased the inventory of popular works like Bunyan's *Pilgrim's Progress* and produced a spate of new materials, including polity manuals, a model church covenant* and confession of faith,* statistical reports, and the first Baptist hymnal (see Hymnody) in the United States. One of the most far-sighted actions of this era was the establishment in 1853 of a historical department, later to become the American Baptist Historical Society.

Under the able leadership of Benjamin Griffith, which began in 1857, the society developed a unique distribution program that included colporteur wagons, boats, sleds, and eventually, in conjunction with the Home Mission Society, railroad cars and airplanes. A missionary department for tracts and books in non-English languages was started, as was a newspaper, *The National Baptist*. Griffith relied heavily on his relatives in the John P. Crozer* family for financial support in launching these endeavors. Griffith also supervised the construction of commodious headquarters in downtown Philadelphia, making that city a national center of Baptist life in the United States.

In 1891 the Baptist Young People's Union* began as an outgrowth of the Publication Society. Again, Benjamin Griffith was in the forefront in responding to the success of other interdenominational groups like the United Society of Christian Endeavor.

The society reached another high point in the 1940s under Luther Wesley Smith's leadership. Smith persuaded J. L. Kraft, a Chicago dairy processor, to provide funds to purchase a bankrupt luxury hotel at Green Lake, Wisconsin, which became the American Baptist Assembly in 1944. The society also merged with the Northern Baptist Board of Education in 1944 to become the American Baptist Board of Education and Publication.

In the reorganization of the American Baptist Convention in 1972, the work of the Board of Education and Publication was folded into the Board of Educational Ministries, ABCUSA.* The Publication Society's corporate name has been retained.

BIBLIOGRAPHY. L. T. Slaght, *Multiplying the Witness: 150 Years of American Baptist Educational Ministries* (1974); D. G. Stevens, *The First Hundred Years of the American Baptist Publication Society* (1925).

W. H. Brackney

American Baptist Seminary of the West. An American Baptist theological seminary affiliated with the Graduate Theological Union (GTU) in the San Francisco Bay area. It is a federation of Berkeley Baptist Divinity School and California Baptist Theological Seminary (CBTS). CBTS was founded in 1944, largely at the instigation of Frederic I. Drexler. Classes were first held at Temple Baptist Church of Los Angeles. The school, which had both a college division and a graduate theological seminary, moved to Covina, California, in 1951. Recognized by the American Baptist Convention in 1958, it was to be "evangelical, academically sound and committed to the Baptist tradition." CBTS was fully accredited in 1962 by the American Association of Theological Schools.

In 1967 a unified board was formed with Berkeley Baptist Divinity School. The Berkeley school was a merger of California College, founded in 1871, and the Pacific Coast Theological Seminary (1884). It had moved to Berkeley in 1904 and was named Berkeley Baptist Divinity School in 1912. It was known for its emphasis on the pastorate and on mission service. On December 27, 1968, the American Baptist Seminary of the West (ABSW) was incorporated as a degree-granting institution.

A distinctive feature of ABSW is its commitment to multicultural programs in preparation for ministry. Two degree programs of ABSW, the master of divinity and the master of arts in religion, are fully accredited by the Association of Theological Schools. ABSW has a Covenant of Cooperation with New College for Advanced Christian Studies, Berkeley, which was established in 1977 as a graduate school for professionals who want to deepen their understanding of Christian life and faith.

BIBLIOGRAPHY. American Baptist Seminary of the West, *Catalogue, 1990-92.*

H. W. Pipkin

American Baptist Theological Seminary. African-American Baptist seminary in Nashville, Tennessee. The seminary was established in 1924 and is jointly owned and supported by the National Baptist Convention, Inc. (*see* National Baptists), and the Southern Baptist Convention.* The initial proposal was first presented in 1913 by E. Y. Mullins,* president of the Southern Baptist Theological Seminary.* World War I and divisions among National Baptists delayed the opening of the school. The original organization involved joint ownership and a board of trustees elected from the National (four trustees) and Southern Baptist (eight trustees) conventions. Southern Baptists contributed over $10,000 per year to the school during the first twenty years of its history. In 1978 the two conventions agreed to form a board of trustees consisting of thirty-two persons, half from the National and half from the Southern Baptist convention. They also established a holding board of eight Southern Baptists and four National Baptists.

BIBLIOGRAPHY. *ESB* 1:43-44; 4:2081-82.

B. J. Leonard

American Bible Society. Nondenominational organization dedicated to distributing the Bible throughout the world. The American Bible Society (ABS) was founded in New York City in 1816. At the time of its formation some 130 Bible societies had already sprung up in twenty-four states or territories. Their purpose was chiefly to supply Americans, especially the many immigrants, with Bibles in their own languages. Although some Bibles were published in America prior to 1816, the American societies received most of their Bibles from the British and Foreign Bible Society.

As the number of societies in America increased, there was a call for a national association that would function as an umbrella for the many regional societies. At first this move was strongly opposed by some local societies, particularly by the Philadelphia Bible Society. However, in May 1816 delegates from the regional societies met in New York and formed the American Bible Society. The British and Foreign Bible Society served as a model for this new organization. Elias Boudinot was chosen as first chairman of the board, which was composed mainly of Christian laymen. The purpose of the ABS was to offer help to the existing societies, not to replace them. Regional societies were encouraged to join the "parent" society (ABS) as auxiliaries. Within a year forty-one societies had become auxiliaries of ABS. The ABS was designed to supply the regional agencies with Bibles and money. The "daughter" societies acted as agents for the ABS, not only in the distribution of the Scriptures but also in the collecting of monies. Eventually, however, most of these auxiliaries disappeared.

As time went on the ABS began to see its mission in other lands more clearly. Working in close cooperation with missionaries of various denominations, the ABS has now printed Bibles in more than a thousand tongues. In 1986 the ABS distributed 289,486,970 Bibles and portions of Scripture. The ABS headquarters are in New York. On the initiative of the ABS, the United Bible Society was formed in 1946 to serve as an umbrella organization over the national societies.

BIBLIOGRAPHY. C. Lacy, *The Word Carrying Giant* (1977).

D. Ewert

American Bible Union. Nineteenth-century Baptist Bible society. The American Bible Union grew out of a controversy over the translation of the Greek verb *baptizō*, which the King James Version translates as "baptize" and Baptists wished to translate as "immerse." The controversy split the American Bible Society* (ABS) and dragged on for more than a decade. The occasion for the controversy was the work of British Baptists in Calcutta, who asked the ABS for help in publishing a second edition of the Bengali New Testament after the British and Foreign Bible Society turned them down because of its policy not to print sectarian versions.

In 1835 the ABS appointed a commission to look into the matter. But the issue created a schism in the ABS board to the embarrassment of all sides, for the battle was fully reported in the secular press. However, the ABS held firm to its policy not to publish sectarian versions and insisted that the Greek verb *baptizō* was simply to be transliterated in English.

The Baptists then formed the American and Foreign Bible Society in 1836. This name offended the ABS, and there was acrimonious debate when both societies applied for a government charter in 1841. Among Baptists too there was sharp disagreement on the name of the Baptist society and on the new society's publication policies. Out of this controversy the American Bible Union was born on June 10, 1850, with the financial backing of William Colgate* and with Spencer Cone, former secretary of ABS, as president.

The policy of the American Bible Union was to circulate "only such versions as are conformed as nearly as possible to the original text." Its avowed object was "to procure and circulate the most faithful versions of the Sacred Scriptures in all languages throughout the world." The rift between Baptists and the ABS was eventually healed, and Baptists in various conventions resumed their earlier place among the most loyal supporters of the ABS.

BIBLIOGRAPHY. J. Edmunds, *Discussion on Revision of the Holy Oracles* (1856); C. Lacy, *The Word Carrying Giant* (1977); W. H. Wyckoff, *Documentary History of the American Bible Union,* 4 vols. (1857-1867).

D. Ewert

Americans United for Separation of Church and State. An organization promoting a policy of strict separation of church and state. Americans United for Separation of Church and State (AUSCS; also called Protestants and Other Americans United for Separation of Church and State) began as a coalition of liberals and conservatives, under the leadership of the Southern Baptist Joseph Dawson,* who opposed the Supreme Court's decision in *Everson* v. *Board of Education* (1947) to allow federal assistance in transporting children to parochial schools. In that year the group issued a manifesto that clearly stated its rejection of any use of public funds for religious purposes, its opposition to any efforts to breach the "wall" of separation between church and state, and its belief that the greatest threat to religious liberty* lay in "clericalism," or the manipulation of political power by churches for their own ends. Not surprisingly, this view of church-state relations brought the AUSCS into frequent conflict with the Catholic Church. This conflict came to a head during John F. Kennedy's 1960 presidential campaign, when AUSCS issued its "questions for a Catholic candidate," which called for the candidate to clarify his stance on the relationship of church and state.

AUSCS experienced rapid growth under Glen Archer, who served as executive director from 1948 to 1975. It now claims a membership of 50,000, with headquarters in Washington, D.C., and 115 local chapters. In addition, it maintains an archive of some 30,000 volumes on church-state issues and seeks to educate the public on the importance of church-state separation for religious freedom. These include a monthly magazine, *Church and State,* books, pamphlets, films, speakers and a yearly national conference. It has also been involved in lobbying efforts in Washington, D.C., and in various court cases involving alleged violations of separation of church and state.

BIBLIOGRAPHY. L. P. Creedon and W. D. Falcon, *United for Separation: An Analysis of POAU Assaults on Catholicism* (1959); C. S. Lowell, *Embattled Wall—Americans United: An Idea and a Man* (1966).   R. P. Hesselgrave

Anabaptists. Free church movement originating in Zurich, Switzerland, but soon appearing in varying manifestations throughout Europe. The Swiss reformer Ulrich Zwingli (1484-1531) carried out his reformation of the Zurich church in cooperation with the city council. Several of his more radical followers, including Conrad Grebel (c. 1498-1526) and Felix Manz (c. 1498-1527), became impatient with the pace and nature of the reform. Streams of anticlericalism combined with regional calls for local control of economic and church life brought urban radicals and rural agitators into a cooperative effort. They urged Zwingli toward a more thoroughgoing reform, one that would not be tied to a quest for the approval of the civic authorities.

Eventually the question of baptism emerged as a central issue; the radicals fruitlessly called on Zwingli to give up infant baptism in favor of believer's baptism, which they understood to be the New Testament practice. The first adult believers' baptisms were carried out in the home of Manz's mother on January 21, 1525. Over the next few weeks and months several dozen such baptisms were administered to adult believers on the basis of their repentance and confession of faith. The city council saw these acts as rebaptisms—the term *anabaptist* means "rebaptizer"—and hence illegal. The council carried out a largely successful campaign against the believer's baptism movement in Zurich, culminating in the execution by drowning of Manz on January 5, 1527. The movement did spread, however, throughout German-speaking Switzerland.

The Anabaptist reformation was not limited to Switzerland. The same impulses that produced Anabaptism in Zurich eventually emerged elsewhere in similar though not causally connected forms. The south German reformer Balthasar Hubmaier (c. 1480-1528) instituted an Anabaptist reformation in the city of Waldshut in April 1525. Forced out of the city by the Hapsburg rulers, he spent a short time in Zurich in prison before making his way to Nikolsburg in Moravia. There he pastored an Anabaptist community and wrote numerous pastoral and theological works. He was captured and burned at the stake in Vienna in February 1528. Another form of Anabaptism was also prevalent in Moravia, that of the Hutterian or communitarian Anabaptists, known for their holding goods in common and for their missionary work. Other Anabaptists in central Europe included the itinerant leaders Hans Denck (c. 1500-1527), Hans Hut (d. 1527) and Pilgrim Marpeck (d. 1556).

Another center of Anabaptist activity was in northern Europe, especially from Strasbourg to the Netherlands. A dominant figure among these Anabaptists was Melchior Hofmann (c. 1495-1543), an earlier follower of Luther who spent the last years of his life in prison in Strasbourg. Noted for his apocalyptic ardor and near-docetic Christology, Hofmann fueled much of the fervor for radical Christianity in the second generation of the movement. An extreme form of Anabaptism was found in the Anabaptist kingdom of Münster in Westphalia, which was crushed by the princes in 1536. After Hoffman and Münster, the major leader of northern Anabaptism was Menno Simons (c. 1496-1561), whose consistent and stable leadership proved decisive in the emergence of a largely peaceful form of Anabaptism.

There was considerable diversity among the Anabaptists. Many practiced community of goods; most did not. Most second-generation Anabaptists were nonviolent and suffered considerable persecution from the mainline churches, both Protestant and Catholic. A true, pure church was a major concern, one that would be free from moral impurities. Religious liberty was foundational to the Anabaptists, and their commitment to a church free from governmental influence eventually laid the foundation for the separation of church and state in later times. Morally earnest Christians, they tended toward ethical legalism even as they stressed discipleship. Most tended toward a very strict reading of the New Testament as the basis for their views.

Baptist scholars disagree as to the relationship between Anabaptists and the Baptist movement. Some claim more direct ties, while others point to a more "spiritual kinship."

BIBLIOGRAPHY. C. J. Dyck, gen. ed., *Classics of the Radical Reformation* (1973-); W. R. Estep, *The Anabaptist Story* (1975); G. H. Williams, *The Radical Reformation* (1992).

H. W. Pipkin

Anderson College. An institution of higher education of the South Carolina Baptist Convention. Anderson College was opened as a four-year college for women in 1912 after several attempts to establish higher educational institutions for women in Anderson had failed. In an effort initiated by the Chamber of Commerce in 1910, the South Carolina Baptist Convention was offered thirty-two acres of land and 100,000 if it would open a college in Anderson. The convention accepted the offer, appointed trustees and obtained a charter in 1911.

The college operated as a four-year institution for women until 1930, when it became a two-year college. Annie Dove Denmark became president of Anderson in 1928 and was the first woman to serve as president of a college in South Carolina. It was due to her tight financial management that

the school survived the Depression. In 1931 men were admitted for the first time as day students. Anderson continued as a coeducational junior college until 1990, when it secured permission from the South Carolina Baptist Convention to become a four-year institution. The first bachelor's degrees to be granted since 1930 were awarded in 1992.

BIBLIOGRAPHY. H. I. Hester, *They That Wait: A History of Anderson College* (1969); J. King, *A History of South Carolina Baptists* (1964).

G. Clayton

Andover Newton Theological School. Seminary located in Newton Centre, Massachusetts, and related to both the American Baptist Churches in the USA* and the United Church of Christ. The product of affiliation (1931) and formal merger (1965) between two of the oldest seminaries in the United States, Andover Newton represents a continuous tradition of scholarship and innovation in the preparation of persons for ministry. Founded in 1807 by orthodox Congregationalists who objected to Harvard's liberal drift, Andover Theological Seminary* was the first professional school for the training of clergy in New England; Newton Theological Institution,* established nineteen years later, was the first Baptist graduate institution. Both were influential in creating national standards for modern theological education, including the "professional" faculty and the familiar three-year course of diversified graduate study.

The combined schools have continued to provide national leadership in theological education, in 1931 beginning the first program of clinical pastoral education in the United States. During the 1970s Andover Newton initiated a pioneering project in the area of lay ministries, established the internationally known "teaching parish" method for field education and became one of the first institutions in the country to offer the doctor of ministry (D.Min.) degree. During the 1980s the school committed itself to becoming a "multiracial, multicultural, international" institution by establishing black and Hispanic ministries programs and a required course dealing with racism, sexism and other divisive social issues.

Presently Andover Newton maintains close ties with both affiliated denominations, although members of the United Church of Christ predominate. The student and faculty population is strongly ecumenical, composed of representatives from over forty different religious bodies; the school intentionally seeks to provide a forum for serious theological discussion between liberals and conservatives. Andover Newton is a participant in and founding member of the Boston Theological Institute (1968), a consortium of nine theological schools in the Boston area, and shares cooperative programming with Boston and Emmanuel Colleges, both Roman Catholic institutions.

See also ANDOVER THEOLOGICAL SEMINARY; NEWTON THEOLOGICAL INSTITUTION.

BIBLIOGRAPHY. Andover Newton Theological Seminary, *Catalog 1992-1993.*

E. C. Nordbeck

Andover Theological Seminary. The first graduate school in New England for the training of clergy, founded by a coalition of "Old Calvinist" and "New Divinity" Congregationalists in 1807 to counter Harvard's drift toward Unitarianism. Andover was a pioneer in "professionalizing" modern theological education; its founders emphasized advanced biblical studies and replaced the typical system of ministerial apprenticeship with a demanding three-year regimen of graduate work led by faculty with different theological specialties. Here the modern missionary movement began, and throughout the century a disproportionate number of Andover men staffed mission posts worldwide.

Located in northeastern Massachusetts on the campus of Phillips Academy (a preparatory school where boys had learned "true Piety and Virtue" since 1778), Andover initially educated zealous Congregationalists as well as a few Baptists and young men of other denominations eager to uphold the bulwarks of orthodoxy. To ensure the latter, faculty were required to subscribe to the famous Andover Creed, an essentially Calvinist document with Hopkinsian modifications. By the end of the century, however, Andover's faculty— like Congregationalists in general—had largely abandoned the Calvinism* of the institution's founders and openly embraced liberal theological ideas. The famous "Andover controversy" of the 1880s, centering on the doctrine of "future probation" as it related to missions, brought notoriety to the school and a decline in enrollment.

In 1908, prompted by a desire to broaden the curriculum and offer instruction in a less isolated environment, the trustees voted a move to Cambridge and a plan of affiliation with Harvard Di-

vinity School; the institutions were to share resources but remain structurally separate. In 1922 plans to merge the two schools were legally voided, however, when Andover's board of visitors invoked the ancient (and long-ignored) requirement that faculty subscribe to the Andover Creed. Freed from this requirement by the courts in 1931 after a five-year suspension of programming, the Andover trustees accepted an invitation to affiliate with Newton Theological Institution. Known thereafter as Andover Newton Theological School,* the two institutions shared resources for more than thirty years while remaining legally separate. During this period the student body grew, with Congregationalists replacing Baptists as the dominant group; the combined faculties gained a national reputation for scholarly excellence and innovation in areas such as clinical pastoral education and pastoral counseling. In 1965 a formal merger was effected.

See also ANDOVER NEWTON THEOLOGICAL SCHOOL.

BIBLIOGRAPHY. J. K. Morse and Jedidiah Morse, *A Champion of New England Orthodoxy* (1939); L. Woods, *History of Andover Theological Seminary* (1884).

E. C. Nordbeck

Anthony, Alfred Williams (1860-1939). College professor and Free (Will) Baptist* minister. A native of Providence, Rhode Island, and a 1883 graduate of Brown University,* Anthony received his theological training at Cobb Divinity School and the University of Berlin. After pastoring Essex Street Free Baptist Church in Bangor, Maine, from 1885 to 1888, he taught New Testament at Cobb from 1890 to 1908. From 1908 to 1911 he taught Christian literature and ethics at Bates College in Lewiston, Maine. He served as special joint secretary of the General Conference of Free Baptists and the American Baptist Foreign Mission Society* (1911-1915), contributing to the eventual merger of Free Baptists and Northern (later renamed "American") Baptists. From 1912 to 1916 he also chaired a commission on state and local federations under the auspices of the Federal Council of Churches. Between 1918 and 1923 he served as executive secretary of Northern Baptists' Home Missions Council. Throughout this time he was also a trustee of Bates College and the now-defunct Storer College. Anthony wrote several books, including *An Introduction to the Life of Jesus* (1896), *The Method of Jesus* (1899), *The Conscience and Concessions* (1918) and *Bates College and Its Background* (1936), as well as many brochures and pamphlets on church and denominational administration.

A. M. Manis

Antimission Movement. An intense movement, primarily on the American frontier in the early nineteenth century, objecting to organized denominational efforts to send missionaries. The movement was centered among Baptists.

Two important Baptist antimission statements were the Kehuckee* Declaration (1827) and the Black Rock Address (1832). In the Kehuckee Declaration, churches in a North Carolina association voted to "discard all Missionary Societies, Bible Societies, and Theological Seminaries." Five years later, ultraconservative churches meeting at Black Rock, Maryland, issued a statement condemning all missionary societies, Bible societies, Sunday schools, church colleges and seminaries, and protracted meetings.

Antimissions seldom stood alone; almost always those who opposed missions also opposed other "modern innovations" such as Sunday schools, theological education, revival meetings and even Bible societies that printed and distributed Christian literature. Motives for the antimissions movement varied. Some objected because their extreme Calvinism,* with its emphasis on predestination, led them to believe mission activity was irrelevant. Others feared that the denominational organization needed for missionary work might compromise the independence of each church. Some objected to the financial basis of missions, while others feared that the educational standards required for mission appointees might reflect badly on the uneducated frontier preachers.

Leaders of antimissionism included John Taylor,* Alexander Campbell* and Daniel Parker.* Taylor grew up in Virginia and later became a prosperous farmer-preacher in Kentucky. His 1819 pamphlet *Thoughts on Missions* ridiculed missionary societies and their appointees and greatly retarded mission work on the frontier.

Campbell, best known for his "reformation" which led to the Church of Christ movement, objected to missionary societies because no such organization is specifically mentioned in the Bible. Through his preaching and his paper *Millennial Harbinger,* Campbell wielded great influence on the frontier.

Parker issued a monthly paper, the *Church Advocate,* in which he opposed missions, theolog-

ical education and all other "human efforts" for the gospel. His 1826 publication *Views of the Two Seeds* gives his most extreme antimission views. Parker was active in Illinois, Tennessee and Texas and spread his views widely.

Baptists lost many churches and members to the antimission movement, but in time most Baptists accepted missionary effort. Remnants of the antimission Baptists are found today in small groups like the Primitive Baptists.*

See also CAMPBELL, ALEXANDER; PARKER, DANIEL; PRIMITIVE BAPTISTS; TAYLOR, JOHN.

BIBLIOGRAPHY. H. L. McBeth, *The Baptist Heritage* (1987); W. W. Sweet, ed., *Religion on the American Frontier: The Baptists* (1931).

H. L. McBeth

Arlington Baptist College. *See* BIBLE BAPTIST SEMINARY.

Arminianism, Baptist Views. The theological ideas attributed to the Dutch theologian Jacob Arminius have produced a variety of responses from Baptist groups in America. Free Will Baptists* have identified themselves most extensively with Arminian views. They affirm the relationship between prevenient grace, that enabling grace by which sinners reach out to God, and saving grace, by which God reaches out to sinners. They insist that Christ's atoning death was potentially for all persons (general atonement) and is actualized through repentance and faith, the terms of salvation and election. They stress the role of free will and human participation in the salvific process. Free Will and other Arminian Baptists also acknowledge the possibility that persons who freely choose grace can freely reject it later on, thus "falling from grace." Other Baptist traditions, such as the Primitive* and Old Regular* Baptists, repudiate any hint of Arminianism as a contradiction of the theology of Calvinism* and the New Testament. They deny that sinful human beings have the free will to choose grace until God has infused such grace through regeneration. Only then are repentance and faith possible.

Still other Baptist groups occupy varying degrees of middle ground regarding Arminian theology. Individuals and groups within the Southern* and National Baptist* conventions as well as the American Baptist Churches in the USA* reflect degrees of Calvinist or Arminian emphasis. For example, Southern Baptists generally reject the Arminian idea of falling from grace, preferring instead to speak of "the eternal security of the true believer." At the same time they seem most comfortable with a more Arminian approach to evangelism, missions, general atonement and the role of free will (prevenient grace) in salvation. Revivalism and other methods of mass evangelism influenced the gradual Arminianization of previously Calvinistic Baptists in American religious life. A resurgence of Reformed Baptists* reflects growing reaction against Arminianism in various Baptist churches.

See also CALVINISM AMONG BAPTISTS.

BIBLIOGRAPHY. B. J. Leonard, "Getting Saved Southern Baptist: An Evangelical Sacramentalism" (typescript, 1987); H. L. McBeth, *The Baptist Heritage* (1987).

B. J. Leonard

Armitage, Thomas (1819-1896). Baptist historian and pastor. Born in England, Armitage began his pastoral career in the Methodist Church of England in 1835 at age sixteen. Immigrating to the U.S. in 1838, he served as a Methodist Episcopal pastor in New York until 1848. He then joined the Baptist Church after becoming convinced of the doctrine of believer's baptism* by immersion. Subsequently he was pastor of Washington Avenue Baptist Church, Albany, New York (1839-1848), and served nearly forty years as pastor of the Fifth Avenue Baptist Church of New York City (1848-1896). A contemporary Baptist, William Cathcart, suggested that Armitage was "regarded by many as the foremost man in the American pulpit."

In 1850 Armitage led in the formation of the American Bible Union and served as its second president. This organization advocated translating the Greek word *baptizō* as "immersion" rather than "baptism." Armitage is best known, however, for his publication of *A History of the Baptists* (1887). While not claiming an unbroken succession of organized Baptist churches all the way back to Christ (as did the "Landmarkers"*), Armitage attempted to trace the continuation of Baptist teachings (that is, certain biblical truths) from the New Testament to the present.

BIBLIOGRAPHY. J. F. Eller, *Thomas Armitage, D.D., the Man, the Preacher, the Leader* (1896).

H. L. McBeth

Armstrong, Annie Walker (1850-1938). Leader of the Southern Baptist* Woman's Missionary Union.* Born into a prosperous, traditional Baltimore family, she joined a local Baptist church around the age of twenty. She and her sister Alice, neither of whom ever married, became involved in the woman's missionary movement* which was sweeping the country during the 1870s and 1880s. At Richmond in 1888, Annie Armstrong led the way in forming the Woman's Missionary Union. From her election as corresponding secretary in 1888 until she left that position in 1906, Armstrong continued to exert her influence in shaping the union, both in its publications and in its missionary offerings. She was instrumental in instituting the famous Lottie Moon* Christmas Offering among Southern Baptists.

Perhaps more than any other person in the convention's history, Armstrong helped advance the cause of Southern Baptist home and foreign missions. Talented, but at times struggling with her leadership role, she is representative of many late-nineteenth-century women who felt torn between the opportunities for leadership in church and society and the traditional roles of women. Today her name is honored among Southern Baptists by the Annie Armstrong Offering for Home Missions.

See also WOMAN'S MISSIONARY UNION.

BIBLIOGRAPHY. A. Hunt, *History of Woman's Missionary Union* (1976); B. Sorrill, *Annie Armstrong: Dreamer in Action* (1984).

M. G. Bell

Armstrong, Laura Dell Malotte (1886-1945). Southern Baptist* missions* leader. Armstrong served on the executive board of the Missouri Baptist General Association from 1919 to 1936 and on the executive committee of the Southern Baptist Convention from 1927 to 1945. For the last ten years she was the board's only female member. She also served as a member of the executive committee of the Baptist World Alliance.* Armstrong is best known for her leadership in the Woman's Missionary Union.* She headed the statewide organization at the Baptist World Congress in Berlin in 1934 and in Atlanta, Georgia, in 1939. As Woman's Missionary Union president and chairman of the board of trustees of its Training School, she guided the erection of a new facility outside Louisville and proposed a $10,000 fundraising drive to benefit black Southern Baptist colleges and churches.

BIBLIOGRAPHY. K. Mallory, "Mrs. Frank W. Armstrong," *Royal Service* 40 (July 1945):3-4.

M. L. Bendroth

Asher, Jeremiah (1812-1865). African-American Baptist minister who protested racial discrimination in northern Baptist churches. Born free in New Haven, Connecticut, on October 13, 1812, Asher was converted at about fourteen years of age and joined the white First Baptist Church. In 1839 this church ordained him to preach. For two months he received private instruction from Quakers in Providence.

Asher protested the segregated "Negro pew" in First Baptist Church. As a compromise, the church agreed to allow blacks to sit anywhere in the gallery. Instead, in 1840 Asher organized an independent black Baptist church out of the white First Baptist Church in Providence, Rhode Island, and served the church for nine years. He assumed the pastorate of all-black Shiloh Baptist Church in Philadelphia and built a "commodious house of worship." In 1849 Asher visited England, Scotland and Ireland and was well received in Baptist and independent churches and schools. While there, he raised $2,000 toward his church's mortgage and noticed that public and religious facilities were racially integrated. In church "he never was pointed to a corner in the gallery." Upon his return to the United States he wrote a narrative, *Incidents in the Life of the Rev. J. Asher* (1850), detailing his life experiences.

BIBLIOGRAPHY. M. C. Sernett, ed., *Afro-American Religious History* (1985).

L. H. Williams

Association of Baptists for World Evangelism. Independent Baptist* foreign mission society. The fundamentalist-modernist controversy in the Northern Baptist Convention (*see* Fundamentalism; American Baptist Churches in the USA) contributed to the formation of the Association of Baptists for Evangelism in the Orient (ABEO) in 1927. The founder, Raphael C. Thomas, a veteran medical missionary in the Philippines under the American Baptist Foreign Mission Society* (ABFMS), launched the new faith mission following disagreements with ABFMS policies on doctrine and evangelism.* In 1928 Thomas and other former ABFMS missionaries returned to the Philippines to begin their new work. At home, ABEO opened a headquarters in Philadelphia and chose Lucy Peabody* as its first president.

For over a decade, ABEO concentrated on its Philippine field. In 1939 it extended its operations into Peru and changed its name to the Association of Baptists for World Evangelism (ABWE) to reflect a new scope of ministry. During and after World War II, ABWE developed additional stations in South America and Asia. In more recent years the mission has initiated new efforts in Africa, Australia and Europe. In 1971 ABWE moved its home office to Cherry Hill, New Jersey. Today it primarily engages in church planting, theological education, medicine and Bible translation. ABWE employs over 450 full-time missionaries in over twenty countries, handles a total annual income of $10.5 million and is affiliated with the Fellowship of Missions, a fundamentalist agency (*see* Fundamentalism) based in Cleveland, Ohio.

BIBLIOGRAPHY. H. T. Commons, *Heritage and Harvest* (1981); W. W. Kempton, "The Faithfulness of God," *The Message* 45 (Spring 1987):2-5.

J. A. Patterson

Associations, Baptist. Baptists' first ecclesial bodies beyond the local church, indicating a belief in the interdependence as well as independence of the churches. Consisting of delegates from Baptist churches with a common theology, associations developed formally among both Particular* and General* Baptists in England in the 1640s and 1650s. Informal cooperation, however, may be dated as early as 1626. General Baptists established the first association in America, perhaps as early as the 1670s. But the Philadelphia Association,* founded by the Particular Baptists* in 1707, was far more influential, setting the pattern for associational life in America. Baptists adopted this pattern, called "the Philadelphia Tradition," throughout the country—the Charleston Association (1751) in the South, the Warren (1767) in New England and the Elkhorn (1785) on the Kentucky frontier. Under Shubal Stearns,* the Separate Baptists established the Sandy Creek Association in 1758 near Greensboro, North Carolina.

While the purpose of associations was often vaguely defined as "to promote the interest of the Redeemer's kingdom and the good of the common cause," four main objectives, remaining basically intact to the present, characterized the organizations: (1) to promote fellowship among the churches, (2) to maintain uniformity in faith and practice among the churches, (3) to provide counsel and assistance to the churches, and (4) to establish a structure through which churches could cooperate in their broader ministries. Practical factors were unquestionably the primary reasons for forming associations, but Baptists justified the existence of associations on biblical and theological as well as pragmatic grounds.

Meeting usually on an annual basis, early associations provided inspiration through sermons and worship, answered vexing questions (called "queries") submitted by churches and individuals, wrote to their churches "circular letters" which both reflected and shaped Baptist church life, adopted confessions of faith, warned churches of vagabond ministers, collected and preserved valuable statistical data from the churches, and developed a network of communication with other associations which fostered a denominational unity and consciousness. Most of Baptists' early advocacy of religious liberty, education and missions came through their associations.

In terms of polity, Baptists view associations as autonomous bodies functioning in an advisory role for the churches. Historically, however, associational "advice" has had muscle in it. Local churches and individual Baptists, especially in the eighteenth and early nineteenth centuries, were hesitant to spurn associational direction, if for no other reason than that they wanted to retain membership in the body. In the end, however, Baptists have always been far more interested in the freedom and independence of the local church than in extending the powers of associations and other denominational bodies. Most associational constitutions have consumed more space indicating what an association cannot do than clearly stating what it can do.

Without question, the association, next to the local church, became the most important factor in the development and organization of the Baptist denomination in America prior to the organization of the Triennial Convention* in 1814. Although still very much present in Baptist life, associations have been dislodged from their earlier prominence by the development of state, regional and national conventions.

BIBLIOGRAPHY. F. W. Sacks, *The Philadelphia Baptist Tradition of Church and Church Authority: 1707-1814* (1989); W. B. Shurden, *Associationalism Among Baptists in America: 1707-1814* (1980); B. R. White, ed., *Associations Records of the Particular Baptists of England, Wales and Ireland to 1660* (1971, 1973, 1974).

W. B. Shurden

Augusta Institute. *See* MOREHOUSE COLLEGE

Averett College. A liberal arts college in Danville, Virginia, affiliated with the Baptist General Association of Virginia (BGAV). Spawned by an antebellum educational reform movement, civic pride, missionary fervor and fear of Northern antislavery sentiment, the school opened its doors in 1859 as Union Female College. Jointly supported by three Baptist associations, the school was known as Roanoke Female College from 1864 to 1917, when the name was changed to honor two early coprincipals, brothers Samuel Wootton Averett (1873-1887) and John Taylor Averett (1873-1892). Instruction was divided into three phases: preparatory, emphasizing elementary liberal arts education, collegiate, which added courses in philosophy and sciences, and "ornamental," with a typical finishing-school emphasis on music and art.

In 1917 the school changed its status to that of junior college. During the presidency of Curtis V. Bishop (1936-1966), Averett doubled the size of its physical plant and library, and it renewed its senior college status under Conwell A. Anderson (1966-1978). In 1978 and 1979 Averett began offering master's degrees in education and business administration. By 1992, under President Frank R. Campbell (1985-), Averett had grown to 1,440 students and strengthened its connections with the BGAV.

BIBLIOGRAPHY. J. I. Hayes, *A History of Averett College* (1984).

A. M. Manis

Ayer, William Ward (1892-1985). Fundamentalist Baptist pastor, evangelist, radio and Bible conference speaker (*see* Fundamentalism). Born in Shediac, New Brunswick, Canada, Ayer ran away from home some time after the death of his mother in 1897. Converted at a 1916 Billy Sunday revival meeting in Boston, Ayer later attended Moody Bible Institute, graduating in 1919. He went on to serve Baptist churches in Mason City (c. 1919-1920) and Atlanta, Illinois (1920-1922), and Valparaiso (1922-1927) and Gary, Indiana (1927-1932), as well as the nondenominational Philpott Tabernacle in Hamilton, Ontario (1932-1936).

He is best remembered as minister of Calvary Baptist Church, New York City (1936-1949). Under Ayer's leadership the church grew from 400 to 1,600 members, with some 5,000 people professing conversion and as many as a quarter of a million persons listening to him each week over radio station WHN (later WMGM). In 1947 a radio poll to discover "New York's Number One Citizen" placed Ayer third behind Francis J. Spellman and Eleanor Roosevelt, but ahead of Harry Emerson Fosdick.* He served as trustee of Bob Jones University (which awarded him a D.D. in 1937) and Eastern Baptist Theological Seminary* and was elected the first president of the National Religious Broadcasters.

Among his more controversial views were his belief that America should take an unequivocal stand against Russian atheism, his assertion that the success of Fulton J. Sheen had been overestimated and overpublicized, and his conviction that the Roman Catholic Church was the enemy of religious liberty.* Ayer wrote ten books, among

them *Questions Jesus Answered* (1941) and *God's Answer to Man's Doubts* (1943).

Ayer resigned as minister of Calvary Baptist Church in 1949, desiring to give greater time to evangelism and Bible conference work. But he continued his radio ministry independently of the church. During his active ministry Ayer traveled widely, making evangelistic trips to England and to Central and South America. Ayer was a well-known spokesperson for fundamentalism, although he chose to work within the framework of the Northern Baptist Convention (*see* American Baptist Churches in the USA).

BIBLIOGRAPHY M. Larson, *God's Man in Manhattan* (1950).

C. A. Russell

B

Babcock, Rufus (1798-1875). Baptist minister in the North. Born in Colebrook, Connecticut, Babcock graduated from Brown University* (B.A., 1821) and studied theology under William Stoughton in Washington, D.C., while serving as a tutor at Columbian College* (1821-1823). Babcock was active in a variety of leadership roles in American Baptist* life in the first half of the nineteenth century. He served as pastor in Baptist churches at Poughkeepsie, New York (1823-1826), and Salem, Massachusetts (1826-1833), before becoming the second president of Waterville College of Maine (now Colby College) from 1833 to 1836. He later served as pastor of Spruce Street Baptist Church, Philadelphia (1836-1840), followed by a pastorate in Paterson, New Jersey (1840-1875).

Babcock served as president of the American Baptist Publication Society* and corresponding secretary of the American Bible Society* and the American Sunday School Union. A prolific writer, he founded and edited from 1841 to 1845 *The Baptist Memorial,* a monthly journal that encouraged an awareness of denominational heritage through biographical sketches and current religious news. Other works included *Memoirs of Andrew Fuller* (1830) and *Forty Years of Pioneer Life: Memoir of John Mason Peck* (1864). His major contribution to his denomination was in advocating interdenominational cooperation in areas of common mission, an emphasis that helped Northern Baptists overcome their sectarian tendencies.

BIBLIOGRAPHY. H. S. Burrage, *History of Baptists in Maine* (1904); *DARB; NCAB* 8.

C. D. Weaver

Backus, Isaac (1724-1806). Baptist minister and champion of religious liberty* during the Revolutionary era. Born in Norwich, Connecticut, into the ruling elite of Puritan Connecticut, he imbibed the principles of Calvinism* as a New England farm boy and learned that religious training and the laws of the state maintain the good order of society. The crumbling of these social foundations came in the 1740s with the turbulent Great Awakening. Seventeen-year-old Isaac was "born again" without unusual emotion, but he confessed that he was "enabled by divine light" to see "the riches of God's grace."

Backus soon plunged into itinerant evangelism. Near Middleborough, Massachusetts, he found a gathering of converts who were anxious to have a revivalistic pastor, so he was ordained* to serve the church. Slowly he came to Baptist beliefs. After agonizing prayer* and intense Bible study he, along with six fellow church members, was immersed on profession of faith in Christ. For five years the Titicut church tried to live in peace as a mixed fellowship. But finally Backus followed his conscience and, with his wife and four others, formed a Baptist church, the First Baptist Church in Middleborough.

Freed of his indecision, Backus plunged into evangelistic tours, pastoral responsibilities and, most importantly, the cause of religious freedom. As spokesman for the Warren Association of Baptists, Backus wrote tracts, drew up dozens of petitions and carried on a constant warfare of words in newspapers, public disputes and private letters. In 1773 his most important tract, *An Appeal to the Public for Religious Liberty Against the Oppression of the Present Day,* appeared—the best exposition of the eighteenth-century evangelical concept of separation of church and state. Backus lived to see the birth of the United States and found comfort in the nation's adoption of the First Amendment guaranteeing religious freedom. It is estimated that Backus traveled over 67,000 miles and preached nearly 10,000 sermons in the course of his nearly sixty years of ministry.

BIBLIOGRAPHY. *DAB* I; *DARB;* W. G. McLoughlin, *Isaac Backus and the American Pietistic Tradition* (1967); W. G. McLoughlin, *New England Dis-*

sent, 1630-1833: The Baptists and the Separation of Church and State, 2 vols. (1971); W. G. McLoughlin, ed., *The Diary of Isaac Backus,* 3 vols. (1979).   B. L. Shelley

Baldwin, Thomas (1753-1825). Pastor and apologist. Formerly a politician, Thomas Baldwin moved to become pastor at one of New England's premier Baptist churches, Second Baptist, Boston.

As pastor in Boston, Baldwin participated in several of the major denominational events and institutions of his long era of ministry. He was in 1802 one of the founders of the Massachusetts Baptist Missionary Society* and for the next two decades the editor of its widely circulated magazine. He was also a founder of the Newton Theological Institution* and a charter member of educational and tract societies across New England. It was his influence that caused Mary Webb* to begin the first women's missionary society in the United States.

Baldwin was one of the significant controversialists of his day. He debated with Congregationalists on matters concerning the church and baptism, holding that faith, not the covenant, was the basis of membership. In a major tract, *Christian Baptism* (1812), he argued that believer's baptism by immersion was the only valid mode. He died August 19, 1825.

BIBLIOGRAPHY. W. H. Brackney, *The Baptists* (1988); D. Chessman, *Memoir of Rev. Thomas Baldwin D.D., Together with a Funeral Sermon* (1826).   W. H. Brackney

Baptism. The initiation rite practiced by most Christian churches in which water is applied to the participant. The rite is related to certain spiritual truths bound up with one's new status, including death and new life, cleansing from sin and the presence of the Spirit.

New Testament Background and History. The term *baptism* is a transliteration from the Greek words referring to the action of washing with or plunging into (literally, "surrounding with") water. While some scholars have tried to trace the early Christian practice to various sources, including Jewish and pagan rituals, the church has claimed the New Testament precedent of Jesus' baptism by John the Baptist (Mt 3:13) and Jesus' command to baptize disciples (Mt 28:19) as the origin and authority for the Christian rite.

The practice of both John the Baptist and the early church seems to have included the dipping of the participant in the baptismal water (as in Acts 8:38-39), although it is possible that the practice of pouring water over the participant had already been introduced. In the early church the name of "the Lord Jesus" (Acts 19:5) or the trinitarian formula (Mt 28:19) was invoked at baptism, for by this rite the participant was symbolically placed "into the Lord."

The New Testament employs several models from the Old Testament to indicate the meaning of baptism, including the exodus (1 Cor 10:1-2), circumcision (Col 2:11-12) and the flood (1 Pet 3:19-20). But of greater importance for Christian baptism than these Old Testament events is the paradigm of Jesus' death and resurrection (Rom 6:3-5). The rite of baptism indicates a person's union with Christ and the spiritual realities of the forgiveness of sins (Acts 2:38; 1 Pet 3:21) and the reception of the Spirit (1 Cor 12:13).

By extension this union with Christ also includes union with the body of Christ, the church (1 Cor 12:13). It also symbolizes the confirming of a covenant with God, for the rite is an outward pledge of a person to God made possible by the salvation that comes through the resurrection of Jesus (1 Pet 3:21). This baptismal confession is subsequently reaffirmed through participation in the Lord's Supper (1 Cor 10:14-21).

In each of these senses, baptism is a visual word of proclamation, declaring the death and resurrection of Christ on behalf of sinners and the baptized person's participation in Christ. At the same time, the practice of the rite issues a call for response. The baptizing community is called to nurture its own and to complete the mandate to baptize all nations (Mt 28:19-20). Onlookers are called to make the same confession being declared by the rite. And the participant is called to walk in newness of life, reaffirming in daily living the baptismal vow (Rom 6:3-8).

In linking the participant with Christ's death and resurrection, baptism carries an eschatological orientation. It points beyond initiation into the Christian life to the process of sanctification and the continual renewal of the believer by the Spirit (Rom 8:10; 2 Cor 3:18). This process will one day result in a final, total transformation at the Lord's return (Rom 8:11; 1 Cor 15:51-57).

Specific instructions for baptism were developed in the patristic era. The *Didache,* for example, stipulated the type of water to be employed (preferably a running stream of cold water). Later writings reveal the growth of an involved initiation process, as the church sought to incorporate a large number of converts from pagan backgrounds. Sometime after the second century, the baptism of infants and the mode of sprinkling were introduced. However, believer's baptism (the rite as a profession of the personal faith of the participant) and immersion (placing the participant fully under water) continued in general use up to the Middle Ages. Eventually the sprinkling of infants gained ascendancy throughout the church, a practice that the Protestant Reformers affirmed against the so-called Anabaptists* of the sixteenth century. Nevertheless, believer's baptism and immersion have been seen as valid options by nearly all Christian traditions and are the sole practice of several Protestant groups.

Baptism in Church Traditions. Christian churches have understood the meaning of baptism in various ways. While all declare baptism to be both a divine and a human act, pedobaptist groups (those who practice infant baptism) have tended to emphasize the side of the divine action, whereas adherents to believer's baptism stress the human response. The divine agency involved in baptism is variously interpreted. According to one view, that of baptismal regeneration, the rite works regeneration as God produces through the act what baptism signifies. The Roman Catholic and Eastern Orthodox churches tie the Spirit's regenerative action closely to the act itself *(ex opere operato)*. Some Episcopalians and Confessional Lutherans understand the regenerative nature of baptism more in covenantal terms, as the rite places one within the church covenant (Episcopal) or as it constitutes God's covenantal promise of life (Lutheran). An understanding akin to baptismal regeneration is also maintained in a believer's baptism context by certain followers of the nineteenth-century American churchman Alexander Campbell.*

Traditional Roman Catholic theology speaks of the efficacy of baptism in remitting original sin and the actual guilt brought by sin. At the same time, the virtues of faith, hope and love are poured into the participant. The Orthodox Church, in contrast, speaks of the regeneration worked in baptism in terms of divinization. The participant partakes of the divine nature and from that point on carries the very life of God.

Many Protestants deny any direct correlation between baptism and the regeneration of the participant. For some, including many Lutherans, the rite is rather the sign of God's claim on an individual prior to personal response. Churches in the Reformed tradition, while accepting this emphasis, tend to see the significance of baptism in terms of covenant theology. Baptism is the sign and seal of the covenant that God makes with his people or that God's people make with their Lord. Some (like low-church Episcopalians and many Methodists) emphasize the conditional nature of this covenant, requiring future repentance and faith. Other Reformed bodies highlight the permanent nature of the covenant in the case of God's elect.

The concept of baptism as covenant is present among some who practice believer's baptism as well. However, they tend to emphasize the human response to the covenant sealed by the rite. Two alternative but interrelated outlooks on baptism have developed out of this understanding. Some describe baptism as a significant, divinely given means of responding personally to the gospel. Others view it as a public testimony to an inner spiritual transformation. In either case, baptism is linked to discipleship. It is a public affirmation of one's conscious decision to place oneself under the lordship of Jesus. For this the baptism of Jesus serves as a model, and the disciple is often said to be "following the Lord in baptism."

Related to this discussion of the theology of baptism is the question of terminology. The normal word for a sacred rite in the Orthodox Church is *mystery,* emphasizing the mystery of God's love and grace proclaimed by the church. Most churches in the Western tradition refer to the rite as *sacrament.* Although there are differences concerning the definition of the term, it is generally meant to suggest a close connection between the sign and the reality it signifies.

Many in the baptistic tradition reject the term *sacrament* in favor of *ordinance.** The word *sacrament,* they claim, carries the "magical" understanding of medieval Catholic theology, in which the rites of the church were supposed to infuse divine grace into the recipient. *Ordinance* avoids this danger. The term is derived from *ordain,* suggesting that these rites are ordained or commanded by Jesus. Participation in them, therefore, symbolizes the obedience of the disciple to the Lord and corresponds to the personal and voluntary character of the sacred practices emphasized by believer's baptism.

Some Christian groups focus more on the underlying spiritual reality symbolized by baptism than on the rite itself. In the Holiness and Pentecostal movements the baptism of the Spirit tends to be separated from water baptism entirely and linked with a "second work of grace" experienced subsequent to conversion and initiation. This experience of Spirit baptism is viewed as more significant than human rites such as water baptism. For the Evangelical Free Church of America, baptism is optional and not required for local church membership. The Salvation Army and the Society of Friends do not practice water baptism at all, the spiritual reality (Spirit baptism) has eliminated the need for its symbol.

Baptism and the American Churches. Baptism has been controversial throughout much of Christian history. Controversy has been especially acute in America, where Christian groups with widely divergent views have flourished, coexisted and competed. The debate over the role of baptism in the life of American churches goes back to colonial New England.

In the first half of the seventeenth century the Puritan settlers of Massachusetts developed a distinctive form of church life known as the "New England Way." Full communicant status in the congregations required not only the older requisites (acceptance of the doctrines of the church and baptism) but also verbal evidence of a religious experience that had made the candidate aware of his or her elect status. In this way the Puritans attempted to produce and maintain churches composed of the elect only (regenerate church membership). At the same time the Puritans sought to develop a Christian commonwealth ordered according to divine law, in which civil government acknowledged and protected true religion.

As the seventeenth century unfolded, the New England Way faced dissension and challenge. The first leading dissenter was Roger Williams.* Soon after his arrival in Massachusetts, Williams concluded that the principle of regenerate church membership required believer's baptism. Although he was banished from Massachusetts, his thinking made inroads throughout New England.

The New England Way faced other challenges as church membership declined. The Puritans had simply assumed that most of the children born to the elect, if brought into the covenant through infant baptism, would later experience a confirmation of their own elect status and thereby be eligible for church membership. When the numbers of nominal Christians swelled, however, the problem of the status of the seed of the elect became acute. In response, the Halfway Covenant was adopted in 1657, whereby those who had been baptized in infancy but who could not give evidence of election could bring their children for baptism but could not receive Communion or vote in congregational meetings.

The face of American religion was radically changed by the Great Awakening of the 1740s and the resultant rise of evangelical fervor. The Awakening led to division in the colonial churches and to the formation of separate congregations by many who were converted during the revival. The renewed commitment to regenerate church membership that characterized the Separates, or revivalists, led to a reopening of the question of baptism. Many adopted believer's baptism and eventually joined the Baptists.*

The nineteenth century was characterized by lively debates between Baptists and pedobaptists, and by the birth of new developments that affected the older denominations. One such development, the Restoration Movement, arose in western Virginia, Tennessee and Kentucky. At the turn of the century Thomas Campbell was instrumental in forming the Christian Association of Washington with the watchword "Where the Scriptures speak, we speak; where they are silent, we are silent." He and his son Alexander broke with Presbyterianism and became convinced that believer's baptism by immersion was the only scriptural initiation rite. After joining the Baptists in 1813 Alexander Campbell became a controversial leader in the region. He and his followers saw themselves as "Reformers," desiring "the restoration of the ancient order of things." Baptist leaders, however, accused Campbell of teaching baptismal regeneration. Certain churches and associations withdrew fellowship from the Campbellites, and separate Campbellite churches were organized, generally known as the Disciples of Christ or the Christian Church. A second development, the Landmark movement,* nearly divided the Southern Baptist Convention.* James M. Pendleton* in an essay raised the issue of the status of non-Baptist clergy. The Big Hatchie Association, meeting at Cotton Grove, Tennessee, in 1851, declared all non-Baptist churches to be religious societies whose clergy should not be recognized and whose members should not be addressed as "brethren." The term *Landmarkism* was derived from the republication of Pendleton's essay by James R. Graves* in 1854 under the title *An Old Landmark Reset.* The movement focused on five major doctrines: an unbroken succession of true churches from the Jerusalem Church to the Baptists, no church apart from local churches, the rejection of alien immersion (baptism administered in any church except a Baptist congregation), closed Communion (only the faithful members of the celebrating local congregation are admitted to the Lord's Supper) and a rejection of cooperative mission programs.

Although the tide in the Southern Baptist Convention had turned against the Landmarkers by 1862, the controversy simmered for many years, until a separate Landmark denomination was formed early in the twentieth century. Landmarkers continue to maintain that the divine pattern for baptism includes a proper candidate (a believer), mode (immersion), design (a picture showing forth the gospel) and administrator (one whose authority is derived from a scriptural church).

As the nineteenth century drew to a close, the debates of the earlier era began to subside. The rise of Protestant theological liberalism* led to a deemphasis on traditional doctrine and a reduction of the role of the sacraments. In liberal theology, baptism lost its stature as a regenerative rite or a sign of the covenant. Instead it was viewed as a formality for church membership or, in the case of infant baptism, a dedicatory rite for parents. Likewise the nondenominationalism of liberalism called into question the importance of church divisions based on theology or polity.

Although many of the older questions persist into the twentieth century, the outlook of baptismal controversies has been reshaped by a new interest in ecumenism. The establishment of the Faith and Order Commission in 1927 is a striking example of this shift in outlook. The work of the Commission came to a climax in a widely disseminated document, *Baptism, Eucharist and Ministry,* which seeks to articulate a basic agreement among the churches on these three topics. The understanding of baptism reflected in the document is inclusive. The act is seen as both a divine gift and a human response. Churches are invited to see believer's baptism and infant baptism as "equivalent alternatives." At the same time, faith is declared to be necessary for the reception of the salvation set forth in baptism. In the case of infants, this personal response, which is integral

to baptism, is to be offered later in the person's life. *Baptism, Eucharist and Ministry* holds forth the hope that the divisions produced or enhanced by divergent understandings of baptism can be overcome. The current cooperative mood, whether among churches committed to future organizational union or among those loosely allied in evangelical organizations, calls on all traditions to learn from each other while offering their own tradition as a contribution to the whole church.

See also GRAVES, JAMES ROBINSON; LANDMARK MOVEMENT; ORDINANCES; PENDLETON, JAMES MADISON.

BIBLIOGRAPHY. *Baptism, Eucharist and Ministry,* Faith and Order Paper 111 (1982); G. R. Beasley-Murray, *Baptism in the New Testament* (1981); C. E. Braaten and R. W. Jenson, eds., *Christian Dogmatics,* 2 vols. (1984); D. Bridge and D. Phypers, *The Water That Divides* (1977); G. W. Bromiley, *Children of Promise* (1979); A. M. Coniaris, *Introducing the Orthodox Church: Its Faith and Life* (1982); M. J. Erickson, *Christian Theology,* vol. 3 (1985); J. D. C. Fisher et al., "Baptism," *The New Westminster Dictionary of Liturgy and Worship,* ed. J. G. Davies (1986); S. J. Grenz, *Isaac Backus—Puritan and Baptist* (1983); J. A. Hardon, *The Catholic Catechism* (1966); P. K. Jewett, *Infant Baptism and the Covenant of Grace* (1978); D. Moody, *Baptism: Foundation for Christian Unity* (1967); W. M. Nevins, *Alien Baptism and the Baptists* (1951); L. H. Stookey, *Baptism: Christ's Act in the Church* (1982).

S. J. Grenz

Baptism, Baptist Views. Baptism of believers by immersion is the act that gave Baptists* their name and that has become their most visible mark. Although John Smyth,* an Englishman and their first leader of record, baptized himself and the remainder of his congregation by affusion (pouring) in Amsterdam, as was the practice of the Mennonites, both the General* and Particular* Baptists were baptizing by immersion by the year 1642. However, the Particular Baptist Confession of 1644 was the first confession* that gave explicit instructions for baptizing by immersion and explained its symbolism. Since then, Baptists have baptized only by immersion.

Contrary to popular opinion, Baptists have never insisted that baptism is necessary for salvation or that it imparts saving grace. Some Baptists have insisted that baptism is invalid unless received at the hands of one who also has been baptized by immersion. Baptists consider baptism an act of confession, of obedient discipleship and of church membership. The theological basis for baptism as generally practiced by Baptists involves responsible discipleship; there must be a degree of maturity on the part of the candidate so that the act of baptism may be preceded by repentance and personal faith in Christ. Immersion depicts dying to the old life and rising to live a qualitatively different life according to the teachings of Christ. It is a kerygmatic or gospel-proclaiming act, with the "Christ event" portrayed by the candidate in the waters of baptism. It also has eschatological significance, since it points toward the final resurrection of the believer.

In recent years a quasi-sacramental theology of baptism has been developing among some English Baptists. By default, other Baptists seem to have slipped into a rather careless pattern of accepting young children, incapable of making their own confessions of faith, for baptism. There is also an almost complete lack of understanding of baptism as a church ordinance in which baptized persons recognize their obligations as part of the community of faith. In some churches the acceptance of new members on the basis of their infant baptism has also become common. If these trends continue, it appears only a matter of time until Baptists will have forsaken their most distinguishing visible characteristic.

See also DAPTISM; ORDINANCES, BAPTIST VIEWS.

BIBLIOGRAPHY. N. Maring and W. Hudson, *A Baptist Manual of Polity and Practice* (1991); D. K. McCall, ed., *What Is the Church?* (1958).

W. R. Estep

Baptismal Font. A vessel containing water used for baptism.* The term is derived from the Latin *fons,* meaning "a spring of water." The shape and meaning of the baptismal font have changed considerably through the centuries of church history. In the early church the font was large enough for an adult to step down into it for immersion or affusion. The advent of infant baptism introduced the font as an elevated basin in which a child could conveniently be immersed. Later still the change from immersion to affusion as a mode of baptism introduced a font shaped like a small basin or a cup. The prominence of the font in church furnishings varies widely. In some traditions it is a rather ornate vessel mounted on a pedestal, while in others it is a simple small cup viewed only during baptism.

See also BAPTISM; BAPTISTERY.

BIBLIOGRAPHY. F. Bond, *Fonts and Font Covers* (1908); J. G. Davies, *The Architectural Setting of Baptism* (1962).

M. G. Bell

Baptist (the Name). The name Baptist is derived from the particular practice that distinguishes this free church communion from churches that practice pedo- or infant baptism. In the early seventeenth century, the English Baptists, although similar to separatist Puritans in many beliefs and practices, departed from them on the matter of baptism,* after determining that the normative New Testament practice was believer's baptism. At first they probably baptized by affusion, or pouring water over the head, but by the 1630s baptism by immersion became the more normal mode.

Believer's baptism had been reinstituted on the Continent by the Swiss Anabaptists* in 1525 and soon emerged throughout Europe. The term *anabaptist,* meaning rebaptizer, was a pejorative expression applied to those who eschewed the baptism of infants in favor of believer's baptism. Pedobaptists asserted that the radicals were rebaptizing those who had been baptized as children, while the baptists believed they were giving true baptism for the first time. There were imperial laws against rebaptism that called for the death penalty.

When the English Baptists began to practice believer's baptism, they were accused of being Anabaptists, a term they clearly wished to avoid. The London Confession of 1644, for example, was entitled "The Confession of Faith, of those Churches which are commonly (though falsely) called Anabaptists." The seventeenth-century anti-Baptist Thomas Bakewell wrote a polemical tract against this confession entitled "An Answer or Confutation of divers errors broached and maintained by the seven churches of Anabaptists contained in those articles of their confession of faith." For understandable reasons early Baptists preferred other terms such as Brethren or the Church of the Baptized Way, and it was only in the eighteenth century that the term came to be widely used by Baptists themselves. The German term for Anabaptist, *Wiedertäufer,* has in recent years been shortened to the simple term *Täufer* (baptizer, or baptist) and is often used by modern German-language Baptists to describe themselves.

See also ANABAPTISTS; BAPTISM; BAPTIST CHURCHES.

BIBLIOGRAPHY. H. L. McBeth, *The Baptist Heritage* (1987).

H. W. Pipkin

Baptist Argus. A weekly Baptist newspaper published in Louisville, Kentucky, from October 28, 1897, to August 10, 1919. Born in the midst of the Whitsitt* Controversy at Southern Baptist Theological Seminary,* the paper was founded by seminary professors J. R. Sampey,* A. T. Robertson* and others. Pro-Whitsitt, the *Argus* was clearly a rival paper to the *Western Recorder,* whose editor, T. T. Eaton,* was ardently anti-Whitsitt. J. N. Prestridge became editor, M. P. Hunt associate editor, and Thomas D. Osborne news editor.

Originally intended to promote all areas of Kentucky Baptist and Southern Baptist* work, the paper also became an organ of Baptists worldwide. Prestridge sent copies of the paper to prominent Baptists around the world, asking in return that they give him their news at least once a year. An editorial appeared in the January 14, 1904, issue entitled "Why Not a World's Baptist Conference?" The next year, in 1905, the Baptist World Alliance* was organized in London. By 1908 the name of the paper had been changed to *Baptist World.* In 1919 the *Western Recorder* and the *Baptist World* merged into a single paper for Kentucky Baptists, retaining the name *Recorder.*

BIBLIOGRAPHY. F. M. Masters, *A History of Baptists in Kentucky* (1953); J. R. Sampey, *Memoirs of John R. Sampey* (1947).

W. B. Shurden

Baptist Bible College. A Bible school founded and supported by the Baptist Bible Fellowship,* Springfield, Missouri. The college was established in 1950 as a result of a schism between Texas fundamentalist J. Frank Norris* and certain of his associates. The dispute began over Norris's control of the Bible Baptist Seminary founded in First Baptist Church, Fort Worth, Texas, in 1939. Norris's desire to control the seminary led to his decision to fire the president, George Beauchamp Vick,* replace most of the trustees and propose a new set of bylaws. Vick and others organized the Baptist Bible Fellowship and moved it to Springfield, Missouri. At the same time they established a new school, also in Springfield. This institution became a center for this segment of Baptist fundamentalism,* educating and helping to network succeeding generations of pastors and church workers, among them Jerry Falwell, pastor of Thomas Road Baptist Church, Lynchburg, Virginia. The school maintains a student body of almost 3,000 students. It is an accredited Bible school with primary focus on church-related vocations and fundamentalist theology.

BIBLIOGRAPHY. H. L. McBeth, *The Baptist Heritage* (1987).

B. J. Leonard

Baptist Bible Fellowship. A confederation of independent, fundamentalist* Baptist churches for mutual fellowship and encouragement. The Baptist Bible Fellowship was formed in 1950 as a result of a dispute between Texas Baptist fundamentalist J. Frank Norris* and several of his associates, including Noel Smith and George Beauchamp Vick.* The dispute centered around Norris's autocratic leadership and his control of the Bible Baptist Seminary,* a school related to the First Baptist Church of Fort Worth, where Norris was pastor. Vick and other protesters moved to Springfield, Missouri, where they founded another school, Baptist Bible College,* a newspaper, *Baptist Bible Tribune*, and a fellowship of like-minded churches.

The leaders made it clear that the organization was not a denomination but a New Testament fellowship of independent Baptist congregations. It would be, in the words of one leader, "a separate, distinct, new, independent, Fundamental, premillennial, old-fashioned, Baptist, missionary fellowship." The fellowship helped to promote independent Baptist doctrines and practices with particular emphasis on evangelism, revivals, church growth and Sunday-school attendance.

Many of the congregations associated with the fellowship—First Baptist Church of Hammond, Indiana, and Thomas Road Baptist Church of Lynchburg, Virginia—claimed to have some of the largest Sunday-school and church memberships in the United States. While making no claim to dictate policy to local churches, the fellowship reflects the fundamentalist doctrines and conservative political viewpoints that characterize its constituency. During the 1960s this included opposition to the civil rights movement, to the work of Martin Luther King Jr. and to the election of John F. Kennedy as U.S. president. While rejecting designation as a denomination, the fellowship reflects denominational elements in its support for an educational institution and its function as a source of identity and networking for independent Baptist churches and pastors.

BIBLIOGRAPHY. H. L. McBeth, *The Baptist Heritage* (1987); "Reasons for Baptist Bible Fellowship," *Baptist Bible Tribune,* June 23, 1950.

B. J. Leonard

Baptist Bible Institute. *See* NEW ORLEANS BAPTIST THEOLOGICAL SEMINARY

Baptist Bible Tribune. A fundamentalist Baptist newspaper based in Springfield, Missouri. The *Baptist Bible Tribune* was founded in 1950 as a result of a split between Texas fundamentalist J. Frank Norris* and his associates, including Noel Smith and George Beauchamp Vick.* Those who opposed Norris helped to form the Baptist Bible Fellowship* and the *Baptist Bible Tribune.* The paper's first edition appeared on June 23, 1950.

James O. Combs, the newspaper's first editor, shaped its direction as a major source of news and information for independent Baptist churches. Indeed, the paper helped to link these fiercely autonomous congregations by promoting common beliefs and practices, evangelism, church growth, and doctrinal rigorism. The paper also reflected a strongly conservative political perspective, attacking liberalism in the church and the society. During the 1960s Combs opposed the election of John F. Kennedy as a Catholic president, the civil rights movement as a violation of biblical mandates regarding the mixing of the races, and the work of Martin Luther King Jr.,* whom Combs and others accused of theological and political liberalism. The paper was also a frequent critic of the liberalism of the Southern Baptist Convention* and its sacrifice of doctrinal integrity for denominational unity. While it applauded the fundamentalist/conservative control of the SBC in the 1980s, it discouraged independent Baptist churches from joining the denomination.

BIBLIOGRAPHY. H. L. McBeth, *The Baptist Heritage* (1987); B. J. Leonard, "A Theology for Racism: Independent Baptists and the Civil Rights Movement" (typescript, 1988).　　　B. J. Leonard

Baptist Bible Union of North America. An organization of radical fundamentalists formed in 1923 as a reaction against modernism in the Northern Baptist Convention (NBC; *see* Fundamentalism; American Baptist Churches in the USA). Although the major complaint of the union was liberalism within the Northern convention, the group also included Southerners such as J. Frank Norris* and Canadians such as T. T. Shields,* who was the first president. It was felt that the NBC was under liberal control from the beginning and that the majority of graduates from Northern seminaries were liberals. Issues included modernist influences, schools, teaching

materials, evolution, the Social Gospel* and open membership. The Northern Baptist Foreign Mission Society was a major concern for the Baptist Bible Union (BBU), as was McMaster University.* "Information Concerning the Baptist Bible Union of North America with By-Laws and Aims and Confession of Faith" (1926) asserted that "the Holy Bible was written by men supernaturally inspired; that it has truth without any admixture of error for its matter" (p. 15). The New Hampshire Confession* with a premillenial emphasis was adopted.

At first the BBU was a movement, but it quickly evolved in an organizational direction as Shields gained greater influence. It was his desire to see a continentwide structure that would embrace both Northern and Southern conventions as well as Canada. But the union did not last long. A recommendation from 1932, adopted the following year, issued in the creation of the General Association of Regular Baptist Churches.*

BIBLIOGRAPHY. R. G. Delnay, "A History of the Baptist Bible Union" (doctoral dissertation, Dallas Theological Seminary, 1963).

H. W. Pipkin

Baptist Board of Foreign Missions. The foreign mission society of Baptists in the first half of the nineteenth century. After Ann* and Adoniram Judson* and Luther Rice* adopted believer's baptism on their trip to India in 1813, they moved their mission work to Burma. Adoniram Judson wrote to Boston asking if there was a Baptist missionary society that would support their work, and Rice returned to the United States to secure such support as could be found. Rice's efforts led to the creation on May 21, 1814, of the General Missionary Convention of the Baptist Denomination in the United States of Ameria for Foreign Missions, which came to be known as the Triennial Convention.*

This mission organization was in many ways the impetus to the formation of a unified Baptist denomination in America. The president of the convention was Richard Furman* of Charleston, South Carolina; the secretary was Thomas Baldwin* of Boston. The membership was open to Baptist delegates from missionary societies and other religious bodies. In 1820 a board of twenty-one commissioners to act for the convention was created. It was called the Baptist Board of Foreign Missions in the United States. This pattern continued to serve the Triennial Convention* for thirty-two years.

The organization represented certain new departures for overseas mission work. First, it was a Baptist organization, not a nondenominational one—unusual for American mission boards. Second, not only were the missionaries to be persons of mature spirituality, but they were to be in good standing with a local congregation. After the Southern Baptists* split over the issue of slavery in 1845, the name was changed the following year to the American Baptist Missionary Union. In 1910 it became the American Baptist Foreign Mission Society. The present-day successor is the Board of International Ministries, ABC/USA. In 1992 there are 156 missionary personnel in twenty-one countries representing American Baptists.

See also FURMAN, RICHARD; RICE, LUTHER; TRIENNIAL CONVENTION.

BIBLIOGRAPHY. R. G. Torbet, *Venture of Faith: The Story of the American Baptist Foreign Mission Society and the Woman's American Baptist Foreign Mission Society, 1814-1954* (1955).

H. W. Pipkin

Baptist Center for Ethics. An organization founded by moderate Southern Baptists to give attention to ethical concerns. The center was founded in 1991 to offer Baptist churches guidance on ethical issues and in response to the changing agenda of the Southern Baptist Convention's* Christian Life Commission.* Founding documents noted that it was established "in the Baptist heritage of soul freedom, local church autonomy, personal and social responsibility, while it retains an ecumenical spirit." Robert Parham was appointed the first executive director. Based in Nashville, Tennessee, the center provides a variety of services for churches, including an annual national conference on specific ethical issues, regional conferences and local church resources. A tape series for churches examines issues of the environment, peacemaking and racism. The organization also seeks to develop and facilitate new networks among Baptist groups and the broader Christian community.

BIBLIOGRAPHY. R. Parham, "The History of the Baptist Center for Ethics," in *The Struggle for the Soul of the SBC,* ed. W. Shurden (1993).

B. J. Leonard

Baptist Church of Christ. *See* DUCK RIVER (& KINDRED) ASSOCIATION

Baptist Churches. Members of a Christian denomination that originated within seventeenth-century English Puritanism. Puritans believed that the established Church of England demonstrated far too few signs of the true church of Christ. As a territorial church, the Church of England welcomed sinners in a neighborhood to worship just as readily as it welcomed saints. Puritans believed that the church should be congregations of the saints, men and women who could testify to the grace of God in their lives.

Baptists, at first a handful of radicals on the fringe of the Puritan movement, agreed with the Puritan majority in their criticism of the Anglican Church, but they disagreed with most Puritans at two important points. (1) They said that not only should church membership be limited to those families who could testify of the grace of God, but even children of believers should be denied baptism and church membership until they too could personally confess their faith in Christ. (2) They argued that God had instituted the state as well as the church, and that the two were designed by God to serve two distinct purposes. While the state was intended to bear the sword of justice, the church was designed to worship, preach and grow by voluntary means alone, free of the state's power.

The name Baptist came from the group's insistence that baptism be limited to those old enough to confess faith in Jesus Christ. But perhaps more significant was the view of the church as a community of Christian believers gathered by the witness of the Spirit, not by the state.

In the United States, by 1984, scholars could identify fifty-two distinct Baptist groups with a total membership of just over 30 million, the largest Protestant denominational family in North America. The largest Baptist convention is the mammoth Southern Baptist Convention,* numbering almost 14 million. It is followed by two predominantly black Baptist conventions: the National Baptist Convention, U.S.A., Inc., with an estimated 6 million members, and the National Baptist Convention of America, with an estimated 3.5 million members (*see* National Baptists).

The multiplicity of Baptist groups in America is traceable to four primary developments in Baptist life. (1) Baptists started with two distinct theological groups, Calvinists* (or Regular Baptists*) and Arminians (or General Baptists*). (2) Baptists have separated over the use of "means" in church activity, thus producing missionary and primitive* (or antimission*) bodies. (3) Baptists have divided between those with Northern cultural roots and those with Southern cultural roots. (4) In the twentieth century Baptists have separated over the issues of centralized denominational structures and theological inclusivism (or liberalism*).

Colonial Period. While some Baptists immigrated to the New World from England and Wales, many more adopted Baptist views after their arrival in the American colonies. Henry Dunster,* the first president of Harvard College, and Roger Williams,* the founder of Rhode Island Colony, are representatives of the latter group.

Williams, shortly after his banishment from the Massachusetts Bay Colony for preaching "new and dangerous opinions," led in the establishment of the first Baptist church in America. The location was Providence, Rhode Island; the year was 1639. Less than a year later Williams came to the conclusion that all existing churches lacked proper foundations and that the true church could only be reestablished by a new dispensation of apostolic authority.

Williams's defection left the Providence church without adequate leadership, but a short distance away, at Newport, Rhode Island, between 1641 and 1648 John Clarke* established another congregation with Baptist convictions. Due to Puritan opposition, however, the Baptist witness in New England remained weak throughout the seventeenth century.

Baptists found a more favorable atmosphere in the Middle Colonies. In 1707 five churches in New Jersey, Delaware and Pennsylvania united to form the Philadelphia Baptist Association.* This first association in America enabled Baptists to launch a vigorous missionary effort. By 1760 the Philadelphia Association extended from Connecticut in the North to Virginia in the South. In 1751 Baptists in the South formed the Charleston Association, and others soon followed.

Most of this growth is traceable to the colonial revival called the Great Awakening that took place during the decades preceding the American Revolution. In addition to strengthening the existing "regular" Baptist churches, the revival drew to Baptist churches in New England large numbers of awakened believers from established Puritan Congregationalism. These revivalistic believers were called Separate Baptists.* Through the ministry of Shubal Stearns,* the revivalistic spirit spread to the South and marked the region for generations to come. Stearns was a New England Separate Baptist who moved to Sandy Creek,

North Carolina, in 1755 and initiated a widespread revival that eventually penetrated the entire Piedmont area.

At the same time Baptist work began in Canada. Ebenezer Moulton, a Baptist emigrant from Massachusetts, organized a church in Nova Scotia in 1763. The earliest churches in Ontario were planted by United Empire Loyalists who crossed the border following the American Revolution. Still other churches were started by immigrant Baptists from Scotland and by missionaries from Vermont and New York.

The Nineteenth Century. Scholars have estimated that at the outbreak of the American Revolution, Baptist congregations numbered 494. Twenty years later, in 1795, Isaac Backus,* a leader of Baptists in New England, estimated that Baptists could claim 1,152 churches. Thus, on the threshold of the nineteenth century Baptists were poised to make a major contribution to American life.

Their first need, however, was some unifying cause. This came in the form of the missionary challenge. Early in the century the newly formed Congregational mission board sent Adoniram Judson* and Luther Rice* to India as its first missionaries. En route to India, however, both men came to the Baptist conviction that only believers should be baptized. Upon their arrival in Calcutta they agreed that Judson should go on to Burma and that Rice should return to America to enlist support for missions among Baptists. As a result, in 1814 Rice succeeded in rallying Baptists in the formation of a General Convention of the Baptist Denomination. Since it met every three years, most Baptists called it the Triennial Convention.*

Initially the convention tried to support home missions, education and publications, as well as foreign missions. In 1826, however, the convention decided to limit its role to foreign missions. Other independent societies were formed to meet the needs of home missions, publications and education.

Many Baptists, however, especially on the Southern frontier, objected to these new agencies on the grounds that they were without biblical precedent. The sovereign God of the Bible, they said, had no need of these modern "means" to reach the lost. This resistance to voluntary societies gave birth to the Primitive* or antimission* Baptists. Their strict Calvinism gave rise to their "hard shell" label.

The Primitive Baptist protest was a regional crisis. The greatest challenge to the new Baptist unity was the slavery controversy that enveloped the whole country by midcentury. During the decade prior to 1845 Baptists considered various compromises for the proslavery and antislavery parties in their ranks, but all proposals proved unacceptable. As a result, in 1845 Southern churchmen organized the Southern Baptist Convention* in Augusta, Georgia. The division between North and South was consolidated in 1907, when eight once-independent agencies joined in the formation of the Northern Baptist Convention (later renamed American Baptist Churches in the USA*).

As early as the eighteenth century, black Baptists organized independent local congregations. The first black Baptist church was organized around 1773 at Silver Bluff, across the Savannah River from Augusta, Georgia. Others soon followed in Virginia, Kentucky and other states. The great influx of blacks into Baptist churches, however, awaited the Emancipation Proclamation.

The lack of formality in Baptist churches, together with their absence of ritual and the democratic spirit in their congregations, appealed to black believers more than the formality and hierarchy of priestly denominations. Within fifteen years after the Civil War, nearly one million black Baptists were worshiping in their own churches.

In 1866 black leaders organized a state convention in North Carolina, and in 1880 the first national organization was formed at Montgomery, Alabama, called the Foreign Mission Baptist Convention. The National Baptist Convention was created at Atlanta, Georgia, in 1895 (see National Baptists). Early in the twentieth century (1915), however, a dispute over the adoption of a charter and control of a publishing house led to the two largest conventions of black Baptists today.

The Twentieth Century. After 1900, Baptists in the South as well as the North were divided by theological controversy and the growth of denominational bureaucracies. In 1905 churches located primarily in Texas, Oklahoma and Arkansas—called Landmarkers*—protested the "conventionism" of the Southern Baptist Convention. The result was the American Baptist Association,* whose adherents by 1980 numbered about 200,000. Later, in the 1950s, another conservative group arose from Southern fundamentalism*: the Baptist Bible Fellowship.* By 1980 membership within the fellowship was an estimated 750,000.

In Northern Baptist circles, theological differences centering in the fundamentalist-modernist debate generated two conservative bodies: the

General Association of Regular Baptist Churches* in 1932 (240,000 in size by 1980) and the Conservative Baptists* in the 1940s (210,000 by 1980). A third conservative body in the North, the Baptist General Conference,* traces its roots to nineteenth-century Swedish immigrants in the Midwest. General Conference churches, counting about 120,000 members in 1980, were scattered across the North and the West.

Twentieth-century theological controversy was also evident among the 220,000 Baptists in Canada.* In 1944 three regional conventions—Atlantic Provinces, Ontario and Quebec, and Western Canada—formed the Baptist Federation of Canada. Conservatives, however, objected to the presence of theological liberalism in the older conventions and created several separate bodies.

In 1953 the Fellowship of Evangelical Baptist Churches in Canada united most of the conservatives in eastern Canada; then in the 1960s two conservative bodies in western Canada joined the fellowship. In 1980 these shifts and mergers resulted in 127,000 members within the Baptist Federation and 47,000 within the Fellowship of Evangelical Baptists, the second largest group in Canada.

BIBLIOGRAPHY. W. H. Brackney, *The Baptists* (1988); *ESB;* W. L. Lumpkin, ed., *Baptist Confessions of Faith* (1963); H. L. McBeth, *The Baptist Heritage: Four Centuries of Baptist Witness* (1986); R. G. Torbet, *A History of the Baptists* (1950); A. W. Wardin Jr., *Baptist Atlas* (1980); J. K. Zeman, ed., *Baptists in Canada* (1980).

B. L. Shelley

Baptist Faith and Message. A Southern Baptist confession of faith.* Although founded in 1845, the Southern Baptist Convention* had no formal confession of faith until 1925. That document, known as the Baptist Faith and Message, closely paralleled the New Hampshire Confession of Faith* (1833). Theologically, the document reflects a modified Calvinist* perspective with statements on Scripture, salvation, the church, election, perseverance, religious liberty* and other doctrines. The momentum for a confession was influenced by the fundamentalist-modernist controversy of the 1920s.

A revision of the confession was approved in 1963, written in response to another theological controversy, this one involving the historical-critical method of biblical studies. That method was evident in a controversy surrounding Ralph Elliot and his book *The Message of Genesis*, published by Broadman Press.* The revision of the confession included a section on academic freedom and responsibility. During the 1980s fundamentalist* efforts to gain control of convention agencies led to a renewed emphasis on the confession, particularly its statement on Scripture. While the document does not specifically address the question of biblical inerrancy,* fundamentalists sought to define it as an inerrancy statement to be imposed on all convention employees in seminaries and other agencies. The role of the confession continued to evolve throughout the later twentieth century.

BIBLIOGRAPHY. *ESB* 1, 3; B. J. Leonard, *God's Last and Only Hope: The Fragmentation of the SBC* (1990).
B. J. Leonard

Baptist Foreign Mission Convention of the United States of America. Southern-based African-American organization formed in 1880 in Montgomery, Alabama, for overseas, particularly African, missions. Organized efforts among African-American Baptists for African missions date back at least to 1815, with the founding of the Richmond African Baptist Missionary Convention. This organization worked closely with the Triennial Convention* and subsequently with the Southern Baptist Convention. After the Civil War, independent black Baptist state conventions emerged, and African missions occupied a central place on their agendas. In the 1870s William W. Colley, an African missionary jointly supported by the Southern Baptist Convention* and the Virginia Baptist State Convention, grew weary of racial discrimination on the mission field at the hands of white mission supervisors. Convinced that African-American Baptists could best carry out the goal of African evangelization in a separate organization, Colley in 1880 helped establish the Baptist Foreign Mission Convention (BFMC).

The BFMC sent six missionaries to the African continent in 1883 and 1884, including Colley and his wife. Other missionaries soon followed. But the death or withdrawal from the field of a number of missionaries and a declining base of financial support contributed to the demise of the group. Nevertheless, the BFMC was one of three major groups consolidating in 1895 to form the oldest continuing black Baptist national organization, the National Baptist Convention (*see* National Baptists), and effectively became its foreign mission board.

BIBLIOGRAPHY. L. Fitts, *A History of Black Baptists* (1985); L. G. Jordan, *Negro Baptist History* (1930); S. D. Martin, *Black Baptist and African Missions* (1989); J. M. Washington, *Frustrated Fellowship* (1986).
S. D. Martin

Baptist General Conference. Baptist denomination. The Baptist General Conference originated in the great evangelical revival of the nineteenth century. Its specific roots were in Swedish Pietism. Simple biblical faith, dedicated evangelism, rejection of formalism and a demand for a regenerate clergy were the trademarks of the Baptists in the Scandinavian homeland.

The first Swedish Baptist congregation in America was founded in 1852 at Rock Island, Illinois, by Anders Wiberg and Gustaf Palmquist. Known for their energetic witness to newly arrived Scandinavian immigrants, by 1871 the Swedish Baptists had grown to 1,500 members in congregations dispersed over seven states. The church grew with the influx of Swedish immigrants in the late nineteenth century, and by 1902 there were 22,000 members in 324 churches. A Canadian branch was established at Winnipeg in 1894.

The national body became known as the Swedish Baptist General Conference in 1879. Prior to World War II the conference maintained its ethnic identity, though English gradually replaced Swedish in worship services. In 1940 the denomination's official organ, *Nya Wecko-Posten,* was renamed *The Standard.* In 1945 the conference, by then numbering 40,000 adherents and more comfortable with its American identity, dropped *Swedish* from its title.

The conference operates Bethel Theological Seminary* and Bethel College in St. Paul, Minnesota, originally founded in Chicago during the late nineteenth century by pastor John Alexis Edgren.* The college began as a Bible and missionary school in 1922 and started its four-year liberal arts program in 1947. The conference also operates a foreign missions program reaching Asia, Africa and Latin America. In 1980 the conference recorded a total of 135,000 members in 779 churches.

BIBLIOGRAPHY. N. Magnusson, *How We Grew: Highlights of the First Hundred Years of Conference History* (1988); A. Olson, *Seventy-five Years: A History of Bethel Theological Seminary* (1946).
J. E. Johnson

Baptist General Tract Society. *See* AMERICAN BAPTIST PUBLICATION SOCIETY.

Baptist Hymnal, The (1991). A Southern Baptist Convention* (SBC) hymnal, the largest hymn collection to be produced by Baptists since the mid-nineteenth century (*The Psalmist** [1843] was larger). Published in response to a pressing need to make available new materials from charismatic renewal groups, ethnic churches and Christian artists, as well as late-twentieth-century "mainline" hymnists, it was the result of two years of work by a representative committee of ninety-eight persons. Its theological stance is conservative, every line of each included item having been measured against the Baptist Faith and Message Statement adopted by the SBC in 1963.

New features of the hymnal include divider pages with visual symbols (stained-glass window art), titles accompanied by biblical explanations, "classic" examples of highly favored praise songs and Scripture choruses, recently composed hymns for the ordinances and other Baptist emphases such as the priesthood of all believers,* and Christian "pop" numbers (various "praise choruses," for example). The contributions of some fifty contemporary Southern Baptists appear alongside a good selection of universally accepted hymns from the contemporary ecumenical community.

BIBLIOGRAPHY. W. L. Forbis, "Currents and Cross Currents Impacting Hymnal Formation: The New Baptist Hymnal, Issues and Answers," *RE* 87 (Winter 1990):75-88; C. M. Roper, C. R. Young and L. Madden, "The Baptist Hymnal (1991): Three Perspectives," *SBCMJ* 9 (1992):24-37.

H. T. McElrath

Baptist Joint Committee on Public Affairs. The BJC is composed of representatives from various national cooperating Baptist bodies in the United States and deals exclusively with issues pertaining to religious liberty* and its political corollary, church-state separation. Constituent members include American Baptist Churches in the USA,* Baptist General Conference,* National Baptist Convention of America, National Baptist Convention, U.S.A., Inc. (*see* National Baptists), National Missionary Baptist Convention (*see* Missionary Baptists), North American Baptist Conference,* Progressive National Baptist Convention, Inc. (*see* National Baptists), Religious Liberty Council, Seventh Day Baptist* General Conference and various Southern Baptist state conventions, associations and churches.

Headquartered on Capitol Hill, Washington,

D.C., the BJC represents its constituent Baptist groups before Congress, the Supreme Court and the federal agencies. Because of the congregational autonomy of individual Baptist churches, the BJC does not purport to speak for all Baptists.

The BJC's predecessor, the Committee on Public Relations, was established in 1936 and was chaired by Rufus W. Weaver.* The BJC opened a full-time Washington office in 1946 as the Joint Conference Committee on Public Relations. The current name of the agency was adopted in 1950. Because of disagreements, including issues of church-state philosophy, the Southern Baptist Convention* severed its relationship with the BJC in 1992. Over the years, the BJC has broadened its membership, and despite the changing views of many Baptists and others, it has continued to defend what it regards as the historic Baptist concepts of religious liberty and church-state separation.

Those who have served as BJC executive directors are J. M. Dawson* (1946-1953), C. Emanuel Carlson (1957-1971), James E. Wood Jr. (1972-1980) and James M. Dunn (1981-).

BIBLIOGRAPHY. *ESB* 2:1123-24; 3:1925-27; 4:2429-30; S. L. Hastey, "A History of the Baptist Joint Committee on Public Affairs, 1946-1971" (Th.D. dissertation, Southern Baptist Theological Seminary, 1974).

J. B. Walker

Baptist Jubilee Advance. A five-year endeavor by seven major Baptist bodies of North America, commemorating the founding of the Triennial Convention* in 1814. A Joint Committee on the Baptist Jubilee, formed in 1956, drew up yearly guidelines, set themes for emphasis each year and met twice a year to provide coordination. Evangelism was to be the primary focus. Each body determined its own approach, and most utilized traditional methods. The American Baptist Convention, however, led by Jitsuo Morikawa, director of evangelism, attempted an innovative program. His vision of the church as a servant people called for combining personal evangelism with lay witness in their vocations and concern for social justice. Although his plan evoked opposition, it had a lasting impact on the denomination. The climax of the Jubilee Advance came at Atlantic City, New Jersey, where the Southern Baptist and American Baptist conventions held their separate annual meetings and representatives of the seven bodies shared in joint convocations.

BIBLIOGRAPHY. E. G. Ernst, "The Baptist Jubilee Advance in Historical Context," *Foun,* January 1966; D. C. Wooley, ed., *Baptist Advance* (1964).

N. H. Maring

Baptist Mid-Missions. Independent Baptist foreign missionary agency. The founder of Baptist Mid-Missions, William C. Haas, first sailed to Africa in late 1911 under the Africa Inland Mission, with the primary goal of reaching the Zande tribe in the Belgian Congo. Following some exceptional achievements in reducing tribal languages to writing, Haas joined Ralph Buxton and C. T. Studd, English missionaries who were establishing the Heart of Africa Mission (later the Worldwide Evangelization Crusade). After several years of linguistic and evangelistic ministry, Haas returned to the United States to build support for a new mission to French Equatorial Africa. On October 15, 1920, the General Council of Cooperating Baptist Missions of North America was organized at Elyria, Ohio. The new mission sent six missionaries to Africa on a project known as the Mid-Africa Mission. Haas died in 1924 and was buried in Africa.

In addition to an expanding work in Africa, the agency eventually opened new stations in Central and South America, the Caribbean, Europe, Asia, Australia and the Pacific islands. The name Baptist Mid-Missions replaced its unwieldy predecessor in 1953. The mission emphasizes evangelism, church planting, theological education, medicine and Bible translation. Since 1983 C. Raymond Buck has served as mission president and supervises over 600 full-time missionaries in more than thirty countries and a total annual income of almost 17 million. The home office is in Cleveland, Ohio, and the mission is affiliated with the Fellowship of Missions, a group of eleven mission societies in the fundamentalist/separatist tradition, also based in Cleveland.

J. A. Patterson

Baptist Missionary Association. An organization that traces its structural origins to 1893 and the Texas Baptist Convention. There some churches voiced disagreement with convention policy regarding methods of missions and paid secretaries. The differences in methodology continued until 1899, when a large number of churches and people withdrew and formed the Baptist Missionary Association. By 1904 some 500 churches, mostly in east Texas, had aligned with the new group.

A similar group in Arkansas began in 1901 as the State Association of Missionary Baptist Churches in Arkansas. The move can be dated to 1888 at the state convention of Arkansas Baptists, when the debate was also over boards and paid secretaries. In 1902 in Antioch Church in Little Rock, twenty churches met and formed the General Association of Arkansas Baptists. A major leader of the group was Ben M. Bogard,* who had come from Kentucky to Searcy, Arkansas, to pastor a church.

In 1905 the Arkansas group joined in Texarkana with other groups from Mississippi, Texas and Oklahoma and adopted the name General Landmark Baptist Churches of the United States. In addition to the previous states mentioned, messengers came from Missouri, Tennessee, Colorado and Kentucky. A Statement of Principles was adopted, and over 500 churches accepted it.

The break with so-called Convention Baptists was completed in the 1920s. The Arkansas and Texas groups merged in 1924 and thereafter were called the American Baptist Association.* Twenty-two associations had been formed by 1921, with more than 500 churches and 34,000 members in Arkansas.

In 1949 the Ben Bogard group separated itself from the BMA in Texas, and in 1950 a new group, the North American Baptist Association, was formed in Little Rock. In 1968 its members took the name Baptist Missionary Association of America (BMAA). The remaining group was the American Baptist Association (ABA). The division was the result of a dispute over the Articles of Agreement adopted in 1924 regarding voting messengers from the local churches: was a messenger required to be a member of the church being represented? Debates also arose over questions of support for colleges and seminaries: were they to be supported by the association or by one church? Both bodies are outspoken proponents of fundamentalist and Landmark* views.

See also AMERICAN BAPTIST ASSOCIATION; BOGARD, BENJAMIN MARCUS; LANDMARK BAPTISTS.

BIBLIOGRAPHY. *EAR* 1:373; *Yearbook of the Baptist Missionary Association of America, 1991.*

J. T. Greer

Baptist Missionary Magazine. The *Baptist Missionary Magazine* is the oldest religious magazine with continuous publication in the Western hemisphere. It was first published in 1803 as *The*

Massachusetts Baptist Missionary Magazine, with the purpose of promoting the work of the Massachusetts Baptist Missionary Society "in the new settlements within the United States; or further, if circumstances shall render it proper . . . [providing] such other information respecting the general state of religion, as may be thought interesting to the community at large." Subsequently the publication became known as *The American Baptist Magazine and Missionary Intelligences* (1817); *The Baptist Missionary Magazine* (1824); *Missions,* after merging with *Home Missions Monthly* (1910); *Mission* (1967); and *The American Baptist,* after merging with *Crusader* (1979).

Until 1835 the magazine was the organ of both home and foreign missions, but in 1836 it became for many years strictly a publication for foreign missions, edited by the corresponding secretaries of the American Baptist Foreign Missionary Society.* After 1893 the office of editorial secretary was created. In 1897 the magazine was enlarged and became the first missionary periodical in America to make extensive use of photographs in the manner of secular periodicals.

The current publication, *American Baptist IN MISSION,* provides the members of the American Baptist Churches in the USA* and others "with up-to-date news about the ministries and mission . . . American Baptists are carrying out in local churches, regions, and through national mission boards."

BIBLIOGRAPHY. *The American Baptist* (1992); *The Massachusetts Baptist Missionary Magazine* 1 (1803); R. G. Torbet, *Venture of Faith* (1955).

C. A. Russell

Baptist Peace Fellowship of North America. The BPFNA was formed in a March 30-31, 1984, meeting of American and Southern Baptists in Louisville, Kentucky. The twenty-six people who attended represented two constituencies: the steering committee of the (American) Baptist Peace Fellowship, which originated as the Baptist Pacifist Fellowship in 1940 in what was then called the Northern Baptist Convention; and the volunteer staff and other readers of the *Baptist Peacemaker,** a journal founded by Southern Baptists in Louisville. The goal of the meeting was to create a multiracial network linking Baptists from the many separate conventions in Canada, the United States, Mexico and Puerto Rico who were concerned about justice and peace issues.

The organization's purpose is "to unite and enable Baptist Christians to make peace in our warring world." Special emphases include communicating a biblical understanding of peacemaking as being more comprehensive than opposing war and including "caring for the weak, the poor, the despised—all who suffer violence, including creation itself"; influencing Baptist institutions by creating and sustaining a grassroots movement, based in local churches, of Baptists committed to peacemaking; and providing practical handles and ideas for involvement.

The BPFNA publishes two periodicals, *Baptist Peacemaker,* a quarterly journal, and *PeaceWork,* a newsletter, along with other special resources, including a three-volume book series entitled *Dreaming God's Dream: Celebrating the Life and Legacy of Martin Luther King Jr.*

Its other projects include overseas Friendship Tours to countries where there is conflict; "Baptist Pen Pals for Peace," linking Baptist young people; concert tours by Baptist musical groups from Russia and from Cuba; and an annual conference. The group has also organized International Baptist Peace Conferences (in Sweden, 1988; in Nicaragua, 1992).

BIBLIOGRAPHY. P. Dekar, "For the Healing of the Nations: The Story of the Baptist Peace Fellowship," *AB,* March 1992; K. Sehested, "Are We Facing a New Moment in Baptist History?" in *Seek Peace and Pursue It: Proceedings from the 1988 International Baptist Peace Conference,* ed. H. W. Pipkin (1989); K. Sehested, "Baptist Peacemakers in North America: A Story, a Strategy and a Theology," *FM,* Fall 1986; K. Sehested, "Baptists and Peacemaking," *TEc,* May-June 1988.

K. Sehested

Baptist Peacemaker. The *Baptist Peacemaker* journal was founded in 1980 by an ad hoc group of Southern Baptists in Louisville, Kentucky, as a communication tool to link Southern Baptists concerned about peacemaking. The idea for such a periodical developed after a 1979 convocation on peacemaking organized by students and professors at Southern Baptist Theological Seminary* and local clergy and lay leaders. The success of that convocation—the first of its kind within Southern Baptist circles—convinced the planning group that the issue needed greater attention.

For nine years the quarterly journal—supported entirely by readers' contributions—was based at Deer Park Baptist Church in Louisville and produced by an all-volunteer staff. Production was transferred to the Baptist Peace Fellowship of North America in 1989.

Initially the journal's principal concern was the prospect of nuclear war and the need, from a Christian perspective, for disarmament and non-violent resolution of international conflict. Later the topical focus expanded to include attention to a variety of justice issues.

BIBLIOGRAPHY. P. Cole, "The Baptist Peacemaker: Ten Years and Growing," *BP,* Spring 1990; *ESB* 4; P. Womack, "Founding of the *Baptist Peacemaker"* (interview with R. Parham, archives of the Baptist Peace Fellowship of North America, 1990).   K. Sehested

Baptist Student Union. The name applied to most Southern Baptist student programs conducted on college and university campuses. The Southern Baptist Convention* assigned the national coordination of Baptist Student Union (BSU) work to the Sunday School Board* in 1928. The board's student ministry department relates to BSUs on about 1,050 campuses in the United States and in several foreign countries, through publications (such as *The Student*), consultants and other program support. Each BSU ministry operates through a BSU Council (composed of students); a salaried or volunteer director of student ministries; a Baptist student center, a special building for BSU activities; and a program of student ministries in each Baptist state convention. BSU provides opportunity for student fellowship, spiritual growth and missions involvement.

BIBLIOGRAPHY. *ESB* 1:124-25; 3:1599-1600; 4:2108.   C. W. Deweese

Baptist Sunday School Board. As the world's largest publisher of religious materials, this Southern Baptist Convention* (SBC) agency's work is guided by the following vision statement: "We will assist local churches and believers to evangelize the world to Christ, develop believers, and grow churches by being the best worldwide provider of relevant, high-quality, high-value Christian products and services." In addition to providing church literature, books, Bibles, audiovisuals, music and recordings, computer hardware and software, and church supplies, the board develops and promotes education and service programs for churches. In addition, it operates a national chain of more than sixty Christian bookstores and two national conference centers, at Glorieta, New Mexico, and Ridgecrest,

North Carolina.

Organized in 1891, the Baptist Sunday School Board (BSSB) conducts programs of work assigned to it by the SBC. These include church programs and services development, Sunday-school development, discipleship training development, family ministry development, church media library development, church recreation development, church architecture service, conference center operation, bookstore operation, Broadman publishing, Bible publishing, cooperative work with state conventions, Southern Baptist Convention support, and Sunday School Board general management.

Employing about 1,900 persons, the BSSB has an annual budget exceeding $200 million. The agency is financially self-supporting through the sale of products. Its facilities in Nashville, Tennessee, encompass more than 1 million square feet of floor space. The BSSB's chief executives have included J. M. Frost* (1891-1893, 1896-1916), T. P. Bell (1893-1896), I. J. Van Ness (1916-1935), T. L. Holcomb (1935-1953), James L. Sullivan (1953-1975), Grady C. Cothen (1975-1984), Lloyd Elder (1984-1991) and James T. Draper Jr. (1991-).

BIBLIOGRAPHY. "General Information: The Sunday School Board of the Southern Baptist Convention" (background news sheets updated regularly by the BSSB's Office of Communications); W. B. Sherden, *The Sunday Board: Ninety Years of Service* (1981).   C. W. Deweese

Baptist Theological Seminary at Richmond. Baptist school governed by an independent, self-perpetuating board to provide advanced theological education for men and women preparing for Christian ministry.

The beginnings of the Baptist Theological Seminary at Richmond (BTSR) were related to pressures being placed on the six Southern Baptist seminaries and particularly to the fundamentalist* takeover of Southeastern Seminary,* Wake Forest, North Carolina, in October 1987. After exploring various alternatives, the theological education committee of the Southern Baptist Alliance* recommended that a new seminary be established in Richmond, Virginia, joining Union Theological Seminary, Presbyterian School of Christian Education and the School of Theology of Virginia Union University as a part of the Richmond Theological Consortium.

On March 2, 1989, in Greenville, South Carolina, the alliance voted to constitute a provisional board of trustees to establish a theological seminary in Richmond. The board elected as chair Mary Strauss of Hagerstown, Maryland, developed a mission statement, named the school Baptist Theological Seminary at Richmond, elected Morris Ashcraft to be acting president and officially requested membership in the Richmond Theological Consortium. After Ashcraft spent over a year laying the groundwork for the new school, the board appointed a committee to search for a full-time president.

The board named Thomas H. Graves as the seminary's first president and faculty member January 7, 1991. On March 16, 1991, upon Graves's recommendation, the board authorized the hiring of adjunct faculty, approved the opening of the school for classes in the fall of 1991 and brought the number of permanent faculty members to three. The school officially opened on September 10, in space leased from the Presbyterian School of Christian Education, with an enrollment of thirty-two students.

By the 1992-1993 academic year, the school had grown to eighty-six students, eight adjunct faculty members, five full-time staff members and six permanent faculty members. Support for the school also grew. In 1991 the Baptist General Association of Virginia (BGAV) had approved a resolution of affirmation and placed the school in its budget. In 1992 the BGAV named the seminary a "shared ministry" and increased its funding. The Cooperative Baptist Fellowship* had also placed the seminary in its budget. In addition, support came from numerous individuals and churches. Thus by the end of 1992 the seminary appeared able to achieve its objective of providing an alternative Baptist theological education.

BIBLIOGRAPHY. *Baptist Theological Seminary at Richmond Catalog 1992-93*; T. H. Graves, "The Early History of Baptist Theological Seminary at Richmond" (paper presented at Mercer University, October 9, 1992).

G. T. Halbrooks

Baptist Theological Seminary—Luther Rice Seminary. Baptist seminary named for the famous nineteenth-century Baptist missionary and chartered by the state of Florida on June 14, 1962, in Jacksonville. Committed to the doctrinal beliefs and mission of the Southern Baptist Convention,* all full-time faculty of the Baptist Theological Seminary—Luther Rice Seminary (LRS) are Southern Baptists. The seminary is accredited by

Transnational Association of Christian Schools and is a member of the Florida Association of Colleges and Universities and the Association of Christian Schools International. Its purpose is to train students in the evangelical Christian ministry, and it is committed to the doctrine of scriptural infallibility. Through the Lay Institute, Luther Rice Bible College and the seminary, several standard degrees are offered, from a certificate to the extended doctor of ministry degree.

Robert Witty, pastor of Central Baptist Church, Jacksonville, was the founder and inspiration for the seminary. It opened for classes on September 11, 1962, in the Central Baptist Church, with the initial faculty consisting of volunteer Southern Baptist pastors. Until 1968 the seminary was directed by trustees, with Witty as chairman and a succession of three part-time presidents. In 1968 Witty became the part-time president and Fred Williams became chairman of the trustees. From 1970 to 1982 Witty served as the first full-time president and later as chancellor. During his presidency the seminary purchased its first property, expanded its external degree program and built the Bertha Smith Library. Gene Williams succeeded Witty as president. In 1988 property in Atlanta, Georgia, was donated to the seminary, which announced a move to the Georgia campus in 1992. The majority of LRS students participate in the external off-campus program begun in 1964, which serves students in the United States and over fifty foreign countries. The seminary produces a quarterly publication, *The Pioneer.* James Bryant followed Williams as president.

J. F. Loftis

Baptist Union Theological Seminary at Chicago. Also called the Morgan Park Baptist Seminary, this institution became the University of Chicago's Divinity School* in 1890. The Baptist Theological Union of the Northwest formed in 1860 to respond to the call for theological education issuing from the ministerial students at the original University of Chicago (began 1858; failed 1886). The union was chartered by Illinois in 1865 for founding and supporting a theological institution. Classes began in 1866. Church historian G. W. Northrup from Rochester Theological Seminary* was hired in 1867. He was made president in 1869 and served until the 1890 merger with the new University of Chicago. The seminary had 20 students its first year, increasing to 13 faculty and 190 students by 1891. A Scandinavian department was added in 1873, forerunner of Bethel Theological Seminary.* Baptist Union Theological Seminary moved to Morgan Park in 1877.

John D. Rockefeller,* for nine years vice president of the union, agreed to contribute $200,000 to the seminary if it would combine with the new University of Chicago. The seminary did so, ending twenty-five years of independent existence. Two of the first three presidents of the university came from the Divinity School.

See also UNIVERSITY OF CHICAGO, THE DIVINITY SCHOOL.

BIBLIOGRAPHY. BE 212-14; T. W. Goodspeed, A History of the University of Chicago (1916).

W. L. Allen

Baptist World Alliance. An international fellowship of Baptist organizations. The Baptist World Alliance, the first international Baptist organization of its type, was formed in 1905 at a meeting in Exeter Hall, London. The primary purposes of the alliance include safeguarding and maintaining religious liberty* everywhere, propagating Baptist principles and tenets of faith, arranging and conducting preaching* missions throughout the world, gathering and disseminating Baptist news, and coordinating relief efforts as occasions arise. Between 1905 and 1985 the Baptist World Alliance has held fifteen world congresses, usually at five-year intervals.

At present the Baptist World Alliance consists of 136 bodies in ninety-four nations and dependencies. This includes about 126,000 churches with a total membership of over 32 million. Recently the alliance has been engaged in projects such as providing Bibles and commentaries in translation to the states of the former Soviet Union, providing relief and development assistance to Nicaragua, Argentina, Bangladesh, Lebanon and Zaire, and conducting friendship tours to Russia and China. Gerhard Class was the general secretary of the Baptist World Alliance until his death in March 1988.

Two historic Baptist commitments have received the attention of the Baptist World Alliance: religious liberty and congregational autonomy. The preamble of its constitution states that the alliance may "in no way interfere with the independence of the churches or assume the administrative functions of existing organizations."

The major periodical of the alliance is The Baptist World, and its headquarters are in McLean, Virginia. It was located at the Baptist Church House in London until 1941, when for safety reasons it was moved to Washington, D.C. Denton Lotz is currently general secretary.

BIBLIOGRAPHY. F. T. Lord, Baptist World Fellowship (1955); J. Nordenhaug et al., Baptists of the World, 1950-1970; W. B. Shurden, ed., The Life of Baptists in the Life of the World (1985).

G. W. Carlson

Baptist Young People's Union. A federation of organizations for Baptist young people in the United States and Canada which was organized in 1891 at Chicago's Second Baptist Church. The organization emerged out of the Christian young people's movement of the late nineteenth and early twentieth centuries, which also spawned the Young Men's Christian Association (YMCA). The Baptist Young People's Union (BYPU) assisted Baptist young people in their spiritual development and biblical knowledge, enhanced their unity and provided instruction in Baptist history and doctrine.

The last decades of the nineteenth century witnessed the proliferation of Baptist organizations for young people in local churches. Baptist leaders such as F. L. Wilkins encouraged a meeting of representatives from these local organizations in order to form a national union. Wilkins was elected the first general secretary at the organizational meeting in 1891.

After 1910 the work of the national BYPU was gradually absorbed by the individual Baptist denominations. The Northern Baptist Convention (see American Baptist Churches in the USA) maintained the national organization. Other Baptist denominations created their own youth organizations patterned after the BYPU. Southern Baptists, for example, maintained a BYPU organization until 1934, at which time the Baptist Training Union was established.

BIBLIOGRAPHY. H. L. McBeth, The Baptist Heritage: Four Centuries of Baptist Witness (1987); S. D. Beasley, "The Development of the Church Training Department of the Southern Baptist Convention: An Historical Review" (Ed.D. dissertation, Southern Baptist Theological Seminary, 1988).

R. Nash

Baptistery (also Baptistry). Term referring to the place of baptism.* The changing practices concerning baptism in church history have been reflected in the various architectural settings for the rite. The term carries at least three distinct meanings: (1) a round or polygonal building used for baptismal services in the early and medieval church; (2) an area in a church building containing a font for use in baptism; (3) a large tank, often below floor level, utilized by churches practicing immersion. In churches within the Baptist tradition, the baptistery is located behind the chancel and may be entered by steps descending into the water on either side. Catholic churches have generally placed the baptistery in a location apart from the main sanctuary, and other denominations have adopted a variety of locations, each seeking to enhance the meaning of the rite by its architectural setting.

See also BAPTISM; BAPTISMAL FONT.

BIBLIOGRAPHY. K. F. Brown, *Baptism Through the Centuries* (1965); J. G. Davies, *The Architectural Setting of Baptism* (1962).

M. G. Bell

Barnes, William Wright (1883-1960). Minister and church historian. William Wright Barnes was born on February 28, 1883, in Elm City, North Carolina, and died April 6, 1960, in Fort Worth, Texas. Barnes was converted in 1898 at the age of fifteen and shortly afterward was baptized in Elm City Baptist Church. He was ordained six years later, on July 31, 1904. He received his A.B. and A.M. degrees from Wake Forest College. After a year in the Divinity School of the University of Chicago* and two years in the Southern Baptist Theological Seminary,* he received the Th.M. degree in 1909, and the Th.D. in 1913. He also pursued postdoctoral studies at Columbia University in 1919-1920.

W. W. Barnes and Ethel Lee Dalrymple were married on October 20, 1909, in Amory, Mississippi. He began his teaching career as director of the Cuban American College in Havana, Cuba. He succeeded A. H. Newman as professor of church history at Southwestern Baptist Theological Seminary,* Fort Worth, in 1913 and continued teaching there until 1953. He also served as chairman of the theological faculty from 1924 to 1949. Barnes was heavily involved in denominational affairs during these years. He wrote several articles and two books, the more important of which was *The Southern Baptist Convention, 1845-1953* (1954).

See also SOUTHWESTERN BAPTIST THEOLOGICAL SEMINARY.

BIBLIOGRAPHY. W. W. Barnes, *The Southern Baptist Convention, 1845-1953* (1954); *ESB* 4:1608.

W. R. Estep

Barton, Arthur James (1867-1942). Baptist pastor and temperance leader. Born February 2, 1867, near Jonesboro, Arkansas, Barton was the son of William H. and Eliza (Morgan) Barton. He earned the A.B. degree from Southwestern Baptist University (now Union University*), Jackson, Tennessee, in 1891. Barton held pastorates in five states, the most significant being in Alexandria, Louisiana (1918-1924), and Wilmington, North Carolina (1930-1942). He was an executive with the Home and Foreign Mission boards and with the Arkansas, Texas and Missouri state conventions. Barton's most significant work was in the area of temperance. Nationally, he was instrumental in shaping legislation that would become the Eighteenth Amendment. Within the Southern Baptist Convention* (SBC), Barton served without compensation as chairman of the Social Service Commission (now the Christian Life Commission*) from its inception in 1914 until his death. He wrote the annual reports of the commission to the SBC and articles for Baptist state papers on social ministries. Barton died July 19, 1942, in Nashville, Tennessee.

See also CHRISTIAN LIFE COMMISSION.

BIBLIOGRAPHY. J. L. Eighmy, *Churches in Cultural Captivity* (1972); *ESB* 1:156.

A. L. Pratt

Batten, Samuel Zane (1859-1925). A leading American Baptist spokesman in the Social Gospel* movement. He worked in the Social Service Commission of the American Baptists in the first decade of the twentieth century and concerned himself especially with the relation of the gospel to labor and industry. On his recommendation a full-time position was created in the American Baptist Publication Society* (ABPS) that devoted itself to social issues. After 1912 he was Secretary of Social Education, ABPS; he reorganized his division in 1920 as the title of Department of Social Education and remained there until his death in 1925. He was active in war and peace issues during and after World War I, worked as a supporter of the League of Nations and was particularly active in the last years of his life on behalf of temperance and Prohibition. In general he was a leading spokesman for the creation of "a more Christian social order." He wrote numerous books in support of Social Gospel themes, including *The New Citizenship: Christian Character in Its Biblical Ideals, Sources and Relations* (1898); *The Social Task of Christianity: A Sum-*

mons to the New Crusade (1911); The Christian State: The State, Democracy and Christianity (1909); The New World Order (1919); and If America Fail: Our National Mission and Our Possible Future (1922).

H. W. Pipkin

Baylor, Robert Emmett Bledsoe (1793-1873). Lawyer and judge, Texas Baptist leader and educator. Born to Walker and Jane Bledsoe Baylor on May 10, 1793, in Lincoln County, Kentucky, Robert Baylor left school to join the army during the War of 1812. After the war he read law and served in the Kentucky legislature. He moved to Alabama and served in the legislature there before being elected to Congress in 1828. In 1839 he became a Christian and was ordained as a Baptist minister. That same year he moved to Texas, where he served as a judge for the Third Judicial District and on the Republic of Texas's Supreme Court. With William Tryon and James Huckins, Baylor organized the Texas Baptist Education Society in 1841 and chartered Baylor University* in 1845, giving the first $1,000 that the university received. He taught law there, served as university president more than once and was a trustee. He died in Washington County in 1873.

BIBLIOGRAPHY. E. W. Baker, To Light the Ways of Time (1987); ESB 1:150.

R. Beck

Baylor University. Baptist General Convention of Texas educational institution. With a 1992 enrollment of over 11,000 at the 300-acre main campus in Waco and at campuses in Dallas and San Antonio, Baylor is the world's largest Baptist educational institution.

The Texas Baptist Education Society voted in 1844 to "found a Baptist university in Texas." Judge R. E. Baylor and two appointees of the American Baptist Home Missionary Society—William Tryon and James Huckins—lobbied the Ninth Congress of the Republic of Texas for the charter. The oldest continuously chartered university in Texas and one of the oldest coeducational universities in America, Baylor opened at Independence, Texas, in 1846, with Henry Lea Graves as the first president and with twenty-four students. In 1886 Baylor University and Waco University, a Baptist school, consolidated and were rechartered as Baylor University at Waco.

Baylor has a college of arts and sciences, a graduate school which awards twelve Ph.D.s and

more than sixty M.A.s per year, and schools of business, education, law, music and nursing. With a 1992 operating budget of 130 million and an endowment of more than 270 million, Baylor continues on a sound financial basis.

The university houses the world's largest collection of Elizabeth Barrett and Robert Browning materials and maintains the John K. Strecker Museum of Natural History. Students come from all fifty states and more than forty foreign countries. President Herbert Reynolds has been chief officer since 1981. From 1886 on the Baptist General Convention of Texas (BGCT) elected Baylor's trustees. However, in 1990 the trustees altered the school's charter, creating a self-perpetuating Board of Regents. They said this was necessary to protect Baylor from a takeover by fundamentalists. The more than 11,000 messengers to the 1991 BGCT meeting voted by a two-to-one margin to elect 25 percent of Baylor's regents, recommend to the board another 50 percent and allow Baylor to choose the remaining 25 percent. They voted to eliminate the board of trustees completely.

BIBLIOGRAPHY. E. W. Baker, To Light the Ways of Time (1987); ESB 1:150-53; 4:2117-18.

R. Beck

Beebe, Gilbert (1800-c. 1881). Baptist preacher and writer. Reared on a farm in Connecticut and baptized at the age of eleven, he was ordained in 1824 and soon began a fifty-year pastorate of the New Vernon Baptist Church in New York. Many Baptists of the time were engaged in promoting revivals and societies to advance religion, education and reforms. Many other Baptists, however, resisted changes that conflicted with their predestinarian theology. Beebe, in contrast to his fellow pastor and close friend Zealots Grenell, espoused the Old School Baptist movement and was one of its chief advocates for fifty years. He asserted that revivals, Sunday schools, theological seminaries, Bible and mission societies, temperance, and the antislavery movement were human inventions not taught by the Bible or the confession of faith. Beebe helped prepare the definitive "Black Rock Address" in 1832, edited Signs of the Times and reported traveling 200,000 miles to preach 10,000 sermons.

See also ANTIMISSION MOVEMENT.

BIBLIOGRAPHY. L. O. Grenell, Life and Labors of Zelotes Grenell (1885); B. C. Lambert, Rise of Anti-Mission Baptists (1980).

N. H. Maring

Beeson Divinity School. A theology school based at Samford University,* a Baptist institution in Alabama. The divinity school was founded in 1988-1989 through an initial seven-million-dollar grant from Ralph Waldo Beeson, a Presbyterian businessman and longtime benefactor of Samford University. The school was named for Beeson and his father, John Wesley Beeson. The full bequest exceeded 43 million dollars. While Baptist-based and governed by trustees of Samford University, the divinity school maintains chairs filled by representatives of numerous denominational traditions. It offers the master of divinity, master of theological studies and doctor of ministry degrees. Under the terms of Beeson's bequest, the school serves a maximum of 180-200 students. Under the leadership of Timothy George, founding dean, it has developed an identity as an evangelical educational community.

BIBLIOGRAPHY. Samford University, *Catalog, 1993-94.*   B. J. Leonard

Beissel, Johann Conrad. *See* GERMAN RELIGIOUS SOCIETY OF THE SEVENTH DAY BAPTISTS (EPHRATA)

Belmont University. A four-year liberal arts university located in Nashville, Tennessee, and operated in cooperation with the Tennessee Baptist Convention. The school was established in 1865 as Ward Seminary, a school for women. Another school for women, Belmont College, was founded in Nashville in 1890. In 1913 the two schools combined to form Ward-Belmont College for women, which continued until its purchase in January 1951 by Tennessee Baptists. The school then took the name Belmont College. In September 1951 Belmont College opened as a junior college with Warren F. Jones, president of Union University in Jackson, Tennessee, serving as acting president. R. Kelly White was elected in August 1952 as the first president. In 1959 Belmont became an accredited senior college offering bachelor's degrees. Graduate degrees have been offered since the opening of the Jack C. Massey Graduate School of Business in 1986. The university has a sizable resident population but also has a strong program for part-time students, especially in business.

BIBLIOGRAPHY. *ESB* 1, 3, 4.
                                              C. Blevins

Benedict, David (1779-1874). Baptist minister and historian. Born on October 10, 1779, in Nor-walk, Connecticut, Benedict began preaching to a Baptist congregation in Pawtucket, Rhode Island, while a student at Brown University.* Ordained in 1806 after his graduation, he continued as pastor for another twenty-three years. An amateur historian, he traveled and corresponded extensively, ultimately giving up his pastorate to write Baptist history. Using his own materials as well as those gathered by Morgan Edwards,* Isaac Backus* and John Asplund, he highlighted the changes in American Baptist life during the nineteenth century. He particularly noted changes in preaching and worship styles, missionary and educational concern, and congregational practices. He was a successionist who claimed to be able to trace Baptists back through the medieval sects to the first century. A trustee of Brown University for fifty-six years, he died in Pawtucket on December 5, 1874.

See also BROWN UNIVERSITY.

BIBLIOGRAPHY. D. Benedict, *Fifty Years Among the Baptists* (1860); D. Benedict, *A General History of the Baptist Denomination in America and Other Parts of the World,* 2 vols. (1813); D. Benedict, *History of All Religions* (1824).
                                              A. M. Manis

Bethel Academy. Bethel Academy was begun in 1905 by a group of Baptist General Conference* (then Swedish Baptist General Conference) pastors and laypeople. It was first housed in the Elim Baptist Church of Minneapolis and later acquired its own building in the St. Anthony Park area of St. Paul. Its first principal was Arvid Gordh. In 1914 it was combined with the denominational seminary to form Bethel Academy and Seminary. The combined institution came under the official control of the conference, and a campus was established in the Midway section of St. Paul. With the rising educational level of the population, the prerequisite for entry into the seminary became two years of college. Consequently, Bethel Junior College was opened in 1931. This, together with the presence by then in most Minnesota communities of accredited high schools, obviated the need for an academy, and with a declining enrollment, the school closed its doors in 1936.

See also BETHEL THEOLOGICAL SEMINARY.
                                              M. J. Erickson

Bethel Theological Seminary. A theological seminary owned and operated by the Baptist

General Conference. It was founded by John Alexis Edgren* in 1871 in Chicago and became the Scandinavian department of the Baptist Union Theological Seminary. It was moved to St. Paul from 1884 to 1886 and to Stromsburg, Nebraska, from 1886 to 1888. It then returned to Chicago, where it became the Swedish department of the Baptist Union Seminary, which in 1892 became the Divinity School of the University of Chicago.* In 1914 it was moved to St. Paul, where it was joined with Bethel Academy, later Bethel Junior College and finally Bethel College. In 1965 it moved to a 214-acre wooded lakeside campus in suburban St. Paul. In 1977 an extension was opened in San Diego—the first extension campus in the United States to offer the M.Div. degree completely in extension.

Bethel Seminary is governed by the same board of regents as Bethel College and shares a president and business and development departments, but has a separate faculty, academic administration, calendar and curriculum. It is fully accredited by the North Central Association of Schools and Colleges and the Association of Theological Schools in the United States and Canada. Although it is a Baptist school and all of its full-time faculty members must be members of a Baptist General Conference church, approximately one-half of its students are non-Baptists. It is a member of the Minnesota Consortium of Theological Schools.

BIBLIOGRAPHY. Bethel Theological Seminary, *Catalogue 1991-92.*

M. J. Erickson

Bible Baptist Seminary. An educational institution founded by J. Frank Norris* to serve the needs of Southern fundamentalists.* In 1939 Norris and his close associate Louis Entzminger* established the Fundamental Baptist Bible Institute. Located at Norris's First Baptist Church of Fort Worth, Texas, the institute served the growing ranks of the World Fundamental Baptist Missionary Fellowship, which had been established in 1933 as the Premillennial Baptist Missionary Fellowship* by Norris, C. P. Stealey and others.

The institute was renamed the Bible Baptist Seminary in 1944 and claimed to be "the only seminary in the world teaching the whole English Bible." The curriculum was mostly practical, emphasizing preaching the English Bible and building Sunday schools. Students did not pay tuition or need a college degree to enter. In the 1940s

the student body ranged between 200 and 300 per year. An early graduate was John Birch, who was killed while serving as a missionary in China and after whom the John Birch Society was named. In 1948 Norris named G. Beauchamp Vick* president of the seminary, but he never relinquished control. When Norris fired Vick without the board's knowledge or approval, a number of pastors broke with Norris, formed the Baptist Bible Fellowship* and started a school of their own, the Baptist Bible College* of Springfield, Missouri.

The Bible Baptist Seminary is now located in Arlington, Texas, and has been renamed Arlington Baptist College.

See also BAPTIST BIBLE FELLOWSHIP; NORRIS, J. FRANK

BIBLIOGRAPHY. B. V. Bartlett, *A History of Baptist Separatism* (1972); G. W. Dollar, *A History of Fundamentalism in America* (1973).

T. P. Weber

Billington, Dallas Franklin (1903-1972). Baptist preacher. Born in a log house in western Kentucky and raised in a devout Christian home, Billington did not respond to the gospel until the age of twenty one, when he was converted at a tent meeting in Paducah, Kentucky, where he had been invited by his fiancée, Nell Stokes. In 1927, having moved to Akron, Ohio, to gain employment, during a serious illness of his infant son Billington acknowledged God's call to preach. In June 1934 he was invited to organize a group of people into a Baptist church. Beginning with thirteen people meeting in an elementary school and an offering of $1.18, the Akron Baptist Temple was born. Under Billington's ministry over the next thirty-eight years, the church grew to 16,000 members, with physical assets of several million dollars. The church was among the first to have its own television studio. Its radio, television and missionary outreach made its ministry worldwide. In 1968 the church was recognized by *Christian Life* magazine as having the world's largest Sunday school. Billington had heart trouble beginning in 1941, and he died of a heart attack on August 26, 1972, at age sixty-nine. His only son, Charles, who had served as associate pastor for twenty-four years, succeeded him as pastor of the Akron Baptist Temple.

BIBLIOGRAPHY. G. Dollar, *A History of Fundamentalism* (1973).

E. L. Towns

Billy Graham Evangelistic Association. Evangelistic organization founded in 1950. The Billy Graham Evangelistic Association (BGEA) was established to answer criticism leveled against Billy Graham's* crusade ministry at a time when his evangelistic endeavors were attracting national attention. It operates Billy Graham's ministry in a businesslike way and serves as a nonprofit entity to receive donations for crusades and related ministries. The BGEA also took on the work of planning and coordinating Graham's evangelistic meetings throughout the world and oversaw the expansion of the evangelist's ministry. Four decades later, the organization, which established headquarters in Minneapolis and maintained offices in other cities around the world, coordinated and supervised a large and varied range of religious activities. With its agents and subsidiaries the BGEA produced the *Hour of Decision* radio program, television programs of Graham's crusades, documentary and evangelistic films produced by World Wide Pictures, *Decision* magazine, which was published in six languages and had a monthly circulation of four million, books and pamphlets, and recordings. It sponsored a series of international and regional conferences on evangelism, beginning in 1966 with the World Congress on Evangelism in Berlin. In addition, the BGEA, through its counseling department, responded to 250,000 letters and 6,000 calls a year, and through a World Emergency Fund distributed $4-5 million a year for relief. The association was instrumental in the founding of *Christianity Today* magazine (1956), Wheaton College's Billy Graham Center (1978) and The Cove, a Christian retreat center (1988). Graham's considerable achievements and popularity must be attributed not only to his straightforward preaching but also to the superb organizational support rendered by the BGEA.

BIBLIOGRAPHY. W. Martin, *A Prophet with Honor: The Billy Graham Story* (1991); J. C. Pollack, *Billy Graham: The Authorized Biography* (1966).

D. G. Hart

Binns, Walter Pope (1895-1966). Preacher and educator. Binns was born in Washington, Georgia, on September 18, 1895, and was ordained to the ministry in 1918 at West End Baptist Church in Atlanta. He was awarded an A.B. degree and honorary doctorate by Mercer University* and also attended Southern Baptist Theological Seminary* in Louisville, Kentucky. He married Blanche Mallory of Macon, Georgia, in 1918, and they had four children.

Binns served briefly as an army chaplain at the end of World War I. He pastored churches in Atlanta, Georgia; Laurenceville, Kentucky; Moultrie, Georgia; La Grange, Georgia; and Roanoke, Virginia. He was president of William Jewell College,* Liberty, Missouri, from 1943 to 1962. Binns also served as a trustee of Mercer University, was a member of the executive committees of the Southern Baptist Convention* and the Baptist World Alliance,* and was chairman of the Baptist Joint Committee on Public Affairs* and the executive committee of Americans United for Separation of Church and State. Binns died December 3, 1966, in Falls Church, Virginia.

BIBLIOGRAPHY. W. P. Binns, *My Life Story* (1968).

J. B. Walker

Bishop, Josiah. African-American Baptist minister. A former slave and gifted preacher, Bishop served as pastor of the racially mixed Court Street Baptist Church in Portsmouth, Virginia (1792 or 1795 to 1802). But after several years, opposition arose in relation to the role played by blacks. It was suggested that the church segregate, with Bishop becoming pastor of a separate black branch. According to Mechal Sobel, the church's white historians have argued that Bishop was only the pastor of the black members. However, there is strong evidence to the contrary. Regardless, Bishop resigned by 1802, moved to Baltimore and worked among black Baptists there.

Later Bishop assumed the pastorate (1810-1813) of the newly organized Abyssinian Baptist Church, a black congregation in New York City, which would become quite prominent. Interestingly, Bishop's new church also was the outgrowth of racial controversy. Seeking equality in the Gold Street Baptist Church, the black members had withdrawn from the church. At this time in the North it was uncommon for blacks to withdraw from predominantly white churches, because whites viewed separate black churches as politically and socially threatening.

BIBLIOGRAPHY. M. Sobel, *Trabelin' On: The Slave Journey to an Afro-Baptist Faith* (1979); C. G. Woodson, *The History of the Negro Church* (1921). L. H. Williams

Black Churchmen of the American Baptist Convention. Black caucus within the American Baptist Churches in the USA.* The Black Churchmen of the American Baptist Convention

(BCABC) was started as an informal organization in 1963. By May 1968 a formal organization had been developed and a manifesto of twelve demands presented to the General Council of the American Baptist Convention (GCABC). The BCABC contended that in spite of the representation of 400 churches, with a membership of over a quarter of a million, black American Baptists were excluded, especially from national boards and staff, regional and institutional positions, and there was virtually no black contribution to policymaking.

Historically, the BCABC also was informed by the National Committee of Black Churchmen (NCBC), which was organized in 1966. Consisting primarily of black clergy serving in white denominations, the NCBC soon became responsible for developing "black caucuses in every major white denomination," including the BCABC.

Although the GCABC accepted the twelve demands, the BCABC remained as an organization within the American Baptist Convention. In recent years, the BCABC's name has been changed to the Black American Baptist Caucus (BABC), several personnel and staff positions in the denomination have been filled by blacks, and there have been two black ABC presidents, including Thomas Kilgore Jr. (elected in 1971) and James A. Scott, the current president. The current president of the BABC is Gellette O. James of San Fernando, California.

BIBLIOGRAPHY. Black American Baptist Caucus, *Newsletter,* Winter 1992; M. E. Owens files, *AB,* April 1992; G. S. Wilmore, *Black Religion and Black Radicalism: An Interpretation of the Religious History of Afro-American People,* 2nd ed. (1983).
L. H. Williams

Blue Mountain College. A four-year women's college located in Blue Mountain, near Tupelo, Mississippi. Founded in 1873 by minister and Civil War general Mark Perrin Lowrey, the school, whose faculty was composed of Lowrey and his two daughters, provided academic, social and spiritual education for its initial fifty students. Modena Lowrey Berry served as "Lady Principal" and then as vice president until 1934, and General Lowrey's sons and grandson held successive presidencies until 1960. Since then Wilfred C. Tyler (1960-1965) and E. Harold Fisher (1965-) have served as president. Historically balancing liberal arts and vocational studies, today the college offers the B.A., B.S., B.S. in education and

bachelor of music degrees with majors in biblical studies, fine arts, language and literature, combined sciences, education and psychology, and social sciences. The faculty numbers thirty-five, and chapel attendance is required of full-time students three times a week.

BIBLIOGRAPHY. *Blue Mountain College Catalogue, 1990-1992;* R. N. Sumrall, *A Light on a Hill: A History of Blue Mountain College* (1947).
A. M. Manis

Bluefield College. Southern Baptist educational institution. The Baptist General Association of Virginia selected Bluefield as the site for a junior college in southwest Virginia in 1919. Fundraising and the construction of facilities took time, and the school opened in 1922. It had been intended to be a men's college, yet the original class was coeducational. Women lived on campus beginning in 1951. As a junior college the school was known for its preengineering program, and it has traditionally trained a high percentage of Baptist ministers. The college began offering four-year degrees in 1975 and has since added over twenty majors.

Bluefield College has had seven presidents: R. A. Lansdell (1922-1926), J. Taylor Stinson (1926-1927), Oscar E. Sams (1927-1930), J. Taylor Stinson (1930-1934), Edwin Wade (1934-1946), Charles L. Harman (1946-1972), Charles L. Tyer (1972-1988) and Roy Dobyns (1989-). A small college (285 students, 1955; 330 students, 1988), it experienced significant growth in the early 1990s, doubling the enrollment in the drive to reach the trustees' goal of 750.

BIBLIOGRAPHY. Bluefield College, *Catalogue 1991-1992.*
C. D. Weaver

Board of Educational Ministries, ABCUSA. A program board of the American Baptist Churches in the USA* (ABCUSA). The Board of Educational Ministries (BEM) evolved from the General Tract Society organized in 1824. Initially "its sole object [was] to disseminate evangelical truth, and to inculcate morals, by distribution of tracts." A convenient evangelistic tool, tracts focused on the urgency of becoming a Christian and on personal piety and morality. Colporteurs carried tracts in neckpacks and saddlebags to the most sparsely settled areas of the North, South and West. As modes of transportation changed, distribution of tracts and other literature became better organized, utilizing specially designed wagons, trains and automobiles. The chapel car, one notable means, resembled a Pullman sleeper and was equipped with living quarters for the "Sunday-school missionary" and spouse as well as a pulpit and seats for an audience. The first such car, *Evangel,* was put into service in 1891, and eventually six more were used in out-of-the-way places, giving mobility and visibility to the Baptists and their message.

By 1840 the society expanded its objective and became the American Baptist Publication Society* (ABPS). As converts multiplied and new churches were organized, books were needed to instruct new members in Christian teaching and Baptist traditions. Inexpensive books on doctrine, denominational history and biography were distributed by colporteurs. Also, hymnbooks, periodicals and even scholarly journals were published. To promote appreciation of the Baptist heritage, the American Baptist Historical Society was formed in 1853. Closely related to the Publication Society were the American and Foreign Bible Society (1837) and its offshoot, the American Bible Union (1850), both of which merged with ABPS in 1880. In 1879 it was stated: "It is at once a Bible Society, Book Concern, Tract Society, Colporteur Agency, and Sunday School Union of the Baptists." The ABPS was not divided by the slavery issue which split the home and foreign mission societies, and it continued to provide most of the religious literature used by Baptists in the South long after the Civil War. The ABPS proved the most important influence in shaping an identity for Baptists of the United States, giving them a basic unity of doctrine and practice in the nineteenth century. This influence extended beyond the United States as materials and funds were sent to missions in Germany, France, Sweden, Greece and elsewhere.

Sunday schools had been a primary interest of the Tract Society, and the ABPS was long considered as "pre-eminently a Sunday-School Society." Over the years the ABPS reflected trends in the broader Sunday-school movement, developing new objectives, methods, literature, theories of education and patterns of organization. Lesson materials specifically designed for Sunday schools were developed, with Bible lessons provided in 1868, separate books for teachers and pupils in 1870, the Uniform Lesson Series in 1872 and Graded Lessons in 1909. Special departments emphasized children's work, young people's work and adult work. The Baptist Young People's

Union* (BYPU) was organized in 1891, and a separate Young People's Department was created in 1914. In 1912 a Department of Social Services was established to foster a Christian approach to social and economic conditions. In 1911 the Department of Education was formed to cover the whole range of religious education, including teacher training, all the age groups, weekday schools, Vacation Bible Schools,* training institutes, and work with immigrants and blacks.

Meanwhile, the American Baptist Board of Education was formed in 1888 to coordinate and strengthen colleges. Including Baptists of both North and South, it was concerned to meet the growing need for pastors. Attention was concentrated at first on strengthening existing colleges in the West and on establishing the University of Chicago, which opened in 1892. The Board of Education counseled schools on finances and developed the Institutional Support Process to help schools raise funds. Having inherited responsibilities in behalf of Negro colleges begun by the American Baptist Home Mission Society during Reconstruction, it sought to develop leadership in black churches and educational institutions. Campus ministry became another major responsibility of the board. In 1944 the Board of Education merged with ABPS as the American Baptist Board of Education and Publication (ABBEP). In 1947 the Commission on the Ministry was organized to deal specifically with ministerial education, recruitment and ordination standards.

In 1972 the ABBEP became the Board of Education Ministries of ABCUSA. It publishes a wide range of educational and program materials, books and leadership-development resources. It relates in various ways to twenty-six schools, colleges and seminaries, publishes *The American Baptist* and has administrative responsibilities for the American Baptist Assembly, Green Lake, Wisconsin; American Baptist Men; American Baptist Women's Ministries; and the American Baptist Historical Society.

BIBLIOGRAPHY. L. C. Barnes et al., *Pioneers of Light* (1924); S. Fleming, "Board of Education and Theological Education, 1911-1963," *Foun,* January 1965; N. H. Maring and W. S. Hudson, *A Baptist Manual of Polity and Practice* (1990).

N. H. Maring

Board of International Ministries, ABCUSA.
Foreign mission agency of the American Baptist Churches in the USA.* In 1812 Adoniram Judson*

and Luther Rice* sailed for India under the American Board of Commissioners for Foreign Missions, were converted en route to the Baptist view of baptism* by immersion and soon resigned their appointments with the ABCFM. Judson and his wife, Ann Haseltine Judson,* started a Baptist mission in Burma, while Rice returned to the United States to raise support. Baptists in America responded by organizing in 1814 the General Missionary Convention of the Baptist Denomination in the United States for Foreign Missions, or Triennial Convention.* In 1820 a board of twenty-one commissioners, called the Baptist Board of Foreign Missions in the United States,* was created to act for the convention. In 1826 the board became a voluntary society, and the American Baptist Foreign Mission Society* (ABFMS) was thus created.

Baptist missions functioned through the American Baptist Foreign Mission Society and the Triennial Convention until 1845, when a conflict primarily over slavery led to the formation of the Southern Baptist Convention.* In 1846 Baptists in the North restructured their program as the American Baptist Missionary Union* (ABMU). During the nineteenth century new fields were opened in Europe, Asia, Africa and Central America.

In 1910 the ABMU reverted to its old name, American Baptist Foreign Mission Society, and nine years later it became more fully integrated into the Northern Baptist Convention (organized in 1907). Meanwhile, new ministries commenced overseas, particularly in Central America and the Philippines. However, the board suffered setbacks with fundamentalist* defections to Baptist Mid-Missions* (1920), the Association of Baptists for World Evangelism* (1927) and the Conservative Baptist* Foreign Mission Society (1943). In 1973 the ABFMS was brought under the Board of International Ministries of the American Baptist Churches in the USA, and it currently employs almost 200 missionaries and reports an annual income of over $10 million.

See also AMERICAN BAPTIST FOREIGN MISSION SOCIETY; AMERICAN BAPTIST MISSIONARY UNION; BAPTIST BOARD FOR FOREIGN MISSIONS; TRIENNIAL CONVENTION.

BIBLIOGRAPHY. R. G. Torbet, *Venture of Faith: The Story of the American Baptist Foreign Mission Society and the Women's American Baptist Foreign Mission Society, 1814-1954* (1955); H. C. Vedder, *A Short History of Baptist Missions* (1927).   J. A. Patterson

Board of Men's Work, Baptist General Conference. *See* NATIONAL MEN'S FELLOWSHIP OF THE BAPTIST GENERAL CONFERENCE

Board of National Ministries, ABCUSA. Originally called American Baptist Home Mission Society (ABHMS), it was organized in 1832 to meet the challenges of westward migration, growing cities and needs of ethnic minorities. In 1817 John Mason Peck* began a pioneer ministry in Missouri, Illinois and Indiana. Organizing Sunday schools, churches, associations, and Bible and mission societies, editing a Baptist paper and founding a seminary, he helped establish the ABHMS. For years that agency united Baptists of North and South in efforts to Christianize the West.

During and after the Civil War its major ministry aimed to provide churches, ministers and education for slaves and freedpersons. Continued ministry in the South after the Civil War provoked resentment which led to agreements in 1894 concerning work with African-Americans. Immigrants poured into the United States, and seminaries equipped leaders for bilingual ministries with many ethnic groups. Interest in ministry with Native Americans, begun by Isaac McCoy in 1817, was renewed in Oklahoma, where Bacone College was organized in 1876; other missions were established elsewhere. Beginning in 1877 the Woman's American Baptist Home Mission Society reinforced the ABHMS. Majoring in evangelism and church planting, the societies employed missionaries, subsidized pastors' salaries and after 1866 supplied funds for buildings. Almost 90 percent of all ABC churches constituted after 1865 have been assisted by the Home Mission societies.

The societies have adapted to changing needs with creative programs. To assist small rural churches, emphasis was placed upon improved leadership, utilizing special institutes, a Town and Country Department, and a conference center at Green Lake, Wisconsin. Among the approaches developed to meet the changing demands of urban and suburban ministries have been institutional churches, bilingual ministries, Christian centers, Christian Friendliness Missionaries, community witness, urban convocations and the Juvenile Protection Program. Supplying chaplains for the military and for prisons, hospitals and retirement homes, as well as pastoral counselors, has been another area of service.

Evangelism and organizing new churches have always been primary aims, but concomitant with winning people to faith in Jesus Christ is a concern for social justice. Thus the Council for Christian Social Progress, organized in 1941, was incorporated into the ABHMS in 1973. The organizational pattern of the society has varied as structures have been adapted to meet the challenges of evangelism, church extension and ministries to public sectors of society. "Grow by Caring" was introduced in 1982 as a new approach to evangelism, and Macedonia Ministries aimed at renewal of church life. In 1954 a denomination-wide program, Churches for New Frontiers, was launched to support church extension, and in 1984 a plan to start 500 new churches in ten years was begun.

The American Baptist Extension Corporation makes funds available for church construction. Since 1948 the society has sponsored settlement of over 60,000 refugees from nineteen countries. Concern for social justice and involvement in the civil rights movement have helped to make the ABC ethnically very diverse. It has been committed to carrying out its mission in cooperation with other Christians. Since the reorganization of the American Baptist Churches in 1972 it has been called the Board of National Ministries.

See also AMERICAN BAPTIST CHURCHES IN THE USA.

BIBLIOGRAPHY. G. P. Beers, *Ministry to Turbulent America* (1957); M. N. Wenger, "Objective: North America," *Chron*, January 1957; C. L. White, *A Century of Faith* (1932).

N. H. Maring

Board of Women's Work. Agency of the Baptist General Conference* (BGC). The Board of Women's Work, first known as the Women's Commission, was adopted in 1945 as the women's department of the Baptist General Conference. Its first executive secretary came in 1960. Missions education and projects were fostered in keeping with the dynamics of the BGC, sending missionaries to home and world fields beginning in the mid-forties. The board sponsored the Girl's Missionary Guild as part of this emphasis. By the 1970s women's needs were recognized, and the program expanded to develop each woman's potential under God in maturity and ministry to people in the United States and abroad. Under the direction of Dorothy Dahlman, five basic areas of emphasis, with projects in each of them, became the basis for local church leadership training: spiritual

growth, evangelism, missions, service and hospitality. Women were trained and resources provided to use the gifts of women in ministries that would enhance the growth of the church. The director in 1992 was Pamela Heim.

C. Allen

Boardman, George Dana (1801-1831). Pioneer Baptist missionary to Burma. Born in Livermore, Maine, Boardman graduated from the Maine Literary and Theological Institute (now Colby College) and taught there from 1822 to 1823. Feeling an imperative call to foreign missionary service, he attended Andover Theological Seminary* and was sent by the Baptist Missionary Board to Burma in 1825. He served in Calcutta until 1827 and then founded the station at Moulmein, Burma. In 1828 he founded a station at Tavoy, where he inaugurated extensive educational work. Boardman baptized Kyo Tha Byu, the first convert among the Karen people; this man became the first of many effective evangelists among a people whose own religious legends had prepared them in an extraordinary way to receive the gospel. Boardman died at Tavoy at the end of a jungle tour among the Karens. His wife, Sarah Boardman (see Sarah Hall Boardman Judson), stayed on to continue work in Burma, and in 1834 she married Adoniram Judson,* founder of the Burma mission.

BIBLIOGRAPHY. *AAP* 6; J. C. Robbins, *Boardman of Burma* (1940).

D. M. Stowe

Bogard, Benjamin Marcus (1868-1951). Pastor, evangelist, debater and Landmark* leader. Born March 9, 1868, near Elizabethtown, Kentucky, Bogard attended college in Georgetown, Kentucky, and Bethel College, Russellville, Kentucky (1889-1891). He married Linnie Onida Meachmam Owen in 1891. Bogard's first pastorate was Rocky Ridge Baptist Church, Trigg County, Kentucky. Other pastorates were Princeton (1892-1894), Harmony and Fulton (1894), and Wingo (1895), Kentucky; First Baptist Church, Charleston, Missouri (1895-1899); and First Baptist Church, Searcy, Arkansas (1899-1903). While at Searcy, Bogard published his first book, *Pillars of Orthodoxy: Or, Defenders of the Faith* (1901). Bogard led the "anti-Corresponding Secretary" movement at the Arkansas Baptist State Convention in 1901. He helped form the General Association of Arkansas Baptist Churches (April

10-11, 1902) and the General Association of Baptists (November 24-26, 1905). The General Association of Baptists, now the American Baptist Association* (ABA), is a Landmark body representing churches in twelve states. Bogard also founded the Sunday-school literature arm of the ABA and served as editor of the *Missionary Baptist Searchlight.*

From 1904 to 1920, Bogard alternated between independent evangelistic work and pastorates in Argenta (now North Little Rock), Arkansas (1903-1904); Itasca, Texas (1912-1914); and Texarkana, Arkansas (1914-1919). In 1920 Bogard became pastor of Antioch Missionary Baptist Church, Little Rock, where he remained for twenty-seven years. Bogard was a pioneer radio minister in Arkansas, airing the first weekly religious radio program in Little Rock. He authored *The Baptist Way-Book; A Manual Designed for Use in Baptist Churches* (1945). He was founder and president of the Missionary Baptist Seminary associated with the Antioch Church. Bogard died May 29, 1951, in Little Rock, Arkansas.

BIBLIOGRAPHY. L. D. Foreman and A. Payne, *The Life and Works of Benjamin Marcus Bogard,* 3 vols. (1965); E. G. Hinson, *A History of Baptists in Arkansas* (1979).

A. L. Pratt

Boyce, James Petigru (1827-1888). Southern Baptist* educator, theologian and seminary founder. Born in Charleston, South Carolina, Boyce was educated at Charleston College, Brown University* and Princeton. Princeton professor Charles Hodge helped shape Boyce's appreciation for Reformed theology. Boyce's conversion to Christianity in 1846 led him to religious studies and the decision to enter the ministry. After serving as pastor of First Baptist Church, Columbia, South Carolina, and as professor of theology at Furman University,* in 1859 Boyce helped to found the Southern Baptist Theological Seminary* in Greenville, South Carolina. He served as professor and chairman of the seminary faculty until his death in 1888. Boyce was chief fundraiser for the seminary and a proponent of theological education for all Southern Baptist ministers. Under his guidance the fledgling seminary survived the Civil War years and a move to Louisville in 1877. Boyce's moderate Reformed theology left its imprint in the seminary's doctrinal statement, "Abstract of Principles," and in his book *Abstract of Systematic Theology,* published in

1887. Boyce was also president of the Southern Baptist Convention 1872-1879 and 1888.

BIBLIOGRAPHY. J. A. Broadus, *Memoir of James Petigru Boyce* (1893); *DAB* I.

B. J. Leonard

Boyd, Richard Henry (1843-1922). Pastor, denominational leader, publisher, businessman, banker. Born enslaved in Mississippi, Boyd attended Bishop College in Marshall, Texas, after Emancipation. He organized the first black Texas Baptist association in 1870, founded churches and became a leader in the black state Baptist convention. With the establishment of the National Baptist Convention in 1895 (*see* National Baptists), Boyd headed its publishing board, building a successful enterprise with funds he raised, and then incorporated it under his own name. The ensuing incorporation controversy eventuated in the formation of the Boyd-led National Baptist Convention of America in 1916. Boyd also presided over a company that manufactured the first black dolls in 1911, and he helped found and served as president of the Citizens Savings Bank and Trust Company in Nashville.

BIBLIOGRAPHY. *DAB* II; L. G. Jordan, *Negro Baptist History* (1930); R. W. Logan and M. R. Winston, *Dictionary of American Negro Biography* (1982); O. D. Pelt, *Ralph Lee Smith: The Story of the National Baptists* (1960); J. M. Washington, *Frustrated Fellowship* (1986).

S. D. Martin

Brantly, William Theophilus, Jr. (1816-1882). A distinguished Baptist minister in both the North and South, Brantley was the son of William Theophilus Brantley Sr.,* pastor of First Baptist, Augusta, Georgia.

Brantley was caught in the whirlwind of regional relationships during the Civil War era. He began his ministry in his father's church, following his education at New England's Brown University.* After a brief teaching career at the University of Georgia, he became minister at Tabernacle Baptist in Philadelphia, one of the city's stronger Baptist congregations. The impending military conflict, however, caused him to resign and return to his native Georgia.

During the war he preached in a number of outlying places in the vicinity of Atlanta and later was pastor at Second Baptist, Atlanta. In 1871 he returned North to Baltimore's Seventh Baptist Church. In the course of the 1860s he advocated states' rights and Unionism, accommodating himself to increasingly progressive political positions.

BIBLIOGRAPHY. W. H. Brackney, *The Baptists* (1988); W. T. Brantly, *Our National Troubles* (1860). W. H. Brackney

Brantly, William Theophilus, Sr. (1787-1845). Born January 23, 1787, in North Carolina and educated at South Carolina College, W. T. Brantly first served as a pastor in Beaufort, South Carolina, where he became one of the state's best preachers. In 1819 he was named head of Richmond Academy at Augusta, Georgia, where again his oratory was foremost. He started what became First Baptist Church,* Augusta, and built an impressive meetinghouse.

After Philadelphia's First Baptist Church* suffered a split over Henry Holcomb's* disagreements with the General Missionary Convention and Holcomb died in 1826, Brantly was called to that historic pulpit. He won the hearts of the differing factions and renewed the congregation; in eleven years he baptized over 600 persons.

In 1837 he accepted the call to Charleston's First Baptist Church,* where he also served as president of the College of Charleston—both prestigious roles in Old Charleston's social register. Ironically, Brantly died just as the division between Northern* and Southern* Baptists reached its climax. He died March 28, 1845.

BIBLIOGRAPHY. W. H. Brackney, *The Baptists* (1988). W. H. Brackney

Brethren, Church of the. *See* DUNKERS

Brewton-Parker College. The only private, denominational senior college in Georgia south of Macon. Brewton-Parker College was chartered as Union Baptist Institute and established in 1905 at Ailey-Mt. Vernon on fifteen acres partly donated by African-American farmer W. C. Crawley. Established to offer secondary education, the school was renamed Brewton-Parker Institute in 1912 and came to be supported by twenty-one Baptist associations in south Georgia. In 1927, first- and second-year college courses having been added, the name was changed to Brewton-Parker Junior College. All secondary instruction was discontinued and ownership was transferred in 1948 to the Georgia Baptist Convention. The Southern Association of Colleges and Schools extended senior college accreditation in 1986 based on a bachelor of ministry degree. Between 1983 and

1992 total net assets increased 49 percent. Including an off-campus correctional system program, Brewton-Parker had a fall 1991 enrollment of 2,147.

BIBLIOGRAPHY. Brewton-Parker College, *Catalog 1990-91.* W. L. Allen

Brisbane, William Henry (1806-1878). Pastor, journalist and humanitarian. William Henry Brisbane was born October 12, 1806, into a Southern aristocratic family; as a young man he studied medicine. He enjoyed preaching and was ordained to the Baptist ministry in 1835 in Beauford, South Carolina. His political views took a radical turn when he encountered the work of Francis Wayland, after which he developed antislavery views and set his own slaves free.

Under local pressure, Brisbane left the South to edit an abolitionist newspaper in Cincinnati, Ohio. Encountering new opposition to his work, he moved again to Wisconsin, where he mingled with national antislavery leaders and launched several forays into the South to denounce slavery. During the Civil War he served as a chaplain, and afterward he worked for the improvement of freedpersons. After the war he worked for the federal government in South Carolina and part-time in the Baptist ministry.

BIBLIOGRAPHY. W. H. Brackney, *The Baptists* (1988). W. H. Brackney

Broaddus, Andrew (1770-1848). Baptist pastor and associational leader. Born in Caroline County, Virginia, Broaddus rarely ventured outside his native state. He was largely self-educated, but his father, John Broaddus, probably tutored him for a time. Though his family was of Episcopal background, Andrew Broaddus came under the influence of Theodore Noel, pastor of the Upper King and Queen Baptist Church, by whom he was baptized (1789) and ordained (1791). A good number of children were born of four marriages; Broaddus was severely criticized for his third marriage, to the sister of his deceased wife.

Broaddus served as pastor of several rural churches in Virginia, including Salem (from 1820) and Upper King and Queen (from 1827). His son and grandson succeeded him at Salem, providing a continuous ministry for over a century. An active leader and often moderator of the Dover Association, Broaddus resisted the views of Alexander Campbell* and his followers in associational conferences, numerous articles and a book entitled *The Extra Examined* (1831). Regarded as a superb preacher and biblical expositor, he declined invitations from influential city churches and remained a rural pastor.

A frequent contributor to the *Religious Herald* and author of several books, Broaddus may be best remembered for three collections of hymns: *Collection of Sacred Ballads* (1790), *The Dover Selection of Spiritual Songs* (1828) and *The Virginia Selection of Psalms, Hymns and Spiritual Songs* (1836). A few of his own compositions appear in these works.

BIBLIOGRAPHY. *AAP* 6; J. B. Jeter, *The Sermons and Other Writings of the Rev. Andrew Broaddus with a Memoir of His Life* (1852); J. B. Taylor, *Virginia Baptist Ministers* (1860).

C. L. Howe

Broadman Press. Trade name of the general book publishing program of the Sunday School Board (SSB) of the Southern Baptist Convention* (SBC). Broadman catalogs also list church supplies and audiovisuals. The name Broadman derives from joining portions of the last names of John Albert Broadus* and Basil Manly Jr.,* secretary and president, respectively, of the first SSB (existed 1863-1873). The first books published with the Broadman imprint appeared in 1934.

Broadman has published thousands of books in numerous subject areas. Major, multivolume publications have included the *Encyclopedia of Southern Baptists* (4 vols., 1958-1982), the Broadman Bible Commentary (12 vols., 1969-1972; vol. 1 revised in 1973), the BibLearn Series for children (24 vols., 1976-1979), the Layman's Bible Book Commentary (24 vols., 1978-1984), the Meet the Missionary series for children (20 vols., 1982-1986), the Layman's Library of Christian Doctrine (16 vols., 1984-1988), and the Bible-and-Me Series for preschoolers (24 vols., 1988-). The New American Commentary (40 vols., 1991-1998), based on the New International Version of the Bible, is among the largest publication projects ever attempted by Broadman. This commentary is based on a conservative, inerrantist viewpoint.

Products released by Broadman have exerted important influences on Southern Baptist Bible study, theology, church administration, history, deacon programs, pastoral ministry, evangelism and missions, ethics, age-graded church organizational leadership, prayer, preaching, and many practical aspects of discipleship and personal faith. Broadman has also provided numerous textbooks for colleges, universities and seminaries.

Occasionally Broadman books have been the focus of controversy. Examples include (1) Ralph H. Elliott's *The Message of Genesis* (1961), whose alleged liberal content led both to the blocking of a reprint by the SSB in 1962 and the dismissal of Elliott from his faculty post at Midwestern Baptist Theological Seminary,* also in 1962, (2) volume 1 (1969) of the Broadman Bible Commentary, removed from distribution and rewritten after the SBC voted in 1970 that the volume should be revised to reflect a more conservative perspective, and (3) the SSB's centennial history (prepared by H. Leon McBeth), whose publication was blocked in 1990 by trustees who alleged that the volume showed partiality to the administration of then-current SSB president Lloyd Elder, who was forced into early retirement in 1991.

BIBLIOGRAPHY. *Broadman Catalog; ESB* 1:194; 3:1620-21; 4:2130.

C. W. Deweese

Broadus, John Albert (1827-1895). Seminary professor and Southern Baptist* minister. Reared in Virginia in a home marked by a high degree of culture and spiritual devotion, Broadus was converted at sixteen years of age. Following his graduation from the University of Virginia in 1850 (M.A.), he became a tutor in Latin and Greek at the university while serving as pastor of the Baptist Church of Charlottesville. Later Broadus became one of the four original faculty members of the Southern Baptist Theological Seminary,* originally established at Greenville, South Carolina, in 1859. For the next thirty-six years, from 1859 to 1895, he served as professor of New Testament interpretation and homiletics, interrupted only by the seminary's closure during the Civil War, when he served a stint as chaplain in Robert E. Lee's army. After the war he and his colleagues reopened the seminary, which moved to Louisville, Kentucky, in 1877. There Broadus was to serve for several years as president (1889-1895).

Of his numerous books, pamphlets and tracts, he is best known for his introduction to homiletics, *On the Preparation and Delivery of Sermons* (1870), which became a textbook in many denominational seminaries and remains in print even today. His *Commentary on the Gospel of Matthew* (1886) was esteemed for its careful scholarship, and his *Harmony of the Gospels* (1893) was to achieve a long and distinguished reputation. In 1889 he delivered the Beecher Lectures on Preaching at Yale, the first Southern Baptist to do so. Known for his biblical scholarship and homiletical skills, Broadus was invited to serve on other theological faculties, but he was consistently loyal to his calling of nurturing a blend of scholarship and erudition in the Southern Baptist ministry.

See also SOUTHERN BAPTIST THEOLOGICAL SEMINARY.

BIBLIOGRAPHY. *DAB* II; *DARB; ESB* 1; W. A. Mueller, *A History of Southern Baptist Theological Seminary* (1959); *NCAB* 18; A. T. Robertson, *Life and Letters of John A. Broadus* (1901).

W. R. Estep

Brooks, Walter Henderson (1851-1945). Prominent African-American Baptist pastor, author and spokesman. Brooks was born into slavery in Richmond, Virginia, on August 30, 1851. He remained a slave until his emancipation in 1865. He entered Lincoln University the following year, graduating in 1872 with the A.B. degree. The son of Christian parents, Brooks was converted in 1867 but not baptized until 1873, when he united with the First African Baptist Church of Richmond. Following his ordination in 1876, he accepted a call to the pastorate of the Second Baptist Church of Richmond. From 1874 to 1876 and again from 1880 to 1881, Brooks served as an agent of the American Baptist Publication Society.* During Brooks's lengthy pastorate at the Nineteenth Street Baptist Church in Washington, D.C., from 1881 until his death in 1945, he entered the most notable period of his career. He achieved national prominence through his involvement with the promotion of African-American education and social improvement, the temperance movement, and the advancement of separate denominational structures for black Baptists.

BIBLIOGRAPHY. W. H. Brooks, *The Pastor's Voice* (1945); J. M. Washington, *Frustrated Fellowship: The Black Baptist Quest for Social Power* (1986).

B. C. Leslie

Brotherhood Commission, SBC. Missions support, education and action agency of the Southern Baptist Convention* (SBC) for men and boys. Organized in 1907 as the Laymen's Missionary Movement, SBC, it was renamed Baptist Brotherhood of the South in 1927 and took its current

name in 1950. Age-graded church programs exist for Royal Ambassadors* (grades 1-9), High School Baptist Young Men, Collegiate Baptist Young Men, Baptist Young Men, Baptist Men and Senior Baptist Men. The commission helps coordinate World Missions conferences, involves thousands of people in mission action projects and sponsors a major disaster-relief program. Executives have included J. T. Henderson (1908-1938), Lawson H. Cooke (1938-1951), George W. Schroeder (1952-1971), W. Glendon McCullough (1971-1978), James H. Smith (1979-1991) and James D. Williams (1991-). Commission offices are located in Memphis, Tennessee.

BIBLIOGRAPHY. *Brotherhood Means Missions* (1987); *ESB* 1:196-99; 3:1, 621-1424; 4:2131-33.

C. W. Deweese

Brown, John Newton (1803-1868). Minister. Brown was born in New London, Connecticut, in June 1803 and died May 14, 1868, in Germantown, Pennsylvania. Educated in Hamilton, New York, he was ordained in Buffalo (1824) and became pastor at Moulden, Massachusetts, three years later. Brown became professor of theology and pastoral relations in the New Hampton Institution, New Hampshire. In 1849 he became editorial secretary of the American Baptist Publication Society.* He is best remembered for his part in the revision of the New Hampshire Confession of Faith.* In 1833 the confession was approved by the board of the convention and recommended to the churches. Twenty years later Brown revised it and added two articles, "Repentance and Faith" and "Sanctification," making a total of eighteen articles. Because of its modified Calvinism and its lack of any reference to the universal church, it became the most popular confession among Baptists in the United States. Brown was also the editor of the *Encyclopedia of Religious Knowledge* (1858), which became a widely used work of reference in the nineteenth century.

See also CONFESSIONS OF FAITH; NEW HAMPSHIRE CONFESSION.

BIBLIOGRAPHY. W. H. Brackney, *The Baptists* (1988).

W. R. Estep

Brown, Joseph Emerson (1821-1894). Southern lawyer, politician and businessman. Reared in northwest Georgia, where he received a rudimentary education; in 1840 he entered Calhoun Academy in Anderson, South Carolina. Returning to Georgia, he passed the bar in 1845, after which he graduated from Yale Law School. Elected in 1857, he was the wartime governor of Georgia. Though he was a strong supporter of states' rights, slavery and secession, he often opposed the policies of Jefferson Davis. After the war he supported Congressional Reconstruction, served as a judge, and was U.S. Senator from 1880 to 1891. He became wealthy in business and gave $50,000 to the University of Georgia and a like amount to the Southern Baptist Theological Seminary* to endow a chair in theology. Smaller amounts went to Mercer University* and to his home church, Second Baptist, Atlanta. For nineteen years he was a trustee of SBTS, being president of the board from 1883 to 1894.

BIBLIOGRAPHY. *DAB* II.

N. H. Maring

Brown University. An institution of higher education founded by colonial Baptists. Founded at Warren, Rhode Island, the College of Rhode Island was a Baptist response to earlier collegiate formation. Concern over the initial charter presented to the legislature, which seemed to vest control in Congregationalist interests, led in 1764 to a revised charter that placed the institution squarely in Baptist hands. From its beginnings the college espoused principles of religious liberty.* No religious tests were required of either students or faculty, and by 1770 Jews were also allowed as students, though Roman Catholics, deists and atheists were still proscribed. All of the school's presidents, however, were Baptist ministers until well into the twentieth century.

In 1765 James Manning,* a Baptist minister, was appointed as first president, and the first class was graduated in 1769. The college moved to Providence in 1770. In 1776 the last commencement until after the Revolutionary War was held. Subsequently the college was used as a barracks and hospital by the Continental and French armies and was badly damaged. In the 1780s a lack of students and funds created additional problems. In gratitude for a $5,000 gift from Nicholas Brown, an alumnus, the name of the college was changed to Brown University in 1804.

Academically, Brown reached its nineteenth-century apex during the innovative presidency of Francis Wayland.* Among his accomplishments were the introduction of a largely elective curriculum and a program of instruction that allowed students to finish in three years. Women were first admitted in 1891. The university has offered

graduate instruction since 1897 and grants degrees through the doctoral level.

BIBLIOGRAPHY. W. C. Bronson, *The History of Brown University, 1764-1914* (1914).

F. M. Perko

Bryan, Andrew (1737-1812). Pioneer black Baptist minister. Born in slavery at Goose Creek, South Carolina, Bryan was brought to a plantation near Savannah, Georgia. Near the age of thirty-five he was converted to Christianity by George Liele,* who evangelized along the coastal plantations. Beginning his own ministry, Bryan and his brother, Sampson, were brought before city authorities and whipped for refusing to discontinue their work. He and his followers were forbidden to hold services at night, but they were able, with owners' permission, to meet during the day, and Bryan's master opened his barn at Brampton for their use.

In 1788 Abraham Marshall, a white Baptist minister, accompanied by Jesse Galphin (or Jesse Peter), a black associate, visited the congregation. After examination they baptized forty to sixty people and ordained Bryan—an early, if not the first, ordination of an Afro American. The First Colored (later African) Baptist Church of Savannah erected its first building in 1794, and the membership grew to 850 by 1802. After purchasing his freedom, Bryan was able to extend his ministry, organizing a Second African Baptist Church with Henry Francis, a slave, as pastor. He then went on to organize a Third Church in another part of town. Widely known by Baptists in England and in North America, Bryan died in October 1812, having been active in the ministry until the end of his life.

BIBLIOGRAPHY. J. M. Simms, *The First Colored Baptist Church in North America* (1888); M. Sobel, *Trabelin' On: The Slave Journey of an Afro-Baptist Faith* (1979).

W. B. Gravely and C. White

Bucknell University. Institution of higher learning founded by Pennsylvania Baptists. In 1845 the Northumberland Baptist Association of north-central Pennsylvania, under the leadership of James Moore II, undertook to establish an educational center of higher learning that would offer broad-based educational opportunities and promote denominational ideals among the young. The result was an academy that met in the basement of the Baptist church of Lewisburg,

Pennsylvania. The academy was chartered on February 5, 1846, as the University of Lewisburg. A permanent college campus building was erected in 1848. Howard Malcolm, the first president, was chosen in 1851. Women were officially admitted to the university in 1883 (a separate school for women had existed under the auspices of the university since 1852). The school was renamed Bucknell University in 1886, after William Bucknell of Philadelphia, a respected patron and trustee. In 1990 the university enrolled over 3,500 students and employed 250 faculty members.

BIBLIOGRAPHY. J. O. Oliphant, *The Rise of Bucknell University* (1965); J. J. Zimmerman et al., *All Our Past Proclaims Our Future* (1981).

B. C. Leslie

Buhlmaier, Marie (1859-1938). Baptist home missionary. Born in Heilbronn, Germany, Buhlmaier came to the United States with her family in 1868. With only three years of schooling, she had to go to work at age ten. Confirmed in the Lutheran Church in 1873, she was baptized into the German Baptist Church the same year. At age fifteen she became a church worker for the First Baptist Church of Harlem, New York. In 1893 she became a missionary to German immigrants in Baltimore for the Home Mission Board of the Southern Baptist Convention.* A gifted speaker, she also wrote *Along the Highway of Service* (1924).

N. A. Hardesty

Burroughs, Peleg (1748-1800). Clergyman and merchant. Burroughs was born in Newport, Rhode Island, on June 5, 1748, and died at Tiverton, Rhode Island, on August 8, 1800. He was the son of Samuel and Mary Greene Burroughs and was married to Kezia Burdick West in 1772. They had ten children. He had no formal education.

Raised within the Second Baptist Church (General Six Principle*) of Newport, Burroughs was immersed in 1767. His wife, however, never renounced her Seventh Day Baptist* views. Burroughs started to preach in 1772 and was pastor of the Tiverton First Baptist (Old Stone) Church (then General Six Principle) from 1775 until his death. He was ordained to the ministry in 1780. For many years he was co-owner of a general store in Tiverton. Although he sympathized with American views during the Revolution, he was a pacifist. From 1778 to 1797 he maintained a detailed diary, which was published in the twentieth

century. The records of the church throughout most of his ministry have been preserved.

R. G. Gardner

Burton, Ernest Dewitt (1856-1925). Baptist biblical scholar and president of the University of Chicago. Born in Granville, Ohio, Burton graduated from Denison University (B.A., 1876) and as a young man taught school in Michigan and Ohio, after which he studied for the ministry at Rochester Theological Seminary* (B.D., 1882). At twenty-seven he was elected to the chair in New Testament at Newton Theological Institute* (1883). It was at the reorganized University of Chicago, however, that Burton made his major contribution. In 1892 he became the head of the department of New Testament and early Christian literature. In this capacity he edited *Biblical World* and the *American Journal of Theology* and wrote widely in the field of New Testament studies. Upon Harry Pratt Judson's retirement in 1923, Burton became president of the university (1923-1925).

Few writers surpassed Burton's usefulness in producing New Testament scholarship. He was among the first to develop the field of biblical theology as a historical discipline, presenting the thesis that the books of the Bible represent a historical process. He paid particular attention to the environment of the biblical writers and the context of extracanonical literature. With E. J. Goodspeed, Burton edited *Harmony of the Synoptic Gospels* (1920), and he organized *A Sourcebook for the Study of the Teaching of Jesus in Its Historical Relationships* (1923), which provided a new approach to the contemporary quest for a unified life of Christ. Burton's work in New Testament paralleled that of William R. Harper* in Old Testament and Semitics and Shailer Mathews in historical theology in the well-known University of Chicago Divinity School.*

BIBLIOGRAPHY. *DAB* II; T. W. Goodspeed, *Ernest Dewitt Burton* (1926).

W. H. Brackney

Bushyhead, Jesse (1804-1844). Cherokee minister, interpreter, lobbyist and chief justice. Born in the Cherokee Nation, September 1804, Bushyhead received his education from Presbyterian missionaries but converted to Baptist doctrines and worked under the leadership of the Baptist missionary Evan Jones. Bushyhead worked as an interpreter and itinerant preacher, became the first ordained Cherokee minister and founded the first indigenous Cherokee church at Amohee, Tennessee. He was appointed as a justice to the Cherokee Supreme Court and later served as chief justice. Described as the most noble-looking and eloquent man in the Cherokee Nation, he was active as a lobbyist to Congress in opposition to removal.

In 1844 abolitionists of the Northern United States published false information that Bushyhead owned slaves and asked whether a slave-holder should be employed by the Baptist Mission Board. This action called forth the "Alabama Resolutions," which prompted the split of 1845 between Southern and Northern Baptist churches. That same year, on July 17, Bushyhead died in Westville, Oklahoma, of "prairie fever" before word of the controversy reached him.

BIBLIOGRAPHY. W. McLoughlin, *Cherokee and Missionaries, 1789-1839* (1984); W. N. Wyeth, *Poor Lo!* (1896):60-62.

W. A. Horton

C

California Baptist College. Educational institution founded by the Southern Baptist Convention* of California. The school began operation in 1950 at El Monte, but in 1955 moved to the present sixty-acre campus in Riverside, sixty miles from downtown Los Angeles. Enrollment has increased from 120 students to about 700, who come from throughout the United States and twenty foreign countries. Its purpose is to offer a broad liberal arts education in a Christian environment. The curriculum includes seventeen major areas of study, with special strength in the fields of education, behavioral sciences, music, business administration and religion. A master's degree is offered in marriage, family and child counseling. The college is accredited by Western States Association of Schools and Colleges, and it holds associate membership in the National Association of Schools of Music. It is also certified by the California Board of Education for teacher education. To nurture spiritual life, a Baptist Student Union program, directed by a campus minister, is maintained. Chapel services are held once a week and on special occasions; attendance is required of students carrying seven or more units. A set of expectations for student conduct is based on "the historic tenets of the institution and Southern Baptist traditions."

BIBLIOGRAPHY. California Baptist College, *Catalogue, 1991-92.*   N. H. Maring

Call to the Ministry, Baptist Views. The call to the ministry is second only to the conversion* experience as a significant religious experience among Baptists. This view of the call to the ministry has influenced their understanding of the role and expectations of the minister. But Baptist views of the call experience have differed according to time period, educational level, theological-ecclesiological tradition and geographical location.

Eighteenth-century Regular Baptists* were rep-resentative of a strong Calvinistic theology that emphasized that ministers were appointed by Christ and chosen and set apart by the church through fasting, prayer and the imposition of hands by the eldership. Ministers were responsible for preaching and the administration of the ordinances. This tradition did allow for others to preach if enabled by the Holy Spirit and with the consent of the church. Ministers were to be called out of local congregations, which had the power and privilege of seeking candidates who feared God, were born again of the Spirit, led blameless lives, were strong in the faith, desired to glorify God and save souls, and had a capacity to learn and teach.

Candidates for ministry who exhibited the gifts and graces for the work were selected and put on private trial for a season. If edifying, they were then allowed to preach in public. If the public preaching produced results, then the candidate was asked to articulate an inward call. For this tradition, the call to the ministry was primarily shaped by the unanimous consent of the local church, which was the primary instrument of conveying the will of God to those called out. While the individual had to be able to profess a personal call, the identification and evaluation of the acceptability of gifts for the ministry were the duty of the church, association and presbytery. Education was viewed as an appropriate enhancement of the call experience. For these Calvinistic Baptists, the call was primarily a corporate experience.

Baptists shaped by the revivalistic tradition emphasized individualism and evangelical fervor. Call for these Baptists was an internal and experiential rather than a professional choice. Emphasis was on the charismatic gift affirmed by the local congregation. Candidates were to have an ever-deepening conviction of the soul, the ability to speak with conviction, and a useful ministry and good character. An inward call was essential, and the church's external approval became an added assurance.

Twentieth-century Baptists expanded the concept of call to all believers endowed with spiritual gifts for service, with the office of pastor determined by a local body. The call of God was an outward call from the church, while an inward call was an inner assurance on the part of individuals that they were complying with God's will. Theological education was expected for those entering the vocation of minister. Baptists seek to hold in tension the role of the Holy Spirit in an inward, individualistic, self-authenticating call with the outward call of the local church and the desire for an educated ministry.

BIBLIOGRAPHY. H. B. Foshee, *Broadman Church Manual* (1973); A. C. Loveland, *Southern Evangelicals and the Social Order, 1800-1860* (1980), N. H. Maring and W. S. Hudson, *A Baptist Manual of Polity and Practice*, rev. ed. (1991).

J. F. Loftis

Calvin, John (1509-1564). French Protestant Reformer and theologian. Along with Martin Luther of Germany and Ulrich Zwingli of Zurich, Calvin is known as one of the greatest Reformers of the sixteenth century.

Born in France and educated at the Universities of Paris and Orleans, Calvin became a Protestant in 1534. In 1536 he published his *Institutes of the Christian Religion,* a brilliant outline of Protestant theology. He constantly revised and enlarged this work until the definitive edition of 1559, and it became the most influential theological treatise of the Reformation.

Calvin settled in Geneva, Switzerland, from 1536 to 1538 and from 1541 to 1564, with a brief interval in Strasbourg from 1538 to 1541. In Geneva, Calvin shaped the doctrines and structures of Protestantism. He is particularly identified with the doctrine of predestination. His legacy is seen in the Reformed tradition of Protestant churches. Calvin also helped shape Western views on politics, economics and marriage. Many, however, regard Calvin as a cheerless theologian who introduced a note of rigid legalism into Protestantism.

Calvin's Reformed version of Protestantism spread in Switzerland, the Netherlands and England. From England it was transported to the American colonies, where it helped shape Christianity in the United States and Canada.

See also CALVINISM AMONG BAPTISTS.

BIBLIOGRAPHY. G. Harkness, *John Calvin: The Man and His Ethics* (1958); J. T. McNeill, *The History and Character of Calvinism* (1964).

H. L. McBeth

Calvinism Among Baptists. The views of John Calvin,* Protestant Reformer, influenced Baptist theology and practice more than any other of the great Reformers.

Of the two groups of English Baptists (General* and Particular*) that emerged in the early seventeenth century, the Particular were more Calvinistic. Their confessions* of 1644 and 1689 reflect their commitment to Calvinistic theology. For a time in the eighteenth century, under the leadership of John Gill, Particular Baptists embraced an extreme form of "hyper-Calvinism." These extreme views were modified by Andrew Fuller, pastor in Kettering, and by William Carey,* the pioneer Baptist missionary to India.

Both General and Particular Baptists made their way to colonial America. The Calvinistic or Particular Baptists founded churches in Rhode Island (1639), Massachusetts (1663), Maine (1682) and South Carolina (1696). These quickly became the mainstream of Baptists in America. In 1707 they formed the influential Philadelphia Baptist Association,* a group that eventually covered several states and wielded vast influence. The Philadelphia Confession of Faith, printed by Benjamin Franklin in 1742, reflects modified Calvinism. That association provided cohesion, and its confession spread Calvinistic views among most Baptists in America.

The New Hampshire Baptist Confession* of 1834 also picked up Calvinistic teachings. Though it originated in New England, the New Hampshire Confession blanketed the South and fixed Calvinist views upon Baptists in that region.

Several movements arose to challenge or soften Calvinism among Baptists. The older General Baptist influence, though outnumbered, never disappeared. The rise of the Free Will Baptists,* led by Paul Palmer* in North Carolina from 1727, and a later movement led by Benjamin Randall* in New Hampshire from 1783, challenged Calvinist theology among Baptists. The rise of the intensely revivalist Separate Baptists,* especially as led by Shubal Stearns* in North Carolina in the 1750s, further eroded Calvinist hegemony.

In the twentieth century, Calvinist emphases have been retained but muted somewhat in most of the mainline Baptist groups in America. Major theologians like William Newton Clarke* and A. H. Strong* in the North, along with E. Y. Mullins* and Walter T. Conner* in the South, modified Calvinism to make more room for personal decision and experience in religion. The emergent organized evangelism, especially as led by Lee Rutland Scarborough* in the Southern Baptist Convention,* did not abandon Calvinism but turned the spotlight on other dimensions of the Christian faith.

More intense Calvinistic emphases continue in some smaller Baptist groups, including the Primitive Baptists,* the Regular Baptists,* the Reformed Baptists* and some of the fundamentalist groups. There is also a small but intense resurgence of Calvinism in recent years, especially in the General Association of Regular Baptist Churches* in the North and in the Southern Baptist Convention.

BIBLIOGRAPHY. H. L. McBeth, *The Baptist Heritage* (1987); T. J. Nettles, *By His Grace and for His Glory* (1986). H. L. McBeth

Cameron, Robert (c. 1845-c. 1922). Canadian Baptist minister and prophetic writer. Originally from Brantford, Ontario, Cameron was a prominent figure in the Niagara Bible Conference. He first embraced and then rejected strict dispensationalism's doctrine of a secret and imminent return of Christ before the tribulation of the last days. In 1884 he questioned the increasing dominance of this pretribulation view at the conference, maintaining his own posttribulation premillennial eschatology.

Despite differences over eschatology, Cameron worked closely with A. J. Gordon,* a historic premillennialist. Following Gordon's death, Cameron took over the editorship of *The Watchword,* a leading millenarian journal. He cooperated with James H. Brookes, a dispensationalist who edited another prophetic magazine, *The Truth.* Following Brookes's death, Cameron purchased this journal and merged the two publications to form *The Watchword and Truth.* In 1902 he published a strong attack on the pretribulationist view, which led to an aggressive assertion of the full dispensational position by opponents. Cameron expounded his millenarian views in two books, *The Doctrine of the Ages* (1896) and *Scriptural Truth About the Lord's Return* (1922).

BIBLIOGRAPHY. E. Sandeen, *The Roots of Fundamentalism* (1970). D. M. Lewis

Campbell, Alexander (1788-1866). A founder of the Disciples of Christ, editor and college pres-

ident; born in Ireland, September 12, 1788, to Jane and Thomas Campbell. Thomas, an Anti-Burgher Seceder Presbyterian minister, came to Pennsylvania in 1807; his family tried to follow in 1808. Delayed by shipwreck, Alexander attended the University of Glasgow and was influenced there by Greenville Ewig and the Haldane movement. He left the Seceders while at Glasgow.

Thomas had also left the Seceders and in his 1809 *Declaration and Address of the Christian Association of Washington, Pennsylvania,* called for the use of New World freedom to restore primitive Christianity as the basis of unity, "that the world might believe" the gospel. Joining his father in 1809, Alexander Campbell made this his life's work. In 1811 he married Margaret Brown. Her family farm in Brook County, [West] Virginia, became his permanent home.

After 1812, the year of his ordination by the Brush Run Church (formerly the Christian Association), Alexander's insistence that baptism* was the immersion of penitent adult believers marked him as the new leader in the movement and led to a brief relationship with Baptists. Between 1815 and 1830 the Campbells were part of the Redstone (Pennsylvania) and Mahoning (Ohio) Baptists associations.

In debates with Presbyterians John Walker (1820) and William MacCalla (1823), Campbell championed a "baptist" position. But many Baptists soon eschewed him as a "water regenerationist." Campbell debated the "infidel" Robert Owen in 1829 and the Roman Catholic archbishop John Purcell in 1837. He also spoke as a delegate to the Virginia constitutional convention of 1829.

Campbell edited and published the monthly serials *The Christian Baptist* (1823-1829) and *The Millennial Harbinger* (1830-1863), which, along with his debates, an edition of the New Testament and *The Christian System* (1839), were among his primary publications.

In 1832 Campbell's followers united with many of those of Barton Warren Stone. Campbell was the founder (1840) and president (to 1866) of Bethany College. In 1849 the first national convention of the Disciples (in Cincinnati) elected the absent Campbell president of their new American Christian Missionary Society, and he served until his death in 1866.

BIBLIOGRAPHY. R. Richardson, *Memoirs of Alexander Campbell,* 2 vols. (1868).

A. L. Dunnavant

Campbell University. A Baptist university in Buies Creek, North Carolina. The school was originally founded in 1887 by James Archibald Campbell as Buies Creek Academy, a high school. Campbell owned and operated the academy until 1925, when it was bought by the North Carolina State Baptist Convention. In 1926 it became Buies Creek Junior College. The school was renamed for Campbell in 1927, and he continued as president until his death in 1934, when he was succeeded by his son Leslie H. Campbell. The school continued to maintain a high school until after World War II. In 1979 it became a university, now offering more than thirty major areas of study including liberal arts, law, education and business administration. The school is widely recognized for its law school and its trust management major. Norman A. Wiggins has been president of the university since 1967.

BIBLIOGRAPHY. *ESB* 1, 4.

B. J. Leonard

Canadian Baptist Federation. A loose confederation of four autonomous Baptist conventions/unions. The founding denominations are the United Baptist Convention of the Maritime (now Atlantic) Provinces (560 churches, 62,000 members), the Baptist Convention of Ontario and Quebec (382 churches, 46,000 members), and the Baptist Union of Western Canada (162 churches, 21,000 members). In 1970 the Union d'Eglises Baptistes Françaises au Canada, or Union of French Baptist Churches in Canada (22 churches, 1200 members) joined the federation. Previously known as the Baptist Federation of Canada (1944), the federation has held its current name since 1983.

Atlantic Baptists trace their history to the late 1800s, when British Empire Loyalists emigrated following the American Revolution. Growth attributable to the Alline* revivals and Free Will Baptist* missionary enterprise eventually resulted in an Arminian stream, which coalesced with Calvinistic* Baptists to form the United Baptist Convention of the Maritime (now Atlantic) Provinces in 1905-1906. In Upper and Lower Canada, Baptist emigrants from Britain and the United States, the majority Particular Baptists,* eventually organized the Baptist Convention of Ontario and Quebec (1888). Baptist witness in Western Canada began in Manitoba in 1873 through the initiative of Ontario missionaries, and in British Columbia in 1875 with American Baptist support. In 1907-1909

four provincial conventions founded the Baptist Union of Western Canada. The Union d'Eglises Baptistes Françaises au Canada (1969) is the indigenous product of the historic Grand Ligne Mission. Canadian Baptists support four theological colleges, one junior college and two lay training institutes.

In the 1840s and in the decade of the 1900s, attempts were made to unite Baptists in Canada. However, it was only in 1944, in Saint John, New Brunswick, that the federation emerged as a national coordinating agency. The structure is "presbygational," with a twenty-six-member council nominated by the convention/unions, but it is consensual in practice. An inspirational Triennial Assembly elects officers but lacks legislative or fiscal authority. In the 1920s the fundamentalist*-modernist controversy produced schisms from the Baptist Convention of Ontario and Quebec as well as the Baptist Union of Western Canada. In 1965 the resulting conservative communions organized a second indigenous Baptist denomination, the Canada-Wide Fellowship of Evangelical Baptist Churches. The Canadian Baptist Federation, through its Canadian Baptist Relief and Development Fund, cooperates with the Canadian Baptist Overseas Mission Board and numerous relief agencies overseas. In Canada the federation serves as the voice of Canadian Baptists before governments, and it provides ministerial support services and limited publication assistance. The federation's headquarters are in Mississauga, Ontario.

BIBLIOGRAPHY. J. E. Harris, *The Baptist Union of Western Canada* (1976); S. Ivison and F. Rosser, *The Baptists in Upper and Lower Canada Before 1813* (1946); E. Levy, *The Baptists of the Maritime Provinces, 1753-1946* (1946); H. Renfree, *Heritage and Horizon: The Baptist Story in Canada* (1988); E. A. Therrien, *Baptist Work in French Canada* (1954).

W. E. Ellis

Canadian Baptists. There are about 2,000 Baptist congregations in Canada, with a total membership of around 230,000. The 1981 Canadian census reported 696,850 persons as Baptist, including children and adherents.

In contrast to those of the United States, Baptists in Canada, with the exception of the provinces of Nova Scotia and New Brunswick, are a small minority (2.9 percent of the population) and yet the largest evangelical denomination in

Canada. They share their distinctive beliefs and practices with Baptists in the United States, but congregations and denominational bodies differ among themselves in interpreting particular doctrines and in their attitudes to such issues as ecumenical cooperation and moral standards. Regional loyalties, conflicting American and British influences, diverse ethnic origins and the fundamentalist*-modernist controversy of the 1920s have contributed to dividing Canadian Baptists into two larger and several smaller bodies.

1. The Canadian Baptist Federation (CBF) is the largest body (1,125 churches and 135,000 members) and represents the mainstream Baptist tradition. Organized in 1944 as the Baptist Federation of Canada (BFC) and renamed CBF in 1983, it coordinates programs in national, international and interdenominational spheres but also provides opportunities for consultation and cooperation in other areas of work. Regionalism has prevented the CBF from functioning as a national denomination. Most programs are administered by one of the four constituent bodies: the United Baptist Convention of the Atlantic Provinces (UBCAP, organized 1906, 550 churches, 67,000 members), Baptist Convention of Ontario and Quebec (BCOQ, organized 1888, 390 churches, 47,000 members), Baptist Union of Western Canada (BUWC, organized 1909, 160 churches, 21,000 members) or Union of French Baptist Churches (UFBC, organized 1969, 25 churches, 1,000 members).

The Baptist movement in the Maritimes began in the 1760s under the influence of New Light and Baptist preachers from New England. Repeated revivals produced church growth unmatched elsewhere in Canada. In Ontario and English-speaking Quebec, Baptists suffered from conflicting influences brought by ministers and immigrants from the United States (predominantly Regular Baptists* practicing closed Communion), England (open Communion), Scotland (revivalist tradition) and later immigrants from elsewhere. The earlier tensions were overcome when the Baptist Convention of Ontario and Quebec was formed in 1888, only to reappear during the fundamentalist-modernist controversy in the 1920s (*see* Shields, Thomas T.). Black Baptists, many of whom originally were slaves who escaped from the United States, have maintained a distinct piety and separate organizations in the Maritimes (African Association) and Ontario (Amherstburg Association).

Baptists have pioneered in Protestant mission to French Canadians in Quebec since the 1830s (Grande Ligne Society, 1855), but persecution and lack of resources hindered growth until the "quiet revolution" in French Canada during the 1970s. Baptist missionaries arrived late in the prairies (Winnipeg, 1875) and in British Columbia (Victoria, 1876). Denominational growth was further impeded by schism in the 1920s and economic factors during the Depression of the 1930s.

2. The Fellowship of Evangelical Baptist Churches in Canada (FEBCC), the second largest group (an estimated 475 churches and 56,000 members), was formed in 1953 through the merger of two groups that appeared in Central and Western Canada (*see* Shields, Thomas T.) after the fundamentalist-modernist controversy: the Union of Regular Baptist Churches of Ontario and Quebec (1927) and the Fellowship of Independent Baptist Churches of Canada (1933). In the 1960s, Regular Baptist churches in Western Canada joined the FEBCC. In recent years a few churches have been planted in the Atlantic provinces. About ten churches in Ontario, led by Jarvis Street Baptist Church in Toronto, continue a separate Association of Regular Baptist Churches (Canada).

3. The multiracial and multicultural mosaic of Canadian society has been mirrored in a variety of ethnic Baptist churches for more than a century. German-speaking and Swedish-speaking congregations appeared in Central and Western Canada in the 1850s and 1880s respectively. Originally they maintained dual affiliation with one of the Canadian conventions and with ethnic conferences in the United States. Several factors led to severance of links with the Baptist Convention of Ontario and Quebec and the Baptist Union of Western Canada in the 1930s. Churches in both ethnic groups are now English-speaking, and the two conferences have formalized their independent status in Canada: Baptist General Conference of Canada* (BGC, originally Swedish, 75 churches, 6,000 members) and North American Baptist Conference in Canada (NABC, originally German, 120 churches, 18,000 members). Many other ethnic churches appear and disappear, reflecting the changing patterns of Canadian immigration. Through the years, churches related to the Canadian Baptist Federation have assisted new Canadian work among immigrants in more than thirty languages. Of all Baptist churches in Canada, the Chinese are now the fastest growing.

Oddly enough, Baptists have largely ignored the native Canadian peoples.

4. Other Baptist groups include the Canadian Convention of Southern Baptists (CCSB, 80 churches, 5,000 members), which was organized in 1985 after three decades of slow invasion of Western and Central Canada by missionaries sent by churches affiliated with the Southern Baptist Convention* in the United States. Other Baptist bodies in the United States, such as Bible Baptists and Seventh Day Baptists,* have also expanded their work into Canada in recent years. In the Maritimes the Alliance of Reformed Baptist Churches, founded in 1888 as part of the holiness movement, united with the Wesleyan Methodist Church in 1966 and then became part of the Wesleyan Church in a subsequent merger with the Pilgrim Holiness Church in 1968. The Primitive Baptist* Conference of New Brunswick emerged in the 1870s and recently linked up with the Association of Free Will Baptists* in the United States.

Canadian Baptists remain divided over relations with cooperative Baptist and ecumenical organizations. Only the Canadian Baptist Federation and North American Baptist Conference belong to the Baptist World Alliance.* The conventions and unions that form the Canadian Baptist Federation were among the founding bodies of the Canadian Council of Churches in 1944. Since 1980 only the Baptist Convention of Ontario and Quebec retains membership in the Canadian Council of Churches, while the Baptist Union of Western Canada and the Baptist General Conference joined the Evangelical Fellowship of Canada. No Canadian Baptist body has ever held membership in the World Council of Churches.*

In the nineteenth century Canadian Baptists made major contributions to the clarification of church-state relations and to higher education. Even though they relinquished control of three universities (Acadia, McMaster and Brandon), the various conventions and conferences now operate two colleges, eleven seminaries, and several Bible schools and lay training centers.

With contrasting political convictions, several Baptists have given leadership in federal and provincial governments: prime ministers Alexander MacKenzie (1822-1892), Charles Tupper (1921-1915) and John George Diefenbaker (1957-1963); premiers of Alberta, William Aberhart and Ernest Charles Manning, and of Saskatchewan, Thomas Clement Douglas.

See also BAPTIST CHURCHES.

BIBLIOGRAPHY. P. R. Dekar and M. J. S. Ford, eds., *Celebrating Canadian Baptist Heritage* (1985); J. H. Watt, *The Fellowship Story* (1978); J. K. Zeman, ed., *Baptists in Canada* (1980); J. K. Zeman and W. Klaassen, eds., *The Believers' Church in Canada* (1979); J. K. Zeman and G. A. Rawlyk, *Baptists in Canada: A Bibliography* (1988).

J. K. Zeman

Carey, William (1761-1834). Baptist missionary and founder of the Baptist mission enterprise. Born in Paulerspury, North Hampton, England, on August 17, 1761, he died in Serampore, India, June 9, 1834. Carey is frequently referred to as the "father of the modern mission movement." Although he was inspired by the heroic efforts of the Moravians to carry the gospel to various parts of the world, it was his unique contribution that sparked the modern mission movement. His initial treatise *An Enquiry into the Obligations of Christians to Use Means for the Conversion of the Heathens* (1792) became the catalyst. Because his own Particular Baptist* denomination was divided over the necessity of sending missionaries to preach the gospel in the remote parts of the world, Carey and a few fellow ministers formed a society for this purpose on October 2, 1792. This became the pattern for other denominations, which on the basis of voluntary support formed similar missionary societies.

Carey and his wife became one of the first two missionary couples sent out by the new Baptist society, and in spite of difficulties and tragedies, including his wife's loss of sanity, Carey gained a knowledge of many languages and established a model mission station in Serampore. Belatedly, the British government, which had shut him out upon his arrival in Calcutta, recognized his genius, and for thirty years he taught the Bengali and Sanskrit languages in Fort William College of Calcutta. He also became world-renowned for his contributions as a botanist. The Bible was translated under his direction into forty-two Asian languages. With the help of national converts, Carey and his colleagues William Ward and Joshua Marshman established twenty churches in India. A college was founded at Serampore in 1812.

Beyond the direct missionary involvement of Bible translation, preaching and teaching, Carey was influential in getting laws passed prohibiting some of India's most deplorable social evils, such as sacrificing infants to the gods, abandonment of unwanted babies and the aged, and suttee (the burning of widows alive on the bodies of their deceased husbands). The forty-one years of Carey's life in India had lifted him from obscurity as a onetime cobbler and Baptist pastor in England to the world's stage as the most influential missionary of his generation. Although he did not see the fruition of his ecumenical ideas in his own lifetime, future generations would remember that it was Carey who first proposed a regular international conference of representatives of mission societies for mutual support, fellowship and the sharing of information. Little did John Ryland know when he wrote in his diary, "Today I baptized a poor journeyman cobbler," that he had baptized one whose life and ministry would affect the course of Christian history as few have.

BIBLIOGRAPHY. T. George, *Faithful Witness: The Life and Mission of William Carey* (1991); *RE,* Winter 1992.

W. R. Estep

Carnell, Edward John (1919-1967). Evangelical theologian and educator. Born in Antigo, Wisconsin, Carnell grew up in a Baptist parsonage. He attended Wheaton College (B.A., 1941), where he was influenced by Gordon H. Clark, a Christian rationalist dedicated to the defense of orthodoxy. Carnell received his seminary education at Westminster Theological Seminary (Th.B., Th.M., 1944) and concentrated on apologetics under Cornelius Van Til. He later studied at Harvard University (Th.D., 1948), writing his dissertation on the theology of Reinhold Niebuhr. His second doctorate, in philosophy, came from Boston University (Ph.D., 1949), where he studied under E. S. Brightman and wrote his dissertation on "The Problem of Verification in Søren Kierkegaard."

In 1945 Carnell commenced his teaching career at Gordon College and Divinity School as professor of philosophy and religion. Three years later he moved to California to join the faculty of the newly founded Fuller Theological Seminary. During his nineteen years at Fuller he served in several positions. He was president of the school from 1954 to 1959 and at the time of his death was professor of ethics and philosophy of religion.

Carnell became one of the leaders in the intellectual awakening of conservative evangelicalism in America after World War II. His influence was extended through nine books. His *An Introduction to Christian Apologetics* (1948) argued that Christianity satisfies the demands of reason, while two later books, *Christian Commitment* (1957) and *The Kingdom of Love and the Pride of Life* (1960), broadened his apologetic to include "knowledge by acquaintance."

BIBLIOGRAPHY. G. M. Marsden, *Reforming Fundamentalism: Fuller Seminary and the New Evangelicalism* (1987); R. Nelson, *The Making and Unmaking of an Evangelical Mind: The Case of Edward Carnell* (1988); J. A. Sims, *Edward John Carnell: Defender of the Faith* (1979).

B. L. Shelley

Carroll, Benjah Harvey (1843-1914). Southern Baptist* pastor, educator and controversialist. Born in Mississippi, Carroll received formal education at Baylor University* (then Waco University). During the Civil War he served in the Texas Rangers as well as in the Confederate Army. After the war he served various Baptist churches in Texas, including First Baptist Church in Waco (1871-1899). In 1899 he became corresponding secretary for the Texas Baptist Education Commission. During the years 1872 to 1905 he taught theology at Baylor and then organized Baylor Theological Seminary in 1905. The seminary was chartered as Southwestern Baptist Theological Seminary* in 1908 and moved to Fort Worth in 1910. Carroll was president of the seminary until his death in 1914. A popular preacher, Carroll was an able spokesman for Southern Baptist doctrine and polity, promoting evangelism and attacking heresy. Largely self-educated, he wrote extensively, with some thirty-three volumes published.

BIBLIOGRAPHY. R. A. Baker, *The Southern Baptist Convention and Its People, 1607-1972* (1974); W. W. Barnes, *The Southern Baptist Convention, 1845-1953* (1954); J. M. Carroll, *Dr. B. H. Carroll, the Colossus of Baptist History* (1946).

B. J. Leonard

Carroll, James Milton (1852-1931). Minister and educator. Born in Monticello, Arkansas, on January 8, 1852, he died in Fort Worth, Texas, on January 11, 1931. Carroll was six years old when his family moved to Texas. He married Sudie Wamble when nineteen. Two years later (1873) he entered Baylor University* at Independence, Texas, from which he graduated with an M.A. degree. Carroll was founder and first president of San Marcos Academy. For a brief period he was also president, first of Oklahoma Baptist University* and later of Howard Payne College.* He was the first secretary of the Texas Baptist Education Commission. He enjoyed a national reputation as an ornithologist. His literary productions include a collection of lectures on the history of Baptists, *The Trail of Blood* (1931), a biography of his more famous brother, *B. H. Carroll, the Colossus of Baptist History* (1946), *Texas Baptist Statistics* (1895) and *A History of Texas Baptists* (1923), which was his finest work.

See also CARROLL, BENJAH HARVEY; LANDMARKISM.
BIBLIOGRAPHY. *ESB* 1:233-34.

W. R. Estep

Carson-Newman College. A four-year liberal arts college located in Jefferson City, Tennessee, and operated in cooperation with the Tennessee Baptist Convention. The East Tennessee Baptist Educational Society was organized in 1849 to study the possibility of establishing an institution for educating young people, especially future ministers. The society founded the school in Mossy Creek (presently Jefferson City) in 1851 as Mossy Creek Missionary Baptist Seminary. William Rogers was chosen as the first president. Because of its liberal arts curriculum, the name was changed in 1855 to Mossy Creek Baptist College.

The college was located in a crucial area of Union territory during the Civil War. As a result of the war the school closed in 1862, and college buildings were converted into quarters for Union soldiers. The soldiers stayed for about three years, leaving behind severely damaged buildings and a school without adequate funds. Two years later, in 1868, the college was financially able to open its doors again. In 1880 the school was renamed Carson College to honor a generous donor, James Henderson Carson of Dandridge. In 1889 Carson College merged with Newman Baptist Female College (also named for a generous donor, the William Cate Newman family) and became Carson-Newman College, a coeducational institution. In 1919 the school became associated with the Tennessee Baptist Convention.

The college experienced great financial stress during the Depression of the 1930s, but following World War II it benefited from a growing enrollment. The 1960s and 1970s were a time of expanding curriculum, and in 1987 a graduate program in education was initiated.

BIBLIOGRAPHY. I. N. Carr, *History of Carson-Newman College; ESB* 1, 3, 4. C. Blevins

Carter, James Earl, Jr. (1924-). Businessman, farmer, statesman, Baptist layman and thirty-ninth U.S. president. Born in Plains, Georgia, Jimmy Carter (as he prefers to be known) is the eldest of four children of James Earl and Lillian Gordy Carter. He grew up near Plains, where his father both farmed and operated a small country store. He was appointed to the U.S. Naval Academy in 1942, graduated in 1946, married his hometown sweetheart, Rosalynn Smith, shortly thereafter and spent the next seven years in the U.S. Navy. However, in 1953, following the death of his father, he resigned his commission and returned to Plains to take over the family farm.

After a profitable stint as a businessman-farmer and considerable experience in local politics, Carter in 1962 ran a successful campaign for election to the Georgia State Senate, where he served two terms (1963-1967). In 1966 he unsuccessfully sought the Georgia governorship, but in 1970 he won election to that office. On completing his term as governor in 1975, Carter began to run for the presidency. On most issues, his campaign was built on moderate positions, and he set a moral tone for the election by promising never to lie to the American people and to institute a compassionate and responsible government. This gained him the support of many people who were looking for a change in leadership after the Vietnam War, the Watergate scandal and the ignominious resignations of Vice President Spiro Agnew and President Richard Nixon.* Despite fears aroused by the fact that he was a self-acknowledged evangelical Christian, a Southerner and a nonestablishment outsider, he won the presidency in 1976.

Carter's administration (1977-1981), like his earlier legislative and gubernatorial career, received mixed reviews. He never was able to seize the economic initiative in domestic affairs, and the country suffered increasing inflation, unemployment and federal deficits during his tenure in office. He succeeded in some matters, such as civil service reform, environmental legislation and an energy program.

In foreign affairs, Carter inaugurated full diplomatic relations with the People's Republic of China in 1979, persuaded Israel and Egypt to sign the Camp David peace accord in March 1979 and tried, with limited success, to establish human rights as a basic element of American policy. He signed the SALT II Treaty in 1979 but failed to secure Senate ratification. His successful push for confirmation of the Panama Canal treaties in 1977 was criticized by the political right as a sellout of American interests; he received little support for his boycott of the 1980 Summer Olympic Games in Moscow in retaliation for the 1979 Soviet invasion of Afghanistan; and his handling of the Iran hostage crisis in 1979-1980 was perceived by many as bungled.

Much of the 1980 presidential campaign was played out under the cloud of the hostage problem, and Carter was criticized by his Republican opponent, Ronald Reagan, for ineptitude and a lack of leadership. In addition, many evangelicals who had supported Carter in 1976 drifted away to the Reagan camp. Reagan was swept into office in a landslide victory.

In 1981 Carter returned to Plains. In the years following he wrote his memoirs, oversaw the development of his presidential library in Atlanta, taught and lectured on public affairs in various universities around the country, worked in his local Baptist church, served as a special envoy to various Latin American countries and promoted Habitat for Humanity, a Christian organization that provides low-cost housing for the poor.

Having burst onto the national stage in 1976, the much-publicized "Year of the Evangelicals," Carter displayed a combination of straightforwardness, an aura of moral rectitude that exemplified traditional values and a transparently authentic religious faith that struck the right note for the time. Carter was perhaps the most dedicated Christian ever to occupy the White House, and along with Abraham Lincoln and Woodrow Wilson, he was certainly one of the most theologically perceptive. Conversant with the work of such noted theologians as Reinhold Niebuhr and Søren Kierkegaard, Carter was also steeped in the teachings of the Bible. He had professed faith in Christ in 1935 at age eleven, and he had been baptized and had become a member of a Southern Baptist* church shortly thereafter. He has been a Sunday-school teacher since 1936 and a deacon since 1958. Sometime in late 1966 or early 1967, following his defeat in his first try for the governorship of Georgia, he experienced a spiritual crisis that led to a rededication of his life to Christ and eventually to a commitment to fulfill his Christian vocation through politics.

Carter thus brought with him to the presidency a faith that was an integral part of his personal identity. On church-state issues, for example, he adhered to the traditional Baptist insistence on a high wall of separation, even refusing to hold worship services in the White House. His Baptist faith also taught him that Christians are on earth to serve; thus he considered himself, as president, the "First Servant" of the nation. His personal style—marked by enormous self-discipline, a commitment to hard work, orderliness and fiscal responsibility—largely reflected his evangelical worldview. His dedication to social justice also flowed from his Christian faith. Most of all, his biblical faith dictated restraint in the use of power.

Essentially Niebuhrian in his understanding of the complexity of ethical issues, Carter's "Christian realism" sometimes led him to appear indecisive because he understood the irony of how humans are often in the most danger of being wrong when they think they are absolutely right. He frequently cited a paraphrase of Niebuhr when articulating his own political philosophy: "The sad duty of politics is to establish justice in a sinful world."

The supreme irony of Carter's presidency may have been the reaction to his energy address, known as "the malaise speech," delivered in prophetic civil-religion language on national TV in July 1979. The president used the occasion to talk of a national moral and spiritual crisis, and to call on his fellow Americans to repent of the sins of materialism and consumptionism and to be prepared to sacrifice in order to resolve the energy crisis and restore national vigor. Carter's loss in the 1980 election was, in part, a reflection of public rejection of his prophetic civil religion in favor of Reagan's politics of nostalgia for a bygone era of respected might and limitless plenty.

BIBLIOGRAPHY. J. T. Baker, *A Southern Baptist in the White House* (1977); J. Carter, *A Government as Good as Its People* (1977); J. Carter, *Keeping Faith: Memoirs of a President* (1982); J. Carter, *Why Not the Best?* (1975); R. B. Flowers, "President Jimmy Carter, Evangelicalism, Church-State Relations and Civil Religion," *JCS* 25 (Winter 1983):113-32; E. C. Hargrove, *Jimmy Carter as President* (1988); R. G. Hutcheson Jr., *God in the White House* (1988); R. L. Maddox, *Preacher at the White House* (1984); W. L. Miller, *Yankee from Georgia: The Emergence of Jimmy Carter* (1970); R. V. Pierard and R. D. Linder, *Civil Religion and the Presidency* (1988); W. G. Pippert, ed., *The Spiritual Journey of Jimmy Carter* (1979); G. Smith, *Morality, Reason and Power: American Diplomacy in the Carter Years* (1986); D. Winter, "The Carter-Niebuhr Connection," *NJ* 10 (February 4, 1978):188-92. R. D. Linder

Carver, William Owen (1868-1954). Southern Baptist* pastor, professor and missiologist. Born in Tennessee, Carver graduated from Richmond College, Richmond, Virginia (M.A., 1891), and the Southern Baptist Seminary, Louisville, Kentucky (Th.M., 1895; Th.D., 1896). After serving several pastorates in Virginia, Tennessee and Kentucky, Carver joined the faculty of the Southern Baptist Theological Seminary* in 1896. In 1899 he offered the seminary's first course in missions and comparative religion. In 1900 he became head of the missions department, a position he held until his retirement in 1943.

Carver helped to establish the Woman's Missionary Union Training School* at Southern Baptist Seminary in 1907. In 1953 the school's name was changed to the Carver School of Missions and Social Work.* An ecumenical churchman, Carver sought to interpret the Baptist missionary imperative within the mission of the whole church. He published twenty books, many of which helped shape Southern Baptist theology of missions* in the twentieth century. These include *Missions in the Plan of the Ages* (1909) and *Christian Missions in Today's World* (1942).

BIBLIOGRAPHY. W. O. Carver, *Out of This Treasure* (1956); C. U. Littlejohn, *History of the Carver School of Missions and Social Work* (1958).

B. J. Leonard

Carver School of Missions and Social Work (1953-1963). A Southern Baptist* higher education institution in Louisville, Kentucky. Operated from 1907 as the Woman's Missionary Union Training School,* the school became coeducational and the name was changed to reflect a revised curriculum in 1953. The name honors William O. Carver,* who was influential in the school's formative years and was its first professor. The school offered biblical and theological studies in conjunction with the neighboring Southern Baptist Theological Seminary,* as well as courses in missionary education, social work, personal evangelism, church music, public speaking and religious education. The school also operated a social service center, called the Good Will Center, in which students received practical training in social work. Degrees offered were a bachelor's and master's in religious education. In 1957, due to financial strain, ownership and management of the school were transferred from the Woman's Missionary Union to the Southern Baptist Convention.* The Good Will Center property

was transferred to the Home Mission Board* of the Southern Baptist Convention.

The school sought accreditation by the Council on Social Work Education but could not be accredited unless it was housed in a university or college. When it became apparent that accreditation would not be possible, the school was merged with Southern Baptist Theological Seminary in 1963. The social work program remained a part of the seminary's School of Religious Education until 1984, when the seminary trustees granted the program school status. The Carver School of Church Social Work was accredited by the Council on Social Work and Education in February 1987.

BIBLIOGRAPHY. *ESB* 3:1639-40; C. Littlejohn, *History of Carver School of Missions and Social Work* (1958).   T. L. Scales

Cary (Carey), Lott (c. 1780-1828). African-American Baptist missionary. Born a slave in Charles City County, Virginia, Cary worked in Richmond tobacco warehouses. In 1807, after hearing a sermon on John 3:16, he was converted and swore off "profanity and intoxication." Gary joined the biracial First Baptist Church, learned to read and write, and became a lay preacher. Officially licensed in 1813—the year he also bought his freedom—Cary helped found the Richmond Baptist Missionary Society, which, with the American Colonization Society (ACS) and the Triennial Convention* of Baptist churches, authorized in 1819 his trip to Africa. Cary surrendered leadership in the First Baptist Church of Richmond to go to Sierra Leone early in 1821, accompanied by another black Baptist, Colin Teague (or Teage).

Early in 1822 the colonists moved to found the colony of Liberia. Over the next six years Cary lost his wife, survived a conflict with Jeduhi Ashmun (the white agent of the ACS), gave military and administrative leadership to the colony and became a lay medical practitioner. Ordained before his departure for Africa, he established churches and schools among the local inhabitants. An explosion during one of several conflicts with local tribes took Cary's life in November 1828. Black Baptists in America sixty years later named their foreign missionary organization for Cary.

BIBLIOGRAPHY. M. M. Fisher, "Lott Cary, the Colonizing Missionary," *JNH* 7 (1922):380-418; W. A. Poe, "Lott Cary: Man of Purchased Freedom," *CH* 39 (1970):49-61.

W. B. Gravely and D. Nelson

Case, Shirley Jackson (1872-1947). Baptist New Testament scholar. Born in New Brunswick, Canada, Case was educated at Acadia University (A.B., M.A.) and Yale Divinity School (B.D., Ph.D.) and then became professor of New Testament and early church history at the University of Chicago Divinity School* (1908-1938) and dean after 1933. Case refined the "socio-historical-environmental" method of the Chicago School, which viewed religious movements and theology mainly as products of their social settings. Contrary to the views of A. Schweitzer, Case believed that he could find the historical Jesus and contended that the Jesus of history was in fact the Christ of faith (in *The Historicity of Jesus*, 1912; *Jesus: A New Biography*, 1927).

In his study of Christian origins he emphasized the importance of understanding the social environment of early Christians over analyzing the documents of the New Testament (*The Evolution of Early Christianity*, 1914) and viewed the development of theology as "transcendental politics." Thus Case stood midway between skeptics who accounted for Christianity's emergence without a historical Jesus and conservatives who viewed Christian origins in purely supernaturalistic terms.

BIBLIOGRAPHY. *DAB* IV; W. Hynes, *Shirley Jackson Case and the Chicago School: The Socio-Historical Method* (1981).

. T. P. Weber

Catechisms, Baptist Use of. Baptists have used catechisms as important pedagogical and evangelistic tools. Among the Particular Baptists,* Henry Jessey* wrote a series of four catechisms in 1652 entitled *A Catechism for Babes, or Little Ones*. In 1680 Hercules Collins adapted the Heidelberg Catechism for Baptist use, in a work entitled The Orthodox Catechism. In 1693 the London Particular Baptists requested William Collins and Benjamin Keach* to produce a catechism built on the Westminster Shorter Catechism. Thomas Grantham in 1687 published a catechism for the General Baptists entitled St. Paul's Catechism and built on the six principles of Hebrews 6. Dan Taylor wrote A Catechism or Instruction for Children and Youth for the New Connection of General Baptists. Keach's catechism, also known as *The Baptist Catechism,* became the most influential and popular among Baptist catechisms. C. H. Spurgeon* in England and the churches of the Philadelphia* and Charleston as-

sociations in the United States used versions of it. Baptists in the South employed catechisms for the religious instruction of slaves, one by E. T. Winkler of Charleston being entitled *Notes and Questions for the Oral Instruction of Colored People*. In her evangelistic work among the Chinese, Lottie Moon* used a catechism written by Mrs. T. P. Crawford.* The Sunday School Board* of the Southern Baptist Convention* published catechisms by both J. P. Boyce (1864) and John R. Broadus* (1892).

BIBLIOGRAPHY. H. L. McBeth, *A Sourcebook for Baptist Heritage* (1990).

T. J. Nettles

Cauthen, Baker James (1909-1985). Southern Baptist* missionary, educator and missions executive. Born in Huntsville, Texas, Cauthen was licensed to preach at age sixteen and ordained in 1927. He received his education from Stephen F. Austin College (B.A., 1929), Baylor University* (M.A., 1930) and Southwestern Baptist Theological Seminary* (Th.M., 1933; Th.D., 1936).

While serving as pastor of the Polytechnic Baptist Church, Fort Worth (1933-1939), he was also professor of missions at Southwestern Baptist Theological Seminary* (1935-1939). Offering themselves as missionaries, he and his wife served in China from 1939 to 1945. He was then elected secretary for the Orient (1945-1953) and executive secretary of the Foreign Mission Board of the Southern Baptist Convention (1954-1979). His service in the calling of missions encompassed more than forty-six years.

With a longer tenure than any of his seven predecessors as head of the mission board (twenty-six years), Cauthen led Southern Baptists in building one of the largest missionary forces among Protestant denominations, from 908 missionaries in 1954 to 3,008 in 1979, located in ninety-four countries. Missions funding grew from $6.7 million (1954) to $76.7 million (1979).

Cauthen challenged Southern Baptists, "God has not given us our current resources that we may use them upon ourselves." His goal was 5,000 missionaries in 125 countries by the year 2000, with 10,000 lay volunteers. He urged major thrusts into urban areas and among students, increases in overseas churches, leadership training, greater use of media, and more attention to health care, disease prevention, world hunger and disasters. His vision and achievements earned him the honor of a missionary statesman.

BIBLIOGRAPHY. J. C. Fletcher, *Baker James Cauthen: A Man for All Nations* (1977).

W. M. Patterson

Central Baptist College. The Baptist Missionary Association of Arkansas sought an institution of higher learning to educate preachers and "young people in general." By 1950 the group began the Arkansas Extension School of Jacksonville Baptist College (Jacksonville, Texas) at Temple Baptist Church in Little Rock. Support for a college grew, and in 1952 the group purchased the campus of a female college in Conway, Arkansas, from the Arkansas Baptist State Convention. The school opened that fall as Conway Baptist College, with five faculty members.

In 1962 the name was changed to Central Baptist College. In 1977 the college was accredited with the American Association of Bible Colleges. Currently enrollment is approximately 300 students, and both associate and bachelor's degrees are offered, along with one-year certificates in business. Graduate degrees are offered in biblical studies and pastoral studies.

J. T. Greer

Central Baptist Theological Seminary. Founded in 1901 in Kansas City, Kansas, it was the first theological seminary west of the Mississippi. In 1917 a Women's Missionary Training School was added. Describing itself as "affiliated with the American Baptist Churches in the USA,* ecumenical, and evangelical in spirit," the school is accredited by North Central and the Association of Theological Schools. Established to provide ministers for many small churches in a region where theological education was inaccessible for most pastors, the seminary early had a precarious existence and survived by the sacrificial labors of faculty members and spouses and a few loyal contributors. Today, finances are stable, with about $3 million in endowment and a steady income from the Central Region of ABCUSA, strong ties having been maintained with these churches.

Until 1956 the seminary served both Northern and Southern Baptists.* When a formal, cooperative arrangement with the Southern Baptist Convention (SBC) was proposed, the SBC declined the offer and proceeded to establish Midwestern Baptist Theological Seminary* not far away. An exodus of Southern Baptist trustees, faculty, and students ensued, leaving a legacy of ill feelings.

Central's main purpose is to prepare parish ministers, but there is a strong emphasis on overseas missions and ministries to Native Americans. For persons unable to attend seminary in residence for the full three years, a "Long Distance Learning" program makes courses available by means of videotapes and simultaneous telephone conference calls, but one year in residence is required to obtain a degree. In recent years enrollment has fluctuated from around 100 to 200.

BIBLIOGRAPHY. F. C. Means, *Founders of Central* (1962); *The Voice*, September 1991.

N. H. Maring

Charismatic Movement Among Baptists. The revival of Pentecostal experience that entered mainline Protestant denominations and Catholicism in the 1960s has had a mixed reaction among Baptists. More than that of most denominations, Baptist leadership across the theological spectrum has heavily criticized the charismatic movement. The Southern Baptist Convention* (SBC) has responded to charismatics with increasing hostility. Beginning in the late 1960s, several books by prominent Baptist professors repudiated Pentecostal theology. Fundamentalist leader W. A. Criswell* called speaking in tongues "gibberish" and the movement "near heresy." In the 1970s five associations in four states excluded charismatic churches, while other associations adopted resolutions of denunciation. In July 1987 the Home Mission Board* voted to restrict its missionaries from practicing speaking in tongues.

During the 1970s SBC charismatics organized several regional meetings and then held a National Southern Baptist Charismatic Conference in 1975. While mainline Baptist historians have suggested that the movement peaked among Baptists in 1975, charismatics continue to meet together occasionally for "Fulness" Conferences. Don LeMaster, pastor of West Lauderdale Baptist Church of Florida and spokesman for many charismatics, heads Fulness Ministries and publishes *Fulness* magazine. The number of charismatic churches in the SBC at present is estimated to be about 200.

Charismatics in the American Baptist Churches in the USA* (ABC) first organized in 1968. Led by Kenneth L. Pagard, the American Baptist Charismatic Fellowship of Pasadena sponsored gatherings and had display booths at convention meetings. Since 1975, annual summer conferences have been held at a denominational campground. The most prominent ABC charismatic is

Howard Irvin, professor at Oral Roberts University and important author of works dealing with charismatic theology.

There are two Baptist Pentecostal denominations. The Pentecostal Free-Will Baptist Church, with headquarters in North Carolina, had 13,000 members in 150 churches in 1979. A smaller group from South Carolina, the Free-Will Baptist Church of the Pentecostal Faith, is an offshoot of the former body.

Several prominent charismatic leaders have Baptist backgrounds, including Pat Robertson and James Robison.

BIBLIOGRAPHY. S. M. Burgess and G. B. McGee, *Dictionary of Pentecostal and Charismatic Movements* (1988); C. Howe, *Glimpses of Baptist Heritage* (1981); V. Synan, "Baptists Ride the Third Wave," *Charisma and Christian Life* 12, no. 5 (1986):52-57.   C. D. Weaver

Charleston Southern University. Formerly Baptist College of Charleston; an institution of higher education of the South Carolina Baptist Convention. As early as 1952, the Baptists in the lower part of South Carolina began to agitate for the establishment of a Baptist college in their section of the state. A motion to study the establishment of such a school was first made during the 1956 meeting of the South Carolina Baptist Convention. In 1958 the convention agreed to consider supporting a college for the lower part of the state if Baptists of the region would meet certain financial conditions. A charter was granted in 1960.

In 1964 the South Carolina Baptist Convention voted to accept the Baptist College of Charleston. The first president was John Asa Hamrick, who as pastor of First Baptist Church, Charleston,* was a leader of the campaign to establish the school. Classes were held initially in January 1965 at the First Baptist Church of North Charleston. In September 1966, classes were held for the first time on the new 500-acre site. In 1984 a master's program was added in education and the M.A.T. and M.B.A. degrees in 1990. In November 1990 the school's name was changed to Charleston Southern University.

BIBLIOGRAPHY. *ESB* 3, 4; J. M. King, *A History of South Carolina Baptists* (1964).

G. Clayton

Cherokee Baptist Convention. The Cherokee Baptist Convention was organized in 1854 as a sponsoring group for the proposed Cherokee Baptist College of Cassville, Georgia. The body was composed of Georgia, Alabama and Tennessee churches and associations that held pro-Landmark* views. For varying lengths of time eight associations participated in its life. At its height, in about 1860, the convention comprised more than 250 churches, with a membership of about 15,540. In ten years the body met eleven times— usually in Cassville, Rome or Cedartown. J. R. Graves,* A. C. Dayton* and J. M. Pendleton* all attended at least one plenary session. The convention owned and supported two colleges (Cherokee Baptist College for young men in Cassville and Woodland Female College in Cedartown); fostered the *Landmark Banner and Cherokee Baptist;* helped to support E. L. Compere, a part-time missionary to the Cherokees in the Indian Territory; and enthusiastically supported the Confederacy. A meeting of the convention was scheduled for Cartersville in 1864, but the presence of federal troops rendered this impossible. Hope persisted that the body might be reactivated after the war—a hope that died in the late 1860s, along with the convention.

R. G. Gardner

Cherokee Baptist Female College. *See* SHORTER COLLEGE

Chowan College. A two-year liberal arts college owned by North Carolina Baptists. The school, located in Murfreesboro, North Carolina, was established in 1848 as a female academy by the Chowan Baptists Association. Early in its history the institution was supported through a stock company. By 1878 it had come under the jurisdiction of the North Carolina Baptist Convention. In 1911 it was named Chowan College and its ties to the state Baptist convention were solidified. The school was made coeducational in 1925 and became a junior college in 1937.

Financial problems led to the closing of the college from 1943 until 1949, when it was reopened with renovations to existing facilities. The school is known for its programs in business and secretarial studies as well as in art and advertising.

BIBLIOGRAPHY. *ESB* 1, 4.

B. J. Leonard

Christian Life Commission, SBC. A commission of the Southern Baptist Convention* with responsibility for ethical, social and political issues.

Southern Baptists were often hesitant to address the social implications of the gospel, frequently because they felt that doing so would interfere with the evangelistic mandate and also because confronting social issues meant confronting racial questions. In 1907, however, a Committee on Civic Righteousness urged the SBC to take seriously the call for earthly righteousness. In 1915 the Social Service Commission was founded, originally charged with providing information on temperance, morality and other ethical issues for Southern Baptist churches. Under the leadership of A. J. Barton,* the Social Service Commission built a constituency by opposing liquor sales throughout the South. By 1947 the name had been changed to the Christian Life Commission. Directors included Hugh A. Brimm, Acker C. Miller, Foy D. Valentine, Larry Baker and Richard Land.

In 1961 the agency was charged to aid churches in understanding the moral imperatives of the gospel and to guide Southern Baptists in responding to moral and social concerns. The organization responded with educational materials for churches on such issues as alcohol, gambling, family relations, race, peace, hunger, economics, aging and pornography. In 1959 the Commission submitted a statement that protested "the violence in all its ugly forms that is being used against the Negro people in the current segregation issue or at any other time." Throughout the 1960s, under the leadership of executive secretary (director) Foy Valentine, the commission experienced significant controversy due to its support for the civil rights movement and racial equality in the United States. In 1965 a motion to abolish the commission was overwhelmingly rejected by messengers from churches meeting at the annual convention in Dallas. Many Southern Baptists were divided over the commission's work. Some felt it should concentrate on issues of personal morality—alcohol, pornography, gambling—while others applauded its emphasis on corporate morality—race, war, poverty and hunger.

By the 1970s and 1980s the commission was a focal point of debate among SBC moderates and fundamentalists in the battle to control the convention (see Fundamentalism). As fundamentalists gained control of the denomination, the work of the commission was refocused with particular concern for the abortion debate. While continuing to offer responses to issues of hunger and race, the commission gave significant emphasis to the prolife position regarding abortion. When the Southern Baptist Convention withdrew its support for and participation in the Baptist Joint Committee on Public Affairs,* the Washington-based Baptist lobby, the Christian Life Commission was charged with providing political information and carrying out lobbying on behalf of the SBC through a new Washington office. The commission conducts an annual spring conference which focuses on specific issues of moral and social concern. It publishes a monthly newsletter, *Light.*

BIBLIOGRAPHY. *ESB* 1; H. L. McBeth, *The Baptist Heritage* (1987).

B. J. Leonard

Church Homecomings. A Southern tradition of reunion of present and former members of a local congregation, usually celebrated annually on a designated Sunday. Typically the celebration begins with morning worship, followed by a "dinner on the grounds," and concludes in the afternoon with congregational singing and "special music" in the Southern gospel style. Reflecting the tradition's rural origins, most homecomings occur in late July or early August, a time originally designated because the crops were laid by.

In the South, church homecomings have great sentimental value because of the interrelatedness of church, community and family in rural areas. The event not only allows church members to celebrate their spiritual heritage but also provides a setting for families and members of a bygone community to reminisce. Because many rural churches are surrounded by a cemetery, the occasion frequently provides an opportunity for rituals of respect at the graves. Today the homecoming provides a link to the distinctive cultural values of the rural South.

BIBLIOGRAPHY. G. K. Neville, "Homecomings," *ERS.*

M. G. Bell

Churching, Baptist Practice of. The act of expelling individuals from church membership, as practiced primarily by some traditional Baptist denominations in central Appalachia. Although not as harsh as the Amish tradition of "shunning," "churching" (better known as "exclusion") removes the errant individual from the church roll and disallows her or his participation in Communion, foot-washing* and all worship leadership. Depending on the particular Baptist sect, "churched" individuals may be allowed to attend services, but strictly as nonmember celebrants, denied the right to sit in "members only" sections.

For Regulars,* Separates,* Old Regulars,* Unit-eds* and Primitives* (plus some Free Will* and Missionary Baptists*), "churching" may result from doctrinal errancy and also from insufficient attendance, drunkenness, other objectionable so-cial behaviors, divorce and remarriage ("double-marriage"), violations of secular law, and even gossiping, backbiting and similar practices de-structive of fellowship harmony. When a church belongs to an association, "excluded" becomes the status of the individual throughout that asso-ciation, meaning that if the person seeks mem-bership in another affiliated fellowship, he or she must return to the original church for reinstate-ment and a letter of dismissal in good standing. This local church control of the process also re-sults in the absence of any appellate process.

Today "churching" occurs less frequently than was the case in late nineteenth- and early twen-tieth-century Appalachian Baptist communities, where secular misbehavior was as often the jus-tification for such action as were church matters, but surveys of annual association minutes for such traditional Baptists as those mentioned above show the practice to be very much alive.

BIBLIOGRAPHY. H. Dorgan, *Giving Glory to God in Appalachia: Worship Practices of Six Baptist Denominations* (1987); H. Dorgan, *The Old Reg-ular Baptists of Central Appalachia: Brothers and Sisters in Hope* (1989); also see the Appalachian Collection, Appalachian State University, Boone, North Carolina.   H. Dorgan

City Mission Societies. Organizations for relig-ious work in inner cities. As cities burgeoned with immigrants and people from rural areas, as well as seamen and other transients, many single-purpose societies were formed to minister to the growing populations. By 1870 it was clear that new approaches and more efficient methods were needed, and Baptists led in the develop-ment of new approaches to urban ministry. Be-ginning with Cleveland (1868), cities of all sizes consolidated previous organizations into a single City Mission Society, to be involved in evangel-ism, starting new churches, erecting buildings, disseminating literature and ministering to the new immigrant groups.

When the Northern Baptist Convention was formed in 1907, the City Societies became "affil-iating organizations," with the same status as state conventions. After numerous attempts to create standards, "Standard Mission Society" became the main classification that decided the status of such a body in the renamed American Baptist Conven-tion (1950). Criteria were size of city, number of churches and members, full-time staff, coopera-tion with the convention in budget matters, and so on. More attention was gradually given to plan-ning strategies and to encouraging churches to look beyond their own doors to attack social problems as well as continue the core traditional functions.

In 1972 the American Baptist Churches in the USA* (ABCUSA) reorganized with thirty-seven re-gions, states and City Societies. There were nine of the latter, and they have the same status as do, all other regions. Sharing in the budget covenants with ABCUSA, cooperating with national boards and the general secretary, they have responsibility for developing plans and implementing pro-grams of the national body.

BIBLIOGRAPHY. N. H. Maring and W. S. Hudson, *A Baptist Manual of Polity and Practice* (1991); D. A. McQueen, "History of City Mission Societies, American Baptist Convention," *Chron,* January 1954, January 1956; G. D. Younger, "Urban Min-istry in American Baptist Churches" (typescript, December 1992).

N. H. Maring

Clarke, John (1609-1676). Baptist minister, co-founder of Rhode Island Colony and advocate of religious freedom. Clarke was born in Suffolk County, England, and while his educational expe-rience remains unknown (he may have studied at the University of Leiden), he was well versed in theology, languages and medicine. Emigrating to Massachusetts Bay in 1637, Clarke championed the cause of Anne Hutchinson in the antinomian controversy. Searching for refuge from persecu-tion, with the help of Roger Williams,* Clarke and several other settlers purchased land from the In-dians on the island of Aquidneck in Narragansett Bay, where they established the town of Ports-mouth in 1638. By 1639 he had helped found Newport on the land now renamed Rhode Island. Clarke became the minister of the local congre-gation, which became identified as a Baptist church by 1644. Calvinist* by persuasion, the con-gregation followed Clarke in professing Particular Baptist* beliefs.

In 1651, while leading a prayer meeting* in the home of a blind Baptist by the name of William Witter in Lynn, Massachusetts, Clarke and two young men, John Crandall and Obadiah Holmes,* were arrested and imprisoned for conducting an unauthorized worship service. They were sentenced to be fined or whipped; Clarke's fine was paid, but Holmes was publicly flogged. Out of this experience Clarke published in England an account of his persecution in Massachusetts Bay Colony, *Ill Newes from New England, or a Narrative of New England's Persecutions* (1652).

In 1652 Clarke traveled with Roger Williams to London in an attempt to secure a new charter for Rhode Island Colony. While Williams returned to Rhode Island in 1654, Clarke remained in England until he succeeded in securing the charter from Charles II in 1663. Not only did the charter confirm their right to the land, but it gave the colonists permission to attempt "a lively experiment" in which they could enjoy complete religious liberty.* *Ill Newes* had done much to secure British sympathy for the Rhode Island colonists.

After his return from England in 1664, Clarke was elected to the General Assembly (1664-1669) and was later elected to three terms as deputy governor (1669-1672). Throughout his years in the colony he served as pastor of the Newport Baptist Church while practicing medicine to support himself. Clarke and Williams shared the same convictions regarding religious liberty and the separation of church and state, though Clarke was more influential in the development of the Baptists in the colony.

See also WILLIAMS, ROGER.

BIBLIOGRAPHY. *AAP* 6; T. W. Bicknell, *Story of Dr. John Clarke* (1915); *DAB* II; *DARB;* E. S. Gaustad, *Baptist Piety* (1978); *NCAB* 7; W. Nelson, *The Hero of Aquidneck and Life of Dr. John Clarke* (1938).   W. R. Estep

Clarke, William Newton (1841-1912). Baptist minister and theologian. Born in Cazenovia, New York, Clarke graduated from Madison (now Colgate Baptist*) University and Theological Seminary in New York. He pastored Baptist churches in Keene, New Hampshire (1863-1869), Newton Centre, Massachusetts (1869-1880), and Montreal, Quebec (1880-1883). He then taught New Testament interpretation at the Baptist Theological School in Toronto (1883-1887). After a brief pastorate in Hamilton, New York (1887-1890), he became professor of theology at Colgate Theological Seminary (1890-1908), where he became a leader in the New Theology.

Unable to use any available textbook, Clarke wrote America's first systematic theology from a liberal perspective (*An Outline of Christian Theology,* 1898). Following Schleiermacher, he believed that the starting point for theology was "religious sentiment," not the irreducible facts of Scripture. Since all theology grew out of religious experience, all the world's religions contain some truth. He rejected older views of biblical inspiration and condemned orthodoxy's "proof-texting" method. He claimed to take the Bible "as it is" and argued that the Scriptures should inspire theology, not be its source (*The Use of the Scriptures in Theology,* 1905, and *Sixty Years with the Bible,* 1912).

Though his *Outline* included traditional categories, Clarke often replaced technical terms with simpler, more dynamic ones and redefined historic doctrines in accordance with his scientific and critical approach to the Bible. Underlying his method was the assumption that the ultimate arbiter of theological truth is the Holy Spirit working in individuals, culture and all humanity. Clarke also showed a keen interest in foreign missions, as evidenced in *A Study of Christian Missions* (1900). Rejecting traditional motives for saving the lost, he suggested that missionaries should call the world to Christ and Christian civilization because of their superiority over other alternatives.

BIBLIOGRAPHY. E. S. Clarke, *William Newton Clarke* (1916); *DAB* II; *DARB; NCAB* 22.

T. P. Weber

Clearwaters, Richard Volley (1900-). Baptist preacher and educator. Born in Wilmot, Kansas, Clearwaters graduated from Moody Bible Institute (1924) and went on to earn degrees from Northern Baptist Theological Seminary* (Th.B., 1928; B.D., 1931). He also attended Kalamazoo College (B.A., 1930) and the University of Chicago Divinity School* (M.A., 1931). Clearwaters served churches in the Northern Baptist Convention (*see* American Baptist Churches in the USA), becoming pastor of Fourth Baptist Church, Minneapolis, Minnesota (1940-1982). He was president of the Iowa Baptist Convention (1937-1939) and served on the board of trustees of Northern Baptist Theological Seminary.

Apart from his pastoral ministry, Clearwaters served as dean and professor of practical theology of Northwestern Theological Seminary and then, in 1956, became founder and president of Central Baptist Seminary in Minneapolis, which was housed in his church. He also founded and served as first president of Pillsbury Baptist Bible College, Owanatonna, Minnesota. He received honorary degrees from Northern Baptist Theological Seminary, San Francisco Conservative Baptist Theological Seminary and Bob Jones University.

E. L. Towns

Clough, John Everett (1836-1910). Baptist missionary to India. Born in western New York, Clough graduated from Upper Iowa University in 1862, was ordained two years later and went to India to serve in the Telegu Mission. He settled in Ongole, Madras Presidency, in 1866 and promptly founded a church as he ministered among the outcaste Madigas. His relief work during the terrible famine of 1876-1878 was much respected among the people, and after assuring himself of the sincerity of their conversion, he and his assistants baptized some 9,000 persons in a six-month period as his influence spread through 400 villages. His congregation totaled 21,000 members five years later, before it was divided for sake of convenience. He became well known at home through his reports and addresses while on furlough, and he contributed to the growing popularity of foreign missions. He retired in 1905 and died five years later in Rochester.

BIBLIOGRAPHY. E. R. Clough, *John E. Clough* (1902); J. E. Clough, *Social Christianity in the Orient;* (1901) *DAB* II.

R. T. Handy

Cockrum, William M. (1837-?). General Baptist* churchman and philanthropist. Colonel William M. Cockrum, son of prominent General Baptist layman Colonel J. W. Cockrum, was himself an influential General Baptist benefactor, especially of Oakland City College.* Born in Oakland City, Indiana, on December 3, 1837, Cockrum distinguished himself during the Civil War as commanding colonel of the Forty-second Indiana Regiment. Following the war he went on to establish himself as a businessman, politician and civic leader in southern Indiana.

Following several unsuccessful attempts to establish a General Baptist institution of higher learning, Cockrum and his wife, Lucretia, donated ten acres of land for a campus in his hometown of Oakland City on August 5, 1885. Not only did Cockrum donate the land, but he was also instrumental in securing gifts and donations to finance the college, which commenced classes in April 1891.

BIBLIOGRAPHY. O. Latch, *History of the General Baptists* (1954); A. D. Williams, *Benoni Stinson and the General Baptists* (1892).

L. C. Shull

Colgate, Samuel (1822-1897). Industrialist and bibliophile. Born March 22, 1822, in New York City, the son of William Colgate* the soap manufacturer, Samuel Colgate was self-educated. He assumed control of the Colgate Palmolive Peet Company in 1857 and served as president for forty years.

Colgate was devoted to Baptist missions and education. From 1885 to 1888 he was president of the American Baptist Home Mission Society.* He was a member of the board of trustees of Madison, later Colgate Baptist University,* for nineteen years.

In 1887 he was asked to give a speech on the rise of women's missions and could not locate sufficient data. This led to a collection of Baptist books, pamphlets and reports that constituted the Samuel Colgate Baptist Historical Collection, first housed in his home at East Orange, New Jersey. Colgate gave the collection of almost a quarter-million items to Colgate University in 1892.

In 1946 a chapel on the campus of Colgate Rochester Divinity School* in Rochester, New York, was dedicated in Colgate's honor.

BIBLIOGRAPHY. S. T. Hardin, *The Colgate Story* (1959).

W. H. Brackney

Colgate, William (1783-1857). Prominent American Baptist layperson and philanthropist. Born in Hollingbourne, England, Colgate was the founder of the Colgate Palmolive Peet Soap Company and an active lay leader in several local New York City churches. He also was the leading contributor to the Triennial Missionary Convention.* From 1829 to 1852 he was a member of the board of managers of the General Missionary Convention (later the American Baptist Foreign Mission Society*). Likewise, he was a life member of the American Baptist Missionary Union* and served as treasurer of the American Baptist Home Mission Society* (1836-1842 and 1845-1846). His son, Samuel Colgate,* later became president of the Home Mission Society. Along with his brother James, Samuel endowed Madison (later Colgate Baptist*) University and the University of Rochester.

BIBLIOGRAPHY. W. H. Brackney, *The Baptists* (1988); S. T. Hardin, *The Colgate Story* (1959).

L. H. Williams

Colgate Baptist University. Baptist university founded in 1819 as the Hamilton Literary and Theological Institution. In becoming Colgate University the school evolved through several stages. Baptists on the New York frontier desired a training school for mission pastors in the region. In 1817 leaders assembled at Hamilton, New York, and formed the Baptist Education Society of the State of New York. Its principal purpose was to foster a school, which was organized on the literary and theological model pioneered that same year among Baptists in Waterville, Maine.

From 1820, when classes began, to its reorganization in 1846, the institution trained missionary pastors in a three year course that included theological as well as arts courses. Among Hamilton's outstanding students were Jabez Swan and Jacob Knapp,* evangelists, and Jonathan Wade and Eugenio Kincaid, two of the first missionaries to Burma. In 1833, in part in response to the postundergraduate programs at Newton* and Andover* in New England, the theological program was separated out as a department. An illustrious faculty of the early years counted in its ranks Asahel and Nathaniel Kendrick,* Daniel Hascall, Barnas Sears and Thomas J. Conant.*

One of the deficiencies the institution suffered in its early years was its inability to confer degrees. A plan in the 1840s involved Columbian College* in Washington, D.C., which conferred arts degrees; this proved to be unsatisfactory. In 1846 the school was chartered as Madison University, named for the county in which it was situated. This allowed only for baccalaureate degrees; the first master's degrees were conferred in 1852. Major controversy erupted in 1847 when proponents of a scheme to relocate the university in Rochester divided the faculty and the community. The plan failed.

Madison University was a major educational center for Baptist pastors and missionaries throughout the nineteenth century. Adoniram Judson* spent his first missionary furlough on campus in 1845. The Samuel Colgate* Baptist Historical Collection, established in 1888 and presented to the university, became an important scholarly resource.

In response to two generations of benevolence from the Colgate family totaling over $600,000, the trustees adopted the name Colgate in 1890. In 1928 when Colgate Theological Seminary was merged with Rochester Theological Seminary,* the university ceased to be a church-related institution.

See also COLGATE ROCHESTER DIVINITY SCHOOL; COLGATE, SAMUEL.

BIBLIOGRAPHY. S. W. Taylor, *Historical Sketch of Madison University* (1852); H. D. Williams, *A History of Colgate University, 1819-1969* (1969).

W. H. Brackney

Colgate Rochester Divinity School. Colgate Rochester Divinity School (CRDS) is the result of the 1928 merger of Colgate and Rochester seminaries. From 1847 the two schools had shared a sometimes competitive but mostly congenial history, which brought them to consider a merger. Under the able leadership of President Albert W. Beaven, Rochester Seminary invited Colgate Seminary to consider moving its program to an urban center in the 1920s. The result was a new institution on a new campus, occupied in 1932.

During its first three decades, CRDS developed a reputation as an ecumenical divinity school on the model of the University of Chicago Divinity School,* the alma mater of many of its illustrious faculty. A substantial endowment was amassed during the presidency of Wilbur E. Saunders. Significant research capability was brought to the institution when the Samuel Colgate* Baptist Historical Collection was merged with the American Baptist Historical Society, becoming the largest corpus of Baptistiana in existence.

In the turbulent 1960s the Divinity School underwent profound change. A faculty position for African-American studies was approved, and the school was the scene of a major protest and "lockout" by black students. One of the faculty members, William Hamilton, was distinguished for his writing in the "Death of God" movement. An emphasis on women in ministry was realized when the Baptist Missionary Training School of Chicago moved to Rochester in 1961. Faculty and trustees further fulfilled their ecumenical vision by inviting Crozer Theological Seminary in Pennsylvania and Bexley Hall Divinity School in Ohio to join CRDS in a cluster at the Rochester site. Later, St. Bernard's Seminary of the Catholic Diocese of Rochester was added to the Rochester Center for Theological Studies.

BIBLIOGRAPHY. O. D. Judd, *An Historical Sketch of Colgate Rochester Divinity School* (1963).

W. H. Brackney

Colored Baptist Association, Friends to Humanity. Early African-American Baptist association. The Colored Baptist Association of Illinois and Friends to Humanity (CBAFH) was organized on April 27, 1839, in St. Clair County, Illinois; in 1852 the name was changed to the Wood River Association (WRA). Founded by John Livingston, a free black preacher, and Alfred H. Richardson, a free black layperson, CBAFH/WRA grew from five to ten churches between 1839 and 1862, including four missions in Racine, Wisconsin, and Leavenworth, Kansas, and the membership increased from 64 to over 400.

Modeled after white Baptist associations, the CBAFH emphasized mutual aid, domestic missions, temperance, family worship and education. Like earlier black Baptist associations, the CBAFH was an antislavery society. In 1843 the CBAFH organized the Colored Baptist Home Missionary Society, which led to the founding of the Western Colored Baptist Convention and included representatives from seven states. In 1864 the WRA helped to form a regional convention, which was known as the Northwestern and Southern Baptist Convention, with representatives from eight states.

BIBLIOGRAPHY. C. E. Lincoln and L. H. Mamiya, *The Black Church in the African American Experience* (1990); 1888 Minutes, Wood River Baptist Association.   L. H. Williams

Columbian College. Baptist-sponsored college for classical and theological training. From its founding in 1821 by the Triennial Convention,* the college was linked to the Baptist missionary movement. The Triennial Convention, which was founded in 1814 to support missions,* had expanded its purpose in 1817 to include the support of education. The vision of Luther Rice,* William Staughton, Richard Furman* and other Baptist leaders was to establish a national Baptist institution of higher education in the U.S. capital. It would serve as a unifying force for the widely scattered denomination, and it would support missions and provide instruction in classical studies and theology. William Staughton moved his small seminary from Philadelphia to Washington to merge with the college, and he became the school's first president.

The Baptists failed to fulfill their purpose in Columbian College, however, due largely to poor timing and inadequate financial management. The school was founded during a particularly difficult economic time; thus many pledges for support failed to materialize. Individual state loyalties were stronger than national loyalties in many

areas, and there was still skepticism among many Baptists about higher education in general. But above all, Luther Rice and other leaders were not cautious enough in proceeding with building projects. Contracts were made before adequate funds were received, and when the financial resources failed to materialize, the project failed.

In 1825 the theological department separated to form the Newton Theological Institution* in Massachusetts, and a year later, in 1826, the Triennial Convention voted to sever ties with Columbian College, although it maintained Baptist influence in retaining its right to nominate trustees. Rice's reputation was damaged because of the financial collapse of the college, and he spent the rest of his life traveling throughout the country raising financial support for both missions and the college. In 1852 the Maryland Baptist Union Association took partial control of the college, but the financially crippled school eventually was rescued by Congress and came under U.S. government control. In 1874 the college was renamed Columbian University. In 1903 it became known as George Washington University, and in 1904 its remaining ties with the Baptists were severed.

BIBLIOGRAPHY. W. H. Brackney, *The Baptists* (1983); W. H. Brackney, ed., *Baptist Life and Thought, 1600-1980* (1983); H. L. McBeth, *The Baptist Heritage* (1987).

T. R. McKibbens and A. M. Manis

Columbian Star. Along with the *Latter Day Luminary,* the *Columbian Star* was one of the first Baptist newspapers in the United States. Founded in 1822 in Washington, D.C., and later moved to Philadelphia, the paper was bought by Georgia Baptist leader Jesse Mercer,* who became its editor from 1833 to 1840. After its removal to Georgia, the paper was renamed the *Christian-Index.* Under Mercer's leadership the paper gave strong, even militant, responses to opponents of missions and education in Baptist work. In 1841 Mercer donated the paper to the Georgia Baptist Convention, which has continued to use it as its official organ. Throughout most of the twentieth century, under editors Louie Newton and Jack U. Harwell, the *Index* was a progressive influence among Southern Baptists.

BIBLIOGRAPHY. H. L. McBeth, *The Baptist Heritage* (1987); A. H. Newman, *A History of the Baptist Churches in the United States* (1894); *History of the Baptist Denomination in Georgia* (1881).

A. M. Manis

Committee on the Religious Instruction of the Colored People. A committee of the Southern Baptist Convention* overseeing work among the freed slaves after the Civil War. In its report to the 1866 convention, the committee recommended that every church establish a Sunday school for freedpersons. The committee called for white pastors to offer theological and other kinds of instruction to black ministers. They further encouraged the establishment of day schools for black children with Southern Baptist young people serving as teachers. Responding to what they saw as "northern encroachment" into their territory, they stated that "while we are not opposed to any right-minded man aiding in this important work, it is our decided conviction, from our knowledge of the character of these people . . . that this work must be done mainly by ourselves." In these ways Southern Baptists sought to keep black Baptists "in their place," conducting their church life in ways not threatening to the Southern way of life.

BIBLIOGRAPHY. *Proceedings of the Southern Baptist Convention,* 1866.

A. M. Manis

Conant, Thomas Jefferson (1802-1891). Educator and biblical scholar. A Vermonter, Thomas J. Conant was educated at Middlebury College and taught for a time at Columbian College in Washington, D.C., and Waterville College in Maine. Conant was known as a thoroughgoing scholar among his contemporaries, and this was reinforced when he quit his teaching at Waterville to live in Boston and use the libraries to study Eastern philosophy. In 1825 he became professor of biblical literature at Hamilton Literary and Theological Institute (*see* Colgate Baptist University) and spent twenty-five years there. In 1850 he joined the new faculty at the Rochester Theological Seminary,* from which he retired in 1890.

Conant, joined by his wife, translated and revised Gesenius's *Hebrew Grammar,* producing an edition that was used by most students of the era. He became the senior scholar in the translation project of the American Bible Union, a Baptist body conceived by William Colgate* and others.

BIBLIOGRAPHY. T. J. Conant, "Inaugural Address Delivered in the Chapel of the Hamilton Literary and Theological Seminary," August 19, 1835; *DAB.*

W. H. Brackney

Cone, Spencer Houghton (1785-1855). Pastor and denominational leader. An actor by training, Spencer Cone left his profession for duty in the War of 1812, where he made important friendships in the federal government. After the war he took on churches in the Washington area, distinguishing himself as a Baptist minister. On that experience he was subsequently invited to New York's prestigious Oliver Street Church in 1823.

Among the members of Oliver Street was William Colgate.* Deacon Colgate and pastor Cone were among the most prominent leaders of American Baptist* missionary and educational enterprises. Cone was active in the American Baptist Foreign Mission Society* and was particularly interested in the work of Johann Oncken and Isaac McCoy. As a member of the board of the Home Mission Society,* he was sympathetic to the Southern position and urged an amicable settlement short of schism. As a leader in the American Bible Society* movement of his day, he stoutly defended the Baptist position on baptism and helped to organize a new translation of Scripture. Cone died August 28, 1855.

BIBLIOGRAPHY. W. H. Brackney, *The Baptists* (1988); E. W. Cone, *Life of Spencer H. Cone* (1851).

W. H. Brackney

Confessions of Faith, Baptist. Confessions of faith have both reflected and influenced the doctrinal positions of Baptists in America. Drawn up by individuals, churches, associations and conventions, confessions have expressed the beliefs of the Baptists who wrote or adopted them. American Baptists inherited their confession-writing tendencies from English Baptists, who prepared confessions as far back as the early 1600s. Baptists have typically described confessions as voluntary, nonbinding, fallible statements of faith, and they have basically opposed creeds, since they imply unwarranted finality and ultimate authority in matters of faith or practice.

In 1742 the Philadelphia Baptist Association* adopted the first major Baptist confession of faith in America. The confession, with its strongly Calvinistic* thrust, was based heavily on the 1677 Second London Confession of English Baptists. Two new articles provided for the singing of "psalms, hymns, and spiritual songs" in public worship and for the "laying on of hands (with prayer) upon baptized believers." Other key associations adopted this confession, such as that of

Charleston in South Carolina in 1751 (without the article on laying on of hands) and that of Warren in Rhode Island in 1767. The Philadelphia Confession was the most influential one among Baptists in America in the 1700s and early 1800s.

In 1833 the Board of the Baptist Convention of New Hampshire approved a confession that eventually superseded Philadelphia's as the most widely spread doctrinal statement of Baptists in America. Reflecting a mild form of Calvinism, this confession gained popularity (often with the addition of two new articles, "Repentance and Faith" and "Sanctification") with inclusion in key Baptist church manuals in the late 1800s and adoption by many Landmark* Baptists, who admired its emphasis on the local, visible church and its silence on the doctrine of a universal church.

The New Hampshire Confession* served as the basis for the revised and expanded Baptist Faith and Message Statement* adopted in 1925 by the Southern Baptist Convention* (SBC). Then in 1963 the SBC adopted a revised Baptist Faith and Message Statement that reduced the 1925 version from twenty-five articles to seventeen. The 1963 confession was conservative and expressed mild Calvinism. Both the 1925 and 1963 statements arose to clarify SBC positions in response to controversy. The statements contained the same introduction, which insisted that the confessions should not be used as creeds. Despite this safeguard, however, a major Baptist historian has claimed that "the 1963 confession has become more creedal than any other in Baptist history" (see H. L. McBeth, *The Baptist Heritage* [1987], p. 686).

Free Will Baptists* utilize a "Treatise" approved in 1935 and revised in 1948. Its basic doctrines come from an Arminian* theology. Fundamentalist Baptist groups such as the American Baptist Association,* the Conservative Baptist Association of America* and the Baptist Bible Union of America utilize confessions that affirm biblical inerrancy, literal creation accounts, a personal devil and perseverance of the saints (*see* Fundamentalism). Baptist diversity in America is reflected in the variety of confessions used by Baptist groups.

BIBLIOGRAPHY. W. L. Lumpkin, *Baptist Confessions of Faith* (1969).

C. W. Deweese

Congress of National Black Churches. An Af-

rican-American ecumenical organization. Organized December 1978, the Congress of National Black Churches (CNBC) consists of blacks holding membership in the seven largest all-black denominations in the United States (African Methodist Episcopal Church, African Methodist Episcopal Zion Church, Christian Methodist Episcopal Church, National Baptist Convention, U.S.A. Inc., National Baptist Convention of America, Progressive National Baptist Convention [*see* National Baptists] and the Church of God in Christ). The CNBC's purpose is one of long-range black social and economic development within the United States and Africa. Its program is based on black ecumenical collective action, especially in the areas of banking, education, insurance, purchasing and communications. The CNBC also operates within the context of the National Council of Churches. John Hurst Adams, an African Methodist Episcopal bishop, served as the first chairperson. Currently the CNBC maintains a national headquarters in Washington, D.C., and H. Michael Lemmons is executive director. It holds annual conventions and meetings and publishes a quarterly periodical called the *Newsletter.*

BIBLIOGRAPHY. D. M. Burek, ed., *Encyclopedia of Associations* (1991); M. E. Sawyer, "Black Ecumenical Movements: Proponents of Social Change," *RRR,* December 1988.

L. H. Williams

Conner, Walter Thomas (1877-1952). Baptist theologian and educator. Born in Rowell, Arkansas, Conner lived most of his life in Texas. Ordained in 1899, he attended Simmons College and graduated from Baylor University* (A.B., 1906), Baylor Theological Seminary (Th.B., A.M., 1908), Rochester Theological Seminary* (B.D., 1910) and Southern Baptist Theological Seminary* (Th.D., 1916; Ph.D., 1931). He studied briefly at the University of Chicago.

Conner served as pastor of several small churches, but his greatest contributions came through thirty-nine years of teaching (1910-1949) at Southwestern Baptist Theological Seminary.* A frequent contributor to theological journals, a popular teacher and a dedicated scholar who stayed abreast of theological developments, Conner published fifteen books, including *A System of Christian Doctrine* (1924), *Revelation and God* (1936), *Christian Doctrine* (1937), *The Faith of the New Testament* (1940), *The Gospel of Re-*

demption (1945), *The Work of the Holy Spirit* (1949) and *The Cross in the New Testament* (1954), edited by Jesse J. Northcutt.

Strongly influenced by professors John S. Tanner at Baylor, Augustus H. Strong* at Rochester and E. Y. Mullins* at Southern, Conner took a conservative but progressive approach to theology. He essentially set forth a strong Christocentric theology rooted in the Incarnation and atonement. He viewed Scripture as authoritative for faith and practice but defended no fixed view of inspiration. Through his teaching and writing he shaped the theology of thousands of Southern Baptists,* becoming one of the most influential and respected Southern Baptist theologians of the twentieth century.

BIBLIOGRAPHY. S. A. Newman, *W. T. Conner: Theologian of the Southwest* (1964); J. J. Northcutt, "Walter Thomas Conner, Theologian of Southwestern," *SwJT* 9 (Fall 1966):81-89.

C. L. Howe

Conservative Baptist Association of America. An association of approximately 1,200 Baptist churches chiefly in the Northern and Western areas of the United States. Organized in Atlantic City, New Jersey, in 1947, the Conservation Baptist Association of America (CBA) is closely allied with CBInternational Mission to the Americas, Southwestern Bible College in Phoenix, Arizona, and three theological seminaries: Denver Seminary (Colorado), Western Seminary (Portland, Oregon) and Eastern Conservative Baptist Seminary. The seven organizations constitute the Conservative Baptist "movement." Total membership of the churches in the association is approximately 230,000, but thousands more in other congregations provide financial support for the missions and schools and add to the total strength of the movement. Conservative Baptists prefer to speak of their movement rather than their denomination because the CBA creates only a loose affiliation for its churches. Unlike most denominations, it has no unified budget for its cooperating agencies. Each of the schools and mission societies has its own budget and board of directors. Structurally, then, Conservative Baptists operate more as cooperating interdenominational agencies than as a traditional denomination.

The association emerged from the fundamentalist*-modernist controversy within the Northern Baptist denomination (now American Baptist Churches in the USA*). As early as 1921 conservative pastors within the convention attempted to establish doctrinal standards for the missionary agencies of the Northern Baptist Convention. But several votes at annual conventions (1922-1925) proved fruitless. Then, in 1943, after renewed but unsuccessful attempts to create theological tests for the Northern Baptist missionary program, several hundred conservative churches formed the Conservative Baptist Foreign Mission Society. Pastor Richard Beal at the First Baptist Church of Tucson, Arizona, and Pastor Albert Johnson at Hinson Baptist Church in Portland, Oregon, assumed the leadership in this action.

The conservative association of churches was organized when it became apparent, at the Northern Baptist Convention meeting at Grand Rapids, Michigan (1946), that the older convention would not tolerate a competing missionary agency within its structures. In the following years hundreds of Northern Baptist churches left their national convention to join the conservatives. In Minnesota and Arizona, conservatives even captured the state conventions of the denomination.

Conservative Baptist agencies grew rapidly during the first fifteen years of independent ministry, but in the late 1950s internal conflict developed over acceptable affiliations outside the movement. The vast majority of Conservative Baptist churches cooperated with other denominations and parachurch agencies in the National Association of Evangelicals, and especially with the Billy Graham Evangelistic Association.* A militant minority within Conservative Baptist circles, however, insisted that such cooperation was dangerous and to be avoided. These were the fundamentalists within Conservative Baptist circles. After seven years of intense debate over separation, the militant minority, consisting of about 200 churches, found a new home in fundamentalistic circles.

During the 1970s Conservative Baptist schools and mission agencies shared in the resurgence of evangelicalism highlighted by the election of Jimmy Carter* to the presidency. In more recent years Conservative Baptists have supported annually nearly 1,000 career and short-term missionaries through their foreign and home missionary societies and have enrolled over 1,000 students in their three seminaries.

BIBLIOGRAPHY. B. L. Shelley, *Founded on the Word, Focused on the World: The Story of CBFMS* (1978); B. L. Shelley, *A History of Conservative Baptists* (1971); A. W. Wardin Jr., *Baptists in Oregon* (1969).

B. L. Shelley

Conservative Baptist Fellowship. *See* NATION-AL FEDERATION OF FUNDAMENTALISTS OF THE NORTHERN BAPTISTS.

Consolidated American Baptist Missionary Convention. A black Baptist convention organized in 1866, focused on missionary work among Southern blacks in the aftermath of the Civil War, and terminated in 1879. Perhaps the first truly national organization of black Baptists, the Consolidated American Baptist Missionary Convention (CABMC) began in Richmond, Virginia, in 1866, resulting from a merger of the American Baptist Missionary Convention (1840) and the Northwestern and Southern Baptist Convention (1864). The CABMC's primary mission was the organization of religious life among Southern blacks, most of them formerly enslaved, but it also exhibited missionary interest in Haiti and Africa. Among its most influential leaders and officers were Richard DeBaptiste, Rufus Lewis Perry and William P. Brooks.

After thirteen years of struggle, the CABMC collapsed in 1879 because of the lack of financial support and internal, sectional dissensions. Despite its short life, the CABMC played an instrumental role through its missionary and church work in keeping alive the vision of a national black Baptist convention and helping to shape a sense of black identity and responsibility in ecclesiastical and political affairs.

BIBLIOGRAPHY. L. G. Jordan, *Negro Baptist History* (1930); S. D. Martin, *Black Baptists and African Missions* (1989); O. D. Pelt and R. L. Smith, *The Story of the National Baptists* (1960); J. M. Washington, *Frustrated Fellowship* (1986); C. G. Woodson, *History of the Negro Church* (1921, 1972).

S. D. Martin

Continental Baptist Churches. Association of Reformed Baptist* churches. In the late 1970s a group led by Ron McKinney became interested in Reformed Baptist theology. In order to nurture this common interest, the group convened an annual Council on Baptist Theology at Plano, Texas, from 1980 to 1982. In the summer of 1983 the group met in Wheaton, Illinois, and formally organized an association named Continental Baptist Churches (CBC). What began as an association of approximately twenty churches has dwindled to six churches located in New York, Virginia, Michigan and Indiana. At the present time, Allen Smith, a pastor in Roanoke, Virginia, is the leader of the association. The CBC publishes a newsletter and continues to sponsor an annual meeting. Continental Baptist Churches has distant ties to the larger Reformed Baptist movement known as Sovereign Grace.

BIBLIOGRAPHY. M. McCulley, *Studies in History and Ethics* (1983).

A. L. Pratt

Conversion, Baptist Views. The need for a regenerate church membership—a congregation of Christian believers—has been a hallmark of Baptist doctrine from the beginning of the movement. Consequently, Baptist groups have stressed the necessity of conversion, a personal experience of divine grace through faith in Christ, for all persons who would belong to a Baptist church. Baptism was to be administered only to those who could testify to a work of grace within.

While Baptists agree on the need for conversion, they do not always agree on the process whereby conversion is secured. The Regular* (Calvinistic*) Baptists believed that conversion was entirely the work of God. Preachers were called upon to declare the word of grace and redemption which the Spirit would use to awaken the hearts and minds of the elect. Conversion was often a rather lengthy process of struggling against grace. Elect individuals might refuse grace for a time, but ultimately its irresistible mercy would prevail. Primitive* and Old Regular* Baptists went beyond this modified Calvinism to suggest that conversion was such a work of God that revivals, evangelism and Sunday schools aimed at securing conversion were useless human efforts.

Nineteenth-century revivalism was influential in promoting a more Arminian* approach to conversion, with greater emphasis on free will, human choice and the participation of the sinner in the conversion process. Preachers declared that Christ had died for all persons. All were *potentially* in the elect and could actualize election through repentance and faith. By the twentieth century, many Baptist groups were promoting a process of personal conversion whereby sinful individuals recognized a need for Christ, confessed personal sins and "invited" Jesus into their hearts as "Savior and Lord." Such conversion was often described as a dramatic event when one turned from sin to salvation, a life-changing experience. Free Will Baptists* affirmed this process while insisting that believers could "fall away" from salvation if they chose to do so later on.

Southern Baptists* were among those groups that denied that falling away was possible for the true believer. They retained a belief in the perseverance of the saints, often popularly referred to as "once saved, always saved."

Another concern involved the time of conversion. In the colonial and frontier periods, conversion and baptism usually occurred during the adolescent or adult years. Some Baptists emphasized the importance of adult believer's baptism over the baptism of children. By the late nineteenth and early twentieth centuries, however, some groups began to promote the need for child evangelism, insisting that tenderhearted children were ripe for conversion. Another factor in child evangelism was the question of the "age of accountability," that nebulous time when children become accountable for their moral and spiritual actions and decisions. The concern for children was also evident in the stress on Christian nurture, training children from infancy so as to lead them to faith in Christ. Thus many Baptists testified to dramatic conversion experiences, while others, particularly those converted in childhood, claimed to have known and loved Jesus for as long as they could remember.

During the later twentieth century, child baptism created theological problems for many Baptist groups, particularly Southern Baptists. Adults baptized in childhood sometimes doubted the validity of their salvation since it was clouded in memory and understanding. Thus many adults received "rebaptism," repudiating earlier baptism and conversion for a more adult response to the Christian gospel. Likewise, as traditional revivalistic methods of promoting conversion have become less viable, many Baptists have begun to ask questions about the nature of conversion, its meaning and its role in Baptist life. As Baptists enter the twenty-first century, conversion remains both a doctrine and a dilemma for many groups.

BIBLIOGRAPHY. B. J. Leonard, "Getting Saved in America: Conversion Event in a Pluralistic Culture," *RE*, Winter 1981; H. L. McBeth, *The Baptist Heritage* (1987). B. J. Leonard

Conwell, Russell Herman (1843-1925). Inspirational lecturer and writer, Baptist pastor. Born near Worthington, Massachusetts, Conwell attended Wilbraham Academy and Yale College (1860-1862) before enlisting in the Union Army during the Civil War. He graduated from Albany Law School in 1865 and worked as a lawyer and traveling journalist. Among his legal clients was Mary Baker Eddy, founder of Christian Science.

In 1882 Conwell became pastor of the Baptist Temple. By 1893 the church had over 3,000 members, a new building with a gymnasium and reading rooms. It also had a large Sunday school and two hospitals, making it the largest Protestant church in America. Conwell founded Temple University when he began teaching evening classes for workers who desired an education but could not afford it. In 1969 the Conwell School of Theology, associated with Temple University, merged with Gordon Divinity School to form the Gordon-Conwell Theological Seminary.

Conwell wrote over thirty inspirational books but is best remembered for "Acres of Diamonds," the sermonic lecture he delivered over 6,000 times nationwide. Contemporaries believed he "addressed more people than any man of the past century." The central theme of "Acres of Diamonds" summarizes Conwell's message: it is one's Christian responsibility to become wealthy in order to help the cause of Christ. As in Andrew Carnegie's "Gospel of Wealth," the rich were to be wise stewards. Unlike Carnegie, however, Conwell announced that wealth was available to all—there were "acres of diamonds" in everyone's own backyard.

Conwell echoed a long tradition, dating back to Puritanism, of popular religious notions concerning success, health and wealth. His popularization helped mold twentieth-century expression of these ideas by religionists like Bruce Barton, Norman Vincent Peale and Robert Schuller, as well as entrepreneurs such as W. Clement Stone (founder of *Success Magazine*).

BIBLIOGRAPHY. D. W. Bjork, *Victorian Flight: Russell Conwell and the Crisis of American Individualism* (1979); A. R. Burr, *Russell H. Conwell and His Work* (1926); R. H. Conwell, *Acres of Diamonds, with His Life and Achievements by Robert Shackleton* (1943); *DAB* 11; *DARB*; *NCAB* 3.

J. R. Wimmer

Cooperative Baptist Fellowship. A national organization of moderate Southern Baptists* for missions and other cooperative endeavors. Southern Baptist (SBC) moderates met in Atlanta in August 1990 to discuss forming a new way of working together after a decade of confrontation with SBC fundamentalists* over control of the parent denomination. Having been largely unsuccessful in their efforts to defeat or negotiate with fundamentalists, some 3,000 moderates gathered for reevaluation and dialogue. This meeting produced momentum that led to the founding of the Cooperative Baptist Fellowship (CBF) at a gathering of over 6,000 persons in Atlanta in 1991.

The fellowship, governed by a coordinating council composed of lay and clergy representatives from churches and regions, defines itself as a missionary organization providing cooperative options for churches and individuals. Funding is provided for various Baptist and ecumenical endeavors, including theological education, missions, evangelism, ethics and women in ministry. As of 1994 contributors could choose among several funding plans, one of which contributes to existing Southern Baptist agencies. Most of the contributors come from Southern Baptist churches. Many of those churches now provide alternative giving plans whereby members may choose to send money through the traditional SBC Cooperative Program* of giving or through the Cooperative Baptist Fellowship. While the CBF is not an official denomination and tends to function according to the society method of funding specific programs directly and individually, it remains to be seen how long it can or will be permitted to function alongside Southern Baptist institutions. Its national offices are in Atlanta, Georgia, and its annual convocation is held in May.

BIBLIOGRAPHY. D. Vestal, "The History of the Cooperative Baptist Fellowship," in *The Struggle for the Soul of the SBC,* ed. W. Shurden (1993).

B. J. Leonard

Cooperative Program, Southern Baptist Convention. A denominational funding program through which Southern Baptist* churches send money to help finance the ministries of state Baptist conventions and the Southern Baptist Convention (SBC). The most influential factor in the adoption of the Cooperative Program (CP) by the SBC in 1925 was the 75 Million Campaign of 1919-1924. Intended to raise $75 million for denominational work (followed by pledges totaling $92.6 million), the campaign actually raised only $58 million, thus leaving in serious debt most Southern Baptist institutions and agencies—state and southwide—which had planned to receive shares of the full $75 million.

With remarkable success, the CP advanced to the point that CP receipts reported by state conventions in 1990 totaled $364,461,354, with $140,710,282 of that amount going to SBC causes. Across the years the CP has aided denominational unity, provided a single vehicle for funding the denomination's work, enabled each church member and each church to support the denomination's total ministries, and facilitated budgetary planning.

The Stewardship Commission, SBC, and stewardship offices in state Baptist conventions hold primary responsibility for CP promotion. The annual denominational calendar includes CP Day (third Sunday in April) and CP Month (October). CP has been the primary channel for funding Bold Mission Thrust, a twenty-five-year plan of Southern Baptists to share the gospel with everyone on earth by the year 2000.

Controversy and a breakdown of trust at key points in SBC life since 1979 have created a major threat to the future of the CP and of Bold Mission Thrust. There is a growing tendency of some individuals, churches and state conventions to consider alternate funding mechanisms that support ministries with which they more readily identify.

By the latter twentieth century, controversy related to biblical inerrancy and control of the Southern Baptist Convention significantly affected the Cooperative Program, with churches both fundamentalist and moderate "designating" funds to specific agencies they supported and away from others (*see* Cooperative Baptist Fellowship). While it continues to function as the denomination's primary funding mechanism, the CP mirrors transitions in the SBC structure and organization.

BIBLIOGRAPHY. R. A. Baker, "The Cooperative Program in Historical Perspective," *BHH,* July 1975, pp. 169-76; *ESB* 1:323-24; 3:1666; 4:2174-75.

C. W. Deweese

Cotton Grove Resolutions (1851). Statement of Landmark Principles. Landmarkism,* led by J. R. Graves,* ignited over the issue of alien immersion, the acceptance of baptism by a pedobaptist minister. After ridiculing the position of John L. Waller, editor of the *Western Recorder,* in a newspaper debate, Graves called for a meeting at Cotton Grove in western Tennessee to discuss the true Christian-Baptist position. The meeting, held June 24, 1851, issued a statement of five principles for the New Testament (Baptist) church: non-Baptist "societies" could not be recognized because they possessed different governments, officers and doctrines from those found in

Scripture; these societies could not be called churches; their ministers could not be recognized as valid ministers; pulpit affiliation or other church activities of their ministers could not be recognized; and these non-Baptists could not be called "brethren" since they did not have the doctrine of Christ. These resolutions were the earliest organized effort of the Landmark movement.

See also GRAVES, JAMES ROBINSON; LANDMARKISM.

BIBLIOGRAPHY. H. L. McBeth, *The Baptist Heritage* (1987). C. D. Weaver

Council on Christian Social Progress. Baptist ethics agency. From its early years, the Northern Baptist Convention (*see* American Baptist Churches in the USA) exhibited an interest in the relation between religion and contemporary social concerns. Walter Rauschenbusch* and Samuel Zane Batten* assisted in the formation of a convention committee to address social issues as early as 1914.

Several committees were combined in 1940, and the Council on Christian Social Progress was formed as a bureau of the convention. Its mandate was "to address neo-paganism and assist impoverished and exploited humanity." The council was composed of seventeen members drawn from all the national societies and the state and city organizations. Its first task was to appraise social needs and prepare suitable resolutions to the convention. The council agreed to adhere to a five-point system that stressed Christian character, the ethics of Jesus and historic Christian principles.

Over its twenty-one-year span of influence, the council investigated and produced reports on alcohol, narcotics, prostitution, gambling, domestic relations, international order, church-state issues and civil liberties. In conjunction with the American Baptist Publication Society,* primers on timely subjects were produced. Following World War II, the council particularly focused on coal and auto strikes, the high prices of consumer goods, peace, and children's and women's rights. When the denomination was reorganized in 1961, the council's work was assigned to the Division of Christian Social Concern. In 1972 a second reorganization took place, and that division's work was broken up between the Statement of Concerns Committee of the Office of the General Secretary and the Board of National Ministries.* Prominent names associated with the council include Frank W. Padelford, John W. Thomas and Elizabeth J. Miller.

BIBLIOGRAPHY. *Annual of the Northern Baptist Convention,* 1940-1972.

W. H. Brackney

Covenants, Baptist Church. A church covenant is a series of written pledges focusing on conduct and lifestyle which church members voluntarily make to God and one another. Baptist churches in early America tended to use covenants. Pre-1830 trends included the following: (1) most churches wrote their own covenants, although some used standard covenants, (2) churches linked covenantal faithfulness to church discipline, (3) Baptists generally signed covenants, and (4) Baptists used covenants in such settings as constituting new churches, receiving and baptizing new members, and monthly covenant meetings.

The most important trend since the 1830s has been the increased standardization of covenants. The primary cause has been the proliferating publication of standard (or model) covenants in church and ministers' manuals, hymnals, church minute books, encyclopedias, pocket cards and wall charts. J. Newton Brown's* covenant in his *The Baptist Church Manual* (1853) became and remains the covenant most widely used by Baptists in the United States and in some other countries. Brown based his covenant on the covenant adopted by the New Hampshire Baptist Convention in 1833 (*see* New Hampshire Confession of Faith).

The use of covenants declined in the 1900s for several reasons. First, churches tended to adopt uniform covenants that did not meet their unique needs, instead of creatively thinking through and writing individual covenants. Second, Baptists resisted a legalistic application of covenants. And third, a general secularizing process invaded Baptist life; covenants, like church discipline, have fallen victim to this development. But influenced by the "church renewal movement" of the 1960s and 1970s, some Baptists have expressed a revitalized interest in covenants in recent years.

BIBLIOGRAPHY. C. W. Deweese, *Baptist Church Covenants* (1990).

C. W. Deweese

Cox, Joseph B. (1830-?). Major Joseph B. Cox was a prominent General Baptist* layman, contributing to both its educational and its publishing institutions. Born to parents who were members of the founding congregation of General Baptists, Cox received his military title during service in the Civil War. After completing a formal education at Cincinnati Business College, Cox distinguished himself in Vanderburgh County, Indiana, in business and politics. Among other responsibilities, he served as county sheriff, county treasurer and U.S. surveyor of customs.

Having amassed a considerable estate, Cox was a principal benefactor of Oakland City College.* He also was a stockholder and manager of an early General Baptist publication, the *Herald*. His reputation of being a well-educated and highly successful man while at the same time having a generous and sterling character was well deserved.

See also GENERAL BAPTISTS; STINSON, BENONI.

BIBLIOGRAPHY. A. D. Williams, *Benoni Stinson and the General Baptists* (1892).

L. C. Shull

Craig, Elijah (1743-1808). Pioneer farmer, preacher and educator in Virginia and Kentucky. Born in Orange County, Virginia, he was a brother of Baptist ministers Joseph and Lewis Craig.* Encouraged by Samuel Harris in 1765, Elijah held meetings in his tobacco barn before he was baptized in 1766. With little formal education, he was ordained pastor of the Blue Run Church in 1771. Craig was twice briefly imprisoned for Baptist preaching. Numerous times he was delegated a spokesperson for Separate Baptists* to the Virginia General Assembly. In 1786 he moved to Kentucky near what is now Georgetown, establishing a classical school there in 1788. He continued to preach and was active in the Elkhorn Association until his death at Georgetown in 1808, but his ministerial influence decreased as his businesses prospered. Credited with inventing bourbon whiskey, he also started the first sawmill, paper mill and rope works in Kentucky.

BIBLIOGRAPHY. *ESB* 1:327; R. B. Semple, *A History of the Baptists in Virginia* (1810); J. H. Spencer, *A History of Kentucky Baptists* (1885).

W. L. Allen

Craig, Lewis (1741-1824). Pioneer preacher in Virginia and Kentucky. Born in Orange County, Virginia, he was the brother of Baptist ministers Joseph and Elijah Craig.* Lewis Craig, convicted in 1765 under the preaching of Samuel Harris, began public testifying before his conversion. After assurance but before baptism (1767), he was

indicted for "preaching contrary to law." His defense converted one of the jurors, John Waller. In 1768 and again in 1771, Craig was imprisoned briefly because of his religious views, gaining much sympathy for his cause. Ordained in 1770 to the pastorate of the Upper Spotsylvania Church (Craig's Church), he traveled often and widely, founding several churches in Virginia.

In the fall of 1781 Craig, with most of his congregation, moved into central Kentucky. This entourage, called the "Travelling Church," settled as the Gilberts Creek Church, south of the Kentucky River in Garrard County territory, in December 1781. Two years later most of the congregation moved again with Craig to Fayette County, where they constituted the South Elkhorn Church. There Craig was instrumental in founding the Elkhorn Association (1785), the first in Kentucky. Economic losses forced a move in 1792 to Braken County (now Mason County), where he founded a church near Minerva the following year and organized the Braken Association in 1799. Having predicted the circumstances of his own death, he died suddenly in 1824.

BIBLIOGRAPHY. G. W. Ranck, *The Travelling Church* (1891); L. N. Thompson, *Lewis Craig* (1910).

W. L. Allen

Cramp, John Mockett (1796-1881). Canadian Baptist* leader and educator. Born in the Baptist parsonage at St. Peter's, Ramsgate, England, to Thomas and Rebecca Cramp, John was educated at Stepney College, Regent's Park. Between 1818 and 1844 he had pastorates at Dean Street Chapel, Southwark, St. Peter's and Hastings. A prolific writer, he published thirty-five works, as well as hundreds of articles, and edited the *Baptist Magazine* from 1825 to 1828. He was president of the English Baptist Union from 1837 to 1838.

After serving as president of Canada Baptist College, Montreal, from 1844 to 1849, Cramp edited several papers and in 1851 became president of Acadia College, Wolfville, Nova Scotia. The "Second Founder" of the college, he rebuilt its financial and faculty resources between 1851 and 1869. He taught every subject there at some time, while preaching every Sunday, writing and maintaining a massive correspondence. He became a Maritime Baptist leader and also gave direction to the temperance and education causes. His best-known work was his *Baptist History from the Foundation of the Christian Church to the Close of the Eighteenth Century* (1869), which was translated into German. As an educator, denominational leader and historian, he shaped a generation of Maritime Baptist scholars and pastors as he helped integrate the British and American traditions.   R. S. Wilson

Crawford, Alexander (c. 1785-1828). Pioneer Baptist preacher on Prince Edward Island. Born on the island of Arran, Scotland, Crawford joined the Baptistic Haldane movement (1800) and attended the Haldane brothers' seminary in Edinburgh, following them when they became Baptists (1808). Alexander and his wife, Jane, emigrated to Yarmouth, Nova Scotia, in 1810. There he taught school but found little fellowship with the local revival-oriented Baptists led by Henry Alline's* disciple Harris Harding.

In 1812 Crawford visited Prince Edward Island, where he performed the first adult believer's baptism* and founded a Baptist church at Three Rivers, Montague. In 1815 he moved to Prince Edward Island and taught school in Charlottetown. In 1818 he settled on a farm in Tryon and served as an itinerant preacher. He helped found churches at Three Rivers, Tryon, East Point, Lot Forty-Eight, Cross Roads and Belfast. Because he believed that prayer, praise, reading of Scripture, salutation, breaking of bread, offering, exhortation and discipline should be observed every Sunday by believers only, he did not join the local churches. He published his views on baptism in *Believer Immersion as Opposed to Unbeliever Sprinkling* (1827). Both the Baptists and the Disciples of Christ look to him as their founding father on Prince Edward Island.

R. S. Wilson

Crawford, Isabel Alice Hartley (1865-1961). Woman's American Baptist Home Mission Society* (WABHMS) missionary to Elk Creek, Oklahoma, 1893-1895; to Saddle Mountain, 1895-1906; and lecturer for WABHMS, 1906-1918. Isabel Crawford was born on May 26, 1865, the fifth child of John and Sarah Hackett Crawford. She graduated from the Baptist Missionary Training School in Chicago in 1893. While in Chicago she served as a missionary in the red light district. Hoping to be a missionary to Africa, India or China, Crawford was moved instead by the needs of American Indians. Chief Lone Wolf of the Kiowas asked for help from Christians, and American Baptists responded by sending Crawford, Hattie Everts and a minister to Elk Creek. Crawford be-

came an outspoken advocate for the Indians and after a short time was transferred to Saddle Mountain. There she ignored custom and assisted an unordained interpreter in administering the Lord's Supper, causing quite a stir among Indian and white Baptist officials. Believing that Indians had the right as well as the duty to partake of the elements, Crawford submitted her resignation to resolve the issue.

After leaving the reservations, Crawford lectured on and promoted Indian rights and Baptist missions.* In 1918 she moved to the Allegheny Indian Reservation in western New York. There she was involved in a dispute between Presbyterians and Baptists over the ownership of Red Horse Church. She gained support from the tribes, confronted her superiors and won the dispute.

The "Jesus Way Woman," as the Indians named her, was buried in Saddle Mountain Reservation under a stone on which is inscribed "I dwell among my own people."

BIBLIOGRAPHY. W. H. Brackney, *The Baptists* (1988); S. Mondello, "Isabel Crawford: The Making of a Missionary," *Foun,* October 1978, pp. 322-39; idem, "Isabel Crawford and the Kiowa Indians," *Foun,* January 1979, pp. 28-42; idem, "Isabel Crawford: Champion of the American Indians," *Foun,* April 1979, pp. 99-115.

C. Blevins

Crawford, Tarleton Perry (1821-1902). Southern Baptist missionary to China and leader of a Landmark* spinoff movement which took his name, "Crawfordism." Crawford was born in Georgia and graduated from Union University in Murfreesboro, Tennessee. He was appointed by the Foreign Mission Board* of the Southern Baptist Convention* (SBC) as a missionary to China in 1851; a few weeks later he married Martha Foster. The Crawfords worked in Shanghai for eleven years, after which they moved to Tengchow.

Crawford developed extreme Landmark views of missions,* denying that mission boards or societies had authority to appoint missionaries. He believed all such boards should be abolished and only churches should appoint missionaries. Crawford also taught that missionaries should subsist at absolute poverty levels and that they should find ways to earn their own livelihood on the field. His views on nonsupport intensified after his own extensive, and sometimes ethically questionable, investments in China afforded him financial independence.

In 1892 Crawford published his militant pamphlet *Churches, to the Front!* This launched what he called the Gospel Mission* movement, in contrast to what he considered the unbiblical plan of working through mission boards. For some years Crawford went his own way, refusing all directives from the Foreign Mission Board (though continuing to accept his salary). After years of patience, the Foreign Mission Board eventually severed all ties with Crawford and repudiated his movement.

BIBLIOGRAPHY. H. L. McBeth, ed., *A Sourcebook for Baptist Heritage* (1990).

H. L. McBeth

Creeds. *See* CONFESSIONS OF FAITH, BAPTIST

Criswell, W(allie) A(mos) (1909-). Southern Baptist* minister. Born in El Dorado, Oklahoma, Criswell escaped early family poverty and graduated magna cum laude from Baylor University* in 1931. He continued his education at Southern Baptist Theological Seminary* in Louisville, Kentucky, where he earned his Th.M. (1934) and his Ph.D. (1937). The author of nearly fifty books, Criswell is considered one of the most influential fundamentalist* ministers in the latter half of the twentieth century. The hallmark of Criswell's theology is his belief that the Bible is inerrant,* as expressed in his book *Why I Preach That the Bible Is Literally True* (1969).

After pastoring in Chicasha (1937-1941) and Muskogee (1941-1944), both in Oklahoma, the thirty-four-year-old Criswell accepted the August 1944 call of First Baptist Church of Dallas. An expository preacher, Criswell places great emphasis on evangelism. During his decades of strong conservative leadership the church has grown nearly fourfold to a membership, on paper at least, of around 26,000. His sermons have been broadcast live over radio and television throughout the Southwestern region of the United States. In the late 1960s his influence in mainstream Southern Baptist life reached its height when he served two years as president of the Southern Baptist Convention (SBC). During the 1980s Criswell was at the center of the inerrancy* party in the SBC and its effort to control convention agencies. By the 1990s he had retired as pastor but continued preaching in selected services and assisting in Criswell College,* an undergraduate institution sponsored in part through First Baptist Church, Dallas.

BIBLIOGRAPHY. B. Keith, *W. A. Criswell: The Authorized Biography* (1973); C. A. Russell, "W. A. Criswell: A Case Study in Fundamentalism," *RE* 81 (1984):107-31; M. G. Toulouse, "W. A. Criswell," in *Twentieth Century Shapers of American Popular Religion,* ed. C. H. Lippy (1989).

M. G. Toulouse

Criswell College. A degree-granting Bible college in Dallas, Texas, founded and operated in connection with the First Baptist Church of Dallas. The school was founded in 1970 under the name Criswell Bible Institute. Its purpose at that time was to train laypeople as well as full-time church workers. In 1977 the academic offerings were expanded, and the school was called the Criswell Center for Biblical Studies. Further expansion as a degree-granting institution led to the present name, Criswell College, in 1985. By 1992 two men had served as president: H. Leo Eddleman (1972-1974) and Paige Patterson (1975-1992). Criswell College offers master's degrees in several fields and since 1985 has been accredited by the Southern Association of Colleges and Schools (SACS). It is also accredited by the American Association of Bible Colleges (AABC).

At its peak the school reported twenty-four full-time professors and nearly 400 students, but as of 1992 those figures were much lower. The school is named for its founder, W. A. Criswell,* long-time pastor of First Baptist Church in Dallas. The school also has the Criswell College Wallace Library, operates the Criswell Radio Network and issues a semiannual journal, the *Criswell Theological Review.* The school's publication division also issued the *Criswell Study Bible* in 1979. In 1991 the school moved to its own renovated campus, including a 1,500-seat auditorium, in facilities formerly owned by Gaston Avenue Baptist Church.

BIBLIOGRAPHY. P. D. Jacobs, "The History and Development of the Criswell College, 1971-1990" (Ph.D. dissertation, University of North Texas, 1991).

H. L. McBeth

Crozer, John Price (1793-1866). An industrialist who modernized the textile industry in the Delaware Valley region. A Quaker by upbringing, John P. Crozer was converted at sixteen under the ministry of William Staughton* of Philadelphia. Staughton interested Crozer in voluntary organizations, and Crozer spent the remainder of his life aiding Baptist benevolent organizations. He was particularly interested in Sunday schools and was on the board of managers of the American Baptist Publication Society* for a number of years, under the leadership of his son-in-law Benjamin Griffith.

At the outbreak of the Civil War, Crozer established an academy for training ministers in the Middle States. In conjunction with the University of Lewisburg (a Baptist institution), he constructed an impressive edifice in Upland, Pennsylvania, near his home and factory. During the war it was used for a prison, and Crozer died before his dream of a school could be realized. He died March 11, 1866. His widow, Sallie K. Crozer, and son, Samuel P. Crozer, established in 1867 a theological seminary in his honor (see Crozer Theological Seminary).

BIBLIOGRAPHY. W. H. Brackney, *The Baptists* (1988); J. W. Smith, *Life of John P. Crozer* (1867).

W. H. Brackney

Crozer Theological Seminary. An American Baptist-related theological school now located on the campus of Colgate Rochester Divinity School* in Rochester, New York.

Crozer was founded in 1867 by the family of John Price Crozer,* a textile manufacturer of Upland, Pennsylvania. The school was actually an outgrowth of the theological division of the Baptist University of Lewisburg, Pennsylvania (later named Bucknell* in honor of Crozer's son-in-law).

Under the able forty-two-year presidency of Henry Griggs Weston (1867-1909), Crozer built a strong reputation as the mainstream, pastorally oriented institution of the Philadelphia region. It also attracted numerous faculty and Baptist students from the upper Southern states.

After 1910 the curriculum was substantially reorganized to reflect the newest thrusts of European historical and biblical scholarship. Faculty members like Milton S. Evans, Henry C. Vedder and Morton Scott Enslin placed Crozer squarely in the tradition of schools like the University of Chicago Divinity School,* as well as in the storm center of the fundamentalist* debate of the mid-1920s. Reaction to Crozer's perceived liberalism led directly to the establishment of Eastern Baptist Theological Seminary,* in part with Crozer retired faculty.

Crozer struggled for an identity after World War

II. In the 1960s a degree program in social change was instituted in honor of one of the school's outstanding graduates, Martin Luther King Jr.* Declining assets, coupled with the desire of some denominational educators to cluster seminaries, led to Crozer's removal to Rochester, where its programs are integrated with Colgate Rochester* and Bexley Hall (Episcopal) seminaries.

BIBLIOGRAPHY. *The Voice* 60 (July 1968).

W. H. Brackney

Curry, Jabez Lamar Monroe (1825-1903). Baptist leader, author and statesman. Born to a prosperous farming family, Curry spent his early years in Georgia and Alabama. Raised in a non-Christian home, he was converted and baptized at age twenty-one. Graduating from Harvard Law School, Curry distinguished himself as a U.S. congressman for the state of Alabama from 1857 to 1861 and as a member of the first Confederate Congress at Richmond. Curry was ordained in 1866 and began to preach regularly, although he never accepted a pastorate. Instead he dedicated himself to the cause of Baptist higher education, serving briefly (1865-1868) as president of Howard College (now Samford University*) and from 1868 to 1881 as a teacher at Richmond College (University of Richmond*). He also served for twelve years as president of the Foreign Mission Board* of the Southern Baptist Convention.* In 1885 he was appointed U.S. ambassador to Spain. In later life Curry became an outspoken and influential advocate for state-sponsored education and was particularly committed to advancing the educational opportunities of the Southern black population. He was the author of numerous books, including a biography of William Gladstone.

BIBLIOGRAPHY. E. A. Alderman, *J. L. M. Curry: A Biography* (1911); G. B. Taylor, *Virginia Baptist Ministers,* series 5 (1915).

B. C. Leslie

Curtis, Thomas Fenner (1815-1872). A teacher and preacher whose memory was eclipsed after his advocacy of historical-critical study of the Bible. Born in England, Curtis came to the United States in 1833. After graduating from Bangor Theological Seminary (Maine) in 1839, he held pastorates in Georgia and Alabama. A delegate from the Baptist Church at Tuscaloosa, Alabama (along with fellow members Basil Manly Sr.* and J. L. Dagg*), to the organizational meeting of the

Southern Baptist Convention,* he was one of four appointed to prepare the "Address to the Public." He was a member of the first Board of Domestic Missions and served as its corresponding secretary from 1852 to 1853. From 1849 to 1852 he taught theology at Howard College (now Samford University*), and in 1855 he accepted a similar post at what is now Bucknell University.*

Having an inquiring mind, Curtis adopted Bushnellian ideas on Christian nurture and open Communion views. He was a pioneer among evangelicals in the United States in espousing a historical-critical approach to the Bible. He wrote: "For many years I conscientiously and earnestly struggled to maintain the current theories of the Infallibility of Scripture Inspiration until all possibility of doing so reasonably and honestly was gone." Maintaining that his new views were compatible with evangelical theology, he published *The Human Element in the Inspiration of the Sacred Scriptures* (1867). Despite his former reputation for piety, character and scholarship, he was denounced in book reviews and editorials by fellow Baptists, and doors to further employment were closed to him. He died in Cambridge, Massachusetts.

BIBLIOGRAPHY. Bangor Theological Seminary, *Historical Catalogue, 1816-1916; ESB* 3:1673.

N. H. Maring

Cushing, Ellen Howard (1840-1915). Missionary to Burma, American Baptist* educator.

Born August 29, 1840, in Kingston, Massachusetts, Ellen was a teacher in Boston until she went in 1862 to the sea islands of South Carolina to serve as a superintendent of two cotton plantations employing free blacks. There she met J. M. Fairfield, whom she married in 1863. In 1865 he was drowned in a shipwreck and she returned to Boston, taking charge of the "Home for Little Wanderers" until 1866, when she married Josiah Cushing and sailed for Burma as a missionary to the Shan people. Cushing prepared school texts in the Shan language and collaborated with her husband in translating Scriptures. The Cushings periodically lived apart in order to serve several villages at once. Because of her profound courage and independence, she is distinguished among early Baptist missionary women. Ellen Cushing and her son Herbert (b. 1872) returned to the United States in August 1880 due to her poor health, leaving Josiah Cushing to finish the translations. From 1892 to 1900 Cushing served as preceptress of the Baptist Training School for Christian Workers in Philadelphia (named Cushing Junior College in 1966). Her husband died while on furlough in 1905, and Cushing returned to Burma (1905-1908) to finish his translations. She died April 30, 1915, in Providence, Rhode Island.

BIBLIOGRAPHY. W. St. John, *Josiah Nelson Cushing* (1912); W. S. Stewart, *Early Baptist Missionaries and Pioneers,* vol. 2 (1925).

T. L. Scales

D

Dagg, John Leadley (1794-1884). Baptist minister, educator and theologian. Born at Middleburg, Virginia, the oldest of eight children, he was baptized in 1812 by the Ebenezer Baptist Church and ordained in 1817. Although his formal education was limited, Dagg possessed genuine intellectual gifts and a strong desire to learn. Thus, other than having six or seven years of formal schooling, he was largely self-taught in his mastery of Latin, Greek, Hebrew and higher mathematics.

Dagg served several churches in Virginia and for nine years (1825-1834) was pastor of the Fifth Baptist Church in Philadelphia. Because of difficulty with his throat, however, he then withdrew from the pastorate and gave himself to teaching, educational administration and writing. He became head of the Haddington Institution near Philadelphia and then, in 1836, the Alabama Female Athenaeum in Tuscaloosa. From 1844 to 1854 he was president of Mercer University* in Penfield, Georgia. He remained there as professor of theology until 1856.

During his years as an educator Dagg wrote essays dealing with the ordinances and with the Bible: *An Essay in Defence of Strict Communion* (1845), *A Decisive Argument Against Infant Baptism* (1849) and *Origin and Authority of the Bible* (1853). His more influential books on theology were written after his retirement: *A Manual of Theology* (1857), *A Treatise on Church Order* (1858), *The Elements of Moral Science* (1860) and *The Evidences of Christianity* (1869). Through these volumes he became recognized as a theologian and exerted wide influence on his former students and other Baptists. Whether in writing or in teaching, Dagg's aim was to assist in the preparation of ministers. His theology may be described as essentially biblical and moderately Calvinistic, and it earned him the reputation as the pioneer Baptist theologian in America.

BIBLIOGRAPHY. *DAB* III; R. G. Gardner, "John Leadley Dagg," *RE* 54 (1957):246-63.

W. M. Patterson

Dallas Baptist University. Baptist General Convention of Texas (BGCT) educational institution. Originally Northwest Texas Baptist College in Decatur, founded in 1892, Dallas Baptist University (DBU) came into existence when the BGCT bought Northwest's property for $7,000 in 1897. Jesse L. Ward, pastor of First Baptist of Decatur, B. H. Carroll of Waco and J. M. Carroll of Dallas organized the purchase. As Decatur Baptist College, the school opened in 1898 with seventy-five students and B. F. Giles as president. Decatur Baptist became the world's first junior college; Texas Baptists intended it to be a feeder for Baylor University.*

In the early 1950s Baptists in the Dallas area began discussing with administrators the possibility of relocating the school. The college moved in 1965 to a 200-acre site in southwest Dallas, and in 1967 it became a four-year institution with an enrollment of 900 students.

In the 1970s and early 1980s, under the leadership of Charles P. Pitts, William E. Thorn and W. Marvin Watson, the college gained university status and increased its annual budget from $900,000 to more than $4 million. Enrollment grew to more than 1,000 students.

President Gary R. Cook subsequently led DBU to an enrollment of more than 2,200 students from twenty-eight states and thirty-one countries. The 1989-1990 budget was more than $12 million, with a university endowment of more than $7 million. Dallas Baptist University continues to grow in student and financial strength.

BIBLIOGRAPHY. Baptist General Convention of Texas, *Texas Baptist Annual* (1990); *ESB* 1:357; 4:2179-80.

R. Beck

Danish-Norwegian Baptist Conference of North America. Baptist immigrant union. From the mid-nineteenth-century beginnings of Scandinavian Baptist life, the scattered Norwegian and Danish immigrants combined not only in local churches but also on the state or regional level. The earliest such conference, the Danish-Norwegian Baptist Conference of the North-Western States, which organized in 1864, was composed of the churches of Wisconsin, Michigan and Illinois. Other cooperative efforts included the Western, Minnesota, South Dakota and Washington conferences.

There was also an ongoing sense of a need for cooperation at the national level. On June 13, 1879, delegates of the three Scandinavian groups met at Village Creek, Iowa, and organized the Scandinavian Baptist General Conference of America (SBGC). The Danes and Norwegians seem not to have met with the Swedes again, however, and the SBGC became the Swedish Baptist General Conference. A second abortive attempt to organize the Danes and Norwegians nationally occurred in June 1893, but nothing substantive was accomplished until 1910. In March and again in September of that year, delegates, mostly Danish, from the various state and district conferences met to discuss whether to organize a Danish-Norwegian general conference. At the September meeting, after much debate, the forty-eight Danish churches organized the Danish Baptist General Conference. Later that autumn (November 17) the forty-one Norwegian congregations formed the Norwegian Baptist Conference of America.* Both conferences eventually merged with the American Baptists*—the Norwegian Conference in 1956 and the Danish three years later.

BIBLIOGRAPHY. I. Fredmund et al., *Seventy-five Years of Danish Baptist Missionary Work in America* (1931); P. A. Stiansen, "Contributions of the Norwegian Baptist Conference of America," *Chron* 20 (January 1957):44-48; P. Stiansen, *History of the Norwegian Baptists in America* (1939). N. A. Magnuson

Dargan, Edwin Charles (1852-1930). Minister, teacher, editor and author. A graduate of Furman University* and the Southern Baptist Theological Seminary,* he later received honorary degrees from Washington and Lee University and Baylor University.* His Baptist pastorates included four Virginia churches (1877-1887), the longest being First Church, Petersburg (1881-1887); a church in Dixon, California (1887-1888);

Citadel Square Church, Charleston, South Carolina (1888-1892); and First Church, Macon, Georgia (1907-1917). He made many of his most significant contributions during his fifteen-year service (1892-1907) as professor of homiletics at Southern Baptist Theological Seminary and his ten-year ministry (1917-1927) as editorial secretary of the Sunday School Board* of the Southern Baptist Convention* (SBC). He was a member of the International Sunday School Lessons Committee (1918-1928), serving as its chairman from 1920 to 1921.

Selected books by Dargan include *Ecclesiology: A Study of the Churches* (1897), *The History of Preaching* (vol. 1, 1905; vol. 2, 1912), *The Doctrines of Our Faith* (1905), *An Exposition of the Epistle to the Romans* (1914), *The Changeless Christ and Other Sermons* (1918), *The Art of Preaching in the Light of Its History* (1922) and *The Bible Our Heritage* (1924).

Partly in honor of Dargan, the Dargan-Carver Library, the joint library of the Sunday School Board, SBC, and the Historical Commission,* SBC, was dedicated on June 16, 1953. This joint arrangement continued until early 1985, when the Historical Commission moved its part of the library to its new quarters in the SBC Building in Nashville, Tennessee. The Sunday School Board then renamed its library the E. C. Dargan Research Library.

BIBLIOGRAPHY. *ESB* 1:348.

C. W. Deweese

David, William J. (1850-1919). Baptist missionary to Nigeria. Reared in Mississippi, he graduated from Mississippi College* (1869) and Crozer Theological Seminary* (1874). In the latter year the Foreign Mission Board* of the Southern Baptist Convention* appointed him to reestablish the mission in Africa, which had been closed because of the Civil War at home and tribal wars in Africa. David soon decided to close the mission in Liberia and concentrated on work with the Yorubas in Nigeria, establishing centers at Abeokuta and Ogbomosho. He came home in 1878 because of illness but returned the following year with a wife. After his wife and child died, he again came home, but in 1886 he went back to Africa, taking materials for a church building at Lagos. In 1889 he moved to the United States for health reasons and never returned to Africa. The mission in Nigeria survived, although for years it had a precarious existence.

BIBLIOGRAPHY. G. W. Sadler, *A Century in Africa* (1950).
N. H. Maring

Dawson, J(oseph) M(artin) (1879-1973). Southern Baptist* minister, denominational executive and advocate of civil liberty. Born in Corsicana, Texas, Dawson graduated from Baylor University* in 1904 and later received honorary doctorates from Baylor (1916) and Howard Payne College* (1936). During pastorates at several Texas churches, including thirty-five years at First Baptist Church of Waco, Dawson also participated in numerous aspects of Southern Baptist denominational life, such as the convention's executive committee, its Relief and Annuity Board and the Baylor board of trustees.

Dawson was best known as an outspoken representative of the Baptist position on religious freedom, peace, social justice and civil liberty. He was the first executive director of the Baptist Joint Committee on Public Affairs* (1946-1953), an agency serving as a united lobby for various Baptist denominations in behalf of religious liberty* and separation of church and state. Dawson was particularly concerned that Baptists know and understand their heritage as defenders of religious liberty. He wrote twelve books and innumerable articles on social issues, and his *Baptists and the American Republic* (1956) is a classic statement of the Baptist role in shaping the nation. The J. M. Dawson Institute of Church-State Studies at Baylor University is named in his honor.

BIBLIOGRAPHY. J. E. Wood Jr., "The Legacy of Joseph Martin Dawson, 1879-1973," *JCS* 15 (1973):363-66.
B. J. Leonard

Dayton, Amos Cooper (1813-1865). Author and promoter of Landmarkism.* Originally a Presbyterian, Dayton, along with J. R. Graves* and J. M. Pendleton,* promoted the Baptist Landmark movement in the nineteenth century. He encouraged the spread of Landmark views when he served as president of the Bible Board from 1854 to 1858 and then through the Southern Baptist* Sunday School Union, which formed in Nashville in 1857. The author of thirteen books and many articles, Dayton is perhaps best remembered among Baptists for his novel *Theodosia Ernest: Or, Heroine of Faith* (1857). This novel, which focused on the struggles of a young Presbyterian girl to find the "true church" among Baptists, was used to popularize the limited ecclesiological focus of Landmarkism.

BIBLIOGRAPHY. R. Baker, *The Southern Baptist Convention and Its People, 1607-1972* (1974); H. L. McBeth, *The Baptist Heritage* (1987).
K. Smith

Deacon. Baptists in America have viewed deacons as officers in local churches since the 1600s. Although extant records relating to seventeenth-century deacons are limited, the records of two important Baptist churches, First Boston (formed in 1665) and Pennepack in Pennsylvania (formed in 1688), show deacons experiencing probationary election, ordination* and church discipline, preparing for and distributing the Lord's Supper,* and signing a church covenant.*

Materials about deacons grew rapidly in the 1700s as the number of churches and deacons expanded. Baptists typically described deacons as "table servers." The ministry of serving tables centered on meeting needs relating to the Lord's Supper, the poor and the minister. Deacons continued to be ordained. Whereas pastors were to focus on the "ministry of the word and prayer," deacons were to tend to the "outward concerns" or "temporal affairs" of the church. Deaconesses existed in some churches, especially among the Separate Baptists* in the South. Deacons became more involved in church business and management from the 1770s onward as the number of churches increased and there was an inadequate supply of ministers.

Many of the emphases of the 1700s continued into the 1800s, and the role of deacons as church business managers expanded. A pivotal publication that shaped this trend was R. B. C. Howell's *The Deaconship* (1846). This influential book described deacons as "the financial officers of the church" and as "a BOARD OF OFFICERS, or the *executive board* of the church, for her temporal department."

Although this pattern persisted well into the 1900s, recent publications have tended to accent the spiritual and pastoral ministries of deacons rather than the administrative. Howard B. Foshee's *The Ministry of the Deacon* (1968) strongly urged this new approach to deacon life. Henry Webb's *Deacons: Servant Models in the Church* (1980) described the deacon's role in terms of a "servant model." Robert L. Sheffield's *The Ministry of Baptist Deacons* (1990) viewed deacons as partners with the pastor in leadership, corporate worship, personal witnessing and caregiving.

Baptists have experienced an increase in the

number of women deacons, many of whom are ordained. While this practice dates from the late 1800s, it has flourished among some Baptist groups in the latter twentieth century.

BIBLIOGRAPHY. C. W. Deweese, *The Emerging Role of Deacons* (1979); L. E. May, ed., "Baptist Deacons: A Story of Service," *BHH,* April 1990.

C. W. Deweese

Decatur Baptist College. *See* DALLAS BAPTIST UNIVERSITY

Denison University. Former Baptist educational institution. The product of Baptist interest in higher education in the 1800s, Denison University was founded in 1831 upon the vote of the Ohio Baptist Education Society. The school was named the Granville Literary and Theological Institution and was located on a farm outside Granville, Ohio, in order for students to combine work and study. The institution was formed to serve the educational needs of the rapidly growing western part of the country. The literary emphasis, it was hoped, would train schoolteachers and business leaders. The theological emphasis would focus on the training of Baptist ministers. In 1845 the school became Granville College and dropped its manual labor emphasis. A final name change occurred in 1856 as the school expanded and moved to town, becoming Denison University in honor of its chief benefactor.

BIBLIOGRAPHY. W. H. Brackney, ed., *Baptist Life and Thought, 1600-1980* (1983); R. G. Torbet, *A History of the Baptists* (1963).

C. D. Weaver

Denominationalism Among Baptists. Despite their vigorous centrifugal forces, the historic and jealously guarded emphases of voluntarism, congregationalism and individualism, Baptists developed an explicit denominational awareness early in their history. Baptist denominationalism was facilitated by at least three factors. One, Baptists developed an ecclesiology that, while highlighting the independence of local churches, never overlooked the interdependence of those churches. Second, Baptist churches recognized a theological kinship with other local church groups which drew them together for confessional purposes. Third, and most important, Baptist churches aligned themselves with each other informally and formally for practical purposes.

Individual Baptist churches and their ministers aided each other in seventeenth-century America in constituting churches, ordaining ministers and defending Baptist principles. Maintaining close contact through correspondence, they requested one another's spiritual support through prayers, reported their state of persecution or peace, admonished to church unity and sought advice. A major factor that gave pioneer Baptists a very definite, though unorganized, corporate consciousness was their distinctive doctrinal emphasis on believer's baptism* by immersion and religious liberty.* In a period when religious discrimination and infant baptism were the order of the day, these ideas were dangerously novel, but they also served as catalysts in unifying Baptists.

In the early eighteenth century, "church councils" became a regular feature of Baptist church life. Neighboring churches would send representatives to form a council for arbitrating some internal dissension in the life of a troubled church. Lack of formal organization did not mean lack of cooperation among Baptist churches in the colonies. Following the rise of church councils, Baptist associations began developing by the turn of the eighteenth century. Associations* represented the first formal Baptist denominational organizations beyond the local church level. By 1800 two other organizations arose among Baptists. The first, called a general committee or general committee of correspondence, a precursor to late state conventions, brought representatives from associations together. These general committees acted as bonds of union and centers of information for Baptists in regional areas. In 1802 a new means of Baptist cooperation emerged known as the society, a voluntary association of Baptists committed to a single cause such as education or missions.

Baptists began to issue calls for national denominational unity as early as 1766, when Samuel Jones,* on behalf of the Philadelphia Association,* suggested the union of Baptist associations in America. In 1770 Morgan Edwards* echoed that call for national unity in the first volume of his history of American Baptists. But the national organizational unity did not come until the formation of the Triennial Convention* under Luther Rice* in 1814. In 1821 the first state Baptist convention was organized in South Carolina. By 1905 Baptists from different denominational families had created the Baptist World Alliance.*

BIBLIOGRAPHY. W. H. Brackney, *The Baptists* (1988); W. B. Shurden, "The Baptist Drive for Denominational Unity," *QR* 40 (October-December 1979):50-55.

W. B. Shurden

Denver Conservative Baptist Seminary. An evangelical seminary with historic ties to the Conservative Baptist* movement. As a result of the fundamentalist*-modernist controversy in the Northern Baptist Convention (NBC; *see* American Baptist Churches in the USA), a few hundred congregations withdrew in the late 1940s to form the Conservative Baptist Association when the NBC refused to recognize the newly organized Conservative Baptist Foreign Mission Society.

Because of their experience in the NBC, Conservative Baptists kept their movement institutionally decentralized. Thus when Conservative Baptists in Colorado founded the Conservative Baptist Theological Seminary in 1950, it was structurally independent. A self-perpetuating trustee board purchased the old Bonfils mansion in the Capitol Hill section of Denver, called Carey S. Thomas as president, hired a small faculty (mainly recruited from Northern Baptist Theological Seminary* in Chicago) and enrolled thirty-one students.

From the beginning, militant Conservative Baptist pastors criticized the seminary's nonseparatist stance and its hiring of nondispensationalist faculty. Vernon Grounds, the seminary's second president (1956-1979), maintained the school's independence and its growing identification with the "new evangelical" attempt to reform fundamentalism.

Because the decentralized Conservative Baptist movement provided no regular denominational funding for the seminary, survival depended on expanding its constituency. Under president Haddon Robinson (1979-1991), the seminary changed its name (officially to Denver Conservative Baptist Seminary, but more popularly to Denver Seminary) and promoted itself as "an evangelical seminary in the Baptist tradition." Thus, without repudiating its historic ties, the seminary attracted a wide variety of students. In the mid-1990s only a third of its 600 M.Div., M.A. and D.Min. students were Baptists. Under president Edward Hayes (1993-) the seminary was recognized by the Evangelical Presbyterian Church for the training of its ministers.

T. P. Weber

Dixon, Amzi Clarence (1854-1925). Baptist pastor and evangelist. Born in Shelby, North Carolina, Dixon attended Wake Forest* College (B.A., 1875) and studied theology for six months under John A. Broadus* at the Southern Baptist Theological Seminary,* then in Greenville, South Carolina. Following several early pastorates in North Carolina (Bear Marsh and Mount Olive, 1874-1875; Chapel Hill and Ashville, 1876-1882), Dixon became pastor of Immanuel Baptist Church in Baltimore (1882-1890). During this period Dixon became a popular Bible conference speaker in America and England (he traveled as a delegate to the 1889 World's Sunday School Convention in London), and his reputation as an effective evangelist spread. In 1893, while pastor of the Hanson Place Baptist Church in Brooklyn (1890-1901), he preached with Dwight L. Moody in Moody's World's Fair evangelistic campaign.

After pastoring the Ruggles Street Church in Boston for several years (1901-1906), Dixon was called as pastor to Moody's Chicago Avenue Church in Chicago (1906-1911). However, his most prestigious pulpit was Spurgeon's Tabernacle in London, where he pastored from 1911 until 1919. A committed churchman, Dixon headed the London Baptist Association from 1915 to 1916 and attended Baptist World congresses in London in 1905 and in Stockholm in 1923.

After returning from London in 1919, Dixon spent several years in an itinerant evangelistic and Bible teaching ministry across the United States. During this time he lectured for several months at the Bible Institute of Los Angeles and conducted a preaching tour of mission stations in Japan and China. His last pastorate was at University Baptist, Baltimore (1921-1925).

Dixon was a staunch fundamentalist* and premillennialist* and an opponent of Darwinism and biblical criticism. His most noteworthy contribution to the fundamentalist cause was his role as the first executive secretary and editor of *The Fundamentals,* a twelve-volume defense of the basic doctrines of conservative orthodoxy. Dixon oversaw the publication of the first five volumes of the series, which appeared between 1915 and 1920. Above all of his accomplishments, Dixon regarded his first love as evangelism.

BIBLIOGRAPHY. H. C. A. Dixon, *A. C. Dixon: A Romance of Preaching* (1931); *NCAB* 39.

P. C. Wilt

Dobbins, Gaines Stanley (1886-1978). Southern Baptist* educator and denominationalist. Born July 26, 1886, in Langsdale, Mississippi,

Dobbins by age eighteen was a master printer, Associated Press correspondent and news magazine editor. At Mississippi College* (B.A., 1908) he turned to Christian ministry. Graduating from Southern Baptist Theological Seminary* (Th.D., 1914), he left brief pastorates in Mississippi to go to the Southern Baptist Sunday School Board* in 1916, editing its missions journal for sixteen years. He became professor of church efficiency and Sunday-school pedagogy at Southern Baptist Theological Seminary* in 1920. Before retirement in 1956 his positions there included first dean of religious education, publicity director, development officer, treasurer and interim president. From 1956 to 1966 he taught at Golden Gate Baptist Theological Seminary,* and he remained active in ministry until his death September 22, 1978, in Birmingham, Alabama. Dobbins's thirty-two books and over 4,900 articles significantly influenced Southern Baptist journalism, administrative organization, religious education and practical ministries.

BIBLIOGRAPHY. *ESB* 4:2187-88; "Religious Education: Festschrift for Gaines S. Dobbins," *RE* 75 (Summer 1978).

W. L. Allen

Dual Alignment. The practice in which a Baptist congregation maintains an official relationship with two or more denominations. In this arrangement the congregation participates in several denominational systems and is considered a member of each of these denominations. In most cases the churches establish membership in two distinct Baptist denominations. In certain border regions, between North and South, congregations may hold membership in both the American Baptist Churches in the USA* (ABC) and the Southern Baptist Convention* (SBC). That arrangement exists in First Baptist Church, Washington, D.C. A growing phenomenon involves dual alignment between traditionally white and African-American churches. For example, Sixth Avenue Baptist Church, Birmingham, Alabama, a historic black congregation, is now related to both the National Baptists* and the SBC. Some churches also have membership with non-Baptist groups. Riverside Church,* New York City, maintains membership in both the ABC and the United Church of Christ.

BIBLIOGRAPHY. N. Maring and W. S. Hudson, *A Manual of Baptist Polity and Practice* (1991).

B. J. Leonard

Duck River (& Kindred) Association of Baptists (Baptist Church of Christ). A group of independent Baptists located in Tennessee. The Duck River Association of Christ was formed in 1826 when one-third of the Elk River Association of Primitive Baptists* left over Arminian* doctrines and the teachings of Alexander Campbell.* Soon the phrase *of Christ* in the name was dropped. Their beliefs and practices were similar to those of Old Regular Baptists* and United Baptists.* They were often called "the Baptist Church of Christ." By 1828 twenty-three churches located in Bedford, Cannon, Coffee, Franklin, Rutherford and Warren counties, Tennessee, were members of the new association. Some Duck River Baptists believed in missions, educating ministers and using Sunday-school literature; others opposed these practices. The result was an 1843 split in which both groups claimed to be the Duck River Association. One group was known as "Missionary," the other as "Separate." The Separate group declined in number, later joining with similar associations to form the General Association of Baptists. The Missionary group established Mary Sharp College (1851-1896), the Duck River Male Academy (1854-1908) and the Tennessee College for Women (1905-1946). In 1877 the Missionary association voted to "become auxiliary to the Tennessee Baptist Convention."

By 1945 the Duck River Missionary Association had thirty-nine churches before fifteen churches asked to be dismissed. Dismissal was granted, and the New Duck River Association was organized in October 1945. By 1976, on its 150th anniversary, the Duck River Missionary Association had thirty-four churches and two missions with 10,238 members. In 1992 there were thirty-seven churches and one mission with 12,995 members in Coffee, Franklin and Grundy counties. Association offices are located in Tullahoma, Tennessee.

BIBLIOGRAPHY. E. Templin, *History of Duck River Baptist Association and Churches, 1826-1976* (1976).

C. Blevins

Dungan, Thomas (?-1688). Colonial Baptist leader. Born in Ireland, Dungan fled to New England sometime before 1684 to escape persecution. He settled in Newport, Rhode Island, where there was freedom of conscience under the leadership of John Clarke* and Roger Williams.* In 1684, however, he and his family moved to Cold

Spring, Pennsylvania, which only two years earlier had passed the "Great Law" of 1682 which recognized God as the only Lord of conscience and provided that no one would be "molested or prejudiced for his or her Conscientious persuasion or practice."

Dungan became the first Baptist minister in Pennsylvania, established the first Baptist church in Pennsylvania at Cold Spring, in Bucks County, and died in 1688. The church he led survived until about 1702.

He is best remembered among Baptists as the person who baptized Elias Keach,* who became the most influential early Baptist minister in Pennsylvania and founded the Pennepek church, which became the mother and grandmother of many Baptist churches, including the venerable First Baptist Church of Philadelphia.*

BIBLIOGRAPHY. H. L. McBeth, *The Baptist Heritage* (1987).   T. R. McKibbens

Dunkers. Also known as Conservative Dunkers, German Baptist Brethren and Church of the Brethren. The Brethren originated in 1708 in Schwarzenau, Germany, with a group of eight people who left the state church to form a church which would more completely follow the teachings of the New Testament. They were pacifists, opposed taking oaths, dressed very conservatively, and believed that only believers should be baptized. One distinctive belief regarded Communion, which they insisted should be in the evening, should include foot-washing,* eating a meal, and sharing bread and wine and should never be observed more than twice a year. Another unique practice was their baptism, which was conducted by immersing the person three times forward. Because of this custom they were often called *tunken* or *Tunkers* in Germany. Fleeing persecution, the group left Germany for Philadelphia in 1719. They spread to Pennsylvania, Maryland, Virginia and the Carolinas. They opposed slavery and war, refusing to fight in the American Revolution. In America the *T* in *Tunkers* became a *D,* and the Brethren were often called Dunkers although they preferred the name Brethren. By the nineteenth century the name German Baptist Brethren was more common.

In the 1880s the group split over Sunday schools, revival meetings and a paid, educated ministry. The group opposing these practices became known as the Old German Baptist Brethren. The progressive and larger group kept the name German Baptist Brethren, changing it in 1908 to Church of the Brethren.

With headquarters in Elgin, Illinois, the Brethren had a membership of 200,000 by 1974.

BIBLIOGRAPHY. *EAR* 1:342; *ERS.*

C. Blevins

Dunster, Henry (1612-1659). Colonial Baptist leader. Born in England, Dunster was educated at Cambridge University and emigrated to Boston in 1640. He immediately joined the Puritan Church in Cambridge, where he submitted his "Confession of Faith and Christian Experience."

For twelve years he led Harvard College by developing its philosophy of education, writing its rules of admission and its requirements for graduation, and modeling the college on his own experience at Cambridge University.

Sometime before 1651 Dunster came to the Baptist position on the question of believer's baptism.* In 1653 he went public with his Baptist sentiments by preaching on the subject of infant baptism from the pulpit of the Puritan Church. The following May he was tried by the General Court, which instructed the overseers of the college "not to admit or suffer any such to be continued in the office or place of teaching, educating, or instructing . . . that have manifested themselves unsound in the faith"—an obvious reference to Dunster. He was therefore forced to resign the presidency and was banished from Cambridge. He eventually moved with his family to Scituate, in Plymouth Colony, where he preached and served the Independent Church until his death in 1659.

BIBLIOGRAPHY. H. L. McBeth, *The Baptist Heritage* (1987).

T. R. McKibbens

E

Eager, George Boardman (1847-1929). Southern Baptist* pastor and educator. Born February 22, 1847, in Jefferson County, Mississippi, Eager joined the Confederate Army at sixteen and served in combat as a courier. He graduated from Mississippi College* in 1872 and Southern Baptist Theological Seminary* in 1876. For the next twenty-five years he held a series of prominent pastorates in Virginia, Tennessee and Alabama. In 1901 he became professor of biblical introduction and pastoral theology at Southern Seminary, editing the *Review and Expositor** and becoming the seminary's first professor emeritus upon his retirement in 1920. He died in Jacksonville, Florida, on March 21, 1929. Fellow professor W. O. Carver* called Eager "the embodiment of that chivalry which was the Old South," and Carver's wife remarked that the seminary could well afford to pay Eager's salary "just to enable the students to see what a true Christian gentleman was like."

BIBLIOGRAPHY. *ESB* 1:382; "George Boardman Eager: An Appreciation of Life and Work" (memorial by associates, family and friends, n.d.), Southern Seminary Library, Louisville, Kentucky.

W. L. Allen

East, James Edward (1881-1934). African-American Baptist missionary and corresponding secretary of the National Baptist Convention, U.S.A., Inc. Foreign Mission Board (*see* National Baptists). Born on January 27, 1881, in Huntsville, Alabama, the son of former slaves, East enrolled in the Missionary Training Institute in Nyack, New York, and graduated from Virginia Seminary (1909) in Lynchburg. That same year he and his wife sailed for South Africa, where he served as pastor of a church in Rabula, returning to the United States in 1920. East became corresponding secretary of the Foreign Mission Board in 1921 and served during a period that was difficult for African-American missionaries because of the European colonization of Africa. East died in office in 1934. At that time there were 105 mission stations, 25 day schools and 7 boarding schools, 41 teachers and over 3,000 schoolchildren.

BIBLIOGRAPHY. L. Fitts, *A History of Black Baptists* (1985); *NBV*, October 13, 1934; O. D. Pelt and R. L. Smith, *The Story of the National Baptists* (1960).

L. H. Williams

East Texas Baptist University. Baptist General Convention of Texas educational institution. In 1912 the Baptists of Marshall, Texas, received the charter for the College of Marshall. The school had a multidenominational council until the Baptist General Convention of Texas assumed ownership in 1914. The school opened in 1917 as a junior college with an associated academy. Thurman C. Gardner was the first president. In 1944 the college went to four-year status and changed its name to East Texas Baptist College.

The college achieved university status in the 1980s and maintains a strong emphasis on preparation for ministry. More than one-fourth of the students are training for Christian ministry. President Robert E. Riley directs the university with a budget of over $7.5 million, an endowment of more than $9 million and an enrollment of more than 1,000 students.

BIBLIOGRAPHY. J. H. Boyd, *History of the College of Marshall* (1944); *ESB* 1:383-84.

R. Beck

Eastern Baptist Theological Seminary. Theological seminary affiliated with American Baptist Churches in the USA.* The seminary was organized in March 1925 in Philadelphia by fundamentalists* in the Northern Baptist Convention (NBC). Eastern's founders identified with the early fundamentalists, who were irenic in spirit and represented a moderate conservatism. As fundamentalism became increasingly separatist, belligerent and anti-intellectual, the seminary maintained its moderate stance, declining to follow the Conservative Baptist* secession from the NBC after 1946. Opposing widespread reductionist approaches to Bible and theology and shortcut ministerial training by Bible schools, Eastern aimed to educate ministers to combine evangelical theology and sound learning.

Eastern opened in September 1925, having secured approval as a seminary of the NBC. In the first year there were nine full-time professors and 100 students. Among the most influential founders were Curtis Lee Laws,* Harry W. Barras, Gordon H. Baker and James A. Maxwell. Scholarly president Austen K. deBlois, dean Carl H. Morgan and professors W. W. Adams, Barnard C. Taylor, Donald R. Gorham, Wilber T. Elmore and W. Everett Griffiths did much to realize the school's ideals in the early years. A collegiate department, begun in 1932, was chartered in 1952 as a separate college, Eastern College, on its own campus in St. Davids, Pennsylvania.

The seminary is fully accredited. In 1939 it moved to its present location, where a chapel, donated by Marguerite T. Doane, was dedicated in 1951. Affiliated with the American Baptist Churches in the USA, the school is "broadly ecumenical in spirit and practice." In 1993-1994 about half the 380 degree students were non-Baptists, with non-Baptists also represented on the faculty and board of directors. Support comes from Baptist and non-Baptist sources. The student body is ethnically diverse and international, as is the faculty. Strong ties exist with African-American and Hispanic churches. By the early 1990s women had come to make up about one-third of the student body, and many students were training for a second career.

Although new degree programs have been developed, such as the master of arts in theological studies (MATS), the M.Div. is still taken by a majority of students. Joint programs (the M.Div.-M.B.A. and M.Div.-M.S.W.) are offered in conjunction with other schools, and a D.Min. in marriage and family is also offered. Three endowed lectureships enrich the curriculum: Swartley (preaching), Torbet (church history) and Rutenber (theology). An urban ministries program offers experience in inner-city service, an extension program takes theological education to bivocational pastors in West Virginia, and Eastern's School for Christian Ministry offers certificate courses for laypersons in area churches.

BIBLIOGRAPHY. A. K. deBlois, *The Making of*

Ministers (1936); G. L. Guffin, ed., *What God Hath Wrought: Eastern's First Thirty-five Years* (1960). N. H. Maring

Eaton, Thomas Treadwell (1845-1907). Southern Baptist* pastor and editor. Born in Murfreesboro, Tennessee, Eaton taught for five years at Union University, a local Baptist college where his father served as president. In 1881, after pastoring churches in Tennessee and Virginia, he became pastor of Walnut Street Baptist Church in Louisville, Kentucky. In 1887 he took on the additional responsibility of editing the Kentucky Baptist newspaper, *The Western Recorder*. Eaton served in both of these capacities until death. As editor of *The Western Recorder*, Eaton increasingly gained a reputation as the successor to J. R. Graves* in the Landmark* movement. His powerful journalistic influence forced W. H. Whitsitt* to resign as president of Southern Baptist Theological Seminary* in Louisville. Whitsitt's assertion that Baptists began in seventeenth-century England undercut the Landmark notion of an unbroken succession of Baptists since the early church. The fall of Whitsitt demonstrated both the influence of Eaton and the strength of Landmarkism among Southern Baptists.

BIBLIOGRAPHY. W. J. Leonard, *Community in Diversity: A History of the Walnut Street Baptist Church* (1990); W. Mueller, *A History of the Southern Baptist Theological Seminary* (1958).
M. G. Bell

Ecclesiology, Baptist. Baptist understanding of the nature of the church. The doctrine of the church has been a foundational and distinctive concern of Baptists and was a major factor in the emergence of Baptists. Early Baptist confessions show an interest in both the visible, local and the invisible, universal church. The London Confession of 1644 spoke of the church as "a spirituall Kingdome" which had been redeemed by Christ and which was visible as a separate community, called by the Spirit of God. The church was composed of those who had been baptized on the basis of a visible profession of faith and who were joined to the Lord and each other "by mutual agreement, in the practical injoyment of the Ordinances, commanded by Christ their head and King" (London Confession, 1644).

Believer's baptism was essential to the emphasis on a regenerate membership. Also integral to the early Baptist understanding of church was separation from the civil government. The Second London Confession of 1677, which was to be very influential among early American Baptists, described the "Catholick or universal Church," the invisible church composed of all Christian believers of all time.

For Baptists the church is the people of God, a fellowship of believers with Christ as head. Alternatively, the church is spoken of as the body of Christ. Baptists intend the church to be based on Scripture and often speak of "the New Testament church." They understand the church to be a worshiping community, a witnessing community concerned for evangelism and growth, and a ministering community to those outside the church. Maring and Hudson identify the distinguishing marks of a Baptist church as follows: "a regenerate membership safeguarded by believers' baptism; congregational polity, coupled with an associational principle; and the necessity of freeing the church from interference by the civil government" (N. H. Maring and W. S. Hudson, *A Baptist Manual of Polity and Practice* [1963], p. 15).

Although local churches are autonomous, it was early recognized that cooperation was important. The 1644 confession affirmed that the particular congregations were "by all meanes convenient to have the counsell and help one of another in all needfull affaires of the Church." The ecclesial organizations through which independent congregations cooperated were called "associations," which may have been modeled in part originally on the associative organization of Cromwell's New Model Army. The specific nature of associations has varied in place and time, but typically they do not infringe on the independence of the local congregation.

The officers of a local church are ordained and lay. The ordained cleric was earlier called pastor, bishop, elder or preacher. The lay deacons assist the pastor in the temporal affairs of the church. In some Baptist denominations the clergy are ordained by the local congregation; in others they are ordained by associations or the national denomination. The Baptist ministry is always informed by a commitment to the priesthood of all believers.* There are two ordinances* among Baptists, baptism* and the Lord's Supper.* Some Baptist groups have traditionally observed footwashing* as a third ordinance.

Baptists have varied patterns of involvement in national and international organizations. Many Baptist denominations have membership in the national council of churches in their country, and a few Baptist denominations are members of the World Council of Churches. The Baptist World Alliance,* an organization of 163 national Baptist groups, is not, strictly speaking, an ecclesial organization and does not have authority over local denominations and congregations.

The Landmark* movement among Baptists has generally opposed the notion of the universal or invisible church. Where Landmarkists have been influential, there has been little or no participation possible for the church beyond the local congregation.

BIBLIOGRAPHY. S. Grenz, *The Baptist Congregation* (1985); W. S. Hudson, *Baptist Concepts of the Church* (1959); W. Lumpkin, *Baptist Confessions of Faith* (1959); D. K. McCall, comp., *What Is the Church?* (1958). H. W. Pipkin

Ecumenism, Baptist Attitudes. Baptists generally have shown considerable hesitancy about mergers with other communions, including other Baptists. In line with the free church tradition, they have favored ecumenical models that do not bind them structurally. As in many other areas of belief and practice, however, they have displayed immense diversity in their attitudes toward ecumenical endeavors. (1) Most Baptists participate in ecumenical activities at the local level with other Protestants, Roman Catholics, Orthodox and even persons of other religious faiths. Activities in which they join comfortably vary widely, but they include regional ministries, dialogues, social services, evangelistic meetings and joint worship. Although many Baptists still entertain some suspicion of Roman Catholics, they have altered their views markedly since the Second Vatican Council (1962-1965). (2) Baptists diverge sharply on membership in local, national or international ecumenical organizations such as councils of churches. Because local ecumenical organizations are somewhat more loose-knit, Baptists, either individually or by congregations, join these more readily. Several national Baptist bodies such as the Baptist Union of Great Britain and Ireland, the American Baptist Churches in the USA,* the German Baptist Union and the Nigerian Baptist Convention hold membership in both their national councils and in the World Council of Churches. But the Southern Baptist Convention,* the largest Baptist body in the world, abstains from membership in either on the grounds that such decisions must be made by local congregations, though the convention participates in the North American Baptist Fellowship and the Baptist World Alliance.* (3) Diverse as they are, Baptists feel more comfortable in strictly Baptist organizations such as the Baptist World Alliance, but even there they are ecumenically cautious. Differences of doctrine, ecclesiology, polity and psychological/sociological backgrounds throw stumbling blocks in the path of fuller involvement. A narrow ecclesiology known as Landmarkism,* which emphasizes the local congregation as the only valid expression of the church, has exerted a negative influence on ecumenism, especially in the southern United States and in other countries where Southern Baptists have had influence.

BIBLIOGRAPHY. *BHH* 25 (July 1990); W. R. Estep, *Baptists and Christian Unity* (1966); E. G. Hinson, "Southern Baptists and Ecumenism: Some Contemporary Patterns," *RE* 66 (Summer 1969):287-98; G. Igleheart and W. J. Boney, eds., *Baptists and Ecumenism* (1980).

E. G. Hinson

Edgren, John Alexis (1839-1908). A nineteenth-century clergyman in the Swedish Baptist* General Conference of America and founder of what today is Bethel Theological Seminary.* Born in Varmland, Sweden, February 20, 1839, he served as an officer in the Union Navy during the U.S. Civil War. He was converted during a storm at sea in 1857 and was baptized the following year and joined the Mariner's Baptist Church in New York. He was a brilliant student, knew at least sixteen spoken and sixteen unspoken languages, and was an accomplished Egyptologist as well as an excellent painter. He studied at Princeton Seminary, the Baptist Seminary in Hamilton, New York, and the Baptist Union Seminary in Chicago. He was a missionary to Sweden, taught at the Baptist Seminary in Stockholm and served as pastor in Uppsala. While pastoring a Swedish Baptist congregation in Chicago and editing a paper for his fellow Swedish Baptists, he felt the need to begin a seminary for his countrymen, which opened in the fall of 1871 with one student.

The school experienced difficult financial times, and because of ill-health Edgren had to relinquish work at the school in 1887. He retired to Oakland, California, where he spent his last years writing books, translating portions of the Bible and painting. A number of his paintings are in the archives of the Baptist General Conference at Bethel Theological Seminary in St. Paul. He died January 26, 1908, and is buried in Berkeley.

BIBLIOGRAPHY. A. Olson, *A Centenary History As Related to the Baptist General Conference of America* (1952).

M. J. Erickson

Education Commission, SBC. Higher education agency of the Southern Baptist Convention* (SBC). Organized in 1951, the commission promotes cooperation between SBC agencies and sixty-five colleges, universities, academies and Bible schools related primarily to state Baptist conventions. The commission coordinates a placement registry and scholarship and loan programs, and works with regional and national accrediting associations. Publications include *The Southern Baptist Educator* (monthly) and *Directory of Southern Baptist Colleges and Schools* (biannually). The agency conducted a National Conference on Faith and Discipline in Birmingham, Alabama, in June 1992 for the faculty and administration of Southern Baptist schools and colleges. The commission had no employed staff until 1951. Commission executives have included R. Orin Cornett (1951-1959), Rabun L. Brantley (1959-1970), Ben C. Fisher (1970-1978) and Arthur L. Walker Jr. (1978-1993). Commission offices are located in the SBC Building in Nashville, Tennessee.

BIBLIOGRAPHY. *ESB* 1:392-94; 3:1685-86; 4:2191-92.

C. W. Deweese

Edwards, Morgan (1722-1795). Baptist preacher, evangelist, historian and educator. Born in Trevethin, Wales, of Anglican parents, Edwards was educated at Bristol Baptist College (1742-1744). After becoming a Baptist at age sixteen, he began ministering in Lincolnshire (1744-1751), Cork, Ireland (1751-1760), and Sussex (1760-1761), although he was not ordained until 1757. Edwards subscribed to the Particular Baptist* London Confession of 1689.

On the recommendation of John Gill, he served for ten years as pastor of the Philadelphia church, beginning in 1761. Immediately assuming an active role in the Philadelphia Baptist Association,* Edwards served as clerk, moderator, evangelist and historian. During the Revolutionary War he came under sharp criticism and travel restrictions for his Tory views, being perhaps the only Baptist leader holding such views at the time. Edwards left the Philadelphia church in 1781, in part for "using intemperately an antidote" and in part for his friendship with the universalist Elhanan Winchester, whose views Edwards did not share.

Edwards's travels for the Philadelphia Association provided the opportunity to collect the historical information later published in his valuable *Materials Towards a History of the Baptists* (2 vols., 1770-1792), used since his time by historians of the era. His concern for an educated American Baptist clergy were fulfilled with the aid of James Manning* and Hezekiah Smith* in the founding of Rhode Island College (Brown University*). Edwards traveled through the North and in England, preaching and soliciting funds and books for the college. He also petitioned the Massachusetts delegates to the Continental Congress in support of the separation of church and state.

BIBLIOGRAPHY. *AAP* 6; D. H. Ashton, "Morgan Edwards, First Historian of American Baptists," *Chron* 14 (April 1951):70-79; *DAB* III; T. B. McKibbens and K. L. Smith, *The Life and Works of Morgan Edwards* (1980).

L. W. Hähnlen

Elders and Eldresses, Baptist Views. The title *elder* has been applied to a minister of a church by Baptists in America since the 1700s. *Elder* was synonymous with the terms *pastor, minister, bishop, teacher, overseer* and *preacher.* Elders were primarily responsible for preaching and observing the ordinances* but were often responsible for the business affairs of church also. The position of ruling elder among Baptists of the eighteenth century was different from ministerial elder; ruling elders assisted the pastor in maintaining the order and government of the church. Ruling elders became prominent because the office was supported by the influential church discipline of the Philadelphia Baptist Association* and had the support of important Baptist leaders like Morgan Edwards.* Eighteenth-century Baptist ministers also needed assistance in administrative work. Ruling elders were ordained like the other officers of the church with fasting, prayer and imposition of hands. Their office related only to rule and order, however, not teaching. If they had the gift of teaching, they were to be ordained again to a different office. Ruling elders were distinct from ministers and deacons. Scriptural references used to justify the office of ruling elder were Romans 12:8, 1 Corinthians 12:28, 1 Timothy 5:17 and Hebrews 13:7, 17.

In the eighteenth century many Baptist churches also had eldresses. This was especially true of Separate Baptists.* The eldresses led in prayer, teaching and consultation with women regarding matters of the church. Eldresses cared for sick women and assisted in the baptism of women. They reported the concerns of the women to the elders. Eldresses' election and ordination was much like that of elders. A distinction was made between eldresses and deaconesses. With the merger of Regular* and Separate* Baptists in the late eighteenth century, the leadership role of women diminished.

The position of ruling elder declined in the nineteenth century due to a concern about the biblical basis for the office and the lack of its inclusion in the Charleston church discipline, the Philadelphia Confession of 1742 and the New Hampshire Confession of Faith (1833). The function of the ruling elder was superseded by those of trustees and deacons. The title *elder* gave way to *reverend* by the late nineteenth century. In the late twentieth century, however, the role of elder has reemerged, causing some controversy regarding congregational rule.

BIBLIOGRAPHY. C. W. Deweese, "Baptist Elders in America in the 1700's: Documents and Evaluation," *QR* 50 (October-December 1989):57-65; R. Mathis, "Elders in Baptist Churches," *TE* 42 (Fall 1990):23-27; H. L. McBeth, *Women in Baptist Life* (1979).

J. F. Loftis

Engberg, Petrus Engelbrekt (1847-1916). Swedish Baptist* Sunday-school missionary in the Eastern United States. Born in Sundsvall, Sweden, on October 3, 1847, raised in a devout home and widely traveled in Europe and North America as a young man, Petrus Engberg began witnessing to his newfound faith immediately following his conversion (January 15, 1876). Baptized not long thereafter, he soon accepted a call to pastor the church at Hernosand where he had been converted. He emigrated to America in 1881. On August 17, 1889, he entered the Sunday-school ministry that was to be his life work; for the first fifteen years he was primarily involved in New England, and for the next twelve in New York. Although without formal training, he accomplished a larger work than any other Swedish Baptist Sunday-school missionary; in his twenty-five years' summary in 1914, two years before his death, he reported having made 26,282 visits to homes, distributed nearly 83,000 tracts and organized 116 Sunday schools, out of which developed 30 churches. Engberg died on September 26, 1916.

BIBLIOGRAPHY. J. E. Klingberg, "P. E. Engberg," *Nya Wecko Posten Illustrated Kalendar 1917* (1917):120-33; A. Olson, *A Centenary History As Related to the Baptist General Conference of America* (1952). N. A. Magnuson

Entzminger, Louis (1878-1956). Fundamentalist* Baptist educator and Sunday-school organizer. After serving state Baptist conventions in Florida and Kentucky, in 1913 Entzminger accepted the invitation of J. Frank Norris* to come to First Baptist Church, Fort Worth, Texas, to build a great Sunday school.

Using no curriculum except the King James Version of the Bible and stressing a program of visitation and follow-up, Entzminger built up the Sunday school at First Baptist, Fort Worth, from 250 in 1913 to over 5,000 by the mid-1920s. In 1923 he supported Norris, T. T. Shields* and W. B. Riley* in the founding of the Baptist Bible Union of North America,* which included fundamentalists from the Northern, Southern and Canadian Baptist conventions; Entzminger preached at its organizing meeting.

In 1939 Entzminger urged Norris, who was at first opposed to the idea, to establish at Norris's church the Fundamental Baptist Bible Institute, which was renamed the Bible Baptist Seminary* in 1944. Under Entzminger's influence the school centered its curriculum on preaching from the English Bible and developing strategies for large Sunday schools. Even when others abandoned the controversial Norris, Entzminger remained loyal. His *The J. Frank Norris I Have Known for Thirty-four Years* (1947) presented the "Texas Tornado" in the best possible light. When old allies split from Norris's World Baptist Fellowship in 1950 to form the Baptist Bible Fellowship,* Entzminger stayed behind. His primary contribution to Baptist fundamentalism was his emphasis on big Sunday schools, which became typical of independent Baptist fundamentalists.

BIBLIOGRAPHY. J. O. Combs, *Roots and Origins of Baptist Fundamentalism* (1984); G. Dollar, *A History of Fundamentalism in America* (1973).
T. P. Weber

Ephrata Community. *See* GERMAN RELIGIOUS SOCIETY OF THE SEVENTH DAY BAPTISTS (EPHRATA)

Eschmann, John. A German Baptist* who did missionary work in North America. Baptist work in Germany began in the 1830s and spread to German immigrants in North America in the early 1840s. Working independently were a number of German Baptists, including Konrad Fleischmann,* who started a church at Philadelphia in 1843; Alexander von Puttkammer, who founded Baptist churches in Buffalo and Albany, New York; and William Grimm, who organized a Baptist church in Manitowoc, Wisconsin. Another pioneer worker among German immigrants in America was John Eschmann, who had pastored a Dissenter church outside Zurich, Switzerland. He arrived in America in the 1840s and founded a Baptist church in New York City in 1847, which marked the beginning of extensive missionary work among the German population there. His and the others' churches joined together to form the German Baptist Conference in 1851. Because of the movement's rapid spread, the German Baptists divided their work into Eastern and Western conferences. When the division proved unwieldy, they reunited in 1865 to form the North American Baptist Conference.*

BIBLIOGRAPHY. D. C. Woolley, ed., *Baptist Advance* (1964). T. P. Weber

Evangelical Baptist Church, Inc., General Conference of the. Baptist Holiness/Pentecostal group organized in 1935 by William Howard Carter, a Free Will* Baptist minister in Goldsboro, North Carolina. Carter differed with some of his fellowship who had become pentecostal, insisting on "speaking in tongues" (glossolalia) as the evidence of the baptism of the Holy Spirit. Formerly known as the Church of the Full Gospel, Inc., the denomination is Wesleyan-Arminian* in theology, emphasizing the new birth experience (justification), sanctification, baptism of the Holy Spirit, though not necessarily with glossolalia, and divine healing. The body accepts the designation *fundamentalist,* affirming biblical inerrancy, the bodily resurrection of Christ, a premillennial Second Coming and baptism by immersion. The body holds its annual conference during the third week in October and is headquartered at Goldsboro. The Evangelical Baptist Church retains close fellowship, primarily by pastoral exchanges, with the Wilmington Conference of the Free Will Baptist Church. At its peak the denomination had 2,200 members in thirty-one churches, but since Carter's death in 1980, most of its churches have disbanded or become independent. In 1992 there remained about 100 members in two congregations, one in Goldsboro and the other in Sumter, South Carolina.

BIBLIOGRAPHY. C. H. Jacquet Jr., *Yearbook of American and Canadian Churches* (1990); F. S. Mead and S. S. Hill, *Handbook of Denominations in the United States*, 9th ed. (1990).

A. M. Manis

Evangelicalism, Baptist. Baptists reflect a wide range of understandings of and attitudes toward evangelicalism. (1) Most Baptists would acknowledge themselves as evangelicals in the sense of being heirs of the Protestant Reformation. In terms of their history they would have to think of themselves as second-generation Protestant evangelicals by way of Puritanism. Baptists strongly influenced by Landmarkism,* however, often deny this connection, tracing the Baptist tradition by way of independent sects back to the apostolic church. (2) Some Baptists define themselves as evangelicals in terms of American Protestant fundamentalism* and its roots in Protestant scholasticism of the seventeenth century. Those who espouse this interpretation emphasize doctrinal purity. Normally they cite belief in the inerrancy of the Scriptures, literal virgin birth, substitutionary atonement, physical resurrection and literal Second Coming as the principal tests of faith. In the late twentieth century several social and political issues such as opposition to abortion, support of a strong military defense and prayer in public schools have also gained a prominent place. (3) Other Baptists consider themselves evangelicals as fosterers of personal conversion and cultivation of the inner life. As heirs of the Puritans, they emphasize heart religion manifested in transformed lives and a quest for social transformation. Frequently meeting opposition to their efforts to win converts, they have accentuated the voluntary* principle and religious liberty.* In America the First Great Awakening* (1720-1760) and Frontier Revivals (1790-1820) generated an intense concern for evangelism and missions. Many Southern Baptists* would consider these two items the chief criteria for being evangelical. (4) In response to rather ambiguous and diverse usages, some Baptists designate themselves as evangelicals in the sense of faithfulness to the gospel (*euangelion*) both personally and socially. Most of them would include concern for the hungry, the homeless, the oppressed, victims of injustice and other needy persons as a criterion for faithfulness; not just saying, "Lord, Lord," but doing the will of God is the test.

BIBLIOGRAPHY. M. W. Belew, *A Missions People* (1989), H. Cook, *What Baptists Stand For*, rev. ed. (1957); J. L. Garrett, E. G. Hinson, J. Tull, *Are Southern Baptists Evangelicals?* (1983); B. Ramm, *The Evangelical Heritage* (1973).

E. G. Hinson

Evans, Christmas (1766-1838). Welsh Baptist pastor and evangelist. Evans was known by many as the greatest Welsh preacher of the nineteenth century. Born on Christmas Day in Cardiganshire, he worked as a farmhand for several years before entering the ministry in 1789 as an itinerant evangelist. While Evans's education was modest, his rhetorical abilities were widely recognized. A highly dramatic style, sometimes elevated to the bizarre, as well as an artful use of imagery contributed to the great popularity of his preaching. His translated sermons were printed in religious periodicals and widely circulated by American publishers during the Second Great Awakening. Evans was also known as an influence of moderation upon the harsh Welsh Calvinism of his day. From 1791 to 1826 he served as a pastor in Anglesea. In 1832 he returned to North Wales and died in Swansea.

BIBLIOGRAPHY. T. M. Bassett, *The Welsh Baptists* (1977); J. Cross, *Sermons of Christmas Evans* (1850); J. Davis, *Memoir of the Rev. Christmas Evans* (1840).

B. C. Leslie

Exclusion. *See* CHURCHING, BAPTIST PRACTICE OF.

F

Federal Council of Churches, Baptist Participation. Baptist participation in the Federal Council of Churches was uneven from the beginning. Samuel Zane Batten, director of the Office of Social Education for the American Baptist Publication Society* saw the Federal Council as a way for him to further the causes for which he was working. He served on committees with the Federal Council. The first recording secretary elected to the council was Rivington Lord, pastor of First Free Baptist Church of Brooklyn, New York. The Northern Baptist Convention (see American Baptist Churches in the USA) was a charter member of the council, voting in resolution 5 of the inaugural meeting of the American Baptist Convention in 1908 "that we desire to co-operate in every way practicable with all the people of God in the establishment of the kingdom of righteousness on earth, and accordingly instruct the Executive Committee to appoint our quota of representatives to the Federal Council of the Church of Christ in America."

The Southern Baptist Convention* (SBC) did not participate in the Federal Council, generally reflecting the conservative evangelical state of the denomination and the influence of the Landmarkist* movement. In 1914 the SBC adopted "The Pronouncement on Christian Union and Denominational Efficiency," which reflected an individualistic and radical congregational view of salvation and church life. Thereafter Southern Baptists devoted their energies to denominational programs. Conservative Baptists were likewise opposed to the council. One of the council's most outspoken opponents was J. Frank Norris,* fundamentalist pastor of First Baptist Church, Fort Worth, who called the council "modernistic and communistic" and widely circulated sermons that he had preached against it.

Today, several Baptist bodies participate in the National Council of Churches,* founded out of the Federal Council and the Evangelical Alliance in 1950.

BIBLIOGRAPHY. *Annual of the American Baptist Convention,* 1908; J. F. Norris, *The Federal Council of Churches Unmasked* (1939); C. E. Tulga, *The Case Against the Federal Council of Churches* (1948). H. W. Pipkin

Female Missionary Society, Baltimore. A society organized by a group of Baptist women to support foreign missions. In 1822 the Baltimore Female Judson Society was formed in response to Ann Haseltine Judson's* appeal for financial support for her Bible school efforts in China. The name of the society was changed to the Baltimore Female Missionary Society sometime before 1835. At that time Mrs. N. D. Crane was secretary and Mrs. James Wilson was treasurer. The society prayed for the missionaries and continued to meet needs on the mission field, particularly those of women. The society is credited with encouraging the development of many more missionary societies in Maryland.

BIBLIOGRAPHY. J. T. Watts, *The Rise and Progress of Maryland Baptists* (1953); B. S. White, *Our Heritage* (1959). S. L. Still

Female Missionary Society, Richmond. First Baptist women's missionary society formed in the South to support foreign missions. The society formed in the spring of 1813 at the Richmond Baptist Church in response to Mary Webb's* plea published in *The Massachusetts Baptist Missionary Magazine.* Webb, secretary of the Boston Female Missionary Society for Missionary Purposes, encouraged women to meet on the first Monday afternoon of each month to pray for missionaries. The first recorded director was Mrs. William Crone, who began service in 1823, but it is believed that Mrs. John Bryce gave strong leadership in the first decade of the society's existence. The society was generous to Luther Rice,* supported the first ordained Baptist preacher in China, Yong Sun Sang, and aided needy churches. The society is credited for setting the example of supporting missions which led to the formation of the Woman's Missionary Union.* In 1844 the society became an auxiliary to the Southern Baptist Convention,* and it was disbanded in 1884.

BIBLIOGRAPHY. J. Mather, *Light Three Candles* (1972); B. S. White, *First Baptist Church Richmond: 1780-1955* (1955).

S. L. Still

Ferrill, London (Loudin) (?-1854). Black Baptist minister. Born a slave in Hanover County, Virginia, Ferrill was rescued from drowning at the age of eleven, an event that precipitated his religious conversion. As a young man he gained a reputation as an unordained slave preacher, claiming fifty converts. Freed upon the death of his owner, Ferrill moved with his wife to Lexington, Kentucky. There he began to compete with an older black freelance preacher called Old Captain. Ferrill sought the sanction of the white First Baptist Church, which sponsored his ordination* and the membership of his First African Church in the Elkhorn Association in 1822. Thirty years later, still an auxiliary of the white Baptists, the congregation was the largest in the state, numbering 1,820 members. Respected by whites and especially by younger blacks, Ferrill became a man of wealth and fame, even drawing a salary from the city because of his influence over his own people. Adapting to the circumstances of the upper South, Ferrill performed slave marriages with the stipulation "until death or distance do them part," and he left behind a prayer blessing "the white people who have always treated me as though I was a white man." His pastorate of thirty-two years ended at his death on October 12, 1854.

BIBLIOGRAPHY. W. J. Simmons, *Men of Mark* (1887); M. Sobel, *Trabelin' On: The Slave Journey of an Afro-Baptist Faith* (1979).

W. B. Gravely and C. White

Fielde, Adele (1839-1916). Baptist missionary to China. As a young woman Fielde became engaged to a Baptist missionary candidate to Siam. She agreed to marry him and join him in Southeast Asia, but upon her arrival in Siam in 1865 she was informed that he had died. Fielde stayed and conducted missionary work for several years, until she was dismissed from the mission for unbecoming conduct—dancing and card-playing with members of the diplomatic community.

On her return trip to America she visited China,

where she caught the vision for missionary work among Chinese women. Having pled with her directors to reinstate her, in 1872 she returned to China and began training Chinese women to become Bible women—lay Bible teachers and assistants to missionaries. She organized a school, wrote textbooks, taught classes and conducted field training. During her twenty-year term of service she trained some 500 women to evangelize and train their own people. After she retired from active missionary service, she began a career of research and writing.

BIBLIOGRAPHY. F. B. Yoyt, " 'When a Field Was Found Too Difficult for a Man, a Woman Should Be Sent': Adele M. Fielde in Asia, 1865-1890," *His,* May 1982.

R. A. Tucker

First African Baptist Church, Savannah, Georgia. The church widely regarded as the oldest black Baptist congregation in the United States. Officially organized by Andrew Bryan around 1788, this congregation emerged against the background of evangelical Christianity in the middle eighteenth century and independent black church movements in South Carolina and Georgia. The church increased its membership greatly, within decades producing several other congregations.

In the early 1830s the original First African divided into two factions, one retaining the original name and located on Franklin Square and the other eventually named First Bryan Baptist Church and located in the Yamacraw area of Savannah. First African, for two centuries a leading church in the state, is a historical landmark competing with First Bryan as the oldest continuous congregation of independent black Baptists in the world.

BIBLIOGRAPHY. C. M. Wagner, *Profiles of Black Georgia Baptists* (1980); J. M. Washington, *Frustrated Fellowship* (1986); C. G. Woodson, *History of the Negro Church* (1921, 1972); brochure, First African Baptist Church.

S. D. Martin

First Baptist Church, Augusta, Georgia. Historic Baptist church. This church owes its origin to the Baptist Praying Society of Augusta, which was organized on March 25, 1817, by eighteen people, ten women and eight men. The Praying Society was constituted a church two months later with the assistance of Abram Marshall. The church was supplied irregularly by Marshall but did not have a full-time minister until William T. Brantly Sr.* assumed the post in the fall of 1819. Brantly led in formally reorganizing the church on January 20, 1820; a new constitution was written and a new building begun in February 1820. The church had a number of prominent Baptist leaders as ministers, including William T. Brantly Jr.* (1840-1848) and Lansing B. Burrows (1883-1899). The Southern Baptist Convention* was organized in the church on May 8-12, 1845. William Bullein Johnson* was elected first president of the SBC.

BIBLIOGRAPHY. A. O. Jones, *History of the First Baptist Church Augusta, Georgia, 1817-1967* (1967).   G. Clayton

First Baptist Church, Charleston, South Carolina. The oldest Baptist church in the South. First Baptist Church, Charleston, dates its beginning to the organization of a Baptist church in Kittery, Maine, by the Reverend William Screven* in 1682. Screven and most of the members migrated to Charleston in 1696. There they were joined by other Baptists living in the area to form the Charleston Baptist Church. The church was given a lot in 1699, and by 1701 the first building was constructed on the site that the present building occupies. In 1749 Oliver Hart* came from Philadelphia to become pastor of the church. He brought with him the wisdom and experience of the Philadelphia Baptist Association.* In 1751 Hart led in organizing the Charleston Baptist Association. He fled Charleston when the British captured the city during the American Revolution. Richard Furman* succeeded Hart in 1787 and remained at the church until 1825. During Furman's tenure, the architect Robert Mills was employed to design a new sanctuary. This edifice, dedicated in 1822, survives to the present.

A succession of outstanding ministers followed Furman, including Basil Manly Sr.,* W. T. Brantly Sr.,* E. T. Winkler, A. J. S. Thomas and Lewis Hall Shuck. H. A. Tupper and James Petigru Boyce* were products of the congregation. First Baptist, Charleston, represents and has carried on the best of the English Regular* or Particular* Baptist traditions.

On September 21, 1989, Hurricane Hugo hit Charleston, and the Mills sanctuary sustained extensive damage. A restoration costing approximately $1.5 million was completed in approximately one year. A rededication service was held in the sanctuary on November 4, 1990.

BIBLIOGRAPHY. R. A. Baker and P. J. Craven Jr., *Adventure in Faith: The First 300 Years of First Baptist Church, Charleston, South Carolina* (1982).   G. Clayton

First Baptist Church, Philadelphia, Pennsylvania. The antecedent congregation to the First Baptist Church of Philadelphia was formed at Pennepack in January 1688 under the leadership of Elias Keach.* The Philadelphia congregation was formed in 1698, separating from Pennepack and becoming a separate entity in 1746. Messengers from the Philadelphia church were received at the next annual Philadelphia Baptist Association* meeting, the association having been established in the church in 1707. Jenkin Jones served as pastor from 1746 to 1760. The Welshman Morgan Edwards* assumed the role of permanent pastor in 1761, serving with distinction until 1772. The extent of the Welsh population of Philadelphia is signaled by the fact that First Baptist held separate Welsh-language worship services until 1841. Edwards was the principal mover in the founding of Rhode Island College, which became Brown University.* Edwards is also renowned for his collecting of Baptist history materials from New Hampshire to Georgia.

BIBLIOGRAPHY. W. W. Keen, *The Bi-centennial Celebration of the Founding of the First Baptist Church of the City of Philadelphia* (1899); R. Torbet, *A Social History of the Philadelphia Baptist Association, 1707-1940* (1944).

H. W. Pipkin

First Baptist Church, Providence, Rhode Island. By some counts, the first Baptist church in America. Roger Williams's* commitment to soul liberty and belief that the magistracy should have no control over people's consciences led him to flee Puritan Massachusetts Bay Colony, eventually settling on land purchased from the Narragansett Indians, a settlement he called Providence. In 1639 Williams and eleven others were immersed according to their understanding of the New Testament baptismal practice. Williams likely saw in believer's baptism* the positive expression of his principle of voluntarism* in religion. Although Williams did not himself remain a Baptist, the First Baptist Church of Providence dates its origins from these events. Though Baptists were the only Christian confession in Providence for some time, the church suffered from divisions in the early years. James Manning, who served as pastor from 1771 to 1791, was the first college-educated pastor. The distinctive steepled meetinghouse that was to serve as landmark and gathering place for church and society in Rhode Island was erected in 1774-1775. The period of 1790-1890 was the time of greatest influence of the church, both nationally and locally.

BIBLIOGRAPHY. H. M. King, *The Mother Church* (1896); H. M. King, comp., *Historical Catalogue of the Members of the First Baptist Church in Providence, Rhode Island* (1908); J. S. Lemons, *The First Baptist Church in America* (1988).

H. W. Pipkin

First Great Awakening, Baptist Participation. The First Great Awakening was a series of revivals beginning about 1726 that spread from New Jersey, throughout the colonies, north to New England and south to Georgia. The movement was related to contemporary religious awakenings in Britain and the Continent. An important link was the English Calvinist evangelist George Whitefield, who preached throughout the colonies.

Although Baptists did not have much to do with the origins of the revivals, they profited considerably from them. Characteristics of the awakening included emphases on the confession of sin, the need for a radical conversion and the high emotionalism of experiential religion. Not only did many Baptist churches grow significantly during the awakening, but many already existing churches moved into the Baptist camp. Divisions were also a factor among Baptists during this highly emotional time of growth. Regular Baptists* generally opposed the emotional manifestations, while the Separate Baptists* saw the movement as an authentic expression of God's work.

It would be hard to overestimate the significance of the First Awakening for Baptists. Not only did Baptist churches flourish during this time, but they grew in political power as well, particularly in Virginia. In fact, the migration of Baptists to the Southern colonies during the Great Awakening precipitated the numerical emergence of Baptists in the region. Baptists also grew in number in New England during this time. The Philadelphia Baptist Association* was active during the revivals, often sending evangelists to other regions. Four churches were founded by the association along the Atlantic coast, as far south as Charleston, South Carolina. The note-worthy evangelists of the Separate Baptists, Shubal Stearns* and Daniel Marshall,* settled on Sandy Creek in what is now Randolph County, North Carolina. From this settlement spread a particularly emotional brand of revivalistic Baptists. With the growth of Baptist churches in the South came the emergence of a variety of theological persuasions, both Calvinistic* and Arminian.* Several new and influential Baptist associations also emerged during this time.

See also MARSHALL, DANIEL; STEARNS, SHUBAL.

BIBLIOGRAPHY. C. C. Goen, *Revivalism and Separatism in New England, 1740-1800* (1962); R. T. Handy, *A History of the Churches in the United States and Canada* (1976); W. Lumpkin, *Baptist Foundations in the South: Tracing Through the Separates the Influence of the Great Awakening, 1754-1787* (1961).

H. W. Pipkin

Fish, Henry Clay (1820-1877). Baptist pastor, educator and historian. Born the son of a Baptist pastor in Halifax, Vermont, on January 27, 1820, Fish developed an intense piety and hunger for learning. After teaching for several years in Massachusetts and New Jersey, he prepared for the ministry at Union Theological Seminary* in New York City. Upon graduation in 1845 he was ordained and became the pastor of the Baptist church in Somerville, New Jersey. In 1851 he began a twenty-seven-year pastorate of the First Baptist Church of Newark. His interest in education persisted, and he served for many years as the secretary of the New Jersey Baptist Education Society. In these roles he stimulated among Northern Baptists a concern for a better-educated ministry. Conferred the D.D. by the University of Rochester, he was a prolific writer. For more than twenty years he published at least one volume a year, usually of a historical nature. He died in Newark, still serving as pastor, on October 27, 1877.

BIBLIOGRAPHY. *BE;* H. C. Fish, *History and Repository of Pulpit Eloquence* (1857); H. C. Fish, *The Price of Soul-Liberty and Who Paid It* (1860).

A. M. Manis

Fisher, Miles Mark (1899-1971). Prominent African-American Baptist minister, theologian and historian. Born on October 29, 1899, in Atlanta, Georgia, Fisher was the son of former slaves. He graduated from Morehouse College* (A.B., 1918), Northern Baptist Theological Seminary* (B.D.,

1922) and the University of Chicago (M.A., 1922; Ph.D., 1938).

Fisher was pastor of White Rock Baptist Church in Durham, North Carolina (1932-1964). Using a Social Gospel* approach, White Rock's program included an employment agency, recreation, relief and day care. Fisher was an outstanding preacher and for more than thirty years taught at Shaw University. But his lasting contribution was as a scholar, and he wrote several books on black Baptists: *Lott Carey, the Colonizing Missionary* (1922), *A Short History of the Baptist Denomination* (1933) and *Negro Slave Songs in the United States* (1953).

BIBLIOGRAPHY. L. H. Davis, "Miles Mark Fisher: Minister, Historian and Cultural Philosopher," *NHB* 46 (January-March 1983); *EBA.*

L. H. Williams

Fleischmann, Konrad Anton (1812-1867). Founder of the German Baptist* Conference. Born in Nuremburg, Germany, on April 18, 1812, Fleischmann was raised Lutheran. At age nineteen he experienced a religious awakening through contact with Swiss Separatists. Soon after joining a Separatist church he requested baptism by immersion, a decision considered optional by the Separatists. He received theological instruction in Bern while serving as pastor of a small church. In 1839 he arrived in New York to begin work among German immigrants. Fleischmann moved to Philadelphia in 1842 after earning a reputation as an effective preacher and evangelist. The following year he established a German-language church which gradually came to identify itself as Baptist, thus becoming the first German Baptist church in America. In 1851 he led in the organization of the first conference of German Baptists in North America, predecessor of the North American Baptist Conference.* Fleischmann served as host pastor and secretary of the first conference and remained an influential leader of the movement up to his death on October 15, 1867.

BIBLIOGRAPHY. F. H. Woyke, *Heritage and Ministry of the North American Baptist Conference* (1985).

B. C. Leslie

Florida Baptist Theological College. Founded in Lakeland, Florida, in 1943 as the Baptist Bible Institute for older ministers who lacked education. Classes met in the First Baptist Church until land and buildings were acquired. By 1947, 100 students were enrolled. Leon M. Gambrell

was the first president (1943-1952).

In 1948 the institute was included in the annual offering for state missions. In 1952 Arthur H. Stainback became president, and in 1953 the school moved to Graceville, Florida. In 1957 the institute came under the control of the Florida Baptist Convention. While James E. Sutherland was president (1957-1977), the school grew in enrollment and building expansion.

Under President Joseph P. DuBose (1977-1990), the name was changed to Florida Baptist Theological College. Thomas A. Kinchen became president in 1990. The school offers six degree programs and has a student enrollment of 443, a budget of $960,816 and $609,354 in endowment.

BIBLIOGRAPHY. *ESD* 1, 3, 4; E. E. Joiner, *A History of Florida Baptists* (1972); Statistical Reports to SBC Education Commission.

E. E. Joiner

Foot-Washing, Baptist Practice of. A form of Christian communion practiced by traditional Baptists—Primitives,* Regulars,* Old Regulars,* Separates,* Uniteds,* and some Free Wills,* Missionaries* and Independents.* It is usually conducted once a year, immediately following the church's sacramental service, and involves mutual exchanges in the bathing of another communicant's feet, always followed by an embrace and frequently by tearful comments of support and fellowship.

The Christian practice of "foot-washing" derives from the narrative of the Last Supper provided in John 13:4-15. In that account Christ is depicted as rising from the table, girding himself with a towel, pouring water into a basin and then proceeding to wash each disciple's feet. John's narrative of this event concludes with the following statement by Christ: "Ye call me Master and Lord: and ye say well; for so I am. If I then, your Lord and Master, have washed your feet, ye ought to wash one another's feet. For I have given you an example, that ye should do as I have done" (Jn 13:13-15 KJV).

For several traditional Baptist sects, verse 15 makes foot-washing an ordinance, obligating observance of the practice. Frequently held during the summer, when weather allows more people to attend, the event may occasion a daylong celebration—the regular Sunday service, followed by Communion and foot-washing rites that extend far into the afternoon. All of this is concluded by "dinner on the ground" and perhaps by an afternoon "sing" or one or more creek baptisms.

BIBLIOGRAPHY. H. Dorgan, *Giving Glory to God in Appalachia: Worship Practices of Six Baptist Subdenominations* (1987); H. Dorgan, *The Old Regular Baptists of Central Appalachia: Brothers and Sisters in Hope* (1989); C. B. Hassell, *History of the Church of God from the Creation to A.D. 1885; Including Especially the History of the Kehukee Primitive Baptist Association* (1886).

H. Dorgan

Ford, Reuben (1742-1823). Baptist pastor and apologist for religious liberty.* Converted in 1762 under George Whitefield, Ford began his career as a lay exhorter. He was baptized in 1769 and two years later established and was ordained by the church at Goochland, Virginia. Ford also assisted in the founding of Licking Hole Church and served the Dover Association as its clerk for thirty years. Additionally, much of his career was spent clarifying church-state relations through his contacts with Patrick Henry, Thomas Jefferson and James Madison. Ford contributed to the Baptist cause in Virginia, both directly and indirectly, in the elimination of compulsory tax support for the clergy (1776), the guarantee of religious freedom (1785) and the return of glebe lands to the public domain (1799). He also played a major role in the union of the Separate* and Regular* Baptists in 1787. Ford contributed to Baptist liturgy by writing a service for the solemnizing of marriage, based on the Book of Common Prayer.

BIBLIOGRAPHY. R. B. Semple, *History of the Baptists in Virginia,* rev. ed. (1972).

L. H. Hähnlen

Fortress Monroe Conference. A consultation at Fortress Monroe, Virginia, between representatives of the Southern Baptist Convention* (SBC) and the American Baptist Home Mission Society* (ABHMS) on September 12-13, 1894, to seek cooperation on two issues: ministry to African-Americans in the South, and the territorial limits of Northern and Southern Baptists. The significance of this conference is to be found in the easing of strained relations between Northern and Southern Baptists.

One source of the strain was that following the Civil War, Northern Baptists had come into the South with home missionaries, focusing on establishing schools to meet the educational needs of freed African-Americans. Southern Baptists resented this "invasion" of their field of ministry. A second source of the strain was territorial overlap of the work of the two groups.

With, as the Southern Baptists reported, "full, frank, free discussion on all questions presented," the conferees began by resolving "to avoid discussion of past issues" and addressed themselves "to the task of securing for *the future* such co-operation as may be found practicable." The Joint Committee unanimously agreed on three issues. First, the ABHMS would retain control of the African-American schools, but the SBC, through the Home Mission Board,* would appoint local advisory committees while also seeking support for the schools from the Baptists of the South. Second, the two groups would cooperate in mission work to African-Americans in the South. Three, concerning territorial limits of each group, neither was to begin new work in areas already occupied by the other, and all antagonisms were to be avoided where geographical overlap already existed. Initiating a new period of comity agreements, the Fortress Monroe Agreement was nevertheless rescinded by a joint committee in 1909.

BIBLIOGRAPHY. R. A. Baker, *Relations Between Northern and Southern Baptists* (1948); H. L. McBeth, *A Sourcebook for Baptist Heritage* (1990).

W. B. Shurden

Fosdick, Harry Emerson (1878-1969). Liberal* Baptist preacher. Born in Buffalo, New York, Fosdick was educated at Colgate University* (B.A., 1900), where he was mentored by William Newton Clarke,* the foremost Baptist liberal theologian of the period. Fosdick later referred to Clarke as his "spiritual godfather" and translated Clarke's teachings into his own famous dictum "We must distinguish between abiding experiences and changing categories." Fosdick subsequently studied at Union Theological Seminary,* New York, and Columbia University. At Union he was influenced by the writings of Walter Rauschenbusch* on the Social Gospel.*

After his ordination to the Baptist ministry, Fosdick's first pastorate was Montclair Baptist Church, Montclair, New Jersey (1904-1915), where he came to be known as an outstanding preacher. He served as a chaplain in France in 1918 and then became pulpit minister at First Presbyterian Church, New York City (1918-1925).

There he gained national attention on May 21, 1922, when he preached his most famous sermon, "Shall the Fundamentalists Win?" Ivy Lee, a

Presbyterian layman, published and distributed the sermon under the title "The New Knowledge and the Christian Faith." The sermon was intended as a plea for greater tolerance and understanding between fundamentalists* and liberals. But Fosdick identified three central issues where fundamentalists needed to be more tolerant. He suggested that belief in the virgin birth was unessential, the inerrancy* of the Bible was incredible to the modern mind, and the expectation of a literal second coming of Jesus Christ was outmoded and needed rethinking. Fosdick warned fundamentalists that they could not "drive out from the Christian churches all the consecrated souls who do not agree with their theory of inspiration" and concluded by encouraging Christian fellowship that is "intellectually hospitable, open-minded, liberty-loving, fair, tolerant." The sermon made Fosdick the focal point of controversy within the Presbyterian Church of the U.S.A. In 1924 he was asked to become a member of the Presbyterian Church; however, being a Baptist minister, he declined and resigned his ministry at First Presbyterian Church.

At the urging of James C. Colgate and John D. Rockefeller Jr.,* Fosdick became pastor of Park Avenue Baptist Church in 1925. By 1930 the congregation had erected a new building named Riverside Church.* Fosdick insisted that the ministry of Riverside Church be nonsectarian. The program was one of Christian personalism, a people-centered ministry emphasizing personal spiritual growth and social consciousness. Riverside Church developed a large church school and nursery school and provided playground and gymnasium facilities for young people. A department of social service was organized to help find jobs for those hurt by the Depression. Between 1930 and 1935 some 7,000 unemployed individuals found work through the church. Organizations such as the Riverside Symphony Orchestra, the Business and Professional Women's Club, the Riverside Guild (which served more than 300 teenagers), and the Riverside Men's Class were established. Fosdick was a renowned preacher and for years gave out his message of Christian personalism to millions of listeners via a radio program entitled *National Vespers.* His ministry also reached millions through published works such as *The Meaning of Prayer* (1915), *The Meaning of Faith* (1917), *The Meaning of Service* (1920) and *The Modern Use of the Bible* (1924). Throughout much of his ministerial career (1908-

1946) Fosdick was also professor of practical theology at Union Theological Seminary. He retired from Riverside in 1946 but maintained an active role in the causes of world peace and racial justice until his death in 1969.

BIBLIOGRAPHY. *DAB* 8; *DARB;* H. E. Fosdick, *The Living of These Days: An Autobiography* (1969); R. M. Miller, *Harry Emerson Fosdick: Preacher, Pastor, Prophet* (1985); *NCAB* E.

C. W. Whiteman

Foster, George Burman (1858-1918). Liberal* theologian. Born in Alderson, West Virginia, he graduated from West Virginia University with A.B. and A.M. degrees. He was ordained to the Baptist ministry in 1879, graduating from Rochester Theological Seminary* in 1887. He served for a time as pastor at First Baptist Church, Saratoga Springs, New York. After studying in Germany in 1891-1892, he became assistant professor of philosophy at McMaster University until 1895. He then became assistant professor of systematic theology in the University of Chicago Divinity School* and professor of philosophy of religion in the department of comparative religion of the university, a position he held until his death in 1918. His liberal views brought much conflict, and he was often attacked by the clergy of Chicago and elsewhere. He pastored a Unitarian church in Madison, Wisconsin, during the last few years of his life, in addition to his teaching. He published numerous scholarly articles and four significant books, two posthumously edited.

BIBLIOGRAPHY. G. B. Foster, *The Finality of the Christian Religion,* 2nd ed. (1909); G. B. Foster, *The Function of Religion in Man's Struggle for Existence* (1909); A. Gragg, *George Burman Foster: Religious Humanist* (1978); A. E. Haydon, ed., *Friedrich Nietzsche* (1931); D. C. Macintosh, ed., *Christianity in Its Modern Expression* (1921).

H. W. Pipkin

Franklin College of Indiana. A four-year Baptist college in Franklin, Indiana. Franklin College is in voluntary affiliation with the American Baptist Churches in the USA* and the American Baptist Churches of Indiana. The college currently has an enrollment of 850 students.

The fifth oldest institution in the state of Indiana, Franklin College was established in 1834 by several Baptists in the central Indiana area who saw the need for a Baptist institution of higher learning. Founders included Eliphalet Williams, a home missionary of the American Baptist Home Mission Society* and pastor of the First Baptist Church of Franklin; Lewis Morgan, a Baptist pastor in Indiana; and Ezra Fisher, another local minister.

The Indiana High School Press Association has its national offices at Franklin College.

BIBLIOGRAPHY. Franklin College Board of Trustees, *First Half Century of Franklin College, 1834-1884* (1884); Franklin College of Indiana, *1990-91 Catalog.*   R. Nash

Free Will Baptists. Arminian* Baptist group. Formed in the eighteenth century in opposition to Calvinist* predestination among Regular Baptists,* Free Will (or Freewill) Baptists arose in the United States from two streams. Paul Palmer* formed General Baptist* churches in North Carolina in the 1720s. These churches held a doctrine of "free will"—that is, freedom of any to believe in Christ—as opposed to the Calvinist doctrine of predestination of the "elect" to salvation. In time most of these early "Freewillers" succumbed to the intense proselytism of the Regular (Calvinist) churches of the Philadelphia Baptist Association.*

In 1780 another stream of Free Will Baptists arose in New England, led by Benjamin Randall.* Converted in George Whitefield's revivals, Randall joined the Baptists in 1776 but broke with them in 1779 over predestination. In 1780 he formed a church of seven members at New Durham, New Hampshire, the first of many Free Will Baptist churches in New England. In time the Calvinism of Regular Baptists moderated, diminishing the justification for Free Will Baptists. In 1911 most Free Wills in the North merged into the Northern Baptist Convention.

Remnants of the Palmer and Randall lines reestablished contact, however, and in 1935 representatives from both groups met in Nashville, Tennessee, to form the National Association of Free Will Baptists (NAFWB). They adopted a confession of faith in 1935 and established a college in Nashville in 1942. The Free Wills are distinguished from other Baptists by their intense conservatism, centralized organizational structure and the practice of foot-washing.* In 1981 the NAFWB reported 216,848 members in 2,479 churches. The United American Free Will Baptist Church (1867) and the General Conference of Original Free Will Baptists (1962) represent smaller groups with similar emphases.

See also BAPTIST CHURCHES; RANDALL, BENJAMIN.

BIBLIOGRAPHY. W. F. Davidson, *The Free Will Baptists in America, 1727-1984* (1985).
                                        H. L. McBeth

Freedmen's Institute. A ministry of the American (Northern) Baptist Home Mission Society* among black Southerners during the Reconstruction period. Not conceding home mission work in the South to the war-weary Baptists of that region, in 1863 the Home Missionary Society began working in the Southern district. By 1869 one-third of its missionaries worked in the South. Among its concerns was the establishment of the Freedmen's Fund, designed to work particularly among Southern freedpersons. Its programs included the Freedmen's Institute, a mobile teaching organization that instructed black Baptist ministers and laypersons in the essentials of Baptist thought and polity. By 1879 the society's superintendent of Missions to the Freedmen reported that institutes held in every Southern state had instructed a total of 1,119 ministers and deacons. In 1881 the program became a summer program of the black colleges founded in this period to which Northern Baptists had contributed financially. These educational activities of the Home Mission Society, even more than their evangelistic efforts, antagonized many Southern Baptists, who were suspicious of any "Yankee" work in the South and particularly work with blacks. The Freedmen's Institute thus exacerbated hostilities between Southern and Northern Baptists in the late nineteenth century.

BIBLIOGRAPHY. R. A. Baker, *Relations Between Northern and Southern Baptists,* 2nd ed. (1954).
                                        A. M. Manis

Frost, James Marion (1848-1916). Southern Baptist* pastor and Sunday School Board* executive. Born and raised in Georgetown, Kentucky, the son of a pastor, Frost graduated from Georgetown College and was ordained, having accepted the pastorate of First Baptist, Maysville, Kentucky, on the same day in 1870. Frost served a succession of churches in Kentucky, Virginia and Alabama.

Frost captured the attention of Southern Baptists in 1890 by announcing through the *Religious Herald* and other Baptist papers that he would propose forming a denominational Sunday School Board to the upcoming Southern Baptist Convention. Then pastor of Leigh Street Baptist Church in Richmond, Virginia, Frost discovered strong opposition to his resolution among many Baptist editors and pastors. The convention in Fort Worth, Texas, set up a Sunday School Committee instead of a board. However, at the next convention (1891) in Birmingham, Alabama, Frost made a similar proposal that was adopted without debate after a heated discussion in committee. The board was established in Nashville, Tennessee, and Frost, after much persuasion, agreed to lead the enterprise as secretary. Eighteen months later he resigned to become pastor of First Baptist, Nashville, but he returned in 1896 to lead the board for two decades. Under his leadership the board gained denominational confidence, developed into publishing curriculum materials and books, and launched programs designed to strengthen Sunday schools and the denomination. In time the board produced income for the convention and served as a source of unity for the entire denomination. Today the board is the largest denominational publishing agency in the world.

BIBLIOGRAPHY. R. Baker, *The Story of the Sunday School Board* (1966); J. M. Price, *Baptist Leaders in Religious Education* (1943).

C. L. Howe

Fuller, Ellis Adams (1891-1950). Southern Baptist* pastor, evangelist and seminary president. Born April 1, 1891, in Cross Hill, South Carolina, Fuller graduated from Presbyterian College, Clinton, South Carolina (A.B. 1912), and Southern Baptist Theological Seminary,* Louisville, Kentucky (Th.M. 1921), where he also completed all but the dissertation for a Ph.D. Fuller was a public-school teacher and bivocational pastor (1912-1917), pastor in South Carolina (1922-1925), superintendent of the Home Mission Board's* department of evangelism (1925-1928) and pastor of Atlanta's First Baptist Church from 1928 until he accepted the presidency of Southern Seminary in 1942. In 1950 he suffered a heart attack while preaching and died October 28 in San Diego, California. During his tenure at Southern, Fuller led in establishing a school of church music, in increasing faculty from eleven to twenty-six, in erecting eighteen new buildings and in enlarging the student body by two-thirds.

See also SOUTHERN BAPTIST THEOLOGICAL SEMINARY.

BIBLIOGRAPHY. *ESB* 1; "In Memoriam: Ellis Adams Fuller, 1891-1950, President of Southern Baptist Theological Seminary 1942-1950," *RE* 48 (January 1951). W. L. Allen

Fuller, Richard (1804-1876). Prominent Baptist pastor and leader in the formation of the Southern Baptist Convention.* Born into a wealthy family in South Carolina, Fuller was educated at Harvard. In 1847 he came as a pastor to Baltimore, where he served for the rest of his life. Raised in the South and educated in the North, he had a rare perspective on the national tensions leading up to the Civil War.

In 1844 Fuller entered a journalistic debate over slavery with Francis Wayland,* who was then president of Brown University.* Out of this debate came his defense of slavery, *Domestic Slavery Considered as a Scriptural Institution* (1845). Fuller was active in the denominational life of the newly formed Southern Baptist Convention, serving as president of the convention for two years, preaching the first annual sermon in 1846 and avidly supporting theological education for all ministers.

BIBLIOGRAPHY. J. H. Cuthbert, *Life of Richard Fuller* (1879); *DAB* IV.

M. G. Bell

Fulton Confession, Primitive Baptists. Articles of faith adopted November 18, 1900, at Fulton, Kentucky, by fifty-one Primitive Baptist* elders representing congregations in Alabama, Arkansas, Georgia, Indiana, Illinois, Kentucky, Mississippi, Missouri, Tennessee and Washington. The document was a reprinting—with accompanying Primitive Baptist interpretations—of the 1689 expanded version of the London Confession, originally adopted in 1644 by seven Particular Baptist* churches of that city. This 1689 document also was the base for the Philadelphia Confession, accepted in 1742 as the beliefs of the Philadelphia Baptist Association.*

Designed to prevent disunity in Primitive ranks, Fulton Confession expresses a Calvinistic* faith characterized by affirmative positions on the sovereignty of God; the infallibility of Scripture; the immutable nature of humankind's Fall and sinfulness; the causative relationship of God to righteousness but the noncausative relationship of God to sin; the particularity of election; the finality of justification, sanctification and the resulting state of grace; and the certainty of salvation for the elect. In addition, the document takes firm positions on baptism* by immersion, closed Communion, the unacceptability of "double marriage" and a number of issues related to church structure and governance.

This document has never been accepted by all Primitive Baptists, and some Primitive churches in central Appalachia are not aware of its existence.

BIBLIOGRAPHY. R. A. Baker, *Baptist Source Book* (1966); W. L. Lumpkin, *Baptist Confessions of Faith* (1959); *Those Things Most Surely Believed Among Us: The Primitive Baptist Confession of Faith of 1900, Fulton, Kentucky* (1900).

H. Dorgan

Fundamental Baptist Bible Institute. *See* BIBLE BAPTIST SEMINARY

Fundamentalism, Baptist Views. The Baptists, along with the Presbyterians, exerted a major influence upon the birth, growth and development of fundamentalism. This influence was the result of the impact of persons, organizations, schools, newspapers and magazines.

Traditional Baptist principles loaned themselves quite naturally to the support of fundamentalism. These included an emphasis on regenerate membership, which dovetailed with the fundamentalist stress on conversion and the methodology of revivalism; the authority of the Bible, to be read and interpreted by the individual, which left the door open for the fundamentalist understanding of biblical inerrancy;* and the autonomous nature of Baptist polity (*see* Ecclesiology), which enabled an ultraconservative theological tendency to grow rapidly and made it difficult for denominational officials to exercise any control over local churches and clergy. Fundamentalism continues to be largely associated with Baptist-related congregations and ministers, especially those of America's largest Protestant denomination, the Southern Baptist Convention.*

To the extent that millenarianism contributed to the roots of fundamentalism, Baptists made their early impact through such persons as A. J. Gordon (1836-1895), pastor of the Clarendon Street Baptist Church in Boston; George C. Needham (1846-1902), evangelist and Bible conference leader; Arthur T. Pierson (1837-1911), a Presbyterian minister who "was rebaptized and became in fact, if not in name, a Baptist"; and Isaac M. Haldeman* (1845-1933), a Baptist pastor who served the First Baptist Church of New York City for over fifty years. When the series of booklets known as *The Fundamentals* * was published from 1910 to 1915, the theologically moderate E. Y. Mullins,* Baptist educator and onetime

pastor, was among the contributors. It remained for Curtis Lee Laws,* Baptist editor of the conservative Baptist publication *The Watchman-Examiner,* * to coin in 1920 the word *fundamentalist* and to define *fundamentalists* as those ready "to do battle royal for the [doctrinal] Fundamentals of the faith."

In the North in the twentieth century, the leading proponents of fundamentalism were Baptists. They included J. C. Massee (1871-1965), a pastor and denominational leader who eventually disassociated himself from political fundamentalism; John Roach Straton* (1875-1929), the outspoken minister of Calvary Baptist Church in New York City; W. B. Riley* (1861-1947), longtime pastor of the First Baptist Church in Minneapolis, publisher of *Christian Fundamentals in School and in Church* and founder of the Northwestern Bible and Missionary Training School, as well as the World's Christian Fundamentals Association; and T. T. Shields,* (1873-1955), pastor of the Jarvi Street Baptist Church, Toronto, onetime president of Des Moines University in Iowa, and publisher of *The Gospel Witness*. Despite their aggressive leadership, the Baptist fundamentalists failed to capture the Northern Baptist Convention in either the 1920s or the 1940s (*see* American Baptist Churches in the USA). As a result some groups broke away from the convention, including the Baptist Bible Union* of 1922, which evolved into the General Association of Regular Baptist Churches* (1932) and the Conservative Baptist Association of America* (1947).

In the South in the twentieth century, prominent Baptist leaders of fundamentalism have included J. Frank Norris* (1877-1952), W. A. Criswell* and Jerry Falwell (1933-). Norris was the irascible minister of the First Baptist Church in Fort Worth, Texas, publisher of *The Fundamentalist* and the one who gave fundamentalism its "rough-hewn" image, in part because of his shooting of an unarmed man in his study in 1926. Criswell, a prominent preacher and orator, served the First Baptist Church of Dallas for many years and for two terms was president of the Southern Baptist Convention. Falwell, the pastor of the unaffiliated Thomas Road Baptist Church in Lynchburg, Virginia, has been a television evangelist and is the founder of Liberty University (formerly Liberty Baptist College) and the Moral Majority* (1979-1989), a right-wing political action group. The Moral Majority announced that it was prolife, pro traditional family and traditional morality, and pro-American. In 1980 and 1984 Criswell and Falwell joined other forces to help bring Ronald Reagan to the U.S. presidency. Since the late 1970s, Baptist fundamentalists, led by "architects" Criswell, Paul Pressler (a prominent judge from Houston) and Paige Patterson (former president of Criswell College* in Dallas and more recently the president of Southeastern Baptist Theological Seminary in Wake Forest, North Carolina), have been successful in gaining control of the Southern Baptist Convention. Recent presidents of the denomination have been fundamentalists; by virtue of their office they have had great influence over the appointment of denominational officials, including the trustees of denominational colleges and seminaries. Critics feel that, in turn, the trustees exert considerable influence on professors, frequently viewing them as instruments to indoctrinate students rather than academicians to lead them in a search for truth. From a fundamentalist perspective, truth has already been discovered.

In general, Baptist fundamentalists have had greater influence in the South than in the North, although their impact has been nationwide. What is also very clear, however, is that wherever fundamentalism has gone it has been characterized not only by opposition to Protestant liberalism but also by division and splintering between moderates and extremists within its own ranks. Recent illustrations include the formation of the moderate Cooperative Baptist Fellowship* and the moderate Southern Baptist Alliance* with its own seminary in Richmond, Virginia.

BIBLIOGRAPHY. E. G. Hinson, ed., "Fundamentalism and the Southern Baptist Convention," *RE* 79 (Winter 1982); B. J. Leonard, *God's Last and Only Hope: The Fragmentation of the SBC* (1990); G. M. Marsden, *Fundamentalism and American Culture* (1980); M. E. Marty, *Modern American Religion,* vol. 2, *The Noise of Conflict, 1919-1941* (1991); C. A. Russell, *Voices of American Fundamentalism* (1976); E. R. Sandeen, *The Roots of Fundamentalism* (1970).

C. A. Russell

Fundamentalist, The. A tabloidlike newspaper originally published and edited by J. Frank Norris* (1877-1951), the controversial fundamentalist* pastor of First Baptist Church, Fort Worth, Texas (1909-1952), and simultaneously of Temple Baptist Church, Detroit, Michigan (1934-1947). The earlier names of the publication were *The Fence Rail* (1917-1921) and *The Searchlight*

(1921-1927). Norris used this vehicle to publish his flamboyant, hard-hitting sermons, to expose what he felt to be the existence of sin in individuals and in society, and to bring to his readers news of events in the world of fundamentalism itself, especially in the South.

The Fundamentalist became a fierce competitor to *The Baptist Standard,* the publication of the Southern Baptist Convention in Texas. Norris had once served as the *Standard's* business manager and editor but was crowded out because of his showmanship and differing ideas about the denomination. In Norris's day, some claimed that *The Fundamentalist* developed into the religious journal most widely circulated in the South, with approximately 80,000 readers. Between 1934 and 1947 alone, when Norris was serving his two congregations in Fort Worth and Detroit, it was reported that 18 million copies of *The Fundamentalist* were published. *The Fundamentalist* continued after Norris's death, although less well known, and remains today the organ of the World Baptist Fellowship,* one of the groups emanating from Norris's own loosely bound "fellowship" of churches.

BIBLIOGRAPHY G. W. Dollar, *A History of Fundamentalism in America* (1973); C. A. Russell, *Voices of American Fundamentalism* (1976).

C. A. Russell

Fundamentalist Baptist Fellowship. A movement of conservatives in the Northern Baptist Convention (*see* American Baptist Churches in the USA). In 1921 a group that came to be called the Fundamentalist Fellowship sought to rid Northern Baptist Convention schools of liberal teachers. Meeting prior to the national conference of the convention, they planned a strategy for imposing their views on the denomination as a whole. To this end they prepared a confession of faith known as the Goodchild Confession, based on the Philadelphia and New Hampshire* confessions. Their plans were shattered, however, by committee reports and parliamentary maneuvers. In 1922 the denomination affirmed the New Testament as its only rule of faith in order to avert the adoption of a fundamentalist statement. Fundamentalists could muster only one-third of the voting participants for their doctrinal standard.

The Fundamentalist Fellowship never again had the opportunity to capture the convention or put its policies into effect. Several smaller groups emerged from the convention in the late 1920s, but the Fundamentalist Fellowship itself stayed within the denomination until the 1940s. In 1943 the fundamentalists, in protest of the policies of the convention's foreign mission society, organized the Conservative Baptist Foreign Mission Society and laid the foundation for the Conservative Baptist* movement. A separatist wing among the conservatives continued the critical influence of the Fundamentalist Fellowship until 1965, when it withdrew and adopted the name Fundamental Baptist Fellowship. Offices for the fellowship were in Chicago until 1970; for the next two years they were located in Denver, but in 1972 the headquarters was moved back to Chicago.

See also NATIONAL FEDERATION OF FUNDAMENTALISTS OF THE NORTHERN BAPTISTS.

BIBLIOGRAPHY. G. M. Marsden, *Fundamentalism and American Culture* (1980); B. L. Shelley, *A History of Conservative Baptists* (1981).

E. L. Towns

Fundamentalist Fellowship. *See* FUNDAMENTALIST BAPTIST FELLOWSHIP; NATIONAL FEDERATION OF FUNDAMENTALISTS OF THE NORTHERN BAPTISTS.

Fundamentals, The. *The Fundamentals: A Testimony to the Truth* was a set of twelve booklets, each about 125 pages, setting forth the theological issues of the day from an orthodox Protestant standpoint by a galaxy of sixty-four authors from British and American backgrounds (eleven of them American Baptists). Through the generosity of two wealthy laymen from Los Angeles, Lyman and Milton Stewart, these booklets were sent over a five-year period (1910-1915) to some 3 million people. Every pastor, evangelist, missionary, theological professor, theological student, Sunday-school superintendent, YMCA and YWCA secretary, and religious editor in the English-speaking world received a copy. Among the authors were prominent scholars including James Orr, W. H. Griffith Thomas, Benjamin B. Warfield and E. Y. Mullins.* The various writers defended traditional Christian doctrine, especially the authority of the Bible (some were inerrantists, some were not) and asserted the testimony of personal experience in confirming Christian belief. Their tone was moderate, in contrast to the stridency of the later leaders of fundamentalism. The significance of *The Fundamentals* is that it represented a united, interdenominational effort of millenarians, with strong premillennial* interests, and nonmillenarians to unite in the defense of conservative-evangelical Christianity. Some scholars feel that the dissemination of *The Fundamentals* marked the beginning of fundamentalism as a movement. Yet the publication of *The Fundamentals* failed to check the spread of theological liberalism, which had been its original goal, and the division between the millenarians and the nonmillenarians soon became even more intense.

BIBLIOGRAPHY. S. E. Ahlstrom, *A Religious History of the American People* (1972); G. M. Marsden, *Fundamentalism and American Culture* (1980); E. R. Sandeen, *The Roots of Fundamentalism: British and American Millenarianism, 1800-1930* (1970). C. A. Russell

Furman, Richard (1755-1825). Early eighteenth-century Baptist leader in the South. Considered the most important Baptist leader of the antebellum South, Richard Furman was converted in 1771 by the revivalistic Separate Baptists.* The "boy evangelist" began preaching at age sixteen; he was pastor of the High Hills of Santee Church, in South Carolina, from 1774 to 1784 and of First Baptist, Charleston*—the most prominent Baptist church in the South—from 1787 until his death.

Furman was a pioneer denominational statesman. He was the first president of the Triennial Convention,* the first national body of Baptists in America (1814-1820); the first president of the South Carolina Baptist Convention, the first state convention of American Baptists (1821-1825); and the moderator for more than twenty-five years of the Charleston Baptist Association. In addition, Furman was most responsible for developing the organizational concepts that prevailed in the creation of the Southern Baptist Convention* (1845). Opposed to separate societies, in 1817 Furman convinced the Triennial Convention to support ministerial education in addition to missions.* Although this plan later was discarded, the South Carolina State Convention was organized along Furman's plan of a centralized convention that would support multibenevolence.

Having had little formal education himself, Furman was the "apostle of education" among Baptists in the South. He led Charleston Baptists to set up an education committee in 1790 and personally directed the work for thirty-four years. Furman's 1817 plan of education adopted by the Triennial Convention led to the formation of Columbian College* (George Washington University). Furman University,* the first Baptist college in the South, was named in his honor.

A leading advocate of religious liberty* in colonial South Carolina, Furman was also an aristocratic slaveowner who in 1822 wrote the classic Southern biblical defense of slavery.

BIBLIOGRAPHY. H. T. Cook, *A Biography of Richard Furman* (1913); *DAB* IV; *DARB; NCAB* 12; J. A. Rogers, *Richard Furman: Life and Legacy* (1985).   C. D. Weaver

Furman University. Educational institution founded in 1826 in Edgefield, South Carolina, by the South Carolina Baptist Convention (SCBC) as Furman Academy and Theological Institute. It was named in honor of Richard Furman,* a minister and an early advocate of ministerial education. The first classes were held in January 1927 under Joseph Warne, the first principal. Warne resigned after a year and a half, and in January 1829 the students were placed under the care of the Reverend Jesse Hartwell at his home near the High Hills of Santee Baptist Church in Sumter County. Hartwell suffered financial ruin but managed to keep the school operating for five years.

Furman reopened in 1837 near Winnsboro, South Carolina, as a manual labor school called simply Furman Institution and a theological institute and an English and classical school. The manual labor feature failed, and the classical school closed. Theological education alone was offered for nine years, from 1839 to 1848. Furman was moved to Greenville in 1851 and was chartered as Furman University. James C. Furman, son of Richard, was elected first president. Southern Baptist Theological Seminary* was organized in Greenville in 1859; Furman contributed to it its theological library and part of its endowment.

The Greenville Baptist Female College, later called Greenville Women's College, was begun by the South Carolina Baptist Convention in Greenville in 1854 to provide an educational institution for women. It was merged with Furman in the 1930s to create a coeducational institution.

Furman began a law school in 1921; it operated for eleven years but closed in 1932 because of the financial pressures of the Depression. After the merger with Greenville Women's College, Furman operated on two campuses near downtown Greenville. In 1950 Furman purchased about 900 acres north of the city on which to build a new campus. Ground was broken in 1953 and construction was begun. The move to the new campus was gradual. The 1961-1962 school year finally united everyone on the new campus. Development of the new campus continued with the addition of new buildings for physical education, music and art, as well as an infirmary and a stadium.

Furman's relationship with the SCBC since the 1920s has been characterized by struggles over heresy, fraternities, dancing and federal aid. The fundamentalist takeover of the Southern Baptist Convention* and similar moves in the South Carolina Baptist Convention prompted a group of alumni to urge Furman to break ties with the SCBC. On October 15, 1990, the Furman trustees voted to sever ties with the SCBC and declared that the board alone would elect its members.

During the SCBC meeting in November 1990, a committee was appointed to study the Furman matter. A compromise was reached and presented to the 1991 annual meeting. However, a substitute motion to take Furman to court to determine the legality of the trustees' action passed by a slim margin. Efforts to avoid legal action continued. At the urging of a group of thirty-four prominent ministers, the president of the convention called a special session to be held in Columbia, South Carolina, on May 15, 1992. At this meeting, a vote was taken to cut all legal and financial ties with Furman.

BIBLIOGRAPHY. A. S. Reid, *Furman University: Toward a New Identity, 1925-1975* (1976).
                        G. Clayton

G

Galusha, Elon (?-1856). Baptist pastor of New York. Elon Galusha was a prominent Baptist minister in New York during the first half of the nineteenth century. He was the son of Jonas Galusha, a governor of Vermont and a member of the Shaftsbury Church, the first Baptist church in Vermont. The younger Galusha entered the ministry as a young man. He served many years at Whitesborough, near Utica, New York. Subsequent pastorates included Utica, Rochester, Perry and Lockport, all in New York. Active at all levels of Baptist life, Galusha served as the president of the Baptist Missionary Convention of New York. According to William Cathcart, Galusha was one of the best-known men in his state and was an extremely powerful and eloquent preacher. He died January 6, 1856, in Lockport, New York.

BIBLIOGRAPHY. *BE.*

C. D. Weaver

Gambrell, James Bruton (1841-1921). Southern Baptist* pastor, editor and denominational leader. Born in South Carolina and raised in Mississippi, Gambrell served in the Confederate Army. After he married Mary T. Corbell in 1864, the couple settled in Mississippi. Ordained in 1867, he served churches at West Point and Oxford before becoming editor in 1877 of the *Baptist Record,* a position he held for fifteen years. Gambrell then became president of Mercer University* (1893-1896) before moving to Texas in 1896 as superintendent of missions. He became editor of the *Baptist Standard* in 1910 and four years later was elected executive secretary of the Texas Convention. Gambrell also served four terms as president of the Southern Baptist Convention (1917-1921). He died a few months after returning from a visit with European Baptists. Known for his practical wisdom and keen wit, Gambrell stressed cooperation within Southern Baptist life and isolation from ecumenical* involvement.

BIBLIOGRAPHY. B. J. Leonard, "The Southern Bap-

tist Denominational Leader as Theologian," *BHH* 16 (1980):23-32, 61, 63; E. C. Routh, *Life Story of Dr. J. B. Gambrell* (1929).

C. L. Howe

Gano, John (1727-1804). Baptist pastor, itinerant evangelist in the South and Revolutionary War chaplain. Born of Huguenot and English stock in Hopewell, New Jersey, Gano was converted in his early youth. After study with Presbyterian pastors, including one of the Tennents, he became a Baptist and was immersed, joining the Hopewell church. His call to the ministry confirmed, Gano was ordained in 1754 and conducted a missionary tour of the South. His longest pastorate was in New York City (1762-1787), interrupted by service as chaplain in the New York Brigade, where he served with George Washington. It was popularly believed that Gano baptized Washington, but there is no evidence that this took place. While in New York Gano served as a regent of the University of New York and a trustee of King's College (Columbia). He was also associated with the new Rhode Island College (later Brown University*), addressing commencement in 1771. In 1788 Gano left New York for Kentucky, settling as pastor at Town Fork, near Lexington.

In 1754 Gano began a series of trips into the South as an evangelist of the Philadelphia Baptist Association,* distinguishing himself as a warm-hearted preacher and peacemaker among the struggling churches. He was instrumental in establishing and reorganizing churches conforming to Regular Baptist* (Calvinist*) order.

BIBLIOGRAPHY. *AAP* 6; L. C. Barnes, *The John Gano Evidence of George Washington's Religion* (1926); *DAB* IV; J. Gano, *Biographical Memoirs of the Rev. John Gano of Frankfurt, Written by Himself* (1806). L. W. Hähnlen

Gardner, Charles Spurgeon (1859-1948). Southern Baptist pastor, author and seminary professor. Gardner was born February 28, 1859, in Gibson County, Tennessee. Beginning in 1887, he attended three higher-education institutions— Union University* in Tennessee, the University of Richmond* in Virginia and Southern Baptist Theological Seminary* in Louisville, Kentucky— for a total of seven years, but received no degree. Gardner was pastor of several churches in Tennessee (1884-1894), then of First Baptist Greenville, South Carolina (1894-1901), and Grace Street in Richmond, Virginia (1901-1907). In 1907 he became professor of homiletics and ecclesiology at Southern Seminary. He retired in 1929 and died April 1, 1948, in Richmond, Virginia.

Gardner broadened ministerial preparation in practical disciplines at Southern by introducing courses in Christian sociology, psychology and ethics as they related to preaching. Advocating "open-minded conservatism," he wrote *The Ethics of Jesus and Social Progress* (1914) and *Psychology and Preaching* (1918).

BIBLIOGRAPHY. J. B. Weatherspoon, "Charles Spurgeon Gardner," *RE* 52 (April 1955); E. R. Whaley, "The Ethical Contribution of Charles S. Gardner" (Th.M. thesis, Southern Baptist Theological Seminary, 1953).

W. L. Allen

Gardner-Webb University. A Baptist liberal arts school in Boiling Springs, North Carolina. Founded in 1905 by two local associations, Kings Mountain and Sandy Run, the school opened as a high school in 1907. By 1923 it was providing higher education as Boiling Springs Junior College. The high school continued until 1948. The school was renamed Gardner-Webb in 1942 in honor of two prominent benefactors, Oliver Max Gardner, former governor of North Carolina, and his wife, Faye Webb Gardner.

The school became a four-year college in 1969. It offers degrees of A.A., B.S., B.A., M.A. and M.Div. The latter degree is offered through a divinity school begun in 1993. This is the first divinity school to be established in a North Carolina Baptist college or university. The university has long been known for its program in community service. Gardner-Webb occupies a 1,200-acre campus.

BIBLIOGRAPHY. *ESB* 1, 4.

B. J. Leonard

Garrison, William Lloyd (1805-1879). Baptist layman and abolitionist editor. Born on December 10, 1805, in Newburyport, Massachusetts,

he served in early life as an apprentice printer. He then edited several newspapers in New England, followed in 1829-1830 by a coeditorship of Benjamin Lundy's Baltimore-based journal, *Genius of Universal Emancipation.* He converted to the advocacy of immediate emancipation without colonization. After a libel suit, he parted with Lundy and began his own antislavery journal, *The Liberator,* in 1831. Harsh and uncompromising, he raised moral questions of slavery to new urgency. In 1833 he helped form the American Antislavery Society, but increasingly he alienated other "Christian abolitionists" by his acceptance of feminism, pacifism and anticlericalism. In the 1850s he denounced the Constitution as a "covenant with death and an agreement with Hell." A radical Baptist with perfectionist and postmillennial views, he called for true Christians to "come out" of the proslavery churches. This emphasis prompted Southern defenses of slavery as a "positive good." In 1859 his pacifism was strained in his defense of John Brown's raid, which he paradoxically viewed as "the sublime platform of nonresistance." He ceased publication of his newspaper in 1865 after Emancipation, but continued his work through the agenda of the Radical Republicans.

BIBLIOGRAPHY. G. M. Fredrickson, *William Lloyd Garrison* (1968); J. L. Thomas, *The Liberator: William Lloyd Garrison* (1963).

A. M. Manis

General Association of Regular Baptist Churches. A fundamentalist* and separatist Baptist denomination located primarily in the Northern United States. Throughout the decade of the 1920s and even earlier, a radical right-wing rebellion was brewing within the Northern Baptist Convention (now the American Baptist Churches in the USA*). Charging the convention with numerous errors—"modernism" which both denied the truth of the Bible and refused to adopt a creedal statement, "unitarianism" which denied the deity of Jesus, "ecclesiasticism" which denied congregationalism and an equal representation for the churches in the convention's assemblies—the fundamentalists first followed a strategy of "purging" Northern Baptists of those leaders who placed in jeopardy the spiritual life of the denomination. During the effort at "purging," two fundamentalist organizations, forerunners to the General Association of Regular Baptist Churches (GARB), developed among Northern

Baptists. These two groups were the Fundamentalist Fellowship (1920), a moderately fundamentalist group, and the Baptist Bible Union* (BBU; 1923), a more militant faction.

When it became obvious to the leadership of the BBU that "purging" or changing the denomination from within would not be an effective strategy for accomplishing their purposes, they decided to separate from the parent body. Thirty-four delegates from eight states gathered at the Belden Avenue Baptist Church in Chicago in May 1932 for what was the last meeting of the BBU and the first of the GARB. Concerned that the name Regular might wrongly associate them with the small group of Regular Baptists* in the South, the founders of the GARB nevertheless chose the term because it was already in use by fundamentalist Baptists in Canada and Michigan. Moreover, the name was selected to distinguish between those holding the regular, historic Baptist position and those "irregular" Baptists who were corrupted by modernism.

In 1934 the GARB adopted the Articles of Faith, a confessional statement modeled after the New Hampshire Confession of Faith* but containing explicit teachings regarding premillennialism. Subscription to the confessional document is required of all churches desiring membership and of every voting messenger to the association, which meets annually. Dual alignment* with other Baptist bodies is not permitted, and churches entering the GARB must withdraw fellowship and cooperation from any group that permits "modernism."

Rather than creating its own denominational agencies, the GARB has opted to conduct missionary and educational work through "approved" institutions. Church government is rigorously congregational, but a Council of Eighteen is elected to make recommendations for the work of the association. With the home office in Schaumburg, Illinois, the GARB had 1,582 affiliated churches in 1990. The denomination publishes the *Baptist Bulletin,* a monthly periodical. The GARB is a major representation of those Baptists in America who are fundamentalist in theology and separatist in methodology.

BIBLIOGRAPHY. H. L. McBeth, *The Baptist Heritage* (1987); F. S. Mead and S. S. Hill, *Handbook of Denominations in the United States* (1990); J. M. Stowell, *Background and History of the General Association of Regular Baptist Churches* (1949).   W. B. Shurden

General Baptists. Baptists named for their adherence to the Arminian* doctrine of general atonement, which claims that Christ died for all persons. Their first church was gathered in 1608 or 1609 by John Smyth* and Separatists* who had followed him in exile to Amsterdam. When Smyth sought closer ties with local Mennonites, Thomas Helwys* led a schismatic group to Spitalfields (London), where they planted the first Baptist church in England (1612). Growing to forty-seven churches by 1650, General Baptists formed a national general assembly by 1654 and issued the Standard Confession (1660) and the Orthodox Creed (1678). Their earliest American churches resulted from schisms in Particular*-General churches: Providence (1652), Newport (1665) and Swansea (c. 1680). Also known as Six-Principle Baptists,* they held Arminian doctrine, opposed singing in worship and required hands to be laid upon new converts.

General Baptists formed what is perhaps the first (temporary) Baptist association* in America (c. 1670) and the first Baptist churches in New York (1714), Virginia (1714) and North Carolina (1727). Suffering from doctrinal ambiguity, diminishing evangelism, hesitancy to organize, untrained ministers and proselytizing by Regular* Baptists, they became almost extinct by 1800. A new movement, led by Benoni Stinson* after 1822, culminated in the formation of the General Association of General Baptists (1870). With headquarters at Poplar Bluff, Missouri, it covers sixteen Midwestern states, publishes *The General Baptist Messenger,* supports Oakland City (Indiana) College* and maintains boards for home and foreign missions, ministers' aid, publications, education and women's work. In 1987 there were 879 American churches with 73,515 members, and 14,820 members overseas.

BIBLIOGRAPHY. T. A. Laslie, *Laslie's History of the General Baptists* (1938); O. Latch, *History of the General Baptists* (1954); B. R. White, *The English Baptists of the Seventeenth Century* (1983).
J. T. Spivey

General Conference of the Evangelical Baptist Church. *See* EVANGELICAL BAPTIST CHURCH, INC., GENERAL CONFERENCE.

George, David (c. 1742-1810). Black Baptist pastor. David George was the pastor of Silver Bluff Church in Aiken, South Carolina (near Augusta, Georgia), organized in 1773 as the first

Baptist church founded by and composed of all black members. George was born in Essex County, Virginia. He was converted in 1772 by the black missionary preacher George Liele.* Wait Palmer, an itinerant black preacher, baptized George and seven others, who then constituted the Silver Bluff Church. Liele encouraged George, who had begun exhorting his fellow slaves, to pastor the church. With the help of white children, George learned to read the Bible. When the British invaded Savannah in 1779, George's master, George Gauflin, fled his Indian trading post and deserted his slaves. George and several others were sent by the British to Nova Scotia in 1783. In Canada George continued preaching and established black Baptist congregations in Nova Scotia and New Brunswick. In 1792 he and practically his whole congregation moved to Sierra Leone. There George organized a Baptist church of almost 200 members.

BIBLIOGRAPHY. E. G. Wilson, *The Loyal Blacks* (1976). C. D. Weaver

George Washington University. *See* COLUMBIAN COLLEGE.

German Baptist Brethren. *See* DUNKERS.

German Baptist Churches in North America, General Conference of. The major conference of German-language Baptists in America and Canada. The pioneer of German Baptists in America was Konrad Anton Fleischmann,* a native of Nuremberg who was converted to believer's baptist views in Switzerland in 1831. He came to America in 1839 and began preaching among German immigrants, soon receiving appointment from the American Baptist Home Mission Society,* though he was apparently reluctant to be too closely identified with the Baptist denomination. In 1842 he relocated in Philadelphia, where he remained until his death. His church affiliated with the Philadelphia Baptist Association* in 1848.

The first conference of German pastors and coworkers was held in Philadelphia in 1851, and the second in Rochester the following year. A German-language Baptist periodical was soon published. An early leader of work among German settlers was Augustus Rauschenbusch, professor in the German department of Rochester Theological Seminary.* The work of evangelization of Germans continued, especially in the West. By 1865 the work had grown to such an extent that it was feasible to form the General Conference of German Baptist Churches in North America, the organizing meeting being held in Wilmot, Ontario. There were 137 German-language Baptist churches by 1882, with a membership of 10,334. By 1889 there were 171 churches with a total membership of 14,807.

At first the German churches identified themselves with English-language associations, but as the work grew they moved toward forming their own. The language barrier was a major factor in this development. The continued use of German was encouraged in the churches; it was asserted that the Old World language was necessary to the evangelization of German settlers. A concern for overseas mission was apparent in the sending of two missionaries in 1891 to serve under the Cameroon Baptist Mission, a semi-independent mission that was related to the Baptists of Germany. After the Northern Baptist Convention (*see* American Baptist Churches in the USA) was founded in 1907, the German Conference continued its relationship to the parent denomination as a foreign-language group within the convention.

In 1946 the General Council of the German Baptists took action to incorporate as North American Baptists, Inc. In 1949 the denomination moved into its new seminary, North American Baptist Seminary,* in Sioux Falls, South Dakota. The first full-time denominational administrator, Frank H. Woyke, was elected in 1946. While the process of Americanization has continued and the denomination has lost much of its German identity, the North American Baptist Conference* still maintains its separate identity as a denomination, if not strictly speaking an ethnic church.

BIBLIOGRAPHY. F. H. Woyke, *Heritage and Ministry of the North American Baptist Conference* (1979). H. W. Pipkin

German Religious Society of Seventh-Day Baptists (Ephrata). An eighteenth- and early-nineteenth-century religious society. The founder was Johann Conrad Beissel (1691-1768), a radical Pietist who left his native Germany because of persecution for his religious beliefs. He founded the community in 1732. In 1736 it was first called Ephrata, a scriptural reference to Bethlehem which had mystical import for Beissel. There were both celibates and married householders in the community. In addition to the ordinance* of believer's baptism, Ephrata observed foot-washing* and the love feast. Seventh-day (Saturday) worship was a characteristic of the community, which was also strongly committed to religious liberty.* Beissel's mystical tendencies were likely derived in part from the German Pietist Jakob Boehme. In its early years the movement appealed strongly to residents of eastern Pennsylvania, especially Lutherans and Reformed. Singing was an important component of life in Ephrata, and numerous hymns were produced by the community. The religious education of children was a priority, and it has been suggested that the movement played an important role in the evolution of the Sunday school in America.

The community declined during the last quarter of the eighteenth century. The celibate community ended in 1814, and the property was given over to a German Seventh Day Baptist congregation, which itself ceased to exist in 1934.

BIBLIOGRAPHY. J. E. Ernst, *Ephrata* (1963); F. E. Stoeffler, *Mysticism in Colonial Pennsylvania* (1950).   H. W. Pipkin

Girls Auxiliary. Southern Baptist* missions organization for girls. In 1909 the Junior Young Woman's Auxiliary was formed by the Woman's Missionary Union* (WMU) for preteen and young teenage girls. At the 1913 meeting of the WMU the group was given official recognition, and in 1914 the group changed its name to Girls Auxiliary. In 1924 the Girls Auxiliary was divided into Junior Girls Auxiliary (ages 9-12) and Intermediate Girls Auxiliary (ages 13-16).

Forward Steps, a ranking system for the recognition of specific achievements such as Scripture memorization and an understanding of denominational operations, was created in 1928 by Juliette Mather. The girls were recognized by their churches in coronation services.

The group grew to be WMU's second largest organization, with an enrollment of more than 350,000 before the reorganization of WMU in 1970, which changed the name to Girls in Action and the ages to 6-11 years.

BIBLIOGRAPHY. C. B. Allen, *A Century to Celebrate: History of Woman's Missionary Union* (1987); A. Hunt, *History of Woman's Missionary Union* (1964).   S. L. Still

Goble, Jonathan (1827-1896). First Baptist missionary to Japan. Born on a farm at Wayne, New York, on March 4, 1827, Goble early ac-

quired his lasting reputation as a temperamental rowdy. He professed conversion while serving a two-year sentence in Auburn Prison (1846-1848). Sensing a call to missions, he joined the Marine Corps in 1851 and visited Japan with Matthew Perry's expedition of 1853-1854. A journal he kept aboard ship is preserved at William Jewell College.* He entered the academy of Madison (Colgate*) University in 1855 but was expelled the next year for getting married (to Eliza Weeks). He audited courses at Madison off and on until 1859, when he was appointed a missionary by the American Baptist Free Mission Society.

During his first term in Japan (1860-1871), Goble largely supported himself by various trades while translating the four Gospels and Acts into Japanese. He began his second term (1873-1883) under appointment of the American Baptist Missionary Union,* which dismissed him within a year for scandalous behavior. Though fiercely independent, he served effectively as chief colporteur for the American Bible Society* from 1879 to 1882.

Goble returned to America a widower and broken in health. He died penniless on May 1, 1896, in St. Louis. The "poor Baptist missionary" was widely acclaimed in America as inventor of the *jinrikisha* (rickshaw). In Japan he is noted for his 1871 translation of Matthew's Gospel, the oldest extant Scripture portion published in that country.

BIBLIOGRAPHY. F. C. Parker, *Jonathan Goble of Japan: Marine, Missionary, Maverick* (1990); K. Seat, ed., "Jonathan Goble's Book," in *Transactions of the Asiatic Society of Japan*, 3rd ser., 16 (1981):109-52.   F. C. Parker

Going, Jonathan (1786-1844). Pastor, educator and missions executive. Born in Reading, Vermont, on March 7, 1786, he was converted in 1805 while a freshman at Brown University* and was baptized by Stephen Gano. After graduating in 1809, he remained to study theology with Brown's president, Asa Messer. In 1811 he was ordained pastor of the Baptist church in Cavendish, Vermont, and married Lucy Thorndike. During his next pastorate, in Worcester, Massachusetts (1815-1832), Going gained prominence as an able promoter of Sabbath schools, ministerial education, temperance reforms and missionary endeavors. Inspired by years of correspondence with John Mason Peck* and their joint tour of the Midwest in 1831, he led in establishing the American Baptist Home Mission Society* in 1832 and served as its corresponding secretary until 1837. He then moved to the Granville (Ohio) Literary and Theological Institution (now Denison University*) as second president and professor of theology, guiding the school through economic crises until the closing weeks of his life. He died in Granville on November 9, 1844.

Going held honorary degrees from the University of Vermont (A.M., 1812) and Waterville (Maine) College (D.D., 1832). He contributed to the founding of Hamilton Theological Institute and the Western colleges of Shurtleff, Franklin and Kalamazoo. A large man with an iron constitution, he was noted for his executive ability, public spirit, ready wit and frequent use of anecdotes.

BIBLIOGRAPHY. *AAP* 6; *DAB* IV; A. Fisher, "Discourse on the Life, Character and Services of Rev. Jonathan Going, D.D.," in *Minutes of the Worcester Baptist Association,* 1846, 20-36.

F. C. Parker

Golden Gate Baptist Theological Seminary. Southern Baptist* expansion into California convinced some pastors of the need for a theological school to train leaders. Isam B. Hodges, pastor of the Golden Gate Baptist Church of Oakland, enlisted Dallas G. Faulkner, pastor of the First Southern Baptist Church of San Francisco, to support such an endeavor. Their two churches elected trustees to begin the Golden Gate Baptist Theological Seminary in 1944. The school began with seven students meeting for classes in the Golden Gate Church but expanded as the local association and then the state convention provided support. Hodges (1944-1946) and B. O. Berring (1946-1951) served as the first two presidents.

The Southern Baptist Convention accepted ownership and control of the seminary in 1950 and constructed a beautiful campus on Strawberry Point in Marion County; the school moved to this location in 1959. Harold K. Graves provided leadership as president (1951-1977) during the relocation and expansion, and was followed by William M. Pinson Jr. (1977-1981), Franklin D. Pollard (1983-1986) and William O. Crews Jr. (1986-). The school functions as one of six Southern Baptist theological seminaries, offers multiple degree programs in theology, Christian education and church music, and is accredited by the Association of Theological Schools and the regional accrediting body. Courses of study are offered in several off-campus locations as well as on the campus in Mill Valley. The ethnic diversity of the student body (40 percent nonwhite) reflects the diversity of Southern Baptists in California and of the state itself. A Center for Multi-cultural Ministry has been established to aid training and ministry in a multicultural mission field.

BIBLIOGRAPHY. Golden Gate Baptist Theological Seminary, *Catalogue, 1992-93.*

C. L. Howe Jr.

Goodchild, Frank Marsden (1860-1928). Pastor and editor. A graduate of Bucknell University* and Crozer Seminary,* Frank M. Goodchild served as pastor at Amenia, New York; Spruce Street, Philadelphia; and Central Baptist, New York City, where he spent nearly three decades. In New York Goodchild was considered a powerful pulpiteer and sparring partner with Cornelius Woelfkin* and Harry Emerson Fosdick.*

Goodchild wrote a regular column for *The Watchman-Examiner* in which he defended fundamentalist* views. He held that all Baptists should be willing to affirm the infallibility of Scripture, supernaturalism and historic Baptist principles. He repeatedly asserted that fundamentalists were not schismatics.

Goodchild wrote that Baptist educators had a greater responsibility to "common honesty" than to academic freedom. He defended the right of a school to establish a doctrinal basis and was probably an author of the statement adopted by Eastern Baptist Theological Seminary* in 1925.

The Committee on Fundamentals in the Northern Baptist Convention (*see* American Baptist Churches in the USA) offered Goodchild the position of general secretary of the association. Due to ill-health, he declined, and it was not offered to anyone else.

BIBLIOGRAPHY. Frank M. Goodchild, *Aspects of Fundamentalism* (1927); "Frank M. Goodchild: An Appreciation," *Bap,* April 14, 1928.

W. H. Brackney

Goodspeed, Edgar Johnson (1871-1962). Baptist educator and New Testament scholar at the University of Chicago Divinity School.* The son of an aide to William Rainey Harper* and John D. Rockefeller* in the founding of the university and its divinity school, Goodspeed was "born to the Baptist blue" and kept loyalty to the tradition and the Northern Baptist Convention (*see* American Baptists in the USA). Viewed as a modernist by the fundamentalist* faction during denominational struggles of the 1920s, he was definitely of the liberal element, though of a personally moderate mien and outlook. Goodspeed studied at Denison University* and under Harper at Yale, and then took his Ph.D. at the young University of Chicago in 1898. Harper sent his protégé to study with Adolf Harnack in Germany, after which Goodspeed went to Egypt to visit archaeologists. This experience helped him learn devotion to detail in the world surrounding the Bible.

Goodspeed was a widely recognized scholar with an extraordinary gift for relating the findings of research in nonacademic language. With colleague J. M. P. Smith he prepared *The Complete Bible: An American Translation* (1939). It was the bestseller of the University of Chicago Press. While pursuing technical scholarship, Goodspeed produced popular works such as *How to Read the Bible* (1946) and *An Introduction to the New Testament* (1937). He is also remembered for the discovery of a Byzantine manuscript with features dating to the thirteenth century and for his classic edition of this work.

BIBLIOGRAPHY. J. H. Cobb, *A Biography and Bibliography of Edgar Johnson Goodspeed* (1948); J. Cook, *Edgar Johnson Goodspeed: Articulate Scholar* (1981); E. Goodspeed, *As I Remember* (1953). M. E. Marty

Gordh, Arvid (1872-1940). Pastor and educator among the Swedish Baptists* in America. Born in Goteborg, Sweden, on November 15, 1872, he emigrated to Brooklyn, New York, as a young man. He was converted at the age of nineteen and was baptized into the membership of the Swedish Baptist Church in Brooklyn. He was educated at Gordon Bible School, the Swedish Baptist Seminary in Chicago, Bethel Seminary in Stockholm and Newton Centre Theological Institution, receiving the Th.D. degree from Southern Baptist Theological Seminary.* He served pastorates in Sweden; Brockton, Massachusetts; and New York City. He became the first principal of Bethel Academy* in Minneapolis, serving from 1905 until 1912. Later he was called to Bethel Theological Seminary,* where he served as dean from 1922 to 1925 and as professor of New Testament until his death January 4, 1940. In his preaching and teaching he emphasized the necessity of the Spirit-filled life.

M. J. Erickson

Gordon, Adoniram Judson (1836-1895). Baptist minister and missions* leader. After completing his education at Brown University* and Newton Theological Institution,* in 1863 Gordon became the pastor of the Jamaica Plain Baptist Church in Massachusetts. In 1869 he became pastor of the Clarendon Street Church in Boston, where he labored until his death.

In the twenty-five years that Gordon pastored the Clarendon Street Church, he transformed it into one of the leading missions-minded churches in America and a leading fundraiser for Baptist foreign missions. But the church's mission involvement was not limited to overseas. In 1877 Dwight L. Moody held a revival near the church that inspired the congregation to minister to alcoholics, the homeless and other needy people in Boston. Gordon himself began the Boston Industrial Temporary Home as a social service for unemployed men.

The last decade of Gordon's life brought an increased devotion to foreign missions. Active in the American Baptist Missionary Union* (ABMU), Gordon played a key role in its adoption of the British Livingstone Inland Mission as its Congo mission in 1884. In 1888 he was elected chairman of the ABMU's executive committee. As chairman of the ABMU, Gordon guided the denomination's missions for seven years. His other mission activity included attendance at the London Centenary Conference in 1888 and associate editorship of *The Missionary Review of the World.* Above all of these efforts, Gordon is best remembered for founding, in 1889, the Boston Missionary Training School, the forerunner of Gordon College and Gordon-Conwell Theological Seminary.

Gordon was a prolific writer on Christ's Second Coming. In 1878 he founded *The Watchword,* a journal to help believers "looking for that blessed hope, and the glorious appearing of the great God and our Savior Jesus Christ." His works on spirituality and theology included *Ecce Venit—Behold He Cometh* (1889), *The Holy Spirit in Missions* (1893), *How Christ Came to Church* (1893) and his most famous book, *The Ministry of the Spirit* (1894).

Well known for his emphasis on the Holy Spirit and his advocacy of faith healing, Gordon was also a leading evangelical supporter of women's suffrage and of women's work in the Prohibition movement. In 1894 he wrote *The Ministry of Women* in defense of women's right to preach,* prophesy and teach men in the church. From its opening, the Boston Missionary Training School had a majority of women students studying to be missionaries, evangelists and city workers. Gordon received heavy criticism for supporting "shortcut" training for ministry, but he encouraged the multiplication of Christian workers by any means so as to prepare for Christ's Second Coming. Despite his denominational ties, he supported the emerging Bible schools and faith missions of the 1890s.

A close associate of evangelist Dwight L. Moody, Gordon was a leader in the emerging fundamentalist* movement as it was exemplified in the Niagara and prophetic Bible conferences. Gordon was one of the most influential evangelicals of the late nineteenth century, and his popularity permitted him to bridge the ranks of separatist fundamentalists and denominational loyalists. After his death, friends renamed his missionary training school in his honor.

BIBLIOGRAPHY. *DARB;* E. B. Gordon, *Adoniram Judson Gordon: A Biography* (1896); *NCAB* 11; D. L. Robert, "The Legacy of Adoniram Judson Gordon," *IBMR* 11 (October 1987):176-81; C. A. Russell, "Adoniram Judson Gordon: Nineteenth-Century Fundamentalist," *ABQ* 4 (March 1985): 61-89; *The Watchword,* 1878-1895.

D. L. Robert

Gospel Mission Controversy. The Gospel Mission controversy arose in China over the teachings of Tarleton Perry Crawford* (1821-1902). The Crawfords began their missionary work in Shanghai under the auspices of the Foreign Mission Board* of the Southern Baptist Convention.* Eleven years later, after moving to Tengchow, Shantung Province, Crawford seems to have been embroiled in one controversy after another, some of which arose out of his investments in various business enterprises. His financial independence gave him an opportunity to express his convictions on local church support and criticism of the Foreign Mission Board. His views were similar to those of J. R. Graves,* if not derived from him. In a tract entitled *Churches, to the Front!* published in China in 1892, he called for severe limitation of the authority of all conventions and their boards on the mission field. However, he did see value in associations of churches, for interchange of views on matters of common concern, for gathering information regarding the condition and work of the various churches, for stimulating their religious zeal and

Christian fellowship, and for keeping the unity of the faith in the bonds of gospel love, purity and peace.

Some of his ideas anticipated modern missionary emphases on self-propagation, indigeneity and self-support, but his combative personality militated against a widespread acceptance of his teachings. A separate Gospel Mission Association of Chinese Baptist churches was formed by a few missionaries and Chinese who adhered to Crawford's principles, but it failed to prosper.

See also CRAWFORD, TARLETON PERRY.

BIBLIOGRAPHY. R. A. Baker, *The Southern Baptist Convention and Its People, 1607-1972* (1974); T. P. Crawford, *Churches, to the Front!* (1892).

W. R. Estep

Gospel Standard Baptists. *See* STRICT AND PARTICULAR BAPTISTS.

Gould, Thomas (?-1675). Early colonial Baptist pastor from Boston. Gould (Goold) first came to notice through his association with Henry Dunster,* ousted president of Harvard College (1654), over the issue of infant baptism. In 1655, under the influence of Dunster and convinced of the error of the practice, Gould refused to have his first child baptized. Gould separated himself from the Charlestown church and met with other Baptist dissenters in his home, being charged in 1665 with schism. In 1666 he and others were fined and required to post bond; failing to pay, they were imprisoned. When the desired conformity to church law was not secured, Gould left for Noddle's Island (East Boston). Despite continuing threats of persecution, Gould ministered to the Baptists of the area. A modest permanent meetinghouse was erected in 1678 in Boston.

BIBLIOGRAPHY. I. Backus, *History of New England with Particular Reference to the Denomination of Christians Called Baptists* (1796); A. H. Newman, *A History of the Baptist Churches in the United States* (1894).

L. W. Hähnlen

Graham, William (Billy) Franklin (1918-). International evangelist. Born near Charlotte, North Carolina, Graham was raised in a moral home atmosphere by his churchgoing parents, William Franklin Graham, a dairy farmer, and Morrow Coffey Graham. At age sixteen Graham was converted to Christ during an evangelistic campaign led by Mordecai F. Ham, a hard-driving evangelist. In 1936 Graham began classes at Bob Jones College, Cleveland, Tennessee, but he transferred to Florida Bible Institute in Tampa in January 1937. When a young woman broke an engagement with him, Graham felt deeply troubled. He was also struggling with a call to a preaching ministry. One evening in March 1938, on the eighteenth green of a golf course near the Florida Bible Institute, Graham surrendered himself to a life of gospel preaching. In the summer of 1938 he preached his first revival at East Palatka Baptist Church, Florida, and some time later he was ordained as an evangelist by the St. John's Baptist Association of Northern Florida. These events were the beginning of his lifelong denominational identity as a Southern Baptist.*

Between 1940 and 1943, Billy Graham attended Wheaton College, Wheaton, Illinois. There he met Ruth Bell, the daughter of Dr. and Mrs. Nelson Bell, Presbyterian missionaries to China. The couple were married in 1943. Following a brief pastorate at an independent Baptist church in Western Springs, Illinois, in 1944-1945 Graham became an evangelist for Youth for Christ, an organization recently formed by Torrey Johnson. In 1946-1947 Graham made two trips to England for evangelistic tours, the first with Johnson, the second with Cliff Barrows. He also served as the president of Northwestern Bible College in Minneapolis, Minnesota, for a time (1947-1951).

Graham's evangelistic efforts in Los Angeles (1949) brought him to national attention. Just before the campaign he had experienced doubts about the full authority of Scripture. At Forest Home Camp, however, he committed himself completely to a belief that the Bible is the very Word of God. Thereafter he became even more determined to preach what "the Bible says." The Los Angeles crusade seemed to be winding down until William Randolph Hearst gave his newspaper people the order to "puff Graham." Suddenly the crusade was the subject of numerous newspaper articles, and Graham appeared on the front pages of *Time, Newsweek* and later *Life* magazines.

In 1950 Graham founded the Billy Graham Evangelistic Association,* and *The Hour of Decision* went on the air on November 5 of that year. He continued to preach in crusades, often making allusion to the threat of communism. In 1954 the Graham team ministered in England with remarkable results. This crusade ushered Graham

onto the international stage. In those years he published two important books, *Peace with God* (1953) and *The Secret of Happiness* (1955). In 1956 he was a major force in establishing the publication *Christianity Today.* Graham's stature within American society led him to become an unofficial spiritual adviser and confidant to many U.S. presidents, beginning with Dwight D. Eisenhower.

Criticism began to mount regarding the evangelist's positive stance on cooperative evangelism—meaning Graham's policy of working cooperatively with nonevangelical mainline churches. This criticism came to a head in the summer of 1957 in the wake of the New York Crusade, one of the first nationally televised crusades. A number of fundamentalists* broke with Graham because they believed that "decision cards" were not necessarily going to conservative churches for the follow-up of converts and that the evangelist gave too prominent a position to Protestant liberals during the crusade.

Graham became involved in launching a number of important congresses on evangelism, including Berlin (1966), Lausanne (1974), Itinerant Evangelists (1983) and Itinerant Evangelists (1986). These congresses encouraged Christian leaders from many nations to pursue world evangelization.

Characterized by sterling integrity and a genuine humility, Graham has weathered criticism by not responding to it and has remained one of the most respected public figures of his generation and the most influential evangelical of the twentieth century. He has preached the gospel to more people than any evangelist in the history of the church, reaching nearly 100 million individuals in person and untold numbers by radio and television throughout the world. During his meetings 2 million individuals have come forward in response to his invitation* to accept Christ.

While Graham has never emphasized his denominational affiliation, he has maintained membership in First Baptist Church, Dallas, Texas, since 1953. He has been a frequent speaker at Baptist conventions and convocations and at international meetings of the Baptist World Alliance.* Both Southern Baptist Theological Seminary* and Beeson Divinity School* maintain Billy Graham chairs of evangelism.

See also BILLY GRAHAM EVANGELISTIC ASSOCIATION.

BIBLIOGRAPHY. M. Frady, *Billy Graham, a Para-*

ble of American Righteousness (1979); W. G. McLoughlin, *Billy Graham: Revivalist in a Secular Age* (1960); W. Martin, *A Prophet with Honor: The Billy Graham Story* (1991); R. V. Pierard, "Billy Graham and the U.S. Presidency," *JCS* 22 (1980):107-27; J. Pollock, *Billy Graham: The Authorized Biography* (1966); J. Pollock, *Billy Graham, Evangelist to the World: An Authorized Biography of the Decisive Years* (1979).

J. D. Woodbridge

Grand Canyon University. A Christian liberal arts school owned and operated by the Arizona Southern Baptist Convention. The institution was chartered August 1, 1949, and opened shortly afterward with 16 faculty and about 100 students in temporary quarters at Prescott with Willis J. Ray as president (1949-1950). Two years later it moved to a permanent campus in Phoenix. From a program intended primarily for preachers, the school expanded its offerings to include teacher education, science, nursing, business, music and the arts, becoming a university in 1989. The North Central Association of Colleges and Schools accredited the institution in 1968, and a variety of bachelor's and master's degree programs are maintained. Bill R. Williams became the school's president in 1978. The university provides a Christian atmosphere, a diverse liberal arts curriculum, a strong athletic program, and national and international programs to increase global awareness.

BIBLIOGRAPHY. Grand Canyon University, *Catalogue, 1992-93*.

C. L. Howe Jr.

Grand Island College. American Baptist* College located in Grand Island, Nebraska, from 1892 to 1931. Concern for a Baptist college in Nebraska dates from the earliest years of the state convention. In 1870 a report was issued suggesting that a college be founded in Nebraska only if there were adequate support for such an enterprise. The Nebraska Baptist Seminary was founded in 1880 and lasted some five years before being closed by the state convention due to internal difficulties. The city of Grand Island offered land and buildings toward the founding of a new college, which came to fruition in 1892 under the direction of the American Baptist Education Society.* Enrollment was much lower than anticipated, however, and the school experienced continual financial difficulties exacerbated by a severe regional drought and the consequent de-

parture of thousands of Nebraskans to the East. George Sutherland provided significant leadership as president from 1893 to 1911. By 1910 the total enrollment of the college was 262. Indebtedness and a declining enrollment eventually led to the decision to merge the college with Sioux Falls College, which union was realized in 1931 in North Dakota.

BIBLIOGRAPHY. S. Fleming, *American Baptists and Higher Education* (1965); G. Sutherland, *A History of Grand Island College* (1935).

H. W. Pipkin

Granville Literary and Theological Institution; Granville College. *See* DENISON UNIVERSITY; GOING, JONATHAN.

Graves, James Robinson (1820-1893). Southern Baptist* preacher, editor and publisher who led in the formation of the Landmark* movement. Born into a Congregational family in Vermont, he joined a Baptist congregation at age fifteen. Growing up in a poor farming family, Graves received little formal education. He applied himself diligently to private studies, however, and became a schoolteacher, finding work first in Kingsville, Ohio (1840-1842), and then in Jessamine County, Kentucky (1842-1843). In 1842 he was ordained into the Baptist ministry, and he preached in Ohio for a short period (1843-1845) before taking a teaching position in Nashville, Tennessee, in 1845.

Soon after moving to Nashville, Graves became pastor of a church, and by 1848 he was the editor of *The Tennessee Baptist*. His chief contribution to Baptist life and history was through his career in journalism. By the eve of the Civil War, *The Tennessee Baptist* had the largest circulation (13,000 in 1859) of any denominational paper in the South. Not only did it serve the Baptists of Tennessee, but it was also the denominational journal for Mississippi, Louisiana, Arkansas and most of the lower Mississippi Valley. Graves also formed a publishing company which became one of the most influential and prolific religious presses in the South during the second half of the nineteenth century.

During the decade before the Civil War, Graves became the dominant figure of a developing movement in Baptist life known as Landmarkism. In 1851 he convened a meeting at Cotton Grove, Tennessee, that formulated the chief tenets of the movement, the foundational premise being the sole validity of Baptist churches as true churches of Christ, joined in unbroken succession since the New Testament era. Throughout the latter half of the nineteenth century, Landmarkism became the most potent force in the Southern Baptist Convention, especially in the old Southwest. The sectarian tendencies of the movement continue to characterize many aspects of Southern Baptist life, particularly in rural churches of the mid-South and the lower Mississippi Valley. Graves's book *Old Landmarkism: What Is It?* (1880) is a classic pronouncement of this doctrine.

BIBLIOGRAPHY. *DAB* IV; *DARB;* O. L. Hailey, *J. R. Graves: Life, Times and Teaching* (1929); J. E. Tull, *Shapers of Baptist Thought* (1972).

M. G. Bell

Great Awakening. *See* FIRST GREAT AWAKENING; SECOND GREAT AWAKENING.

Griffin, Mildred. African-American foreign missionary. She was recruited by the Foreign Mission Board (FMB) of the National Baptist Convention, U.S.A. Inc. (*see* National Baptists)* while a member of the New Hope Baptist Church in Wichita. She had earlier graduated from East High School and the Normal School of Kansas and had received training in the College of Kansas. Along with several other missionaries, she sailed on December 23, 1928, for the Suehn Industrial Mission located sixty-five miles from Monrovia, Liberia; they arrived on January 19, 1929.

Griffin's correspondences (1929-1939) with FMB corresponding secretaries James E. East* and Joseph H. Jackson* were regularly recorded in *The Mission Herald.* The Suehn Mission had been started in 1912 by Emma B. Delaney as an industrial school for girls. By the time of Griffin's arrival it was a coeducational secondary school consisting of three buildings. She was placed in charge of the junior high. In 1938 she reported 165 students from various tribes. In addition to academics, the students were taught farming and animal husbandry, which made the mission almost self-sufficient.

After serving for ten years, in 1939 Griffin married the Reverend U. S. Bowen and moved to Topeka. In her final letter she thanked the FMB for a positive African missionary experience and compared the FMB favorably with other boards, especially for regularly meeting budgets and salaries.

BIBLIOGRAPHY. *The Mission Herald,* September-October 1939, pp. 13-14; *Wichita Eagle,* February 20, 1939.   L. H. Williams

Griffin, Susan Elizabeth Cilley (1851-1926). The first fully recognized ordained woman in the Baptist ministry. Born February 28, 1851, Libby Griffin, as she was known, was raised in the Free Will Baptist* tradition and originally went to India as a Free Will missionary. She was taken ill at Midnapore in 1880 and returned to the United States. During her recuperation in Michigan she met and married Zebina Griffin, a furloughing missionary, and the couple returned to India for work at Balasore. A second furlough was taken in 1893. While they were in New York State, the Elmira Heights Baptist Church called the two couple, and Libby Griffin was ordained that year. They served at Elmira and several other small churches throughout the decade. During this period Griffin also edited a children's magazine. Her ordination was later recognized by the Northern Baptist Convention after its merger with the Free Baptist General Conference (*see* American Baptist Churches in the USA).

A subsequent tour of mission in India found the Griffins working at a school for various religious groups at Santipore. After the 1911 merger of the Free Baptist General Conference and the Northern Baptist Convention, Griffin devoted her efforts to the union of the two denominations' women's groups. She was a frequent speaker at rallies and a close confidante of Helen Barret Montgomery* and Susan B. Anthony. In her last position, with Keuka College, she again was pastor of a local church in the town of Keuka Park, New York. She died January 5, 1926.

BIBLIOGRAPHY. W. H. Brackney, *The Baptists* (1988); Z. F. Griffin, *The Biography of Libby Cilley Griffin* (1927).   W. H. Brackney

Griffith, Benjamin. *See* AMERICAN BAPTIST PUBLICATION SOCIETY.

H

Haldeman, Isaac Massey (1845-1933). Baptist pastor. Born in Concordville, Pennsylvania, Haldeman received his education at West Chester Academy and was ordained to the Baptist ministry in 1870. After serving Northern Baptist churches in Chadds Ford, Pennsylvania (1871-1875), and Wilmington, Delaware (1875-1884), he was called to the First Baptist Church of New York City, where he remained until his death nearly fifty years later.

Because Haldeman was an outstanding pulpit orator, his parishioners often found standing room only at the rear of the church. Haldeman was deeply committed to the fundamentalist* crusade against "worldliness" in any of its forms, but especially in the theater. A dispensationalist, he espoused radical cultural pessimism. In *The Signs of the Times* (1910) he provided a popular reading of prophecy and current events, indicating that the end of history was near. Haldeman had no time for reform movements, arguing that such efforts were like setting staterooms in order as the ship sinks.

Haldeman was also active in the fundamentalist-modernist controversy, contending with fellow Baptists Cornelius Woelfkin,* Harry Emerson Fosdick* and Walter Rauschenbusch.* He authored scores of books and pamphlets, most of which were derived from sermons preached in his church. In 1909 William Jewel College* conferred on him an honorary degree of D.D.

BIBLIOGRAPHY. G. Marsden, *Fundamentalism and American Culture* (1980); *NCAB* 15.

P. C. Wilt

Ham, Mordecai Fowler (1877-1961). Fundamentalist* Baptist evangelist and pastor. Reputed to be a descendant of a line of Baptist ministers going back to Roger Williams*—a claim that cannot be proved—Ham was born in Allen County, Kentucky. After attending Ogden College in Bowling Green, Kentucky, he pursued a business career in Chicago (1897-1900). He left business to enter the ministry in Bowling Green and was ordained in 1901.

Concern for evangelism led him into a life of itinerant ministry through the Southern United States, holding citywide meetings. At the close of his ministry he claimed 1 million converts, including Billy Graham,* who had made a decision at the Charlotte, North Carolina, meetings in 1934. Ham utilized the radio extensively in gaining publicity for his campaigns. He left his evangelistic campaigns for a brief term as pastor of the First Baptist Church of Oklahoma City (1927-1929) and later served as president of the Interdenominational Association of Christian Evangelists (1936). He campaigned fervently against evolution, communism and liquor interests. In 1935 he was awarded a doctor of divinity degree by Bob Jones College.

BIBLIOGRAPHY. E. E. Ham, *Fifty Years on the Battle Front with Christ: A Biography of Mordecai F. Ham* (1950). R. T. Clutter

Hamilton Literary and Theological Institution. *See* COLGATE BAPTIST UNIVERSITY.

Hancock, Gordon Blaine (1884-1970). African-American Baptist minister, college professor and social activist. Born on June 23, 1884, in Ninety-six Township, South Carolina, Hancock graduated from Benedict College (A.B., 1911; B.D., 1912), Colgate Baptist University* (A.B., 1919; B.D., 1920) and Harvard (M.A., 1921). Between the time of Booker T. Washington* and Martin Luther King Jr.,* Hancock was perhaps the most prominent black spokesperson in Virginia and one of the most prominent Southern black leaders. In 1921 he organized the department of economics and sociology at Virginia Union and became dean of the seminary in 1940. In the 1920s he coined the phrase "the double-duty dollar," advocating black self-help and economic solidarity. In 1939 he delivered the keynote speech, entitled "The Color Challenge," before the Baptist World Alliance* meeting in Atlanta. In 1969 Colgate conferred an honorary doctorate upon him. He died in July 1970.

BIBLIOGRAPHY. R. Gavins, "Gordon Blaine Hancock: A Black Profile from the New South," *JNH* 59 (July 1974); R. Gavins, *The Perils and Prospect of Southern Black Leadership: Gordon Blaine Hancock, 1884-1970* (1977).

L. H. Williams

Hannibal-LaGrange College. Liberal arts college affiliated with the Missouri Baptist Convention. LaGrange College, LaGrange, Missouri, was founded in 1858 by the Wyaconda Baptist Association. In 1928 the residents of Hannibal, Missouri, pledged $232,000 for a campus and buildings. LaGrange College subsequently moved to Hannibal and became Hannibal-LaGrange College. Ownership of the college was conveyed to the Missouri Baptist Convention in 1957. Hannibal-LaGrange College merged with St. Louis College in 1967, forming Missouri Baptist College;* but the merger was dissolved in 1973. The college was accredited as a four-year institution in 1975. A fire destroyed Hannibal-LaGrange's administration building in June 1989. The opening of a new administration building in late 1992 completed a building program that included the "Tech Center" and a sports complex. In the early 1990s Paul Brown was president of Hannibal-LaGrange, which had 37 full-time faculty members and 951 students enrolled in undergraduate programs.

BIBLIOGRAPHY. *ESB* 1:597.

A. L. Pratt

Hardin-Simmons University. Baptist General Convention of Texas educational institution. Founded in 1891 as Abilene Baptist College by the Sweetwater Baptist Association, the school was designed to provide quality Christian education and training for those called to the ministry. James B. Simmons, a New York minister, donated $5,000 to complete the first campus building, and the trustees changed the school's name to Simmons College. The school opened in 1892 on a forty-acre campus with Owen Clinton Pope as president.

In 1925, with the addition of an M.A. program, the college became Simmons University. John G. Hardin of Burkburnett, Texas, gave the school

$900,000 in 1934, and the trustees voted to change the name to Hardin-Simmons University (HSU). The Baptist General Convention of Texas became the owner-operator of the school in 1941.

President Jesse Fletcher reorganized the university in the 1980s. The university now includes schools of music, education, nursing, business and finance, and a College of Arts and Science.

HSU built the Logsdon School of Theology in the late 1980s with a substantial gift from the Logsdon family. In 1990 the school enjoyed a $28 million endowment and operated with an $18 million budget; student enrollment came to about 2,000. The school maintains a strong commitment to ministerial education. The president in the early 1990s was Lanny Hall.

BIBLIOGRAPHY. Baptist General Convention of Texas, *Texas Baptist Annual* (1990); A. Y. Stackhouse, *Hardin-Simmons University* (1991).

R. Beck

Hardshell Baptists. A pejorative title often applied, in a nonspecific fashion, to highly traditional Baptist denominations and sects, particularly Primitives* but also occasionally Regulars,* Old Regulars,* Uniteds* and others influenced by the doctrines of limited atonement and predestination. During the nineteenth century antimission* controversy, *hardshell* was often applied to the antimission Baptists along with the less prejudicial titles "Old Baptists," "Old School Baptists" and "Primitives."

Although users of the term may imply only a degree of traditionalism in excess of mainline Baptist practice, there are specific doctrines, fellowship mores and worship forms that have become associated with the label: Pauline mandates relative to gender roles, "natural water" baptism, foot-washing, prohibitions against musical instruments, the practice of lined singing, particular election, a "preservation of the saints" doctrine that denies the possibility of backsliding and restoration, the right to pass judgment on both spiritual and secular behavior of members, the right to exclude errant individuals from membership, sanctions against divorce and remarriage ("double marriage"), the prohibition of its ministers' formal participation in any interdenominational worship, and a host of other beliefs and behaviors that together tend to create a spirit of rigidity and insularity.

Primitive Baptists are often offended by the

term, and since the word does tend to be pejorative, it should be used—if at all—with great care and sensitivity, in particular avoiding stereotyping that lumps together a wide range of traditional but disparate Baptist groups.

See also PRIMITIVE BAPTISTS.

BIBLIOGRAPHY. R. A. Baker, *A Baptist Source Book* (1966); W. M. Patterson, "Small Baptist Groups in Kentucky," in *Baptists in Kentucky, 1776-1976*, ed. L. T. Crismon (1975); O. W. Taylor, *Early Tennessee Baptists, 1769-1852* (1957).

H. Dorgan

Harper, William Rainey (1856-1906). A native of New Concord, Ohio, and child graduate of Muskingum College, Harper went on to become a prodigious Semitic scholar at Yale and then, in a contest-filled partnership with Baptist layman John D. Rockefeller,* founded the University of Chicago in 1891. It replaced the failed Old University of Chicago and brought in the Baptist Union Theological Seminary as the University of Chicago's Divinity School.*

As university president, from the first day Harper encouraged people of non-Baptist, and indeed non-Christian, orientation to teach and study at Chicago. While favoring the Baptist ministerial cause, he also insisted that his divinity school would prepare seminary, college and university teachers, again including non-Baptists.

Harper's was an expansive, restless vision that would encompass faith and reason, religion and science, love for biblical and Baptist traditions and a free academic spirit born of the Enlightenment. Even while busy raising funds, he remained a teacher of Hebrew with a large and devoted following. He founded a university press, various extension programs, journals, efforts at the Chautauqua Institution, and home study out reach endeavors, all to support his faith that democracy, citizenship and learning would profit from biblical and theological inquiry.

Inevitably he came to be the object of suspicion among more conservative and denominationally minded Baptists, but he died of cancer at age fifty, a generation before the battles he helped start came to a head in the Northern Baptist Convention (*see* American Baptist Churches in the USA). While always available to promote his causes and piety in Baptist circles, he kept up his scholarship, particularly displayed in his *Critical and Exegetical Commentary on Amos and Hosea* (1905).

BIBLIOGRAPHY. *DCA;* T. W. Goodspeed, *William Rainey Harper* (1928).

M. E. Marty

Hart, Oliver (1723-1795). Baptist pastor and founder of the Charleston Association. Hart was converted at age seventeen and baptized at Southampton, Bucks County, Pennsylvania. He was ordained to the ministry by the same church in the midst of the First Great Awakening.* After years of active participation in the Philadelphia Baptist Association,* Hart moved to Charleston in 1749 to become pastor of the renowned Charleston congregation, the oldest in the South (see First Baptist Church, Charleston); he served there for thirty years. In 1751 he led in the formation of the Charleston Association, the first Baptist association in the South. Hart modeled the confessional stance as well as the operational form of the association after those of the Philadelphia Association.

Hart's political activities as a patriot made it necessary for him to flee the British in 1780. He then accepted the pastorate of the Baptist church at Hopewell, New Jersey, where he remained until his death. Hart was author of numerous pamphlets and sermons.

BIBLIOGRAPHY. W. H. Brackney, *The Baptists* (1988); L. L. Owens, *Oliver Hart, 1723-1795: A Biography* (1966); L. Townsend, *South Carolina Baptists, 1670-1805* (1978).

B. C. Leslie

Hatcher, William Eldridge (1834-1912). Baptist minister and editor. Born and raised in Virginia, Hatcher attended the schools of Bedford County prior to studying at Richmond College (B.A., 1858). After graduating in 1858, he accepted a call to the Baptist Church in Manchester, Virginia. In 1867 he became pastor of Franklin Square Baptist Church in Baltimore, but in 1868 he returned to Virginia to become pastor of First Baptist of Petersburg. In 1875 he assumed the pastorate of Grace Street Church in Richmond, where he remained for twenty-six years. Hatcher maintained a variety of other activities during his pastoral career. From 1882 to 1885 he was editor of and a frequent contributor to the *Religious Herald*. In 1888 he went to Europe, where he visited numerous preacher friends, including Charles Spurgeon.* In 1899 he championed the cause of William H. Whitsitt,* the Southern Baptist Theological Seminary* professor who fell into controversy because of his criticism of the popularly held view that Baptist churches and believer's immersion had been maintained in unbroken succession throughout church history. Hatcher was instrumental in arranging for Whitsitt's call to Richmond College (now the University of Richmond*). A gifted preacher and master pulpiteer, Hatcher was known in the South for his leadership in Baptist circles.

BIBLIOGRAPHY. *DAB* IV; E. B. Hatcher, *Wm. E. Hatcher* (1915); W. E. Hatcher, *Along the Trail of the Friendly Years* (1910).

R. R. Mathisen

Hawaii Baptist Academy. A college preparatory school in Honolulu owned and operated by the Hawaii Baptist Convention. Hawaii Baptist Academy began in 1949 with seventh and eighth grades directed by the first principal, Hugh Pendleton McCormick, a former missionary to Nigeria, and eventually expanded to include a full elementary and high-school curriculum. Stanley A. Sagert directed the academy for almost two decades, and Dan Kong, an experienced pastor and educator, became president in 1989.

The academy occupies four locations for the high-school, junior-high and elementary grades, recently acquiring fifteen acres at a cost of $17 million for the Leeward Oahu Elementary Campus. A board of directors elected by the executive board of the convention administers operations, and a mainland advisory council provides support. Enrollment numbers about 1,000 students, two-thirds of whom are non-Christian, so the academy serves an evangelistic purpose as well as providing a fully accredited school with outstanding academic programs.

C. L. Howe Jr.

Hays, Lawrence Brooks (1898-1981). Lawyer, congressman and Southern Baptist Convention* president. Raised in Russellville, Arkansas, and a graduate of the University of Arkansas (1919) and the Law School of George Washington University (1922; *see* Columbian College), Hays married Marion Prather in 1922. For two decades thereafter he practiced law in Russellville and Little Rock, engaged unsuccessfully in political campaigns for governor and congressman, and filled several appointive posts in his native state. From 1943 to 1959 he served as U.S. congressman from the fifth district of Arkansas.

An active advocate of civil rights for all citizens,

Hays opposed the views of Governor Orval Faubus during the school desegregation crisis in Little Rock (1958); this position brought his defeat for reelection by a strong segregationist candidate. President Dwight D. Eisenhower appointed him to the board of the Tennessee Valley Authority (1959-1961), after which he served as a special presidential assistant for President John F. Kennedy (1961-1963) and President Lyndon B. Johnson (1963-1964).

Hays maintained an active church involvement throughout his career. He was president of the Southern Baptist Convention for two terms (1957-1959) and a vice president of the National Council of Churches* (1969). He directed the Ecumenical Institute at Wake Forest University* for five years (1969-1974) and published several books, including *The Baptist Way of Life* (1963) with John Steely and an autobiography, *Politics Is My Parish* (1981).

C. L. Howe Jr.

Heck, Fannie Exile Scudder (1862-1915). Longtime president of the Woman's Missionary Union* (WMU), an auxiliary to the Southern Baptist Convention.* She was born June 16, 1862, in Mecklenberg County, Virginia. Her family followed her father from town to town in his wartime travels as a lieutenant colonel. After the war the Hecks settled in Raleigh, North Carolina, where her father resumed his law practice and Fannie Heck attended Professor Hobgood's Seminary for Young Women. Later she graduated from Hollins Institute near Roanoake, Virginia.

Heck was active in church and community work, teaching a boys' Sunday-school class and serving as vice president of the Southern Sociological Congress. She was elected president of the North Carolina WMU at its formation in January 1886 and served in that office until her death. She was also president of the conventionwide WMU from 1892 to 1894, 1895 to 1899 and 1906 to 1915. She served a total of fifteen years as president—the longest tenure in WMU history—with interruptions for reasons of health and conflict with WMU corresponding secretary Annie Armstrong* over the formation of the Woman's Missionary Union Training School* at Louisville, Kentucky (Armstrong did not support it). Heck is considered one of the founders of the school (1907), and she pioneered in the area of Christian social action by beginning WMU's "personal service" program in 1909.

Heck wrote "The Woman's Hymn," the official

hymn of WMU, numerous articles and pamphlets, and four books: *In Royal Service* (1913), *Everyday Gladness* (1915), *Sunrise and Other Poems* (1916) and *The Pageant of the Golden Rule* (1916). After a long illness, Heck died in her Raleigh home on August 25, 1915.

BIBLIOGRAPHY. C. Allen, *Laborers Together with God* (1987); W. C. James, *Fannie E. S. Heck: A Study of the Hidden Springs of a Rarely Useful and Victorious Life* (1939).

T. L. Scales

Helwys, Thomas (c. 1550-c. 1615). General Baptist* minister. Born into a landed family in Nottinghamshire, he was admitted to Gray's Inn, the British legal society, in 1593. In 1607 Helwys was part of a group of Separatists who, with John Smyth, went to Amsterdam. By 1609 their search for the "true church" led them to embrace the principle of baptism* of believers only (though not by immersion). After baptizing himself, Smyth baptized Helwys and others within their congregation. Later, after Smyth questioned his baptism and moved to join with the Waterlander Mennonites, Helwys and others separated from him and returned to England. They settled at Spitalfields outside London in 1611 and established the first identifiable General Baptist church on English soil.

Helwys is believed to have been the primary author of "Declaration of Faith of English People Remaining at Amsterdam" (1611). He also wrote several books and treatises; his *A Short Declaration of the Mistery of Iniquity* (1612) is recognized as one of the earliest pleas for liberty of conscience published in England. Both Helwys and his wife, Joan (Ashmore) Helwys, whom he married in 1595, suffered persecution for their views. Joan Helwys was under arrest at York Castle in 1608, and Thomas Helwys was imprisoned in Newgate Prison in 1615 and died in or around 1616.

BIBLIOGRAPHY. T. Crosby, *The History of English Baptists,* vol. 1 (1738); H. L. McBeth, *The Baptist Heritage* (1987); W. T. Whitley, *A Baptist Bibliography,* vol. 1 (1916). K. Smith

Hiscox, William (?-1704). First pastor of the first Seventh Day Baptist* church in America. Hiscox was converted to sabbatarian views by Stephen Mumford, a member of the Bell Lane Seventh Day Baptist Church in London, who came to Newport, Rhode Island, in 1664 and affiliated with the existing First Baptist Church of Newport, led by John Clarke.*

In 1671 a sharp controversy arose among the Baptists in Newport regarding sabbatarian beliefs, and the result was a withdrawal of seven members, led by William Hiscox, to form their own church, which became known as the First Seventh Day Baptist Church of Newport—the first church of that faith in America.

The little church in Newport grew, both by the coming of Seventh Day Baptists from England and by frequent conversions within the colony. Known as a man of great ministerial gifts and skilled in debate, Hiscox served as pastor of the church for thirty-three years until his death in 1704.

BIBLIOGRAPHY. H. L. McBeth, *The Baptist Heritage* (1987). T. R. McKibbens

Hispanic Baptist Theological Seminary. A theological school in San Antonio, Texas, for the training of Mexican Baptist pastors. This school was founded as the Mexican-American Baptist Bible Institute by the San Antonio Baptist Association. The first classes in Spanish were held during the winter of 1947 at the Palm Springs Baptist Church under the direction of Paul Siebenmann. In 1949 C. G. Carter was elected the first president. Other presidents have been H. B. Ramsour, Daniel J. Rivera and Joshua Grijalva. From 1947 to 1962 the school was owned and operated by the San Antonio Baptist Association in cooperation with the Baptist General Convention of Texas (BGCT). The school outgrew the resources of a single association and in 1963 came under the auspices of the BGCT.

A major change came in 1981, when the school was merged with Southwestern Baptist Theological Seminary* in Fort Worth and took the name Hispanic Baptist Theological Seminary (HBTS). Though the school continued on its own campus and with its own faculty and administration, it became an integral part of the Fort Worth seminary. However, those ties were severed in 1989, when HBTS reverted to the sponsorship of the State Missions Commission of the BGCT.

HBTS offers programs of study in theology, religious education and church music. In 1990 the school reported a faculty of nine, plus other staff. Enrollment approaches 200.

BIBLIOGRAPHY. J. Grijalva, *A History of Mexican Baptists in Texas, 1881-1981* (1982).

H. L. McBeth

Historical Commission, SBC. History agency of the Southern Baptist Convention* (SBC). Chartered in 1951, the commission provides historical publications and services and operates the Southern Baptist Historical Library and Archives (SBHLA). *Baptist History and Heritage* is the commission's quarterly journal. Services include annual historical conferences, microfilm, research, and assistance to church, association and state Baptist history programs. The SBHLA contains the world's largest collection of resources on Southern Baptists. Annual awards include the Norman W. Cox Award (best article published), Davis C. Wooley Award (best achievements in state Baptist history) and Distinguished Service Award (honoring a career of service). The Southern Baptist Historical Society is auxiliary to the commission. Commission executives have included Norman W. Cox (1951-1959), Davis C. Wooley (1959-1971) and Lynn E. May Jr. (1971-). Commission offices and the SBHLA are located in the SBC Building in Nashville, Tennessee.

BIBLIOGRAPHY. L. E. May Jr. and C. W. Deweese, "Southern Baptists' History Agency; Forty Years of Service, 1951-1991," *BHH,* April 1991, pp. 6-19.

C. W. Deweese

Holliman, Ezekiel. Early American Baptist leader. Little is known about him beyond his association with Roger Williams* in establishing the first Baptist church in America. According to John Winthrop, a woman named Scott had "been infected with Anabaptistry" and moved to Providence. "Mr. Williams," he stated, "was taken (or rather emboldened) by her to make open profession thereof, and accordingly was rebaptized by one Holyman, a poor man late of Salem. Then Mr. Williams rebaptized him and some ten more." Holliman (Holyman) and others had followed Williams from Salem to Providence. That he had been at odds with the Salem Church after Williams's forced departure is indicated in the Massachusetts General Court Records of 1638: "Ezekiel Holliman appeared upon summons, because he did not attend the public assemblies, and for seducing many, was referred to the ministers for conviction." He moved to Newport in 1640 and later went to Warwick.

BIBLIOGRAPHY. J. Winthrop, *Journal* (1825).

N. H. Maring

Holman, Russell (1812-1879). Baptist pastor, missionary and denominational leader. A native of Massachusetts, he attended Brown University* in the late 1830s. He moved to Kentucky, pastored two churches and was ordained in 1840. In the early 1840s he went to New Orleans as a missionary of the American Baptist Home Mission Society* and founded the first Baptist church in that city. One of his major ministries included service as corresponding secretary of the Domestic (Home) Mission Board* of the Southern Baptist Convention* (1845-1851 and 1857-1862). Between 1851 and 1856 he taught mathematics at Howard College (now Samford University*) and pastored several Alabama churches. His latter years included service as an evangelist in the Confederate Army (1862-1865), as an agent for the Domestic Mission Board in Missouri and New Orleans (1865-1866), and as a pastor of churches in Illinois, Kentucky and Missouri (1867-1876). A stroke of paralysis in 1876 ended his active career.

BIBLIOGRAPHY. *BE; ESB* 4:758.

C. W. Deweese

Holmes, Elkanah (1744-1832). Early Baptist home missionary and preacher. He served as military chaplain to the New Jersey militia during the Revolutionary War. He pastored in New Jersey, Connecticut and New York and is recorded as having preached at the Philadelphia Baptist Association* on October 7, 1788. The New York Baptist Association, which had assumed responsibility for mission to the American Indians as early as 1796, appointed Holmes as one of the earliest Baptist missionaries to Indians in western New York. Reports and greetings from Indian chiefs came to the association over the next few years. Holmes's work was supported by churches in New York and New Jersey. He worked with the interdenominational New York Mission Society but broke with it in 1808 over the issue of baptism. His support was then taken over by the New York Baptist Mission Society with assistance from the Massachusetts Baptist Missionary Society. Holmes was located in Canada during the War of 1812 and played the role of an American patriot. His Calvinist* views are reflected in his *A Church Covenant, Including a Summary of the Fundamental Doctrines of the Gospel* (1818).

BIBLIOGRAPHY. W. H. Brackney, *The Baptists* (1988); N. Maring, *Baptists in New Jersey* (1964).

H. W. Pipkin

Holmes, Obadiah (c. 1607-1602). Colonial Baptist minister. Born near Manchester, England,

Holmes immigrated to Massachusetts in 1638. The following year he and his family settled in Salem, where he joined the Congregational church and worked as a glassmaker. In 1645 he moved to Rehoboth in Plymouth Colony and quickly became critical of church practices. When he became a Baptist in 1650, the Rehoboth church excommunicated him and the Plymouth General Court indicted him. As a result he moved his family to Newport, Rhode Island, where he joined the Baptist church pastored by John Clarke.*

In 1651 Holmes, Clarke and John Crandall traveled to Massachusetts Bay Colony to help a blind and aged fellow Baptist. But they were promptly arrested in Lynn, then put on trial in Boston for promoting Anabaptism.* The trio was fined and ordered to leave the colony, but when Holmes refused to comply, he was imprisoned and eventually "well whipped" in public. After his release he returned to Newport, where he was ordained to the ministry (1652) and served the church as pastor for nearly thirty years.

Holmes's greatest legacy was his *Last Will and Testimony* (1675), which remains the best example of Baptist theology, preaching style, piety and family life to come out of the seventeenth century.

BIBLIOGRAPHY. E. S. Gaustad, ed., *Baptist Piety: The Last Will and Testimony of Obadiah Holmes* (1978).   T. P. Weber

Home Mission Board, SBC. With roots in the Massachusetts Baptist Missionary Society (1802) and the American Baptist Home Mission Society* (1832), the Home Mission Board (HMB), called initially the Board of Domestic Missions, was established as part of the Southern Baptist Convention* (SBC) in 1845. Because Baptists of the South were accustomed to carrying on home missions through state conventions and associations, the HMB struggled in its early years to win acceptance. The situation, complicated by the presence of Northern Baptist missionaries in the South after the Civil War, became so desperate that the SBC faced the possibility of discontinuation of the HMB in 1882. A turnaround in the HMB's fortunes came in 1882 with the election of I. T. Tichenor* as its executive and the removal of the board from Marion, Alabama, to Atlanta, Georgia. Ten years after his election, in his report to the SBC in 1892, Tichenor gave a glowing, but realistic, assessment of the progress of the HMB, saying,

"The board has demonstrated its right to live, and has won the confidence of the denomination."

While the HMB certainly had made a remarkable recovery by the end of the nineteenth century, it was not without some serious difficulties in the first half of the twentieth century. Several suggestions for its radical alteration, even abolition, came as late as 1959; financial troubles, including an almost $1 million embezzlement by its treasurer, plagued the board until 1943; and controversial and courageous HMB leadership on social issues in the 1960s and 1970s made it suspect among many Southern Baptists. Withstanding all such difficulties, the board has coordinated and spearheaded diverse mission efforts of the SBC. Much of the Southern Baptist expansion in the United States since the middle of the century is due to the ministry of the HMB.

BIBLIOGRAPHY. R. A. Baker, *The Southern Baptist Convention and Its People* (1974); A. B. Rutledge, *Mission to America: A Century and a Quarter of Southern Baptist Home Missions* (1969).

W. B. Shurden

Homecomings. *See* CHURCH HOMECOMINGS.

Horton, Walter Marshall (1895-1966). Neoorthodox theologian. Born in Somerville, Massachusetts, Horton was educated at Harvard (B.A., 1917), Union Theological Seminary,* New York (B.D., 1920, S.T.M., 1923), and Columbia University (M.A., 1920; Ph.D., 1926). He also studied at the Sorbonne, the University of Strasbourg and the University of Marburg. Ordained a Baptist minister in 1919, Horton began his teaching career at Union Theological Seminary (1922-1925) but soon moved to Oberlin College Graduate School of Theology, where he spent the rest of his career as Fairchild Professor.

Horton began his active professional career amidst the transition from liberal thought to neoorthodox theology—or, as in the title of one of his books, *Realistic Theology* (1934). In 1931 he published *A Psychological Approach to Theology,* in which he analyzed religious experience in terms of its behavioral dimensions, integrating moral values and human development with traditional theological doctrines such as theism, sin, salvation and human destiny. Always aware of the limitations of psychology, Horton attempted to reconnect theology and the sciences in the wake of the disintegration of the liberal tradition after World War I. He is rightly regarded as a parent of the field of pastoral psychology.

Later, in the 1950s, Horton made a second important contribution in creating an ecumenical theology (*Christian Theology: An Ecumenical Approach*, 1955). Determining denominational theological education and theologies to be inadequate, he found in the universal necessity of religion and the commonality of Christian doctrinal expression a need for a more universal Christian faith. He believed, for instance, that the Christian unity of the Roman Catholic Church together with the Christian liberty of Protestantism provided a model for a historically valid ecumenical theology. A friend of Paul Tillich and Gustaf Aulén, Horton was also a leading advocate of the role and work of the World Council of Churches.* As one of the first proponents of the psychological basis for theology and as a vigorous advocate of an ecumenical approach to theological inquiry, Horton broke new ground in twentieth-century American theology.

BIBLIOGRAPHY. "The Man of the Month," *Pastoral Psychology* 7 (November 1956).

W. H. Brackney

Houghton, William Henry (1887-1947). Fundamentalist* Baptist minister and president of Moody Bible Institute. Born in South Boston, Massachusetts, Houghton was educated in Boston and Providence, Rhode Island. In 1901, at the age of fourteen, he was converted in an evangelistic meeting in Lynn, Massachusetts. In his earlier years he pursued an interest in music and drama, but in 1909, under the preaching of a Nazarene pastor, he was convicted of his life of disobedience, gave up his stage career and soon enrolled in Eastern Nazarene College. After no more than six months at college (c. 1910), he was invited by Reuben A. Torrey to be his evangelistic and Bible conference song leader. Torrey looked after his further instruction in the faith and served as his mentor in succeeding years.

Houghton was ordained a Baptist minister in 1915 and served churches in Canton (1915-1917), New Bethlehem (1918-1922) and Norristown (1922-1924), Pennsylvania. During his years at Bethlehem he published some successful tracts and began a short-lived periodical, *The Baptist Believer;* at Norristown he increasingly became involved in evangelistic endeavors. An evangelistic campaign in Ireland in 1924 was followed by further successful pastorates at the Baptist Tabernacle in Atlanta, Georgia (1925-1930), and Calvary Bap-

tist Church in New York City (1930-1934), where he succeeded John Roach Straton.* Finally, in 1934 he became president of Moody Bible Institute, where he succeeded James M. Gray.

At Moody he built up the faculty and student body (from 848 in 1934 to 1,428 in 1945) and edited and expanded the circulation of *Moody Monthly* (from 35,000 in 1934 to 75,000 in 1945). Houghton, with Irwin A. Moon, initiated the idea of a periodic meeting of Christians involved in science, which eventually became the American Scientific Affiliation. Moon carried out a novel form of evangelism called "sermons from science," which under Houghton's leadership developed into the Moody Institute of Science. Houghton was a passionate leader and tireless worker, and his years at Moody were a significant chapter in the institution's life. Houghton died in Los Angeles in 1947 after several months of coronary problems.

BIBLIOGRAPHY. W. M. Smith, *A Watchman on the Wall: The Life Story of Will H. Houghton* (1951).

D. G. Reid

Houston Baptist University. Baptist General Convention of Texas educational institution. Houston Baptist University (HBU) is the only Texas Baptist university started by the Baptist General Convention. Founded in 1960 as a liberal arts school twelve miles from downtown Houston, HBU has grown from a student body of 196 in 1963 to more than 2,400 in 1990.

President William H. Hinton led the 200-acre school for many years. HBU achieved full accreditation in 1968 and moved to university status in 1973. As the school grew, business, nursing and education programs were added. In 1990 HBU offered more than sixty undergraduate areas of study and six master's degrees.

President E. D. Hodo has committed the university to utilize the latest available educational technology. He manages a budget of more than $17 million and an endowment exceeding $28 million.

BIBLIOGRAPHY. *ESB* 4:2277; Baptist General Convention of Texas, *Texas Baptist Annual,* 1990.

R. Beck

Hovey, Alvah (1820-1903). Baptist educator. Hovey is best remembered for his far-ranging influence as an educator and president of the Newton Theological Institution* (now Andover Newton Theological School*). He was born in

Chenango County, New York, on March 5, 1820, but his family soon moved to Thetford, Vermont. When Hovey was sixteen he obtained permission from his father to leave home for further education. He eventually earned degrees from Dartmouth College and Newton Theological Institution.

In 1849 he was invited to join the faculty in Newton, where he began a fifty-four-year teaching career, during thirty of which he served as president (1868-1898). He was eclectic in his academic interests, teaching at one time or another church history, theology, ethics and biblical studies.

His published books include *Manual of Systematic Theology and Christian Ethics* (1877), *Manual of Christian Theology* (rev. ed. 1900), *God with Us* (1872), *Studies in Ethics and Religion* (1892), *A Memoir of the Life and Times of Isaac Backus* (1858) and *Barnas Sears, a Christian Educator: His Life and Work* (1902).

T. R. McKibbens

Howard College. *See* SAMFORD UNIVERSITY.

Howard Payne College. A Baptist coeducational college in Brownwood, Texas. The school was founded in June 1889 by the Pecan Valley Baptist Association, led by J. D. Robnett, pastor of First Baptist Church in Brownwood. Robnett secured a substantial gift from his brother-in-law Edward Howard Payne of Fulton, Missouri, and the college was named for that donor. The school opened its doors in 1890, and John D. Robnett Jr. was the first graduate in 1895.

The original seven acres of the campus has more than doubled and in 1992 included twenty-three permanent buildings. The Walker Memorial Library serves also as a selective U.S. government document depository; in 1992 it included over 45,000 items. In 1953 the Daniel Baker College was consolidated with Howard Payne, further enlarging the campus. In 1974 the trustees changed the name of the school to Howard Payne University.

Howard Payne University is noted for the Douglas MacArthur Academy of Freedom, providing honors courses for various career tracks, including military.

BIBLIOGRAPHY. B. M. Hitt, *History of Howard Payne College* (1951).

H. L. McBeth

Howell, Robert Boyte Crawford (1801-1868). Southern Baptist* pastor and denomina-

tional leader. Born in North Carolina and raised an Episcopalian, Howell became a Baptist in 1821. After attending Columbian College,* Washington, D.C., he entered the ministry, first as a pastor and later as a home missionary. In 1835 Howell became pastor of First Baptist Church, Nashville, Tennessee. That same year he began publication of *The Baptist,* a monthly periodical addressed primarily to Baptist churches in Tennessee.

Howell was one of the leading figures in the formation of the Southern Baptist Convention in 1845 and was its second president. A proponent of theological education among Baptists, he was instrumental in the founding of various Baptist institutions, including Southern Baptist Theological Seminary* (1859). Howell also addressed numerous controversies in Southern Baptist life and is best known for his opposition to the movement called Old Landmarkism* and its effort to trace Baptist churches directly to New Testament times. He wrote numerous books on Baptist history and theology, among them *The Cross* (1854), *The Early Baptists of Virginia* (1876) and *The Evils of Infant Baptism* (1854).

BIBLIOGRAPHY. J. W. Barton, *Road to Augusta: R. B. C. Howell and the Formation of the Southern Baptist Convention* (1976); *DAB* V.

B. J. Leonard

Huey, Mary Alice (1877-1960). Baptist missionary to China. Born February 25, 1877, in Jefferson County, Alabama, Huey was educated at Judson College* and in 1904 became one of the first students at the training school for women at Louisville, Kentucky (later Woman's Missionary Union Training School*). In July 1907 Huey was appointed by the Foreign Mission Board* of the Southern Baptist Convention* to serve in Laichow, China. She worked among the women and children of Laichow as the principal and Bible teacher at a girls' school. In 1926 Huey returned to the United States to care for her parents. She remained at home for six years and then returned to China to continue her work until 1940. During World War II the situation became extremely difficult for missionaries in China, and in 1941 Huey transferred to the Hawaiian Mission at Honolulu, where she carried out pioneer evangelistic work until her retirement in 1946. She died in Bessemer, Alabama, on April 16, 1960.

BIBLIOGRAPHY. V. Wingo, "Pioneers! O Pioneers!" *WMU Training School Alumnae Bulletin,* August 1947; *The Commission,* July 1960.

T. L. Scales

Hymnody, Baptist. Baptist immigrants in mid-seventeenth-century America were divided between the two traditions prevailing at the time in England: the Particular Baptists* (Calvinistic*) and the General Baptists* (Arminian*). Though English Particular Baptists were the first promoters of congregational hymn-singing, while the General Baptists forbade it, in America this distinction was not so firmly drawn. There is some evidence that these early Baptists may have sung from some of the various psalters then available: the Anglo-Genevan (1556 and later), Sternhold and Hopkins (1562 and later) and Ainsworth (1612). However, since the Baptists were subject to persecution at the hands of the New England ecclesiastical powers, it is unlikely that they made use of the *Bay Psalm Book* (1640).

Apart from psalters, Baptists sang from hymn collections brought from England. Among these was *Spiritual Melody* (1691) by the pioneering Benjamin Keach.* Elias Keach,* who arrived in America in 1686, shared his father's enthusiasm for singing in public worship. Welsh Baptists also, who immigrated to the middle colonies in the early eighteenth century, brought with them a strong singing tradition.

However, it was not until the later eighteenth century that Baptists began to compile their own hymnbooks. Their first publication was a 1762 reprint of a 1750 collection made in London by Benjamin Wallin. The first truly American Baptist hymnal, *Hymns and Spiritual Songs,* was published in Newport in 1766 by Samuel Hall.

Several other hymn collections by Baptists appeared before the turn of the century. Many, like *Baptismal Hymns* (1791), compiler unknown, were intended for singing at the administration of baptism.* Hymns for the Lord's Supper* were also a prominent feature of these early compilations. The Federal Period saw the ascendancy of the psalms and hymns of Isaac Watts, which achieved almost canonical status in the late eighteenth century. Baptist publications were salable only if they were promoted as supplements or appendices to Watts's works. John Rippon, leading London Baptist figure of his time, pastor, historian and publisher, released in 1787 *A Selection of Hymns from the Best Authors,* intended to be an *Appendix to Dr. Watts' Psalms and Hymns,* and its com-

panion tune book in 1793. This anthology became so popular that several reprints were made not only in England but also in the United States. Baptists in America thus became familiar with the vast store of British evangelical hymnody through "Rippon's Watts." In 1818 James Winchell, pastor of the First Baptist Church, Boston, published a collection that became known as "Winchell's Watts" and was widely used among New England Baptist churches. Few Baptists, however, wrote original hymns during this period. The works of those who did write were undistinguished, with the possible exception of the lyrics of colonial pastor John Leland.

Baptist associations began producing hymnals in the late eighteenth and early nineteenth centuries. The first of these voluntary groupings of cooperating churches, the Philadelphia Baptist Association,* authorized *A Selection of Psalms and Hymns* to be prepared by Samuel Jones* and Burgis Allison in 1790. In 1828 the large Dover Association (Virginia) asked Andrew Broaddus* to compile *The Dover Selection of Spiritual Songs.* In a second edition Broaddus included an appendix of representative hymns by Wesley, Montgomery, Newton and others, in addition to those by Baptists such as Fawcett, Medley and Stennett.

During the nineteenth century Baptist creativity was evident along two lines of development: folk hymnody appearing in shape-note tune books and Sunday-school songs and gospel hymns produced in songsters and "juvenile" collections. The first stream is represented by three prominent shape-note tune books, *The Southern Harmony* (1835) compiled by William "Singing Billy" Walker, *The Sacred Harp* (1844) by Benjamin Franklin White and E. J. King, and *The Social Harp* (1855) by John G. McGurry—the compilers of all three being Baptists. The Sunday-school hymn and gospel song stream was fed by several Baptists, many of whom were composers as well as compilers of collections. The principal figures were William B. Bradbury (China, "Jesus Loves Me"), Woodworth, ("Just As I Am Without One Plea"), Robert Lowry (Hanson Place, "Shall We Gather at the River"), Philip P. Bliss (Wonderful Words, "Sing Them Over Again to Me") and William Howard Doane, known for his tunes to Fanny Crosby texts ("Near the Cross," "I Am Thine," "To God Be the Glory").

Other Baptist hymnists of the "romantic century" include Lydia Baxter ("Take the Name of Jesus with You"), Annie Sherwood Hawks ("I

Need Thee Every Hour"), Sylvanus Dryden Phelps ("Saviour, Thy Dying Love") and Samuel F. Smith ("The Morning Light Is Breaking"; "My Country, 'Tis of Thee").

The first important Baptist denominational hymnals were *The Psalmist** (1843) and *The Baptist Hymnal* (1883), both published in Philadelphia by the American Baptist Publication Society.* These were large books, the goals of which were to appeal to Baptist worshipers in both the Northern and Southern regions of a divided denomination. Both set high standards but failed to reach their goal because of broad differences in the worship styles of the two regions. *Baptist Psalmody* (Charleston, 1850), published by the Southern Baptist Publication Society as the first hymn collection for the Southern Baptist Convention,* was edited by Basil Manly Sr.* and Basil Manly Jr.* to meet the needs of Southern churches.

Greatly affected in their hymn-singing habits and repertoire by revivalism, Southern Baptists became increasingly active in hymnbook publishing and gospel-song production in the twentieth century. A major contribution toward bringing Southern Baptists into the mainstream of hymnody was *The Baptist Hymn and Praise Book* (1904), edited by Lansing Burroughs. This trend was continued when *The New Baptist Hymnal* was released jointly by the Northern and Southern publishing houses in 1926; however, it failed to gain widespread acceptance in the South.

Southern Baptist tastes were more fairly represented by the song collections of Robert Coleman, a Baptist layman publishing in Dallas, and by *The Broadman Hymnal* (1940), edited by B. B. McKinney, gospel-song writer and denominational executive. *The Broadman Hymnal,* made up predominantly of gospel songs, brought a degree of unanimity to the congregational singing of Southern Baptists. At the same time Northern Baptists joined with the Christian Churches (Disciples of Christ) in publishing *Christian Worship* (1941) and *Hymnbook for Christian Worship* (1970). Both reflected mainline ecumenical hymnody but made little Baptist contribution to it and showed limited concern for gospel hymnody.

In the latter half of the twentieth century Southern Baptists produced three hymnals that were widely accepted throughout the denomination and beyond: *Baptist Hymnal* (1956), edited by W. Hines Sims, *Baptist Hymnal* (1975), edited by William J. Reynolds, and *The Baptist Hymnal** (1991), edited by Wesley L. Forbis. Each of these hymnals reflected the influence of changes in musical worship styles and tastes of its times and sought to keep pace with the varied needs of an increasingly diverse denomination. This was partially accomplished by their inclusion of a constantly growing number of Baptist text and tune writers. However, no Southern Baptist text or tune has become a part of the common repertoire of the major denominations. The most widely known twentieth-century hymn by a Baptist is without doubt Harry Emerson Fosdick's* "God of Grace and God of Glory."

Baptists may have made their greatest contribution to hymnody by their labors in the field of hymnology. The presence in the late twentieth century of several Baptist scholars active in this field may point to the realm of the most potent influence of Baptists in the wider world of Christian hymnody.

BIBLIOGRAPHY. *ESB* 1:661-62, 3:1765-67, 4:2280-81; H. L. Eskew, "Southern Baptist Contributions to Hymnody," *BHH* 19 (January 1984):27-35; W. L. Hooper, *Church Music in Transition* (1963); W. J. Reynolds, "Baptist Hymnody in America," in *Handbook to the Baptist Hymnal* (1992); P. A. Richardson, "Baptist Contributions to Hymnody and Hymnology," *RE* 87 (Winter 1990):59-74.   H. T. McElrath

I

Ide, George B. (1804-1872). Distinguished Baptist clergyman. Reared in Vermont, he was the son of a Baptist pastor. Graduating from Middlebury College, having become a religious skeptic, he aspired to a career in law. However, influenced by his earlier home environment, Christian friends and evangelical preaching, he was converted, felt called to the ministry and was ordained. He became a popular preacher, noted for eloquence, revivalistic fervor and intellectual gifts.

After pastorates in Vermont, Albany and Boston, he went to First Baptist Church, Philadelphia,* for fourteen years. Called then to First Baptist Church, Springfield, Massachusetts, he served there for twenty years until his death. An ardent proponent of missions,* education, Sunday schools and other progressive movements, he was noted for his role in expanding the General Tract Society into the American Baptist Publication Society,* as a mediator between proslavery and antislavery parties in the Triennial Convention,* and as author of several books.

BIBLIOGRAPHY. *BE.*

N. H. Maring

Independent Baptists. A collection of fiercely autonomous local congregations, fundamentalist* in theology, Baptist in polity, and separatist in their response to denominational and ecclesiastical relations. While Baptist churches historically have reflected a high degree of congregational autonomy, the independent Baptist movement is a fairly recent phenomenon developing out of the fundamentalist-modernist controversy of the early twentieth century. Among its early leaders were J. Frank Norris,* W. B. Riley* and T. T. Shields.* Rejecting denominational organizations as modernistic and unscriptural, these persons helped form loosely organized "fellowships" for mutual encouragement and spiritual support. These organizations included the Baptist Bible Fellowship,* the Baptist Bible Union,* the Southwide Baptist Fellowship,* the World Baptist Fellowship* and the General Association of Regular Baptist Churches.*

The World Baptist Fellowship has its antecedents in Norris's battles with the Southern Baptist Convention* and his founding of the Premillennial, Fundamental Missionary Fellowship in 1931. The Baptist Bible Fellowship was established in May 1950 out of a split between Norris and his followers over control of the Bible Baptist Seminary,* a Bible school founded in First Baptist Church, Fort Worth, Texas. While these groups are spread throughout the United States, they are concentrated in the Fort Worth-Dallas area, Springfield, Missouri, and the Southern states.

The local congregation is the center of the independent Baptist movement and is the primary source of ecclesiastical authority. Independent churches reject denominations as a threat to congregational autonomy. Theologically the churches are fundamentalist, affirming the inerrancy* of Holy Scripture, the virgin birth, the substitutionary atonement and the bodily resurrection of Christ. Premillennial* eschatology is also an important tenet. Churches emphasize the need for biblical separatism, distancing themselves from any persons or communions that are not themselves fundamentalist and independent. They reject mission* boards and fund missionaries only through local churches. They also renounce other denominational elements such as stewardship campaigns, Sunday-school literature and bureaucratic organizations. Their ecclesiology is generally Landmark* in orientation, centered in the idea that the New Testament church is known only in its local expression. They deny that Baptists are Protestants and claim to trace their lineage back to John the Baptist.

Independent Baptists are highly evangelistic, promoting revival campaigns and large Sunday schools. Many independent churches claim huge memberships. These include First Baptist Church, Hammond, Indiana; Tennessee Temple Baptist Church, Knoxville, Tennessee; and Thomas Road Baptist Church, Lynchburg, Virginia. The latter church was founded by Jerry Falwell and became the center of his widely known television ministry. Independent Baptist ministers tend to dominate churches through authoritarian leadership and charismatic personality.

Independent Baptists have made extensive use of the media—radio, television and newspapers—to promote their causes. Their newspapers provide spiritual guidance, news and commentary for circulation throughout their congregations. These periodicals have included *The Sword of the Lord, The Baptist Bible Tribune* and *The Fundamentalist.*

In certain regions, particularly Appalachia, independent Baptist churches are those that exist entirely unto themselves with no other ecclesiastical ties and relationships.

BIBLIOGRAPHY. J. O. Combs, ed., *Roots and Origins of Baptist Fundamentalism* (1984); G. Dollar, *A History of Fundamentalism in America* (1973); B. J. Leonard, "Independent Baptists: From Sectarian Minority to 'Moral Majority,' " *CH,* December 1987.   B. J. Leonard

"Inerrancy Controversy," SBC. The longest and most serious internal denominational conflict ever suffered by the Southern Baptist Convention* (SBC). Two factions, fundamentalists* and moderates, polarized the SBC from 1979 to 1990, and results linger to the present. With numerous antecedents, the conflict began in earnest on June 12-14, 1979, at the annual meeting of the SBC in Houston, Texas. Three fundamentalist leaders emerged at that meeting and skillfully guided the fundamentalists to triumph over moderates for twelve years. Those three were Paige Patterson, then president of Criswell Center for Biblical Studies in Dallas, Texas (*see* Criswell College); Paul Pressler, a layman from Houston, Texas; and Adrian Rogers, pastor of Bellevue Baptist Church in Memphis, Tennessee. Each served a crucial role in the fundamentalist victory. Patterson, a professor, was the theological architect; Pressler, a judge, was the political strategist; and Rogers, an effective and popular preacher without whom the fundamentalists might never have won, stirred to action mass SBC audiences.

Beginning in the spring of 1979, Pressler and Patterson designed and announced a ten-year plan whereby fundamentalists could gain control of the SBC. Garnering a following by proclaiming that liberalism had invaded the entire denominational system—seminaries, colleges, universities, publication agencies, denominational press—they discovered that they could use the appointive powers of the SBC presidency to dominate the denomination. Following the 1979 election of Rogers as SBC president, every one of the seven presidents through the election in 1990 was a fundamentalist who used presidential powers to stack the boards of all trustee agencies, something never before done in SBC history. By 1990 virtually every SBC agency's board of trustees was dominated by hard-line fundamentalists. While the political key to the fundamentalist victory was the election of the SBC president and subsequent trustee appointments, the rallying cry was "the inerrancy of the Bible"—hence the popular name of the controversy. The strife focused, however, on far more than the nature or interpretation of the Bible. One issue, generic in character, hung as a colossal canopy over all the contention. That issue was "control versus freedom"—no new conflict in Baptist history. Fundamentalists argued for stricter controls in light of what they believed was too much freedom, while their moderate counterparts lobbied for freedom in the face of what they thought was a non-Baptistic and paralyzing control. This central issue could also be described as "conformity versus liberty" or "uniformity versus diversity." Fundamentalists were more interested in theological conformity and denominational uniformity, while moderates were more interested in liberty of conscience and denominational diversity.

The "control versus freedom" war played itself out in numerous smaller battles. Biblically, the two groups disputed the nature and interpretation of the Bible; theologically, they wrangled over the role of women and pastoral authority; educationally, they argued over both the content and the methodology of theological education; ethically, they disagreed over the implications of religious liberty* and the separation of church and state, particularly as those principles related to prayer in public schools and related national issues; historically and denominationally, they disputed the place of creedalism in Baptist life, the intent and purpose of the SBC, and the freedom or control of the denominational press and the denominational publishing agency; and missiologically, they differed over theological credentials for appointment and the vocational purposes of missionaries. The contrasts could be extended into national politics and other areas.

The results have been (1) a clear win for the fundamentalists, with solid control over all SBC agencies, (2) the exclusion of moderates from all SBC boards and their sure eventual elimination from SBC agencies, (3) the establishment by moderates of new entities such as the Southern Baptist Alliance* in 1987 and the Cooperative Baptist Fellowship* in 1990 (the latter organization containing all the signs of an emerging denomination), (4) the development of new moderate theological seminaries, a publishing agency, an ethics agency and other non-SBC enterprises, (5) the removal of the conflict from the SBC to the state convention level and (6) some signs of institutional decline within the SBC.

See also INERRANCY DEBATE.

BIBLIOGRAPHY. N. T. Ammerman, *Baptist Battles* (1990); J. C. Hefley, *The Conservative Resurgence in the Southern Baptist Convention* (1991); R. James, ed., *The Takeover in the Southern Baptist Convention* (1989); B. J. Leonard, *God's Last and Only Hope: The Fragmentation of the Southern Baptist Convention* (1990).

W. B. Shurden

Inerrancy Debate, Evangelical. One of the most vexing controversies within conservative Protestantism since World War II has focused on the doctrine of biblical inerrancy. In 1949 the Evangelical Theological Society, which gathered academics from various denominational backgrounds, established as its doctrinal basis the inerrancy of the Bible in the original autographs. In the 1950s fundamentalists, most evangelicals and for that matter most Roman Catholics upheld the inerrancy of the Bible. By this they meant that the Bible, when correctly interpreted, is "truthful" regardless of the topic it broaches, whether in the area of doctrine and ethics or that of history and the natural world.

As late as 1975 Martin Marty observed that evangelicals and fundamentalists viewed biblical inerrancy as one of their essential doctrines. A year later, however, Harold Lindsell published *The Battle for the Bible* (1976), in which he chronicled what he believed were defections from the doctrine of biblical inerrancy at evangelical colleges and seminaries. In the late 1950s a small number of evangelical scholars had become uncomfortable with the doctrine, believing that the Bible does in fact contain material errors. They claimed that the doctrine's defenders often practiced a particularly wooden ("literal") exegesis and relied on deductive logic rather than on inductive study of the texts of Scripture to prove their case.

In 1967 Fuller Theological Seminary removed the doctrine of biblical inerrancy from its statement of faith. In response to Lindsell's book, Jack Rogers of Fuller edited *Biblical Authority* (1977) and later, with Donald McKim (now of Memphis Theological Seminary), wrote *The Authority and Interpretation of the Bible: An Historical Approach* (1979). In the latter volume the authors argued that the doctrine of biblical inerrancy had been created in the last decades of the seventeenth century. In 1980 George Marsden proposed that the doctrine had been greatly shaped by the commitment of professors at Princeton Theological Seminary to Common Sense philosophy and that its particular late-nineteenth-century configuration became a defining characteristic of fundamentalism. Critics of the doctrine essayed to demonstrate that Christians of earlier centuries had believed in the Bible's *infallibility*, defined as its capacity to lead us to salvation and right living, but not in its *inerrancy*.

As a foil for these developments, conservatives in the Lutheran Church—Missouri Synod who favored the doctrine of inerrancy gained control of their denomination in the 1970s. In the same decade the International Council of Biblical Inerrancy was established to defend the doctrine. This council held a series of academic and lay conferences and commissioned a series of volumes. It drew up "The Chicago Statement on Biblical Inerrancy" (1978), which was published in the volume *Inerrancy* (1979). This statement represented for large numbers of evangelicals a responsible exposition of the doctrine. In other publications, scholars such as J. I. Packer, Kenneth Kantzer and D. A. Carson argued that the doctrine of biblical inerrancy, carefully defined, represents what the Bible teaches about itself and what the "central tradition" of the Christian churches has maintained. In the late 1980s conservatives in the Southern Baptist Convention* met with success in their attempt to gain control of the convention. They were determined to bring the doctrine of biblical inerrancy back into more prominence in Southern Baptist seminaries. Thus the debate regarding biblical inerrancy showed few signs of slackening at the end of the 1980s.

See also INERRANCY CONTROVERSY, SBC.

BIBLIOGRAPHY. N. Geisler, ed., *Inerrancy* (1979); H. Lindsell, *The Battle for the Bible* (1976); G. Marsden, *Reforming Fundamentalism* (1987); J. Rogers, ed., *Biblical Authority* (1977); J. Rogers and D. McKim, *The Authority and Interpretation of the Bible: An Historical Approach* (1979); J. D. Woodbridge, *Biblical Authority: A Critique of the Rogers/McKim Proposal* (1982).

J. D. Woodbridge

Invitation, Baptist Use of. The "invitation" is that time in evangelical revivals and worship services when individuals are invited to make specific "decisions for Christ" and declare those decisions publicly. The invitation evolved from certain nineteenth-century revivalistic practices such as the "anxious bench" and the "altar call," occasions in which sinners were asked to make public their struggles with sin and search for conversion. The anxious bench was identified with the revivalistic "new measures" of evangelist Charles G. Finney. Altar calls or invitations were also associated with the evangelistic campaigns of Dwight L. Moody, Billy Sunday and Billy Graham.

In Baptist churches, the earliest invitations were probably incorporated into the seasonal protracted revival meetings. Sinners were called to make a public profession of faith in Christ prior to receiving Christian baptism.* So powerful was this act as a way of identifying salvation that many Baptists describe their conversion with such phrases as "when I walked the aisle," "when I came forward," "when I shook the preacher's hand." Invitations were also extended to other spiritual decisions, including the "rededication" of life by professing Christians, the decision to join a particular church and the decision to enter "full-time Christian service" as a minister or missionary. Invitations are usually given at the end of the worship service during the singing of a hymn.

BIBLIOGRAPHY. B. J. Leonard, "Getting Saved in America: Conversion Event in a Pluralistic Culture," *RE,* Winter 1981; H. L. McBeth, *The Baptist Heritage* (1987).

B. J. Leonard

J

Jackson, Joseph Harrison (1900-1990). African-American Baptist clergyman and president of the National Baptist Convention U.S.A., Inc. (NBC; see National Baptists). Born in Rudyard, Mississippi, on September 11, 1900, Jackson graduated from Jackson State College (B.A., 1926), Colgate Rochester Divinity School* (B.D., 1932) and Creighton University (M.A., 1933).

Jackson assumed the pastorate of First Baptist Church in McComb, Mississippi, in 1922. He became pastor of Bethel Baptist Church in Omaha (1926-1934) and then was pastor of Monumental Baptist Church in Philadelphia while serving as corresponding secretary of the NBC's Foreign Mission Board (1934-1941). He also served as pastor of the historic Olivet Baptist Church (1941-1990) in Chicago.

But Jackson's greatest work was as president of the NBC (1953-1982). He was president during the civil rights era and openly criticized Martin Luther King Jr.* and the civil rights movement. Jackson argued for "preparation over protest" and believed that litigation was the best strategy. In 1961 the situation led to a split in the NBC and the founding of the Progressive National Baptist Convention (see National Baptists).

Jackson was also a member of the executive committee of the Baptist World Alliance.* He was the author of several books: *Stars in the Night* (1950), *The Eternal Flame* (1956), *Many But One* (1964) and *A Story of Christian Activism* (1980). On August 18, 1990, he died in Chicago after a brief illness.

BIBLIOGRAPHY. W. H. Brackney, *The Baptists* (1988); *ERS*; P. Paris, *Black Leaders in Conflict: Joseph H. Jackson, Martin Luther King Jr., Malcolm X, Adam Clayton Powell Jr.* (1978).

L. H. Williams

Jackson, Mahalia (1911-1972). African-American gospel singer. Born in New Orleans, the daughter of a Baptist minister, she was reared in a home in which only sacred music was permitted. As a child she sang in the choir at Mt. Moriah Baptist Church. In 1927 she moved to Chicago, joined the Greater Salem Baptist Church choir and became a soloist.

Jackson struggled during the Depression to develop her career. Her musical style was influenced by the emotionalism of her New Orleans Baptist upbringing and the percussion instruments used in Sanctified church worship. For this reason, initially her gospel music was rejected by prominent Baptist churches, especially in the North, where it was considered too jazzy. But her career was invigorated by singing before the National Baptist Convention (see National Baptists) in St. Louis and Indiana, which led to more invitations. In 1934 she made her first gospel recording. In 1954 her next recording, *Move On Up a Little Higher,* brought national fame. It was the first gospel record to sell a million copies. Her first concert in Carnegie Hall (1950) was a sellout, and she toured Europe with much success. In 1963 she sang "I Been 'Buked and I Been Scorned" during the March on Washington. Jackson died in 1972 and was buried in New Orleans.

BIBLIOGRAPHY. *EBA;* M. Jackson with E. M. Wylie, *Movin' On Up* (1966).

L. H. Williams

Jacob, Henry (1563-1624). English dissenter and Independent. Jacob was the leader of an Independent congregation that formed in London in 1616 and from which the origins of Calvinistic* Baptists in England in the seventeenth century may be traced. Prior to 1616 Jacob appears to have been among the Separatists who took refuge in Leiden and may have come under the influence of John Robinson. He served the church in London for six years (1616-1622) before resigning to move to Virginia, where he died in 1624.

BIBLIOGRAPHY. H. H. Brackney, ed., *Baptist Life and Thought (1600-1980)* (1983); H. L. McBeth,

A Sourcebook for Baptist Heritage (1990); R. G. Torbet, *A History of the Baptists*, 3rd ed. (1980); B. R. White, *The English Baptists of the Seventeenth Century* (1983).

K. Smith

Jacobs, Benjamin Franklin (1834-1902). Leader in the Sunday School movement.* Born in New Jersey, Jacobs spent most of his life in Chicago. A Baptist layman, produce dealer and real estate entrepreneur, Jacobs served throughout his life as a Sunday-school superintendent. Locally he helped organize a mission Sunday school, the Chicago YMCA and city and state Sunday-school associations. Nationally, he was the organizing genius of the national Sunday-school convention system and the uniform lesson curriculum system, serving on both the convention executive committee and the lesson committee. Jacobs had a vision of uniting churches around the world through weekly study of the same Sunday-school lesson. Internationally, he helped to found the World's Sunday School Convention system in 1889 and served on its executive committee as both a president and a U.S. secretary.

J. L. Seymour

Jasper, John (1812-1901). A prominent African-American Baptist slave preacher. Born in the Tidewater area of Virginia, he served as a slave for fifty years, twenty-five of those as a preacher. His father, Phillip, had also been a slave preacher. Jasper possessed no formal education, but he could read the Bible. Jasper began preaching in 1839. His slave job required him to work as a steamer in a Richmond tobacco factory, and so he could only preach upon the permission of his master. Nevertheless, he gained fame as a preacher at funerals, which among slaves were festive occasions, and he pastored two Sundays a month in Petersburg. Whenever he preached, large crowds of both races came to hear him. When he became a free man, he started Sixth Mount Zion Baptist Church in Richmond. He later erected a new building, contributed $3,000 of his own money and developed a membership of over 2,000. During his pastorate (1865-1901), Jasper's church was the center of black religious life in Richmond.

Jasper's popularity increased tremendously after slavery. Delivered without notes and in dialect, his sermons seldom exceeded fifty minutes. In his most famous sermon, "The Sun Do Move,"

based on Joshua 10, he described a geocentric universe with four corners and the Lord holding the sun still. William E. Hatcher, a white admirer, wrote a biography entitled *John Jasper: The Unmatched Philosopher and Preacher* (1908). However, college-trained black ministers viewed Jasper as an anachronism.

BIBLIOGRAPHY. W. H. Brackney, *The Baptists* (1988); W. E. Hatcher, *John Jasper: The Unmatched Philosopher and Preacher* (1908).

L. H. Williams

Jemison, David Vivian (1875-1954). African-American Baptist minister and president of National Baptist Convention U.S.A., Inc. (*see* National Baptists). Born in 1875 in Marion, Alabama, Jemison was the son of a former slave. He graduated from Selma University (B.D., 1903), and Emerson Institute (1914) in New York City. He was ordained a Baptist minister in 1898, and in 1903 he became pastor of the Tabernacle Baptist church in Selma, where he served for forty-four years. In 1916 Jemison was elected president of the Alabama Colored Baptist State Convention, a position he retained until his death. From 1931 to 1940 he served as vice president of the National Baptist Convention (NBC). In 1940 Jemison assumed the presidency of the NBC. He also served as a vice president of the Baptist World Alliance* (1950-1954).

Jemison took a strong stand in favor of civil rights. In 1953 his son Theodore led the first national black bus boycott in Baton Rouge, Louisiana. This son became president of the NBC in 1982. In 1953 the elder Jemison resigned as president because of age and poor health, and in 1954 he died.

BIBLIOGRAPHY. W. E. Dinkins, "Divine Purpose and Doctor Jemison," *NBV* 8 (March 1959); S. N. Reid, *History of Colored Baptists in Alabama* (1949).

L. H. Williams

Jessey, Henry (1601-1663). English minister and Independent. Jessey served as pastor of an Independent congregation in London which Henry Jacob had served and to which it is believed the origins of the earliest Calvinistic* Baptists in London may be traced. A Cambridge graduate, he was ordained and succeeded John Lathrop as pastor of the London congregation in 1637. In 1638 some members of the congregation, including Richard Blunt, appear to have decided in favor of believer's baptism strictly by immersion, and by 1640 some members left the congregation and formed another. Jessey was baptized by Hansard Knollys in 1645. It appears, however, that while he was pastor the congregation practiced open membership, allowing both those who had been immersed as adults and those who had been baptized as infants to be members. He wrote several treatises, including *The Lord's Loud Call to England* (1660), which discusses the lack of religious toleration in England during the period.

BIBLIOGRAPHY. J. Ivimey, *A History of the English Baptists* (1811); M. R. Watts, *The Dissenters* (1978); B. R. White, *The English Baptists of the Seventeenth Century* (1983); W. T. Whitley, *A Baptist Bibliography,* vol. 1 (1916).

K. Smith

Jeter, Jeremiah Bell (1802-1880). Southern Baptist* pastor, editor and denominational leader. Born in Bedford County, Virginia, Jeter was converted and baptized during a local revival in 1821 and soon began to preach. Although he was self-taught as a minister, Jeter was a very effective pastor of several large churches, including the First Baptist Church, Richmond, Virginia, where he served for more than thirteen years.

Jeter was also a leading denominational activist. He was involved in the organization of the Baptist General Association of Virginia, attended meetings of the Triennial Convention* and was present at the formation of the Southern Baptist Convention* in 1845. Jeter opposed the efforts of the antimissionary* forces among the Baptists, and he served as the first president of the Foreign Mission Board* of the Southern Baptist Convention (1845-1849).

In his later years Jeter purchased and edited the *Religious Herald,* an influential Virginia Baptist paper. He was an ardent if amiable controversialist, and although he had a personal aversion to slavery, he defended it on the basis of biblical precedent. Jeter also wrote a popular refutation of the views of Alexander Campbell,* *Campbellism Examined* (1855). Jeter was a strong supporter of Richmond College and served, at the time of his death, as president of the board of trustees of the Southern Baptist Theological Seminary.*

BIBLIOGRAPHY. *DAB* V; W. F. Hatcher, *Life of J. B. Jeter* (1887); J. B. Jeter, *Recollections of a Long Life* (1891).

T. F. George

Johnson, Charles Oscar (1886-1965). Baptist

minister. Born in Tennessee and educated at Carson-Newman College* in Jefferson City (B.A., 1910) and Southern Baptist Theological Seminary* (Th.M., 1920), Johnson was ordained in 1909. In 1910 he began the first in a series of pastorates that took him to Baptist churches in Newport Beach (1910-1911) and Los Angeles (1911-1915), California; Campbellsburg, Kentucky (1915-1920); and Tacoma, Washington (1920-1931). Johnson's final pastorate was at Third Baptist Church, St. Louis, Missouri (1931-1958), which under his leadership grew by over 10,000 members.

During his years in St. Louis, Johnson was president of the Metropolitan Church Federation (1936) and served on the city school board (1946-1949). In addition to serving as first vice president of the Southern Baptist Convention* and president of the Northern Baptist Convention (*see* American Baptist Churches in the USA), he was president of the Baptist World Alliance* (1947-1952). Johnson spent the final years of his career as a faculty member of Berkeley Divinity School in California (1958-1960). His sermons were published in five volumes (1953-1958).

B. A. McKenzie

Johnson, William Bishop (1858-?). Black Baptist pastor and denominational administrator. Born in Toronto, Canada, on December 11, 1858, Johnson graduated from normal school (1874) in Toronto, and Wayland Seminary (1879). Baptized at Queen Street Baptist Church in Toronto (1872) and ordained (1879), he assumed the pastorate of First Baptist Church in Frederick, Maryland. Later he accepted the pastorate of Second Baptist Church (1883) in Washington, D.C., which under his leadership became one of the leading churches in the area.

Johnson is best known for his leadership in the founding of the National Baptist Convention (NBC; *see* National Baptists). In 1891 he organized the National Baptist Education Convention,* which in 1895 became the Educational Board of the newly organized NBC. As director, he federated black-owned Baptist schools, gathered educational data, assessed property value and collected $618,333 for their support. However, he resigned this position in 1903. In 1893 he became managing editor of the *National Baptist Magazine* (1894-1901), the first official organ of the NBC.

BIBLIOGRAPHY. W. B. Johnson, *The Scourging of*

a Race (1915); J. M. Washington, *Frustrated Fellowship: The Black Baptist Quest for Social Justice* (1986).   L. H. Williams

Johnson, William Bullein (1782-1862). Southern Baptist* minister and leader. Born on John's Island, South Carolina, Johnson had little formal schooling but was self-educated—even in law. In 1814 he was awarded an honorary M.A. by Brown University. After his conversion in 1804, Johnson became convinced he should enter the ministry. He was ordained in 1806 and became pastor of Eutaw Baptist Church.

Throughout Johnson's several pastorates he maintained an active interest in education, serving as headmaster of a number of schools and as chancellor of the Johnson Female University (1853-1858). He was also one of the founders of Furman Academy and Theological Institution (later Furman University*), from which would come the Southern Baptist Theological Seminary.*

His interest in Baptist missions* led him to suggest the first meeting of the General Baptist Missionary Convention, which was held in Philadelphia. As a result of this meeting the Triennial Convention* was formed, of which he served as president from 1841 to 1844. When a number of Baptists in the South decided to separate from the General Missionary Convention and the American Baptist Home Mission Society,* Johnson led in organizing the Southern Baptist Convention and devised a plan incorporating the associational structure of cooperation rather than the society plan followed in the North.

According to this plan, the Southern Baptist Convention would meet every three years, just as the General Convention did. Originally there were only two boards, a Foreign* and a Home Mission Board,* to which other boards could be added. Johnson has somewhat inaccurately been called the "Father of the Southern Baptist Convention," but there is little doubt that he was the major architect of the Southern Baptist Convention and was its most important spokesman as well as its first president.

See also Southern Baptist Convention.

BIBLIOGRAPHY. R. A. Baker, *The Southern Baptist Convention and Its People, 1607-1972* (1974); *DAB* V; *ESB* 1.   W. R. Estep

Jones, John William (1836-1909). Baptist minister, Confederate soldier and author. Born,

raised and educated in Virginia, Jones graduated from the University of Virginia and later studied at Southern Baptist Theological Seminary.* Soon after his ordination in 1860, he was appointed a missionary to China by the Southern Baptist* denomination. His departure was delayed, however, by the outbreak of the Civil War. When Virginia seceded, he enlisted as a private in the Confederate Army. He saw service in the ranks for a year and then did duty as both regiment chaplain and missionary chaplain. In his volume *Christ in the Camp* (1877) he recorded the history of the famous revival services that swept through Lee's army during the winter of 1862-1863.

During the years following the war he held several pastorates, served as chaplain of Washington College and was an agent for the Southern Baptist Theological Seminary in Louisville. Though ill-health afflicted him in his latter years, he continued to write, lecture and labor in various ways to keep alive interest in the history of the Confederacy.

BIBLIOGRAPHY. *DAB* V.   R. R. Mathisen

Jones, Samuel (1735-1814). Baptist pastor, educator and associational leader. Born in Glamorganshire, Wales, he came with his parents to America in 1737. He graduated from the College of Philadelphia (M.A., 1762). The College of Pennsylvania awarded him the D.D. degree (1788). Ordained on January 8, 1763, he became pastor in the Philadelphia Baptist Association* of the Southampton Church until 1770, and then of Pennepack or Lower Dublin Baptist Church until his death on February 7, 1814.

Jones established in Lower Dublin an academy (1765-1795) that taught classical and theological studies. He also remodeled the draft of the charter of Rhode Island College and wrote a new treatise of discipline for the Philadelphia Association in 1798. Along with the Reverend David Jones and Burgiss Allison, he compiled a collection of hymns for use in the churches. Jones also wrote on various other doctrinal, historical and political subjects.

BIBLIOGRAPHY. *BE; * E. C. Starr, *BB* (1967).   S. A. Yarbrough

Jordan, Clarence (1912-1969). Founder of Koinonia Farm.* Born in Talbotton, Georgia, Jordan studied agriculture at the University of Georgia (B.S., 1933) but resigned his ROTC commission to become a licensed Baptist minister.

While studying at Southern Baptist Theological Seminary* (Th.M., 1936; Ph.D., 1939), Jordan developed strong convictions in favor of pacifism, racial equality and communal living. As director of Sunshine Center in Louisville, he was among the earliest white clergymen to minister to inner-city blacks. In 1942, in company with Martin English, Jordan founded Koinonia Farm on 400 acres near Americus, Georgia. The farm was established as a racially integrated witness of Christian community, brotherhood and peace. Koinonia (Greek for "fellowship") taught local farmers scientific techniques and prospered until its opposition to the postwar draft and racial prejudice brought its members expulsion from the Rehobeth Baptist Church in 1950.

For a decade after 1956 Koinonia suffered from an economic boycott as well as physical violence from its opponents. Jordan's response to the segregated South was his Cotton Patch Version of the New Testament, published in four volumes (1968-1973)—the New Testament translated into Southern vernacular and setting. In 1968 Jordan and Millard Fuller reorganized Koinonia Farm as Koinonia Partners, noted for its Fund for Humanity that provides interest-free capital for low-cost housing.

BIBLIOGRAPHY. J. Hollyday, "The Legacy of Clarence Jordan," *Soj* 8 (December 1979):10-19; D. Lee, *The Cotton Patch Evidence: The Story of Clarence Jordan and the Koinonia Experiment* (1971). D. E. Pitzer

Journeycake, Charles (1817-1894). Baptist statesman of Delaware Indians. Charles Journeycake was born on December 16, 1817, in Upper Sandusky, Ohio. Influenced by his mother, the only Delaware Christian for several decades because of an Indian massacre in 1782, he was converted at the age of sixteen (August 11, 1833) and baptized by the Isaac McCoy mission. He was the first Delaware baptized west of the Mississippi and, according to his biographer, the first Protestant baptized in Kansas.

Journeycake served as an assistant chief beginning in 1855, and subsequently he served as the principal (and last) chief of the Delawares from 1861 to his death. He functioned as an important Indian statesman, making twenty-four trips to Washington, D.C.

Journeycake began preaching soon after his conversion. In 1871 he organized the Delaware Baptist Church at Alluwe, Indian Territory. Journeycake translated and compiled a hymnbook and also translated tracts. His career included itinerant preaching to several different tribes of native Americans. He died on January 3, 1894, in Alluwe.

BIBLIOGRAPHY. H. M. Roark, *Charles Journeycake: Indian Statesman and Christian Leader* (1948). C. D. Weaver

Judson, Adoniram (1788-1850). Pioneer missionary to Burma. Born in Malden, Massachusetts, the son of a Congregational minister, Judson graduated from Brown University* (B.A., 1807) and underwent a profound spiritual experience while attending Andover Theological Seminary* (B.D., 1810). He participated in the formation of the nation's first foreign missionary agency, the American Board of Commissioners for Foreign Missions (ABCFM), and was among the first contingent to go overseas. Judson, with his bride, Ann Hasseltine Judson,* sailed for India in 1812. En route they became convinced of the correctness of the doctrine of baptism* by immersion, and they were baptized shortly after their arrival in Calcutta. Their consequent disassociation from the ABCFM led to the organization of the American Baptist Missionary Union* and their expulsion from India.

Circumstances led to their taking up work in Rangoon, Burma, where Judson, despite restrictive government policies, succeeded in gathering a small group of converts while beginning the difficult task of mastering the language and translating the Scriptures. In 1824 he was imprisoned when war broke out between England and Burma. For twenty-one months he suffered intolerable confinement and deprivation, facing the possibility of imminent death and the knowledge of his wife's hardships, including the unattended birth of their child, smallpox and severe tropical fevers. Ann Judson died in 1826, not long after Judson's release. In 1834 Judson married Sarah Boardman Judson,* the widow of a colleague, but she died in 1845 after having contributed significantly to the monumental translation and literary work that became Judson's legacy to the church in Burma. In 1846 he married a young writer, Emily Chubbuck Judson,* whom he had selected as biographer of Sarah Boardman Judson. Emily sailed with him to Burma in that same year and survived him by only a few years.

Not returning to the United States until thirty-three years after the beginning of his missionary career and having sustained such hardship and loss in pursuit of his calling, Judson became an inspiring example of missionary sacrifice and dedication for several generations of young people. The concrete results of his work were no less impressive, as he left a flourishing church of 7,000 members and more than 100 national ministers among both the Burmese and the tribal peoples of the country—a church that has continued in unbroken succession since his death.

BIBLIOGRAPHY. *AAP* 6; C. Anderson, *To the Golden Shore: The Life of Adoniram Judson* (1956); *DAB* V; *DARB; NCAB* 3; R. Torbet, *Venture of Faith* (1955); F. Wayland, *A Memoir of the Life and Labors of the Rev. Adoniram Judson,* 2 vols. (1853). E. A. Wilson

Judson, Ann Hasseltine (1789-1826). Baptist missionary to Burma. Two weeks after marriage to Adoniram Judson* in February 1812, Ann Hasseltine Judson went with him to India to serve as a Congregationalist missionary. During their journey to India the couple decided in favor of believer's baptism* by immersion, and on reaching India they were baptized by British Baptist missionaries. Resigning from the Congregational mission board, they requested support from Baptists in America. In May 1814 American Baptists formed the General Convention of the Baptist Denomination in the United States of America for Foreign Missions (popularly known as the Triennial Convention*) in order to support the work of the Judsons, as well as other American Baptists serving as missionaries.

Stories of Judson's tireless efforts to seek the release of her husband when he was imprisoned are well known. Primarily as the result of her vast correspondence, she attracted the attention of many Baptists in America and gained much support for American Baptist work in India.

See also FEMALE MISSIONARY SOCIETY, BALTIMORE; JUDSON, ADONIRAM; JUDSON, EMILY CHUBBUCK; JUDSON, SARAH HALL BOARDMAN.

BIBLIOGRAPHY. J. J. Brumberg, *Mission for Life: The Story of the Family of Adoniram Judson* (1980); C. B. Hartley, *The Three Mrs. Judsons, the Celebrated Female Missionaries* (n.d.); J. D. Knowles, *Memoir of Mrs. Ann H. Judson* (1829); H. L. McBeth, *Women in Baptist Life* (1979); H. L. McBeth, *A Sourcebook for Baptist Heritage* (1990). K. Smith

Judson, Edward (1844-1914). The son of Adoniram* and Ann Judson.* Born in Burma, he graduated from Brown University* in 1865. After teaching at a seminary in Vermont he went to Madison University, where he was appointed professor of Latin and modern languages in 1868. He accepted the call of the North Orange (New Jersey) Baptist Church in 1875 and remained there for six years before accepting the pastorate at the Berean Baptist Church, New York City. In time Berean became the Judson Memorial Church on Washington Square, New York.

Judson was renowned as a pastor and preacher, reputedly baptizing 300-400 persons in his first five years of the pastorate. Toward the end of his life he gave numerous courses at the University of Chicago, Columbia, New York University, Union Theological Seminary* and the theological seminary at Colgate University.* He was active in denominational life, serving for a time as president of the American Baptist Missionary Union.* He published two books: *The Life of Adoniram Judson* (1883) and *Institutional Church* (1899). His interests extended beyond the life of the church, however, to the social issues of the time. He was characterized by his biographer as a "social prophet," a ministry that has continued to be characterized in the mission of the Judson Memorial Church.

BIBLIOGRAPHY. C. H. Sears, *Edward Judson: Interpreter of God* (1917).

H. W. Pipkin

Judson, Emily Chubbuck (1817-1854). Baptist missionary and writer. Born in Eaton, New York, on August 22, 1817, to Charles and Lavinia (Richards) Chubbuck, Emily Chubbuck spent her early years in poverty. She taught school from 1832 to 1840 and then went to the Utica Female Seminary. In 1841 she published her first Sunday-school book, *Charles Linn: Or, How to Observe the Golden Rule* (1841). During that time she published several other Sunday-school books, though she became best known for the articles and stories she wrote under a pen name, Fanny Forester.

Adoniram Judson* saw her work and selected her to write the biography of his deceased second wife, Sarah Hall Boardman Judson.* They met in 1845 in Philadelphia, were married on June 2, 1846, and went to Burma in July. After Adoniram's death in 1850, which was followed ten days later by the death of their second child, Emily Judson left India with her only surviving child and with two stepchildren. In addition to the *Memoir of Sarah B. Judson* (1848), Emily published several other books. Her own health failing, she returned to Hamilton, New York, where she died in 1854.

BIBLIOGRAPHY. W. H. Brackney, *The Baptists* (1988); *DAB* X; C. B. Hartley, *The Three Mrs. Judsons, the Celebrated Female Missionaries* (n.d.).

K. Smith

Judson, Sarah Hall Boardman (1803-1845). Baptist missionary. Born in Alstead, New Hampshire, on November 4, 1803, Sarah Hall resided during her youth in Salem, Massachusetts, with her parents, Ralph and Abiah O. Hall. In 1825 she married George Dana Boardman,* and together they went to India as missionaries. After George Boardman died in 1831, Sarah Boardman remained at their mission post. In April 1834 she married Adoniram Judson.* They had eight children, three of whom died in infancy. In addition to writing religious verse, she learned the Burmese language, organized schools and translated *The Pilgrim's Progress* as well as several tracts into Burmese. She died at St. Helena on September 1, 1845.

BIBLIOGRAPHY. *DAB* V, X; C. B. Hartley, *The Three Mrs. Judsons, the Celebrated Female Missionaries* (n.d.); *NAW* 2; A. Wilson, *Ann H. Judson and Mrs. Sarah B. Judson, Missionaries to Burmah* (1852); W. N. Wyeth, *Sarah B. Judson: A Memorial* (1889).

K. Smith

Judson College. Judson Female Institute was organized in 1838 in Marion, Alabama. Named for Ann Hasseltine Judson,* wife of Adoniram Judson,* the school opened on January 7, 1839, under the leadership of Milo P. Jewett. Chartered by the Alabama legislature on January 9, 1841, the institute operated as a privately owned institution with local Baptist trustees. In 1843 the trustees conveyed the title of the school to the Alabama Baptist Convention. Faculty member Elizabeth Sexton Shuck was the first Southern Baptist* missionary from Alabama when she went to China in 1847. The Society of the Alumnae of Judson Female Institute was organized in 1868. In 1904 the name of the institute changed to Judson College. The college was accredited by the Southern Association of Colleges in 1925.

Judson now offers the bachelor of arts and bachelor of science degrees to approximately 400 women. The college is known for its technical communications, fashion and design, and equestrian programs. Judson is the home of the Alabama Woman's Hall of Fame.

BIBLIOGRAPHY. F. D. Hamilton and E. C. Wells, *Daughters of the Dream: Judson College 1838-1988* (1989).

J. F. Loftis

Judson Press. In 1924 the publishing arm of the American Baptist Publication Society* became Judson Press in honor of Adoniram Judson,* the pioneer American Baptist missionary. Since the Judson Centennial of 1914 the name had been associated with the printing house. Judson Press is the official denominational publishing house for the American Baptist Churches in the USA.*

Under the imprint of the Publication Society, the press had produced Sunday-school literature, tracts, scholarly works and doctrinal studies. When the new name was adopted, the society sent a signal in the mid-1920s for the expansion of its publication ministry.

In its six decades of production, Judson Press has produced the American Bible Commentary (8 vols., 1958), three generations of Baptist histories, scholarly monographs and biographies, hymnals, polity and service manuals, systematic theologies, Bible study resources, and foreign-language Bibles. Probably its most costly venture was the printing of a full-sized Russian Bible, completed in the mid-1970s. Among the press's best-received items were the theologies of A. H. Strong* and E. Y. Mullins,* histories by Henry Vedder* and Robert Torbet, W. L. Lumpkin's collection of Baptist confessions of faith,* and Edward Hiscox's manual for churches. Judson Press has also published contract work for the Baptist World Alliance* and various ecumenical bodies. Its hymnal *Christian Worship* was produced jointly with the Disciples of Christ. From 1957 through 1982, the press also published *Foundations: A Baptist Journal of History and Theology.*

In 1962 Judson Press moved to a new printing facility in Valley Forge, Pennsylvania, where it eventually became the seventh largest printer in the region. It regularly printed *The American Baptist Magazine,* oldest of its kind in the United States, plus regional American Baptist newspapers. After World War II, bookstores were operated in Philadelphia, Chicago, Los Angeles and Green Lake, Wisconsin. However, due to the high cost of union contracts and declining orders, in 1984 the printing business was discontinued and manufacturing was sent off site.

Judson Press continues to produce a limited number of materials relating to denominational heritage and general religious interest focused on Baptists. Since 1992 the press has cooperated with Trinity Press and Abingdon Cokesbury for distribution.

BIBLIOGRAPHY. L. C. Barnes, *Pioneers of Light: The First Century of the American Baptist Publication Society, 1824-1924* (1924); L. T. Slaght, *Multiplying the Witness: 150 Years of American Baptist Educational Ministries* (1974).

W. H. Brackney

K

Keach, Benjamin (1640-1704). Pastor of the Horsleydown Church in Southwark and one of the leading English Baptists of the seventeenth century. Born in Stokehaman, England, Keach became a Baptist at age fifteen and began preaching at the age of eighteen. At first a General Baptist,* he became a Particular Baptist* in 1688.

In 1664 Keach was arrested for writing and publishing *The Child's Instructor: Or, A New and Easy Primer,* a book of religious instruction for children. He was tried and found guilty of writing that "believers, or godly men and women only, who can make confession of their faith and repentance," were fit subjects for Christian baptism.

In 1668 Keach moved to London to become pastor of a tiny congregation of Baptists meeting from house to house in Southwark. After the Act of Toleration in 1689, however, the congregation came out of hiding and built a meetinghouse in Horsleydown. Under Keach's leadership the church grew rapidly to nearly a thousand people.

Keach was an able preacher, a prolific biblical scholar, a controversialist and an imaginative writer. Among his forty-three published works, the most widely known were an allegory entitled *The Travels of True Godliness* and a biblical reference work entitled *Tropologia: A Key to Open Scripture Metaphors.* He is also credited for introducing hymn singing to English Baptists, publishing two important Baptist hymnals: *Spiritual Melody* (1691) and *Spiritual Songs* (1696).

BIBLIOGRAPHY. H. L. McBeth, *The Baptist Heritage* (1987). T. R. McKibbens

Keach, Elias (1667-1701). Baptist minister in the middle colonies. The son of the famous London Baptist pastor Benjamin Keach,* Elias Keach, unordained, arrived in Philadelphia in 1686/1687 dressed in the black coat and white collar of a minister. The pretension succeeded, and he was asked to preach. Seized by conviction, however, the young pretender stopped his sermon and confessed his sin. Keach sought the spiritual aid of Thomas Dungan* of Cold Spring, who counseled and baptized him. Returning to Pennepek, Keach gathered a small church, which was constituted in 1688. From Pennepek he traveled to Trenton, Philadelphia, Middletown, Cohansey, Salem and other small communities, preaching to groups of English, Irish and Welsh settlers. According to Morgan Edwards,* these churches met in "General Meetings" held twice a year due to the distances separating the members of this Baptist community. When numbers were sufficient, a church was gathered in each location. Contact between the churches of the area was maintained; this evolved into the Philadelphia Baptist Association,* formally established in 1707. Their doctrine and practice was that of the English Particular Baptists.* Called "the chief apostle of the Baptists in these parts" by Edwards, Keach returned to England in 1692.

BIBLIOGRAPHY. T. Armitage, *A History of the Baptists,* 2 vols. (1892); M. Edwards, *Materials Towards a History of the Baptists,* 2 vols. (1770-1792). L. W. Hähnlen

Kehuckee Baptist Association. Baptist antimissionary* group in North Carolina. Baptist churches were formed along Kehuckee Creek in North Carolina by the 1740s, and in 1769 they formed their own association. In 1803 the Kehuckee Association declared itself in favor of missions,* though some churches in the association opposed organized missions for theological and methodological reasons. Churches in the Chowan area split off from the association in 1805 to form their own association, leaving most of the remaining churches in the Kehuckee group opposed to missions. In 1826 the Kehuckee Association voted to "discard all Missionary Societies, Bible Societies, and Theological Seminaries, and the practices heretofore resorted to form their support, in begging money from the public."

Thereafter *Kehuckeeism* became a synonym for antimissions among Baptists. In 1878 remnants of the Kehuckee Association formed the Kehuckee Primitive Baptist* Association.

BIBLIOGRAPHY. L. Burkitt and J. Read, *A Concise History of the Kehuckee Baptist Association* (1850); G. W. Paschal, *A History of North Carolina Baptists* (1930).

H. L. McBeth

Keithian (Quaker) Baptists. Keithian (Quaker) Baptists existed in Pennsylvania from 1697 to about 1711, named for a man who apparently was never a member of the group. The Quaker leader George Keith (1639-1716) and his party called into question the sufficiency of the Divine Inner Light in salvation, emphasizing instead the role of Christ. They became Separate or Keithian Quakers about 1691, but quickly declined when their leader became an Anglican. During the period of dissolution, four small bands in and near Philadelphia began to practice immersion, observe the Lord's Supper* and wash the saints' feet (*see* Foot-Washing). However, they still retained the simple, pacifist customs of the Quakers, giving reason for their alternate name. In 1700 three churches with thirty-three members probably existed. Ten years later the number had been reduced to one church with ten members. This body likely died the following year. Probably fewer than fifty people ever united with these four churches. Many of their former members entered nearby Seventh Day* and Particular*-Regular* Baptist churches. No Keithian association has been discovered.

BIBLIOGRAPHY. Morgan Edwards, *Customs of Primitive Churches* (1774).

R. G. Gardner

Kendrick, Nathaniel (1777-1848). Baptist pastor and educator. Born in Hanover, New Hampshire, April 22, 1777, Kendrick was raised in the Congregational church. He was converted in a Baptist revival in 1797 and was immersed a few months later. Sensing a call to preach, he was licensed to the ministry in 1803 and was ordained two years later at Lansingburg, New York.

After serving numerous churches in Vermont, Kendrick moved in 1817 to Hamilton, New York, where he helped to organize the Baptist Educational Society of New York. This society was chartered by the state in 1819 and served as the parent organization to the Hamilton Literary and Theological Institution, a seminary that eventually became Madison University (later Colgate University*). Kendrick was appointed professor of systematic and pastoral theology there in 1821. He served as corresponding secretary of the Educational Society from 1834 until his death on February 11, 1848. While a respected theologian, pastor and speaker, Kendrick is remembered especially for his many contributions to the cause of Baptist ministerial education.

BIBLIOGRAPHY. S. W. Adams, *Memoirs of Rev. Nathaniel Kendrick, D.D., and Silas N. Kendrick* (1860).

B. C. Leslie

Kentucky Normal and Theological Institute. *See* SIMMONS, WILLIAM JAMES; SIMMONS UNIVERSITY.

Ketcham, Robert Thomas (1889-1978). Fundamentalist* Baptist minister. A native of Nelson, Pennsylvania, Ketcham lacked a college and seminary education but pastored Baptist churches in Roulette (1912-1915), Brookville (1915-1919) and Butler (1919-1923), Pennsylvania; Niles (1923-1926) and Elyria (1926-1932), Ohio; Gary, Indiana (1932-1939); and Waterloo, Iowa (1939-1948).

He entered the fundamentalist-modernist controversy in the Northern Baptist Convention (NBC) through the circulation of more than 200,000 copies of his pamphlet *A Statement of the First Baptist Church of Butler, Pennsylvania, with Reference to the New World Movement and the $100,000,000 Drive* (1919). A member of the Baptist Bible Union,* Ketcham withdrew from the NBC in 1928 and became president of the newly formed Ohio Association of Independent Baptist Churches. He led in the development of the General Association of Regular Baptist Churches* (GARBC), serving as vice president (1933) and president (1934-1938). He was national representative of the GARBC (1948-1960), editor of the *Baptist Bulletin* (1948-1955) and national consultant to the GARBC (1960-1966). Diagnosed as suffering from conical cornea in 1913, he was near blindness throughout his ministry.

BIBLIOGRAPHY. J. M. Murdoch, *Portrait of Obedience* (1979); R. Rayburn, "The Outworking of Obedience," *The Baptist Bulletin* 31 (March 1966):9-12.

R. T. Clutter

King, Martin Luther, Jr. (1929-1968). Black Baptist minister and civil rights leader. Born and raised in Atlanta, Georgia, King experienced the restrictions of segregation throughout his youth. The son and grandson of Baptist ministers, he himself chose a career in the ministry while a student at Morehouse College* (B.A., 1948). He then studied for the ministry at Crozer Theological Seminary* (B.D., 1951) and did graduate studies in systematic theology at Boston University (Ph.D., 1955).

In 1954 he became pastor of Dexter Avenue Baptist Church in Montgomery, Alabama. A year later he gained national acclaim as president of the Montgomery Improvement Association and the leader of the Montgomery bus boycott. It was during this first major campaign of the modern civil rights movement that King developed his philosophy and tactic of nonviolent protest to bring about social change.

Following the boycott, King became associate pastor of his father's church, Ebenezer Baptist, in Atlanta. In 1957 King participated in the Prayer Pilgrimage to Washington, D.C. The same year he became president of the newly organized Southern Christian Leadership Conference* (SCLC), which served as the coordinating body for local protests and affiliates across the South. Two primary objectives of SCLC were desegregation of public accommodations and voter education and registration of blacks. Major campaigns led by King included the Albany, Georgia, movement in 1962, the Birmingham protest in 1963 and the Selma to Montgomery march in 1965. These events, along with the 1963 March on Washington, contributed to passage of the 1964 Civil Rights Act and the 1965 Voting Rights Act. In 1964 King was named the Nobel Peace Prize recipient.

Recognizing that civil rights statutes were of limited meaning to the poor, after 1965 King turned his attention to economic inequities, particularly in Northern urban areas. His Chicago campaign of 1966 served mainly to reveal the complexity and intransigence of economic problems. King is perhaps best known for his 1963 "I Have a Dream" speech, which reflected the goal of integration, the ideology of reform and the strategy of moral persuasion that characterized the first phase of the civil rights movement. His 1967 "Beyond Vietnam" speech, in which he denounced the Vietnam War, linking the issues of poverty, racism and militarism, is reflective of his movement to a more radical critique of the structures of American society in the last three years of his life. In 1968 King began organizing a Poor

People's Campaign to bring together a coalition of impoverished whites and ethnic minorities to lobby the federal government for an "Economic Bill of Rights." His outspokenness on international issues of peace and imperialism earned him the enmity of many former supporters while intensifying the opposition of others. He was assassinated on April 4, 1968, while in Memphis, Tennessee, to support striking garbage workers. King authored five books: *Stride Toward Freedom* (1958), *Strength to Love* (1963), *Why We Can't Wait* (1964), *Where Do We Go from Here: Chaos or Community?* (1967) and *Trumpet of Conscience* (1968). His birthday, observed on the third Monday in January, became a national holiday in 1986.

BIBLIOGRAPHY. *DARB;* D. J. Garrow, *Bearing the Cross: Martin Luther King Jr. and the Southern Christian Leadership Conference, 1955-1968* (1986); D. L. Lewis, *King: A Biography,* 2nd ed. (1978); S. B. Oates, *Let the Trumpet Sound: The Life of Martin Luther King Jr.* (1985).

M. R. Sawyer

King, Martin Luther, Sr. (1899-1984). Prominent African-American Baptist minister and civil rights leader. Born in Stockbridge, Georgia, on December 19, 1899, he was the second of ten children in a poor rural family. Licensed as a Baptist minister at the age of fifteen, he moved to Atlanta a year later. He graduated from Morehouse College* (B.Th., 1926), and succeeded his father-in-law, Reverend A. D. Williams, as pastor of Ebenezer Baptist Church, where he served from 1932 to 1975.

Under King's leadership, Ebenezer became the largest black church in Atlanta, and King became a leading civil rights leader. He picketed city hall over segregated facilities (1935), challenged restrictions on black voting rights (1936), led a protest to equalize teachers' salaries, and was an early proponent of Atlanta's black and white coalition (1946). Obviously, his early example influenced the civil rights activism of his son Martin Luther King Jr. a decade later. In his autobiography, *Daddy King* (1980), the elder King stated that he had no time to hate the men who assassinated his son (1968) and wife (1974).

Earlier, King had been a member of the governing boards of the National Baptist Convention (*see* National Baptists), Atlanta University and Morehouse College. A supporter of Jimmy Carter's* race for the presidency, he delivered invocations at the Democratic National Convention (1976 and 1980). He also delivered a eulogy at the funeral of Nelson A. Rockefeller (1979). Suffering from chronic heart disease, he died in Atlanta on November 11, 1984.

BIBLIOGRAPHY. *ERS;* C. Goss, "Daddy King—Pastor of the Dream," *Encore* 6 (January 17, 1977); M. L. King Sr., *Daddy King* (1980).

L. H. Williams

Knapp, Jacob (1799-1874). Pastor and evangelist. Jacob Knapp was born December 7, 1799, and was raised in an Episcopalian family in upstate New York. He was converted and baptized in the Masonville Baptist Church there in 1819. Knapp attended the newly organized Hamilton Literary and Theological Institution (*see* Colgate Baptist University) and was graduated in 1824 from the theological course. For a time he served as pastor of the Watertown Baptist Church in New York.

Under the influence of the New Measures of Charles G. Finney, Knapp held his own version of protracted meetings in various small towns in northern New York. He moved to Hamilton in 1835 to confront a center of opposition to his ministry. In this farming village, where Knapp's alma mater had evolved into Madison University, Knapp won adherents and caused schism in the Baptist church. He assumed a strong stance against slavery and sided with those who wanted to remove the university to Rochester for a more urban setting.

In the 1840s Knapp became a nationally recognized evangelist and held meetings in New York, Boston, Philadelphia and Washington, D.C. A flamboyant preacher, he would often refer to his impoverished family circumstances, and this would generate large gifts. His erratic behavior caught up with him in the Boston area in 1844, and he suffered disgrace. Eventually he moved to the Illinois region, where he preached and served as pastor of churches far removed from the controversies of his early career.

BIBLIOGRAPHY. *ABQ* 4 (June 1985):184-200; W. H. Brackney, *The Baptists* (1988).

W. H. Brackney

Koinonia Farm. Established in 1942 by Mable and Martin England and Florence and Clarence Jordan* near Americus, Georgia. Described originally as an "agricultural missionary enterprise," Koinonia sought to improve farm practices and to bridge race relations in the area.

Christian pacifism, simple living and racial reconciliation became the watchwords for Koinonia and stirred opposition in Sumter County. The local Ku Klux Klan visited Koinonia in 1942 to intimidate the residents. The Rehobeth Baptist Church withdrew fellowship from six Koinonians in 1950. Jordan's endorsement of black applicants to a public white university in 1956 precipitated a decade of vandalism, violence, legal investigations and economic boycott against Koinonia. Unable to support itself by farming, Koinonia began a mail-order business for pecan products and fruitcakes.

By 1956 Koinonia's population reached sixty, including fifteen African-Americans. A decade later the population had dropped to two families. In 1968 Jordan and Millard Fuller reincorporated Koinonia Farm into Koinonia Partners and began a low-cost, interest-free building program that has since built 185 houses and revived the community. In the 1970s the number of Koinonians peaked at thirty-six, plus children and volunteers. In 1976 Linda and Millard Fuller left to begin Habitat for Humanity International. In 1979 Koinonia sent three couples to Comer, Georgia, to establish Jubilee Partners, which works primarily with refugees.

Koinonia Partners focuses its efforts on Sumter County, providing jobs for fifty employees in its pecan and farming operations and its child-care center. Koinonians also participate in peace demonstrations and death-penalty vigils. Koinonia observed its fiftieth anniversary in 1992 with a reunion that drew 400 people.

See also JORDAN, CLARENCE.

BIBLIOGRAPHY. D. Lee, *The Cotton Patch Evidence: The Story of Clarence Jordan and the Koinonia Farm Experiment* (1971); K. Weiner, ed., *Koinonia Remembered: The First Fifty Years* (1992).

A. S. Chancey

L

Ladd, George Eldon (1911-1982). Evangelical New Testament scholar. Born in New Hampshire, Ladd was converted in 1929 under the preaching ministry of a female graduate of Moody Bible Institute. Graduating from Gordon College of Theology and Missions (B.Th., 1933), he was ordained a Northern Baptist minister (*see* American Baptist Churches in the USA) and continued his theological studies at Gordon Divinity School while pastoring a church in Gilford, New Hampshire. Following a pastorate in Montpelier, Vermont (1936-1942), Ladd served as minister of Blaney Memorial Church in Boston. Resuming his studies, he took up graduate work in classics, first at Boston University and then at Harvard, where he completed his Ph.D. under Henry J. Cadbury in 1949.

Ladd joined the faculty of Fuller Theological Seminary in 1950. His thirty years at Fuller were characterized by hard work, well-reasoned but passionately held views and a driving, Socratic classroom style. Beyond the classroom he was to have a profound impact on a generation of evangelical biblical scholars. In *The New Testament and Criticism* (1967) he moved evangelical biblical interpretation beyond the horizons of defensive fundamentalism,* accepting the positive gains of modern critical methods while challenging the negative results of critical scholars on their own ground.

Books such as his *Crucial Questions About the Kingdom of God* (1952) established his reputation among conservatives as a proponent of classic premillennialism rather than dispensationalism. His *Jesus and the Kingdom* (1964), later republished as *The Presence of the Future* (1974), was intended to bring him the cherished recognition of the broader community of biblical scholars. Unfortunately, while the book won him prestige within the evangelical community, it was severely criticized from without. His later work *A Theology of the New Testament* (1974) became a benchmark of evangelical New Testament scholarship in America.

BIBLIOGRAPHY. D. A. Hubbard, "Biographical Sketch of Appreciation," in *Unity and Diversity in New Testament Theology,* ed. R. A. Guelich (1978); G. M. Marsden, *Reforming Fundamentalism* (1987); M. A. Noll, *Between Faith and Criticism* (1986). D. G. Reid

LaGrange College. *See* HANNIBAL-LAGRANGE COLLEGE.

Landmark Banner and Cherokee Baptist. Antebellum Baptist weekly newspaper. Always privately owned, but favored by the Cherokee Baptist Convention,* this newspaper was published fairly regularly from October 5, 1859, to November 25, 1865. The name was changed to *Banner and Baptist* in 1861 and to *Baptist Banner* in 1862. Major editors and owners were Jesse M. Wood (1859-1861), Henry C. Hornady (1861-1862), James N. Ells (1862-1865) and Amos C. Dayton* (1863-1864). First printed in Rome, Georgia, it was moved to Atlanta on June 14, 1860, and to Augusta on July 23, 1864. The number of subscribers grew to over 2,000 late in 1860. The periodical included essays and editorials favoring Landmarkism,* Baptist news from the Southeast and numerous articles related to the Civil War, particularly in Tennessee and Georgia. The *Baptist Banner* was discontinued because of the devastation of the war, which rendered it insolvent.

See also LANDMARK BAPTISTS.

BIBLIOGRAPHY. Known extant issues available on microfilm from the Historical Commission, SBC; R. G. Gardner, "Landmark Banner and Cherokee Baptist," *QR* 35 (January-March 1975):57-72. R. G. Gardner

Landmark Baptists. An ultraconservative group within the Southern Baptist Convention* in the nineteenth century. The first organized expression of Landmarkism came in 1851 in the form of the Cotton Grove Resolutions,* named for a meeting place in West Tennessee where J. R. Graves* led a group of ultraconservative Baptists to affirm that Baptists had the only true churches and thus the only true baptism* and Lord's Supper.*

The "Triumvirate" of Landmark leaders included James Robinson Graves* (1820-1893), James Madison Pendleton* (1811-1891) and Amos Cooper Dayton* (1813-1865). It was Graves's polemics in the pulpit and in print that established the militant nature of Landmarkism. His book *Old Landmarkism: What Is It?* provided a popular exposition of Landmark teachings, while his 1893 publication *The Work of Christ Consummated in Seven Dispensations* helped introduce dispensational premillennialism into Southern Baptist life. Pendleton exerted great influence, even into the twentieth century, with his *Church Manual* (1867 and republished many times since), which has been widely used in the South. Dayton wrote widely, including fiction and children's literature. One of his works, less known today, is *Theodosia Ernest* (1856), which tells the story of Theodosia, who discovered that Baptists have the only true church in the world.

The name of the Landmark movement comes from Proverbs 22:28 ("Remove not the ancient landmark, which thy fathers have set," KJV). Pendleton wrote a tract arguing that Baptists could not recognize non-Baptist churches as true churches or non-Baptist ministers as true ministers. Graves published this tract under the title *An Old Landmark Re-set* (1856), and this named the movement. Landmark theology centers on one central concept: the doctrine of the church (*see* Ecclesiology). Landmarkers emphasize the primacy of the *local* church; they do not believe in any universal or invisible church. They believe that Jesus established a Baptist church, that Baptist churches have had an unbroken continuity since the days of the apostles and that therefore Baptists are the only true churches in the world. Since only Baptist churches are true churches, it follows that only Baptist baptism and Baptist Lord's Supper are valid. This led to the Landmark insistence upon "closed Communion" (that non-Baptists must not participate in the Lord's Supper in Baptist churches) and their fierce opposition to "alien immersion" (the idea that non-Baptists might perform valid baptism).

Landmark influence today continues in several smaller Baptist groups such as the Baptist Missionary Association,* the American Baptist Association* and the Baptist Missionary Association of America.* A remnant of Landmark doctrine and practice lingers in other Baptist groups, especially the Southern Baptist Convention.*

See also COTTON GROVE RESOLUTIONS; DAYTON, AMOS COOPER; GRAVES, JAMES ROBINSON; PENDLETON, JAMES MADISON.

BIBLIOGRAPHY. *BHH*, January 1975; J. R. Graves, *Old Landmarkism: What Is It?* (1880); H. L. McBeth, *The Baptist Heritage* (1987).

H. L. McBeth

Landrum, William Warren (1853-1926). Southern Baptist* pastor. William was born at Macon, Georgia; his family later moved to Savannah, Georgia. Baptized on March 25, 1866, he attended Mercer University* and graduated from Brown University* (1872) and Southern Baptist Theological Seminary* (1874). Brown and Washington and Lee universities awarded him the D.D. degree and the University of Georgia the LL.D. degree. Ordained in May 1874, in Jefferson, Texas, he pastored First Baptist, Shreveport, Louisiana, from 1874 to 1876, First Baptist, Augusta, Georgia, from 1876 to 1882, Second Baptist, Richmond, Virginia, from 1882 to 1896, First Baptist, Atlanta, Georgia, from 1896 to 1909, Broadway Baptist, Louisville, Kentucky, from 1909 to 1919 and First Baptist, Russellville, Kentucky, from 1919 to 1926. He declined offers of the presidency of three Baptist educational institutions but served on several denominational boards and in the Baptist World Alliance.* He authored *History, Gospel and Prophecy* and *Our Baptist Message—Its Use and Abuse.*

BIBLIOGRAPHY. *ESB* 2:758; B. J. W. Graham, ed., *Baptist Biography* (1917).

S. A. Yarbrough

Lane, Dutton (1732-?). Separate Baptist* pastor and evangelist. Few details of Lane's life survive. Born November 7, 1732, near Baltimore, he moved with his family at some later date to Virginia. He is variously reported as having been baptized by Daniel Marshall* and Shubal Stearns* in 1758. While not ordained until 1764, Lane was called in 1760 to be the first pastor of the newly constituted Dan River Baptist Church, which R. B. Semple identifies as the first Separate Baptist congregation in Virginia. Marshall and Stearns were frequent visitors to his pulpit. Lane was an active evangelist in the region and aided in the establishment of numerous Separate Baptist churches. He is reported to have suffered much persecution as a result of his ministry, including the violent opposition of his own father, who was subsequently converted and baptized by Dutton Lane himself.

BIBLIOGRAPHY. L. P. Little, *Imprisoned Preachers and Religious Liberty in Virginia* (1938); R. B. Semple, *History of the Baptists in Virginia* (1894, 1976).   B. C. Leslie

Larkin, Clarence (1850-1924). Baptist pastor and author. Born in Chester, Pennsylvania, Larkin briefly worked in his father's feed store before becoming a bank clerk. While a clerk he became involved in the YMCA, through which he was converted. He was confirmed in the Episcopal Church. Larkin enrolled in the Polytechnic College of Philadelphia, from which he received a degree in mechanical engineering (1873). After a short employment in a shipyard, he became supervisor and instructor at the Pennsylvania Institution for the Blind, where he served for three years prior to entering into the business field. While serving in secular occupations he taught Bible classes.

At the age of thirty-two Larkin joined the Baptist Church; he was ordained two years later. He pastored at Kennett Square and Fox Chase, Pennsylvania. He is included in the list of signers of the call for the fundamentalist* preconvention meeting of the Northern Baptist Convention in 1920 at Buffalo, New York (*see* American Baptist Churches in the USA). Subsequent to his ordination Larkin became a premillennialist and published books on prophetic themes. Utilizing his background as an engineer, Larkin included in his books numerous memorable charts, many illustrating prophetic themes. His books include *Dispensational Truth* (1920), *The Book of Revelation* (1919) and *The Book of Daniel* (1929).

R. T. Clutter

Larsen, Iver (1847-1917). Prominent pastor of Danish-Norwegian congregations in Wisconsin and Minnesota. Born in Norway on January 10, 1847, immersed May 31, 1872, in Tramso, Norway, and licensed as a minister at LaCrosse, Wisconsin, 1878, he studied in the Scandinavian department of the Baptist Union Theological Seminary* from 1878 to 1879 and was ordained

in 1880. His pastorates included the Half-Way Creek Church near LaCrosse (1879-1880) and churches in Minneapolis (1880-1882 and 1885-1892), Ocanomowoc, Wisconsin (1882-1885), Clark's Grove, Minnesota (1892-1907), and La-Crosse (1907-1912). The church at Clark's Grove was the oldest, and for many years the largest, Danish Baptist church in Minnesota. At the time of his death, which occurred on March 4, 1917, Larsen was in charge of the Ebenezer Mission in Minneapolis.

BIBLIOGRAPHY. I. Fredmund et al., *Seventy-five Years of Danish Baptist Missionary Work in America* (1913); P. Stiansen, *History of the Norwegian Baptists in America* (1919).

N. A. Magnuson

Latourette, Kenneth Scott (1884-1968). Distinguished scholar of Asian and missions* history. Born in Oregon City, Oregon, Latourette was educated at Linfield College (B.S., 1904) and Yale University (B.A., 1906; M.A., 1907; Ph.D., 1909), where his involvement with the Student Volunteer Movement led him to a brief term of missionary service in China (1910-1912). Returning in ill-health after two years, he turned to an academic career, first at Reed College (1914-1916), then at Denison University* (1916-1921), and finally as professor of missions and Oriental history at Yale Divinity School. There he taught for thirty-two years; he retired near his seventieth year, in 1953, after having contributed a prodigious volume of publications to his two areas of major interest. His works, including histories of China and Japan that by the 1940s had established him as a foremost Asian scholar, have reportedly sold more than a million copies. He held honorary doctorates from seventeen universities, including Oxford, Yale and Princeton. His professional achievement was recognized by his selection as president of the American Historical Association, the American Society of Church History and the American Baptist Association.* Latourette was a committed and active member of the American Baptist Convention,* serving one term as president of that denomination.

Latourette's view of Christian history, which was presented in his presidential address to the American Historical Association and dispersed in his histories, is well illustrated in two monumental series, *History of the Expansion of Christianity* (7 vols., 1937-1945) and *Christianity in a Revolutionary Age: A History of Christianity in the Nine-*

teenth and Twentieth Centuries (5 vols., 1958-1962). Placing the church in the context of unfolding historical developments, Latourette perceived God's work in the world through human institutions. History moves toward the realization of human redemption in sometimes fitful expansions and contractions, but always with assurance of ultimate triumph, with the Christian faith rather than the church as the focus. Latourette's objectivity and comprehensiveness brought him acclaim, though his optimism and confidence have sometimes been considered unduly sanguine and rationalistic, given the historic tragedies his generation witnessed.

BIBLIOGRAPHY. S. Bates, "Christian Historian, Doer of History: In Memory of Kenneth Scott Latourette, 1884-1968," *IRM* 58 (1969):317-26; W. C. Harr, ed., *Frontiers of the Christian World Mission Since 1938; Essays in Honor of Kenneth Scott Latourette* (1962); W. A. Speck, "Kenneth Scott Latourette's Vocation as Christian Historian," *CSR* 4 (1975):285-99.   E. A. Wilson

Laws, Curtis Lee (1868-1946). Baptist clergyman and editor. Born in Loudoun County, Virginia, Laws graduated from Crozer Theological Seminary* (1893) and served important pastorates in Baltimore, Maryland (1893-1908), and Brooklyn, New York (1908-1913), before assuming the editorship in 1913 of the Baptist weekly newspaper *The Watchman-Examiner.** When he took over the paper, it enjoyed the widest circulation of any Baptist periodical in the North, and he used its columns to advance his orthodox evangelical Baptist principles.

As an editor, Laws favored a restoration of historic Baptist identity, affirming the authority of Scripture, the autonomy of local congregations and a mission* imperative for all Christians. He rejected contemporary popular labels like Landmarker,* conservative or premillennialist as being rigid or carrying historical disadvantages. Instead, in an editorial in 1920 he coined the name *fundamentalist** for those "who still cling to the great fundamentals and who mean to do battle royal for the faith." In his later years Laws helped to organize the Eastern Baptist Theological Seminary* in Philadelphia and the Association of Baptists for World Evangelism, both loyal to the Northern Baptist Convention (*see* American Baptist Churches in the USA) but founded on clearly evangelical bases. As pastor, editor and denominational leader, Laws was a prominent leader of

the conservative reaction to modernism in the Northern Baptist Convention from 1920 through the 1940s.

See also FUNDAMENTALISM.

BIBLIOGRAPHY. W. H. Brackney, *The Baptists* (1988); J. W. Bradbury, "Curtis Lee Laws, D.D., LL.D.: An Appreciation," *WE* 34 (July 18, 1946).
W. H. Brackney

Laying On of Hands. A religious rite in which the imposition of hands suggests consecration, blessing and invocation of the Holy Spirit. The New Testament contains evidence of three main usages of the rite: healing, ordination* or setting apart for service, and communication of the Holy Spirit, often in conjunction with baptism.* Among Baptists today, laying on of hands is associated principally with ordaining ministers or commissioning Christian workers. In some groups, like General Six-Principle Baptists* of Rhode Island, laying on of hands is a rite that occurs after baptism to symbolize the impartation of the Holy Spirit. Among Pentecostal Christians the imposition of hands is a rite distinct from water baptism in which a believer is baptized with the Holy Spirit and receives spiritual gifts like the ability to speak in "tongues."

See also CHARISMATIC MOVEMENT AMONG BAPTISTS; ORDINANCES.   J. R. Tyson

Laymen's Foreign Missions Inquiry (1930-1932). An inquiry into missions* conducted by prominent Protestant laypersons. Following the International Missionary Council meeting at Jerusalem in 1928, a number of American lay supporters of missions became concerned over the apparent wane in support for foreign missions. They felt that a reappraisal of mission motives and methods was in order. As a result of a proposal originally put forward by the Northern Baptists (*see* American Baptist Churches in the USA), an inquiry was inaugurated, financed by John D. Rockefeller Jr.* A board of directors composed of laymen from the Northern Baptist, Congregational, Dutch Reformed, Presbyterian Church U.S.A., Methodist Episcopal, Protestant Episcopal and United Presbyterian communions was constituted.

The inquiry was confined to missions connected with churches in Burma, China, India and Japan, and a team of researchers was sent to each of these countries. The collected information was then turned over to a Commission of Appraisal headed by William E. Hocking of Harvard University. After about nine months of visiting the four countries and conducting the study, a report was framed and published as *Re-thinking Missions* (1932). This was supplemented by later publications based on the work of the researchers and the Commission of Appraisal.

The report advocated greater autonomy for the churches in Asia, a strengthening of theological education, greater cooperation and unity, and a unified administration of missions at the "home base:" Most controversial was the liberal attitude toward non-Christian religions and the proposal that Christian missions reinforce the nobler aspects of other religions rather than seeking to convert their adherents. The latter proposal was due largely to Hocking's leadership and helped evoke the response of Hendrik Kraemer at Tambaram in 1938, where he insisted on the uniqueness of the Christian faith (*The Christian Message in a Non-Christian World*, 1938).

BIBLIOGRAPHY. K. S. Latourette, "Re-thinking Missions After Twenty-five Years," *IRM* 46 (1947): 164-70. D. J. Hesselgrave

Laymen's Missionary Movement. An interdenominational program to raise funds for Christian missions.* First proposed by John B. Sleman of Washington, D.C., a participant in the Student Volunteer Movement, the Laymen's Missionary Movement was formally organized in New York City. In the next few years committees of lay leaders were organized to ascertain the amounts of missionary contributions in their respective communities and elicit higher levels of commitment through educational presentations. Such meetings, often conducted as a banquet, were held throughout Canada in 1908 and in seventy-five cities in the U.S. the next year. Dramatic increases in missions receipts after 1906 seem to document the movement's effectiveness. Between 1907 and 1909 Presbyterian giving increased by 240 percent, Methodist by 166 percent and Baptist by 265 percent. Total missionary giving for American denominations increased from $8,980,000 in 1906 to $45,272,000 in 1924.

See also BROTHERHOOD COMMISSION, SBC.

BIBLIOGRAPHY. G. S. Eddy, *Pathfinders of the World Missionary Crusade* (1969); J. R. Mott, *The Decisive Hour of Christian Missions* (1910).

E. A. Wilson

Leachman, Emma (1868-1952). Southern Baptist* social ministries pioneer. A native of Washington County, Kentucky, Leachman attended the Central Teachers College in Indiana. In 1904 she was appointed as the city missionary in Louisville under the Kentucky State Mission Board. She was closely associated with the Woman's Missionary Union Training School,* which was organized in Louisville in 1907. There she taught applied methods in city missions and exerted a formative influence over a generation of students. In 1912 she became director of the Good Will Center, an inner-city settlement house that served as a missions* workshop for the students.

In 1921 "Miss Emma" was appointed as the first general field worker of the Home Mission Board* of the Southern Baptist Convention. In this capacity she traveled widely throughout the South, enlisting support for city missions projects and promoting the cause of Christian social ministries among churches, associations and denominational leaders. She retired from the Home Mission Board because of failing health in 1940. Many of the goals for which Leachman worked are now advanced through the Social Ministries Department of the Home Mission Board and the W. O. Carver School of Church Social Work* at the Southern Baptist Theological Seminary.*

BIBLIOGRAPHY. *ESB* 11; C. U. Littlejohn, *History of the Carver School of Missions and Social Work* (1958). T. F. George

Leavell Family. Eight of the nine sons of George Washington and Corra Alice Berry Leavell of Oxford, Mississippi, served Southern Baptist* churches and agencies. Landrum Pinson, the oldest (1874-1929), was educated at the University of Mississippi and Southern Baptist Theological Seminary.* After engaging in Sunday-school work for several years, he became in 1907 the first secretary of the Baptist Young People's Union* (BYPU). His *B.Y.P.U. Manual* (1907) became the standard guide for this organization. When this work was incorporated into the Sunday School Board* (1918), he directed the department and edited much of the literature.

Frank Hartwell (1884-1949) also graduated from the University of Mississippi (B.S., 1909), as well as Columbia University (M.A., 1925). Mississippi College (1935) and Baylor University* (1945) conferred honorary doctorates upon him. After almost a decade as secretary of the Georgia BYPU, he became the executive leader of the Inter-Board Commission, which was responsible for student work of the Southern Baptist Convention. When this assignment was given to the Sunday School Board (1928), Frank Leavell directed its department of student work. He stressed student conferences and the election of state student directors. He also led the Youth Committee of the Baptist World Alliance* for almost two decades and edited or authored about a dozen books.

Another son, Roland Quinche (1891-1963), also attended the University of Mississippi (B.A.; M.A., 1914) and Southern Baptist Theological Seminary (Th.M., 1917; Th.D., 1925). He served in France for two years (1917-1919) with the YMCA. For the next two decades he was pastor of churches, mostly in Mississippi and Georgia, before becoming the first superintendent of evangelism for the Home Mission Board* (1937-1942). A pastorate (1942-1946) in Tampa, Florida, was followed by his election as president of the New Orleans Baptist Theological Seminary* (1946-1958). He strengthened the faculty and curriculum of this institution and moved the campus to its present location. Roland Leavell published fifteen books, including *Evangelism, Christ's Imperative Commission* (1951).

BIBLIOGRAPHY. *ESB* 2; C. H. Leavell, ed., *Genealogy of the Nine Leavell Brothers of Oxford, Mississippi* (1957). C. L. Howe Jr.

Lee, Robert Greene (1886-1978). Minister and denominational leader. Born in Fort Mill, South Carolina, on November 11, 1886, he died at Memphis, Tennessee, on July 20, 1978. He was baptized on August 5, 1898, into the Fort Mill Baptist Church and in 1910 was ordained by the same church. Lee received the B.A. degree from Furman University* in 1913. He was also the recipient of eleven honorary doctorates. He was married on November 26, 1913, to Bula Gentry, and they had one daughter. Lee was pastor of a number of different Baptist churches, the largest of which was the Bellevue Baptist Church, Memphis, Tennessee, which he served thirty-two years, from 1927 to 1960.

Lee published fifty books of sermons and was president of the Tennessee Baptist Convention (four times) and the Southern Baptist Convention* (three terms). Much in demand as an inspirational speaker, he was especially famous for the sermon "Payday Someday," which he is said to have preached 1,275 times.

BIBLIOGRAPHY. *ESB* 4:2312; J. E. Huss, *Robert Greene Lee: The Authorized Biography* (1967).
W. R. Estep

Leland, John (1754-1841). Baptist preacher and religious libertarian. Reared in Massachusetts as a Congregationalist, Leland was nurtured by Scripture and Bunyan's *Pilgrim's Progress* from an early age. At the age of eighteen he was converted and was baptized by Wait Palmer, a Baptist minister. Leland felt called to devote himself to the ministry and was licensed to preach two years later.

By 1777 he and his new bride had arrived in Anglican Virginia, where he was to spend fourteen years pastoring a number of small Baptist churches (including those located at Mt. Poney, Orange and Louisa) and serving as an itinerant evangelist. Leland's ministry was carried out in the midst of hostility—Baptist preachers had been imprisoned, mobs had broken up worship services, and churches had been shut down by local magistrates—and challenges from fellow Baptists who questioned the regularity of his ordination. The latter obstacle was overcome in 1786 when Leland was ordained again, this time with the proper "laying on of hands."* In the end Leland, a leading Separate Baptist,* became a member and spokesman of the General Committee composed of Separate and Regular Baptists.*

Through his preaching, writing and personal friendship with Thomas Jefferson and James Madison, Leland exercised notable influence in the struggle to disestablish the Anglican Church and establish religious liberty. The General Committee repeatedly circulated petitions to the House of Burgesses for the redress of grievances. Leland led Baptists in support of Jefferson's bill establishing religious liberty* in Virginia. Leland-led Baptists also rallied to the support of Presbyterians, Mennonites and others to defeat the General Assessment Bill which the established church was attempting to promote in the House of Burgesses. Leland, like Isaac Backus,* proposed a bill of rights as an appendix to the Constitution. Apparently he refused to support James Madison's candidacy for Virginia's ratifying convention without assurance that Madison would personally see to the development of such a bill of rights once the constitution was ratified.

In 1792 Leland moved back to Cheshire, Massachusetts, where he spent the next fifty years in itinerant ministry throughout New England as well as in several return trips to Virginia. In Massachusetts and Connecticut he again championed religious freedom and the separation of church and state; he served in the Massachusetts House of Representatives from 1811 to 1813. In addition to his political tracts and articles on behalf of religious liberty, Leland wrote as many as twenty-one hymns.

BIBLIOGRAPHY. *AAP* 6; L. H. Butterfield, *Elder John Leland, Jeffersonian Itinerant* (1953); *DAB* VI; *DARB;* J. M. Dawson, *Baptists and the American Republic* (1956); *NCAB* 5.

W. R. Estep

Levering, Joshua (1845-1935). Baptist denominational leader, civic servant and merchant. Born September 12, 1845, in Baltimore, Maryland, Levering was baptized into the Eutaw Place Baptist Church. Educated in Baltimore private schools, he joined his twin brother and fellow Baptist philanthropist, Eugene Levering Jr., in the family coffee-importation business before withdrawing for public service in 1906. Joshua Levering ran for both governor and president on the Prohibition Party's ticket in 1896 and was active in starting the Interdenominational Laymen's Missionary Movement (1906). He was president of the Baltimore YMCA for seventeen years and was vice president of the American Baptist Publication Society.* Levering also served Southern Baptists* as president of the Maryland Baptist Union Association for eighteen years, trustee of the Foreign Mission Board* for forty-eight years, president of the trustees at Southern Baptist Theological Seminary* for forty years (1895-1935) and president of the Southern Baptist Convention from 1908 to 1911. He died in Baltimore on October 5, 1935.

See also SOUTHERN BAPTIST THEOLOGICAL SEMINARY.
BIBLIOGRAPHY. *ESB* 2; *NCAB* 29.

W. L. Allen

Liberalism, Baptist Views. Baptist views of liberalism have ranged across the entire spectrum from wholehearted support to complete antagonism. Protestant liberalism in the United States sought to build an understanding of faith that utilized the historical approach to the Bible, adopted the evolutionary hypothesis, utilized modern psychological and sociological principles and generally stressed the immanence of God, all within a system that was typically centered in Jesus Christ.

There have been several prominent Baptist liberals. William Newton Clarke* is among the most outstanding voices of evangelical liberalism. He served as pastor, teacher and writer. Among his numerous writings was the influential *An Outline*

of Christian Theology, published first in 1898 and going through some fourteen editions. The *Outline* was the virtual handbook of theological liberalism in the early twentieth century. Perhaps the most prominent of Baptist liberal pastors was Harry Emerson Fosdick,* whose years as pastor at Riverside Church* in New York City (1925-1946) covered, and indeed provoked, much of the conflict between liberals and their opponents. Among the several books that Fosdick published were two classics of American Protestant liberalism, *Christianity and Progress* (1922) and *The Modern Use of the Bible* (1924). There were numerous other Baptist liberals, including George Burman Foster,* Shirley Jackson Case,* Shailer Mathews* and William Rainey Harper* at the University of Chicago. Walter Rauschenbusch,* for many years professor at Rochester Theological Seminary,* was both a theoretician of the Social Gospel* movement and one of America's leading Protestant liberals. His *Christianity and the Social Crisis* (1907) was a programmatic essay for the application of a liberal gospel to the social ills of his day.

By all counts, liberalism was well settled in academic and theological institutions of Northern Baptists. It was less prominent in Southern Baptist* institutions. Crawford Howell Toy,* professor of Old Testament at Southern Baptist Theological Seminary* (1869-1879), was forced to relinquish his post because of his controversial views on the Bible.

As the warfare against liberalism emerged among America's conservative evangelicals, Baptists provided a flourishing home for such resistance. The major source of resistance to liberalism was a group of fundamentalists,* among whom Baptists were conspicuously represented. Among the early attacks on liberalism were those instigated in the 1920s by J. Frank Norris* of Fort Worth, Texas. Another assault by Baptists against liberalism was launched by the Baptist Bible Union of North America,* formed in reaction to liberalism in the Northern Baptist Convention (*see* American Baptist Churches in the USA). Other controversies that illustrate Baptists' negative reactions to liberalism include the 1961 Southern Baptist controversy over the publication of *The Message of Genesis* by Ralph Elliott and the retraction of the Genesis commentary in the Broadman Bible Commentary (*see* Broadman Press) as a result of a 1970 vote at the Southern Baptist Convention (SBC). A systematic campaign against liberalism in denominational structures began in 1979 in the SBC, resulting in the polarization of extremes between moderates and fundamental-conservatives (see "Inerrancy Controversy"). The latter group tends to identify any position as "liberal" that does not espouse an inerrantist approach to Scripture.

BIBLIOGRAPHY. N. T. Ammerman, *Baptist Battles* (1990); W. R. H. Hutchison, *The Modernist Impulse in American Protestantism* (1976); B. J. Leonard, *God's Last and Only Hope: The Fragmentation of the Southern Baptist Convention* (1990); H. L. McBeth, *The Baptist Heritage* (1987).

H. W. Pipkin

Liele, George (c. 1750-1820). Black Baptist preacher. Born a slave in Virginia, Liele was taken by his master to Burke County, Georgia, where he was converted to Christianity in 1772. In 1775 he was ordained to work as a missionary among slaves on surrounding plantations. Among those he converted was David George,* a slave of George Calphin, who ran an Indian trading post at Silver Bluff on the South Carolina side of the Savannah River. David George was designated to minister to Silver Bluff Baptist Church, now regarded as the oldest black church in America. Liele, considered the first formally ordained black minister in America, was freed by his master to carry out his ministry. The attempted reenslavement of Liele following his master's death was prevented by a British officer in Savannah, where Liele preached for the three years of the British occupation during the Revolutionary War. Among the slaves baptized by Liele was Andrew Bryan,* who in 1788 organized the First African Church of Savannah.* In 1783 Liele accompanied the British to Jamaica, traveling as an indentured servant to pay his passage. After securing his freedom in 1784, he obtained permission to preach in Jamaica, becoming the first black American foreign missionary.

BIBLIOGRAPHY. E. A. Holmes, "George Liele: Negro Slavery's Prophet of Deliverance," *Foun* 9 (1966):333-45; C. G. Woodson, *The History of the Negro Church* (1921).

M. R. Sawyer

Lindh, Olof (1835-1912). Prominent Swedish Baptist* pioneer preacher. Born into a devout family in the province of Helsingland, Sweden, on September 24, 1935, Lindh was converted at age twenty-four and baptized soon after on May

8, 1860. He began to witness publicly in 1862 and assumed his first pastorate in 1863 in Hudiksvall.

Lindh emigrated to America in 1866 and helped organize the First Swedish Baptist Church of Chicago in August of that year. He was active in its work and then spent almost a decade in western Illinois and eastern Iowa as a missionary and as pastor in Altona (1867-1868) and in Rock Island-Moline (1870-1876). He returned for a short while to Sweden and pastored there from 1876 to 1879. His ministry resulted in revival both in the United States and in Sweden, with 300 baptisms in Sweden. After returning to America, Lindh served as pastor, preacher, evangelist and organizer of new churches in the Eastern states. Nearly 800 persons were baptized by him, and at least twenty-one churches, eighteen of them in the Eastern states, owed their beginning to him. He continued to preach widely after his retirement in 1900. He died on October 5, 1912, while on a preaching mission in Sioux City, Iowa.

BIBLIOGRAPHY. O. Lindh, *Minnen och Iakttagelser fran en Forfluten Lefnad* (1907); A. Olson, *A Centenary History As Related to the Baptist General Conference of America* (1952).

N. A. Magnuson

Lord, Lucy T. (1817-1853). American Baptist missionary to China. She was born in Buckland, Massachusetts, and raised in Chautauqua County, New York, in a loving family that emphasized the church and education. She attended Franklin Academy in Shelburne Falls, Massachusetts, and Mount Holyoke Female Seminary, from which she graduated in 1840. She taught at Mount Holyoke from 1841 to 1846, and it was during that tenure that she began to feel called to missions. She met her husband, Edward C. Lord, at the 1846 annual meeting of the American Baptist Missionary Union. They married on September 14, 1846, and sailed for China on January 5, 1847. They settled in Ningpo. Lucy Lord learned the Chinese language, translated tracts and corresponded. The Lords had one son, who died in infancy. After five years in China, the Lords returned home because of her poor health. She died in Fredonia, New York, on May 5, 1853.

BIBLIOGRAPHY. L. T. Lord, *Memoir of Mrs. Lucy T. Lord* (1854).

S. L. Still

Lord's Supper, Baptist Views. Traditionally Baptists have viewed the Lord's Supper as a church ordinance* restricted to properly baptized believers and understood primarily as a memorial.

Baptists commonly refer to the Lord's Supper as an "ordinance" rather than a "sacrament" to deemphasize Communion as a means of objective grace under institutional control and to accent obedience to Christ's command. There are three main Baptist viewpoints on prerequisites for Communion. "Open communion" Baptists, dominant among British churches, assume that the oneness of the whole people of God outweighs divisions regarding baptism and invite all professing baptized Christians, including those baptized as infants, to the Supper. "Closed [or close] intercommunion," the majority view in America, closes participation to all except those baptized by immersion upon a profession of faith. "Closed [or close] intracommunion," widespread among Baptists in America influenced by the Landmark* movement, further restricts participation to members of the congregation performing the rite. A kind of open Communion by default is practiced in many nominally closed Baptist communions through omission of instructions to or screening of participants.

Early Baptists interpreted Communion as a complex commemoration with depth (like Calvin*) but gradually limited it to a more one-dimensional commemoration as sign (more Zwinglian). This shift is reflected in Baptist confessions* and through popular clichés such as "The Supper is only a symbol." This trend is reversing as ecumenical twentieth-century Baptist leaders have reasserted the manifold meanings of *anamnēsis* ("remembrance"), amplifying the spiritual presence and communion present in biblical and historical observances of the Supper. Appalachian subdenominations of Baptists—Primitives,* Old Regulars*—often articulate the sacramental nature of the observance.

See also ORDINANCES.

BIBLIOGRAPHY. A. B. Crabtree, "Eucharist in Baptist Life and Thought," in *Eucharist in Ecumenical Dialogue,* ed. L. Swidler (1976); N. H. Maring and W. S. Hudson, *Baptist Manual of Polity and Practice* (1991); W. M. Patterson, "The Lord's Supper in Baptist History," *RE* 66 (Winter 1969).

W. L. Allen

Lott Carey Baptist Foreign Mission Convention. African-American Baptist foreign mission convention. The Lott Carey Foreign Mission Convention (LCBFMC) was organized on December 16 and 17, 1897, at the Shiloh Baptist Church in Washington, D.C., by black Baptists of the Eastern Seaboard who were disgruntled with the policies of the newly organized National Baptist Convention (NBC; *see* National Baptists). However, in recent years the differences have been resolved, and members hold positions in both bodies.

The initial charges leading to withdrawal were brought by the Virginia delegation. The group argued that since its founding in 1895, the NBC had removed all Virginians except one from the Foreign Mission Board, moved its headquarters from Richmond to Louisville, Kentucky, and the Home Mission Board was planning to write and publish its own literature instead of continuing to use the publications of the American Baptist Publication Society.* The Virginia delegation's grievances also were related to longevity of service with the old Baptist Foreign Mission Convention, which was founded in 1880 by William W. Colley, a Virginian. Virginia led in the number of missionaries in Africa and in financial support.

The LCBFMC primarily has done mission work in Africa. It has had mission stations in Liberia, Nigeria, South Africa and Zaire, and has aided missionary work in Haiti, Guyana, India and Russia. By 1923 there was a total of forty-three missionaries, thirty-one in Africa and twelve in Haiti. Beginning in the mid-twentieth century, Wendell C. Somerville served as executive secretary-treasurer for many years. The mission's headquarters are in Washington, D.C.

BIBLIOGRAPHY. L. Fitts, *Lott Carey: First Black Missionary to Africa* (1978); S. D. Martin, *Black Baptists and African Missions: The Origins of a Movement, 1880-1915* (1989); J. M. Washington, *Frustrated Fellowship: The Black Baptist Quest For Social Power* (1986).

L. H. Williams

Louisiana College. Four-year coeducational Baptist college. Louisiana College was founded October 3, 1906, in Pineville, Rapides Parish, Louisiana, and is supported by the Louisiana Baptist Convention. It was established to be the successor to two north Louisiana schools, Mt. Lebanon University (1852) for men and Keatchie College (1857) for women. The convention's Education Commission designated W. F. Taylor as chairman of the faculty, with Claybrook Cottingham and Bruce Benton as the other faculty members. Presidents have included E. O. Ware (1908), C. W. Friley (1909), Claybrook Cottingham (1910), Edgar Godbold (1941), G. Earl Guinn (1951) and Robert L. Lynn (1975). The commission was replaced by a board of trustees under a new charter in 1921. By the 1990s there were five administrative officers and seventy-five full-time faculty members.

The campus has grown from forty to eighty-one acres. The first permanent building was Alexandria Hall (1920), followed by seven other administrative/academic buildings, four residence complexes, three student services buildings and two official residences. With recent construction and remodeling, property values will exceed $35 million.

The school began with nineteen students; graduates now exceed 8,000. It has fifteen academic departments, eleven preprofessional programs, twenty majors and thirty-four concentrations. It offers travel-study programs in England and China as well as an international faculty exchange program.

BIBLIOGRAPHY. Louisiana College, *Catalogue, 1992-93.*   S. F. Anders

Louisville Colored Municipal College. *See* PARRISH, CHARLES H., SR.

Love, Emmanuel King (1850-1900). Denominational leader, pastor, newspaper editor, civil rights advocate and missionary agent for Georgia. Love was born near Marion, Alabama, attended Lincoln University and graduated from Augusta Institute in Georgia in 1877 at the top of his class. He served as missionary agent for the American Baptist Home Mission Society* from 1877 to 1879 and for the American Baptist Publication Society* from 1881 to 1885. He was the pastor of several Georgia churches, including the historic First African Baptist Church in Savannah.* Love helped form and served as president (1889-1891, 1893) of the Baptist Foreign Mission Convention and was also president of the state black Baptist convention. He founded and edited *The Baptist Truth,* edited the *Centennial Record* and was associate editor of the *Georgia Sentinel.* Love authored *History of the First African Baptist Church, from Its Organization, January 20, 1788, to July*

1, 1888. He also championed the causes of black higher education and temperance, and called for the abolition of chain gangs, discrimination in public transportation, lynching, voter disfranchisement and discrimination in jury service.

BIBLIOGRAPHY. *A-AE* 5; *DAB* X; S. D. Martin, *Black Baptists and African Missions* (1989); A. W. Pegues, *Our Baptist Ministers and Schools* (1892); C. M. Wagner, *Profiles of Black Georgia Baptists* (1980); J. M. Washington, *Frustrated Fellowship* (1986).   S. D. Martin

Love, James Franklin (1859-1928). Southern Baptist* pastor, denominational executive and foreign missions leader. Born in Elizabeth City, North Carolina, on July 14, 1859, Love was awarded D.D. degrees from Wake Forest College* and Baylor University.* In addition to pastorates at Rocky Mount and Wadesboro, North Carolina, Love served as the state secretary of missions in Arkansas and as assistant corresponding secretary of the Home Mission Board* of the Southern Baptist Convention (1906-1914).

From 1914 to 1915 he served as home secretary of the Foreign Mission Board* of the Southern Baptist Convention. In 1915 he succeeded J. R. Willingham as the executive secretary of the Foreign Mission Board, a position that he held until his death in 1928.

Love's tenure at the board spanned the difficult period of World War I and the earliest stages of the Great Depression. Financial difficulties plagued the board throughout his tenure. His mission philosophy was informed by the concept of Anglo-Saxon supremacy, which became a primary impetus toward increasing Southern Baptist mission efforts in Europe.

His published works include *The Unique Message and the Universal Mission of Christianity* (1910), *The Mission of Our Nation* (1912), *The Union Movement* (1918) and *The Appeal of the Baptist Program for Europe* (1920).

See also FOREIGN MISSION BOARD, SBC.

BIBLIOGRAPHY. B. J. Cauthen and F. K. Means, *Advance to Bold Mission Thrust: 1845-1980* (1980); *ESB* 2:809.   R. Nash

M

Mabie, Henry Clay (1847-1918). Northern Baptist pastor and missionary leader. Born in Belvedere, Illinois, Mabie was encouraged to go into the ministry by his British pastor, Charles Hill Roe, whose daughter he later married. After attending the University of Chicago and its Divinity School,* Mabie served ably as pastor of Baptist churches in Rockford (1869-1873) and Oak Park (1873-1875), Illinois; Boston (1876-1879); Indianapolis (1879-1883); St. Paul (1885-1888); and Minneapolis (1889-1890). A strong supporter of the missions* cause among Baptists, he attended the World Missionary Conference in London in 1888.

In 1890 he was elected as the home secretary of the American Baptist Missionary Union* (later called American Baptist Foreign Mission Society*). In this capacity he traveled extensively to mission sites around the world. Mabie was also a prolific writer and apologist for the missionary cause. Among his better-known books are *The Meaning and Message of the Cross* (1906), *The Divine Right of Missions* (1908) and *The Task Worth While* (1910).

In matters of denominational controversy, Mabie sympathized with the fundamentalists* against the modernists and protested the move toward centralization in the Northern Baptist Convention (*see* American Baptist Churches in the USA), which, he felt, undermined the voluntary* character of the Missionary Union. In later years Mabie lectured widely in Baptist colleges and seminaries and served as professor at Rochester Theological Seminary.*

BIBLIOGRAPHY. H. C. Mabie, *From Romance to Reality* (1917).

T. F. George

McCracken, Robert James (1904-1973). Baptist preacher. Born in Motherwell, Scotland, McCracken studied at the University of Glasgow (M.A., 1925; B.D., 1928). He then served Marshall Street Baptist Church, Edinburgh, from 1928 to 1932 and Dennistown Baptist Church, Glasgow, from 1932 to 1938. He also taught systematic theology at the Baptist Theological College in Glasgow. In 1937 McCracken served as a delegate to the World Conference on Faith and Order at Edinburgh.

In 1938 he moved to Ontario and became professor of Christian theology and philosophy of religion at McMaster University* in Hamilton (1938-1946). In 1946 he succeeded Harry Emerson Fosdick* as minister of the Riverside Church, New York City,* where he preached until he retired in 1967. During his time at Riverside McCracken taught homiletics at Union Theological Seminary* in New York and delivered the Sprunt Lectures at Union Theological Seminary of Virginia (1952), the Stone Lectures at Princeton Theological Seminary (1954) and the Shaffer Lectures at Yale University (1957).

Among his publications were *Questions People Ask* (1951), *The Making of the Sermon* (1956), *Putting Faith to Work* (1960) and *What Is Sin? What Is Virtue?* (1966). As a preacher, McCracken brought to the American pulpit the gift of classic Scottish oratory combined with an emphasis on the biblical text.

See also FOSDICK, HARRY EMERSON.

BIBLIOGRAPHY. C. Fant and W. Pinson Jr., eds., *Twenty Centuries of Great Preaching* (1971).

D. Macleod

McDaniel, George White (1875-1927). Southern Baptist* preacher and denominational leader. Born in Texas, McDaniel received his formal education at Baylor University* in Texas and the Southern Baptist Seminary* at Louisville, Kentucky. Ordained in 1899, he served as pastor of numerous Southern Baptist churches, including Gaston Avenue Baptist in Dallas and First Baptist of Richmond, Virginia (1902-1927).

McDaniel was an active leader in denominational life, serving in numerous agencies and boards of trustees, including those of Richmond College and the Southern Baptist Seminary. He was also president of the Southern Baptist Convention and the Baptist General Association of Virginia. As a spokesman for his denomination, McDaniel opposed efforts to require Bible reading in Virginia public schools. In 1926 the Southern Baptist Convention approved the "McDaniel Statement," which repudiated the theory of evolution and declared humanity the unique expression of divine creation. All Southern Baptist seminary faculty members were required to subscribe.

BIBLIOGRAPHY. D. S. McDaniel, *George White McDaniel* (1928).

B. J. Leonard

McGlothlin, William Joseph (1867-1933). Southern Baptist* historian and college president. Born near Gallatin, Tennessee, McGlothlin was educated at Bethel College in Kentucky (B.A., 1889; M.A., 1891), the Southern Baptist Theological Seminary* (Th.M., 1894) and the University of Berlin (Ph.D., 1901). After teaching in public schools in Tennessee, at Bethel College and at Bardstown Male and Female Institute, in 1894 he became professor of church history at Southern Baptist Theological Seminary, where he served until 1919. From 1919 until his death in 1933 he was president of Furman University.* An active churchman, he served three terms as president of the Southern Baptist Convention (1930-1933). His major writings include *Baptist Confessions of Faith* (1910), *Infant Baptism in History* (1915) and *The Course of Christian History*. He played a significant role in interpreting Baptist history in the wake of the controversy surrounding the teachings of William H. Whitsitt.*

BIBLIOGRAPHY. *ESB* 2.

E. G. Hinson

Macintosh, Douglas Clyde (1877-1948). Baptist theologian and educator. Born in Breadalbane, Canada, Macintosh was educated at McMaster University* (B.A., 1903) and the University of Chicago (Ph.D., 1909). From his rural Canadian background Macintosh emerged to become one of America's leading philosophical theologians. Influenced by his mother's piety and a familial connection with Wesleyan Methodism, he remained devoted to a vital Christian experience, though his studies in theology and his three-dec-

ade teaching career at Yale Divinity School identified him as a powerful thinker of liberal* Protestantism.

Macintosh studied with significant theologians of his era, including George Herbert Mead and George Burman Foster,* and he also claimed an indebtedness to the German liberal theologian Albert Ritschl (1822-1889). Early in his career he attempted an empirical theology in response to the skepticism and historical relativism of his contemporaries. In several major books he created a theology based on empirically verifiable knowledge in combination with other emerging sciences. He also envisioned a world that could be improved by goodwill and energetic human effort, and his doctrine of Christ stood apart from the logical essentials of Christian belief. Among his published works were *The Reasonableness of Christianity* (1928) and *Theology as an Empirical Science* (1919).

Beyond the classroom, Macintosh was remembered for his celebrated struggle to achieve U.S. citizenship. During World War I he became a critic of U.S. military involvement and was subsequently denied the right to citizenship. The U.S. Supreme Court upheld the decision in 1931.

BIBLIOGRAPHY. *DAB* 4.

W. H. Brackney

McKinney, Benjamin Baylus (1886-1952). Prominent song composer and church music leader among Southern Baptists.* Of humble birth in Heflin, Louisiana, he manifested an unusual talent at any early age. After training in schools in Chicago, he taught on the music faculty of Southwestern Baptist Theological Seminary* from 1925 to 1935 and served as music editor for the Dallas firm of Robert H. Coleman from 1918 to 1935.

From 1935 until his death he worked in Nashville, Tennessee, initially as the first music editor of the Baptist Sunday School Board* and then as the first secretary of the church music department (1941). In these capacities he was editor of numerous hymn collections and promoter of a constantly expanding ministry of music in the churches.

Throughout his career he composed, edited and published some 500 works, including the hymns "Have Faith in God," "Satisfied with Jesus," "Wherever He Leads I'll Go" and "Holy Spirit, Breathe on Me." Since he reflected in his gospel songs a style of theological expression and music that was popular with Southern Baptists, he has been generally considered to be the archetypical "Mr. Southern Baptist Church Music." His untimely death on September 7, 1952, in Bryson City, North Carolina, was the result of an automobile accident.

See also HYMNODY, BAPTIST.

BIBLIOGRAPHY. *Handbook to the Baptist Hymnal* (1992); *The New Grove Dictionary of American Music,* vol. 3 (1986); W. J. Reynolds and A. C. Faircloth, *The Songs of B. B. McKinney* (1974).

H. T. McElrath

McLaurin, John Bates (1884-1952). Canadian Baptist* missionary. Born in India to Canadian Baptist missionaries, he received his high-school education in the United States and Canada and in 1905 graduated in engineering from McMaster University.* In 1906 he began theological training at McMaster Divinity School.

Ordained as a Baptist minister, McLaurin was accepted in 1909 as a missionary to south India. There he exercised a remarkably effective ministry among Telugu-speaking people. He taught for a time at Ramapatnam Theological Seminary and later established the Jeevamruta Seminary in Kakinada. A strong advocate of turning over missionary functions to the indigenous church (especially the task of evangelism), McLaurin was critical of the physical and social distance between missionaries and their Indian colleagues. He supported ecumenical cooperation on the field.

McLaurin was one of Canada's best-known missionaries of the first half of the twentieth century. From 1939 until his death he served as the general secretary of the Canadian Baptist Foreign Mission.

BIBLIOGRAPHY. E. C. Merrick, *J. B. McLaurin: A Biography* (1955).

D. M. Lewis

Maclay, Archibald (1778-1860). Baptist pastor and organizer of benevolent societies. Born in Killearn, Scotland, May 14, 1778, Maclay prepared for the ministry at the seminary of Robert and James Haldane in Edinburgh, graduating in 1802. After serving briefly as pastor of a Congregational church at Kirkcaldy, he sailed for New York City in 1805 to begin a career in overseas missions. He immediately formed a Congregational church, though after three years he led a portion of the church to reconstitute itself as a Baptist congre-

gation, which later became known as Tabernacle Church. Widely regarded as a superior preacher and pastor, he resigned the church in 1837 to begin an even more notable career within numerous benevolent societies and the Bible translation movement. In 1837 he became an agent of the American and Foreign Bible Society* and in 1850 helped organize the American Bible Union. Maclay was founder of the Baptist General Missionary Convention, the American Baptist Home Mission Society* and the New York Baptist Missionary Society.

BIBLIOGRAPHY. I. W. Maclay, *The Life of Rev. Archibald Maclay, D.D., 1776-1860* (1902).

B. C. Leslie

McLure, Maude Reynolds (1863-1938). First principal of the Woman's Missionary Union Training School.* Born April 25, 1863, on an Alabama plantation and educated at home by private instructors, McLure attended Judson College* and a finishing school in Baltimore. In January 1886 she married Thomas E. McLure and moved to Chester, South Carolina, where Thomas died in 1889. In 1904 Maude went with her young son to teach music at Cox College, College Park, Georgia. In 1907 she became the first principal of the Woman's Missionary Union Training School at Louisville, Kentucky, where she was lovingly known as "Mother McLure." In 1912 she distinguished herself among Christian social-service workers by establishing a settlement house (later called Good Will Center), a laboratory for students of missions* and social work. This settlement became a model for Baptist centers across the South. In 1916, McLure, with Kathleen Mallory,* became one of the first two women to address the Southern Baptist Convention.* In 1923 McLure retired to South Carolina, where she lived with her son until his death in 1931; she then moved to Columbus, Georgia, to her niece's home, where she died on April 8, 1938.

See also WOMAN'S MISSIONARY UNION TRAINING SCHOOL.

BIBLIOGRAPHY. C. Allen, *A Century to Celebrate* (1987); *ESB* 2:843-44.

T. L. Scales

McMaster, William (1811-1887). Canadian Baptist* philanthropist. Born in County Tyrone in Ulster, Ireland, McMaster was converted at ten years of age and joined the Baptist congregation in Omagh. The intense faith of the small Irish

Baptist community, under the leadership of Alexander Carson, so formed McMaster that in spite of his later financial, political and social eminence, he never deviated from his earliest convictions. He immigrated to Toronto in 1833 and quickly became a partner and then sole proprietor in a dry-goods firm.

McMaster's entrepreneurial genius soon made him one of the wealthiest men in Toronto. He held numerous business directorates in railways and insurance. In 1867, the year of Canadian Confederation, McMaster became a founding president of the Bank of Commerce, a position that he held for two decades, building it into one of the largest banks in the country. In the same year he was also appointed to the newly formed Canadian Senate.

McMaster was a leader in Toronto's original Baptist Congregation and was involved in the erection of its magnificent building on Jarvis Street in 1875. He helped found Woodstock College, the first Baptist college in Ontario, in 1860 and assisted in moving the theological department to Toronto in 1881. In the year of his death the whole institution moved to Toronto, where McMaster munificently contributed to the land, buildings and endowment for what was named McMaster University.

BIBLIOGRAPHY. *DCB* 11; C. M. Johnston, *McMaster University,* 2 vols. (1976).

I. S. Rennie

McMaster University. Canadian Baptist* university. The roots of McMaster University are to be found in 1838, when the Canada Baptist Mission Society established Canada Baptist College in Montreal. The successor was the Canadian Literary Institute, founded by Robert A. Fyfe in 1857; this eventually became Woodstock College. The offer of a generous gift, plus the proximity to the burgeoning University of Toronto, led Ontario Baptists to move the theological program of Woodstock College to the newly formed Toronto Baptist College.

In 1881 Senator William McMaster,* a banker and commodities merchant, gave a substantial endowment to Toronto Baptist College, and the trustees renamed the school in his honor. University status was granted in 1887. McMaster University was situated in Toronto from 1881 until its relocation to Hamilton, Ontario, in 1930.

During the mid-1920s McMaster became a lightning rod for fundamentalist* Baptists in cen-

tral Canada. In 1925 T. T. Shields,* pastor at Jarvis Street Baptist Church in Toronto, called for an investigation of the university's appointment of L. H. Marshall of Coventry, England, to the chair of pastoral theology. Shields then engaged in a fierce crusade against the university and its chancellor, Howard Widden. Amidst stormy sessions of the Baptist Convention in 1926, Shields was defeated and McMaster's course affirmed. The controversy led to a deep rift in Baptist life and ultimately to the formation of an independent body of Baptists.

After World War II student enrollment grew rapidly at McMaster, and the Baptists realized they could no longer adequately support the university. In 1957 McMaster became a provincially funded institution in which theological education was offered by McMaster Divinity College, a separately chartered, affiliated college of the university.

BIBLIOGRAPHY. C. M. Johnston, *McMaster University,* 2 vols. (1981); A. L. McCrimmon, *The Educational Policy of the Baptists of Ontario and Quebec* (1920). W. H. Brackney

Madison University. *See* COLGATE BAPTIST UNIVERSITY.

Mallory, Kathleen Moore (1879-1954). Leader of Woman's Missionary Union* (WMU), auxiliary to the Southern Baptist Convention.* Born in Dallas County, Alabama, January 24, 1879, Kathleen Moore grew up in Selma, where her father was mayor. She graduated with first honors from Dallas Academy in 1898 and received the A.B. degree from Woman's College of Baltimore (later Goucher College) in 1902. Mallory entered professional WMU work in 1909 as the corresponding secretary for Alabama's organization. In 1912 she was elected corresponding secretary of the national WMU organization, a position she held for thirty-six years (with a title change to executive secretary in 1937). In 1916 Mallory and Maude R. McLure* became the first women to address the Southern Baptist Convention. She wrote *Manual of WMU Methods* in 1917, edited *Royal Service* from 1920 to 1948 and edited the annual WMU *Year Book,* first published in 1912. In 1948 Mallory retired at age sixty-nine, living in Selma, Alabama, until her death on June 17, 1954.

BIBLIOGRAPHY. C. Allen, *Laborers Together with God* (1987); A. W. Ussery, *Kathleen Mallory* (1956). T. L. Scales

Manly, Basil, Jr. (1825-1892). Southern Baptist* educator, preacher, organizer and hymnwriter. Born in South Carolina, Manly moved with his family to Tuscaloosa, Alabama, in 1837. Graduating from the University of Alabama (where his father was president) in 1843, he studied theology at Newton Theological Institute* and Princeton Theological Seminary, graduating from Princeton in 1847. Manly served as pastor of the prestigious First Baptist Church of Richmond, Virginia (1850-1854), but resigned in 1854 to become president of Richmond Female Institute.

In 1859 Manly was asked to compose an "abstract of principles" for the newly formed Southern Baptist Theological Seminary.* His effort reflects the moderate Calvinist* approach to Baptist doctrine. Manly also joined the seminary faculty as professor of Old Testament interpretation. Except for a brief period as president of Georgetown College, Kentucky (1871-1877), Manly spent the remainder of his career at the seminary. Among Manly's publications were *A Call to the Ministry* (1867) and *The Bible Doctrine of Inspiration* (1888). He was a noted hymnwriter and with his father, Basil Manly Sr.,* compiled a collection entitled *Baptist Psalmody* (1850). Manly was also instrumental in the founding of the Sunday School Board* of the Southern Baptist Convention in 1863.

See also MANLY, BASIL, SR.; SOUTHERN BAPTIST THEOLOGICAL SEMINARY.

BIBLIOGRAPHY. *DAB* VI; L. Manly, *The Manly Family* (1930).   B. J. Leonard

Manly, Basil, Sr. (1798-1868). Baptist pastor, educator and Confederate statesman. Born in Chatham County, North Carolina, Manly attended the South Carolina College, graduating in 1821. He soon accepted the pastorate of the Edgefield Baptist Church in South Carolina and became known for his ability as a preacher. In 1826 Manly became pastor of the First Baptist Church of Charleston,* South Carolina, and remained there until 1837, when he became the second president of the University of Alabama. He held this position for eighteen years. In 1855 he returned to the pastorate, accepting the call to Wentworth Baptist Church of Charleston. Four years later he became state evangelist for Alabama Baptists, and from 1860 to 1863 he was pastor of First Baptist Church, Montgomery, Alabama.

Manly was a strong supporter of the secessionist cause, urging separation from the Union, and a leader in the formation of the Southern Baptist Convention.* He was also a strong supporter of theological education and the formation of the Southern Baptist Theological Seminary.*

See also MANLY, BASIL, JR.; SOUTHERN BAPTIST THEOLOGICAL SEMINARY.

BIBLIOGRAPHY. J. P. Cox, "A Study of the Life and Work of Basil Manly, Jr." (Ph.D. dissertation, Southern Baptist Theological Seminary, 1954); *DAB* VI; L. Manly, *The Manly Family* (1930).   B. J. Leonard

Manning, James (1738-1791). Colonial Baptist pastor and first president of Rhode Island College (Brown University*). Born at Elizabethtown, New Jersey, Manning was converted in a Baptist church in his hometown and was subsequently ordained by the church as an evangelist. Manning attended the Hopewell Academy (1756-1758) and graduated from the College of New Jersey (B.A. 1762; M.A., 1765). In 1764 he was asked by the Philadelphia Baptist Association* to assist in the founding of a college to train Baptist ministers. Manning settled in Warren, Rhode Island, where he founded a church and established a Latin grammar school. The college opened with one student, William Rogers, in 1765.

In 1767 Manning founded the Warren Association, the first association of Baptists in New England. After resigning from the Warren church, Manning moved Rhode Island College to Providence, where he assumed the pastorate of the Providence church. President Manning represented Rhode Island at the Continental Congress (1785-1786) and was influential in the ratification of the U.S. Constitution. In 1791 he argued in favor of free public schools.

BIBLIOGRAPHY. *AAP* 6; I. Backus, *History of New England Baptists,* rev. ed. (1871); *DAB* VI.   L. W. Hähnlen

Marney, Carlyle (1916-1978). Southern Baptist* pastor and controversialist. A native of Harriman, Tennessee, Carlyle Marney took degrees from Carson-Newman College* (1938) and the Southern Baptist Theological Seminary* (Th.M., 1943; Th.D., 1946). He had an outstanding pastoral ministry in three notable churches: Immanuel Baptist Church, Paducah, Kentucky (1946-1948), First Baptist Church, Austin, Texas (1948-1958), and Myers Park Baptist Church, Charlotte, North Carolina (1958-1967). During the last decade of his life, he founded and directed the Interpreter's

House at Lake Junaluska, North Carolina, a counseling and continuing-education center for pastors and laypersons.

Marney was recognized as one of the great preachers of his day and was much in demand as a lecturer and conference speaker. Although he never severed ties with his Baptist heritage, Marney moved freely in wider ecumenical circles. While he exerted a great influence on progressive pastors within the Southern Baptist Convention, he became increasingly alienated from the denominational hierarchy. He was an outspoken critic of what he saw as religious institutionalism and its captivity to culture.

Marney was a prolific author. Many of his books reflect his advanced ideas on social ethics and pastoral psychology. His writings include *Beggars in Velvet* (1960), *Structures of Prejudice* (1961), *The Recovery of the Person* (1963) and *Priests to Each Other* (1974). In 1976 Marney was awarded the D.D. by Glasgow University.

BIBLIOGRAPHY. J. J. Carey, *Carlyle Marney: A Pilgrim's Progress* (1980); M. Kratt, *Marney* (1979).

T. F. George

Mars Hill College. A Baptist liberal arts college located in Mars Hill, North Carolina. Situated in the Blue Ridge Mountains of North Carolina, the school was the first educational institution to be founded by Baptists in the western part of the state and is now the oldest private school in the region. It began in 1856 as the French Broad Baptist Institute, named for the Baptist association that founded it. The school endured amid financial struggles until it was forced to close during the Civil War, when troops were housed on its campus. After the war, conditions did not immediately improve, and the school had thirteen presidents during the period 1866-1897, until Robert Lee Moore assumed the office and remained president for forty-one years (1897-1938). Moore's lengthy tenure brought stability and growth to the institution. Mars Hill was a junior college until 1963, when it developed its present four-year status. It occupies a campus of over 200 acres in a scenic section of the state and is owned and operated by the Baptist State Convention of North Carolina.

BIBLIOGRAPHY. *ESB* 1, 4.

B. J. Leonard

Marshall, Andrew (?-1856). Black Baptist* minister. Born in slavery, Marshall was converted and taught in the pioneering black Baptist ministry of his uncle Andrew Bryan* in Savannah, Georgia. Succeeding to the pulpit of the First African Church of Savannah* in 1813, he developed a powerful and popular ministry and remained there for forty-three years. Once his congregation numbered nearly 2,800 members, but he lost the support of many of them in the 1830s when he adopted Campbellite theology (*see* Campbell, Alexander). Charged with antinomianism, Marshall was opposed by a contingent of the congregation, which appealed to the Sudbury Baptist Association to put the church under the authority of the white Baptists of Savannah. In 1837 the schism was healed when Marshall renounced Alexander Campbell's teachings, and his popularity was restored. Having once been whipped for violating the laws of slavery, Marshall became a prosperous man and an astute leader among black Southern Baptists. His congregations held membership in biracial associations, Savannah River and Sudbury, and his services became tourist attractions, earning mention in the travel sketches of European writers Fredrika Bremer and Charles Lyell.

BIBLIOGRAPHY. B. K. Lowe, *History of the First African Baptist Church* (1888); A. J. Raboteau, *Slave Religion* (1978).

W. B. Gravely and C. White

Marshall, College of. *See* EAST TEXAS BAPTIST UNIVERSITY.

Marshall, Daniel (1706-1784). Separate Baptist* preacher and revivalist; organizer of the first Baptist church in Georgia. Born in Windsor, Connecticut, Marshall was a member of the Congregational church. Converted in 1726, he served as a deacon for twenty years. By 1744 Marshall seems to have begun to object to the doctrine of infant baptism,* and in 1745 he heard George Whitefield preach. After the death of his first wife, Marshall in 1747 married Martha Stearns (*see* Marshall, Martha Stearns), sister of Shubal Stearns.* By 1751 both Marshall and Stearns were convinced separatists. Sometime in 1751 or 1752 Marshall, joined by his wife and children, began to travel south. Settling in Pennsylvania, they ministered among the Mohawks until difficulties preceding the French and Indian War forced them southward again. Arriving in Opekon (Winchester), Virginia, in 1754, Marshall found a Baptist church (Mill Creek) affiliated with the Philadelphia Baptist Association.* There he was baptized and licensed to preach, although his enthusiastic manner produced some complaints from the Regular Baptists.* Already middle-aged, Marshall preached throughout southern Virginia and North Carolina, and eventually established a Baptist church in Kiokee, Georgia, in 1772. In 1784 Marshall moderated the first meeting of the Georgia Baptist Association, consisting of six churches.

A man of simple natural gifts, yet a passionate and energetic evangelist, Marshall, with Stearns, was responsible for rapid growth among the Baptists in Virginia and the Carolinas. Because of their emphasis on revivalistic evangelism, the Separate Baptists were suspected of Arminianism,* but it is more accurate to describe their theology as a simple Calvinism* suited to the expanding Southern frontier.

BIBLIOGRAPHY. *AAP* 6; *DAB* VI; W. L. Lumpkin, *Baptist Foundations in the South* (1961); J. Mercer, *History of the Georgia Baptist Association* (1838). L. W. Hähnlen

Marshall, Martha Stearns (18th century). Separate Baptist* leader and preacher. The sister of one evangelist (Shubal Stearns*), wife of another (she married Daniel Marshall* in 1747) and mother of a third, Martha Stearns Marshall is most often identified by the men in her life. The power of her witness and of her leadership ability is credited with converting both her brother and her future husband to the Baptist expression of faith, advocating the Separate Baptist migration from New England to the South, and providing a role model for her son. Neither being jailed in Connecticut for preaching nor the shunning of the Separates by other Baptists because of the "disorder" of their worship (especially women's preaching) deterred Martha Marshall. Robert B. Semple reported in his 1810 *History of the Rise and Progress of the Baptists in Virginia* that "without the shadow of an usurped authority over the other sex, Mrs. Marshall, being a lady of good sense, singular piety, and surprising elocution, has, in countless instances, melted a whole concourse into tears by her prayers and exhortations."

See MARSHALL, DANIEL; STEARNS, SHUBAL

BIBLIOGRAPHY. *BE;* W. L. Lumpkin, *Baptist Foundations in the South* (1961); H. L. McBeth, *Women in Baptist Life;* G. W. Paschall, *History of North Carolina Baptists* (1930); G. Ryland, *The Baptists of Virginia, 1699-1926* (1955); R. B. Semple, *His-*

tory of the Rise and Progress of the Baptists in Virginia (1810); L. Sweet, *The Minister's Wife: Her Role in Nineteenth Century American Evangelicalism* (1983).

P. R. Pleasants

Martin, T(homas) T(heodore) (1862-1939). Southern Baptist* evangelist. A native of Mississippi and son of the celebrated preacher Matthew Thomas Martin, T. T. Martin was one of the most popular and influential Southern Baptist evangelists in the first third of the twentieth century. A graduate of Mississippi College* (1886) and the Southern Baptist Theological Seminary* (1896), Martin pastored churches first in Kentucky and then in Colorado, where he preached to miners in the open air.

Martin's full-time evangelistic ministry began in 1900. Most of his meetings were held in secondhand Barnum and Bailey circus tents that seated 600 to 800 people. Focusing his sermons on the free offer of salvation by grace through faith, he stressed the sovereignty of God and the objectivity of his Word. He disapproved of sensational displays of religious feeling. Martin recruited and trained the Blue Mountain Evangelists, a team of gospel singers and preachers for whom he booked revivals throughout the country.

A strong fundamentalist* and antievolutionist, Martin was a friend of William Jennings Bryan and attended the Scopes Monkey Trial in 1925. An able controversialist himself, Martin attacked William L. Poteat,* president of Wake Forest College, for his liberal theological teachings. At the same time, Martin was a loyal supporter of his denomination. This led him to criticize his fundamentalist ally J. Frank Norris* for his attacks on the Southern Baptist Convention. Martin's most popular sermon was entitled "Going to Hell in Droves." His writings include *God's Plan with Men* (1912), *Redemption and the New Birth* (1913) and *Hell in the High Schools* (1923).

BIBLIOGRAPHY. J. F. Loftis, "Thomas Theodore Martin: His Life and Work as Evangelist, Fundamentalist and Anti-Evolutionist" (Th.M. thesis, Southern Baptist Theological Seminary, 1980); T. T. Martin, *Viewing Life's Sunset from Pike's Peak* (n.d.). T. F. George

Massachusetts Baptist Education Society. A society to help train people for the ministry. The Massachusetts Baptist Education Society was organized on September 24, 1814, but its work had begun a generation earlier with the founding in 1791 of the Baptist Education Fund for the purpose of aiding young men to prepare for the ministry. In 1830 its name was changed to the Northern Baptist Education Society.

The society is now the representative of the American Baptist Churches in Massachusetts, New Hampshire and Vermont in aiding young men and women to prepare for Christian service. Scholarships are granted to properly qualified and accredited students.

Over the years the society has aided thousands of ministers, missionaries, educators and general religious workers to pay for specialized theological education. It has encouraged and aided the establishment and development of many Baptist educational institutions and has sought to create a denominational ideal of ministerial education as worthy and attainable.

T. R. McKibbens

Massachusetts Baptist Missionary Magazine. Baptist missions periodical. Founded in 1803, it grew out of the organization of the Massachusetts Baptist Missionary Society a year earlier. The society had been founded for missionary purposes—"to promote the knowledge of evangelistic truth in the new settlements within these United States; or further if circumstances should render it proper," as was stated in its original constitution.

The magazine became the written organ of the society and a pioneer periodical in the American Baptist world. It was filled with reports from pioneer Baptist missionaries on the American frontier, as well as visions of world missionary activities from articles by William Carey* and later Adoniram Judson* and others.

In 1827 the magazine was taken over by the American Baptist Foreign Mission Society,* and in 1909 its name was changed to *Missions,* and still later to *Mission.* The early issues of the magazine contain extremely important primary material on the role of early Baptists in the missionary movement.

T. R. McKibbens

Massee, J(asper) C(ortenus) (1871-1965). Baptist pastor and evangelist. Born in Marshallville, Georgia, Massee graduated from Mercer University* (A.B., 1892) and spent one year at Southern Baptist Theological Seminary* (1896-1897). Ordained in 1893, he held pastorates in Kissimmee, Florida (1893-1896), Orlando, Flori-

da (1897-1899), Lancaster, Kentucky (1899-1901), Mansfield, Ohio (1901-1903), Raleigh, North Carolina (1903-1908), Chattanooga, Tennessee (1908-1913), Dayton, Ohio (1913-1919), Brooklyn, New York (1920-1922), and Tremont Temple in Boston, Massachusetts (1922-1929). Following a successful pastorate in Boston, where he witnessed a growth of almost 2,500 members, Massee entered a Bible conference and evangelistic ministry. In later years Massee lectured at Eastern Baptist Theological Seminary* (1938-1941) and the Winona Lake School of Theology (1947-1948).

Presiding at the fundamentalist* preconvention meeting at Buffalo, New York (1920), Massee was elected president of the Fundamentalist Baptist Fellowship* within the Northern Baptist Convention (*see* American Baptist Churches in the USA) and called for an investigation of the orthodoxy of Baptist colleges and seminaries. His lack of militancy in fundamentalist causes cost him the support of some of that faction, however, and he resigned his presidency in 1925. Weary of battles within the convention, in 1926 he called for a six-month truce for the sake of reconciliation, after which conflict diminished.

BIBLIOGRAPHY. C. A. Russell, "J. C. Massee, Unique Fundamentalist," *Foun* 12, no. 4 (1969):330-56; C. A. Russell, *Voices of American Fundamentalism* (1976).

R. T. Clutter

Masters, Victor Irvine (1867-1954). Southern Baptist* editor. Masters was born in Anderson County, South Carolina, and attended Furman University* (B.A., 1888; M.A., 1889) and the Southern Baptist Theological Seminary* (Th.M., 1893). Masters was ordained in 1889, and he spent one year pastoring four rural Baptist churches in York County, South Carolina. After graduating from seminary, Masters pastored Rock Hill Baptist Church, Rock Hill, South Carolina (1893), and Pocahontas Baptist, Pocahontas, Virginia (1894-1896). From 1896 to 1900 he was a field reporter for South Carolina's *Baptist Courier.* He then pastored three rural churches in Aiken County, South Carolina. In 1903 he returned to the *Baptist Courier* as an associate editor. Masters was part owner and associate editor of South Carolina's *Baptist Press* (1905-1907), associate editor of the *Religious Herald* of Virginia (1908-1909), superintendent of publicity at the Home Mission Board* of the Southern Baptist Convention (1909-1921), editor of the Board's journal, *The Home Field* (1909-1917), and editor of Kentucky's *Western Recorder* (1921-1942).

While at the Home Mission Board, Masters wrote six books on home mission work, appealing to Southern Baptists to Christianize America. Throughout his editorial career, Masters was especially concerned about the socioeconomic and religious implications of the Catholic presence, as well as the influx of immigrant groups into America. In his editorials Masters warned Southern Baptists about the dangers of liberal theology and the bureaucratization of their denomination. Masters called for laws prohibiting the teaching of evolution in public schools, vigorously opposed the presidential candidacy of Alfred E. Smith in 1928 and was a strong supporter of Prohibition. While Masters could at times be intensely critical of his denomination, he found a lifetime of service within it.

D. B. Whitlock

Maston, T(homas) B(uford) (1897-1988). Christian ethicist, professor and author. Maston was born in Tennessee and graduated from Carson-Newman College* in 1920. His further education included Southwestern Baptist Theological Seminary* (M.R.E., 1923; D.R.E., 1925), Texas Christian University (M.A., 1927) and Yale University (Ph.D., 1939). He married Essie Mae McDonald in 1921, and they had two sons.

Maston taught at Southwestern Baptist Theological Seminary from 1922 to 1963. In his teaching he emphasized biblical and social ethics and thereby helped shape the views of a generation of Southern Baptist ministers on social issues. He was particularly known for his progressive views on race when those views were not popular in the South or among Baptists.

Widely recognized for his scholarship, Maston was also a writer and lecturer of note. He held lectureships in many universities and seminaries in the United States as well as overseas with missionaries and military personnel. His writings include *Of One: A Study of Christian Principles and Race Relations* (1946), *The Christian and the Modern World* (1952), *Right or Wrong?* (1955), *Christianity and World Issues* (1957) and *Biblical Ethics* (1967).

See also SOUTHWESTERN BAPTIST THEOLOGICAL SEMINARY.

BIBLIOGRAPHY. F. Valentine, *T. B. Maston: Shaper of Ethics and Social Concern* (1987).

H. L. McBeth

Mathews, Shailer (1863-1941). Baptist educator, ecumenist and spokesman for theological modernism. Born in Maine, Mathews graduated from Colby College (B.A., 1884) and Newton Theological Institute* (B.D., 1887) before studying briefly at Berlin University (1890-1891). He taught at Colby College (1887-1894) and the University of Chicago Divinity School* (1894-1933), where he served as professor and dean (1908-1933).

Mathews's *The Faith of Modernism* (1924) was American liberalism's* most widely read book in the 1920s. It declared that "modernists as a class are evangelical Christians . . . [who] accept Jesus Christ as the revelation of a Savior God." Their starting point is the "inherited orthodoxy," which Mathews identified as a belief in humanity's need for salvation from sin and death, the fatherly love and forgiveness of the Creator, Christ as the revelation of God and the means of salvation, the persistence of human life after death, and the centrality of the Bible as the record of divine revelation and as a guide for life. But Mathews believed that such convictions needed occasional, and even radical, restatement according to the latest scientific, historical and social standards in order to stay viable (*The Gospel and Modern Man,* 1910). When fundamentalists and other conservatives claimed that Mathews's redefinitions departed from traditional Christianity, he accused them of undercutting the faith's relevance by holding to old patterns of thought.

Mathews also advocated the Social Gospel,* as in *The Social Teachings of Jesus* (1897) and *The Atonement and the Social Process* (1930). As an avid ecumenist and churchman he was president of the Federal Council of Churches* (1912-1916) and promoted the formation of the Northern Baptist Convention (*see* American Baptist Churches in the USA), of which he served as president in 1915.

BIBLIOGRAPHY. C. H. Arnold, *Near the Edge of the Battle* (1966); *DAB* 3; *DARB;* W. R. Hutchison, *The Modernist Impulse in American Protestantism* (1976); S. Mathews, *New Faith for Old: An Autobiography* (1936); *NCAB* 11.

T. P. Weber

Mays, Benjamin Elijah (1894-1984). Minister, educator and black leader. Born in rural South Carolina to former slaves, Mays studied at Bates College (B.A., 1920) and the University of Chicago (M.A., 1925; Ph.D., 1935). Ordained to the

Baptist ministry in 1921, Mays spent his early career pursuing intermittent graduate study, pastoring in Atlanta, teaching at Morehouse* and South Carolina State colleges, serving the Urban League (Tampa, Florida) and the YMCA among Southeastern black colleges, and directing a major sociological study of the black churches. From 1934 to 1940 he was dean of Howard University School of Religion, and until 1967 he served as president of Morehouse College. From 1970 to 1982 he was chairman of the Atlanta Board of Education. A theological liberal who authored several books and numerous articles, an internationally known churchman who held high office in the major ecumenical bodies, and a nationally prominent leader in the struggle for racial justice, Mays was an important influence on Martin Luther King Jr.*

BIBLIOGRAPHY. B. E. Mays, *Born to Rebel: An Autobiography* (1986); B. E. Mays and J. Nicholson, *The Negro's Church* (1933).

D. W. Wills

Mell, Patrick Hues (1814-1888). Minister, educator, writer, denominational leader and parliamentarian. A native of Georgia, Mell attended Amherst College in the early 1830s and received an honorary doctorate from Furman University* in 1858 and from Howard College (Samford University*) in 1869. Ordained to the ministry in 1842, he served as pastor of several Georgia churches. He taught ancient languages at Mercer University* from 1841 to 1855 and served at the University of Georgia as vice chancellor from 1860 to 1872 and chancellor from 1878 to 1888. His denominational leadership included service as moderator of the Georgia Baptist Convention for twenty-five years and president of the Southern Baptist Convention* from 1863 to 1871 and 1880 to 1887. Among his books were *Baptism in Its Mode and Subjects* (1853), *Corrective Church Discipline* (1860) and *A Manual of Parliamentary Practice* (1867). The Southern Baptist Convention used this last book as its rules of order for several years. One writer described Mell as "the prince of parliamentarians."

BIBLIOGRAPHY. P. H. Mell Jr., *Life of Patrick Hues Mell, by His Son* (1895).

C. W. Deweese

Mercer, Jesse (1769-1841). Georgia Baptist preacher-pastor, denominational statesman, historian, hymnologist and philanthropist. Born in Halifax County, North Carolina, on December 16, 1769, Mercer was baptized on July 7, 1787, and was ordained by his father, Silas Mercer, to the Baptist ministry at age nineteen, on November 7, 1789. Pastor for fifty-two years of Georgia Baptist churches (Sardis, 1788-1817; Indian Creek, 1793-1796; Phillips' Mill, 1796-1835; Bethesda, 1796-1827; Powelton, 1796-1827; Eatonton, 1820-1826; Washington, 1828-1841), Mercer compiled a hymnal, *The Cluster of Spiritual Songs,* which was widely used in Baptist churches in the South.

From 1795 to 1839 he held the highest offices in the Georgia Baptist Association, the oldest such body in the state. His *A History of the Georgia Baptist Association,* published in 1838, is one of the most important historical documents ever published about Georgia Baptists. With the founding of the Georgia Baptist Convention in 1822, Mercer was elected president, a post he held for nineteen years until his death.

With pulpit, pen and purse, Jesse Mercer enthusiastically advocated Baptist missions, education, journalism and temperance. By his leadership he saved Georgia Baptists from the destructive antimissions movement.* His commitment to education is embodied in his namesake, Mercer University,* to which he gave much of his sizable estate. In 1833 he bought and edited the *Christian Index,* only to donate it to the Georgia Baptist Convention in 1840. The *Index* still serves as the Georgia Baptist newspaper. By almost any measure, Mercer exerted more influence on white Georgia Baptists than anyone in their history.

See also MERCER UNIVERSITY.

BIBLIOGRAPHY. *BE;* C. D. Mallary, *Memoirs of Elder Jesse Mercer* (1844).

W. B. Shurden

Mercer University. A university owned and operated by the Georgia Baptists. It offers an education in the liberal arts and professional education in law, business, medicine, engineering and pharmacy, and has campuses in Macon and Atlanta. Founded by the Georgia Baptist Convention in 1833 as a manual labor school and named Mercer Institute, it was first located in the tiny rural village of Penfield in Greene County. Josiah Penfield, a Baptist layman from Savannah, Jesse Mercer,* a Baptist minister after whom the school is named, and Adiel Sherwood, the "spiritual father" of the institution, were driving forces in the establishment of the school. Primarily motivated by the need for ministerial education, the found ers never restricted Mercer to that purpose.

Becoming a university in 1839, Mercer moved to Macon in 1871. With the College of Liberal Arts as the centerpiece of the institution, Mercer's evolution into a comprehensive university has been gradual. The Walter F. George School of Law began in 1871, and the Southern School of Pharmacy merged with Mercer in 1959. The School of Medicine admitted its first class in 1982, while the Stetson School of Business began in 1983 and the School of Engineering in 1985. University College, offering programs to nontraditional students in off-campus centers, was established in 1988. Mercer University Press began in 1979, making Mercer the only Baptist university with a large, active press. Today Mercer is the second-largest Baptist-affiliated university in America.

BIBLIOGRAPHY. S. Dowell, *A History of Mercer University* (1958); D. B. Potts, *Baptist Colleges in the Development of American Society, 1812-1861* (1988). W. B. Shurden

Meredith, Thomas (1795-1850). Pioneer Baptist pastor, educator and denominational leader in North Carolina. Born in Bucks County, Pennsylvania, Meredith graduated from the University of Pennsylvania (A.M., 1819). In 1819 Meredith moved to North Carolina, where he emerged as a leading voice among Baptists and was one of the founders of the Baptist State Convention of North Carolina, drawing up its constitution in 1830. He also wrote the address to the public to promote the new convention, explaining its twin objectives of Christian education and missions.* Meredith helped form the Wake Forest Institute (now Wake Forest University*) and served for many years on its board of trustees. In 1832 he launched the *Baptist Interpreter,* which became the *Biblical Recorder* in 1835, and served as its editor until his death. At the state convention in 1838 Meredith introduced a resolution urging the formation of a "female academy." In recognition of his leadership, the Baptist school for women in North Carolina was in 1909 renamed Meredith College.

BIBLIOGRAPHY. G. W. Paschal, *A History of North Carolina Baptists* (1930); G. W. Paschal, *A History of Wake Forest College* (1935). H. L. McBeth

Meredith College. A liberal arts college for women, associated with the North Carolina State Baptist Convention. It was founded in 1891 as Baptist Female University, and its first students began in 1899. In 1909 the name was changed to Meredith College, honoring Thomas Meredith, a founder of the North Carolina Baptist Convention and the state Baptist paper, the *Biblical Recorder.* The school is located in Raleigh, North Carolina, on an over-200-acre campus secured during the administration of president Charles Edward Brewer (1915-1939). Known for its strong liberal arts programs, the college offers various programs in music, education and study abroad.

BIBLIOGRAPHY. *ESB* 1, 4. B. J. Leonard

Mexican Baptist Bible Institute. A school to train Mexican-American Baptist pastors in Texas, founded in San Antonio in 1947. Mexican Baptist leaders in Texas had long felt a need for a school to train ministers. Previous efforts at theological education dated to 1907, when Charles D. Daniel sponsored an annual Bible institute, a kind of pastors' conference lasting about three days. This work lapsed but was later revived under the name Escuela de Profetas (School of the Prophets). A more permanent school was formed in 1947 under the name Mexican Baptist Bible Institute (MBBI). Paul J. Siebenmann and Matias C. Garcia were leaders in this new effort. At first sponsored by the San Antonio Baptist Association, the school opened classes in the Palm Springs Baptist Church of San Antonio. MBBI came under the auspices of the Baptist General Convention of Texas in 1963. Later the school moved to its present campus in south San Antonio, where it occupies seven buildings. In 1981 the school merged with Southwestern Baptist Theological Seminary* in Fort Worth, Texas, and took the name of Hispanic Baptist Theological Seminary. In 1989 the ties to Southwestern Seminary were severed, and the Hispanic Seminary came under the sponsorship of the State Missions Commission of the Baptist General Convention of Texas. Joshua Grijalva was president in the early 1990s.

BIBLIOGRAPHY. J. Grijalva, *A History of Mexican Baptists in Texas, 1881-1981* (1982). H. L. McBeth

Mexican Baptist Convention of Texas. Organization formed in 1910 to encourage fellowship and cooperation among Mexican-American Baptist churches in Texas. Baptist witness among Chicanos in Texas goes back at least to Thomas J. Pilgrim, who formed a Sunday school at San

Felipe in 1828. A few years later James Huckins and William Tryon, missionaries of the American Baptist Home Mission Society,* addressed Chicano as well as Anglo hearers. In 1861 the Baptist State Convention appointed J. W. D. Creath to work among Chicanos, apparently the first missionary to that group.

The first Mexican Baptist church in Texas was formed in Laredo in 1883, and by 1900 there were at least thirteen such churches in the state. At a conference of pastors in 1909 a question arose about linking their churches into a state organization. In answer to the pastors' call, twenty-four churches sent thirty-seven messengers to a meeting on May 25, 1910, at the Primera Iglasia Bautista Mexicana in San Antonio, where they formed the Convención Bautista Mexicana. The first officers included Charles D. Daniel (who stepped aside after two years to encourage Hispanic leadership), D. C. Barocio, B. C. Perez and Gil Villarreal. In 1917 a separate women's organization came into being, and in 1938 the Convención launched its own paper, *El Bautista Mexicana*, which is still published.

After strong beginnings through the 1920s, the Chicano churches suffered when the Depression of the 1930s forced many Hispanics back to Mexico. However, the 1940s brought renewal. In 1941 the Convención employed its first general evangelistic worker, Pascual Hurtiz, who moved to San Antonio to divide his time between pastoring the Iglesia Bautista Zarzamora and working as a general evangelist among the Mexican-American population.

As more Chicanos came to use English, Hispanic and Anglo churches found themselves in closer relationship. Many of the Hispanic churches affiliated with Anglo associations. Talk of merger between the Convención and the Baptist General Convention of Texas increased. In 1961 the conventions entered into a joint program called Unidos en Cristo (Unity in Christ), and in 1964 the merger was completed. However, the Mexican Baptist Convention has continued as an agency for communication and fellowship among the Hispanic churches.

BIBLIOGRAPHY. J. Grijalva, *A History of Mexican Baptists in Texas, 1881-1981* (1982); W. B. Miller, *Texas Mexican Baptist History* (1931).

H. L. McBeth

Meyer, Frederick Brotherton (1847-1929). Baptist pastor, Bible conference speaker and writer. Born in London, Meyer was convinced from his childhood that he would be a preacher. He graduated from London University in 1869 and in his student days there served the Duke Street Baptist Church. Upon graduation he took the position of assistant pastor at Pembroke Chapel, Liverpool (1869-1872), after which he served as pastor at Priory Street Baptist Church, York (1872-1874), Victoria Road Baptist Church, Leicester (1874-1878), Melbourne Hall, Leicester (1878-1888), Regent's Park Chapel, London (1888-1892, 1909-1915), and Christ Church, Westminster Bridge Road, Lambeth (1892-1907, 1915-1920). Meyer served two terms as president of the National Free Church Council (1904, 1924) and one as chairman of the English Baptist Union (1906).

While at Priory Street Church in 1873, Meyer befriended Dwight L. Moody and Ira D. Sankey, who had arrived in England to minister but found that the two men who had invited them had died. Invited to York, Moody found Meyer very helpful in getting his campaign started. This friendship resulted in Moody's inviting Meyer to America in 1891 on what was to be the first of twelve trips. Meyer spoke at the East Northfield Summer Conference for two weeks and proved so popular that he was asked to give postconference addresses. In one meeting at Northfield, J. Wilbur Chapman, who would later become a prominent evangelist, was touched by Meyer's preaching and testified later to a life-changing commitment made there.

Meyer's travels through America often proceeded at an exhausting pace. In one six-week tour he visited thirteen cities covering 3,500 miles and delivered a hundred messages. In his last trip to America, at the age of eighty, his ministry extended over 15,000 miles. His written works also received appreciative attention in the United States, especially his biographies of Bible characters and his expositional and devotional works.

BIBLIOGRAPHY. W. Y. Fullerton, *F. B. Meyer: A Biography* (1929); A. C. Mann, *F. B. Meyer: Preacher, Teacher, Man of God* (1929).

R. T. Clutter

Mid-America Baptist Theological Seminary. Baptist school with unofficial ties to the Southern Baptist Convention.* Chartered in 1971 in Louisiana as the School of the Prophets, the school moved to Little Rock, Arkansas, in 1972. There a charter was granted in March 1972, renaming it Mid-America Baptist Theological Seminary (MABTS). Olivet Baptist Church allowed it to meet in its facilities for three years. When it opened in 1972 there were four professors, including founding president B. Gray Allison, and twenty-eight students. As of 1992 its enrollment was above 400. In 1975 the seminary purchased a Reformed Jewish temple and Hebrew school in Memphis, Tennessee, where it began sessions in October 1976.

Though having no formal affiliation with the Southern Baptist Convention, MABTS employs only Southern Baptist professors, and each trustee is a Southern Baptist layman. The historical context of its establishment was the Broadman Commentary controversy (see Broadman Press). The partial rebuff conservatives experienced in that confrontation settled in the minds of several the need for a seminary openly hospitable to their specific concerns. MABTS requires yearly commitment from its faculty to the Bible as "the verbally inspired Word of God, wholly without error as originally given by God." It also requires an aggressive program of personal evangelism by every student and faculty member.

In 1987 Mid-America opened a branch seminary in Schenectady, New York, which the 1992 catalog describes as a "Bible-believing, Bible-preaching, Bible-teaching, soul-winning branch campus." Academic degrees granted include the M.Div., the Th.D., the D.Min., the associate of divinity and the M.A. in religious education.

BIBLIOGRAPHY. *ESB* 4:2341.

T. J. Nettles

Midwestern Baptist Theological Seminary. Southern Baptist* educational institution. The 200-acre campus is located among rolling hills a few miles north of downtown Kansas City in western Missouri.

The 1957 Southern Baptist Convention authorized the establishment of Midwestern as a means of serving expanding Southern Baptist missions* into the Midwest and Northwest United States. A sense of mission has always been at the heart of the school and is reflected in the vocational choices of many Midwestern graduates.

Some of the identity Midwestern has in the Southern Baptist Convention arose out of past contentions. First the hopes of the century-old American Baptist seminary in Kansas City, Central Baptist Theological Seminary,* for a joint institution were disappointed by Southern Baptist insistence on separate facilities. Then, in 1962, *The Message of Genesis* by Professor Ralph Elliott of

Midwestern Seminary created a storm of controversy among conservative Southern Baptists. The controversy became the occasion of the 1963 revision of the Baptist Faith and Message* statement, which continues to be the Southern Baptist Convention confession of faith.*

Midwestern Baptist Theological Seminary has been guided by Presidents Millard Berquist (1958-1972) and Milton Ferguson (1972-). The seminary has pioneered the doctor of ministry degree among Baptist seminaries and has created flexible schedules for off-campus programs to serve a wider constituency.

BIBLIOGRAPHY. *ESB* 3:1839-43.

F. W. Ratliff

Millennial Harbinger, The. Religious periodical published at Bethany, (West) Virginia, from 1830 to 1870. The founder and principal editor to 1863 was Alexander Campbell.* William Kimbrough Pendleton was the editor from 1864 to 1870. *The Millennial Harbinger* was a monthly of forty-eight pages containing editorial opinion, news of the religious "reformation" (Disciples of Christ) of which Campbell was a principal leader, and general religious news. *The Millennial Harbinger* was the successor to Alexander Campbell's *Christian Baptist* (1823-1829), but the *Harbinger*'s editorial tone was more constructive. Until Alexander Campbell's death in 1866, *The Millennial Harbinger* was probably the most influential periodical in the Disciples movement. After 1866 the journalism of the movement was more sectional, with the rise of the *Christian Standard* in the North and the *Gospel Advocate* in the South. It was a powerful medium in the polemics between Baptists and Restorationists.

See also CAMPBELL, ALEXANDER.

BIBLIOGRAPHY. J. B. Major, "The Role of Periodicals in the Development of the Disciples of Christ, 1850-1910" (Ph.D. dissertation, Vanderbilt University, 1966).

A. L. Dunnavant

Millennialism, Baptist Views. In the history of Baptist theology, millennial views have not played a central or crucial role. Historic Baptist confessions of faith* virtually ignore the subject, though at various times, especially in the twentieth century, millennial views have been divisive. Millennialism concerns the thousand-year reign of Christ connected to his Second Coming. Christians have differed over how literally to take

Christ's millennial reign and when it will occur in relation to Christ's return.

Premillennialists believe that Christ will return before the millennium and set up his earthly reign. The current age is in decline, they believe, with the forces of sin and apostasy gaining strength until the antichrist is revealed. This "man of lawlessness" (2 Thess 2) will deceive the nations and persecute the saints (Mt 24). Finally, the nations will gather for a great battle at Armageddon, at which time Christ will return to rescue (or resurrect) his saints, defeat his enemies, bind Satan and establish his messianic kingdom in Jerusalem. After a thousand years (Rev 20) Satan will be loosed, then defeated and cast into the lake of fire; the general resurrection and last judgment will follow; and the new heavens and new earth will be established. Premillennialists often differ in the details of their interpretation, with dispensationalists arguing for two phases of the Second Coming: Christ coming *for* his saints (the rapture, 1 Thess 4) before the tribulation, and *with* his saints after it.

Postmillennialists take apocalyptic texts less literally. Instead of expecting social and spiritual decline, they predict that revival and reform will bring about the transformation of the world prior to the Second Coming of Christ. This millennial period (not necessarily a literal thousand years) will conclude with a final outbreak of evil forces that will be subdued by the return of Christ. Following the Second Coming will occur the resurrection of the righteous and the wicked, the final judgment and the granting of eternal rewards and punishments. Postmillennialists lean most heavily on Scriptures that teach the gradual growth of the kingdom of God (like the parable of the mustard seed) and those passages that depict the resurrection of saints and sinners as occurring at the same time (Mt 25:31-33; Jn 5:28-29).

Amillennialists (literally, "no-millennialists") take Revelation 20 figuratively and argue that the "millennial" reign of Christ occurs spiritually in the hearts of believers or throughout the entire church age in heaven. Though they deny that there will be a literal reign of Christ on earth, amillennialists still anticipate the Second Coming of Christ, the resurrection of the dead and the last judgment.

All three views have been taught by Baptist preachers and theologians. Premillennialism has had a wide popular following, especially among conservatives and fundamentalists;* William

Miller,* J. R. Graves,* W. B. Riley,* George E. Ladd,* John R. Rice,* Dale Moody, W. A. Criswell* and Millard Erickson are included in their ranks. Postmillennialists have included Andrew Fuller, J. M. Pendleton,* B. H. Carroll,* A. H. Strong,* G. W. Truett,* W. O. Carver* and W. T. Conner* (in his early days). Amillennialism, probably the most widely held view among rank-and-file Baptists, has had its respected defenders: T. T. Shields,* W. T. Conner* (in his latter days), Ray Summers, E. A. McDowell and Herschel Hobbs. Other Baptist theologians, E. Y. Mullins* most notably, refused to choose from the available alternatives and essentially bypassed millennial views.

BIBLIOGRAPHY. M. J. Erickson, *Contemporary Options in Eschatology: A Study of the Millennium* (1977); T. George and D. S. Dockery, eds., *Baptist Theologians* (1990).

T. P. Weber

Miller, William (1792-1849). Baptist farmer-preacher and leader of the Adventist movement. Born in Pittsfield, Massachusetts, the oldest of sixteen children, Miller grew up in Low Hampton, New York. In 1803 he married Lucy Smith and moved to Poultney, Vermont, where he read voraciously in the public library and became a deist. He served two years in the War of 1812, then returned to Low Hampton, where he had a severe spiritual struggle. In 1816 he was converted, joined a Baptist church and undertook an intense study of the Bible. After two years studying biblical prophecies, Miller concluded that the Bible contained a precise outline of future events. Using a literalistic hermeneutic and "millennial arithmetic," Miller concluded that Christ's Second Coming would occur in about 1843. Despite his deepening convictions, Miller did not speak publicly about his beliefs until 1831. Two years later his Baptist church granted him a license to preach. In 1836 he published sixteen of his lectures in *Evidence from Scripture and History of the Second Coming of Christ, About the Year 1843*. Though he spoke across New England, Miller had little impact until 1838, when he joined with a Baptist minister, Joshua Himes, an effective promoter who turned Miller's message into a movement.

The Millerites came from a variety of evangelical denominations, attracted by Miller's biblicism and his intricate message. Miller himself condemned sectarianism and denied that he was trying to start a new church, but by criticizing other clergy and condemning all nonadventists as the "great whore of Babylon," he was largely responsible for the "come-outerism" of his followers. Reluctantly he set dates for Christ's return, finally settling on October 22, 1844. After the "great disappointment," Miller formed the Adventist Church without ever admitting the inadequacies of his hermeneutic. Though personally reserved and quite orthodox in theology, Miller was vilified as a false prophet, and *Millerism* became synonymous with fanaticism.

BIBLIOGRAPHY. S. Bliss, *Memoirs of William Miller* (1853); R. L. Numbers and J. M. Butler, eds., *The Disappointed* (1987).

T. P. Weber

Mission Magazine. *See* MASSACHUSETTS BAPTIST MISSIONARY MAGAZINE.

Missionary Baptist College. *See* SHERIDAN COLLEGE.

Missionary Baptist Institute. With the closing of Sheridan College* in 1934, Missionary Baptists* were keenly aware of the need for higher education for ministers. Antioch Church in Little Rock was the mother church for such a movement and provided the space for the new school, which would open in the same year.

The idea of a local church's supporting the movement was in accordance with the ideals and aims of the American Baptist* Association. Such an arrangement discouraged further "institutionalizing" of the associational movement.

Some of the names associated with the Missionary Baptist Institute were Ben M. Bogard,* C. N. Glover, J. Louis Guthrie and Mrs. J. Louis Guthrie. The first year there were fifty-six students enrolled in the high-school and college programs.

J. T. Greer

Missionary Baptists. Two types of Baptists employ the term *missionary,* using it in opposite ways. Adherents to the first type, influenced by Daniel Parker* and James R. Graves,* represent a resurgence of nineteenth-century Landmarkism.* Opposing any form of convention bureaucracy as a threat to local autonomy, they promote missions* solely through individual churches. Their most conservative branch is the American Baptist Association* (ABA), the product of a merger (1924) between Samuel Hayden's Texas-centered Baptist Missionary Association and Ben Bogard's*

General Association of Arkansas Baptists. With headquarters in Texarkana, Texas, it recently listed over 1 million members and 3,570 churches in the United States and Canada. A progressive branch, which broke away from the ABA in 1950, is now known as the Baptist Missionary Association of America (BMAA). The center of BMAA unity is its seminary in Jacksonville, Texas. Listing 219,697 members and 1,487 churches in twenty-nine states in 1982, it still finds its main strength in the Southwest.

In contrast to the ABA and the BMAA, which have been caricatured as antimissionary,* Baptists of the second type cooperate in conventions that allow them to be involved in more comprehensive mission activities and diverse programs. Many Southern Baptist churches still add *Missionary* to their title in order to show this distinction. The Southern Baptist Convention* has drawn its strength from such missionary groups as the Texas Baptist State Convention (1848), which opposed Parker's antimission movement, the Baptist General Convention of Texas (1885), which resisted Hayden's "anticonvention" party, and the Duck River Baptist Association,* which added *Missionary* to its name (1953) in order to distinguish itself from the "Separate" Duck River Baptists.

See also AMERICAN BAPTIST ASSOCIATION; INDEPENDENT BAPTISTS.

BIBLIOGRAPHY. H. L. McBeth, *The Baptist Heritage* (1987).

J. T. Spivey

Missions, Baptist Views of. Before William Carey* there was no real missionary consciousness among Baptists, and up to 1792 there was no mention of missions in a global sense. Between 1792 and 1814, however, the formation of new associations and societies for the purpose of missions became a reality. With this development and the expanding missions efforts came differing mindsets among Baptists about how to do missions.

Historically, Baptist views of missions have fallen into two broad categories. One of these views is called "the antimission movement."* In this view, only the local church can be involved in any form of mission. A representative board or agency acting on behalf of the church, or a group of churches, would be a negation of biblical ecclesiology* and the autonomy of the local church. This Landmark* perspective represents a minority Baptist view.

The majority view holds to a more cooperative, comprehensive and diverse approach to missions activities and accepts the concept of working through boards and agencies representing the congregations. Realistically, however, the cooperation has tended to be within Baptist denominations themselves and not so much across the lines of Baptist families.

While all Baptist groups hold to a doctrine of justification by faith, there has been great diversity in the manner in which that good news has been proclaimed and lived out. For instance, certain millenarian views held by some Baptist bodies lead them to concentrate on individual and personal salvation in readiness for eternity. Working from the same foundation, many American Baptist* churches have emphasized ministry to the physical needs of humanity as a sign of God's love for the whole person. In the past Southern Baptists* tended to emphasize individual salvation and the planting of churches. More recently, however, greater balance has been achieved in ministry to the whole person through development and relief projects. These divergent views reflect the tension between kingdom views and church views. Those Baptists who view the church as both sign and agent of the kingdom of God—a community of the kingdom as a foretaste of the future—are more comfortable with a comprehensive emphasis in missions endeavors. Whatever the divergence in the implementation of the missions mandate, it is safe to say that missions have been a unifying factor among Baptists.

Sociologically, in the late twentieth century Baptists in America have tended toward specialized, single-issue approaches to missions of a more independent variety. Of the seventy-six U.S. Baptist missions entities listed in the *Mission Handbook* (14th ed., 1989), over two-thirds are independent paradenominational associations. This may be a passing phase, or it may reflect the spirit of a new era of internationalized missions and a blurring of denominational lines. Baptists from diverse groupings welcome the concept of partnering with the larger body of Christ, thereby reflecting reciprocity, humility and unity.

BIBLIOGRAPHY. *DCA*, pp. 744-64; H. L. McBeth, *The Baptist Heritage* (1987); D. Roberts and J. A. Siewert, *Mission Handbook,* 14th ed. (1989); W. Shurden, *Not a Silent People* (1972).

W. R. O'Brien

Mississippi College. A four-year liberal arts college located in Clinton, Mississippi, and operated in cooperation with the Mississippi Baptist Convention. The institution was chartered in 1826 as a municipal school, making it the oldest institution of higher learning in the state. F. G. Hopkins was the first principal, serving from 1826 to 1828. In 1831 the college was the first in the United States to award a degree to a woman. The school remained under municipal control until 1842, when it was given to the Presbyterian Church. The Presbyterians operated the school until the church had financial difficulties; at that point Mississippi College was returned to the original owners. Later in 1850 the Mississippi Baptist Convention took over operation of the institution. Issac Newton Urner served as the first president of the Baptist college, from 1850 to 1867.

During the Civil War troops occupied the campus repeatedly. By the end of the war Mississippi College had lost its endowment and its students, and its buildings were in disrepair. A period of slow recovery followed. The college was once more a stable institution by 1891, and it remained so in the twentieth century, even through the Depression years. John William Provine served as president twice (1895-1898, 1911-1932). Under his leadership the campus facilities, endowment and enrollment were significantly improved. The end of World War II spurred a significant increase in enrollment and expansion of facilities. A graduate program was initiated in 1959, and the graduate school was established in 1975.

BIBLIOGRAPHY. *ESB* 2, 3, 4.

C. Blevins

Missouri Baptist College. An evangelical Christian liberal arts college affiliated with the Missouri Baptist Convention and granting undergraduate degrees and professional certificates. Chartered in 1963, the college at first held classes in Tower Grove Baptist Church and was known as St. Louis Baptist College. The St. Louis College merged with Hannibal-LaGrange College* in 1967. A new institution, Missouri Baptist College, was created, with campuses in Hannibal and St. Louis. The merger was dissolved in 1973, restoring Hannibal-LaGrange College and establishing an independent Missouri Baptist College in St. Louis. The college suspended operations in August 1974 due to financial problems, but St. Louis churches mounted a fundraising campaign that allowed the college to reopen within a month. Full accreditation was granted in 1978. Located on the suburban Creve Coeur campus it has occupied since 1968, Missouri Baptist College has twenty-eight full-time faculty and an undergraduate enrollment of 661 students.

BIBLIOGRAPHY. *ESB* 4:1848-49.

A. L. Pratt

Mobile College. See UNIVERSITY OF MOBILE.

Montgomery, Helen Barrett (1861-1934). Biblical scholar and denominational leader. Born in Kingsville, Ohio, Helen Barrett was a native of Rochester, New York. She began her career as a schoolteacher and moved into religious work with several agencies of the Northern Baptist Convention (*see* American Baptist Churches in the USA). Her marriage to businessman William A. Montgomery provided her with unusual social and leadership opportunities, including friendships with Susan B. Anthony and Frances Willard. Montgomery pioneered several leadership roles, serving as the first female member of the Rochester city school board, the first woman president of a religious denomination (the Northern Baptist Convention, 1921) and the first woman to prepare a translation of the entire New Testament into English.

In Baptist life she promoted international missions* by traveling abroad extensively with colleague Lucy W. Peabody* and by helping to organize permanent support groups like the World Wide Guild and the World Day of Prayer. A licensed minister, she was the chief catalyst in the unification of the Women's Baptist Missionary societies of the East and West into a single agency in 1914. When faced with fundamentalist* reactions in the 1921 annual sessions of the Northern Baptist Convention, Montgomery characteristically reminded delegates of their denominational heritage and responsibilities in mission.

Identifying with the scholarly traditions of her father and brother, Montgomery finished her Centenary Translation of the New Testament in 1924. Her lively style, joined with faithfulness to the original Greek, provided a popular study edition that has seen seventeen printings. She dedicated her work to Judson Press* and its heritage of Bible translation work in missionary endeavor.

A lecturer and writer in great demand in seminaries and churches, Montgomery believed that cooperative denominational missions would kindle and revivify churches that were broken by theological strife. She often rebuked pastors for being lukewarm toward missions and unaware of the global implications of the gospel.

BIBLIOGRAPHY. H. B. Montgomery, *Helen Barrett Montgomery, from Campus to World Citizenship* (1940); *NAW* 2.

W. H. Brackney

Moon, Charlotte "Lottie" Diggs (1840-1912). Southern Baptist* missionary to China. Born and raised on a Virginia plantation, Moon graduated from Albemarle Female Institute in 1861 with a master's degree in classics. Following the Civil War, Moon pursued a teaching career in Georgia, but her heart was in foreign missions.* In 1873 she sailed for China, where she initially taught in a children's school. Finding her life lonely and unfulfilling, she considered marriage as a solution to her problems, but in the end broke an engagement to a brilliant missionary-minded young man because of his views on evolution. With that decision, Moon was determined to continue her mission in China and insisted that she be permitted to conduct the type of work to which she was called, that of evangelism and church planting. She wrote, "What women want who come to China is free opportunity to do the largest possible work. . . . What women have a right to demand is perfect equality." Despite her field director's initial opposition, she successfully conducted evangelistic work, and in 1889 her work in P'ing-tu was described as the Southern Baptist effort's "greatest evangelistic center in all China."

Moon identified closely with the Chinese people, and when a time of great famine inflicted devastation on her Chinese friends, she gave her own food supplies to needy families. She died of starvation on Christmas Eve 1912, an event that stirred the conscience of Southern Baptists at home. The Lottie Moon Christmas Offering for Foreign Missions, inspired by her in 1888 and so named in 1918, has since grown to tens of millions of dollars annually. She is often referred to as the "patron saint" of Southern Baptist missions because of the influence she had on missionary outreach and giving.

BIBLIOGRAPHY. C. B. Allen, *The New Lottie Moon Story* (1980); I. T. Hyatt Jr., *Our Ordered Lives Confess: Three Nineteenth-Century American Missionaries in East Shantung* (1976); *NAW* 2.

R. A. Tucker

Moon, Orianna Russell (1834-1883). Physician and missionary. Orianna Moon was born into a privileged Baptist family on the Viewmont estate in Albemarle County, Virginia. She attended Troy Female Seminary (1850-1851) and earned her medical degree from the Female Medical College of Pennsylvania in 1857. She was the first female physician in Virginia and one of two in the South.

Previously hostile to Christianity, Orianna visited Jerusalem, where she became a Christian, was baptized and served as a medical missionary. Back home, she served in the Civil War as a surgeon in Confederate hospitals, where she met her husband, John Summerfield Andrews—also a physician. They married in 1861 and lived in Richmond, Virginia, in northeast Alabama and finally at Viewmont. They had twelve sons, six of whom died in infancy. Until her death from cancer, Andrews operated a hospital with her husband in Scottsville, Virginia.

BIBLIOGRAPHY. C. B. Allen, *The New Lottie Moon Story* (1980); H. L. McBeth, *Women in Baptist Life* (1979).

S. L. Still

Moore, Joanna P. (1832-1916). Baptist home missionary. In 1863 Moore began her missionary career working in refugee camps for freed slaves under the American Baptist Home Missionary Society.* In 1873 she moved to New Orleans and worked alongside the black Baptist churches there. The newly formed Woman's Baptist Home Missionary Society* supported her with financial help and missionary assistants. Moore is rightly credited as a major figure in Baptist women's home missionary work; her efforts in establishing schools and missions around the South, and enlisting black and white teachers and evangelists, consistently enlarged the missionary society's vision and scope. In 1891 in Little Rock, Arkansas, she established a Training School for Mothers; she also began the Fireside School, a correspondence curriculum published in her magazine, *Hope.* Moore's goal was to strengthen black families through vocational and religious training and to encourage independent black efforts in higher education.

BIBLIOGRAPHY. G. M. Eaton, *A Heroine of the Cross: Sketches of the Life and Work of Joanna P. Moore* (1920); J. Moore, *In Christ's Stead: Autobiographical Sketches* (1902).

M. L. Bendroth

Moral Majority. A conservative political group formed in 1979 by Baptist pastor Jerry Falwell. The Moral Majority was the most visible manifestation of the new religious right, which sought to root out secular humanism and restore Judeo-Christian morality in society. The Moral Majority worked to educate and mobilize conservative citizens (mostly Christians) to elect moral candidates to office, to eliminate such evils as abortion and pornography, and to influence a wide range of public policies through lobbying offices in Washington, D.C. At its peak the organization claimed to have about 4 million members. The president of the Moral Majority from 1979 through 1987 was Jerry Falwell, pastor of a Lynchburg, Virginia, church and host of the religious television program *The Old Time Gospel Hour.* He was succeeded for a time by an associate, Jerry Nims. The headquarters was in Washington, D.C., with a branch office in Lynchburg. The 1987 budget was approximately $8.4 million.

The majority of the supporters were white fundamentalist* Christians living in rural areas and attending independent Bible churches. Falwell also claimed that about 30 percent of the members were Catholics, drawn to the organization by its antiabortion stance. The executive board of the Moral Majority included such theologically and politically conservative leaders as Tim LaHaye, D. James Kennedy, Charles Stanley and Greg Dixon.

The Moral Majority was formed in June 1979 in response to the political activities of feminist and homosexual groups and governmental decisions about abortion, religion in public schools and regulation of private schools. Its political platform was staunchly conservative, supporting a human life amendment, prayer in public schools, stricter limits on pornography, free-enterprise economics, the death penalty, a strong defense, and support for Israel. It opposed the Equal Rights Amendment, pornography, drug use, homosexuality, most government welfare programs, government regulation of private schools, and disarmament.

To achieve these goals the Moral Majority launched a vigorous education campaign involving frequent mass mailings, a newsletter called *The Moral Majority Report,* sporadic radio and TV shows, and occasional rallies. In addition, state organizations were established in all fifty U.S. states, usually led by a fundamentalist pastor.

The group's impact was mixed. Although

generally credited with registering 2-3 million new voters, the group was not a major factor in election outcomes. It was able to keep issues such as abortion and school prayer on the congressional agenda, but the measures were not passed. Local chapters succeeded in restricting pornography sales. Media coverage of the movement was extensive, although usually unfavorable. There was vehement criticism by liberals, who saw the Moral Majority as violating the separation of church and state by trying to legislate a sectarian morality. Although the group was a significant participant in political debates, its base of support generally did not go beyond the limited and politically inexperienced segment of Christian fundamentalists. By 1990 Falwell disbanded the movement; many of its sociopolitical concerns, however, were evident in the Republican platform of 1992.

See also FUNDAMENTALISM; INDEPENDENT BAPTISTS.

BIBLIOGRAPHY. J. Falwell, *Listen, America!* (1980); E. Jorstad, *The Politics of Moralism* (1981); R. Zwier, *Born-Again Politics* (1982).

R. Zwier

Morehouse, Henry Lyman (1834-1917). Baptist minister and missionary statesman. Born in Stanford, New York, Morehouse studied at the University of Rochester (1854-1858) and Rochester Theological Seminary* (1861-1864). He began his ministry in 1864 in East Saginaw, Michigan, as a missionary of the American Baptist Home Mission Society,* later serving as pastor of the East Avenue Baptist Church, Rochester, New York (1873-1879). Morehouse served as the corresponding secretary (1879-1892, 1902-1917) and field secretary (1893-1902) of the American Baptist Home Mission Society and was foremost in the founding of the American Baptist Education Society* (1888), which prepared the way for the founding of the University of Chicago (1890). He was also the author of *Baptist Home Missions in America* (1883). As the most prominent Baptist statesman in home missions of his day, he diligently sought to provide education for immigrants, Native Americans and blacks.

BIBLIOGRAPHY. L. A. Crandall, *Henry Lyman Morehouse* (1919); *DAB* VII; A. H. Newman, *A Century of Baptist Achievement* (1901).

J. M. Glass

Morehouse College. Established as Augusta Institute in 1867, the school was one of several founded by the American Baptist Home Mission Society* (ABHMS) for freed African-Americans. Founded by Richard Coulter, William Jefferson and Edmund Turney with thirty-seven former slaves and three faculty members, the school initially met in the basement of Springfield Baptist Church in Augusta, Georgia. After it moved to Atlanta in 1879 the name was changed to Atlanta Baptist College (1897); finally it was renamed Morehouse College (1913) in honor of Henry L. Morehouse,* corresponding secretary of the ABHMS.

Like many schools established by Northern white denominations for African-Americans after slavery, Morehouse maintained a liberal arts curriculum, and for several decades the faculty and staff were dominated by whites, which led to a controversy between white and black Baptists over control. However, in 1913 John Hope, a faculty member since 1893, emerged as the first black president. Under his leadership Morehouse continued to grow. In 1929 it became a part of the Atlanta University Center, a consortium of black colleges in the area. In 1935 Benjamin E. Mays* assumed the presidency, and under his leadership the school continued to receive national and international recognition. An all-male institution, it has remained one of the best schools for African-Americans in the United States. In the early 1990s Morehouse had seventy-five faculty members and led all black institutions in the percentage of alumni holding the Ph.D. degree. Undoubtedly, its most outstanding alumnus is Martin Luther King Jr.*

BIBLIOGRAPHY. B. Brawley, *History of Morehouse College* (1917); *EBA;* C. D. Lowery and J. Marszalek, eds., *Encyclopedia of African-American Civil Rights* (1992). L. H. Williams

Morgan Park Baptist Seminary. *See* BAPTIST UNION THEOLOGICAL SEMINARY AT CHICAGO.

Morris, Elias Camp (1855-1922). African-American Baptist minister and first president of the National Baptist Convention (*see* National Baptists). Born as a slave near Springplace, Georgia, on May 7, 1855, he began his working career as a cobbler. He finished public school in Stevenson, Alabama, and attended Roger Williams University. Morris was converted in 1874, was called to the ministry in 1875 and served as pastor of the Centennial Baptist Church in Helena, Arkansas, from 1879 to 1922. He was elected president of the Negro Baptist State Convention of Arkansas in 1882, founded Arkansas Baptist College in 1884 and served as president there for two years.

Morris also was a founder of the National Baptist Convention (1895). Earlier he had helped to organize the Foreign Mission Convention of the U.S.A. (1880). Under his leadership, these separate conventions merged and, along with the National Baptist Education Convention, became boards of the newly formed National Baptist Convention, with Morris as president from 1895 to 1922. Guiding the convention during its formative years, Morris led the fight to establish a black Baptist publishing house. However, the NBC split in 1915 over the publishing house, and the new group came to be known as the National Baptist Convention of America. In 1901 Morris published a book, *Sermons, Addresses and Reminiscences*, telling of his experiences. He died in Little Rock, Arkansas, on September 5, 1922.

BIBLIOGRAPHY. W. H. Brackney, *The Baptists* (1988); J. H. Jackson, *A Story of Christian Activism* (1980); J. M. Washington, *Frustrated Fellowship: The Black Baptist Quest for Social Power* (1986).

L. H. Williams

Mullins, Edgar Young (1860-1928). President of Southern Baptist Theological Seminary* and professor of theology. Born in Mississippi and reared in Texas, Mullins was encouraged by his father, a teacher and preacher, to secure a good education. After graduating from Texas A&M University in 1879, he worked as a telegraph operator to secure sufficient means to study law. However, during a revival meeting conducted by lawyer and evangelist William Evander Penn, Mullins was converted. He was baptized by his father on November 7, 1880. Shortly afterward he entered Southern Baptist Theological Seminary to prepare for the ministry (B.D., 1885). Mullins had intended to go as a missionary to Brazil, but on a doctor's advice he decided to stay home and pastor a church in Harrodsburg, Kentucky (1885-1888). During that time he married Isla May Hawley of Louisville (1886). His next pastorate took him to Baltimore, Maryland (1888-1895), where he also studied at Johns Hopkins University (1891-1892). After serving a short time as associate secretary of the Southern Baptist Foreign Mission Board* (1895-1896), Mullins served as pastor of the First Baptist Church at Newton Centre, Massachusetts (1896-1899).

In 1899 Mullins was elected president of the Southern Baptist Theological Seminary in Louisville, Kentucky, succeeding William H. Whitsitt,* who had resigned in the midst of a controversy. Mullins was superbly fitted for such a challenge. The situation stabilized, the controversy died down, and the seminary was soon prospering again. It was Mullins who engineered the move of the campus from downtown Louisville to "The Beeches."

Equally important for Baptists was Mullins's work as a theologian. As seminary president and professor, he was able to foster a new level of theological sophistication among Southern Baptist ministers. Thoroughly committed to the orthodox doctrines of the Christian faith, his systematic theology, *The Christian Religion in Its Doctrinal Expression and the Axioms of Religion* (1917), and other works such as *Why Is Christianity True?* (1905), *The Axioms of Religion* (1908), *Baptist Beliefs* (1912) and *Christianity at the Crossroads* (1924) promoted moderate Baptist views.

As a Southern Baptist* statesman, Mullins led the denomination at a difficult time of controversy over evolution and the rise of the fundamentalist* movement. Under his leadership a revised version of the New Hampshire Confession of Faith* was adopted in 1925—the first confession* ever adopted by the Southern Baptist Convention. In a preface Mullins and his committee defined the role and limitations of a confession of faith for Southern Baptists. The convention, under Mullins's guidance, rejected the evolutionary hypothesis as expounded by Charles Darwin and affirmed the supernatural nature of the Christian revelation while emphasizing that the Bible is authoritative in "religious opinions" alone.

As scholar, administrator and statesman, Mullins was one of the most influential leaders among Southern Baptists in the twentieth century.

See also SOUTHERN BAPTIST THEOLOGICAL SEMINARY.

BIBLIOGRAPHY. *DAB* VII; *DARB; ESB* 2; W. A. Mueller, *A History of Southern Baptist Theological Seminary* (1959); I. M. Mullins, *Edgar Young Mullins: An Intimate Biography* (1929); *NCAB* 21.

W. R. Estep

Myers, Cortland (1864-1941). Fundamentalist* Baptist pastor. Born in Kingston, New York, Myers graduated from the University of Rochester (A.B., 1887) and Rochester Theological Seminary* (1890). Ordained in 1890, he pastored the First Baptist churches of Syracuse (1890-1893) and Brooklyn (1893-1909), New York, and Tremont Temple in Boston, Massachusetts (1909-1921); in 1921 he became pastor of Immanuel Baptist in Pasadena, California. In 1918 he called attention to what he called "false teachers" and "false teachings" in Baptist colleges and seminaries. In that same year he signed the call for the Philadelphia Prophetic Convention, where he was one of the speakers. There he decried German rational theology and claimed it was a contributing factor to World War I. Myers also warned of the dangers of foreign immigration to America. A supporter of the World's Christian Fundamentals Association from its beginning, he signed the call for the preconvention meeting on Baptist fundamentals held in Buffalo, New York, in 1920 and addressed the participants in a talk entitled "Things Not Shaken." A commanding pulpiteer, Myers was known among fundamentalists for his outspoken criticism of modernism.

R. T. Clutter

Myles, John (1621-1683). Pioneering Welsh pastor who settled in colonial New England. Born at Newton, Herefordshire, Myles studied at Oxford in the mid-1630s. With Thomas Proud, in 1645 at Ilston he founded one of the first Welsh Baptist churches. He served as pastor there until 1662, when Charles II's Act of Uniformity forced him to leave his parish. With the Ilston church's records in hand, Myles and a few friends left for New England in 1663. He settled at Rehoboth in Plymouth Colony and soon organized a church there. In 1667 he was fined by the General Court of Plymouth Colony and expelled from Rehoboth for setting up an unauthorized "publicke meeting." Myles and a few church members relocated, then set up the town of Swansea on land granted to them by the Plymouth Colony. During King Philip's War, he moved to Boston and briefly pastored First Baptist Church, then returned to Swansea, where he served the church as pastor until his death.

BIBLIOGRAPHY. I. Backus, *A History of New-England, with Particular Reference to the Denomination of Christians Called Baptists* (1777); *DAB* VII.

T. P. Weber

N

National Association of Baptist Professors of Religion. Beginning in 1928 as an association of Southern Baptist* college professors of religion, the National Association of Baptist Professors of Religion (NABPR) has evolved into a national Baptist body that includes any professor, Baptist or not, teaching religion or related subjects at an accredited college, university, seminary or divinity school. Although it is nonsectarian in membership, the preponderance of members are Baptist, over half of whom teach in the Southeast. With approximately 440 members, the NABPR meets annually with the American Academy of Religion.

The evolution of the organization is reflected in its name changes. From 1928 to 1950 it was known as the Association of Southern Baptist Teachers of Bible and Religious Education, from 1950 to 1958 as the College Association of Baptist Teachers of Religion, from 1958 to 1981 as the Association of Baptist Professors of Religion and since 1981 as NABPR. It is presently housed at Mercer University* in Macon, Georgia. The executive secretary-treasurer is Watson E. Mills, the founder of the national body in 1981 and the guiding hand behind most of its achievements since that time.

While the official purpose is to promote a forum for the exchange of ideas in the teaching of religion, in recent years the NABPR has made its major contribution in the field of publication. In addition to publishing a quarterly journal, *Perspectives in Religious Studies,* the association has published a monograph series of special studies, a dissertation series, a bibliographic series and, in conjunction with Mercer University Press, the *Mercer Dictionary of the Bible* and the forthcoming *Mercer Commentary on the Bible.*

BIBLIOGRAPHY. R. Beck, "A Community of Scholars: A History of the National Association of Baptist Professors of Religion," in *National Association of Baptist Professors of Religion: Directory of Members 1991* (1991); D. J. Harris, "ABPR: Fifty Years," *PRS* 4 (Spring 1977):56; D. J. Harris, "A Historical Sketch of the Association of Baptist Professors of Religion," *QR* 26 (October-December 1966):64.   W. B. Shurden

National Baptist Education Convention. An early African-American Baptist convention which later merged to form the National Baptist Convention. The National Baptist Education Convention (NBEC) was organized by William Bishop Johnson* in 1891 in Washington, D.C. Its purpose was to provide training materials and educational leadership for black Baptist churches. With the founding of the National Baptist Convention (NBC) in 1895, the NBEC became the Educational Board of the newly formed NBC.

As the main force behind the NBEC, Johnson was able to help black Baptists realize their greatest potential and numerical strength. He developed a federation of Baptists schools that were owned, managed and controlled by blacks, and he produced statistical data and raised money for their maintenance and support. He also served as the managing editor of the *National Baptist Magazine,* the first official organ of the NBC. In 1903 he resigned as Educational Board general secretary, after twelve years of service. Very few records and details remain explaining the specific activities of the NBEC. However, a primary source is supplied by Johnson's *The Scourging of a Race* (1915).

See also JOHNSON, WILLIAM BISHOP; NATIONAL BAPTISTS.

BIBLIOGRAPHY. L. Fitts, *A History of Black Baptists* (1985); W. B. Johnson, *The Scourging of a Race* (1915).   L. H. Williams

National Baptist Evangelical Life and Soul-Saving Assembly of the United States of America. An African-American evangelical organization and splinter group of the National Baptist Convention of America. The National Baptist Evangelical Life and Soul-Saving Assembly (NBELSA) was founded in 1920 by Captain Allan Arthur Banks Sr. in Kansas City, Missouri, and served as an educational and evangelical auxiliary of the National Baptist Convention of America (NBCA) until 1936, when it declared itself independent.

Known by its more popular name, the Soul-Saving Mission of the World, the NBELSA began as a city mission, with centers established in various cities throughout the United States. It also engaged in evangelism, charity and relief work. But its greatest work was in the area of Bible correspondence courses. Master's and doctoral degrees were offered to students who completed varying periods (60-120 days) of instruction. A 1952 report listed 644 churches, a membership of 70,843, an age requirement of thirteen and older, and headquarters in Boise, Idaho. A recent address for the NBELSA is 441-61 Monroe Avenue in Detroit, Michigan. This also is the address of Second Baptist Church, pastored from 1947-1968 by Allan Arthur Banks Jr., who served as NBELSA general secretary. According to Nathaniel Leach, Second Baptist Church historian, at his father's death Banks Jr. continued to direct only the correspondence school. Upon Banks Jr.'s death in 1968, his widow, Victoria Banks, continued to operate the correspondence school until her retirement.

BIBLIOGRAPHY. *DCA;* J. P. Guzman, ed., *1952 Negro Year Book* (1952); W. J. Payne, ed., *Directory of African American Religious Bodies* (1991); A. C. Piepkorn, *Profiles in Belief: The Religious Bodies of the United States and Canada* (1979).

L. H. Williams

National Baptist Magazine. First official publication of the National Baptist Convention (NBC). Published between 1894 and 1901, the *National Baptist Magazine (NBM)* began as a quarterly but became a monthly journal in June 1898. The managing editor was William Bishop Johnson,* pastor of Second Baptist Church in Washington, D.C.

The *NBM* played a prominent role in the forming of the National Baptist Convention (NBC) by keeping leaders informed of the importance of attendance at the unification meeting in Atlanta in 1895. However, for reasons remaining unclear, in 1902 the *NBM* was replaced as the official denominational journal and became the special publication of the NBC's Educational Board. But there is no evidence that it ever was published after 1901.

See also NATIONAL BAPTISTS.

BIBLIOGRAPHY. L. Fitts, *A History of Black Baptists* (1985); W. B. Johnson, *The Scourging of a Race* (1915); L. B. Scherer, "The *National Baptist Magazine,*" *Newsletter of the Afro-American Religious History Group of the American Academy of Religion* 6 (Spring 1982).

L. H. Williams

National Baptists. Three predominantly African-American Baptist denominations have taken variations of the name National Baptist: the National Baptist Convention of the United States of America, Inc.; the National Baptist Convention of America; and the Progressive National Baptist Convention, Inc.

The National Baptist Convention of the United States of America, Inc., is the largest black denomination in America and the world. Established in Atlanta, Georgia, on September 28, 1895, it constituted the successful merger of three separate Baptist organizations: the Foreign Mission Baptist Convention of 1880, the American National Baptist Convention of 1886 and the Baptist National Educational Convention of 1893. Under the leadership of Elias C. Morris,* a former slave and Arkansas minister who served the convention as president for twenty-eight years, the convention created foreign missions, home missions and education boards, each of which corresponded to the three organizations that predated the formation of the convention itself. In 1896 the Home Mission Board established a publishing house, which it later, in 1898, incorporated as the National Baptist Publishing Board. By 1958 the convention had over 27,000 ministers, 26,000 churches, 5.5 million members, and foreign missions in Africa, South America, India and numerous other parts of the world. In 1984 it numbered an estimated 7 million members in over 30,000 congregations.

In 1915, however, the convention divided into two separate organizations following a dispute over the ownership of the National Baptist Publishing Board. Under the leadership of R. H. Boyd,* corresponding secretary of the convention's publication board and a skillful businessman, the publishing house had become a highly successful business, raising over $2 million within the first ten years of its existence. Tensions emerged between Boyd and the convention when the publishing house failed to donate its substantial funds to other denominational projects or comply with the charter of the convention. Attempting to establish its legal right to the publishing house, the convention adopted a new charter, redefined the charge of the publishing board and incorporated itself as the National Baptist Convention of the United States of America, Incorporated. Boyd and his constituents rejected the new charter, withdrew the publishing house from the newly incorporated convention and designated themselves the National Baptist Convention of America, Unincorporated. In 1956, approximately forty years later, this relatively new denomination claimed over 2.5 million members and over 11,000 congregations.

These two denominational organizations, the National Baptist Convention of the United States of America, Inc., and the National Baptist Convention of America, Unincorporated, continue to function as distinctive bodies well into the twentieth century, though they share basic Baptist theological beliefs in the authority of the Bible, the lordship of Jesus Christ, the baptism* of believers, the separation of church and state, and the autonomy of local church and state associations.

The Progressive National Baptist Convention, Incorporated, emerged in 1961, following a five-year debate within the National Baptist Convention of the United States of America, Inc., over policies regarding the election of officers and the length of the convention president's term in office. In 1957 J. H. Jackson,* who had already served a four-year term as the convention president, ruled against the 1952 policy restricting a president's term in office to four years. Many in the convention, among them G. C. Taylor, felt that this was a return to practices that predated the 1952 policy, when presidents served for life. This discontent led to heated debates at the 1960 convention in Kansas City, Missouri, and an invitation from a convention member, L. Venchael Booth, for all dissatisfied delegates to attend a meeting at his church, Zion Baptist Church in Cincinnati, Ohio. Thirty-three delegates from fourteen states attended that meeting and formed the Progressive National Baptist Convention, Inc.

Though there is little doctrinal disagreement between the Progressive Convention and its parent body, the two organizations do show dissimilarities at the level of organization. The Progressive Convention elects its officers every two years and limits the convention president's term in office to eight years. In the late 1970s the Progressive Convention was composed of 487 churches and had a membership of over 500,000. By 1984 it had approximately 1 million members.

BIBLIOGRAPHY. *EAR* 1 (1978); O. D. Pelt, *The Story of the National Baptists* (1960); A. C. Piepkorn, *Profiles in Belief: The Religious Bodies of the United States and Canada,* vol. 2 (1978).

M. C. Bruce

National Council of Churches of Christ in the U.S.A. A cooperative ecumenical organization, located at 475 Riverside Drive in New York City, that constitutes the voice of mainline Protestantism. Founded in 1950 through a merger of the Federal Council of Churches of Christ (FCC)* in America (1908) and thirteen other interdenominational agencies, the National Council of Churches of Christ in the U.S.A. (NCCC) is the successor to the FCC. Most of its member denominations are Protestant mainline churches, but it also includes several Orthodox bodies. A majority of Christian communions in the United States, including the Roman Catholic, Southern Baptist, Lutheran Church-Missouri Synod and various evangelical denominations, have not affiliated with the NCCC. The activities of the NCCC reflect the older Social Gospel* orientation of the Protestant mainline churches. Its purpose has been to demonstrate Protestant unity and reform American society by providing its member churches with access to political and economic power. It seeks to bring the truths of the gospel to bear upon societal problems through programs involving evangelism, Christian education, foreign missions,* economic policies, human rights, international affairs and ecumenism.* Throughout the 1960s and 1970s, even though it abandoned the idea of "churches working together for a Christian America," the NCCC championed the civil rights movement and during the latter stages of the Cold War advocated nonmilitary solutions to the tensions generated by the arms race. The lion's share of NCCC activity is conducted by the Church World Service, an international relief and development agency that accounts for approximately 85 percent of the council's budget.

See also FEDERAL COUNCIL OF CHURCHES OF CHRIST.

BIBLIOGRAPHY. S. M. Cavert, *Church Cooperation and Unity in America: A Historical Review, 1900-1970* (1970); R. A. Schneider, "Voice of May Waters: Church Federation in the Twentieth Century," in *Between the Times: The Travail of the*

Protestant Establishment in America, 1900-1960, ed. W. R. Hutchinson (1989).

D. G. Hart

National Federation of Fundamentalists of the Northern Baptists. An alliance that sought to impose fundamentalist* practices and beliefs on the Northern Baptist Convention (*see* American Baptist Churches in the USA). After 1921 the group became known as the Fundamentalist Fellowship. This loosely knit organization grew out of a conference on "Fundamentals of Our Baptist Faith" held at the Delaware Avenue Baptist Church in Buffalo, New York, prior to the annual meeting of the Northern Baptist Convention in 1920. One hundred and fifty clergymen and laymen, concerned by what they felt to be the inroads that theological liberalism was making in the denomination, convened the gathering, which had the announced purpose "to restate, reaffirm, and reemphasize the fundamentals of our New Testament faith." J. C. Massee, pastor of Baptist Temple in Brooklyn, presided at the first session and was elected president of the newly formed federation. The main battlefronts were the orthodoxy of denominational schools (colleges, universities and seminaries), the adoption of a confessional* or creedal statement, and the orthodoxy of home and foreign missionaries.

The federation was successful in forcing the denomination to appoint a committee of nine to investigate the schools and the method of election or appointment of trustees. This committee reported one year later that for the most part the educational institutions were ones of which the denomination could be proud, while legitimate grievances could be referred to the trustees of local institutions. Frustrated with this decision, the federation sought to have the denomination adopt a confession of faith. W. B. Riley,* representing the fundamentalist group, proposed at the annual meeting of the denomination at Indianapolis in 1922 the adoption of the New Hampshire Confession of Faith.* However, a substitute motion, "Resolved, that the Northern Baptist Convention affirm that the New Testament is an all-sufficient ground for faith and practice, and we need no other statement," was adopted by a margin of two to one. Concerning the orthodoxy of missionaries, a commission of seven, after study and investigation, reported in Seattle in 1925 its emphatic approval of the great majority of mis-

sionaries and recommended the discipline of a very few. In all three instances, then, the verdicts had gone contrary to the fundamentalists.

The work of the federation had been hampered by extremists within the group, notably W. B. Riley and John Roach Straton,* whose bitter invectives against opponents, including some fellow fundamentalists, hurt their own cause. In 1923 some of the ultrafundamentalists formed the Baptist Bible Union,* a competing fundamentalist organization led by Riley, J. Frank Norris* and T. T. Shields.* Massee, a moderate fundamentalist, resigned his position as president of the Fundamentalist Fellowship in 1925 and one year later left the political ranks of the fundamentalists altogether, although remaining in the denomination. In 1926, in a major address to the convention, Massee pleaded for an armistice of six months between the opposing forces and the rededication of the denominational "machinery" to the task of evangelism. Weary of controversy, the delegates accepted the suggestion, and Massee was hailed as being responsible for a temporary moderate solution to the crisis. The creation of the General Association of Regular Baptists* in 1932, evolving from the Baptist Bible Union, further drained the ranks of the fundamentalists within the Northern Baptist Convention.

In the 1940s the name frequently employed for the fundamentalists in the Northern Baptist Convention was the Conservative Baptist Fellowship, superseding the earlier titles—National Federation of Fundamentalists and Fundamentalist Fellowship. Again there were unsuccessful attempts to impose a doctrinal test on the denomination and to create competing mission boards within the denomination. Eventually many of the fundamentalists (now going increasingly by the name *conservatives*) left the convention and joined with others in 1947 to form the Conservative Baptist Association of America,* an organization "composed of autonomous Baptist churches without regard to other affiliations."

See also CONSERVATIVE BAPTIST ASSOCIATION; FUNDAMENTALISM; FUNDAMENTALIST BAPTIST FELLOWSHIP.

BIBLIOGRAPHY. G. W. Dollar, *A History of Fundamentalism in America* (1973); G. M. Marsden, *Fundamentalism and American Culture* (1980); C. A. Russell, *Voices of American Fundamentalism* (1976); E. R. Sandeen, *The Roots of Fundamentalism: British and American Millenarianism, 1800-1930* (1970).

C. A. Russell

National Men's Fellowship of the Baptist General Conference. An organization of Baptist General Conference* (BGC) men in support of the BGC mission. It was begun at the 1947 annual meeting in Seattle, which also gave the National Men's Fellowship (NMF) the assignment of supporting the newly begun mission in Alaska. When the BGC constitution was revised at the annual meeting in Omaha, Nebraska (1949), the NMF was incorporated into the Board of Men's Work (BMW), assuming the latter name. BMW projects, besides Alaska, included boys' work, a Mexican mission and summer Bible camps. The BMW's ongoing request for full-time leadership was approved in 1962, confirmed in 1964 and implemented in 1965 with the election of Lloyd Mattson as the first and only secretary of the Board of Men's Work. In 1970 the conference merged three boards—Women's, Men's and Bible School/Youth—to form the Board of Christian Education (BCE). Men's work continued under Mattson until 1972 and then under the secretary of the BCE; it was eliminated with further restructuring of the boards in the 1980s.

BIBLIOGRAPHY. D. Anderson, ed., *The 1960s in the Ministry of the Baptist General Conference* (1971); D. Anderson, ed., *The 1970s in the Ministry of the Baptist General Conference* (1981); D. Anderson, ed., *The 1980s in the Ministry of the Baptist General Conference* (1991); D. Guston and M. Erikson, eds., *Fifteen Eventful Years: A Survey of the Baptist General Conference, 1945-1960* (1961). N. A. Magnuson

National Southern Baptist Charismatic Conference. Baptist charismatic* fellowship. Although the charismatic renewal of the 1970s was denounced by most Southern Baptists,* some charismatic Southern Baptist congregations were formed. Amid intense disfavor, charismatic churches and ministers organized several regional and national conferences for fellowship and encouragement. Ray Lambeth and Trinity Baptist of Fern Creek in Louisville, Kentucky, held two regional meetings. The November 1974 and the February 1975 meetings were attended by 500 and 800 persons respectively. These meetings led Trinity and several other churches to convene the first National Southern Baptist Charismatic Conference in Dallas, Texas, July 21-24, 1976. Over 2,000 persons attended from at least fifteen different states. A second national conference the next year attracted 3,500 charismatics from thirty-seven

states and four other countries. These meetings made no impact on the leadership of the Southern Baptist Convention, nor did they result in a noticeable charismatic voice or presence in denominational life.

See also CHARISMATIC MOVEMENT AMONG BAPTISTS.

BIBLIOGRAPHY. C. L. Howe Jr., *Glimpses of Baptist Heritage* (1981). C. D. Weaver

Neel, Isa-Beall Williams (1860-1953). Southern Baptist* Woman's Missionary Union* (WMU) leader in Georgia. Born June 2, 1860, in Cartersville, Georgia, she studied in Germany after receiving her baccalaureate from Mary Sharp College in Tennessee. After marrying lawyer William Jessie Neel, she lived in Rome, Georgia, where she helped organize the Floyd County Associational WMU. Neel served twenty-one years, from 1911 to 1932, as the fifth president of the Georgia WMU. Neel became the WMU organizer for the Southern Baptist Convention's $75 Million Campaign in 1919 and moved to Nashville for six months to direct the women's campaign. Under Neel's leadership, WMU women pledged and gave $7 million more than their goal of $15 million. Neel stayed active in Georgia WMU even after retiring. The Georgia state missions offering bears her name. She is buried at Oak Hill Cemetery, Cartersville.

See also WOMAN'S MISSIONARY UNION, AUXILIARY TO THE SBC.

BIBLIOGRAPHY. C. Allen, *A Century to Celebrate* (1987); *ESB* 2:947. R. Beck

New Century Movement. Attempt around 1900 to unify the fundraising of the Southern Baptist Convention's* boards and agencies. A resolution called for the 1898 Southern Baptist Convention to give thanks for the past and to plan for the century ahead. A committee headed by Franklin Howard Kerfoot of Georgia was given preparation responsibility. This committee reported in 1899 and 1900. Besides arranging celebration events, it called in 1900 for a two-year campaign focused on "combining the energies of the whole denomination" by enlisting the many churches not giving anything to state, home or foreign missions. A "Committee on Co-operation" was formed to implement this project. It recommended developing a separate agency in Baltimore to coordinate the efforts of state conventions and the two mission boards. Resistance delayed a decision for a year. In 1902 the conven-

tion rejected this early attempt at consolidation.
BIBLIOGRAPHY. *ESB* 2:959-60.

W. L. Allen

New Connection Baptists. A conservative English General Baptist* movement. Following the passage of the Act of Toleration (1689), General Baptists experienced serious spiritual and theological decline, including division over the issue of the deity and humanity of Christ. Dan Taylor, a convert of the Evangelical Awakening, led on June 6, 1770, in the formation of the more evangelical and conservative New Connection General Baptists. He moderated the group for forty-five out of the next forty-six years.

The movement adopted a confession known as the Articles of Religion. The statement took a conservative position on six articles of disagreement with the more liberal General Baptists: the fall of humankind, the nature and perpetual obligations of the moral law, the person and work of Christ, salvation by faith, regeneration by the Holy Spirit, and baptism. In practice the New Connection churches shared decisions, such as pastoral calls, with the association, permitted congregational hymn singing, allowed a greater role for women, including service as deaconesses and prophetesses, and eased the practice of church discipline, especially by allowing marriage outside the fellowship. Under Taylor's leadership the movement grew rapidly. For a time the movement recovered orthodox doctrine, spiritual vitality and meaningful worship. In 1891 the New Connection Baptists united with the Particular Baptists,* forming the Baptist Union of Great Britain and Ireland.

BIBLIOGRAPHY. H. L. McBeth, *The Baptist Heritage* (1987); *SHERK* 11; A. C. Underwood, *A History of the English Baptists* (1970).

S. A. Yarbrough

New Hampshire Baptist Antislavery Society. A single-purpose society organized to oppose slavery in the United States. The society was organized in 1838, when L. E. Caswell of Weare, New Hampshire, issued a report to the state Baptist convention on the inhumane treatment of slaves he witnessed while on a trip to Charleston, South Carolina. His hearers decided to organize a society to use "all Christian means for the immediate overthrow of oppression in the land." The fledgling society passed five resolutions, including one that deemed Southern slavery "op-

posed to the gospel of Christ, and morally wrong," and another that called for "immediate and entire emancipation as the only safe and practicable mode of freeing our nation from the shame and sin of slavery." The society collected funds in efforts to educate Baptists about the evils of slavery. The founding of this society reflected growing antislavery sentiment in New England, where several such societies soon developed. These societies in turn set the stage for the formation of the American Baptist Anti-Slavery Convention* in New York City in 1840.

BIBLIOGRAPHY. W. Brackney, *The Baptists* (1983); W. Brackney, ed., *Baptist Life and Thought, 1600-1980* (1983).

A. M. Manis

New Hampshire Confession of Faith. A widely influential statement of Baptist moderate Calvinism,* originally drafted in 1833. In late-eighteenth-century New Hampshire, support for the previously dominant rigid Calvinism was waning. On June 24, 1830, the state Baptist convention appointed a committee to prepare a declaration of faith and practice consistent with the more moderate views of the churches. This document, which was to have been completed by the following year, was revised by several drafting committees. It was finally approved by the convention board on January 15, 1833, and recommended to the churches for adoption.

After 1850 the confession gained stature in the wider Baptist fellowship. It was disseminated by the publications of influential leaders, including J. Newton Brown,* who had prepared the 1833 draft, the Landmark* Baptist James M. Pendleton* and Edward T. Hiscox, author of a widely used Baptist manual.

During the 1920s the confession became a point of tension among the Northern Baptists (*see* American Baptist Churches in the USA). An attempt by some fundamentalists to secure its adoption by the convention was rejected as a move toward creedalism (*see* Confessions of Faith, Baptist). In 1933 a group of conservative churches withdrew from the Northern Convention to form the General Association of Regular Baptists* and adopted a premillennial version of the confession as their standard. The Southern Baptist Convention* used the confession as the basis for a document published in 1923 under the title Baptist Faith and Message.* This statement was revised in 1963.

The confession is organized according to the

general pattern of the Reformed creeds. The subjects discussed follow the order Scripture, God, Fall, salvation and sanctification, church (including civil government), and last things. Readily evident is the attempt by its drafters to articulate a moderate Calvinism during an era of theological controversy. Calvinist emphases are present but subdued, both in the order in which the articles appear and in the descriptions themselves. Election, for example, is not described until article 9, after statements on the Fall and salvation. Salvation, according to the document, is prevented only by personal voluntary refusal, and the perseverance of the saints means that only those who endure to the end are real believers.

The article on consummation is short and omits any reference to rapture, tribulation or millennium. The opening article contains what is now a classic Baptist statement concerning Scripture: "It has God for its author, salvation for its end, and truth, without any mixture of error, for its matter."

See also BAPTIST CHURCHES; CONFESSIONS OF FAITH; PHILADELPHIA CONFESSION OF FAITH.

BIBLIOGRAPHY. E. T. Hiscox, *The Baptist Directory* (1876); W. L. Lumpkin, *Baptist Confessions of Faith* (1974); W. J. McGlothlin, *Baptist Confessions of Faith* (1911).

S. J. Grenz

New Mexico Baptist College. The Lincoln Association promoted the establishment of a Baptist school in New Mexico and enlisted C. C. Waller of Texas to lead the enterprise. Bids were invited from towns desiring the school, and Alamogordo subscribed $34,000 and a cash bonus of $8,000. Land was secured in Alamogordo, and a two-story building was constructed on a thirteen-acre campus. The association elected trustees, and President Waller enlisted a faculty as seventy-five students registered for the opening of New Mexico Baptist College in 1900. Inadequate finances and frequent changes of administration hampered progress of the school, which was offered to and accepted by the New Mexico Baptist Convention in 1905. Support was not sufficient, however, and the convention released the college back to the association in 1909. Heavily in debt, the college ceased to exist on July 1, 1911.

C. L. Howe Jr.

New Orleans Baptist Theological Seminary. The Southern Baptist Convention* meeting in New Orleans, Louisiana, in 1917, approved the establishment of a Baptist Bible institute and requested its Home Mission* and Sunday School* boards to cooperate with the Louisiana and Mississippi Baptist conventions in creating the institution. Such an endeavor had been discussed for a century, and editorials by P. I. Lipsey in *The Baptist Record* of Mississippi in 1914 had renewed interest for founding a missionary-training school in the crescent city.

Trustees elected by the two state conventions and national boards secured the Sophie Newcomb College property on Washington Avenue, elected Byron H. DeMent as president (1917-1928) and officially opened Baptist Bible Institute on October 1, 1918. From the beginning the institute offered courses of study for both college graduates and those with less formal training, stressing practical experience as well as academic excellence.

William Wistar Hamilton, pastor of the St. Charles Avenue Baptist Church in New Orleans, succeeded DeMent as president after a decade and provided excellent leadership during a time of financial crisis (1928-1942), reducing faculty strength and fighting for the survival of the school. Duke K. McCall then served for a brief period (1943-1946) during World War II, strengthening the faculty, reorganizing the curriculum and changing the name of the school in 1946 to New Orleans Baptist Theological Seminary.

Roland Q. Leavell (president 1946-1958; see Leavell Family) secured seventy-five acres of land on Gentilly Boulevard in New Orleans East and led the school in building and moving to the new campus (in 1953). The seminary was reorganized into three separate schools with distinct faculties and degree programs (theology, religious education and church music), and a School of Christian Training for noncollege graduates functioned for about three years (1956-1958).

H. Leo Eddleman was president during the difficult sixties (1959-1970), continuing the building program and extending accreditation with the appropriate agencies. Grady C. Cothen (1970-1974) led the school in a massive curriculum-revision study that led to abolishing the separate schools and forming five academic divisions. Landrum P. Leavell II (1975-) continued expansion of the New Orleans campus and about a dozen off-campus locations. This fully accredited theological seminary offers a full complement of master's and doctoral programs and has also instituted several bachelor's programs through the reconstituted School of Christian Training. It celebrated its seventy-fifth anniversary in 1992-1993 as the third oldest of six Southern Baptist seminaries.

BIBLIOGRAPHY. *ESB.*   C. L. Howe Jr.

New York Baptist City Missionary Society. One of the earliest attempts by Baptists to organize domestic mission work. The Baptist Society was formed in 1806 by the New York Baptist Association, whose leaders were dissatisfied with the missions of the New York Missionary Society. The original society was supported by Presbyterians and Congregationalists.

Beginning in 1796, the New York Missionary Society took an active interest in the evangelization of the Indians on the Niagara Frontier. The first missionary was Elkanah Holmes,* a Baptist clergyman from New York. Soon, however, Baptist supporters quarreled with pedobaptists and withdrew their support.

In the later nineteenth century, the society concentrated its efforts on urban missions to immigrants and tenement residents. It became one of the approved city societies of the Northern Baptist Convention (*see* American Baptist Churches in the USA) in 1907. When the American Baptist Churches of Metropolitan New York was formed in 1976, the New York Baptist City Mission Society was integrated with the new American Baptist regional organization.

BIBLIOGRAPHY. J. W. Grant, "Elkanah Holmes," in *DCB* 6.   W. H. Brackney

Newman, Albert Henry (1852-1933). Baptist church historian and educator. Born in South Carolina, Newman was educated at Mercer University* and Rochester Theological Seminary,* excelling in Semitic languages and historical studies. In his seminary studies Newman was a favorite of Augustus H. Strong* and was offered his initial teaching position at Rochester. John A. Broadus* and Crawford H. Toy* also sought him for Southern Baptist Theological Seminary,* as did the Morgan Park Seminary in Chicago (*see* Baptist Union Theological Seminary at Chicago). To the surprise of many, in 1881 Newman accepted an appointment at what became McMaster University* in Toronto, Canada (1881-1901). In 1901 he moved to Baylor University* (1901-1908), and he finished his career as dean and later professor of church history at Southwestern Baptist Theolog-

ical Seminary* (1908-1913).

Newman's scholarship explored a variety of topics from New Testament and patristic studies to modern Baptist life. In his *History of Antipaedobaptism* (1897) he traced precursors to baptistic principles through examples of opposition to infant baptism in the early and medieval churches. His one-volume contribution on the Baptists in the American Church History Series in 1901 sounded a note of triumphalism for the once-despised frontier sect in early America. Newman's two-volume *Manual of Church History* (1903) was a standard textbook for the first half of the twentieth century among both Baptist and non-Baptist institutions. Newman was one of the premier church historians of the late nineteenth century and one of a few Baptist educators who rose above regional politics to serve in Northern, Southern and Canadian institutions.

See also SOUTHWESTERN BAPTIST THEOLOGICAL SEMINARY.

BIBLIOGRAPHY. *DAB* I; J. M. Dawson, "Our Greatest Baptist Historian," *WE,* June 29, 1933.

         W. H. Brackney

Newton Theological Institution. The first Baptist graduate school in the United States, founded in 1826 in Newton Centre, Massachusetts, by the New England Baptist Education Society. Newton represented an emerging conviction among Northern Baptists that a classical education was essential for the tasks of evangelism and theological disputation, particularly in a competitive environment where Congregationalism had long been dominant among the well-to-do and upwardly mobile.

Based largely on the model of the Congregationalists' own Andover Theological Seminary* (1807), Newton required a bachelor of arts degree for entrance, admitted only those already engaged in active ministry and anticipated a three-year course of theological study. The Bible, however, replaced the famous Calvinistic Andover Creed as the sole measure of orthodoxy.

Despite promising beginnings, the institution struggled throughout the nineteenth century with low enrollment, inadequate funding and a constituency that was often lukewarm about the benefits of higher education; even so, it established an influential tradition of Baptist theological scholarship. By the end of the century it had become theologically and socially quite liberal,* admitting both women and blacks to study (though not yet into degree programs).

In 1908, troubled by continuing low enrollment, the school affiliated with the Baptist Minister's Training Institute, founded by Newton alumnus and trustee A. J. Gordon.* The union ended amicably in 1914, however, and under President George Horr the school, with minimal success, courted a wealthier, more sophisticated constituency. With Horr's retirement in 1925, former pastor Everett Carleton Herrick assumed the presidency, moving quickly to reestablish ties with local churches and provide a financially sound basis for the school. In 1930 the board of trustees invited Andover Theological Seminary, then struggling with its own finances and future, to affiliate, and a year later the two schools began cooperative programming, with Newton providing its campus and Andover its extensive library resources. The partnership was felicitous; between 1931 and 1965, under the name Andover Newton Theological School,* the schools increased their common enrollment and earned a national reputation for solid scholarship and practical training for ministry. By 1965 Newton and Andover had grown so closely together that a formal merger was effected.

See also ANDOVER NEWTON THEOLOGICAL SCHOOL.

E. C. Nordbeck

Nilsson, Fredrik Olaus (1809-1881). Prominent Swedish Baptist* pioneer preacher. Born July 28, 1809, near the city of Gotenburg on the west coast of Sweden, he became a sailor at age eighteen. He married Ulrika Sofia Olsson in 1845. Converted at age twenty-five, Nilsson soon embarked on aggressive personal evangelism, first in New York City, employed by the New York Tract Society, then in Gotenburg, supported by the Seamen's Friend Society. He also organized temperance societies and distributed many thousands of Bibles and tracts as an agent of the British and Foreign Bible Society. Baptized in 1847 by the German Baptist J. G. Oncken, he began the first Baptist church in Sweden in September 1848 and was ordained the following May. Persecution, imprisonment and banishment from Sweden in 1850 followed—actions that drew the attention and protests of the Protestant world. In 1853, after a two-year ministry in Denmark, he emigrated to the United States, where he labored among Swedish immigrants, evangelizing, planting churches and serving as a missionary-pastor. After working in New York City and in Burlington, Iowa, he

spent five fruitful years in Minnesota, where he was instrumental in the early development of the Houston, Scandia, Chisago Lake and Grove City churches, among others. Following his pardon by King Charles XV in 1860, he returned to Sweden for a seven-year ministry in the Gotenburg area (1861-1868). Returning to the United States, he settled in Houston, Minnesota, first as pastor and then in retirement. Nilsson suffered a lapse of evangelical faith during the last decade of his life but appears to have been restored before his death on October 21, 1881.

BIBLIOGRAPHY. J. O. Backlund, *A Pioneer Trio* (1942); J. Bystrom, *En Frikyrklig Banbrytare* (1910); N. Magnuson, "F. O. Nilsson, Free Church Pioneer," in *Discovering Our Baptist Heritage*, ed. W. H. Brackney (1985).

N. A. Magnuson

Norris, J. Frank (1887-1952). Fundamentalist* Baptist minister. Born in Dadeville, Alabama, Frank Norris moved with his family to Hubbard, Texas, when he was eleven years old. He graduated from Baylor University* (B.A., 1903) and Southern Baptist Theological Seminary* (1905) and was ordained a Southern Baptist* minister in 1899. His first pastorate was the McKinney Avenue Baptist Church in Dallas, Texas (1905-1908), which under his leadership grew from under 100 to over 1,000 in attendance. As editor (1907-1909) of the Texas Baptist newspaper *The Baptist Standard,* Norris became a public figure when he stopped racetrack gambling at the State Fair. During those same years he worked with B. H. Carroll* to found Southwestern Baptist Theological Seminary.* Norris served as pastor of First Baptist Church in Fort Worth, Texas (1909-1952), and in later years served simultaneously as pastor of Temple Baptist in Detroit, Michigan (1935-1948), commuting by air between the two churches. Both were large congregations for their day (memberships of 15,000 and 10,000, respectively) and were built around Norris's forceful personality, sensational tactics, soul-winning fervor, and conservative theological and political views. From 1939 to about 1950 Norris presided over Bible Baptist Seminary,* an undergraduate Bible school located in his Fort Worth church.

In 1917 Norris started a paper first called *The Fence Rail,* later known as *The Searchlight* (1921) and finally as *The Fundamentalist** (1927). Exposing sin, criticizing the Southern Baptist Convention and promoting the fundamentalist cause, he became known by many of his fellow Baptist ministers for his independent spirit and acrimonious behavior. He was expelled from the Pastors' Conference of Fort Worth (1914), the Tarrant County Baptist Association (1922) and the Baptist General Convention of Texas (1924). Norris supported the Baptist Bible Union* until its collapse in 1932 and was an ardent supporter of the World's Christian Fundamentals Association throughout the 1920s, hosting its annual meeting in 1923.

Norris had strong anti-Catholic convictions, which led him in 1928 to campaign for Herbert Hoover and against the Catholic nominee for president, Alfred E. Smith. Earlier, in July 1926, in the heat of anti-Catholic sentiments he had helped stir up in Fort Worth, Norris shot and killed a man who had entered his study to threaten him. Charged with murder, he was found not guilty by the jury, who believed he had acted in self-defense. The incident gave Norris an unfavorable notoriety in the public eye, but among Southern fundamentalists he was regarded as a strong leader and champion of the truth.

See also FUNDAMENTALISM; INDEPENDENT BAPTISTS; VICK, G. BEAUCHAMP.

BIBLIOGRAPHY. *DAB* 5; G. W. Dollar, *A History of Fundamentalism in America* (1973); C. A. Russell, *Voices of American Fundamentalism* (1976); M. G. Toulouse, "A Case Study in Schism: J. Frank Norris and the Southern Baptist Convention," *Foun* 24 (January 1981): 32-53.

D. G. Reid

North American Baptist Conference. A small Baptist denomination of German ethnic heritage. The first conference of German Baptists in North America was held at the First German Baptist Church of Philadelphia in 1851. Konrad Anton Fleischmann,* pastor of the church, was a founding leader of the movement. Fleischmann, like most of his fellow immigrants who constituted the early German Baptists, had roots not among Baptists but within the Lutheran state church of Germany. Disenchanted with the formalism and lifelessness of the religion of his youth, Fleischmann was attracted to the spiritual fervor of the Baptists he encountered while preaching in Philadelphia. The rapid growth of German immigration in the late nineteenth century coupled with the evangelistic efforts of early leaders like Fleischmann resulted in a period of rapid expansion among the German Baptists. Beginning with

only eight churches and 405 members in 1851, the conference numbered 2,600 members in sixty-one churches by 1859. The earliest churches were to be found in major Northern metropolitan centers like New York, Philadelphia and Chicago. Subsequent waves of immigration, however, moved a large percentage of the membership into Kansas, Nebraska, Minnesota, the Dakotas and the western provinces of Canada. The General Conference of German Baptist Churches in North America, forerunner of the current organization, was formed in 1865.

The use of the German language was a significant unifying factor for the small and widely dispersed denomination. The official conference newspaper, *Der Sendbote,* launched into circulation in 1853, was also an important tool for preserving denominational cohesion. The strong desire to preserve the cultural identity of the denomination was a major factor in preventing the German Baptists from merging with the American Baptist* Convention. Use of the German language continued into the twentieth century, though the anti-German sentiment of two world wars and the pressures of cultural assimilation have led to its virtual disappearance from North American Baptist congregations. *Der Sendbote* eventually gave way to the English periodical *The Baptist Herald* (founded in 1923).

Two theological institutions serve the needs of the conference: the North American Baptist Seminary* in Sioux Falls, South Dakota, and the Edmonton Baptist Seminary in Edmonton, Alberta (Canada). The conference also supports an active Board of Missions with a significant missionary presence in Cameroon, Japan, the Philippines and Brazil. The conference currently records a membership of more than 60,000 in 378 churches in the United States and Canada. Conference headquarters are located in Forest Park, Illinois.

See also FLEISCHMANN, KONRAD; GERMAN BAPTIST CHURCH IN AMERICA.

BIBLIOGRAPHY. A. J. Ramaker, *The German Baptists in North America* (1924); *Those Glorious Years: The Centenary History of German Baptists of North America, 1843-1943* (1943); F. H. Woyke, *Heritage and Ministry of the North American Baptist Conference* (1985).

B. C. Leslie

North American Baptist Seminary. One of two theological institutions serving the needs of the North American Baptist Conference* (formerly the German Baptist Church in America*). The North American Baptist Seminary traces its roots to the German department of Rochester Theological Seminary,* founded in 1858. The seminary established the German department as a gesture of support for immigrant German Baptists who were only beginning to organize what would eventually become the North American Baptist Conference. The first class consisted of eight students and the first faculty of only one member, August Rauschenbusch (1816-1899), a converted Lutheran who had been educated in the theological tradition of the German universities. He was also father of the school's most notable faculty member, Walter Rauschenbusch,* best known as spokesman for the Social Gospel* movement.

In spite of considerable financial hardship, the German department expanded, adding both students and faculty. With time, however, the cordial relationship between Rochester Seminary and the German department became less satisfactory. In addition, many within the German Baptist Conference began to petition for a training center more centrally located for the needs of German Baptists. In 1949 the seminary relocated to Sioux Falls, South Dakota, under the name North American Baptist Seminary. A transition to the English language had already been inaugurated early in the twentieth century. The seminary maintains a close affiliation with the North American Baptist Conference, though the current enrollment of approximately 200 students reflects denominational diversity. The seminary's sister institution, Edmonton Baptist Seminary in Edmonton, Alberta, serves the needs of North American Baptist Churches in Canada.

See NORTH AMERICAN BAPTIST CONFERENCE.

BIBLIOGRAPHY. A. J. Ramaker, *The German Baptists in North America* (1924); *Those Glorious Years: The Centenary History of German Baptists of North America, 1843-1943* (1943); F. H. Woyke, *Heritage and Ministry of the North American Baptist Conference* (1985);

B. C. Leslie

North Greenville College. An institution of higher learning affiliated with the South Carolina Baptist Convention. North Greenville began in Tigerville, South Carolina, as a high school sponsored by the North Greenville Baptist Association. The idea of the school was first discussed by the association in 1891. The first students were accepted in 1893, with Hugh Lafayette Brock as principal. In 1905 the Home Mission Board* accepted cosponsorship of the school as a mountain mission school. This support continued until 1929. The school was chartered as a Baptist academy in 1915.

Under the leadership of Murphree Claude Donnan, North Greenville began offering college courses in 1934. It became a junior college in 1936, with Donnan serving as first president. In 1949 the association deeded the property and gave control of the college to the South Carolina Baptist Convention. North Greenville continued to operate as a junior college through the 1991-1992 school year. In June 1992 permission was granted for North Greenville to add a four-year program in church-related vocations. Enrollment for 1991-1992 was 387 students.

BIBLIOGRAPHY. *ESB* 2, 3, 4; J. M. Flynn, *A History of North Greenville Junior College* (1953).

G. Clayton

Northern Baptist Convention. See AMERICAN BAPTIST CHURCHES IN THE USA.

Northern Baptist Theological Seminary. Related to the American Baptist Churches in the USA* (ABCUSA). Founded in 1913 by the pastor, John Marvin Dean, and laymen of the Second Baptist Church in Chicago, Northern was established in Chicago, already the home of the University of Chicago and Moody Bible Institute. The University of Chicago's Divinity School* from its beginning was a graduate school preparing academics rather than pastors; Moody was nondenominational. Baptists were eager for an institution related to the Northern Baptist Convention (now ABCUSA) to provide ministers with both a pastoral education and a Baptist identity. A second concern was for conservative theological education. In this regard Northern was a "via media" between the University of Chicago and Moody. Nevertheless, this conservative stance did not prevent Northern from being attacked as theologically suspect in the denominational controversies of the 1920s and 1940s.

From the beginning Northern has been committed to educating for ministry both women and men of diverse ethnic heritage. The first student enrolled at Northern was Amy Lee Stockton, who was in the first graduating class. Northern absorbed several ethnic seminaries in the 1920s: Norwegian Baptist Seminary in 1921, the Danish seminary in 1925 and the Burmese, Karen and

Telegu seminaries in 1927.

The 1960s brought significant changes to Northern. Conflict over continuing to offer both undergraduate and graduate education served primarily by the same faculty led to the separation of the college program with the founding of Judson College in Elgin, Illinois. Northern celebrated its fiftieth anniversary in 1963 by opening a new facility in Lombard, Illinois.

With enrollment around 200, Northern entered its eightieth year committed to offering "an educational context that is international, interracial and intercultural" through its Hispanic program, cooperative relationship with Baptists in Moscow, ties to African-American Baptist congregations in Chicago and close association with Baptist alumni around the world. This educational context prepares women and men as "leaders for the churches who will be personally whole and spiritually mature, biblically grounded and theologically competent, pastoral, evangelistic and prophetic" in diverse settings through a variety of denominations.

See also AMERICAN BAPTIST CHURCHES IN THE USA.

BIBLIOGRAPHY. J. W. Bradbury, "Northern Seminary's Thirtieth Anniversary," *WE* 1 (November 25, 1943); J. M. Dean, "The Founding of the Northern Baptist Theological Seminary," *The Northern* 1 (1924); H. L. McBeth, *The Baptist Heritage* (1987); J. D. Mosteller, "Something Old—Something New," *Foun* 8 (1965):26-48; Northern Baptist Theological Seminary Mission Statement (1990); W. C. Young, *Commit What You Have Heard: A History of Northern Baptist Theological Seminary, 1918-1988* (1988).

P. R. Pleasants

Northwest Texas Baptist College. *See* DALLAS BAPTIST UNIVERSITY.

Norwegian Baptist Conference of America. Small Baptist denomination of Norwegian heritage. The establishment of the Norwegian Baptist Conference of America (NBCA) on November 17, 1910, in Fargo, North Dakota, represented the climax of over sixty years of Norwegian Baptist work in North America. The first Baptist missionary efforts among Norwegian immigrants were undertaken by the Illinois Baptist Convention with the organization of the Ottawa Baptist Church of La Salle County in 1842. The first baptism in the church was that of Norwegian immigrant Hans Valder,* who became a pioneer Baptist preacher

among Norwegians in North America. Valder, ordained in Ottawa in 1844, organized the Norwegian Baptist Church at Indian Creek in 1848, the first separate Norwegian Baptist church in America.

During the years that followed, the Norwegian Baptists worked closely with Danish Baptists and even combined their earliest efforts at denominational structure. The Danish-Norwegian Conference of the Northwestern States was founded in 1864. Other regional Danish-Norwegian conferences followed. Subsequent efforts toward the establishment of a national Scandinavian Baptist body were frustrated, however, leaving each of the three Scandinavian groups to define its own national body. The Norwegian Baptist Mission Society* organized the 1910 meeting in Fargo that led to the establishment of the NBCA. Important functions of the conference included the publication of the denominational newspaper, *Missonaeren,* the support of a seminary (*see* Norwegian Baptist Divinity School) and the financial support of missionaries. Because the work of the NBCA became progressively more intertwined with the structures and budget of the American Baptist Churches in the USA,* however, the conference resolved to dissolve itself in 1956, distributing its assets to support the work of American Baptists.

See also DANISH-NORWEGIAN BAPTIST CONFERENCE OF NORTH AMERICA.

BIBLIOGRAPHY. P. Stiansen, *History of the Norwegian Baptists in America* (1939).

B. C. Leslie

Norwegian Baptist Divinity School. First separate theological institution of Norwegian Baptists. During the last decade of the nineteenth century, Scandinavian Baptists in America were served primarily by two theological institutions, both affiliated with the Baptist Union Theological Seminary in Morgan Park, Illinois: the Dano-Norwegian Theological Seminary and the Swedish Theological Seminary. When in 1890 the Baptist Union became the Divinity School of the "new" University of Chicago,* the Scandinavians continued to be a part. By 1910, however, the university determined it could no longer afford to support the Scandinavian programs. This decision led to the departure of Swedish and Danish Baptists to build independent seminaries elsewhere. The Norwegians were left to negotiate an arrangement with the university, which led eventually to the establishment of a specifically Norwegian seminary in connection with the Divinity School. In the fall of 1913 the Norwegian Baptist Divinity House of the University of Chicago opened with seven students and with professor Henrick Gundersen as dean. Enrollment grew only modestly, so that between 1913 and 1920 no more than nineteen students attended the school. The low enrollment was a result not only of World War I but also of Norwegian Baptists' distrust of the theology of the Divinity School. Consequently, in 1921 the Norwegian Baptist Divinity House negotiated an end to its relationship with the Divinity School and entered into a tentative affiliation with Northern Baptist Theological Seminary* of Chicago. The Divinity House changed its name to Norwegian Baptist Theological Seminary. In 1922 the Norwegian conference sanctioned the move, and the affiliation with Northern Baptist Seminary became permanent.

See also NORWEGIAN BAPTIST CONFERENCE OF AMERICA.

BIBLIOGRAPHY. P. Stiansen, *History of the Norwegian Baptists in America* (1939); W. C. Young, *Commit What You Have Heard: A History of Northern Baptist Theological Seminary, 1913-1988* (1988).   B. C. Leslie

Norwegian Baptist Mission Society. Immediate predecessor to the Norwegian Baptist Conference of America.* During a period in which Scandinavian Baptists in America were segregating themselves along Swedish, Danish and Norwegian lines, the Logan Square Norwegian Baptist Church of Chicago found itself without any national or regional affiliation. In 1910 the church appointed a committee to propose a regional organization that would advance the missionary efforts of Norwegian Baptist churches in North America. On April 7, 1910, the church announced the formation of the Norwegian Baptist Mission Society, with Peder Stiansen serving as the society's first president. The constitution allowed for individuals as well as churches to become members of the society. While individual memberships were numerous, church memberships never consisted of more than two Chicago churches, Logan Square and Humboldt Norwegian Baptist Church. The society is remembered especially as the organization that called for a nationally represented conference of Norwegian Baptist churches in Fargo, North Dakota, on November 10, 1910. Out of this meeting came the

establishment of the Norwegian Baptist Conference of America, a separate organization with broader responsibilities that endured until 1956. The mission society disbanded, however, after three years of service.

See also NORWEGIAN BAPTIST CONFERENCE OF AMERICA.

BIBLIOGRAPHY. P. Stiansen, *History of the Norwegian Baptists in America* (1939).

B. C. Leslie

Norwegian Baptist Theological Seminary. Theological institution of the Norwegian Baptist Conference of America.* From 1913 to 1921 the Norwegian Baptist Divinity House provided Norwegian-language theological training for Norwegian Baptist ministers in connection with the University of Chicago's Divinity School.* The arrangement proved less than satisfactory, however, for two reasons: the Norwegian churches tended to look with suspicion on the less conservative theology of the Divinity School, and the few Norwegian-American students who did attend mostly lacked the educational preparation necessary to meet the rigorous demands of university classes. In 1921 the Divinity House severed ties with the University to affiliate with Northern Baptist Theological Seminary* in Chicago, an arrangement sanctioned by the Norwegian conference in 1922. With the change of affiliation, the Divinity House became Norwegian Baptist Theological Seminary. Four students made up the beginning class of the new seminary. Henrick Gundersen, dean of the Divinity House, retained leadership of the new institution. Upon Gundersen's death in 1926, Peder Stiansen was appointed the new dean, a position he held until the seminary's dissolution in 1956. A substantial portion of the seminary's financial support was provided by the Board of Education of the American Baptist Churches in the USA (see Board of Educational Ministries, ABCUSA). As use of the Norwegian language declined and as the institutional and budgetary relationship between American Baptists* and Norwegian Baptists became more intertwined, the continued existence of the seminary became unnecessary. When in 1956 the Norwegian Baptist Theological Conference disbanded in order to become a part of the American Baptist convention, the seminary was also dissolved and fully incorporated into Northern Baptist Theological Seminary.

See also NORWEGIAN BAPTIST CONFERENCE; NOR-

WEGIAN BAPTIST DIVINITY SCHOOL.

BIBLIOGRAPHY. P. Stiansen, *History of the Norwegian Baptists in America* (1939); W. C. Young, *Commit What You Have Heard: A History of Northern Baptist Theological Seminary, 1913-1988* (1988).

B. C. Leslie

Oakland City College. A coeducational, four-year liberal arts college and seminary located in Oakland City, Indiana. The college was established in 1885 following a number of attempts by General Baptists* to establish a "seminary of higher learning." Sponsored by the General Association of General Baptists, the school is recognized for ministerial and teacher training.

The college offers a number of undergraduate degree and certificate programs; the Onis G. and Pauline Chapman School of Religious Studies offers a master of divinity degree. The school has a student body of 600 to 800 students, with a full-time equivalent faculty of forty. The college is accredited by the North Central Association and the National Council for Accreditation of Teacher Education.

BIBLIOGRAPHY. O. Latch, *History of the General Baptists* (1954); B. L. Shirley, "A History of Oakland City College, 1885-1957" (M.A. thesis, Indiana State University, 1957).

L. C. Shull

Oklahoma Baptist University. A senior-level coeducational liberal arts college owned and supported by the Baptist General Convention of Oklahoma (BGCO). After failed ventures in Blackwell and Mangum, the BGCO voted in 1906 to establish one Baptist college for the state. George E. McKinnis, Shawnee businessman, was instrumental in the city of Shawnee's being chosen as the site for the school, and in 1910 articles of incorporation were granted. Shawnee contributed the original sixty acres and the first major building. The school actually opened under the presidency of James Milton Carroll in 1910, but closed after a year. It reopened in 1915 after completion of Shawnee Hall, the first building on campus. Of the school's presidents, John Wesley Raley served the longest tenure, a total of twenty-seven years (1934-1961). The 125-acre campus currently has twenty-five major buildings. The

university has an enrollment of approximately 2,200 students. Its curriculum has a reputation for strong general education requirements. Presently the university consists of five schools or colleges: arts and sciences, fine arts, Christian service, nursing and business. It is accredited by the North Central Association of Colleges and Secondary Schools, the National Association of Schools and Music, the National League for Nursing and the National Council for Accreditation of Teacher Education. Trustees are elected by the state convention.

BIBLIOGRAPHY. *ESB* 2, 3, 4; J. M. Gaskin et al., *The View from Bison Hill* (1985); J. Owens, *Annals of OBU* (1956).   S. A. Yarbrough

Old German Baptist Brethren. *See* DUNKERS.

Old Port Comfort Conference. A conference between representatives of the Northern and Southern Baptist conventions held September 27-28, 1911, with a view to working out a comity agreement between the two denominations in the matter of home missions. The creation of the Northern Baptist Convention in 1907 (*see* American Baptist Churches in the USA) created the necessity for such an agreement. The earlier basis of comity agreements between North and South had been reached at the Fortress Monroe Conference* in 1894. Although not exclusively so, the general practice was for mission work to be carried out on a regional basis, the major exceptions being work among black Baptists and some work in the American Southwest, notably New Mexico and Arizona.

A controversy developed over the extension of work in New Mexico by Southern Baptists.* Northern Baptists considered this an infringement of the earlier agreement. At a meeting in Washington, D.C., in April 1909, it was conceded that earlier accords no longer applied. Southern churches claimed responsibility for work in New

Mexico. When Northern churches failed to agree with the settlement, the Old Point Comfort Conference was called, which was followed by a second meeting in Hot Springs, Arkansas, January 24-25, 1912. The comity agreement reached there recognized the autonomy of local Baptist churches, affirmed the interdependence of Baptists and asserted the advisory character of denominational organizations. Underlying the agreement was the consideration that Baptist organizations should not compete unduly with other Baptist groups.

BIBLIOGRAPHY. R. A. Baker, *Relations Between Northern and Southern Baptists* (1948).

H. W. Pipkin

Old Regular Baptists. A central Appalachian denomination with approximately 15,000 formal members who hold to a strongly traditional faith controlled by strictly interpreted Pauline mandates concerning church governance, gender codes and membership relations, who accept a modified Calvinism, and who protect themselves from radical change through an insularity that precludes formal interaction with other Baptist groups. Clustered in a score of counties of eastern Kentucky, southwestern Virginia and southern West Virginia (with outpost churches in Arizona, Florida, Illinois, Indiana, Michigan, North Carolina, Ohio, Tennessee and Washington State), Old Regular fellowships are seldom larger than a hundred members and often smaller than twenty. They trace their origins to a 1801 uniting of the South Kentucky (Separate Baptist*) Association and the Elkhorn (Regular Baptist*) Association, an alliance that first produced the United Baptists* and then—via a slow evolvement—the Old Regular Baptists.

From its inception, this branch of the Baptist faith has been plagued by numerous splits. Old Regular churches collect in associations of like-minded fellowships, the largest of which is the Union Association with 3,135 members in seventy-six churches (1990 statistics), and the smallest and newest of which is Little Dove with thirty-seven members in two churches (1991 statistics). In the early 1990s the remaining fifteen associations—New Salem, Bethel, Friendship, Indian Bottom, Mountain 1, Mountain 2, Mountain Liberty, Mud River, Northern New Salem, Old Friendship, Old Indian Bottom, Philadelphia, Sardis, Thornton Union and Kyova—range in size from fifty-six to three churches.

Old Regulars proudly accept the "peculiar people" title employed by Peter (in the King James Version), doggedly preserving such traditional practices as lined singing, a "God-called and God-equipped" unpaid ministry, extemporized and chanted homiletics, "natural water" baptisms, gender separation in members-only sections, exuberant female shouting, highly tactile fellowshipping, strongly emotional once-a-year footwashings,* frequent memorializations of the dead, prohibitions against Sunday schools, and a host of other worship modes carried over from the eighteenth and nineteenth centuries. Rejecting both particular election and Arminianism,* Old Regulars preach an atonement doctrine tied to a personal call that constitutes an awakening to consciousness of sin followed by a "travel" or "travail" during which the individual, through repentance and belief, moves from "conviction" to "redemption." Christ's atonement therefore is for all who wait, listen and respond. With such an emphasis on the personal nature of a call and on the sinner's duty to wait for its coming, among the Old Regulars baptisms tend to occur much later than they do in many Baptist denominations.

BIBLIOGRAPHY. M. B. Bradley et al., *Churches and Church Membership in the United States, 1990* (1992); H. Dorgan, *Giving Glory to God in Appalachia: Worship Practices of Six Baptist Subdenominations* (1987); H. Dorgan, *The Old Regular Baptists of Central Appalachia: Brothers and Sisters in Hope* (1989); W. M. Patterson, "Small Baptist Groups in Kentucky," in *Baptists in Kentucky, 1776-1976*, ed. L. T. Crismon (1975); R. Short, "We Believed in the Family and in the Old Regular Baptist Church," *SouthEx* 4, no. 3 (1976):60-65; J. Wallhausser, "I Can Almost See Heaven from Here," *Kat,* Spring 1983, pp. 2-10.

H. Dorgan

Olney, Thomas (?-1682). Colonial Baptist leader. Olney was one of several colonists who in 1638 followed Roger Williams* from Salem to Providence, Rhode Island, after Williams's banishment from Massachusetts Bay Colony. In Providence, Olney joined Williams at the first Baptist church established in America. Williams soon stepped down as pastor of that church, and Olney replaced him. In the following decades Olney was involved in several religious and political disputes. In the schism of 1652 he led the "Five Principle Baptists" against William Wickenden and his followers, who insisted on the practice of the laying on of hands* for each member of a congregation. The division lasted seventy years. In 1655 Olney helped lead the opposition to Roger Williams's militia training law, on the grounds that military service violated the teaching of Scripture.

BIBLIOGRAPHY. I. Backus, *A History of New England with Particular Reference to the Baptists* (1796); S. H. Brockunier, *The Irrepressible Democrat: Roger Williams* (1941).

T. T. Taylor

Ordinances, Baptist Views. Baptists observe two ordinances (or sacraments). baptism* by immersion upon profession of faith, and the Lord's Supper,* traditionally understood as a commemorative meal restricted to baptized believers. The proper subject for Baptist baptism is a professed believer in Jesus Christ, and the mode is single immersion in water, an act proclaiming initiation into and identification with Christ's death, burial and resurrection. Observed with varying frequency, usually monthly or quarterly, the Lord's Supper is a remembrance *(anamnēsis)* of Christ's death, with central meanings such as "covenant, church, Christ and communion." While many Baptist churches stress the "memorial" nature of the Supper, others suggest some aspect of Christ's "spiritual presence" in the sharing of bread and cup. Most, but not all, use unleavened bread and nonfermented grape juice as elements. Some Baptist traditions—Old Regular, Primitive and others—view foot-washing* as an ordinance of the church.

The earliest Baptists used the term *sacraments,* but *ordinances* gained dominance as Baptists stressed human obedience to Christ's scriptural commands over against tendencies to view the rites as automatic vehicles of grace. This shift emphasized free personal response to divine initiative but resulted in devaluing the depth of the observances, a diminishment represented by the adjective in a common cliché: "Ordinances are *mere* symbols." Recent evidence suggests a return to a more multidimensional approach by Baptists, some of whom have reembraced and redefined the term *sacraments.* For Baptists the ordinances are never the formal instruments of what they symbolize, but there are varying interpretations of the relationship between the externals of observance and the inner spiritual realities.

Baptist ordinances belong within the life of the church. They symbolize inclusion in the fellowship of believers, which has authority for administration. Normally an ordained minister is the administrator, but any believer designated by the observing congregation may so serve.

See also BAPTISM; FOOT-WASHING; LORD'S SUPPER.

BIBLIOGRAPHY. W. L. Lumpkin, *Baptist Confessions of Faith* (1959); N. H. Maring and W. S. Hudson, *A Baptist Manual of Polity and Practice* (1991); J. E. Tull, "The Ordinances/Sacraments in Baptist Thought," *ABQ* 1 (December 1982).

W. L. Allen

Ordination, Baptist Views. Baptists have often seemed of two minds concerning the ordination of ministers. On one hand they have seemed to minimize ordination, stressing the priesthood of all believers* and attempting to avoid the clerical hierarchy they observe in other Christian traditions. On the other hand, from the early days of the movement they have practiced ordination of persons set aside for specific ministry in the church as evidenced in the laying on of hands.* This dual response to ordination is evident in the fact that many early Baptists in England and America practiced the laying on of hands for both clergy and laity. Many laid hands on all the newly baptized as a sign that all Christians were called to be ministers of the gospel. They also administered the laying on of hands to those who were set aside for particular ministry within the community of faith.

While representatives of the regional associations* might be present at ordinations, the event was essentially a local church experience, with the congregation exercising its authority under Christ to set aside persons for ministry. Usually ordination was given in response to a request from a specific congregation that sought to call individuals as ministers. In the colonial and frontier periods there was a close relationship between the individual's sense of call and the verification of the call by the community of faith. As a part of the ordination process, candidates were often "licensed" by the church as a first step. Licensing allowed the church to observe the individual's gifts and character on the way to ordination. Most churches required some statement of faith, belief and call experience as part of the process. Candidates were asked to "testify" to their conversion, their call from God and their willingness to live according to certain ministerial standards. Pulpit and leadership skills were also taken under consideration by the congregation before a vote to ordain was taken.

By the nineteenth century, the "ordination council" had become a common prerequisite to approval. Candidates met with laity and clergy and were questioned on their doctrinal beliefs and religious experience. Churches could and did refuse to ordain persons whose lives or testimonies were deemed unacceptable. The Landmark* movement among Baptists placed great emphasis on ordination in the proper congregation. Some Landmarkists believed that since only the local church could ordain, a pastor had to be reordained by every congregation served.

In frontier Baptist churches, statements of call often followed a standard form: conversion, religious nurture, mentors and the experience of the mysterious call. Frequently would-be ministers told of their early efforts to "run from God" in an effort to do anything but preach the gospel. Others, hesitant to accept the call, were brought to ordination by the congregation, which recognized their gifts and pressed them into service. The ordination service itself was usually a simple affair, usually including a sermon by the candidate's ministerial mentor and concluding with the laying on of hands. Some congregations also gave the ordinand a new Bible. For many years the laying on of hands was administered only by the ordained ministers and deacons who might be present. More recently, some churches invite all members of the congregation to participate in laying on hands as representatives of Christ and the congregation.

Some Baptist groups—though not all—also practice the formal ordination of laypersons who are elected deacons* by the congregation. This office, while ordained, is perceived as a lay office in the church. As a disciplinary measure, ordination may be revoked by the same church that authorizes it.

In recent years the increase in women's ordinations has caused many Baptist groups to reexamine the practice and its meaning. Some churches ordain women both as ministers and as deacons. Others do not. Likewise, many Baptist groups have begun to ordain persons for various ministries—counseling, music, Christian education—as well as for the pastoral ministry. Some churches require that any person who administers baptism and Communion be ordained. Others accept that tradition but also provide that any Baptist believer authorized by the congregation may perform any task in the believing community.

BIBLIOGRAPHY. B. J. Leonard, *Early American Christianity* (1979); idem, "The Ordination Service in Baptist Churches," *RE,* Fall 1981; N. H. Maring and W. H. Hudson, *A Baptist Manual of Polity and Practice* (1991).

B. J. Leonard

Orthodox Baptist Movement. An independent,* fundamentalist,* premillennial Baptist movement that originated in Ardmore, Oklahoma. The Orthodox Baptist movement began when W. Lee Rector, former instructor at Oklahoma Baptist University, Shawnee, resigned as pastor of the First Missionary Baptist Church, Ardmore, on September 27, 1931. On the same day he and more than 300 members of the church withdrew to organize the First Orthodox Baptist Church, Ardmore. The church called Rector as pastor. He was an outspoken critic of modernism in Baptist literature, life and institutions. His church continued its affiliation with the Enon Baptist Association until 1935.

Rector began publication of *The Illuminator* in 1931. The newsletter's name later was changed to *The Orthodox Baptist.* The movement published a confession* written by Rector entitled Orthodox Baptist Confession of Faith, which reflected fundamentalist theology, premillennial eschatology and independent, congregational ecclesiology.* In 1944 the church organized the Orthodox Bible School. The movement divided the Baptist General Convention of Oklahoma—the only such schism in the convention's history with the possible exception of the controversy over the firing of C. P. Stealey* as editor of the *Baptist Messenger.* The Orthodox Baptist movement spread to a number of states, including Colorado, Texas, Maine, Illinois, Arizona and Kansas. Rector died in October 1945.

BIBLIOGRAPHY. *ESB* 2:1064-65.

S. A. Yarbrough

Ouachita Baptist University. The Arkansas Baptist Convention was organized in 1848. Interest in education began in 1850, when a committee was formed to submit a plan to create a "seminary" to educate ministers. In the meantime, cooperation was established with Louisiana Baptists to educate ministers at Mt. Lebanon University.

In 1860 the convention abandoned the idea of

the college due to the "war clouds." When the convention met in 1867, the $41,000 that had been raised was gone. Between 1870 and 1873, Arkansas sent students to Mississippi College.*

After several attempts, Ouachita College opened at Arkadelphia in 1886 with an enrollment of 100 students and five teachers. The first president was J. W. Conger, who had come to Arkansas from Union College in Tennessee and to Arkadelphia from Prescott. Some did not agree with the coeducational policy, and they established a female school in Conway, Arkansas.

The college endowment began in 1916 with a $21,000 gift from Florence Wilson. John Gardner Lile became endowment secretary in 1918. The college was accredited by the North Central Association of Colleges and Universities in the 1920s. It was suspended twice, due to economics, until 1953, when full accreditation was reestablished.

The first graduate program began in 1921 but ceased in the 1930s. It was revived in 1959, with degrees offered in religion and in American civilization. A master of music education degree was offered in 1961 and in education in 1967. The graduate program was eliminated for the second time in 1991. Ouachita College assumed university status in 1965. The current enrollment is 1,300, with a teaching faculty of 105.

BIBLIOGRAPHY. Ouachita Baptist University, *Catalogue 1991-1992.*

J. T. Greer

P

Palm Beach Atlantic College. A four-year coeducational liberal arts college located in West Palm Beach, Florida. As a result of actions by the Florida Baptist Convention in 1962 and 1963, it was begun in 1968 but was released from convention control in the same year and became autonomous, controlled by local trustees.

The first classes were held in the First Baptist Church, and the first president was Jess Moody, pastor of the First Baptist Church. After Moody resigned, the college was led by Warner Earle Fusslle (1972-1978), George Borders (1978-1981), Claude Rhea (1981-1991) and Paul Corts (1991-).

The college was accredited in 1972, and the first new building, the W. G. Lassiter Jr. Student Center, was constructed in 1983 as part of a long-range plan for a permanent campus on twenty-three acres in downtown West Palm Beach. The first phase of a master plan was completed in 1989, the second in 1991. Enrollment now is 1,892, endowment is $18,961,582, and the budget is $12,660,022.

BIBLIOGRAPHY. *ESB* 3, 4; E. E. Joiner, *A History of Florida Baptists* (1972); Palm Beach Atlantic College, *Academic Catalogue 1992-1993*.

E. E. Joiner

Palmer, Paul (?-c.1750). Colonial Baptist preacher. A native of Maryland, Palmer was baptized in the Welsh Tract Church, Delaware, and ordained in Connecticut. Arriving in North Carolina about 1720, he married Joanna Peterson, a widow, and they had two children. After preaching for several years, he organized the first Baptist church in North Carolina (Chowan County) in 1727. His itinerant preaching resulted in other new congregations. A notable convert was Joseph Parker,* who also became a Baptist preacher. The first Baptist church in Maryland (1742) grew out of converts Palmer baptized at Chestnut Ridge. Arminian* in doctrine, Palmer was a major leader

of the early General Baptists* in America. Neither the year of his birth nor the precise year of his death is known, but he apparently died before 1754.

BIBLIOGRAPHY. H. L. McBeth, *The Baptist Heritage* (1986); G. W. Paschal, *History of North Carolina Baptists* (1930).

W. M. Patterson

Parker, Daniel (1781-1844). Baptist preacher, antimissions* leader, founder of the Two-Seed-in-the-Spirit* Predestinarian Baptists. Born in Virginia and reared in Georgia, Parker lacked formal education. Baptized in 1802, he moved in 1803 to Tennessee, where he was ordained (1806) and served as a pastor. In 1817 he moved to Crawford County, Illinois, where he published his antimission views: *A Public Address to the Baptist Society* (1820), *The Second Dose of Doctrine on the Two Seeds* (1826), *Views on the Two Seeds* (1826) and a monthly paper, *The Church Advocate* (1829-1831). He also served as an Illinois state senator (1826-1827).

Although he has been portrayed as totally unsympathetic toward missions, Parker's writings suggest rather opposition to missionary societies and schemes not under church control. He believed that the society plan of organization represented by the Baptist Triennial Convention* (1814) was not based on Scripture. He was not opposed to "the spread of the gospel" or "itinerant preaching."

Parker's Two-Seed notion was based on Genesis 3:15. He concluded that there are two kinds of progeny, one of God and one of Satan—the elect (God's children) and the nonelect (Satan's offspring). The former are predestined to eternal life, the latter are not. The nonelect may respond to the gospel, but when they do not it is their rebellion that condemns them. Although they are "the seed of the serpent, yet they are human beings, and no less accountable to God."

In 1834 Parker moved to Texas with his congregation, the Pilgrim Predestinarian Regular Baptist Church, the first organized Baptist Church in Texas. His itinerant preaching produced nine other congregations. Parker's efforts touched Baptists in several states and resulted in the formation of a small antimission denomination. A man of great energy, natural ability and uncommon resourcefulness, he was vigorous in the pulpit in denouncing the society method of denominational organization and caused much dissension among Baptists on the frontier.

BIBLIOGRAPHY. *DARB; ESB* 2; O. M. Lee, "Daniel Parker's Doctrine of the Two Seeds" (Th.M. thesis, Southern Baptist Theological Seminary, 1962); H. L. McBeth, *The Baptist Heritage* (1986); A. C. Piepkorn, *Profiles in Belief,* vol. 2 (1978).

W. M. Patterson

Parker, Joseph (1705?-1791?). Free Will Baptist* leader. The first isolated Baptists to settle in North Carolina were gathered into a church at Perquimans, near Chowan, in 1727. These General* or Arminian* Baptists were led by Paul Palmer. Little is known of Joseph Parker's early years, but he and his wife, Sarah, came to this area around 1730 and became converts of Palmer. Parker almost immediately formed a church at Meherrin, which became an outpost and evangelistic hub of the area. He ministered as pastor of this church until 1742, when he petitioned for a grant of 200 acres in Edgecombe. According to Morgan Edwards,* in 1748 he gathered and pastored a church at Lower Fishing Creek, near Enfield. Supporting himself by farming, he disliked the growing population in the area, especially the rising number and influence of the Particular Baptists.* By 1756 many of his "sons in the ministry" and the congregation at Enfield had become Particulars. Parker thus sought new fields south of the Tar River, settling first at Little Contentnea (around 1761) and later at Wheat Swamp, forty miles from New Bern in present-day Lenoir County. Most of his labors were with the congregation at Wheat Swamp, though he occasionally preached at Conetoe Creek and the Pungo River.

As Carolina Baptist life gradually became dominated by the Separates,* Parker and his followers refused to unite with them and assumed the name Free Will Baptists. He died in 1791 or 1792 at Wheat Swamp. The present-day Free Will Baptists of North Carolina have descended from the churches organized by Parker.

BIBLIOGRAPHY. J. T. Christian, *A History of the Baptists of the United States* (1922); G. W. Paschal, *History of North Carolina Baptist* (1930); A. C. Piepkorn, *Profiles in Belief,* vol. 2 (1979).

A. M. Manis

Parrish, Charles Henry, Sr. (1859-1931). African-American Baptist minister, president of two independent all-black Baptist schools, a founder of the National Baptist Convention (*see* National Baptists), and leader in interracial and international Baptist affairs. Born on April 18, 1859, in Lexington, Kentucky, Parrish spent his early years as a slave. He graduated from State University (A.B., 1886; A.M., 1889; LL.B., 1923) in Louisville.

Along with William J. Simmons,* in 1890 Parrish founded Eckstein Norton Institute in Cane Spring, Kentucky. After Simmons's death the same year, Parrish became president; he served from 1890 to 1912. In 1918 Parrish became president of State (later Simmons*) University. However, in 1931 Simmons University closed its undergraduate program, a casualty of the Depression. It would continue only as a theological school, later known as Simmons Bible College. Parrish then helped to facilitate a merger between Simmons's undergraduate program and the University of Louisville, which brought into existence Louisville Colored Municipal College.

Parrish also served as chairman of the newly organized National Baptist Convention Foreign Mission Board. In 1923 he spoke at the Baptist World Alliance* meeting in Stockholm and was elected to the executive board. He was author of several articles and edited *Golden Jubilee of the General Association of Colored Baptists in Kentucky* (1915). He served as president of the joint commission of the American Baptist Theological Seminary* (1914-1924) in Nashville, which was cosponsored by Southern Baptists* and National Baptists. Parrish died in Louisville on April 11, 1931.

BIBLIOGRAPHY. Kentucky Human Rights Commission, *Kentucky's Black Heritage* (1971); N. H. Pius, *An Outline of Baptist History* (1911); W. J. Simmons, *Men of Mark* (1887); L. H. Williams, *Black Higher Education in Kentucky, 1879-1930: The History of Simmons University* (1987).

L. H. Williams

Particular Baptists. Calvinistic* Baptists with origins in English Puritanism. English Particular Baptists, following the doctrine of predestination, believed that God redeems only "particular" individuals. This opposed the Arminian* concept of "general" redemption held by General Baptists* and many Anglicans. Particular Baptists emerged from a Southwark (London) Puritan-Separatist congregation which Henry Jacob* had gathered in 1616. Later known by the last initials of its first three pastors—Jacob, Lathrop and Jessey—the "JLJ Church," which practiced infant baptism, experienced several schisms. During Lathrop's pastorate, Samuel Eaton formed a strictly Separatist church (1633), some of whose members were rebaptized, probably because they rejected Anglican baptism as corrupt. In 1638 the first English Calvinistic Baptists began meeting when six members explicitly favoring believer's baptism left the JLJ Church.

By 1644 seven Particular Baptist churches in the London area were associating together. They issued the London Confession (1644) in order to distinguish themselves from General Baptists and from Anabaptists* on the Continent. To defy increasing Anglican persecution and to show doctrinal solidarity with the Presbyterian-Congregational tradition, they expressed a heightened Calvinism in their Second London Confession (1677, 1688, 1689). A revision of this by Benjamin Keach* and Elias Keach* became the first widely used Baptist confession* in America. There, later known as Regular Baptists* and led by the Philadelphia Baptist Association,* they modified the 1689 confession and produced the Philadelphia Confession (1742). With its softened Calvinism, this became the unifying doctrinal statement for most Baptists in America by 1800.

BIBLIOGRAPHY. T. Crosby, *The History of the English Baptists* (1738-1740); H. L. McBeth, *The Baptist Heritage* (1987); B. R. White, *The English Baptists of the Seventeenth Century* (1983).

J. T. Spivey

Particular-Regular Baptists. The largest colonial American Baptist general body. Baptists in early America were of two major varieties, Calvinistic* Particular-Regular (PR) and Arminian* General.* Founded in 1639, the First Baptist Church of Providence, Rhode Island,* was the first Particular church on the North American continent, no doubt initially containing a mixed congregation dominated by Particular members. All-Particular congregations soon sprang up, and through the eighteenth century the name Particular persisted. However, with the rise of Separate*

Baptist churches in the 1740s, Particular Baptists were frequently designated as Regular.* No change in outlook was signified by the new name. They continued to be somewhat more formal and less revivalistic than their Separate neighbors.

This general group gradually spread, largely along the Atlantic seaboard: in 1700 it had twelve churches with 409 members, and by 1750 813 churches and 57,436 members. In the 1780s Separate Baptists were accepted by the PR associations, accounting for the fact that over 84 percent of all North American Baptists in 1790 were PR.

Associational life came early to the PRs. The Philadelphia Baptist Association* was formed in 1707, followed by seventeen others. Eleven Separate associations became PR in the 1780s.

This group provided an important number of congregations supporting contemporary American* and Southern* Baptist activities. Of the churches existing in 1790, about half remain to the present, of which about 85 percent take some part in the organized convention life that replaced the Triennial Convention.*

BIBLIOGRAPHY. R. G. Torbet, *A History of the Baptists* (1978).

R. G. Gardner

Patterson, Frederic William (1877-1966). Canadian Baptist* leader and university president. Patterson served as pastor of Baptist churches in his native New Brunswick and in western Canada. In 1916 he became editor of the *Western Baptist* and in 1919 secretary of the Baptist Union of Western Canada. In 1922 he was appointed president of Acadia University, Wolfville, Nova Scotia, a Baptist institution founded in 1838. A remarkable fundraiser and organizer, he guided the institution through the turbulent period of the Depression and World War II, retiring in 1948. During his presidency Acadia's enrollment expanded from 307 to 890. Patterson successfully trod a middle path between the pressures of his Baptist constituency and the increasing student demands for freedom from denominational* restrictions. After his retirement he continued to serve the university as fundraiser.

BIBLIOGRAPHY. W. Kirkconnell, *The Fifth Quarter-Century: Acadia University, 1938-1963* (1968); R. S. Longley, *Acadia University, 1838-1938* (1939).

B. M. Moody

Peabody, Lucy Whitehead McGill (1861-1949). Baptist missionary and denominational leader. Born in Belmont, Kansas, she was a schoolteacher at Rochester School for the Deaf from 1879 to 1881 in Rochester, New York, before being appointed a missionary to India by the American Baptist Foreign Mission Society.* On her return to the United States in 1888, she became secretary of the Women's American Baptist Foreign Mission Society* as well as its principal editor. In that capacity and with the support and resources of her spouse, Henry W. Peabody, she became a roving ambassador for mission* endeavor, particularly women's work.

Early in her career as a schoolteacher Peabody had made the acquaintance of Helen Barrett Montgomery,* and the two planned and executed significant advances in Protestant work. In 1913, for instance, they made an extensive tour of mission fields in India, China and Japan, out of which grew study guides on mission work, new funds for overseas women's colleges and a proposal for a World Day of Prayer. The latter began as a vigil involving over seventy countries.

Peabody possessed extraordinary skills in organization and coordinated several worldwide efforts. In 1912 she helped create the Federation of Women's Boards of Foreign Missions. Later in life, at the request of her son-in-law Raphael C. Thomas, who was a missionary in the Philippines, she organized within the Northern Baptist Convention (see American Baptist Churches in the USA) the theologically conservative Association of Baptists for World Evangelism.* This group did much to revive interest in overseas ministry during a period of doctrinal tension. Her enthusiasm for missions was shared in two books: A Wider World for Women (1936) and Just Like You: Stories of Children of Every Land (1937).

BIBLIOGRAPHY. L. A. Cattan, Lamps Are for Lighting: The Story of Helen Barrett Montgomery and Lucy Waterbury Peabody (1972).

W. H. Brackney

Peacemaking Among Baptists. Peacemaking, framed in terms of war and peace, has often been the topic of resolutions in Baptist life. But this general pattern holds true: during peacetime, Baptists have spoken up for peace; during war, support is urged for the nation's leaders and troops.

While there is still a debate over the extent of Anabaptist* influence in the beginning of seventeenth-century Baptist congregational life, the former's pacifist position had minimal impact on either the earliest English Baptist leaders or their heirs in North America. In his twenty-seven-article confession of faith, Thomas Helwys,* pastor of the first Baptist congregation on English soil, expressly allowed believers' use of the sword. Many Baptists were among Cromwell's troops in the English Civil War; and later, in the U.S. Revolutionary War, Baptists' revolutionary fervor gained them a favorable reputation in the new republic. During the U.S. Civil War, Baptists lined up in support of both the Union and the Confederacy.

Some of the strongest antiwar language approved by Baptist bodies came during the period between World Wars I and II. In 1934 Northern Baptists (see American Baptist Churches in the USA) approved a statement to "repudiate all aggressive war." "I will cross no national boundary line to kill and to destroy," signers promised, "nor will I support my government in sending its army or navy to do so." And in 1940 the Southern Baptist Convention* expressed its "utter abhorrence of war as an instrument of International policy" and acknowledged for the first time the rights of conscientious objectors.

There have been exceptions to this pattern, however, including Martin Luther King Jr., who mobilized a powerful civil rights movement based on principles of nonviolence and, from that position, also criticized U.S. involvement in the war in Vietnam.

BIBLIOGRAPHY. P. Dekar, For the Healing of the Nations (1993); C. Howe, "Baptists and Peacemaking," RE, Fall 1982; R. S. Trulson, "Baptist Pacifism: A Heritage of Nonviolence," ABQ, September 1991; H. M. Vose, "Exploring the Baptist Heritage for Insights into the Attitudes of Modern Baptists Toward War and Peace," in Seek Peace and Pursue It, ed., H. W. Pipkin (1989); J. E. Wood Jr., ed., Baptists and the American Experience (1976). K. Sehested

Peck, John Mason (1789-1858). Baptist missionary to the Missouri Territory, journalist and educator. Born in Litchfield, Connecticut, Peck moved with his wife, Sally, to Greene County, New York, in 1811. There they left Congregationalism for Baptist views, and Peck began to preach in small Baptist churches in upstate New York. In 1815 Peck met Luther Rice,* a traveling agent for the newly formed Baptist Triennial Convention,* who encouraged Peck's missionary* interests.

The Pecks were appointed to the St. Louis area in 1817, where they established a mission to the

Missouri Territory. Peck preached, formed churches, organized Sunday schools* (which were then new in America), taught school, formed women's "mite societies" to sponsor mission work, and distributed Bibles and religious literature. In 1827 he founded Rock Springs Seminary, one of the earliest schools west of the Mississippi. In 1832 the seminary moved to Upper Alton, Illinois, and it was renamed Shurtleff College* in 1836. In 1829 Peck launched *The Pioneer,* the first of several papers he sponsored in the West. During the 1820s he advocated tax-supported public schools, temperance societies and the abolition of slavery. Peck helped form the American Baptist Home Mission Society* in 1832 and the American Baptist Historical Society in 1853. His interest in stimulating immigration to the West is evident in two of his publications, *Gazetteer of Illinois* (1834) and *A New Guide for Emigrants to the West* (1836). He was convinced that the West was a place where Christian institutions could nurture democracy.

Peck's fifty-three-volume diary was destroyed, but Rufus Babcock* preserved much of it in preparing Peck's memoirs. Though he had scant formal schooling, in 1852 Harvard University recognized his substantial contributions by conferring on him an honorary degree.

BIBLIOGRAPHY. R. Babcock, ed., *Forty Years of Pioneer Life: Memoir of John Mason Peck* (1864); *DAB* VII; *DARB;* C. Hayne, *Vanguard of the Caravan: Life Story of John Mason Peck* (1931); M. Lawrence, *John Mason Peck: The Missionary Pioneer* (1940).   H. L. McBeth

Pendleton, James Madison (1811-1891).
Baptist pastor, professor and journalist. Born in Spotsylvania County, Virginia, and raised in Christian County, Kentucky, Pendleton attended an academy at Hokinsville, Kentucky. By the age of seventeen he had joined the Baptist Church, and by nineteen (1831) he was licensed and preaching. He was ordained a Baptist minister in 1833, but for several years he taught school and studied theology privately.

Pendleton became one of the better-educated Baptist pastors in western Kentucky, and he was the first in his region to enter the professional ministry. In 1837 he became pastor of First Baptist Church, Bowling Green, Kentucky. There he remained until 1857, when he became professor of theology at Union University, Murfreesboro, Tennessee. The following year he became a joint editor of *The Tennessee Baptist.*

Pendleton, along with A. C. Dayton* and J. R. Graves,* made up the "Great Triumvirate" of a Baptist ecclesiological movement known as Landmarkism.* Pendleton coined the term *Landmark* in 1854 in an article Graves published as a tract entitled *An Old Landmark Re-set* (1856). Both men were alarmed that Baptists were setting aside an old landmark of the faith by participating in pulpit exchanges, union meetings and fraternal relations with other denominations. Pendleton was recognized as the systematist of Landmarkism.

Because of his Union sympathies, with the onset of the Civil War Pendleton withdrew to the North. There he pastored a church at Hamilton, Ohio (1862-1865), and then Upland, Pennsylvania (1865-1883), where he also played a role in founding Crozer Theological Seminary.* In 1883 he returned to Tennessee to live with his sons. Among his several publications were *Three Reasons Why I Am a Baptist* (1853), *Church Manual* (1867) and *Christian Doctrines* (1878).

See also LANDMARK BAPTISTS.

BIBLIOGRAPHY. *DAB* VII; J. M. Pendleton, *Reminiscences of a Long Life* (1891); J. H. Spencer, *A History of Kentucky Baptists* (1886).

M. G. Bell

Perspectives in Religious Studies. A quarterly journal of religion published by the National Association of Baptist Professors of Religion* (NABPR). Proposed by Watson E. Mills in 1971 to enhance the image of Baptist scholarship, to provide a place for young scholars to begin publishing and to share the work of scholars with the public, the journal was approved for publication by the NABPR in February 1972. The inaugural issue appeared in the spring of 1974. Mills became and remained the editor until 1991, at which time Rollin S. Armour assumed that office. Published twice a year from 1974 to 1976, it appeared three times a year from 1976 to 1983. Since 1983 it has been published quarterly.

Under the general supervision of an editorial board chosen by the NABPR, *Perspectives in Religious Studies* seeks to guarantee Baptist scholars a free press by publishing a broad variety of articles reflecting the diverse interests of the sponsoring body. The journal also contains a valuable section of critical reviews of contemporary books in the field of religion. Since 1984, each winter issue of the journal has been a "festschrift" for an outstanding Baptist scholar. Scholars honored have included Frank Stagg, T. B. Maston,* Robert G. Torbet, Dale Moody, Walter J. Harrelson, Penrose St. Amant, Bernard Ramm and Henlee Barnette. Present circulation is approximately 800.

See also NATIONAL ASSOCIATION OF BAPTIST PROFESSORS OF RELIGION.

BIBLIOGRAPHY. R. Beck, "A Community of Scholars: A History of the National Association of Baptist Professors of Religion," in *National Association of Baptist Professors of Religion: Directory of Members 1991* (1991); W. E. Mills, "The NABPR Publications Program," *PRS* 9 (1982):275-82.

W. D. Shurden

Pettingill, William Leroy (1866-1950). Fundamentalist* Bible teacher, author and cofounder of the Philadelphia School of the Bible. Born in New York City, Pettingill was ordained a Baptist minister in 1899 and served at North Church, Wilmington, Delaware (1903-1913). In 1914 he assisted in founding Philadelphia School of the Bible and was dean (1914-1928) during the presidency of C. I. Scofield. Later he served as pastor of First Church, New York City (1948-1950).

Throughout his life Pettingill championed the fundamentalist cause, and for a time he served as vice president of the Independent Fundamental Churches of America. In his preaching, teaching and writing he promoted dispensational premillennialism and was a popular speaker at Bible and prophetic conferences. As editor and author, Pettingill founded two periodicals: *Serving-and-Waiting* (1911) and *Just a Word* (1928). He was one of the consulting editors for the Scofield Reference Bible, and among his numerous works were *God's Prophecies for Plain People* (1923), *By Grace Through Faith Plus Nothing: Simple Studies in Galatians* (1938) and *Simple Studies in the Revelation* (1916).

BIBLIOGRAPHY. S. G. Cole, *The History of Fundamentalism* (1931).

R. L. Petersen

Philadelphia Baptist Association (1707-). Oldest surviving Baptist association* in America. In Baptist polity, an "association" is a regional grouping of churches designed for fellowship, mutual guidance, and cooperation in missions and other endeavors. As early as the 1640s, Baptist churches in England formed such associations, whence the pattern was brought to America. The Philadelphia Association was formed in 1707 with five cooperating churches, none of them more than a few years old. In 1742 the association adopted the influential Philadelphia Baptist Confession of Faith, and in 1764 it sponsored the first Baptist college in America at Providence, Rhode Island (now Brown University*). The association also sponsored an "evangelist at large" to itinerate on the frontier, founding new churches. By the 1750s the association extended from New England to the South, functioning essentially as a national body. It proved vastly influential among Baptists in America through its confession,* moderate Calvinist* theology, organizational pattern and missionary zeal.

BIBLIOGRAPHY. A. D. Gillette, ed., *Minutes of the Philadelphia Baptist Association from 1707 to 1807* (1851); R. G. Torbet, *A Social History of the Philadelphia Baptist Associations, 1707-1940* (1944).

H. L. McBeth

Philadelphia Confession of Faith. See CONFESSIONS OF FAITH, BAPTIST.

Pitt, Robert Healey (1853-1937). Southern Baptist* pastor and editor. Born in Middlesex County, Virginia, Pitt attended Richmond College from 1873 to 1879. He was licensed to preach in 1875 and was ordained in 1877 at Walnut Grove, where he pastored his first church (1878-1879). Other pastorates included Venable Street, Richmond, (twice); Martinsburg, West Virginia; Barton Heights, Richmond; and for eight years Ashland, Virginia. While he was pastor at Venable Street, Pitt began his career at the *Religious Herald.* In 1906 he became owner and editor of the paper.

Pitt's editorials won him acclaim for his progressive social views and for his staunch defense of religious liberty.* He was an advocate of temperance and was a leader in the Anti-Saloon League. Pitt vigorously opposed antievolution laws and compulsory daily Bible reading in public schools. He opposed the presidential candidacy of Alfred Smith in 1928 and expressed caution concerning America's entry into the League of Nations, since several of the participating nations were Roman Catholic. In the 1920s, when fundamentalists* within the Southern Baptist Convention were advocating a firmer expression of doctrinal orthodoxy within educational institutions, Pitt advised mutual respect and tolerance. In 1925 Pitt refused to sign the report of the

Southern Baptist Convention Committee on Baptist Faith and Message.* He believed the report, which was adopted by the convention, constituted a creedal* statement and would lead to division among Southern Baptists.

Pitt held important leadership positions, including the presidency of the Virginia Baptist General Association, presidency of the Virginia Baptist Education Commission, and American secretariat of the Baptist World Alliance,* and for forty years he was a member of the Southern Baptist Foreign Mission Board.*

BIBLIOGRAPHY. *ESB* 2.

D. B. Whitlock

Poteat, Edwin McNeill, Jr. (1892-1955). Baptist pastor, missionary, seminary president and author. Born in New Haven, Connecticut, November 20, 1892, son of the renowned Edwin McNeill Poteat Sr.,* Poteat was reared in New Haven, Philadelphia, and Greenville, South Carolina. He received the A.B. (1912) and A.M. (1913) degrees from Furman University* and the Th.M. degree (1916) from the Southern Baptist Theological Seminary.* On June 17, 1917, he married Wilda Hardman; they had three children.

Following seminary, he was traveling secretary for the Student Volunteer Movement, New York, before going to China, where he served as a Southern Baptist* missionary in Kaifeng (1917-1926) and as associate professor of philosophy and ethics at the University of Shanghai (1926-1929). Upon returning to the United States, he was pastor of Pullen Memorial Baptist Church, Raleigh, North Carolina (1929-1937), and Euclid Avenue Baptist Church, Cleveland, Ohio (1937-1944), before serving as president of Colgate-Rochester Divinity School* (1944-1948).

In 1948 he returned to Raleigh, where he served again as pastor of Pullen Memorial Baptist Church until his sudden death on December 17, 1955. In addition to his effective work as pastor and his writing of books, short stories, poetry and hymns, Poteat was widely recognized for his work regarding separation of church and state, race relations, social ministries, and many other areas of community and church life.

BIBLIOGRAPHY. R. H. Crook, *Our Heritage and Our Hope: A History of Pullen Memorial Baptist Church* (1985); *ESB* 2 (1958); J. O. Kelley, "Edwin McNeill Poteat Jr.: The Minister as Advocate," *Foun* 22 (April-June 1979):152-73.

G. T. Halbrooks

Poteat, Edwin McNeill, Sr. (1861-1937). Baptist pastor, professor and college president. Son of planters James Poteat and Julia McNeill Poteat, he was born February 6, 1861, in Caswell County, North Carolina, where he was reared before receiving the B.A. degree from Wake Forest College* (1881) and his theological degree from the Southern Baptist Theological Seminary* (1884).

Following seminary he was ordained and became pastor in Chapel Hill, North Carolina (1884-1886). After graduate study at Johns Hopkins and the University of Berlin, in 1888 he became pastor of Calvary Baptist Church, New Haven, Connecticut, where he married (1889) Harriet Hale Gordon, daughter of the renowned pastor A. J. Gordon,* and served until leaving in 1898 to become pastor of Memorial Baptist Church, Philadelphia.

In 1903 he became president of Furman University,* Greenville, South Carolina, where he served until 1918; that year he became a promoter of the Laymen's Missionary Movement* and the Interchurch World Movement. The following year he became departmental executive secretary of the General Board of Promotion of the Northern Baptist Convention (*see* American Baptist Churches in the USA).

After the death of his wife, he went to China in 1921 to visit his sons who were serving as missionaries. While there he accepted the offer to become professor of philosophy and ethics at the University of Shanghai, and in 1925 he married Baptist missionary Harriet Brittingham. Upon returning to the United States in 1927, he became interim pastor of First Baptist Church, Richmond, Virginia, for two years and then pastor of Second Baptist Church, Atlanta (1929-1931), which he left to teach ethics and comparative religion at Mercer University.* In 1934 he returned as a professor to Furman University, where he served until his death June 25, 1937, in Durham, North Carolina.

BIBLIOGRAPHY. *ESB* 2; *Who Was Who in America, 1897-1942.*

G. T. Halbrooks

Poteat, William Louis (1856-1938). Baptist professor, college president and educational leader. Son of James and Julia McNeill Poteat, he was born October 20, 1856, in Caswell County, North Carolina, where he was reared on the 2,000-acre family plantation and in Yanceyville. He received the B.A. degree from Wake Forest College* (1877) with the highest average in the senior class, and he returned there to teach languages the following year. In 1880 he began to teach biology, and the following year he married Emma Purefoy; they had three children.

Seeking to increase his skills, Poteat studied the laboratory method of teaching biology at Johns Hopkins and was subsequently credited with being one of the first to introduce it in the South. After studying at the Zoological Institute of the University of Berlin, he was awarded the A.M. degree by Wake Forest College in 1889. He did further work in 1893 at the Marine Biological Laboratory at Woods Hole, Massachusetts.

Following his distinguished work in biology, in 1905 Poteat was named president of Wake Forest College, a position he held until his retirement in 1927. During these years he was active in church and community affairs; he was criticized for accepting and teaching evolution, but he defended the college to the Baptists of North Carolina in a State Convention address on December 13, 1922, in which he summoned them to "welcome truth" because of their faith in "Christ as the theme, origin, and end of all truth." His stand has been cited as one of the major reasons that antievolution legislation was never passed in North Carolina.

In a series of lectures at the University of North Carolina, which were subsequently published as *Can a Man Be a Christian Today?* (1925), he set forth his views on why science and faith were not contradictory. In 1927 he retired from the presidency of the college to become president emeritus and continued teaching biology.

Elected president of the Baptist State Convention in 1936, Poteat is the only person to have served as president of both that body and the North Carolina Academy of Science. He died March 12, 1938, in Wake Forest, North Carolina.

BIBLIOGRAPHY. *ESB* 2; S. C. Linder, *William Louis Poteat: Prophet of Progress* (1966).

G. T. Halbrooks

Powell, Adam Clayton, Jr. (1908-1972). Pastor, newspaper publisher, city council member, Congressional leader and civil rights advocate. Born in Connecticut and raised in New York City, Powell received the B.A. from Colgate Baptist University,* the M.A. from Columbia University and the D.D. from Shaw University in North Carolina. He led protests and boycotts against racial discrimination in public transportation, employment and hospital treatment. Powell assumed the pastorate of the 14,000-member Abyssinian Bap-

tist Church in Harlem in 1937, won a city council seat in 1941, and published and edited a black weekly, *People's Voice*, during the 1940s. In 1944, the 89-percent-black Harlem district sent Powell to the U.S. Congress, where he eventually became chair of the powerful Committee on Education and Labor.

In Congress Powell championed federal support for education, civil rights, minimum wage laws, antipoverty programs and vocational education. Powell called upon blacks to seek political and economic power, diversify their education, and take pride in black history. Perhaps the most powerful black Congressperson in American history, Powell in 1967 was ejected by Congress on ethics charges relating to the misuse of public funds and allegations of slander. Though Congress readmitted him and the Supreme Court ruled his original expulsion unconstitutional in 1969, questions of his seniority and the $25,000 imposed fine were unresolved. Absenteeism from congressional duties led to his 1972 defeat.

BIBLIOGRAPHY. *A-AE* 7; *EBA;* P. J. Paris, *Black Leaders in Conflict* (1978); H. A. Ploski and J. Williams, *The Negro Almanac* (1989).

S. D. Martin

Prayer, Baptist Views. Baptists exhibit most of the approaches to prayer listed by Friedrich Heiler: primitive, ritual, philosophical, mystical, prophetic and public. (1) Most Baptists probably practice the childlike, spontaneous, petitionary prayer Heiler labels "primitive." Behind this lies a naive confidence in God as concerned with and attentive to human need. (2) Despite the passionate opposition of early Baptists to set, formal prayers, so powerfully attested in Bunyan's *I Will Pray with the Spirit,* many Baptists have learned to value the great prayer treasury of Christianity (the Psalms and prayers of the saints) and thence have renewed the use of "ritual" prayer. (3) Some Baptists, such as Harry Emerson Fosdick,* have composed sophisticated treatises on prayer which Heiler would call "philosophical." In such writings they have sought to tilt their readers away from self-centered petitionary models to more altruistic ones. (4) As a consequence of increased ecumenical* sensitivities since the 1960s, many Baptists have placed greater value on the "mystical" or "contemplative" approach to prayer, in which primary emphasis is placed on the transformation of the person praying. Throughout their history Baptists have engaged in meditative exercises using the Bible with a view to seeking God's direction; now they have learned a name for it. (5) Most Baptists would like to think they pray "prophetic" prayers, which, according to Heiler, would be simple, spontaneous prayers, like those of "primitive" folk motivated by need, but not quite so self-seeking. At the heart of the Baptist prayer tradition stands a concern for sincere and heartfelt relationship with God. (6) Baptists reflect much the same diversity in public as in private prayer. Most show continuing hesitancy about the use of formal prayers, but that has diminished among better-educated constituencies.

BIBLIOGRAPHY. C. W. Deweese, *Prayer in Baptist Life* (1986); H. E. Fosdick, *The Meaning of Prayer* (1949); F. Heiler, *Prayer* (1932); E. G. Hinson, *The Reaffirmation of Prayer* (1979).

E. G. Hinson

Prayer Meeting. An informal religious service with emphasis on prayer, in U.S. churches commonly held on Wednesday evenings. Many churches schedule the meeting immediately after a "fellowship supper" or combine it with one. A typical service would include congregational singing of hymns and Bible reading and exposition, as well as prayers. Churches vary widely in their practices, but Baptists have traditionally emphasized spontaneity in prayer. Prayer meetings usually focus on intercession or petitions for individual members, the church, the community and the world. Many Baptist congregations, however, have consciously sought to keep other dimensions of prayer (praise, thanksgiving, dedication and surrender).

Baptist churches, like their Puritan forebears, evolved these gatherings from special prayer meetings held to resolve tensions, to bring comfort to the bereaved, to assist in decision-making and to prepare for other aspects of their work. Many schedule what are often called "cottage prayer meetings" prior to revival meetings to assist in preparation for them. Baptists call less frequently than they once did for extended prayer sessions at associational meetings or conventions.

BIBLIOGRAPHY. C. W. Deweese, *Prayer in Baptist Life* (1986); *ESB* 4:2421.

E. G. Hinson

Preaching, Baptist Approaches to. Historically, Baptists have approached preaching in ways that can be categorized under three topics: apologetics, evangelism and proclamation.

The origin of Baptists as a denomination demanded that early preachers define and defend their existence as a separate group of Christians. Both in England and America, and still in many parts of the world, Baptist preachers approach the preaching task from the standpoint of a defense of their unique positions. Sermons from early English Baptists frequently attempted to clarify the Baptists' positions on infant versus believer's baptism, and some, such as Thomas Helwys,* died in prison for it.

Other subjects for apologetic sermons emerged as Baptists began to distinguish themselves not only from other denominations but also among themselves. Calvinistic* (Particular*) and Arminian* (General*) Baptists often preached in defense of their theological positions and against the other side. No more eloquent example of that tendency can be found than the friendly rivalry between two nineteenth-century English Baptists: Charles Haddon Spurgeon* and John Clifford, who remained friends in spite of their differences.

In colonial America, apologetic preaching was often directed toward the dominant denomination in the region, such as the Puritans in New England and the Episcopalians in Virginia. On the frontier, apologetic preaching tended to focus on the rivalry among competing denominations. This was particularly true between the Baptists and Methodists. Inter-Baptist rivalry also maintained its vigor with sermons preached during various controversies, such as those surrounding the Landmark* movement, the fundamentalist*-modernist debate and the ubiquitous issue of science versus religion.

The second major approach to preaching among Baptists has been that of evangelism. With the exception of the extreme Calvinistic Baptists and some Baptists on the liberal wing of the denomination, evangelism has been a compelling force in preaching. As one leading Baptist preacher in New England remarked, "I have no time to trifle with men's souls by directing them to depend on their own exertions, but I will point them to Jesus" (from Samuel Stillman, *Select Sermons on Doctrinal and Practical Subjects* [1808]). The rapid rise of Baptists in many areas can be attributed in part to aggressive evangelistic preaching.

The third major approach to preaching can be characterized as proclamation, which may include an evangelistic or in some cases even apologetic element, but whose major thrust is the proclamation of the gospel in clear terms for the day in which the sermon is preached. Baptist preaching characterized as proclamation is almost always tied closely to the Bible and has often been expository. In its most powerful form, exposition from the Scriptures has been directly related to current issues and injustices of the society, as was seen clearly in the preaching of Martin Luther King Jr., whose national leadership grew naturally from his experience and commitment as a Baptist preacher.

A growing number of Baptists in America have chosen to approach preaching through the use of the Common Lectionary sponsored by the National Council of Churches. In a spirit of ecumenical* cooperation, they select sermon texts from the suggested lectionary readings for each Sunday of the year on a three-year cycle.

Regardless of the approach, the freedom of Baptists with regard to preaching and the importance of preaching in Baptist worship have encouraged a lively preaching tradition that continues in the modern era.

T. R. McKibbens

Premillennial Baptist Missionary Fellowship. A fundamentalist* organization founded by J. Frank Norris* in 1933. In 1923, Norris joined W. B. Riley* and T. T. Shields* in founding the Baptist Bible Union,* an attempt to unite fundamentalists from the Northern (see American Baptist Churches in the USA), Southern* and Canadian* Baptist conventions. During the 1920s, Norris attacked the Southern Baptist Convention and a number of Baptist institutions, including Baylor University* and Southwestern Baptist Theological Seminary,* for teaching modernism and evolution. Because of his disruptive tactics, Norris was excluded from his local Baptist association, the Texas State Convention, and from the Southern Baptist Convention. When the Baptist Bible Union failed in 1932, Norris was without an institutional base of operations besides his First Baptist Church of Fort Worth.

In 1933 Norris, C. P. Stealey* and others formed the Premillennial Baptist Missionary Fellowship (PBMF) in Fort Worth in order to provide premillennial and fundamentalist Baptists in the South an organization of their own. Norris found it difficult to affiliate with anything he could not control, so in 1938 he accused the PBMF president,

Robert White, of misappropriation of funds, had him removed and had himself put in charge. Under Norris, the PBMF changed its name to the World Fundamental Baptist Missionary Fellowship (FBMF).

To provide pastors for his organization, Norris and Louis Entzminger,* his associate at First Baptist Church, founded the Fundamental Baptist Bible Institute (later renamed the Bible Baptist Seminary*) in 1939, though the school had little academic standing. In 1948 Norris named G. Beauchamp Vick,* his copastor at the Temple Baptist Church in Detroit, president of the seminary. It became quickly apparent, however, that Norris was reluctant to give Vick the needed authority to run the institution. By 1950 the conflict between the two men became public when Norris tried to fire the president without board knowledge and approval. In the ensuing dispute, many pastors in the FBMF sided with Vick and withdrew to form the Baptist Bible Fellowship and start their own school, the Baptist Bible College,* in Springfield, Missouri, under Vick's leadership. Those who remained with Norris renamed their organization the World Baptist Fellowship.*

See also BAPTIST BIBLE FELLOWSHIP; NORRIS, J. FRANK.

BIBLIOGRAPHY. B. V. Bartlett, *History of Baptist Separatism* (1972); J. Falwell, ed., *The Fundamentalist Phenomenon* (1981).

T. P. Weber

Priesthood of All Believers. The cardinal Reformation conviction, long affirmed by Baptists, that says all Christian believers, not merely a select group such as the clergy, are free to be priests *before* God as well as responsible to be priests *for* God. Often called the *universal* priesthood of believers, this New Testament doctrine (1 Pet 2:5, 9; Rev 1:5-6; 5:9-10; 20:6), firmly rooted in the Old Testament (Ex 19:4-6), was rediscovered by Martin Luther, John Calvin* and other Reformers in the sixteenth century. In the seventeenth century John Smyth* and other early Baptists made much of this Protestant concept, bequeathing it to later Baptists, who have traditionally made it a hallmark of their faith.

Baptists have applied this doctrine to their life and faith in several ways. First, in terms of salvation, Baptists stress the privilege of uncoerced personal access to God's grace. The Baptist vision of a believer's relationship to God is personal, voluntary and impossible to delegate to any other human. A strong streak of individualism dominates Baptist life. Second, in terms of church life, Baptists emphasize equal privileges for all "priests." Every "priest" has a vote, and therefore church government is democratic. Moreover, every "priest" in the church has a Bible and the right and responsibility to interpret it. Third, the priesthood of believers means for Baptists that the ministry of the church has been universalized and is no longer the responsibility of the ordained clergy alone. All Christians are priests. And this universal priesthood is not based on heredity, gender, ordination* or office, but on a personal relationship to Jesus Christ and on the gifts the Spirit distributes to each of Christ's followers. Fourth, Baptists have utilized the priesthood of believers in relation to the state to argue for religious liberty,* freedom of conscience and separation of church and state.

The doctrine of the priesthood of believers became entangled in the "Inerrancy Controversy"* among Southern Baptists* in the 1980s. At the Southern Baptist Convention in San Antonio in 1987, messengers adopted a controversial resolution that affirmed pastoral authority at the expense of this historic Baptist concept.

See also INERRANCY CONTROVERSY.

BIBLIOGRAPHY. W. B. Shurden, *The Doctrine of the Priesthood of Believers* (1987); W. B. Shurden, "The Priesthood of All Believers and Pastoral Authority in Baptist Thought," *Faith and Mission* 7 (Fall 1989):24-45.

W. B. Shurden

Primitive Baptists. Baptist churches and associations generally characterized by rigid predestinarianism and a desire to recapture the original faith and order of the New Testament apostles. Emerging in the early nineteenth century, these Baptists used Particular Baptist* confessions to develop a rigid Calvinism* and an opposition to organized missions.* The Kehuckee Baptist Association* (North Carolina), which first articulated its position in 1826, said missionary organizations promoted a nonpredestinarian theology, undermined local church autonomy and encouraged a paid clergy. Most Primitive Baptists oppose church auxiliaries not found in Scripture, such as Bible and tract societies, seminaries and Sunday schools. Their churches group only in associations that meet annually and correspond with each other by letter or messenger. Their church order has been characterized by simple monthly worship meetings, closed Communion (*see* Lord's Supper), refusal to accept members without Primitive Baptist immersion, and untrained, unsalaried, bivocational ministers.

Five main groups survive. The rigidly predestinarian Absoluters publish *Signs of the Times* and *Zion's Landmark.* They had 6,495 members and 380 churches in 1980. Old Liners, who allow human responsibility in predestination, publish *Advocate and Messenger, Baptist Witness* and *The Primitive Baptist* and have 48,980 members and 1,426 churches (1980). Progressive Primitive Baptists, the least rigidly predestinarian, meet weekly, pay ministerial salaries and conduct Sunday schools; they had 11,043 members and 163 churches in 1980. Over 1 million National Primitive Baptists, with headquarters in Huntsville, Alabama, make up the black convention. A few descendants of Daniel Parker's* Two-Seed-in-the-Spirit-Predestinarian Baptists* (c. 1826) still exist in Texas and Louisiana.

BIBLIOGRAPHY. H. L. McBeth, *The Baptist Heritage* (1987); A. C. Piepkorn, "The Primitive Baptists of North America," *CTM* 42, no. 55 (1971); A. C. Piepkorn, *Profiles in Belief,* vol. 2 (1978).

J. T. Spivey

Progressive National Baptist Convention, Inc. *See* NATIONAL BAPTISTS.

Psalmist, The. A collection of hymns considered to be a milestone in American Baptist* hymnody. It was compiled in 1843 by Baron Stow, pastor of the Baldwin Place Baptist Church, Boston; and Samuel Francis Smith, pastor of the First Baptist Church, Newton, Massachusetts. Designed to supersede two other prominent Baptist collections, *Winchell's Watts,* generally used in New England, and *Watts and Rippon,* more popular in the middle states, *The Psalmist* sought to unite the Baptists of the United States in a common usage. It was endorsed by a representative committee of eminent clergymen and was generally received with favor in the Baptist churches of the North. However, its reception in the South was cool because it omitted many of that region's most popular hymns. In an attempt to remedy this weakness, two Southern ministers, Richard Fuller, pastor of the Seventh Baptist Church, Baltimore, and J. B. Jeter, pastor of the First Baptist Church, Richmond, in 1850 edited a supplement of 106 selections.

The leading authors in this supplement were

the Olney hymnists, Newton and Cowper, followed by Watts, Wesley, Doddridge and the Baptists Stennett and Steele. Though the supplemented edition was welcomed by some urban college congregations in the South, it found little use in the rural churches. Musically, *The Psalmist* reflected the influence of Lowell Mason, the chief architect of the typical nineteenth-century American hymn tune. The collection in numerous revisions and reprints continued in use well into the twentieth century.

BIBLIOGRAPHY. H. S. Burrage, *Baptist Hymn Writers and Their Hymns* (1888); H. T. McElrath, "Turning Points in the Story of Baptist Church Music," *BHH* 19 (January 1985):10.

H. T. McElrath

Puerto Rico Baptist Convention. Baptist work in Puerto Rico stems from missionaries under the boards of the American Baptist Home Mission Society* and the Woman's American Baptist Home Mission Society.* The convention was formed in 1902.

The Barranquitas Baptist Academy provides general education for children, especially studies in the English language. The academy also emphasizes Bible study, chapel attendance, Sunday-school classes and devotional meetings. Baptists in Puerto Rico have cooperated in the Evangelical Seminary since its establishment in 1919. Baptist women have been especially active in the Puerto Rico convention, helping young women attend missionary training schools in the States. The convention affiliates with the Evangelical Council of Puerto Rico, a local ecumenical* group.

Southern Baptists* began mission work in Puerto Rico in 1964, centering on American military personnel at Ramey Air Force Base in Aquadilla. The first congregation was gathered there in the 1950s. In 1965 five Southern Baptist churches and five missions formed the Puerto Rico Baptist Association. This association related to the Puerto Rico Baptist Convention rather than the Florida Baptist Convention, as first intended, to avoid unnecessary competition between Northern and Southern Baptists in Puerto Rico. By 1970 this association had four English-speaking churches, five Spanish-speaking churches and about twenty missions. It also sponsored a Spanish Baptist Hour radio broadcast, and the Borinquen Church in Aquadillo sponsors a Bible institute to provide basic theological education for pastors, laypeople and bivocational pastors.

BIBLIOGRAPHY. *ESB* 3:1928-29.

H. L. McBeth

Question in Baptist History, A. Book by William Heth Whitsitt,* published in 1896, providing documentary proof that Baptists had originated in Holland as an English church under the leadership of John Smyth,* a refugee English Congregationalist. Whitsitt also argued that the earliest Baptists were not immersionists but adopted immersion under the leadership of Edward Barber in 1641.

Whitsitt was professor of ecclesiastical history and president of Southern Baptist Theological Seminary,* Louisville, Kentucky. His understanding of Baptist roots ran counter to the views of the movement known as Landmarkism,* which held that an unbroken succession of Baptist churches could be traced from the apostolic era. Once Whitsitt's views became known, calls for his removal from the seminary were made. The attack against Whitsitt was led by T. T. Eaton,* pastor of Louisville's Walnut Street Baptist Church and editor of the *Western Recorder,* the Kentucky Baptist newspaper. Whitsitt was forced to resign from the seminary in 1899.

BIBLIOGRAPHY. J. T. Meigs, "The Whitsitt Controversy," *QR,* January-March 1971.

A. L. Pratt

R

Racial Attitudes, Baptist. Few issues have divided Baptists, reflecting the best and the worst of both individuals and churches, more than the issue of race. Like many Christians in colonial America, Baptists did not address the slavery issue or the spiritual state of the slaves until some time in the eighteenth century. When they did there was division.

In 1711 the Western Association produced a strong proslavery statement, affirming the right of slaveholding church members to discipline runaway slaves and insisting that slavery was sanctioned in Holy Scripture. By the later 1700s, however, antislavery sentiments were evident among various Baptist associations, among them the Baptist General Committee of Virginia, which in 1785 declared slavery "a breach of divine laws." In 1809 Baptist abolitionist David Barrow was dismissed from his association for his antislavery views. He helped organize nine Baptist churches into the Baptized Licking Locust Association, Friends of Humanity, an outspoken opposition to slavery. By 1820, however, Richard Furman,* preacher and first president of the Triennial Convention,* had set forth what became one of the most popular proslavery arguments, with particular insistence on the biblical sanction of the practice. Furman and Northern Baptist Francis Wayland* carried on a lively debate on slavery and the Bible.

In the South, where slavery flourished after the invention of the cotton gin in 1792, Baptists attempted extensive evangelistic work among slaves. Converts were accepted as members of Baptist churches. Church records show that the congregations were sources of discipline against recalcitrant slaves, but on occasion slaves did exercise some recourse against highly abusive masters, often with mixed results. Black Christians with Baptist sentiments were also evident in the "hush arbor" movement, those secret gatherings of believers who met beyond the watchful eyes of the slaveowners.

Following Emancipation and the Civil War, African-American Baptists in the North and South found themselves second-class citizens in the churches and moved to establish their own communities of faith. As segregation was established in Southern law and culture, racial attitudes among Baptists mirrored the society. Many white Baptists accepted and advocated ideas of racial subservience and inferiority. Indeed, certain leaders of the Southern Baptist Convention's* Foreign Mission Board* advocated mission activity to Europe so that the Anglo-Saxon races might be converted and then fulfill their destiny to aid the "darker" (and inferior) races. Some Baptists applied various biblical passages to their views on the separation of the races and their fears that integration would lead to racial intermarriage.

African-American Baptist churches were central to the movement for civil rights and racial justice that began with the Montgomery, Alabama, bus boycott of the 1950s. That pivotal action was led by Martin Luther King Jr.,* pastor of the Dexter Avenue Baptist Church in Montgomery. Many of the leaders of the civil rights movement were pastors and laity of African-American Baptist churches. As the movement reached its height in the 1960s, many white Baptist churches divided over changing racial attitudes and responses to integration.

While segregationist legislation ultimately was abolished and increased racial interaction and dialogue became evident among Baptists, questions remain. Churches continue to remain segregated, and old attitudes die hard. New or growing racial and ethnic minorities—Asians, Hispanics—also entered the Baptist fold, often through chapels and congregations organized for specific language or national groups. Some acknowledged Baptist openness to conversion and evangelism among minorities but expressed concern that they were not welcomed into denominational leadership roles. American Baptist Churches in the USA* has made concerted efforts to extend leadership across racial boundaries. Southern Baptists, often viewed as the least racially inclusive denomination, now claim to have a larger African-American constituency than any other predominantly white Baptist group. Much of this has been accomplished as African-American Baptist churches have joined or become dually aligned* with the Southern Baptist Convention. Meanwhile, African-American Baptist groups continue to welcome small numbers of white members into their fellowships. A growing number of new churches are organizing themselves around interracial congregations.

BIBLIOGRAPHY. J. Eighmy, *Churches in Cultural Captivity* (1972); D. Garrow, *Bearing the Cross* (1993); R. Nash, "The Influence of American Myth on Southern Baptist Foreign Missions, 1845-1945" (Ph.D. dissertation, 1989); J. Washington, *Frustrated Fellowship* (1986).

B. J. Leonard

Radio and Television Commission, SBC. This Southern Baptist Convention* agency proclaims Christ in millions of households weekly through broadcasts it produces and distributes. Organized in 1946 as the Radio Commission, the agency assumed its present name in 1954. The commission presents several radio programs thousands of times each week throughout the United States and also presents the gospel on Armed Forces Radio. It ministers to hundreds of communities across America through the ACTS Satellite Network, chartered in 1983. In April 1991, the commission added FamilyNet, a faith and family programming service designed primarily for broadcast television stations. Produced since the 1940s, *The Baptist Hour* is the agency's flagship program. The agency responds annually to about 100,000 letters in response to its broadcasts. Executives have included Samuel Franklin Lowe (1946-1952), Dupree Jordan (acting director, 1952-1953), Paul Morris Stevens (1953-1979), Jimmy R. Allen (1980-1989), Richard T. McCartney (acting president, 1989-1990) and Jack B. Johnson (1990-). Commission offices are located in Fort Worth, Texas.

BIBLIOGRAPHY. *ESB* 2:1130-31, 3:1932-33, 4:2432-33; S. Gregory, "A Brief History of the Radio and Television Commission Since 1980," *BHH,* January 1992.

C. W. Deweese

Randall, Benjamin (1749-1808). Founder of New England branch of Free Will Baptists.* Born in New Castle, New Hampshire, Randall went to sea with his ship-captain father until he was about eighteen. He later worked as a sailmaker and tailor, showing little interest in religion as a youth. But in 1770, upon hearing of the death of George Whitefield, whom he had heard preach and whom he had ridiculed, Randall reproached himself, saying, "Whitefield is in heaven, and I am on the road to hell." He professed conversion and united with a Congregational church.

In 1776 Randall joined the Baptists and soon embarked on an itinerant evangelistic ministry. Resisting the strict Calvinistic* Baptist emphasis on predestination, he broke from the Regular Baptists* in 1779. In 1780 he formed a church with seven members at New Durham, New Hampshire. In time this church, and many others formed by Randall and his followers, took the name Free Will Baptists to emphasize their belief that any person is free to believe in Jesus Christ. By 1782 there were twelve such churches, and Randall led them to form a Quarterly Meeting, much like an "association" among Regular Baptists. In 1792 the organizational structure was completed with the addition of a Yearly Meeting. Described as having a loud, clear voice, Randall traveled and preached constantly, although he was never sturdy of health. He is best understood as an example of resistance to strict Calvinism in New England.

BIBLIOGRAPHY. J. Buzzell, *The Life of Elder Benjamin Randall* (1827); *DAB* VIII; W. F. Davidson, *The Free Will Baptists in America, 1727-1984* (1985); I. D. Stewart, *The History of the Freewill Baptists* (1862); F. L. Wiley, *Life and Influence of Rev. Benjamin Randall* (1915).

H. L. McBeth

Rankin, Milledge Theron (1894-1953). Southern Baptist* missionary and missions leader. Born in South Carolina, the son of a minister, Rankin graduated from Wake Forest College* and Southern Baptist Theological Seminary,* where he earned a Ph.D.

Rankin went as a missionary to China, and from 1921 to 1935 he was president of Graves Theological Seminary, Canton. Rankin was then elected secretary for the Orient (1935-1944). Early in World War II he was imprisoned by the Japanese for nine months in an internment camp in Hong Kong. From 1945 to 1953 he served as executive secretary of the Foreign Mission Board of the Southern Baptist Convention.*

The beginning of Rankin's tenure coincided with the end of the war, and his goals were to reenter mission fields vacated due to the war, rebuild Baptist work there and provide relief for the hungry, homeless and sick. Three years later (1948) he proposed a bold program of advance to appoint 1,750 missionaries with an annual budget of $10 million. With his vision and leadership, Southern Baptist missions flourished. In 1945 there were 504 missionaries under appointment; by 1953 there were 913.

BIBLIOGRAPHY. B. J. Cauthen, *Advance: A History of Southern Baptist Foreign Missions* (1970); J. B. Weatherspoon, *M. Theron Rankin: Apostle of Advance* (1958).   W. M. Patterson

Rauschenbusch, Walter (1861-1918). Prophet and theologian of the Social Gospel.* Born in Rochester, New York, Rauschenbusch was educated in Germany and the United States and graduated from the University of Rochester (B.A., 1884) and Rochester Theological Seminary* (1886). Following seminary he served for eleven years as pastor of a German Baptist church (*see* North American Baptist Conference) on the edge of "Hell's Kitchen" in New York City. There he encountered the effects of poverty, unemployment, insecurity, malnutrition, disease and crime. Becoming active in social reform work, despite increasing deafness, he sought biblical and theological teachings to counter the individualistic, laissez-faire social philosophies and practices that were rampant in his time. During a leave from his parish in 1891, he engaged in biblical and sociological studies in Germany and found in the doctrine of the kingdom of God, particularly as emphasized by Albrecht Ritschl (1822-1889) and his followers, clues for understanding Jesus' teachings and for bringing his own evangelical faith, scholarly interests and social concerns together. A bilingual writer and active participant in Baptist affairs, in 1897 Rauschenbusch was called back to Rochester Seminary, where he became professor of church history in 1902.

His book *Christianity and the Social Crisis,* written "to discharge a debt" to the working people among whom he had ministered, became a bestseller upon its publication in 1907 and made him in great demand as speaker and author until his death from cancer in 1918. He wrote two other major books. *Christianizing the Social Order* (1912) presented a program of progressive, democratic reformism as moving toward the kingdom of God, interpreted as "the progressive transformation of all human affairs by the thought and spirit of Christ." *A Theology for the Social Gospel* (1917) was an effort to provide a vital systematic theology to undergird the Christian social emphasis. The outbreak of World War I had deeply saddened Rauschenbusch, contributing to his increased awareness of sin in the world and intensifying his stress on the "miraculous" aspects of the kingdom of God as "divine in its origin, progress and consummation."

Rauschenbusch also published many articles and smaller books, notably *For God and the People: Prayers of the Social Awakening* (1910), which shows the depth of his own spirituality, and *The Social Principles of Jesus* (1916), a study book for college students which received the widest circulation of any of his works. Much of Rauschenbusch's work bears the stamp of its time; H. Shelton Smith concluded that he was "the foremost molder of American Christian thought in his generation." But later generations also continued to learn from him; Reinhold Niebuhr called him the "most brilliant and generally satisfying exponent" of social Christianity, and Martin Luther King Jr.* observed that "Rauschenbusch gave to American Protestantism a sense of social responsibility that it should never lose." In Rauschenbusch's life and writings, the personal and social dimensions of the Christian gospel were never separated.

BIBLIOGRAPHY. *DAB* VIII; *DARB;* K. J. Jaehn, *Rauschenbusch: The Formative Years* (1976); P. M. Minus, *Walter Rauschenbusch: American Reformer* (1988); *NCAB* 19; D. R. Sharpe, *Walter Rauschenbusch* (1942).

R. T. Handy

Rebaptism. The performing again of the sacrament or ordinance* of baptism.* Technically *rebaptism* is a misnomer, since Christians believe in a single baptism. Hence rebaptism relates to debate over what constitutes a valid sacrament or ordinance.

A valid baptism is usually held to require three elements: (1) the trinitarian formula, (2) water and (3) faith on the part of the recipient (or, according to some pedobaptists, on the part of the adult sponsors). The Council of Arles (A.D. 314) held that the spiritual state of the celebrant does not invalidate the sacrament. By the sixth century the baptism of infants was popular among Catholics, and it became standard practice during the medieval period. Effusion (pouring) and eventually aspersion (sprinkling) replaced the New Testament mode of immersion. Eastern Orthodox churches continued to baptize persons at various ages by alternate modes.

With the sixteenth-century Reformation, radical reformers in Switzerland, Germany and the Netherlands who were committed to returning to New Testament practices began to question and eventually deny the efficacy of baptisms performed in Catholic and state churches. Anabaptists (from the Greek *anabaptizō*—to baptize again) taught that baptisms were invalid when the church performing them was "no church," or when the recipients, usually infants, had made no conscious act of faith or appropriation of God's grace and redemption. After 1560 most emerging "believers' churches" in the Mennonite and Baptist traditions practiced the "faith baptism" by immersion of freely confessing and believing persons.

In North America many evangelical and believers' churches rebaptize if they determine that personal faith was absent at the time a previous baptism was received. Some churches, especially those that teach baptismal regeneration, hold immersion to be essential for a believer's baptism. A minority of Eastern Orthodox and some Catholic and Anglican strict apostolic successionists reject "alien immersion" or "alien baptism." Alien baptism is any baptism that is not performed within that particular denomination. Alien baptism results in rebaptism of persons who have been baptized as believers by immersion among a minority of Landmark* and Primitive* Baptists in the Southern states, the Pacific Northwest and Western Canada. In recent decades some evangelicals have used rebaptism as a witness to a "recommitment to Christ." This practice is viewed by many as an abuse of the rite.

BIBLIOGRAPHY. G. R. Beasley-Murray, *Baptism Today and Tomorrow* (1966); *BHH* 10, no. 1 (1975); D. Bridge, *The Water That Divides: The Baptismal Debate* (1977); A. Gilmore, ed., *Christian Baptism* (1959).

W. F. Ellis

Redford, Samuel Courts (1898-1977). Professor, college president and home missions executive. Following service as professor at Oklahoma Baptist University* (1923-1925) and at Southwest-

ern Baptist Theological Seminary* (1925-1927), Redford served the Missouri Baptist Convention as stewardship and brotherhood secretary (1927-1930), Southwest Baptist College* as president (1930-1943), and the Home Mission Board* (HMB) of the Southern Baptist Convention* (SBC) as assistant executive secretary-treasurer (1943-1954) and as executive secretary-treasurer (1954-1964). In his position as administrative head of the HMB, he assisted in expanding SBC work to all fifty states; in constituting new Baptist state conventions in Colorado, Indiana, Michigan, Ohio and Utah-Idaho; in establishing HMB relationships with Baptists in Canada and Puerto Rico; and in increasing home missionaries from 936 to 2,353. Redford wrote three books: *Spiritual Frontiers* (1948), *Crusade in Home Missions* (1952) and *Home Missions, USA* (1956).

BIBLIOGRAPHY. *ESB* 4:2434-35.

C. W. Deweese

Redpath, Alan (1907-). Baptist minister, Bible conference speaker and writer. English-born, Redpath was influenced by G. Campbell Morgan and others to leave his position as an accountant in a large English firm and enter the ministry. He pastored the Duke Street Baptist Church in London and built it into a large congregation, then came to America to serve as pastor of Moody Memorial Church in Chicago (1953-1962). Under his leadership Moody Church adopted the "flock" concept of ministry, instituted a Spanish-speaking Sunday-school class and for the first time received blacks into membership. In great demand as a conference speaker, Redpath led in the establishment of the first Mid-America Keswick Convention, held at Moody Church in 1954. In 1962 he resigned the pastorate in Chicago to take a similar position at Charlotte Chapel in Edinburgh, Scotland. He subsequently served as pastoral dean at Capenwray Bible School, Lancashire.

BIBLIOGRAPHY. R. G. Flood, *The Story of Moody Church* (1985). R. T. Clutter

Reeves, James E. (1784-1858). Georgia Baptist pioneer preacher. The son of a Baptist preacher, Jeremiah Reeves, who moved from Halifax County, North Carolina, to Wilkes County, Georgia, in 1784, James Reeves was probably born near the time of the move. Some sources indicate he was born in Guilford County, North Carolina, which would have been on the travel route, while others indicate he was born in Georgia. Three of his brothers, Malachi, Jeremiah and John, also became preachers.

Although not ordained until age thirty, he engaged in active ministry for forty years, laboring in the frontier region of west Georgia. Making his home first in Jasper County, he subsequently preached in Jasper, Butts, Henry, Campbell, Paulding, Carroll, Coweta, Heard and Troup counties in Georgia and in areas of eastern Alabama. Throughout the region, he preached in log cabins of new settlers and in temporary arbors. He supplied the people with Bibles and tracts, organized Sunday schools and temperance societies, and fervently supported missions.* For many of the churches in the region he was not only the pastor but also the founder.

Despite his support of missions, Reeves has been most remembered for the refusal to appoint him a missionary. On August 2, 1844, the Executive Committee of the Georgia Baptist Convention asked the board of the American Baptist Home Mission Society* (ABHMS) to appoint him a home missionary to itinerate in the bounds of the Tallapoosa Association in Georgia. They indicated that he owned slaves and that this was a test to see if the board would appoint a slaveholder.

On October 7 the board refused to act on the application because it introduced the topic of slavery. The Georgia Executive Committee responded by appointing Reeves itself and by withholding its money from the ABHMS. The action of the board of the ABHMS was one of the factors precipitating a call for the separation of Southern Baptists from national missionary organizations.

Reeves was married twice, first to Miss McElroy and then to Mrs. Phillips. He had ten children by his first wife and five by his second. He preached until 1854 and died April 6, 1858, in Carroll County, Georgia.

BIBLIOGRAPHY. *BE;* R. G. Gardner et al., *A History of the Georgia Baptist Association* (1988); *History of the Baptist Denomination in Georgia: With Biographical Compendium and Portrait Gallery of Baptist Ministers and Other Georgia Baptists* (1881). G. T. Halbrooks

Reformed Baptists. Reformed Baptists in America consider themselves the doctrinal heirs of the Particular* Baptists of England and the early Calvinistic* Baptists in America. Experientially, they point to John Bunyan. Practically, the preaching of C. H. Spurgeon* and the Puritans and the missionary* emphasis of William Carey* are paradigmatic of their views. Confessionally, these churches accept the First (1644) and Second (1689) London confessions. Organically, they may be traced to the influence of Rolfe Barnard, a Southern Baptist* evangelist and theology teacher at Piedmont Bible College. In a Sword of the Lord Bible Conference at Toccoa Falls, Georgia, in 1949, Barnard brought about a split in the conference by preaching on "Sovereign Grace and Mercy" from Romans 9. Barnard's numerous appearances in churches in the following years increased the number of ministers adhering to the "doctrines of grace."

Sovereign Grace* Bible conferences and the distribution of literature are the movement's major methods of propagating doctrinal distinctives. The most significant division within the ranks of Reformed Baptists has come from two disputes: disagreement over the perpetuity of the Ten Commandments as an expression of moral law for the Christian, and the nature of elder authority in local churches. Although a strong commitment to local autonomy has caused some to remain apart, over thirty Reformed Baptist churches united to form the Reformed Baptist Mission Services, located in Carlisle, Pennsylvania. David Straub began serving in 1986 as its missions coordinator.

BIBLIOGRAPHY. H. L. McBeth, *The Baptist Heritage* (1988). T. J. Nettles

Reforming Baptists. Reformers, Disciples of Christ, Christian Churches or Churches of Christ, the followers of the former Presbyterian religious reformers Thomas and Alexander Campbell.* In 1815 the Campbells' Brush Run Church joined the Redstone (Pennsylvania) Baptist Association but retained its commitment to the ideals of Thomas Campbell's *Declaration and Address of the Christian Association of Washington, Pennsylvania* (1809). Growing tension in the Redstone Association led its Campbellian congregations to join the Mahoning (Ohio) Baptist Association, which they dominated from 1824 to 1830. In the 1820s many Baptist congregations in the West were brought under Campbellian influence by evangelists Walter Scott, "Raccoon" John Smith and John T. Johnson. In 1829 the differences between the Reformers and other Baptists were sufficiently clear that the Beaver (Pennsylvania) Association could publish a list of Campbellian errors ("Beaver Anathema") to be used by other associations. By 1830 the Reforming Baptists were being excluded from Baptist associations in

Ohio, Kentucky, Pennsylvania and Virginia.

BIBLIOGRAPHY. L. G. McAllister and W. E. Tucker, *Journey in Faith: A History of the Christian Church (Disciples of Christ)* (1975).

A. L. Dunnavant

Regular Baptists. Calvinistic* Baptists opposed to the emotionalism and evangelistic invitations of the First Great Awakening.* In contrast to revivalistic Separate Baptists,* Regular Baptists were more urbane and orderly in worship,* supported educated and salaried ministers and discouraged women from ministering publicly. Initially strongest in the Middle Colonies, they were influenced by the Philadelphia Baptist Association* (1707), from which itinerant preachers planted churches in Virginia (1740s), North Carolina (1750s) and Georgia (1770s) and on the Kentucky-Tennessee frontier (1780s). Also influential were the Charleston (1751), Warren (1767) and Kehuckee (1769) associations.

During the late eighteenth century, a campaign by the Philadelphia and Warren associations to win General Baptists* over to Calvinism resulted in the "reformation" of most General ministers and churches, but most of the members did not follow. Simultaneously, Free Will Baptists* became influential. Reacting to the Arminianism* of the Free Will Baptists, Separates moved closer to the Regulars' Calvinism, which, in turn, was softened by Free Will pressure. By 1800 most Regulars and Separates had merged on the basis of the Philadelphia Confession of 1742.

Today Regular Baptists constitute a cultural-religious movement that preserves rural folkways through monthly worship, plaintive singing, singsong preaching, community gatherings and annual association fellowship. They include Old Regular Baptists,* mainly of Appalachia (1980: 19,770 members, 366 churches); United Baptists, found from Kentucky through Missouri (1980: 53,665 members, 517 churches); and the General Association of (Duck River*) Baptists in Alabama, Tennessee, Georgia and Mississippi (1986: 10,579 members, 81 churches).

BIBLIOGRAPHY. W. L. Lumpkin, *Baptist Foundations in the South* (1961); H. L. McBeth, *The Baptist Heritage* (1987).

J. T. Spivey

Religious Liberty and Baptists. Baptists have consistently advocated religious liberty as one of their primary tenets of faith. In their confessions of faith,* Baptists have maintained that individuals have the right, under God, to choose their own religion without any interference from the secular magistrate or the state. Also, Baptists have protested that any union of church and state poses a threat to individuals' right to free religious choice.

Baptists played an important part in the development of religious liberty in England and in the Puritan Revolution that brought Oliver Cromwell to power. Although Cromwell believed that England should be a Protestant country, his government allowed widespread religious liberty. After Cromwell's death, Charles II assumed the throne and withdrew many of the privileges that Cromwell had granted. Baptists suffered under the renewed persecution. John Bunyan, author of *Pilgrim's Progress,* spent twelve years in Bedford Jail for refusing to swear that he would not preach again. The deposition of James II in 1688 led to the adoption of the Act of Toleration, which granted dissenters, including Baptists, some religious liberty. Yet much discrimination continued. The law prohibited nonconformists from teaching school, attending universities or voting for members of Parliament. Baptists, often in league with other dissenters, continued to protest this second-class citizenship. By 1870 Parliament had removed most of these restrictions.

Roger Williams* and John Clarke* were instrumental in founding Rhode Island as the first American colony with full religious liberty. After William Penn established his colony on similar principles, Baptists grew in the Middle Atlantic region. Baptists formed the Philadelphia Baptist Association* in part to further religious liberty in the New World.

Baptists prospered during the First Great Awakening.* The revivalists' appeal to the individual led many people to adopt Baptist principles. As Baptists grew, the leaders of the established churches took action against them. In New England, where the governments legally established Congregational churches, the usual charge against Baptists was refusal to pay the church tax. Often the courts ordered Baptist property seized and sold at auction to pay the debt. Isaac Backus,* a Massachusetts pastor and member of the Warren Association, became one of the leading advocates of religious liberty in New England. Partly as a result of his writings, the New England establishments gradually faded from the scene.

In Virginia the persecution was more severe.

The law required all non-Episcopal clergy to secure a license from a court to preach. Many Baptists refused to do so. While imprisonment was
the most common punishment for this refusal,
the courts occasionally ordered beatings and other corporal punishment. This persecution fatally
weakened the establishment. Young aristocrats,
including James Madison, "Father of the Constitution," were shocked by the severity of the law
and resolved to end religious persecution. After
the American Revolution, Virginia's legislature
passed Thomas Jefferson's bill for establishing religious freedom (1786), the most comprehensive
guarantee of religious freedom at the time. Baptists were major supporters of this law.

Baptists believed that the Federal Constitution
should contain a Bill of Rights. While the First
Amendment was important to American Baptists,
the actual wording did not grant the full liberty
that Baptists advocated. The First Amendment did
not, for example, restrain the states from passing
laws favoring one religious group or from prohibiting non-Christians from voting. Throughout the
nineteenth century, Baptists agitated for full statements of religious liberty in state constitutions.

In the twentieth century, partly as a result of the
extension of the Bill of Rights to the states, the
courts became the frontier in religious liberty
cases. Baptists followed this development carefully. In 1939, Northern (see American Baptist
Churches in the USA) and Southern Baptists* established the Baptist Joint Committee on Public
Affairs to provide the churches and the courts
with information about current church-state
issues. Later, representatives of other Baptist bodies joined the committee. In addition to serving
as a "friend of the court," the Joint Committee
publishes the *Report from the Capitol* to keep
Baptists informed of contemporary issues. On a
more scholarly level, Baptist Baylor University*
sponsors *Church and State,* the leading journal in
the area of church-state relations.

During the 1980s, the historic Baptists saw the
separation of church and state weakened. Many
conservative Baptists, concerned about the growing secularism of American life, became politically active. While many leaders of the conservative
movement, such as Jerry Falwell, were independent Baptists,* others were affiliated with the more
established conventions. As a result of their pressure, Southern Baptists, the largest Baptist body,
gradually reduced their financial commitment to
the Baptist Joint Committee. The Southern Bap-

tists established their own special interest group
to lobby for legislation supporting their moral
stance.

See also BAPTIST JOINT COMMITTEE ON PUBLIC AF-
FAIRS.

BIBLIOGRAPHY. J. M. Dawson, *Baptists and the
American Republic* (1956); E. G. Hinson, *Soul
Liberty* (1975). G. T. Miller

**Religious/Christian Education, Baptist
Views.** Four dimensions of the Christian life
shape the Baptist understanding of religious education. These include the beliefs (1) that the life
of Jesus Christ best defines the nature of the gospel, (2) that Christ's church is called to offer nurture and formation to the Christian disciple, (3)
that the Christian community itself requires nurture and relational support, and (4) that the
church must promote both personal and corporate experience through Christian spirituality and
worship. While Baptists have not always emphasized those elements equally, they compose a
major part of Baptist approach to the educational
task.

In seventeenth-century England, Baptists first
formed communities of faith to express their approach to discipleship. They identified themselves as an oppressed minority who sought religious liberty* and freedom of conscience for the
practice of their beliefs. They wrote confessions
of faith* as a way of informing each other and
promoting fellowship. Among other things, these
confessions were early documents for promoting
the theological and doctrinal education of a new
constituency. In colonial America, Baptists articulated their beliefs regarding church and state, salvation, freedom and polity in treatises, tracts and
other documents used inside and outside the
churches.

With the organization of the Triennial Convention* in 1814, new societies developed for missionary* activity, evangelism and education. Nineteenth-century Baptists founded educational
institutions that came to provide undergraduate
and graduate education for persons across the
United States. Some of those institutions that have
survived have retained Baptist ties, while others
have not. By the nineteenth and twentieth centuries, Baptist groups had founded societies and
organizations for providing churches with educational materials for evangelism, doctrine, missions and, primarily, the study of Scripture.

One early way of providing doctrinal education

for the young came through Baptist catechisms written by well-known theologians/pastors. In some groups—American,* National* and Southern* Baptists, for example—religious education was offered through published materials and programs written for all age groups in the church. Sunday-school was the major occasion for formal religious education, but other courses of study were also developed. By the mid-twentieth century Baptist seminaries were offering courses of study in religious education, and most later offered degrees in the field. Churches, particularly larger ones, began seeking ministers of religious education whose primary role was developing programs of spiritual and educational formation. With time, some questioned whether these programs created a more static "programmed piety" or nurtured the freedom advocated by Baptist forebears. With changes in denominational identity and loyalty, new strategies for offering religious education are taking shape in home Bible study groups, video classes, and renewed nurture of prayer and spirituality.

BIBLIOGRAPHY. I. V. Cully and K. B. Cully, eds., *Encyclopedia of Religious Education* (1990); A. McClellan, *Meet Southern Baptists* (1978); R. L. and E. Wright, *The Big Little School* (1980).

W. B. Rogers and B. J. Leonard

Review and Expositor. A scholarly journal operated by faculty members at the Southern Baptist Theological Seminary,* Louisville, Kentucky. The journal was founded in 1904 as successor to *The Seminary Magazine,* an earlier faculty-student publication. For some years associate editors included faculty from New Orleans* and Southwestern* Baptist seminaries. Until 1990 the seminary president served as editor-in-chief, with a faculty member as managing editor. In 1990 the journal came under control of a self-perpetuating board selected from the seminary faculty. Published quarterly, the journal generally follows a thematic approach to issues relative to theology and ministry.

BIBLIOGRAPHY. *ESB* 1.

B. J. Leonard

Rhode Island College. *See* BROWN UNIVERSITY.

Rice, John R. (1895-1980). Baptist fundamentalist,* evangelist, editor and controversialist. Born in Texas and raised a Southern Baptist,* Rice attended Decatur (Texas) Baptist College (*see*

Dallas Baptist University), Baylor University* and Southwestern Baptist Seminary.* He left the Southern Baptist Convention in the 1920s and remained an outspoken critic of Baptist denominationalism.

Rice served as pastor of the Fundamentalist Baptist Church in Dallas from 1932 to 1940. In 1934 he founded *The Sword of the Lord,* an "independent Christian weekly" promoting fundamentalist theology and attacking modernism and liberalism in church and government. The headquarters of *The Sword of the Lord* was later moved to Murfreesboro, Tennessee, and Rice continued as its editor and a full-time evangelist until his death. *The Sword of the Lord* soon became an influential fundamentalist periodical, particularly among independent Baptists.

Rice was a colorful preacher and prolific author. He was well known for his polemical response to theological modernism, Catholicism, communism and the civil rights movement, as well as to dancing, smoking, movies and alcohol.

BIBLIOGRAPHY. R. Summer, *A Man Sent from God* (1960).

B. J. Leonard

Rice, Luther (1783-1836). Baptist denominational leader, promoter of missions* and education. Born in Northborough, Massachusetts, Rice studied at Leicester Academy and graduated from Williams College (1810). Ordained for missionary service by Congregationalists, he embarked for India in 1812, along with Adoniram* and Ann Judson.* After intense shipboard study of baptism,* he and the Judsons rejected infant baptism and became Baptists. They were immersed in Calcutta in November 1812 by William Ward, an English Baptist missionary.

Returning to America in 1813, Rice severed ties with the Congregationalists and began to stir up Baptist interest in missions. His extensive travels and enthusiastic preaching resulted in the formation in May 1814 of the General Convention of the Baptist Denomination in the United States for Foreign Missions. Known as the Triennial Convention,* it was the first national body of Baptists in America.

Rice's missionary vision led him to advocate the founding of Baptist colleges, beginning in 1821 with Columbian College* in Washington, D.C. In 1818 he started the *Latter Day Luminary,* a missions monthly and the first national Baptist periodical, and in 1821 he began *The Columbian Star* (1821), a religious weekly. Rice was instrumental in founding the Baptist General Tract Society (1824). His travels were marked with success in raising funds for missions and education.

By the mid 1820s Columbian College faced financial difficulties due to overexpansion, and Rice came under criticism. Powerful personalities, inevitable reaction and ecclesiological differences contributed to the problem. Though Rice was personally vindicated, his influence became circumscribed. Rice left no published works, though his journal and letters remain. However, few men have exerted a greater or more lasting influence on the Baptist denomination. One historian said, "The coming of Luther Rice was the most important event in Baptist history in the nineteenth century." He is buried at Pine Pleasant Church, Washington, South Carolina.

BIBLIOGRAPHY. *AAP* 6; *DAB* VIII; *DARB;* H. L. McBeth, *The Baptist Heritage* (1987); L. Rice, *Dispensations of Providence: Journal and Letters of Luther Rice,* ed. W. H. Brackney (1984); E. W. Thompson, *Luther Rice: Believer in Tomorrow* (1967). W. M. Patterson

Riley, William Bell (1861-1947). Baptist pastor and fundamentalist* leader. Born in Green County, Indiana, less than thirty days before the outbreak of the Civil War, Riley, like Lincoln before him, knew the hardships of life in a Kentucky cabin and of dawn-to-dark hoeing. He found time, however, to join other youngsters on the county courthouse steps to listen to summertime trials and to dream of speaking someday to huge audiences. By sixteen he had become an able public speaker.

In August 1875, during an evangelistic meeting, Riley made a public profession of faith in Christ. After his immersion, he was received into the Dallesburg, Kentucky, Baptist church. In 1879 young Riley entered normal school at Valparaiso, Indiana. He intended to pursue a law career, but "a divine voice" indicated that he should enter the ministry instead. As a result Riley moved to the Presbyterian College at Hanover, Indiana, from which he graduated in 1885. Three years later he earned his theological degree from the Southern Baptist Theological Seminary* in Louisville, Kentucky. He was ordained in 1883, and a series of pastorates along the Ohio River followed. Later he moved to Lafayette, Indiana; Bloomington, Illinois; and Chicago; in 1897 he settled at the First Baptist Church of Minneapolis. After only a short time in the Twin Cities area he founded the Northwestern Bible and Missionary Training School. In 1935 he established Northwestern Evangelical Seminary and in 1944 Northwestern College.

Riley's childhood dream of debating was fulfilled when he entered the modernist-fundamentalist controversy. His most prominent contests were in defense of the Bible against the evolutionary theory. He debated, among others, Maynard Shipley of the Science League of America and J. C. McCabe, the English rationalist.

BIBLIOGRAPHY. *DAB* 4; M. A. Riley, *The Dynamic of a Dream* (1938); C. A. Russell, *Voices of American Fundamentalism* (1976); F. M. Szasz, "Three Fundamentalist Leaders" (Ph.D. dissertation, University of Rochester, 1969).

B. L. Shelley

Riverside Church, New York. Riverside Church was constructed by the Park Street Baptist Church as part of the agreement that brought Harry Emerson Fosdick* to the pulpit. That agreement also provided that the congregation would adopt open membership, that ministers from all denominations might serve and that no denominational title would be used in the official name of the church. Despite the church's nondenominational character, Riverside is affiliated with the American Baptist Churches in the USA* and with the United Church of Christ. The congregation takes its name from its location on Riverside Drive.

John D. Rockefeller Jr.,* the chair of the building committee, purchased the land and made an initial contribution of $10,573,542. Over his lifetime he was to donate more than $32 million to the church. Riverside Church was built in a French Gothic style. The building was designed by Henry C. Pelton of New York and Charles Collens of Boston, and the builder was Mark Eidlitz and Sons—the same firms that had been employed by Park Street Baptist Church to construct an earlier church building.

The church building reflects a blend of tradition and modernity. The French Gothic design mandated a split chancel and a central altar. Many of the figures depicted in the windows are modern religious and secular leaders; unusually, the entrance to the building is from the side.

The church has maintained close ties to Union Theological Seminary,* New York. It is a center of community mission and service with an extensive weekday ministry in the community.

See also FOSDICK, HARRY EMERSON.

BIBLIOGRAPHY. H. E. Fosdick, *The Living of These Days: An Autobiography* (1969).

G. T. Miller

Robertson, A(rchibald) T(homas) (1863-1934). Southern Baptist* Greek scholar, professor of New Testament and author. Son of an impoverished physician, Robertson was converted at thirteen years of age, felt called to the gospel ministry at seventeen and preached his first sermon in a black church in North Carolina. He received his M.A. from Wake Forest College* in 1885. Though hindered by a speech impediment, he nevertheless applied himself with unflagging diligence to preparation for the ministry. At Southern Baptist Theological Seminary,* where he received his Th.M. degree in 1888, he distinguished himself as a brilliant student. In 1894 he married Ella Broadus, daughter of his beloved mentor John A. Broadus.* Robertson became the most widely respected Southern Baptist scholar of his time. His "big grammar," *A Grammar of the Greek New Testament in the Light of Historical Research* (1914), established him as the foremost New Testament Greek scholar of his day. He authored forty-four other books, including four grammars, fourteen commentaries, six volumes of *Word Pictures of the New Testament* (1930) and eleven historical and ten biographical studies. His *A Harmony of the Gospels* (1922) and *Studies in the Text of the New Testament* (1926) became the most widely used of his many books.

Robertson combined a demand for academic excellence and a deep Christian devotion. Upon at least one occasion he worked as a counselor in a revival meeting in Louisville, Kentucky, conducted by Dwight L. Moody, and he was in demand as a speaker at religious assemblies in England and America.

BIBLIOGRAPHY. E. Gill, *A. T. Robertson* (1943); W. A. Mueller, *A History of Southern Baptist Theological Seminary* (1959).

W. R. Estep

Robinson, Ezekiel Gilman (1815-1894). Regarded by some as the foremost Baptist of his day, he was reared in Massachusetts and graduated from Brown University* (1838) and Newton Theological Institution* (1842). After pastorates at Norfolk, Virginia; Cambridge, Massachusetts; and Cincinnati, Ohio, he taught theology and homiletics at Rochester Theological Seminary*

from 1853 to 1872. From 1872 until 1889 he was president of Brown University. His keen intellect, eloquence and commanding presence won him a reputation as a preacher, teacher and scholar. A venturesome thinker, he emphasized the role of experience in his theology, saying, "Thus a man's *real* creed will always be just what he has experienced, and no more." Typical of comments by former students was that of Augustus H. Strong*: "In his classroom I found my intellectual awakening. . . . He taught us to think for ourselves." From 1892 until 1894 he taught ethics and apologetics at the new University of Chicago.

BIBLIOGRAPHY. E. H. Johnson et al., eds., *Ezekiel Gilman Robinson* (1896).

N. H. Maring

Rochester Theological Seminary. Founded in 1850 as a sister institution to the Baptist-related University of Rochester, Rochester Theological Seminary was a leading Baptist urban seminary of the nineteenth century.

Several of the faculty in the theological department at Madison (later Colgate*) University attempted to move that institution from its rural location in Hamilton, New York, to the city of Rochester. This caused quite a stir for four years (1847-1851), before the Madison trustees determined to keep the school in Hamilton. At that decision, a group of supporters of the "removal" laid plans for a new university and theological school in Rochester. Like its predecessor in Hamilton, the seminary was governed by a society called the New York Baptist Union for Ministerial Education. Two Madison University theological professors constituted the first faculty in Rochester, and the first president was Ezekiel Gilman Robinson,* a distinguished professor of theology.

Rochester reached its peak of influence under the forty-year presidency of Augustus Hopkins Strong* (1872-1912). Strong recruited an excellent faculty, the most distinguished of whom was Walter Rauschenbusch.* In 1854 a German department was opened to accommodate the growing need for German Baptist Conference pastors (*see* North American Baptist Conference).

During the early decades of the twentieth century, the Rochester faculty advocated a progressive view of church and society and fostered the Social Gospel,* for which much criticism from the constituency was forthcoming. Among its distinguished graduates were Henry Lyman Morehouse,* E. J. Goodspeed,* Judson Barrett and William Dean, the latter a pioneer missionary to China. Rochester Seminary merged in 1928 with Colgate Baptist Seminary, and the German department eventually became the North American Baptist Seminary,* later located in Sioux Falls, South Dakota.

BIBLIOGRAPHY. J. L. Rosenberger, *Rochester and Colgate: Historical Backgrounds of the Two Universities* (1926).

W. H. Brackney

Rock, Clifton Moore (1876-1936). Baptist leader in New Mexico and Arizona. A Southerner from Asheville, North Carolina, he was hired in 1917 as pastor of Calvary Baptist Church, Phoenix, Arizona, a congregation that had broken away from the more liberal* First Baptist Church. Even so, the church affiliated with the Northern Baptist Convention (*see* American Baptist Churches in the USA). In 1921 a group withdrew from Calvary Church and formed the First Southern Baptist Church, with Rock as pastor. The same year the church joined the Southwestern Baptist Association of New Mexico, which was affiliated with the Southern Baptist Convention* (SBC).

Rock served as president of the New Mexico convention in 1926-1927. In 1928 his leadership was influential in the creation of the Baptist General Convention of Arizona, which affiliated with the SBC in May 1929. He served on the executive committee of the SBC from 1929 to 1936.

BIBLIOGRAPHY. R. A. Baker, *Relations Between Northern and Southern Baptists* (1948); *ESB* 2:1169. H. W. Pipkin

Rock Springs Seminary. *See* SHURTLEFF COLLEGE.

Rockefeller, John D., Jr. (1874-1960). Baptist philanthropist and liberal* church leader. Rockefeller inherited an intense interest in Baptist and Christian affairs from his father. While he was a member of the Fifth Avenue Baptist Church (where he once taught the adult men's class), pastors W. H. P. Faunce and Cornelius Woelfkin* inspired him with a liberal theological vision. In Rockefeller's 1917 article "The Christian Church: What of Its Future?" he stated his vision of what the church needed to do: move beyond its preoccupation with "theoretical" religion to a new devotion to "applied" faith. To support this goal, Rockefeller helped finance such ecumenical ministries as the Institute for Social and Religious Research, Union Theological Seminary* (New

York), the Federal (later National) Council of Churches* and Riverside Church.* In addition, Rockefeller continued to support Baptist enterprises at home and abroad. His contributions to the Northern Baptist Convention's Unified Budget between 1919 and 1933 were between 5.8 and 12.6 percent of the total.

G. T. Miller

Rogerenes. American Baptist general body. An offshoot of the Seventh Day Baptist* movement, the Rogerenes took their name from their founder, John Rogers* (c. 1648-1721). About 1674 he and two others were immersed as members of the Third Baptist Church (Seventh Day) of Newport, Rhode Island, and formed an arm of that congregation in New London, Connecticut. About 1677 the Rogers group became a separate church with about eight members. Gradually the movement spread thinly throughout New England, chiefly among middle- and upper-class whites. About 1709 a small number moved to New Jersey and formed a second church with about ten members, followed in 1734 by others who began a third church with twenty-one members. These three had about eighty members in 1770, their greatest extent, but formed no association.

A generally quiet and unassuming people who gained a reputation for extreme enthusiasm from a few isolated instances, the Rogerenes perpetuated the views of their founder. In Connecticut the consequence was spasmodic persecution. Fines were levied, and property was sold when the Rogerenes would not pay. Often they were whipped, placed in stocks or imprisoned.

The Rogerenes no longer exist. One New Jersey church moved to West Pennsylvania about 1775 and dropped from sight; the other numbered only two members in 1790 and died about the turn of the century. The Connecticut church continued with gradually diminishing vigor until about 1900.

BIBLIOGRAPHY. R. G. Gardner, *Baptists of Early America: A Statistical History, 1638-1790* (1983; rev. ed. 1989). R. G. Gardner

Rogers, John (1648-1721). Founder of Rogerene* Baptists. He was born in Milford, Connecticut, on December 1, 1648, the son of James and Elizabeth Rowland Rogers. He married three times: Elizabeth Griswold in 1670, Mary Ransford in 1699 and Sarah Cole in 1714. He had three children.

Rogers was educated by private tutors. Converted from nominal Congregationalism in 1674 by the Seventh Day Baptists* of Newport, Rhode Island, Rogers led a small group of supporters to form a separate Rogerene Baptist church, centered at New London, in 1677. He practiced believer's baptism* by immersion and strongly supported pacifism and the separation of church and state. He opposed clerical salaries, the use of meetinghouses, formal prayers and other forms of ritualism in worship, slavery, and the use of medicines. Eventually he adopted Sunday as the Christian sabbath but insisted that labor on that day was lawful. He wrote thirteen pamphlets, of which *An Epistle to the Churches of Christ Call'd Quakers* (1705), *The Book of the Revelation of Jesus Christ* (1720) and *John Rogers a Servant of Jesus Christ* (3rd ed., 1754) are most notable. He was repeatedly persecuted by the Standing Order, being twice whipped, fined many times and imprisoned on seven occasions for a total of fifteen years. A man of certainty and courage, Rogers initiated a tiny Baptist general group which disappeared completely by 1900. He died in Mamacock, Connecticut, on October 17, 1721.

BIBLIOGRAPHY. R. Brunkow, *American Writers Before 1800* (1983) 3:1236-38; *DAB* XVI.

R. G. Gardner

Romanian Baptist Association of Chicago. Organization of Romanian Baptist Churches in the U.S.A. Founded on September 1, 1913, in Cincinnati, Ohio, the association combined the efforts of nine churches and one publication, called *The Christian,* later known as *The Illuminator.* Under the leadership of L. A. Gredys, C. R. Igrisan and T. Selegean, other missionary organization were soon formed. These were the Monument of the Gospel, the Romanian Baptist Women's Association and the Romanian Baptist Youth Fellowship. The association printed Romanian translations of the Bible, hymnals, tracts and a *History of Romanian Baptists in America.* The members are located primarily in Michigan, Ohio, Illinois and Indiana. By 1954 the association numbered eleven churches and 970 members, with 1,125 members by 1971.

BIBLIOGRAPHY. *ESB* 2:1173; R. G. Torbet, *History of the Baptists* (1972).

A. M. Manis

Routh, Eugene Coke (1874-1966). A native of Fayette County, Texas, Routh graduated from the University of Texas. Ordained in 1901, he pursued an early ministry in district missions. In 1907 he became editor of the *South Texas Baptist.* In 1912 he moved to the prestigious Texas *Baptist Standard.* He refused to drag the 1920s creationist fight into the paper and in 1928 was dismissed for not defending prominent leaders against J. Frank Norris.* That same year, when Oklahoma Baptists had read too much about the controversy in the *Baptist Messenger,* they called Routh as editor. Routh was a committed traditional Baptist, and his editorial interests were Baptist doctrine, Oklahoma Baptist history and world missions.* His interest in missions led to a four-year term as editor of the *Commission,* the Southern Baptist Foreign Mission Board* magazine. He retired to Lockhart, Texas, in 1948 and died at age ninety-two.

BIBLIOGRAPHY. A. McClellan, *Meet Southern Baptists* (1978). A. McClellan

Routh, Porter Wroe (1911-1987). Southern Baptist* denominational leader. Born in Lockhart, Texas, Routh lived most of his youth in Dallas. In 1928 he moved to Oklahoma, and in 1934 he graduated from Oklahoma Baptist University.* He continued his studies at the University of Missouri and Southern Baptist Seminary,* preparing for foreign missions.* He was appointed to the Baptist publications house in Shanghai, but that door was closed when Japan invaded China. After directing lay missions education for Oklahoma Baptists, he succeeded his father in 1944 as editor of the *Baptist Messenger.* In 1945 he was named chief statistician for the Baptist Sunday School Board,* Nashville, Tennessee. Six years later he became treasurer of the Southern Baptist Convention and head of its executive committee. He retired in 1979 but continued as a volunteer in denominational service. A friend once described Routh as always open to the humblest of people and as one of whom it could be said that, like John Wesley, "the world was his parish."

BIBLIOGRAPHY. A. McClellan, *Meet Southern Baptists* (1978). A. McClellan

Royal Ambassadors. Southern Baptist* missionary organization for boys. The Order of Royal Ambassadors (RA) was founded in 1908 by the Woman's Missionary Union (WMU), Auxiliary to the Southern Baptist Convention* (SBC), at the suggestion of national WMU leader Fannie Heck.* It is an activity-oriented organization of boys' missions groups. Arkansas RA leader G. L. Boles, a Mason, developed a ranking system involving missions projects and secret rituals. By the 1920s a similar system, built around knight errantry and the motto "We are ambassadors for Christ" (2 Cor 5:20), became standard nationally. In 1943 WMU hired James Ivyloy Bishop as full-time RA secretary. Spurred by a debate over Boy Scouts groups in churches, the WMU agreed to transfer RA boys over age nine to the Brotherhood Commission* of the SBC in 1957. In 1970 boys six to nine were similarly transferred. RA groups, grades one through twelve, reported 253,758 members in 1990.

BIBLIOGRAPHY. C. Allen, *Century to Celebrate* (1987), *ESB* 2, 4. W. L. Allen

Rutledge, Arthur Bristow (1911-1977). Southern Baptist* denominational leader. A native of San Antonio, Texas, Rutledge graduated from Baylor University* and held graduate degrees from Southern* and Southwestern* Baptist Theological seminaries. After twenty-seven years pastoring Baptist churches, he became stewardship and missions secretary for the Texas Baptist Convention. Two years later he was called to direct the missions division of the Southern Baptist Home Mission Board.* In 1965 he was elected chief executive of the board. His accomplishments in home missions included reorganizing the staff to assure maximum cooperation with the state Baptist conventions and updating the Southern Baptist home mission profile. During his fourteen-year service in Home Missions, the board was one of the best-run operations in Southern Baptist life. Ill when he retired in 1976, Rutledge died about one year later. He was eulogized as a firm but gentle executive and as consistently fair in all personal relationships.

BIBLIOGRAPHY. *ESB* 4:2444.

A. McClellan

S

Sabbath, Baptist Views. Periodically, Baptists in North America have demonstrated confusion with their observance of the sabbath. A portion of that confusion arises from the struggle to understand New Testament and Old Testament teaching and practice on the subject. Further confusion is evident in the application of laws enacted to enforce the sabbath in the social fabric of a community. With the exception of Seventh Day Baptists,* most Baptist groups have defined Sunday as the sabbath and have worked to preserve its keeping in the broader society. As the fourth commandment of the Decalogue has expressed itself in laws that prohibit labor, business and sports on Sunday, sabbath obligations have become more elusive.

Where Baptists provided a majority presence in towns, counties and states, provincial laws restricting Sunday trading were enacted and enforced during the eighteenth, nineteenth and early twentieth centuries. These laws have been challenged, modified or displaced in the mid- to late twentieth century, a time of economic and cultural transitions; Baptist support for legislation restricting or forbidding liquor and gambling has also been meeting with less success.

The teaching of the church and the rhetoric of the pulpit among Baptists have continued to advocate rest and worship as the proper activities on the sabbath. However, the demands of the economic order, social pressure and the pervasive influence of mass communication have eroded the fidelity among Baptists to those "proper" activities. The impact of these developments on Baptists and Baptist churches has been significant.

BIBLIOGRAPHY. *ESB* 4:135-41.

W. B. Rogers Jr.

Sabbath Recorder. The official publication of the Seventh Day Baptists.* Since the 1820s, Seventh Day Baptists* in America wanted a national publication to bind their movement together. In 1821 the General Conference sponsored *The Seventh-Day Baptist Missionary Magazine,* but it failed in 1825 for financial reasons. From 1830-1839 the denomination was served by *The Protestant Sentinel.* It was succeeded by *The Seventh-Day Baptist Register,* a privately owned weekly that ran for only four years. In 1844 George B. Utter began publishing *The Sabbath Recorder* as a weekly newspaper. By 1850 the periodical had been taken over by the Seventh Day Baptist Publishing Society in New York City, but in 1862 it was repurchased by Utter. Ten years later the American Sabbath Tract Society bought the newspaper and N. V. Hull became editor. Under subsequent editors the *Sabbath Recorder* changed styles and formats. Since 1907 it has been published as a magazine, and it remains the official periodical of the Seventh Day Baptist General Conference.

BIBLIOGRAPHY. D. C. Woolley, ed., *Baptist Advance* (1964). T. P. Weber

Sacred Harp, The. The best-known and most widely used shape-note tune-book to be found in rural America in the nineteenth and twentieth centuries. Compiled in 1844 by Benjamin Franklin White and E. J. King, it was published in Philadelphia by J. C. Collins. So pervasive is the influence of this collection even today that gatherings for singing the kinds of music it contains (folk hymns, fuguing tunes), regardless of what book may be used, are known as "Sacred Harp singings." White is credited with the establishment in 1845 of the Southern Musical Convention, which fostered such singings. These events gradually spread from Georgia to Alabama, west to Texas and Oklahoma, north to Tennessee and Kentucky, and south to Florida.

The book has gone through numerous revisions and editions, four of which remain in twentieth-century use. The most widely known is *The*

Original Sacred Harp, Denson Revision (1936, 1960, 1971), which has tended to replace the others. *The Sacred Harp* is the original source of such tunes as ALL IS WELL ("Come, Come, Ye Saints"), BEACH SPRING ("Come, Ye Sinners, Poor and Needy") and WARRENTON ("Come, Thou Fount of Every Blessing").

BIBLIOGRAPHY. H. Eskew and J. C. Lowney, "Shape-Note Hymnody," in *The New Grove Dictionary of American Music,* vol. 4 (1986); G. P. Jackson, *The Story of the Sacred Harp* (1944).

H. T. McElrath

St. Louis Baptist College. *See* MISSOURI BAPTIST COLLEGE.

Samford University. A Baptist university with ties to the Alabama Baptist Convention. The school was founded in 1841 by Alabama business, education and religious leaders as Howard College, named for John Howard, the English prison reformer. It was located in Marion, Alabama, until 1887, when it was moved to Birmingham. In 1957 the college was moved to its present location and the name was changed to Samford University in honor of Frank Samford, a Birmingham businessman and benefactor. Howard College continues as the School of Arts and Sciences. A teacher education division (now School of Education) was begun in 1914, and a division of pharmacy (now School of Pharmacy) was established in 1927. In 1961 Samford secured the Cumberland School of Law, originally a Tennessee school founded in 1847. Others schools include nursing and business. In 1989 the Beeson Divinity School* was established through the benevolence of Ralph Waldo Beeson, an Alabama Presbyterian who contributed over $43 million to the school. With a student body of over 4,000, Samford is the largest private school in Alabama.

BIBLIOGRAPHY. Samford University, *Catalog, 1993-94;* J. Sulzby, *Toward a History of Samford University* (1986). B. J. Leonard

Sampey, John Richard (1863-1946). President of Southern Baptist Theological Seminary* and professor of Old Testament and Hebrew. Sampey was converted at fourteen years of age and two years later enrolled as a ministerial student in Howard College (now Samford University*), Birmingham, Alabama, from which he graduated with his A.B. degree. He entered the Southern Baptist Theological Seminary in 1882 to prepare for foreign missionary* service, but was persuaded to remain and teach at the seminary upon his graduation in 1885.

Upon John A. Broadus's* death, Sampey succeeded him as a member of the International Sunday School Lesson Committee; he became chairman of the committee in 1921 and served continuously on the committee for forty-six years. He was also one of the founders of the Baptist World Alliance* and throughout his long career continued to take a lively interest in Baptists around the world. Sampey took several preaching tours to Brazil, where he found some fulfillment of his earlier desire to become a foreign missionary.

After Edgar Y. Mullins* died in 1928, Sampey became president of Southern Baptist Seminary (1929). In 1942 he resigned from his post after fifty-seven years of continuous service to the seminary. In his years as professor and president of the seminary he had written several books, including *The First Thirty Years of Southern Baptist Theological Seminary* (1890), *The Ethical Teachings of Jesus* (1909) and *The Heart of the Old Testament* (1922).

An effective churchman, Sampey was elected president of the Southern Baptist Convention* in 1935 and was reelected for two succeeding terms. Internationally, his reputation took him to the Conference on Life and Work in Oxford and the Conference on Faith and Order in Edinburgh in 1937, as well as the Congress of the Baptist World Alliance, where he spoke in 1939.

BIBLIOGRAPHY. *ESB* 2; W. A. Mueller, *A History of Southern Baptist Theological Seminary* (1959).

W. R. Estep

Sanders, Billington McCarty (1789-1852). First president of Mercer University,* president of the Georgia Baptist Convention and editor of *The Christian Index.* Born to Ephraim and Nancy Sanders on December 2, 1789, Sanders was orphaned by age ten and was reared by the Ambrose Jones family. In 1809 he graduated from South Carolina College. After a brief stint as a schoolteacher, Sanders spent twenty years as a farmer and preacher and served one term in the state legislature. In 1831 Sanders was invited to lead a classical and theological seminary for Georgia Baptists. Classes began in 1933, with Sanders serving as administrator, teacher, builder and custodian. In 1836 Mercer Institute became Mercer University, with Sanders as its first president. After his resignation in 1839, Sanders served as treasurer of the college, as secretary and as a member of the board of trustees.

Sanders also served as clerk and moderator in the Georgia Association. In the Georgia Baptist Convention he chaired the executive committee, served as president for six years and edited *The Christian Index*.

BIBLIOGRAPHY. *ESB* 2; C. D. Mallary, *Living and Dying unto the Lord* (1854).

C. Blevins

Savage, Mary (fl. 1790s). Free Will Baptist* preacher. Late in the eighteenth century, New England's Baptists—the region's most dynamic dissenting sect—faced a series of challenges. Among the new anti-Calvinist* groups none proved more disturbing than the Free Will Baptist schismatics. Founded by Benjamin Randall* in 1780, this Arminian sect gained thousands of followers during the next two decades in New Hampshire and Vermont. Mary Savage, originally from Woolwich, Maine, joined the Free Will Baptists and began preaching the gospel in 1791. Though she only served as a minister for about a year, she is credited with being the first Baptist woman preacher. Very little is known about her life, but according to one minister who heard her preach, Savage's special ability was helping the most troubled dissenters reconcile their views with Free Will Baptist beliefs.

BIBLIOGRAPHY. I. D. Stewart, *History of the Freewill Baptists for Half a Century, 1780-1830* (1862). J. M. Craig

Scarborough, Lee Rutland (1870-1945). Minister and educator. He was born in Colfax, Louisiana, on July 4, 1870. In 1874 the Scarborough family moved to Texas, where he was reared on a ranch. He received an A.B. degree from Baylor University* in 1892 and another A.B. degree in 1896 from Yale. From 1899 to 1900 he attended the Southern Baptist Theological Seminary* in Louisville, Kentucky. He married Neppie Warren in 1900, and they had six children.

Scarborough was ordained to the ministry in 1896 and served a number of Baptist churches in Texas as pastor. He was a member of the executive board of the convention and later its president. In 1908 he was called to establish the first chair of evangelism at Southwestern Baptist Theological Seminary.* From 1914 to 1945 Scarborough served as president of the seminary, suc-

ceeding the first president, B. H. Carroll.* He was also the author of a number of books, the best known of which is *With Christ After the Lost* (1953), a textbook on evangelism. He died in Amarillo, Texas, on April 10, 1945.

BIBLIOGRAPHY. *ERS; ESB* 2:1186-87.

W. R. Estep

Screven, William (1629-1713). Colonial Baptist leader. English records indicate that William Screven became a Baptist in 1652 in England. He came to America in 1668, probably to escape persecution under the Clarendon Code. Upon his arrival, Screven moved to Kittery, now part of Maine. He appealed to the crown to separate Maine from Massachusetts because of the religious oppression of the Boston authorities. Screven joined the First Baptist Church of Boston in 1681. For some reason, the Boston congregation rebaptized him. Preaching under a license from that congregation, Screven organized a Baptist church in Kittery in 1682. The church experienced some hardships, including the threat of persecution by the established church. In 1696 Screven and the entire congregation moved to Charleston, South Carolina. Both General* and Particular* Baptists were already present in the region, and these joined with the Kittery congregation to form the First Baptist Church of Charleston,* South Carolina. This congregation is the oldest Baptist church in the South. In 1701 the Charleston congregation constructed its first building.

BIBLIOGRAPHY. H. L. McBeth, *The Baptist Heritage* (1987). G. T. Miller

Second Great Awakening, Baptist Participation. The term "Second Great Awakening" usually refers to the period of religious revival in the United States from 1790 to 1836. There were at least three separate aspects of the Awakening. In the Southwest (Kentucky and Tennessee), large camp meetings provided the occasion for many highly emotional revivals. Approximately 25,000 people attended the revival at Cane Ridge. A more sober—but still emotional—series of revivals occurred in northwestern New York and Ohio. Charles G. Finney (1792-1875), the nation's first professional evangelist, developed his revival techniques, called the "new measures," in this movement. Finney sent a team to prepare an area for a revival. Once he was on the site, Finney's techniques included the invitation, the anxious bench, praying for sinners by name and the use of simple, rhythmic hymns ("gospel music") sung by large choirs. In New England, small revivals occurred in many local congregations. Once converted, the awakened went on to establish voluntary societies to Christianize America, promote such good works as temperance and spread the gospel around the world.

Baptists were deeply influenced by these revival movements. But although they grew continually during this period, winning new converts and building new churches, the most important effects of the revival were not numerical. The new evangelism attracted Baptists because of their reliance on the voluntary* principle in religion. Many Baptists agreed with Francis Wayland* (the president of the College of Rhode Island) that a Baptist church was to be a perpetual revival, devoted to the conversion of sinners.

The style of revivalism that Baptists adopted varied by region. Baptists in the South tended toward the more emotional style of revival associated with the camp meeting. Northern and Western Baptists were more attracted by Finney and the "new measures." The adoption of one style of evangelism did not exclude other styles from later consideration. Frontier churches would often be gathered by the more emotional approach. When a region became more settled, churches shifted toward a new measures style. By 1850, for example, most larger churches had adopted the invitation, the anxious bench and gospel hymns.

The Second Great Awakening inspired Baptists to organize their movement nationally. The first step came when some young Congregational missionaries, Luther Rice* and Adoniram Judson,* became Baptists in India. To support Judson's ministry, Rice returned to America and traveled extensively. At his summons, Baptist met in Philadelphia in 1814 and formed the Triennial Convention.* During the new organization's first decade, it tried to sponsor a wide variety of Baptist benevolence, including home missions and a national Baptist university. The resources of the new body, however, were not sufficient for its dreams. Thus Baptists organized separate societies to provide for home missions, ministerial education and publications. The state conventions, which began to be organized in the 1820s, took the lead in the establishment of colleges and in some local missionary work. When Baptists divided along sectional lines in 1859, the South returned to the older understanding of a single convention for all national enterprises.

BIBLIOGRAPHY. P. Conkin, *Cane Ridge: America's Harvest Time* (1989); W. W. Sweet, *Religion on the American Frontier: The Baptists* (1931).

G. T. Miller

Sellers, Ernest Orlando (1869-1952). Evangelical musician, composer, author and educator. He was born in Hastings, Michigan, October 29, 1869. After an early career in surveying and civil engineering, he became active in YMCA work. Later he moved gradually into full-time educational and evangelistic activities, working for a time on the staff at the Moody Bible Institute in Chicago and leading singing in revival campaigns with well-known evangelists, including R. A. Torrey, Gipsy Smith and J. Wilbur Chapman.

In 1919 Sellers became director of the music department of the Baptist Bible Institute (later New Orleans Baptist Theological Seminary*). Affectionately known as "Uncle Fuller," he exerted a powerful influence on his students and was widely respected among Southern Baptists.* He was known as an author and composer as well as a teacher, with writings including *How to Improve Church Music* (1928) and *Worship: How and Why* (1941). He was a member of the committee that compiled *The New Baptist Hymnal* (1926) and the author of the popular gospel hymn "Wonderful, Wonderful Jesus." He died in retirement at Eola, Louisiana, on October 19, 1952.

BIBLIOGRAPHY. *ESB* 2:1189; *Handbook to the Baptist Hymnal* (1992).

H. T. McElrath

Semple, Robert Baylor (1769-1831). Virginia Baptist denominational statesman, pastor, educator, missions* leader and historian. Born January 20, 1769, in King and Queen County, Virginia, Semple was nurtured in the established church and classically educated for the law. Having been contemptuous of Baptists for a time, in December 1789 Semple was baptized into Upper King and Queen Baptist Church. In 1790 he became pastor of Bruington Church in King and Queen County, a post he held for life. He conducted a school on his farm.

Semple was the most prominent leader of the large Dover Association from the mid-1790s until his death, and of the General Association of Baptists in Virginia from its beginning in 1823. From 1794 he led in the limited second and third of the three statewide Baptist organizations that existed prior to 1823, the General Committee (1784-1799) and the General Meeting of Correspondence (1800-1822).

An organizer of the Triennial Convention* (1814), Semple served on its board and was its president (1820-1831). As board president of Columbian College* (later George Washington University) from 1827 to 1831, he reopened and rescued the institution from the disastrous debt Luther Rice* had incurred for the school. Semple's chief work, the classic *History of the Rise and Progress of the Baptists in Virginia* (1810), is foundational for understanding Virginia Baptist history.

BIBLIOGRAPHY. R. S. Mills, *Robert Baylor Semple: A Study in Baptist Denominational Development* (Ph.D. dissertation, Southern Baptist Theological Seminary, 1986); J. B. Taylor, *Virginia Baptist Ministers,* vol. 1 (1859).

R. B. James

Separate Baptists. Baptists originating among the revivalists of the First Great Awakening.* During the Great Awakening many Baptist churches split into revivalistic (Separate) and antirevivalistic (Regular*) factions. The first identifiable Separate Baptist church resulted from such a schism in Boston in 1743. Many revivalistic New Light Congregationalists also became Separate Baptists. Highly evangelistic and moderately Calvinistic,* Separate Baptists allowed women to preach, practiced "nine rites," and disdained a learned or paid ministry and confessionalism.* Their emotional worship services typically ended with invitations for salvation. Notable pastors included Isaac Backus,* the leading advocate for religious liberty* in Massachusetts, and Richard Furman,* leader of the influential Charleston Association and first president of the Triennial Convention* (1814). Shubal Stearns* and Daniel Marshall* began the first Southern Separate Baptist church (1755) and association (1758) at Sandy Creek, North Carolina.

Differences between Regular and Separate Baptists were pronounced in the South, but barriers to fellowship eroded near the end of the eighteenth century. At that time most Separate Baptists moved toward a stronger Calvinism, adopted the Philadelphia Confession and entered Regular Baptist associations. Churches rejecting that union organized six associations in Tennessee, Kentucky, Indiana and Illinois. These formed the General Association of Separate Baptists (1912), which in 1975 added the Christian Unity Association (of North Carolina and Virginia). Generally conservative in theology, they practice foot-washing* as an ordinance. They maintain a mission board and a ministers' conference, but no central headquarters, colleges or seminaries. In 1979 they numbered ninety-eight churches with about 9,000 members.

BIBLIOGRAPHY. H. L. McBeth, *The Baptist Heritage* (1987); J. O. Renault, "The Changing Patterns of Separate Baptist Religious Life, 1803-1977," *BHH* 14 (October 1979):16-25; R. G. Torbet, *A History of the Baptists,* 3rd ed. (1969).

J. T. Spivey

Seventh Day Baptists. A Baptist group that differs mainly from other Baptists in the observance of Saturday as the sabbath. Seventh Day Baptists first emerged in England in 1650 and in America in 1671. The Seventh Day Baptist General Conference, with headquarters in Plainfield, New Jersey, was organized in 1801. Church membership is according to four prerequisites: regeneration, confession of purpose to follow Christ, believer's baptism and Christian living. The laying on of hands* at joining the church is often practiced, though not required. Worship on the sabbath (seventh day) is presumed. The Seventh Day Baptist Missionary Society was formed in 1818, the Tract Society in 1835. The Seventh Day Baptist World Federation was founded in 1964. It is probable that much of the impact of Seventh Day Baptists in the United States is blunted by the Seventh Day Adventists. *The Sabbath Recorder,** the group's leading periodical, was founded in 1844.

BIBLIOGRAPHY. W. L. Burdick and C. F. Randolph, *A Manual of Seventh Day Baptist Church Procedure* (1926); C. F. Randolph, ed., *Seventh Day Baptists in Europe and America* (1910).

H. W. Pipkin

Sheridan College. One of the early educational institutions of the Missionary Baptists* was the Missionary Baptist College, organized in 1917 in Malvern, Hot Spring County, Arkansas. In 1919 it was moved to Sheridan, the county seat of Grant County.

E. B. Jones was the first president, and the college was housed at the Bib Creek Baptist Church. In 1921 the school purchased eleven acres on which to build a new college. The purpose of the school was to reflect Missionary Baptist teachings, and the rules outlined in the early printed matter for students were strict, with emphasis on personal behavior rather than on doctrinal belief.

The school was divided into six divisions and offered the associate in arts, associate in music and associate in Bible degrees. The two-year college operated until 1934, when it was closed due, in part, to financial problems.

J. T. Greer

Shields, T(homas) T(odhunter) (1873-1955). Canadian Baptist* pastor and fundamentalist* leader. Born in England, the son of a Baptist pastor, Shields was raised in southwestern Ontario and began to preach with only his father's instruction and model as education. The younger Shields's attention to clear, forceful language coupled with an impressive build and voice opened doors to a series of successful pastorates.

In 1910 he became pastor of the largest Baptist church in Canada at the time, Jarvis Street in Toronto. Shields served there for the rest of his life, developing a reputation as the "Canadian Spurgeon." The church grew in numbers, even though it suffered a schism over his leadership in 1921. The church's newspaper, *The Gospel Witness,* under Shields's editorship reached 30,000 subscribers in sixty countries. Shields presided over the Canadian Protestant League in anti-Catholic propaganda during its brief flowering in World War II, and he helped lead two fundamentalist organizations, the Baptist Bible Union* and the International Council of Christian Churches.

Shields is best known, however, for his leadership of fundamentalists in the Baptist Convention of Ontario and Quebec (*see* Fundamentalism). From 1910 to 1926 these Christians opposed a succession of appointments of theological liberals* at the denomination's McMaster University.* Largely unsuccessful in their opposition, a number joined Shields in leaving the denomination in 1927. Many of the disaffected would later form the Fellowship of Evangelical Baptist Churches in Canada, but Shields continued his pattern of refusing to compromise and ended up leader only of a tiny denomination, now known as the Association of Regular Baptist Churches of Canada.

See also CANADIAN BAPTISTS.

BIBLIOGRAPHY. C. A. Russell, "Thomas Todhunter Shields, Canadian Fundamentalist," *Ohio History* 70 (1978):263-80; L. K. Tarr, "Another Perspective on T. T. Shields and Fundamentalism," in *Baptists in Canada: Search for Identity Amidst Diversity,* ed. J. K. Zeman (1980); L. K. Tarr, *Shields of Canada* (1967).

J. G. Stackhouse

Shorter, Alfred (1803-1882). Baptist farmer, merchant and philanthropist. Alfred Shorter was born near Washington, Georgia, on November 23, 1803, into a poor rural family. He received no formal education. Shorter married a widow of some means, Martha Harper Baldwin, who encouraged him to invest her money. In 1837 they moved to Floyd County, Georgia, where they remained for the remainder of their lives. Possessing acute business judgment, Shorter was a trader, farmer, holder of numerous slaves and part owner of several businesses. Quietly active in the Rome Baptist Church, he was a trustee and treasurer. Influenced by Luther R. Gwaltney, his pastor, he took a deep interest in the finances of the college named for his wife and himself. They probably contributed approximately $200,000 in all—roughly equivalent to $2.5 million in today's currency. Martha Shorter died on March 22, 1877, and Alfred Shorter on July 18, 1882, in Rome, Georgia. He had no children, and his estate, reliably estimated to be worth about $700,000, was divided among relatives, friends and Shorter College.*

BIBLIOGRAPHY. K. Coleman and C. S. Gurr, eds., *Dictionary of Georgia Biography,* vol. 2 (1983).

R. G. Gardner

Shorter College. An institution of higher education founded by northwest Georgia Baptists. Combining the generosity of Alfred Shorter* and Martha Shorter with the vision of Luther R. Gwaltney, pastor of the Rome Baptist Church, this institution was founded in 1873 as the Cherokee Baptist Female College. The name was changed to Shorter Female College in 1877 and to Shorter College in 1923. Initially it occupied a small site near the center of town; since 1911 the campus has been at its present location. For the first four decades of its life, the school included preparatory and collegiate departments for females—and sometimes a primary department for both girls and boys. It has been accredited by the Southern Association of Colleges and Schools since 1923 and by the National Association of Schools of Music since 1934. Among its presidents have been Luther R. Gwaltney (1882-1890), Azor W. Van

Hoose (1910-1921), Paul M. Cousins (1933-1948), Randall H. Minor (1958-1982) and James D. Jordan (1987-). College-age males were enrolled in the late 1940s, and the first male was graduated in 1953. Males have made up almost 40 percent of the student body since that time. Eight undergraduate and four master's degrees are offered. Five off-campus centers are maintained. In the fall of 1991 the enrollment was 821, with a full-time equivalency of 731. At the 1992 commencement, 128 degrees were awarded, bringing the 119-year total to 6,001 diplomas and degrees. In 1992 the physical facilities were valued at about $14 million, while the endowment had reached almost $13 million.

BIBLIOGRAPHY. R. G. Gardner, *On the Hill: The Story of Shorter College* (1972).

R. G. Gardner

Shuck, Henrietta Hall (1817-1844). Missionary to China. Born in Kilmarnock, Virginia, Henrietta Hall was reared in a Baptist preacher's home and was interested in mission* work from an early age. When she was seventeen years old, Jehu Lewis Shuck* proposed marriage and a life of missionary service. In September 1835 the Shucks were married, and they soon sailed to China as missionaries appointed by the Triennial Convention.* They spent five months in Singapore learning the language and then went to Macao in September 1836; there Henrietta Shuck opened a school for Chinese children. The couple moved to Hong Kong in March 1842 and began the first evangelical church in China. Henrietta Shuck died November 27, 1844, in Hong Kong during the birth of her fifth child. She had been the first American evangelical woman to serve as a missionary in China.

See also SHUCK, JEHU LEWIS.

BIBLIOGRAPHY. T. S. Dunaway, *A Pioneer for Jesus* (1947); J. B. Jeter, *Memoir of Mrs. Henrietta Hall Shuck* (1846).

T. L. Scales

Shuck, Jehu Lewis (1814-1863). Missionary to China. Born in Alexandria, Virginia, September 4, 1814, and educated at Virginia Baptist Seminary (now University of Richmond), Shuck was appointed a missionary by the Triennial Convention* in 1835. He organized the first Baptist church in China at Hong Kong in 1843. After the death of his wife Henrietta Hall Shuck* in 1844, he returned to the United States for two years,

remarried and in 1846 was appointed to serve in Canton by the newly formed Foreign Mission Board* of the Southern Baptist Convention* (SBC). Shuck was transferred to Shanghai and worked with other Baptist missionaries to organize the first Baptist church there in 1847. In 1851 he returned to the United States after the death of his second wife, and he resigned from the Foreign Mission Board in 1853. He worked with the Board of Domestic Missions (see Home Mission Board) of the SBC from 1854 to 1861, doing evangelism among the Chinese of California. Shuck died August 20, 1863, in South Carolina. Shuck and his first wife are celebrated as the first Baptist missionaries to China.

See also SHUCK, HENRIETTA HALL.

BIBLIOGRAPHY. *ESB* 2:1201-2; T. W. Hall, *I Give Myself: The Story of J. Lewis Shuck and His Mission to the Chinese* (1983).

T. L. Scales

Shurtleff College. Early Baptist educational institution. Shurtleff College was founded by Baptist missionary John Mason Peck.* Peck was educated by William Staughton,* an early Baptist theological educator, in the basement of Staughton's parsonage in Philadelphia. Staughton's method of combining classical and English instruction impressed Peck, who later followed this same model on the frontier.

Peck felt a call to minister in the West. Once he was there, however, the low educational level of many Western Baptist ministers appalled him, and he resolved to elevate their educational attainments. Originally, the Triennial Convention* supported Peck's ministry. When that organization ceased to finance home missionaries, the Massachusetts Domestic Missionary Society and, later, the American Baptist Home Missionary Society* provided funding. After teaching several ministers informally, Peck established the Rock Springs Seminary at Rock Springs, Illinois. The site was far from perfect, and Peck and Jonathan Going,* secretary of the Massachusetts Domestic Missionary Society, sought a more central location. Upper Alton, Illinois, on the banks of the Mississippi, was a natural choice. Alton encouraged students from both Illinois and Missouri to attend.

The school's first years were marked by high expectations and low finances. At one point the school institution contained a medical school, a theological seminary, a preparatory school and a liberal arts college. Largely due to Going's efforts, Benjamin Shurtleff, a Boston physician, donated $10,000 to the school on condition that Western Baptists raise an equal amount. Peck and Going raised the money through direct solicitation and by establishing Western educational societies. These funds enabled the school to call its first president, Adiel Sherwood of Georgia, and to regularize its operations.

G. T. Miller

Simmons, William James (1849-1890). African-American Baptist clergyman, editor and college president. Born a slave in Charleston, South Carolina, on June 29, 1849, Simmons graduated from Howard University (A.B., 1873; M.A., 1881). He was by far the most prominent African-American Baptist clergyman during the final decades of the nineteenth century.

In 1879 Simmons moved to Kentucky, where he remained for the rest of his life. After serving as minister of the First (African) Baptist Church in Lexington, in 1880 he assumed the presidency of the Kentucky Normal and Theological Institute (KNTI) in Louisville. The same year he organized the Colored Press Association, serving as president. In 1882 he became editor-president of the *American Baptist*. By 1884 his school had received university status, and a few years later it attained national recognition. In 1886 Simmons organized the American National Baptist Convention (*see* National Baptists). He also served as the first black secretary of the American Baptist Home Mission Society's* work among African-Americans. Yet Simmons is best known for his *Men of Mark: Eminent, Progressive and Rising* (1887), a biographical dictionary written to dispel beliefs of black inferiority.

On October 30, 1890, Simmons died prematurely of heart failure. A few months before his death he had resigned his position at State University (formerly KNTI) and started an industrial school, Eckstein Norton Institute in Cane Spring, Kentucky. His death sparked a power struggle among black Baptists that lasted for four years. In 1918 State University was renamed in his honor.

See also SIMMONS UNIVERSITY.

BIBLIOGRAPHY. W. B. Johnson, *The Scourging of a Race* (1915); W. J. Simmons, *Men of Mark* (1887); J. M. Washington, *The Frustrated Fellowship: The Black Baptist Quest for Social Power* (1986); L. H. Williams, *Black Higher Education in Kentucky, 1879-1930: The History of Simmons*

University (1987).   L. H. Williams

Simmons College (Texas). *See* HARDIN-SIMMONS UNIVERSITY.

Simmons University. Independent African-American Baptist school in Kentucky. In 1879 the school opened in Louisville as the Kentucky Normal and Theological Institute, with Elijah P. Marrs, a former slave, as president. A year later William J. Simmons,* also a former slave, who held B.A. and M.A. degrees from Howard University, became president. Simmons was responsible for securing financial support from Northern and Southern Baptists. Because of his influence, the National Baptist Convention Foreign Mission Board (1895-1911) was located in Louisville and centered in the school that would later bear his name.

In 1884 the school received university status and its name was changed to State University. After the segregation of Berea College by the Kentucky Supreme Court in 1904, State remained the only black Kentucky school offering a college degree, and it claimed the distinction of being the only black-owned institution in the nation providing college, medical and law degrees. In 1918 Charles H. Parrish Sr. became president and led a movement to rename the school in honor of Simmons. By 1922 there were 467 students in the college department, 33 theological students, property valued at $750,000 and an endowment of $54,000. But the economic crisis of the Depression caused Simmons's demise as a university. After August 1931, Simmons continued to function but only as a theological school (later as Simmons Bible College).

BIBLIOGRAPHY. L. Fitts, *A History of Black Baptists* (1985); W. J. Simmons, *Men of Mark* (1887); L. H. Williams, *The History of Black Higher Education in Kentucky* (1987).

L. H. Williams

Six-Principle Baptists. An Arminian* Baptist tradition maintaining the ordinance* of laying on of hands.* During the Interregnum some English Baptists adopted Hebrews 6:1-2 as a six-point confessional standard: repentance, faith, baptism,* laying on of hands, the resurrection of the dead and eternal life. Debate arose among General Baptists* concerning whether this required a new church ordinance, the laying of hands upon new converts. John Griffith's *God's Oracle and*

Christ's Doctrine (1655) became the definitive defense for churches affirming this. The Standard Confession (1660) required that new believers submit to the laying on of hands in order to "receive the promise of the holy Spirit." But because the general assembly refused to adopt the Six Principles as its only official standard, Six-Principle Baptists separated and established their own assembly (1690). Their theology was Arminian, and they practiced closed Communion.

Six-Principle Baptists appeared at an early date as minorities among the first Baptist churches in America—Providence and Newport—most of whose members were Calvinistic.* By 1652, however, they had become the majority in Providence. By 1665 they had left the Newport congregation and formed a church under William Vaughan. Though some Particular Baptists* in America laid hands on converts and Regular Baptists* sanctioned it in their Philadelphia Confession (1742), this practice was more characteristic of General Baptists. It visibly symbolized the difference between two traditions known as Five-Principle (Particular) and Six-Principle (General) Baptists. By the 1670s several Rhode Island Six-Principle churches had formed what was perhaps the first Baptist association in America. In the 1940s three churches identified as Six-Principle Baptists listed 280 members, living mostly in Rhode Island and Pennsylvania.

BIBLIOGRAPHY. W. L. Lumpkin, *Baptist Confessions of Faith* (1978); H. L. McBeth, *The Baptist Heritage* (1987).   J. T. Spivey

Smith, Elias (1769-1846). Founder of the Christian Connection. Elias Smith began his career in 1790 as a Baptist preacher, but in 1801 he became a Universalist. Within the year he renounced this faith and then helped found the Christian Connection, a radical sect that professed no creed but the New Testament. The "Christians" were similar to other frontier churches that believed in radical religious democracy. As a member of this body, Smith founded the *Herald* newspaper, published every two weeks, at Portsmouth, New Hampshire. In 1817 Smith rejoined the Universalists, and Robert Foster, a member of the Christian Connection, took over the paper. Smith declared his recovered universalism in *The Herald of Life and Immortality,* a briefly published newspaper. The 1817 Universalist General Convention "fellowshiped" Smith as a minister. In 1827 he rejoined the Christian Connection, but

he recovered his Universalist convictions again in 1842.   G. T. Miller

Smith, Hezekiah (1737-1805). New England Baptist pastor. Born on Long Island and reared at Morristown, New Jersey, Smith came under the influence of the Reverend John Gano,* who baptized him and encouraged him to pursue higher education in preparation for the ministry. Consequently, he attended Hopewell Academy and the College of New Jersey, from which he graduated in 1762. Smith went immediately to the South as an itinerant evangelist. He toured for fifteen months and was ordained while in Charleston. After the tour Smith was influential in the founding of Rhode Island College, which later became Brown University.* He served as visiting preacher in many New England churches, and in 1776 he became pastor of a Baptist church in Haverhill, Massachusetts.

During a forty-year pastorate, Smith saw the congregation become a large, influential church. He became a leader of Baptists in the region and a strong proponent of mission* endeavors, giving leadership in establishing eighty-six new churches. He was intensely loyal to the causes of national independence and religious liberty.* Smith took leave from his pulpit during the Revolutionary War to serve as an army chaplain under General George Washington, with whom a close personal friendship developed and was sustained during ensuing years. At age sixty-eight Smith suffered a paralysis; he died on January 22, 1805. His journal, which covered the entire forty-two years of his ministry, is a valuable personal account of the Revolutionary era.

BIBLIOGRAPHY. *AAP* 6; *DAB* IX; R. A. Guild, *Chaplain Smith and the Baptists* (1885).

F. A. Teague

Smith, Samuel Francis (1808-1895). Pastor, editor, author, hymnwriter, educator and missionary statesman. Born in Boston on October 21, 1808, Smith was educated at Harvard College and Andover Theological Seminary.* Though poor health prevented his devoting his career to foreign missions,* he served as editor of the *Baptist Missionary Magazine* and afterward as editorial secretary of the American Baptist Missionary Union.* Among his several books was *Rambles in Mission Fields* (1884), an account of a visit made in 1853 to various mission fields in Europe and Asia.

For eight years (1834-1842) he was minister of

the Baptist church in Waterville, Maine, and professor of modern languages at Waterville (now Colby) College. For twelve years (1842-1854) he was the pastor of the First Baptist Church in Newton, Massachusetts.

In the front rank of American hymnwriters, Smith was the author of over a hundred hymns, twenty-six of which appeared in *The Psalmist,** a collection he compiled along with fellow Baptist Baron Stow.* Among his most widely known hymns are "The Morning Light Is Breaking" and "My Country, 'Tis of Thee," now regarded as America's national hymn. He died at Newton Centre, Massachusetts, on November 16, 1895.

BIBLIOGRAPHY. H. S. Burrage, *Baptist Hymn Writers and Their Hymns* (1888); *Handbook to the Baptist Hymnal* (1992); C. W. Hughes, *American Hymns Old and New* (1980) 2:554.

H. T. McElrath

Smith, Sarah Julia Guthrie (1827-1901). Baptist philanthropist. Born in Louisville, Kentucky, March 4, 1827, she was the daughter of Kentucky statesman and financier James Guthrie (1792-1869), who was secretary of the treasury under President Franklin Pierce. She was baptized at Walnut Street Baptist Church in Louisville on June 7, 1851, and remained a member of that church fellowship throughout her life. She married John Lawrence Smith, scientist and teacher, on June 24, 1852.

A benefactor of Baptist institutions, Sarah Smith particularly gave to those for orphans and seminarians. In 1869 she gave property in Louisville, plus $5,000, for the Louisville Baptist Orphans' Home (later to become Spring Meadows). In 1888 she pledged $50,000 to John Albert Broadus* for a library at Southern Baptist Theological Seminary,* to be a memorial to her two nieces, Sarah Julia and Mary Elizabeth Caperton (daughters of her sister Mrs. John Caperton), and her two nephews, William Beverly and Lawrence Smith Caldwell (sons of another sister, Mrs. William B. Caldwell). That library building was completed and dedicated in May 1891. Smith died in Louisville on July 24, 1901. In 1926, when the seminary moved from downtown Louisville to 2825 Lexington Road, the library wing of Norton Hall was designated Memorial Library in recognition of her original gift.

BIBLIOGRAPHY. W. A. Mueller, *A History of Southern Baptist Theological Seminary* (1959).

S. F. Anders

Smyth, John (c. 1570-1612). Smyth, often called the Se-Baptist (self-baptizer), founded the General* or Arminian* Baptist movement. Smyth attended Christ College, Cambridge, a radical Puritan college. In 1600 he became lecturer (preacher) at Lincoln. Shortly afterward Smyth adopted Separatist principles and joined the congregation at Gainsborough. In 1607 or 1608, probably because of the threat of persecution, Smyth moved with his congregation to Amsterdam, one of the few cities in Europe with almost complete religious freedom.

In Holland Smyth merged two lines of thought. The first was a logical elaboration of the Separatist position. If the Church of England was a false church, then the sacraments that it administered were also invalid. By this criterion the baptism* that Smyth and his people had received was invalid. At the same time Smyth began to visit with the Waterlander Mennonites. These Anabaptists* believed that baptism should be reserved for believers who made a public confession of faith. On this ground as well, Smyth reasoned that he and his people were not baptized. In 1609 Smyth acted on these convictions by baptizing himself and those members of the congregation who agreed with his position.

One year later (1610) Smyth began negotiating with the Mennonites to be received by them. These negotiations split the congregation. One part, led by Thomas Helwys,* returned to England in 1612 and founded a congregation at Spitalfields. This part of the congregation disagreed with the Mennonites' position on the lawfulness of oaths and with the Mennonite doctrine of the "celestial flesh" of Christ (the teaching that Christ's flesh had been specially created by the Father and owed nothing to Mary). Those who remained in Holland were received by the Mennonites after Smyth's death and eventually lost their separate identity.

BIBLIOGRAPHY. H. L. McBeth, *The Baptist Heritage* (1987).

G. T. Miller

Smyth and Helwys Publishing Company. A publishing house organized by Southern Baptist* moderates. The press, named for English Baptist founders John Smyth* and Thomas Helwys,* was founded in 1991 by Cecil Staton and Scott Nash, professors at Brewton-Parker College* in Georgia; James Pitts, chaplain at Furman University*; and Ronald D. Jackson. Its founding purpose was "to offer supplemental and alternative materials for

Baptists who have become increasingly concerned about the future direction of the [Southern Baptist] Convention Press and Broadman* [Press]." The concern was to publish materials for churches disturbed by the fundamentalist* control of the Southern Baptist Convention and provide a vehicle for Baptist authors whose works would probably not be published by SBC-related presses. In 1991 Smyth and Helwys Publishing began production of Formations, a graded Sunday-school curriculum written primarily, but not exclusively, for use in Baptist churches. Also in 1991 the company headquarters moved to Macon, Georgia, with Staton as publisher.

BIBLIOGRAPHY. C. Staton, "The History of Smyth & Helwys Publishing," in *The Struggle for the Soul of the SBC,* ed. W. Shurden (1993).

B. J. Leonard

Social Gospel, Baptist Views of the. Beginning in the early eighteenth century, Baptists in America responded to social needs and issues. Associations from 1720 to the 1830s debated resolutions on temperance, women's rights, membership in secret societies and the impact of new immigrants from Europe. Among the national societies, leaders of church associations reached various conclusions about Native American rights and slavery. Baptists in the Northern states articulated a progressive racial understanding when they supported the work of the American Baptist Home Mission Society* among the emancipated slaves.

A much-accelerated flow of social activism occurred in the 1890s, however, with the work of a seminary professor, Walter Rauschenbusch* of Rochester, New York. As a former pastor in New York's Lower East Side, Rauschenbusch had arrived at distressing conclusions about urban life and social injustice. He and a fraternity of international theorists called the Brotherhood of the Kingdom sought to reinstate the collective principle of the kingdom of God in contrast to contemporary emphases on individual salvation.

In 1907 Rauschenbusch published what would become the Baptist classic of the movement, *Christianity and the Social Crisis.* In it he called for a new definition of the kingdom of God: the reign of God in human affairs. He proposed that society be reorganized according to the will of God, by which he meant that urban poverty, the industrial system, the capitalist economy and the international order should be positively influenced by Christian principles. Both the church and the existing social order should be transformed, and Rauschenbusch thought the working classes the best instrument of social change. The ethics and example of Jesus were to be the model for the process of Christianizing the social order.

Rauschenbusch's writings had their greatest impact on the Northern Baptist Convention (NBC; *see* American Baptist Churches in the USA). Theologians and practioners like Henry Clay Vedder* of Crozer Seminary* and Samuel Zane Batten* of Philadelphia launched the Social Gospel into action. Batten was the catalyst for the formation of the Social Service Commission in 1909, and he later created the social policy of the NBC through the Department of Social Service and Brotherhood. Rauschenbusch's relatives and students also carried forth the principles of the Social Gospel, notably Dores R. Sharpe in the Cleveland Baptist City Society and John E. Clough,* who married Rauschenbusch's sister Emma and pioneered a new social plan among the Telugus in India.

The influence of the Social Gospel could be seen elsewhere in the Baptist family. Southern Baptists, influenced by educators like W. L. Poteat,* in 1907 approved a Committee on Civic Righteousness and, in 1914, a Social Service Commission.* Decades later, a national Christian Life Commission* evolved to help Southern Baptists apply Christian principles to social and moral problems like gambling, alcohol and pornography. In Canada the apostle of the Social Gospel was Tommy Douglas (1904-1984), who witnessed the plight of the working class on the Prairies during the Depression and ultimately produced a national health-care system and pension plan.

The Social Gospel has certainly had its critics in the Baptist family. Conservative writers have opposed the intrusion of Christians into the secular world, premillennialists have challenged the new interpretation of the kingdom of God, evangelicals have antithesized the Social Gospel with the "soul gospel," and capitalist thinkers have taken offense at the incursions of socialism.

BIBLIOGRAPHY. W. H. Brackney, *Baptist Life and Thought, 1600-1980* (1983); R. T. Handy, ed., *The Social Gospel in America, 1870-1920* (1966); P. J. Minus, *Walter Rauschenbusch: American Reformer* (1988); W. Rauschenbush, *Christianity and the Social Crisis* (1907); J. K. Zeman, ed., *Costly Vision: The Baptist Pilgrimage in Canada* (1988).

W. H. Brackney

Social Service Commission, The. Southern Baptist* ethics agency. The Southern Baptist Convention established the Commission on Civil Righteousness in 1907. Soon afterward the commission absorbed the older Committee on Temperance. The commission represented the impact of the Social Gospel* on Southern Baptist thinking. Many Baptists believed that the Social Service Commission was beyond the scope of the convention. But its supporters appealed to the Southern Baptist Convention's constitutional mandate to do whatever was needed to expand the Redeemer's kingdom.

The commission had three primary functions: to explore the moral demands of the gospel, to apply Christian principles to moral and social problems, and to promote temperance. Despite these high-sounding ideals, the work of the commission from 1908 to 1919 was largely confined to temperance, and alcohol and tobacco continue to be primary concerns.

The commission became more influential when J. B. Weatherspoon assumed the chair in 1942. In 1947 the commission circulated a statement on race relations that was preparatory for its leadership in the civil rights crisis of the 1950s. In 1953 the Social Service Commission became the Christian Life Commission.*

G. T. Miller

Soul-Saving Mission of the World. See NATIONAL BAPTIST EVANGELICAL LIFE AND SOUL-SAVING ASSEMBLY OF THE USA.

Southeastern Baptist Theological Seminary. A theological school owned by the Southern Baptist Convention* and located in Wake Forest, North Carolina. The seminary began in 1951 in the Music Building of Wake Forest College,* Wake Forest, North Carolina. It was approved by the Southern Baptist Convention in 1950 as a school that would serve the large numbers of Southern Baptists in the southeastern region of the United States and in response to requests for such an institution from North Carolina Baptists. Sydnor L. Stealey, a professor at Southern Baptist Theological Seminary,* was called as the first president. Stealey recommended that the "Abstract of Principles," the basic doctrinal statement of Southern Baptist Seminary, serve as the doctrinal guide for the new school. When Wake Forest College moved to Winston-Salem, North Carolina, the Wake Forest property was secured and renovated for the seminary in 1956.

The school experienced dramatic growth and by 1986 had an enrollment of more than 1,200 students. In 1987, as a result of the inerrancy controversy* in the Southern Baptist Convention, a fundamentalist*-dominated board of trustees came into conflict with faculty and administration. These differences led to the resignation of Randall Lolley, president of the school, and Morris Ashcraft, the seminary's dean. Faculty members organized a chapter affiliated with the American Association of University Professors and challenged trustee efforts to move the school in a more conservative theological direction. Lewis Drummond was appointed to succeed Lolley. He was succeeded in 1992 by Paige Patterson, president of Criswell College,* Dallas, Texas. In time most of the "moderate" Baptist faculty left the school, which, under Drummond and Patterson, has moved toward a fundamentalist-conservative faculty and orientation. In 1993 the seminary enrolled over 500 students.

BIBLIOGRAPHY. *ESB* 2, 4; B. J. Leonard, *God's Last and Only Hope: The Fragmentation of the Southern Baptist Convention* (1990).

B. J. Leonard

Southern Baptist Alliance. See ALLIANCE OF BAPTISTS.

Southern Baptist College. See WILLIAMS COLLEGE.

Southern Baptist Conference on the Faith of the Founders. This conference, targeting Southern Baptist* pastors, has met yearly since 1983. The clear agenda of the conference is the proposition that evangelical Calvinism* is the most consistent and historically defensible theology for Southern Baptists. Each conference consists of a variety of presentations (historical, exegetical, practical and doctrinal) aimed at the experiential and pastoral application of the doctrines of grace. After meeting since 1983 at Southwestern College in Memphis, Tennessee, the conference began meeting in 1991 on the campus of Samford University* in Birmingham, Alabama. A quarterly journal entitled *The Founders Journal*, edited by Tom Ascol, constitutes the publishing ministry of the conference.

BIBLIOGRAPHY. *The Founders Journal.*

T. J. Nettles

Southern Baptist Convention. Largest Baptist body in the United States. The Southern Baptist Convention (SBC) comprises 15 million baptized believers in 38,000 churches in all fifty states, making it the nation's largest Protestant denomination. Approximately half of all Baptists in the United States belong to churches affiliated with the Southern Baptist Convention.

The convention was organized on May 8, 1845, in Augusta, Georgia. Its separation from the General Missionary Convention of the Baptist Denomination in the United States for Foreign Missions (Triennial Convention*) and the American Baptist Home Mission Society* was due to issues arising out of the abolition movement. Other factors, such as the freedom to carry on missionary activities without regard to the slavery issue and differences over the nature of denominational structure, also contributed.

Theologically, most Southern Baptists are evangelicals and subscribe to the authority of the Bible in determining their ecclesiology* and social action. They baptize* by immersion believers who publicly profess faith, but they hold that neither baptism nor the Lord's Supper* conveys sacramental grace. A heavy evangelistic emphasis has helped to shape the denomination into one of the most aggressive missionary bodies in Christendom. In their doctrine of salvation, Southern Baptists can be generally classified as modified Calvinists,* being heirs of the Free Church tradition which includes both Calvinist and Arminian* strains. Southern Baptists are not bound by a creed, but share a confession of faith* (based on the New Hampshire Confession*) first adopted by the convention in 1925 and revised in 1963.

Southern Baptist worship* is nonliturgical. Preaching is the central act of worship while music constitutes an important element in the worship life of the churches. Great emphasis is placed upon congregational singing. Many churches have a graded choir program and some feature orchestras in addition to pianos, organs and bell choirs.

A strong congregational ecclesiology coupled with a sense of destiny and a conservative theology have helped to determine the convention's relationship with other Christian communions. Southern Baptists have steadfastly refused to join the National* and World Councils of Churches.* Its agencies, however, cooperate with various programs of the National Council of Churches on projects of mutual interest. The Southern Baptist Convention took the lead in bringing disparate Baptist unions and conventions together into the Baptist World Alliance* in 1905.

The organization of the SBC seems simple but is, in reality, very complex. Southern Baptists jealously guard the autonomy of the local church. The local church is the highest judicature in Southern Baptist life. Yet the principle of cooperation commands the loyalty of most Southern Baptists. Local congregations are related to the SBC in the same way they are related to the state conventions and local associations. Congregations also send messengers to area associations and state conventions, each of which is an autonomous body but closely related to the others. The state conventions sponsor educational and benevolent institutions, such as hospitals, orphanages and retirement villages, as well as mission programs within their respective states.

The relationship between the congregations, the state convention and the SBC is both voluntary and financial. Churches may send to the annual meeting of the SBC up to ten "messengers." The number is determined by the size of church membership and the amount of money given to denominational causes. The messengers then report back to their churches on the actions of the annual meeting. The convention has no authority over the churches but is free to recommend and promote convention-wide programs. The churches then may support either completely or partially the programs recommended by the associations, state conventions and the SBC. Without the cooperation and financial support of the local churches the SBC could not function. The work of the convention is delegated to four boards, seven commissions and six seminaries. Of these agencies the Foreign and Home Mission Boards sponsor 7,556 missionaries (1987). Missionary work in the U.S. is performed in eighty-seven different languages under the direction of the Home Mission Board. In 1987 the Foreign Mission Board supported 3,816 missionaries who served in 108 countries.

Responsibility for colleges and seminaries of the denomination is divided between the SBC which sponsors the seminaries and the state conventions that operate the colleges and universities. For the 1986-1987 school year, the fifty-one colleges enrolled 161,108 students and the six seminaries had a total enrollment of 10,910.

Since 1979, the SBC has experienced a period of significant upheaval and division within its ranks related to the questions of biblical inerrancy (*see* "Inerrancy Controversy," SBC), socio-political agendas and denominational control. While no formal schism has occurred, significant fragmentation has taken place at almost every level of denominational life.

See also BAPTIST CHURCHES.

BIBLIOGRAPHY. R. A. Baker, *The Southern Baptist Convention and Its People, 1607-1972* (1974); W. Barnes, *The Southern Baptist Convention* (1954); *ESB* 1-4; H. L. McBeth, *The Baptist Heritage* (1987); *Southern Baptist Convention Annual* (1986).   W. R. Estep

Southern Baptist Theological Seminary. The first of six Southern Baptist seminaries. Founded in Greenville, South Carolina, in 1859 with four faculty members—James Pedigru Boyce,* John Albert Broadus,* Basil Manly Jr.* and William Williams*—the seminary had to shut its doors during the Civil War but reopened in 1866. In 1877 the seminary moved to Louisville, Kentucky, where it could obtain better financial support, and enrollment quickly increased. Always in a precarious position financially, it was rocked by a controversy over Baptist origins when church historian William H. Whitsitt,* the third president (1859-1899), refuted the theory of Baptist church succession from apostolic times to the present. Under E. Y. Mullins* (1899-1928) the seminary regained its equilibrium and became the largest Protestant seminary in the world. Originally located near the center of Louisville, it was moved in 1926 to its present location. The timing of the move and extensive building programs just before Mullins's death in 1928 as the Great Depression struck placed a great strain on its resources, but the debt was paid off during the presidencies of John R. Sampey* (1929-1942) and Ellis Fuller* (1942-1950). Early in the presidency of Duke K. McCall (1951-1982), the seminary experienced another severe test as a result of changes in style of administration resisted by the faculty. It encountered another crisis when fundamentalists established control over its board of trustees during the presidency of Roy L. Honeycutt (1982-1993). Albert Mohler was named president in 1993. In 1992 the seminary enrolled more than 2,000 students.

BIBLIOGRAPHY. *ESB* 2:1269-73, 3:1978-83; W. A. Mueller, *A History of the Southern Baptist Theological Seminary* (1959).

E. G. Hinson

Southern Baptist Women in Ministry. An organization for Southern Baptist* women ministers, ordained and unordained, and their supporters. At the 1982 Theology Is a Verb conference in Charlotte, North Carolina, Nancy Hastings Sehested called for an organization and a newsletter to provide support for Southern Baptist women ministers. After a series of informal planning meetings, Southern Baptist Women in Ministry (SBWIM, originally Women in Ministry, SBC) held its first meeting prior to the 1983 Southern Baptist Convention meeting in Pittsburgh, Pennsylvania. SBWIM continued to meet prior to the SBC meetings until 1991, when annual gatherings were rescheduled to coincide with the Cooperative Baptist Fellowship* assembly. SBWIM has become a nonprofit organization affiliated with the Cooperative Baptist Fellowship and the Alliance of Baptists.* It holds annual meetings for business and worship, sponsors a fall retreat and publishes *Folio,* a quarterly newsletter. Between meetings, the executive board oversees the work of the organization.

BIBLIOGRAPHY. E. S. Bellinger, "More Hidden Than Revealed: A History of Southern Baptist Women in Ministry," in *The Struggle for the Soul of the SBC,* ed. W. Shurden (1993).

R. S. Autry

Southern Christian Leadership Conference. An organization advocating nonviolent social change, particularly in the area of civil rights. Although it was only one of several local desegregation campaigns of the mid-1950s, the Montgomery bus boycott of 1955-1956 was distinctive as the triggering event in the formation of a Southwide nonviolent movement. Sparked by the refusal of Rosa Parks, a black seamstress, to yield her bus seat to a white man as law and custom required, the 381-day boycott led by the Montgomery Improvement Association (MIA) became both a model and an experiential center for the convergence of many local efforts. In January 1957 some sixty people, mostly black ministers, met at the Ebenezer Baptist Church in Atlanta to consider the possibility of continuing the "Montgomery way" in an organized regional association. Subsequent meetings in New Orleans and Montgomery in the same year resulted in the formation of the Southern Christian Leadership Conference (SCLC). Martin Luther King Jr.,* pastor of the Dexter Avenue Baptist Church in Montgomery and president of MIA, was elected president of SCLC.

The guiding principle of SCLC was nonviolence, derived in part from the tactics of Mohandas K. (Mahatma) Gandhi in India, but in a broader sense from the religious faith of its members. The SCLC chose not to be a membership organization but a loose network of "affiliates." At the outset SCLC, with its headquarters on Auburn Avenue in Atlanta, had affiliates in eleven states.

SCLC is best known for its leadership of nonviolent campaigns in Albany (1962), Birmingham (1963), St. Augustine (1964) and Selma (1965). The Birmingham and Selma campaigns were very instrumental in moving Congress to enact the 1964 Civil Rights Act and the 1965 Voting Rights Act. But SCLC also had significant impact through its programs of educational and economic improvement. After 1965 SCLC's efforts to extend its outreach into Chicago (1966) and other Northern cities had less obvious results. King's death slowed the momentum of both the nonviolent movement and SCLC. His successor, Ralph David Abernathy* (president from 1968 to 1977), continued the basic program of nonviolent direct action. Abernathy was succeeded by Joseph E. Lowery, a Methodist minister who began a rebuilding program that had visible results by the end of the seventies. In the early 1980s SCLC campaigned for extension of the Voting Rights Act (1982) and a variety of economic and social reforms. Youth programs were expanded, and SCLC/WOMEN was added. Occasionally SCLC also spoke out on foreign affairs issues, as King had done in opposing the Vietnam War.

BIBLIOGRAPHY. A. Fairclough, *To Redeem the Soul of America: The Southern Christian Leadership Conference and Martin Luther King Jr.* (1987); D. J. Garrow, *Bearing the Cross: Martin Luther King Jr. and the Southern Christian Leadership Conference* (1986); T. R. Peake, *Keeping the Dream Alive: A History of the Southern Christian Leadership Conference from King to the Nineteen-Eighties* (1987).

T. R. Peake

Southwest Baptist University. Liberal arts university affiliated with the Missouri Baptist Convention. The university, located at Bolivar, Missouri, was chartered in 1878 as Southwest Baptist College and opened that same year in Lebanon, Missouri. One year later the college was moved to Bolivar. J. R. Maupin and A. S. Ingman were the school's founders and first presidents. In 1906 the college was forced to surrender its property to

creditors and close. Baptists in Bolivar reopened the school as a junior college in 1913. Since 1928 the college has been owned and controlled by the Missouri Baptist Convention. The college was granted accreditation as a junior college in 1957 and as a four-year institution in 1970. The Missouri Baptist Convention approved the change of the institution's name to Southwest Baptist University (SBU) in 1980. Under the leadership of James L. Sells (president 1968-1979 and chancellor from 1979), SBU has experienced significant growth in the areas of campus development, academic programs and enrollment. The university was included in the John Templeton Foundation Honor Roll of colleges for 1990. SBU has 92 full-time faculty members, 2,918 students enrolled in undergraduate programs and 140 graduate students.

BIBLIOGRAPHY. *ESB* 4:2482-83.

A. L. Pratt

Southwestern Baptist Theological Seminary. Southwestern Baptist Theological Seminary grew out of Baylor University's* department of theology. By 1905 the department had become the Baylor Theological Seminary. The seminary was separated from Baylor University and received a charter under its present name from the State of Texas three years later, on March 14, 1908. In 1910 Southwestern was moved from Waco to Fort Worth, Texas. Although the seminary was affiliated with the Baptist General Convention of Texas, in 1925 ownership of the school was transferred to the Southern Baptist Convention.* Consequently the seminary made the convention's articles of faith, "The Baptist Faith and Message,"* its own. Revised in 1963, this confession continues to serve as the seminary's confessional statement.

From its beginning, the seminary's purpose has been to prepare men and women for vocational Christian ministry. Southwestern is organized into three schools (Theology, Religious Education and Church Music), each with its own faculty and degree programs. Through the years the student body has become increasingly international and interdenominational. In 1991 forty-five different countries were represented in the multiethnic student body, and some thirty-eight denominations. During 1991, 4,034 students were enrolled in classes taught on the main campus and in five off-campus centers. By December 1991 the seminary had graduated a total of 29,843 students.

BIBLIOGRAPHY. *ESB* 2:1275-84.

W. R. Estep

Southwestern Baptist University. *See* UNION
UNIVERSITY.

Southwestern Journal of Theology. Baptist
periodical. In April 1917 the faculty of Southwestern Baptist Theological Seminary* voted to inau-
gurate the *Southwestern Journal of Theology.*
C. B. Williams became the first managing editor.
However, after seven years the *Journal* proved
financially unfeasible. It ceased publication in
1924.

After a hiatus of thirty-four years, the faculty of
the School of Theology voted to reestablish the
Journal James Leo Garrett became the managing
editor of the revived publication. The reappear-
ance of the *Journal* was in response to a need for
a medium through which the faculty could serve
the alumni of the seminary and others. The *Journal* is published three times a year with a circulation of 4,100. A third to a half of each issue is
devoted to book reviews.

BIBLIOGRAPHY. *ESB* 2:1284, 3:1986-87, 4:2485-86.

W. R. Estep

Southwide Baptist Fellowship. A fundamentalist* Baptist organization. In 1956 Lee Roberson,
pastor of the Highland Park Baptist Church of
Chattanooga, Tennessee, and founder of Tennessee Temple Schools, founded the Southern
Baptist Fellowship. The membership consisted
primarily of independent Baptists* and fundamentalist Southern Baptists. In 1963 the organization changed its name to Southwide Baptist Fellowship (SBF).

The SBF is militant, separatistic and premillennial. Its early leaders were famous for their independence, aggressive evangelism and massive
bus ministries. Among these were Roberson;
John R. Rice,* colleague of J. Frank Norris* and
editor of *The Sword of the Lord;* Chicago pastor
Wayne Van Gelderen; and Florida pastor Bob
Gray. At times the 50,000-member First Baptist
Church of Hammond, Indiana, has associated
with SBF.

Headquartered in Laurens, South Carolina, and
drawing most of its support from the South, SBF
currently includes about 2,000 congregations.

BIBLIOGRAPHY. *EAR* 1:381.

T. P. Weber

Speer, Jacob (1801-1884). Elder Jacob Speer,
an influential pastor and a founding father of the
General Association of General Baptists,* was
born in North Carolina in 1801. After a brief attempt at a military career and a conversion in
Tennessee in 1817, he joined a United Baptist
church. The church split over the general atonement issue; Speer stayed with the newly formed
Brawley's Fork Church of Separate Baptists in the
Concord Association of Separate Baptists, who licensed him to preach.

Speer moved to Gibson County, Indiana, in
1829 and began preaching near Princeton. After a
return to Tennessee for ordination, he came back
to Princeton and organized the Enon Baptist
Church.

Following a meeting with Benoni Stinson,*
Speer and congregation joined the newly formed
Liberty Association of General Baptists in 1831.
Before his death on October 13, 1884, Speer was
instrumental in the constitution of seventeen
churches and three associations.

BIBLIOGRAPHY. A. D. Williams, *Benoni Stinson
and the General Baptists* (1892).

L. C. Shull

Spelman College. A black college established
by the Woman's American Baptist Home Mission
Society,* formerly Atlanta Baptist Female Seminary and now Spelman College. It was founded
in 1881 in Atlanta, Georgia, when Frank Quarles,
pastor of the African-American congregation of
Friendship Baptist Church, agreed to let two
white Northern Baptist women, Sophia B. Packard
and Harriet E. Giles, use the basement of the
church to establish a school for African-American
women recently freed from slavery. Almost 100
years later, in 1987, Johnnetta B. Cole was elected
president of Spelman—the first African-American
woman to serve in this capacity. In 1929 Spelman
joined with Morehouse College* and Atlanta University to establish the Atlanta University Center.
Nationally recognized as the oldest and largest
historically black, private, undergraduate liberal
arts woman's college, Spelman has a full-time enrollment of around 1,700. Today Spelman boasts
an International Affairs Center that prepares African-American women to enter the private and international job markets; the Women's Research
and Resource Center for curriculum development
in women's studies, focusing on women of color,
community outreach and research; and the first
law school established in a black college.

BIBLIOGRAPHY. M. N. K. Collison, "At Spelman,"
Chronicle for Higher Education 34 (1987); W. A.
Daniel, *The Education of Negro Ministers* (1925);

J. H. Franklin, *From Slavery to Freedom* (1967); S. D. Martin, "The American Baptist Home Mission Society and Black Higher Education in the South, 1865-1920," *Foun* 24 (1981); S. D. Martin, "Spelman's Emma B. DeLaney and the African Mission," *JRT* 41 (1984); *The Spelman Messenger.*

P. R. Pleasants

Spirituality, Baptist Approaches. The voluntary* principle which stands at the center of the Baptist tradition has encouraged diversity of practice in spirituality throughout Baptist history. (1) Some Baptists use chiefly an *institutional* approach, majoring on attendance at Sunday school and church. Chief elements in the cultivation of the inner life would be Bible study, preaching, hymn singing, corporate prayer and fellowship. Most would also have some family devotions, such as prayer at mealtimes. (2) On the opposite end of the spectrum, others emphasize the *experiential,* whether individually or corporately. Often attracting persons of lower socioeconomic status, these Baptists have valued responsiveness to the Spirit in prayer, singing and preaching and have looked with some suspicion on more formal styles. Revivalism on the American frontier fostered an approach similar to that seen today among Pentecostals. (3) Widespread suspicion of intellectuals notwithstanding, some Baptists take an essentially *scholastic* approach to spirituality, emphasizing assent to doctrinal propositions rather than religious experience or attendance at church. (4) Still others underscore the importance of *social* fellowship, service or activity. Baptists have often said, "It is not what you believe but how you live that counts! If you don't live it, you don't really believe it." Out of this tradition have emerged some notable Baptist social reformers such as William Knibb, Walter Rauschenbusch,* Clarence Jordan* and Martin Luther King Jr.* (5) Where their spirituality has been most wholesome and vital, Baptists have probably achieved some balance between all four approaches.

BIBLIOGRAPHY. W. L. Allen, "Spirituality Among Southern Baptist Clergy As Reflected in Selected Autobiographies" (Ph.D. dissertation, Southern Baptist Seminary, 1984); E. G. Hinson, "Baptist and Quaker Spirituality," in *Christian Spirituality,* ed. L. Dupre and D. E. Saliers (1989); B. J. Leonard, *Becoming Christian: Dimensions of Spiritual Formation* (1990).

E. G. Hinson

Spurgeon, Charles Haddon (1834-1892). Spurgeon was among the most gifted and popular Baptist preachers of all time. His unusual ability to preach with great appeal to the masses, his administrative talents and his literary skill built him a worldwide reputation.

Spurgeon was born in Kelvedon, in Essex, England. He was deeply influenced by his grandfather, who was pastor of an independent church in Stambourne. He dated his conversion to a worship service in a Methodist chapel in Colchester on January 6, 1850. At the age of sixteen he became a Baptist.

After short periods as assistant pastor of the St. Andrews Street Baptist Church in Cambridge and as pastor of the Baptist Church at Waterbeach, he was invited to become pastor of the historic Baptist congregation in Southwark, London. The church, which had been decreasing in numbers, immediately began to grow. In 1861 the Metropolitan Tabernacle was built to accommodate the large numbers, and it was later enlarged.

Spurgeon's sermons and commentaries still maintain a large readership. He founded Spurgeon's College, edited a monthly magazine known as the *Sword and Trowel* and established two orphanages. Theologically conservative, he was unhappy with the theological direction of the Baptist Union and separated from it in 1887 after what has become known as the Downgrade Controversy. Spurgeon's sermons were widely circulated in America. His library is now housed at William Jewell College,* Independence, Missouri.

BIBLIOGRAPHY. C. H. Spurgeon, *The "Downgrade" Controversy* (1978).

T. R. McKibbens

Staughton, William (1770-1829). Pastor and educator. William Staughton was a significant link between the Baptist communities of Great Britain and North America. He was also a prime mover in the development of Baptist voluntary societies.

Staughton emerged on the scene as the youngest member of the organizing group for the Baptist Missionary Society at Kettering, England, in 1792. He was acquainted with William Carey,* Andrew Fuller, John Ryland and John Sutcliff. He was an obvious choice when Richard Furman* of South Carolina wrote for pastoral assistance in 1793.

Staughton did not remain long in South Carolina. He eventually became pastor at First Baptist

Church, Philadelphia,* where he earned a high reputation as an orator. While at Sansom Street Church in that city, he was called to be president of Columbian College* in Washington, D.C., and in 1829 he was called to the same position at Georgetown College in Kentucky.

Staughton used his considerable organizational gifts and British experience to give shape to the early American Baptist voluntary societies. He was the first secretary of the General Missionary Convention, and he organized the first Baptist theological school in America at his Philadelphia home in 1812. He died December 12, 1829.

BIBLIOGRAPHY. W. H. Brackney, *The Baptists* (1988); W. L. Staughton, *Memoir of the Rev. William Staughton, D.D.* (1834).

W. H. Brackney

Stealey, Clarence Perry (1868-1937). Southern Baptist* minister, editor, creedalist and fundamentalist* leader. The pastor of First Baptist Church, Martinsburg, West Virginia (1896-1901), Broadus Memorial Church, Richmond, Virginia (1901-1905), West Washington Baptist Church, Washington, D.C. (1905-1909), and Hudson Avenue Baptist Church, Oklahoma City, Oklahoma (1929-1937), Stealey is primarily remembered as the founder (1912) and editor (1912-1928) of the *Baptist Messenger,* the Oklahoma Baptist newspaper. Through the pages of the *Messenger* he became, along with J. Frank Norris,* the primary Southern Baptist fundamentalist leader of the 1920s. The fact that he, unlike Norris, stayed within the Southern Baptist Convention caused him to have more direct and lasting influence on the convention than Norris. His fight against evolution made him the "father of Southern Baptist creedalism." He was the primary force in 1925 behind the adoption of the convention's first major confession,* the Baptist Faith and Message. Even that confession failed to satisfy Stealey's concerns, so he spearheaded the adoption of the McDaniel Statement, an antievolution statement adopted by the Southern Baptist Convention in 1926.

BIBLIOGRAPHY. D. W. Downs, "The McDaniel Statement: An Investigation of Creedalism in the Southern Baptist Convention" (Th.M. thesis, Southern Baptist Theological Seminary, 1980); W. B. Shurden, "Southern Baptist Responses to Their Confessional Statements," *RE* 76 (Winter 1979):69-84.

W. B. Shurden

Stearns, Shubal (1706-1771). Separate Baptist* leader in North Carolina. Born in Boston, Stearns moved in his youth to Tolland, Connecticut, where he joined the Congregational church. During George Whitefield's second tour of New England in 1745, Stearns was converted. In 1751, after a thorough study of the Scriptures, he became a Baptist and persuaded enough of his fellow church members to withdraw from Congregationalism to form a Baptist church in Tolland. In May the church ordained Stearns as pastor. He served the church for three years.

Seeking a special place to preach the gospel, Stearns moved first to Virginia; then, when he received word about the spiritual hunger of people in the Piedmont section of North Carolina, he moved there. Late in 1755 Stearns led a company of fifteen, including his sister Martha Marshall* and brother-in-law Daniel Marshall,* to Sandy Creek in Guilford (now Randolph) County, North Carolina. Within three years the Sandy Creek Church, started by the New Englanders, had planted two sister churches and formed the Sandy Creek Association.

The key to the growth of these Separate Baptists in the South was Stearns's itinerant ministry. Although he lacked formal preparation for the ministry, he was a man of vision, action and unusual preaching skill. Baptist historian Morgan Edwards* reports that his voice was "musical and strong" and he could use it "to make soft impressions on the heart" or "to throw the animal system into tumults."

Stearns died in 1771, completing his sixteen-year mission to the South. The next year his associates counted 42 churches and 125 ministers who had arisen from the Sandy Creek Church.

BIBLIOGRAPHY. *DAB* IX; *DARB;* M. Edwards, *Materials Towards a History of the Baptists,* 2 vols. (1770-1792); W. L. Lumpkin, *Baptist Foundations in the South* (1961).

B. L. Shelley

Steele, Anne (Theodosia) (1717-1778). Baptist hymnwriter. Born in Broughton, Hampshire, England, in 1717, Steele was the daughter of farmer, timber merchant and Baptist minister William Steele and Anne (Fround) Steele. Apart from a brief period when she attended a boarding school in Salisbury, she lived in Broughton until her death on November 11, 1778. She was baptized on July 9, 1732. Although for most of her life she experienced poor health, she became widely known and appreciated by evangelicals in Britain and America for her religious verse.

In 1760 *Poems on Subjects Chiefly Devotional* by Theodosia was published. In 1780 it was reprinted with a volume called *Miscellaneous Pieces.* Many of Steele's hymns were included in hymn collections that were used by Baptists in Britain and America in the eighteenth and nineteenth centuries.

BIBLIOGRAPHY. J. Ivimey, *History of the English Baptists* (1811) 4:312; Steele Papers, Angus Library, Regent's Park College, Oxford.

K. Smith

Stetson University. Baptist college in DeLand, Florida. Stetson University was established in 1883 by the joint efforts of Henry A. Deland and the Florida Baptist Convention. It includes a college of arts and sciences, a school of business, a school of music, and a college of law. First known as DeLand College, it was renamed John B. Stetson University in 1889 because of the generous support of John B. Stetson, a hat manufacturer from Philadelphia. The school charter centers control in a president, who must be Baptist, and trustees, three-quarters of whom must be Baptists.

Under president John F. Forbes (1883-1904), gifts came from Henry M. Flagler, Andrew Carnegie and John D. Rockefeller Sr., and students were exchanged with the University of Chicago.

President Lincoln B. Hulley (1904-1934) saw the student body grow to 500, accreditation obtained, and the College of Law recognized by the American Bar Association. When William Sims Allen was president (1934-1947), the departments of music and business became coordinate colleges. President J. Ollie Edmunds (1948-1967) brought considerable growth to the school, and the law school was relocated in St. Petersburg. Paul Geren served as president from 1967 to 1969 and was followed by John E. Johns (1970-1976), Pope A. Duncan (1977-1987) and H. Douglas Lee (1987-). The annual budget was over $45 million in 1991, the endowment nearly $37 million, and enrollment around 3,000.

BIBLIOGRAPHY. *ESB* 2:1298-1300, 3:1988-89, 4:2488-89; "The President's Annual Report to the Board of Trustees," *Stetson University Bulletin,* 1991; Stetson University Budget Request, 1991.

E. E. Joiner

Stewardship Commission, SBC. Southern Baptist Convention* (SBC) agency with three program assignments: stewardship development, Cooperative Program promotion, and endowment and capital giving. Chartered in 1960, the commission began full operation in 1961. The agency supports the SBC by assisting churches in leading their members to become good stewards of their possessions. It assists the SBC and Baptist state conventions in raising funds to finance their ministries, including support for the Cooperative Program,* the SBC's primary mission support system, and endowment and capital giving. Promotion of Together We Build, a program designed to help churches raise money for building projects, is the main emphasis of the endowment and capital giving program. Consultants from this program have helped more than 1,600 Southern Baptist churches raise over $6 billion for building and debt-retirement programs. The commission also works with Baptist foundations to encourage church members to invest in God's work through estate planning and wills.

The agency finances its work through Cooperative Program gifts from churches, sales of materials and fees. Commission executives have included Merrill D. Moore (1961-1971), James V. Lackey (1971-1973) and A. R. Fagan (1974-). Commission offices are located in the SBC Building in Nashville, Tennessee.

BIBLIOGRAPHY. *ESB* 3:1989-92, 4:2489.

C. W. Deweese

Stillman, Samuel (1737-1807). Baptist minister. Born and raised in Charleston, South Carolina, in an environment that fostered moral and intellectual growth, Stillman was converted under the preaching of Oliver Hart* and directed his education toward preparation for the ministry. He preached his first sermon in 1758, was ordained the next year and immediately began work as an evangelist. Stillman became pastor on James Island, near Charleston, and served there for about two years. During this period he traveled to Philadelphia, where he met and married the daughter of John Morgan, a noted physician and professor of medicine. While in the region he was awarded honorary degrees from the College of Philadelphia and from Harvard.

In 1761 Stillman moved to Bordertown, New Jersey, and in 1763 to Boston, where he assisted the pastor of Second Baptist Church. In 1765 he became pastor of First Baptist Church of Boston, a post he occupied for the rest of his life. His forty-two-year pastorate was regarded as a remarkable success. The church was in decline when he arrived, but Stillman's emphasis on evangelism and a number of successful revivals ushered in extended periods of growth and progress. The church was held in high regard and was visited by presidents, generals and governors. Stillman died on March 12, 1807, after suffering a paralyzing stroke.

BIBLIOGRAPHY. *AAP* 6; I. Backus, *A History of New England with Particular Reference to the Denomination of Christians Called Baptists* (1871); *DAB* IX.   F. A. Teague

Stinson, Benoni (1798-1869). Elder Benoni Stinson, the founding father of the General Association of General Baptists,* was born on December 10, 1798, in Montgomery County, Kentucky. Raised in difficult circumstances with apparently little education, Stinson was converted, was baptized and in 1820 joined a United Baptist church in Wayne County, Kentucky. On November 1, 1821, he was ordained and accepted the pastorate of the Liberty Church. In 1822 Stinson and his family moved to Vanderburgh County, Indiana, where he joined a new church, New Hope, of the Wabash District Association of United Baptists. There Stinson found Calvinism* to be much more extreme than in Kentucky, where the United Baptists allowed the merger statement "Christ tasted death for every man, shall beno [sic] bearer [sic] to communion." As a delegate to form a new association, Stinson, a strong proponent of general atonement, could not get the statement inserted in the new constitution.

In the fall of 1823 Stinson and half of the New Hope group received permission to "letter-off" and begin a new congregation, the Liberty Church of Christ. Stinson was chosen pastor, and the statement that "Christ tasted death for every man" was adopted. Other groups soon followed suit. In October of 1824, Liberty and three other churches organized the Liberty Association of General Baptists.

The remainder of Stinson's life was spent in preaching and organizing churches. He died in October 1869, just one year prior to the establishment of the General Association of General Baptists in 1870.

BIBLIOGRAPHY. O. Latch, *History of the General Baptists* (1954); L. C. Shull, *The God of Our Fathers* (1983); A. D. Williams, *Benoni Stinson and the General Baptists* (1892).

L. C. Shull

Stow, Baron Steuben (1801-1869). Pastor and missionary statesman. Born June 16, 1801, Baron Stow left his harsh upbringing in New Hampshire to become one of the first graduates of Columbian College* in 1825. The collapse of this first national Baptist institution caused Stow much grief, and he held Luther Rice* accountable for its demise.

During his long tenures in Baldwin Place (1832-1848) and Rowe Street (1848-1867) Baptist churches in Boston, Stow energetically advocated the New England single-purpose, voluntary society plan for benevolent work. His chief interest was in foreign missions,* and he served on the board of the American Foreign Mission Society for twenty-nine years. When the Southern Baptist* board was formed in 1845, it was Stow's plan for a reconstituted American Baptist Missionary Union (*see* American Baptist Foreign Mission Society) that prevailed.

BIBLIOGRAPHY. W. H. Brackney, *The Baptists* (1988); J. C. Stockbridge, *A Memoir of the Life and Correspondence of Rev. Baron Stow, D.D.* (1894).   W. H. Brackney

Stowe, Phineas (1812-1868). Leading Bethel missionary among Boston Baptists. Born in Milford, Connecticut, and educated at the New Hampton Literary and Theological Institute, Stowe served briefly as pastor of the Baptist Church in South Danvers, Massachusetts (1843-1845), before entering "Bethel" work. Many nineteenth-century denominations sponsored Bethel ministries, which included evangelizing sailors, running hospitals and orphanages, and working with prisoners. Stowe pioneered Bethel work among Baptists by forming the Boston Baptist Bethel Society in 1845. With that firm financial base, Stowe founded the Mariner's Exchange, which contained a library, place for worship and kitchen; Quincy House, a halfway house for troubled youth; the Washington Home of Boston for the treatment of alcoholics; and other specialized ministries for prostitutes and gamblers. Stowe's work proves that in the mid-nineteenth century, Baptists could combine evangelistic and social ministries.

BIBLIOGRAPHY. W. H. Brackney, *The Baptists* (1988); H. A. Cooke, *Phineas Stowe and Bethel Work* (1874).   T. P. Weber

Straton, John Roach (1875-1929). Fundamentalist* preacher and social rights activist. Born in

Evansville, Indiana, Straton attended Mercer University* and the Southern Baptist Theological Seminary.* He was ordained a Baptist minister in 1900, later holding pastorates in Maryland, Virginia and Illinois (1905-1917) prior to his outspoken ministry at Calvary Baptist Church, New York City (1918-1929). There he championed Christian fundamentals from the pulpit and founded the Fundamentalist League of Greater New York (1922).

Straton's attack on modernism and his antidenominational policies led to tension within the Baptist World Alliance* and his own withdrawal from the Northern Baptist Convention in 1926 (see American Baptist Churches in the USA). Straton fought political corruption, sought justice for minorities and encouraged censorship of entertainment. In his preaching and social activism he made wide use of the media, including pioneer work in radio broadcasting. His books outline a vision of the kingdom of God on earth, differing from that of Walter Rauschenbusch* in its emphasis on a deeper reality accorded to "regeneration, not reform; soteriology, not sociology." This combination of emphases earned him the titles "Pope of fundamentalism" and "prophet of social righteousness."

BIBLIOGRAPHY. *DAB* IX; C. A. Russell, *Voices of American Fundamentalism: Seven Biographical Studies* (1976).   R. L. Petersen

Strict and Particular Baptists. British and American Baptist general body, also called Gospel Standard Baptists. Arising in opposition to the modified Calvinism* of Andrew Fuller, this Calvinistic group became a distinct entity in mid-nineteenth-century England. Early leaders included William Gadsby, John Kershaw and John Warburton, some of whose books are still available in the United States. In America similar groups are called Reformed* or Sovereign Grace* Baptists and number at least 8,250 members in 275 churches.

BIBLIOGRAPHY. R. G. Gardner, "Baptist General Bodies in the USA," *BHH* 19 (October 1984); S. F. Paul, *Historical Sketch of the Gospel Standard Baptists* (1945); J. Zens, *Reformed and Sovereign Grace Baptists* (1983).

R. G. Gardner

Strong, Augustus Hopkins (1836-1921). Northern Baptist (see American Baptist Churches in the USA) theologian. Born in Rochester, New York, the son of a wealthy newspaperman, the brother of the founder and president of the Eastman Kodak Company and a close friend of John D. Rockefeller, Strong moved easily among the rich and powerful. He bore an authoritative if not aristocratic demeanor that propelled him into positions of ecclesiastical and academic leadership.

After graduating from Yale College in 1857 and Rochester Theological Seminary* in 1859, Strong briefly served Baptist churches in Haverhill, Massachusetts, and Cleveland, Ohio. In 1872 he moved back to Rochester, where he spent the next forty years as president of the seminary and professor of systematic theology. During those years he also served as president of numerous organizations such as the American Baptist Foreign Mission Society* (1892-1895) and the General Convention of Baptists of North America (1905-1910). From about 1885 to 1910 Strong reigned as the most influential Northern Baptist and one of the most influential conservative Protestant theologians in the United States.

Generations of Protestant seminarians began their study of theology with Strong's *Systematic Theology*. First published in 1876, this substantial volume passed through eight editions and thirty printings. But his most creative and speculative work appeared in a series of essays published as *Christ in Creation and Ethical Monism* (1899). Here Strong articulated an idealist metaphysical position similar to those propounded by Hemann Lotze in Germany and Borden Parker Bowne at Boston University. Throughout his long life Strong endeavored to avoid theological controversy, but by 1916 his apprehension over the havoc that modernism seemed to be wreaking on the mission* field prompted him to publish *A Tour of the Missions*. The uncharacteristically polemical tone of this volume, coupled with its revelations of theological drift among Baptist foreign missionaries, did more than a little to precipitate the fundamentalist*-modernist controversy in the 1920s.

Assessments of Strong's work have varied. Some have labeled him an early fundamentalist, others have understood him to be a closet liberal, and still others have concluded he was simply confused. The best explanation seems to be that as he grew older and confronted biblical higher criticism and the arguments for human evolution, he changed his mind in key respects. There is no evidence that he ever seriously compromised, much less jettisoned, any of the cardinal doctrines of Reformed orthodoxy, but he did come to believe that the epistemic foundations of all doctrines, including his own, were conditioned by the historical setting in which they had emerged. So for Strong the challenge was to hold the faith of the fathers intact on one side and the best of modern philosophical, social and scientific thought on the other. To some extent he was a tragic figure, forced to come to terms with seemingly incompatible yet equally cogent conceptual worlds.

BIBLIOGRAPHY. *DAB* IX; *DARB;* C. Douglas, ed., *Autobiography of Augustus Hopkins Strong* (1981); C. F. Henry, *Personal Idealism and Strong's Theology* (1951); *NCAB* 12; G. Wacker, *Augustus H. Strong and the Dilemma of Historical Consciousness* (1985).

G. Wacker

Sunbeams. Southern Baptist* missions* organization for children. The first Sunbeam Band was organized in 1886 by Anna L. Shepherd Elsom at the Fairmont Baptist Church in Nelson County, Virginia. Elsom and her pastor, George Braxton Taylor, planned the structure and purpose for the Sunbeam Band. The children prayed for missionaries, learned about distant places and earned money for missions.

As groups were organized throughout the denomination, "Cousin George," as the children called Pastor Taylor, published the material for Sunbeam leaders in the *Foreign Mission Journal* and answered letters from the children. In 1896 the organization was turned over to the Woman's Missionary Union,* Auxiliary to the Southern Baptist Convention.

During the 1900s the age limitation for group members became eight years and younger, and the curriculum emphasized mission education. Sunbeams was replaced by Mission Friends when the WMU reorganized its age-level structure in 1970.

BIBLIOGRAPHY. C. B. Allen, *A Century to Celebrate: History of Woman's Missionary Union* (1987); R. Watkins, *A Backward Glance* (1987).

S. L. Still

Sunday School Board, SBC. The publishing agency for the Southern Baptist Convention* (SBC), located in Nashville, Tennessee. The present Baptist Sunday School Board (BSSB) was founded in Birmingham in 1891, after several previous publication efforts had failed. Its original task was to publish and distribute Bible study materials for the growing number of Sunday schools in Southern Baptist churches. The board first published books in 1898 and now operates Broadman Press,* a major publishing house.

The board's program assignments have increased over the years as new needs arose in the churches. In 1992 BSSB had responsibility for at least seventeen areas of work, including Sunday school, discipleship training, church architecture, records and statistics, Baptist Student Union,* church music, and church recreation.

In its early years the board struggled for acceptance among Southern Baptists, who had previously obtained Sunday-school materials from the American Baptist Publication Society* of Philadelphia, affiliated with Baptists in the North. By the turn of the century, however, few Southern Baptist churches continued to patronize the Northern publishers.

BSSB began with a borrowed desk in a single room in Nashville, provided rent-free, and the first capital was $5,000 of borrowed money. After four years the board purchased a residence for $10,000, and in 1913 it erected its first major building at the present site on Eighth Avenue. By 1992 the board occupied eight major buildings on about six acres of choice real estate in downtown Nashville, just a few blocks from the Tennessee state capitol.

In 1988 BSSB employed 1,964 persons, with an annual payroll of about $60 million. Of these, 1,333 worked in the Nashville complex, while 636 were scattered across the nation in sixty-three Baptist bookstores and two national conference centers at Ridgecrest, North Carolina, and Glorieta, New Mexico. In 1988-1989 the board operated on a budget of about $176 million. SSB is self-supporting, raising these funds from sales of its literature, books and church supplies.

The BSSB has been headed by James M. Frost* (1891-1893, 1896-1916), Theodore P. Bell (1893-1896), I. J. Van Ness (1917-1935), Thomas L. Holcomb (1935-1953), James L. Sullivan (1953-1975), Grady C. Cothen (1975-1984), Lloyd Elder (1984-1991) and James T. Draper (1991-).

The BSSB has been one focal point of the fundamentalist* movement in the SBC, with fundamentalists seeking to control the board to influence the kind of literature supplied to the churches. The forced resignation of Lloyd Elder in 1991 is usually regarded as the crucial point in fundamentalist control.

BIBLIOGRAPHY. R. A. Baker, *The Story of the Sun-*

day School Board (1966); W. B. Shurden, *The Sunday School Board* (1981).

H. L. McBeth

Sunday School Movement, Baptist. In the historical period from 1750 to 1850, Baptists in New England were cooperatively involved in the Sunday-school societies and unions that gave organizational definition to the Sunday School movement. Along with four other denominations, Baptists supported the expansion of the Sunday school in the Ohio and Mississippi valleys with a missionary zeal.

After the Civil War, Baptists in geographic regions outside the Southern and Southwestern states continued their involvement in the Sunday School movement on an ecumenical basis that was racially inclusive. Within the Southern and Southwestern regions, most Baptist leaders were perplexed by the pluralism of ethnic and cultural mixes in the larger cities of the United States.

From 1891 forward, Baptists were in one of two dominant postures in relationship to the Sunday School movement. One posture continued to be in dialogue with the mainline Protestant denominations. This dialogue is demonstrated in the mutually developed curricular plans for Bible study in the Sunday school embodied in the lesson outlines of the International Lesson Series. It is evident in the emphasis on children and youth in the Sunday school as the primary audiences, the attempt to bring scholarly thinking to influence the content of biblical study, and the desire to address ethical issues with a corporate and personal focus. A second posture among Baptists isolated those congregations from ecumenical dialogue. This isolation is demonstrated in the creation of a single denominational publishing house. It is evident in the emphasis that segregates children's groups from youth groups from adult groups in the Sunday-school organization. This posture attempts to bring organizational techniques and an expansionist mentality to influence the Sunday school. The former posture has tended to emphasize content, the latter to emphasize method.

BIBLIOGRAPHY. R. Lynn and E. Wright, *The Big Little School* (1980).   W. B. Rogers Jr.

Swedish Baptist Conference of the Eastern States. Organization of Swedish Baptists. Conceived in a meeting in Boston of three leading Swedish Baptists in the autumn of 1882, the Swedish Baptist Conference of the Eastern States (SBOES) was organized and had its first meeting in New Haven, Connecticut, on February 11, 1883, with delegates representing churches in New York City, Bridgeport, New Haven, Boston, Worcester, Bridgewater, Providence and New Sweden. Missions* occupied the conference from its inception, with a missionary to immigrant Scandinavians appointed that first year. The 500 members of 1883 increased to 814 two years later, to 1,028 in 1887, and in 1893 to 2,054 in twenty-one churches. The 1893 conference divided its churches into three districts: Eastern (Rhode Island, Massachusetts, New Hampshire and Maine), Central (Connecticut, Eastern New York, New Jersey, and the cities Philadelphia and Wilmington) and Western (western Pennsylvania and New York). Continued growth to 3,499 members in thirty-six churches in 1899, in combination with the long distances, prompted the withdrawal of fourteen churches (1,578 members) to form the New England Conference. The remaining twenty-two churches, with 1,921 members, reorganized, changing the name of the SBOES to the Swedish Baptist New York Conference. Four years later (1903) the churches of western New York and Pennsylvania united with those of Ohio to form the Middle East Conference, bringing the Eastern churches into the groupings that continued to serve them until midcentury. In 1946 the New York Conference changed its name to the Eastern Conference, which in its turn became the Mid-Atlantic (1950); in 1974 the Mid-Atlantic and New England conferences were merged to form the Northeast Conference, which, with its 7,734 members in fifty-eight churches in 1991, approximated the geographical distribution of the original conference of Eastern states.

BIBLIOGRAPHY. J. E. Klingberg, *A Brief History of the Swedish Baptist New York Conference, 1883-1933* (1933); F. J. Liljegren, *A Brief History of the Swedish Baptist Conference of New England, 1899-1939* (1939): A. Olson, *A Centenary History As Related to the Baptist General Conference* (1952).   N. A. Magnuson

Swedish Baptist General Conference. *See* DANISH-NORWEGIAN BAPTIST CONFERENCE OF NORTH AMERICA.

Swedish-American Bible Seminary. The (Swedish) Baptist General Conference* theological seminary during the academic year 1884-

1885. For thirteen years (1871-1884) it existed as the Scandinavian department of the Baptist Union Theological Seminary* in Morgan Park (near Chicago). Then founder John Alexis Edgren* moved the Swedish Seminary to St. Paul as the Swedish-American Bible Seminary (SABS) for the sake of flexibility for development and curriculum, better location, and meeting the spiritual and intellectual needs of the Swedish churches. Meeting in the First Swedish Baptist Church (later Payne Avenue and presently Trinity) of St. Paul, the SABS enjoyed record attendance of forty students during the 1884-1885 school year. Six part-time teachers assisted Edgren with a curriculum similar to that which the school had had in Morgan Park. This successful school year also included a graduating class of five and income that at $40,000 approximated the total for the seminary's previous thirteen years. The Swedish Seminary enjoyed a "glorious revival" and effective ministry in the churches.

Despite that auspicious beginning, there remained some question among Swedish Baptists as to the best location for the seminary. The school accepted an attractive offer from Stromsburg, Nebraska, and moved there as the Central Bible Seminary, occupying a new building in late February 1886. After a brief stay there, however, the Swedish seminary returned to Morgan Park in the autumn of 1888 as the Swedish department of the Baptist Union Theological Seminary. In 1914 the seminary moved back to St. Paul, Minnesota, and it eventually became known as Bethel Theological Seminary.*

BIBLIOGRAPHY. J. A. Edgren, "Facta" (manuscript, 1885); N. Magnuson, *Missionsskolan: The History of an Immigrant Theological School* (1983); A. Olson and V. Olson, *Seventy-five Years. A History of Bethel Theological Seminary* (1946).

N. A. Magnuson

Sword of the Lord, The. *See* RICE, JOHN R.

T

Taylor, George Boardman (1832-1907). Southern Baptist missionary educator. Taylor was the son of James Taylor, the first secretary of the Southern Baptist Foreign Mission Board.* Educated at Richmond College and at the University of Virginia, Taylor was noted for his scholarship and helped to edit the *Christian Review,* the first national Baptist theological journal. Taylor served as a pastor in Charlottesville, Baltimore and Staunton, Virginia. During the Civil War, Taylor was the chaplain of Stonewall Jackson's regiment.

In 1873 the Foreign Mission Board appointed Taylor its first missionary to Italy. Taylor founded that country's first Baptist theological school. He wrote *Italy and the Italians* (1898) and *Life and Times of James B. Taylor* (1872), and the University of Chicago awarded him the doctor of divinity for his contributions to Baptist thought.

G. T. Miller

Taylor, John (1752-1836). Pioneer Baptist preacher, missionary and author. Born in Fauquier County, Virginia, Taylor grew up in that region, joined a Baptist church at age twenty and started preaching shortly thereafter. In 1779 he moved west to Kentucky to engage in pastoral work. During the 1880s he became a strong opponent of mission* endeavors in the whole region then known as the West and was a frequent spokesman in opposition to the work of the Baptist Luther Rice.* He also opposed the anti-Baptist activities of Alexander Campbell.* Taylor's work was characterized by the starting of new churches on the frontier and then the pastoring of each new church for a number of years. He is credited with being the major force in the establishment of several Baptist churches in Kentucky, including the Clear Creek church (1785), the Bullittsburg church (1795), the Corn Creek church (1802), the Frankfort church (1816) and the Buck Run church (1818).

Taylor published *History of Ten Churches* (1823), which gives unique insight into the functioning of frontier churches, and *Thoughts on Missions* (1820), which was written to oppose mission work in the West. He also wrote several short biographies of frontier churchmen. Taylor died at Frankfort, Kentucky.

BIBLIOGRAPHY. *BE; DAB* VIII; *ESB* 2; W. L. Lumpkin, *Baptist Foundations in the South* (1961).

F. A. Teague

Testimony Meetings. To "testify" is to give witness to the joy of religious salvation, the rewards of righteous living and the personal assurance of eternal life. A testimony meeting is a special service, either planned or impromptu, conducted in Missionary,* Independent,* Free Will,* Separate* and other Baptist fellowships, including many rural Southern Baptist* churches. It is a largely unstructured happening, devoted to singing, prayer, perhaps a short sermon and then congregational testimonies. Because of their intimate nature, these events become highly emotional and spiritually contagious, and some erupt into shouting and other impassioned expressions of joy.

Testimony became a part of the highly exuberant and personal religious expression that arose from the camp-meeting base of Protestantism in America. Accounts of nineteenth-century revivals are replete with descriptions of extended sessions of testimony, particularly by new converts, who generally were expected to affirm publicly the blessings their salvation had bestowed. Women in particular found the testimonial to be a satisfying outlet for expression, especially in those Baptist denominations that sharply restricted all forms of female church leadership.

BIBLIOGRAPHY. D. D. Bruce Jr., *And They All Sang Hallelujah: Plain-Folk Camp-Meeting Religion, 1800-1845* (1974); J. T. Titon, *Powerhouse for God: Speech, Chant and Song in an Appalachian Baptist Church* (1988).

H. Dorgan

Theological Education in the Northern Baptist Convention. A Northern Baptist (*see* American Baptist Churches in the USA) educational survey. This 1945 book, written by Hugh Harthorne and Milton C. Froyd, surveyed the theological education of Northern Baptist ministers. The study showed that many Baptist ministers had not completed a four-year college degree followed by a three-year seminary program. Hence Harthorne and Froyd recommended that the various state conventions move toward establishing this standard. The study also revealed that while two-thirds of Northern Baptist churches were rural, the urban churches provided the bulk of the denomination's recruits. The picture of the denomination's seminaries was bleak. The survey noted that most Baptist seminaries badly needed greatly increased funding and a more professional program.

The Harthorne and Froyd study was foundational for the development of Northern (later American) Baptist ministerial education in the 1950s and 1960s. The schools, flush with new students paid for by the GI Bill, expanded their offerings, built new facilities and improved their quality. By the mid-1960s, the denomination had adopted the report's recommended standards for ordination, although conventions continued to make exceptions, especially in rural areas.

G. T. Miller

Theological Educator, The. A semiannual journal published by the faculty of New Orleans Baptist Theological Seminary.* An anniversary bulletin published for the fiftieth anniversary of the school (1967-1968) was the first issue, and Dean J. Hardee Kennedy encouraged production of an annual issue. A second issue was published in 1969, with single issues printed thereafter annually through 1972. In 1973 *The Theological Educator* began to be published twice a year, with a fall issue focusing on a book of the Bible and a spring issue covering a variety of topics of interest to church leaders. The journal was produced by a committee through 1975, when Fisher Humphreys became editor. Paul Robertson accepted the editorship in 1990 after the resignation of Humphreys. Normally the journal contains appraisals, features, major articles and book reviews from a variety of sources and perspectives. A special issue in 1993 focused on the seventy-fifth anniversary of the seminary.

C. L. Howe Jr.

Thiessen, Henry Clarence (1883-1947). Evangelical biblical scholar and educator. Born in Hamilton, Nebraska, Thiessen served as a Baptist pastor in Pandora, Ohio, from 1909 to 1916, and then became an instructor (1916-1923) and principal (1919-1923) of Fort Wayne Bible School. He then attended Northern Baptist Theological Seminary (Th.B., 1925) and taught there as an assistant professor (1925-1926). He earned further degrees from Northwestern University (A.B., 1927), Northern Baptist Seminary (B.D., 1928) and Southern Baptist Theological Seminary* (Ph.D., 1929), where he studied under A. T. Robertson.* He was then dean of the College of Theology at the Evangelical University in New Jersey (1929-1931), professor at Dallas Theological Seminary (1931-1935) and successively associate professor of Bible and philosophy (1935-1936), professor of New Testament literature and exegesis (1936-1946), and first dean of the Graduate School (1946) at Wheaton College. He accepted a call to become president of Los Angeles Baptist Seminary with the hope of finding relief from the asthmatic attacks that had troubled him in Illinois. Thiessen authored the widely used *Introduction to the New Testament* (1943) and *Introductory Lectures in Systematic Theology* (1949; rev. ed. 1979). A conscientious and exacting scholar with a dispensational orientation, Thiessen specialized in New Testament studies.

E. E. Cairns

Thurman, Howard (1900-1981). A renowned Baptist minister, ecumenical leader, mystic and author. Born on November 18, 1900, in Daytona Beach, Florida, Thurman was reared by his grandmother, a former slave. He attended Florida Baptist Academy in Jacksonville from 1915 to 1919. In 1919 he was licensed as a Baptist minister. He graduated from Morehouse College* (A.B., 1923). In 1925 he was ordained, and the next year he graduated from Rochester Theological Seminary* (1926). He served as pastor of the Mount Zion Baptist Church in Oberlin, Ohio (1926-1928), and taught at Morehouse and Spelman* (1928-1931).

In 1935 Thurman encountered Mohandas K. (Mahatma) Gandhi during a tour of India. Gandhi aroused Thurman's interest in studying the relationship between the teachings of Jesus and the disinherited. The trip also encouraged him to help organize an interracial church, the Church for the Fellowship of All People, in San Francisco in 1944. In 1953 he became dean of Marsh Chapel at Boston University. He retired in 1964.

Thurman was a prolific writer. He wrote nineteen books and pamphlets, fourteen chapters in various books, and twenty-one addresses and sermons. Some of his most outstanding works were *The Greatest of These* (1944), *Jesus and the Disinherited* (1949), *The Inward Journey* (1961), *The Search for Common Ground* (1971) and *With Head and Heart* (1979), his autobiography. He was the recipient of numerous honors and awards and lectured in over 500 schools. Thurman died in San Francisco on April 10, 1981.

BIBLIOGRAPHY. *EARE; ERS;* J. G. Melton, *Religious Leaders of America* (1992); H. A. Ploski and J. Williams, eds., *The Negro Almanac* (1988).

L. H. Williams

Tichenor, Isaac Taylor (1825-1902). Southern Baptist* preacher, educator, agriculturalist and denominational leader. Born in Spencer County, Kentucky, young Tichenor was a popular preacher, sometimes called "the boy orator of Kentucky." In 1847 he became a representative of the American Indian Mission Association. A year later he was ordained and became pastor of a Baptist church in Columbus, Mississippi. He served as pastor of First Baptist Church, Montgomery, Alabama, from 1852 to 1867.

During the Civil War, Tichenor was both a chaplain and a combat soldier, fighting at the Battle of Shiloh. After the war he served as president of the Alabama Agricultural and Mechanical College, later Auburn University, from 1871 to 1882. His agricultural and industrial expertise were widely recognized. In 1882 Tichenor assumed leadership of the Home Mission Board* of the Southern Baptist Convention. During his seventeen years in that position Tichenor strengthened the mission board financially and extended its ministry among African-Americans and Native Americans, as well as in Appalachia. His work helped to stabilize the Southern Baptist Convention after the Civil War.

BIBLIOGRAPHY. *DAB* IX; J. S. Dill, *Isaac Taylor Tichenor: The Home Mission Statesman* (1908).

B. J. Leonard

Tithe, Baptist Views. The tithe is the giving of a tenth of one's personal income to God, usually through a local church. Tithing is a part of the larger subject of stewardship. Most Baptists consider tithing to be biblical, based primarily on Old Testament law, and cite passages like Leviticus 27:30-32, Numbers 18:26 and Deuteronomy 14:22, 28-29. New Testament references in support of the tithe are few, but include those calling for consistency in complying with the entire scope of the law as in Matthew 23:23 or emphasizing meeting the needs of the church as in 1 Corinthians 16:2.

Colonial Baptists were adverse to the tithe because of its similarity to the state tax on ministers. With the advent of the nineteenth-century missions* movement, tithing gained more support. With the Laymen's Missionary Movement* of the 1890s and special emphases like the Southern Baptist Convention's* $75 million campaign, Baptists began to focus more on the tithe as a systematic means for financial support. The Depression took its toll on tithing, but the post World War II period saw a resurgence in tithing emphasis with campaigns like "A Million Southern Baptists Tithers for Christ," which used stewardship cards, tithing covenants and tithers' visitation plans in 1947. Baptists maintained that the tithe was an ideal minimum standard for giving, representing an outward expression of an inward spiritual experience.

During the twentieth century the concept expanded beyond money to include a tithe of one's talents and time. A disagreement arose among Baptists as to the benefits of tithing. Some maintain that only spiritual blessings occur with tithing, while others believe that material blessings also increase. The tithe is rarely specifically mentioned in Baptist confessions* or church covenants.* A notable exception is the 1948 revision of the Treatise and the Faith and Practices of the Free Will Baptists.*

BIBLIOGRAPHY. *BHH* 21 (January 1986); *RE* 70 (Spring 1973).

J. F. Loftis

Toy, Crawford Howell (1836-1919). Baptist professor of Old Testament and Hebrew. Raised in Virginia, Toy graduated from the University of Virginia in 1856 and taught for three years at the Albemarle Female Institute in Charlottesville, Virginia, before entering Southern Baptist Theological Seminary* in Greenville, South Carolina. His plans to become a missionary to Japan were interrupted by the Civil War, when he served for a time as a chaplain in the Confederate Army. After the war he became a member of the faculty of the University of Virginia, teaching Greek for a year (1865-1866), followed by two years of graduate stdy in Berlin (1866-1868). In 1869 Toy became professor of Old Testament interpretation at Southern Baptist Theological Seminary.

It soon became evident, however, that Toy had embraced Darwin's theory of evolution and favored the Kuenen-Wellhausen theory of Pentateuchal criticism. He was asked by the trustees of the seminary to cease teaching these theories, but in spite of growing dissatisfaction on the part of the trustees, he persisted and was finally forced to resign in 1879. Toy left the seminary without bitterness and spent the following year as literary editor of the New York *Independent* before becoming Hancock Professor of Hebrew and other Oriental languages at Harvard University in 1880. A regular contributor to scholarly journals, he authored several books, including *Quotations in the New Testament* (1884), *Judaism and Christianity* (1890), *A Critical and Exegetical Commentary on the Book of Proverbs* (1899) and *Introduction to the History of Religions* (1913). At Harvard Toy became a recognized scholar in his field, giving three decades (1880-1919) to his teaching and scholarship both in the university and in the Divinity School.

BIBLIOGRAPHY. R. A. Baker, *The Southern Baptist Convention and Its People, 1607-1972* (1974); *DAB* IX; *DARB*; W. A. Mueller, *A History of Southern Baptist Theological Seminary* (1959); *NCAB* 6.

W. R. Estep

Triennial Convention. First national organization of Baptists in the United States. Founded in Philadelphia on May 18, 1814, by thirty-three delegates from eleven states, it was officially named the General Missionary Convention of the Baptist Denomination in the United States for Foreign Missions, and its first president was Richard Furman* of South Carolina. It met every three years—hence the name Triennial Convention. The leading spirit in its formation was Luther Rice,* who challenged Baptists to organize in order to sponsor Adoniram and Ann Judson,* American missionaries working in India and, later, Burma.

Although its primary impulse was foreign missions,* in 1817 its work was broadened to include home missions and education. In that year John Mason Peck* and James Welch were appointed as missionaries to Missouri, and in 1818 Columbian College* was founded.

In 1826 the convention returned to its first emphasis of foreign missions. The ministry of home missions was picked up by the formation of the American Baptist Home Mission Society* in 1832. In 1845 the Triennial Convention was renamed the American Baptist Missionary Union,* and in 1910 it became the American Baptist Foreign Mission Society.* In 1845 Baptists in the South separated from this body and organized the Southern Baptist Convention.*

BIBLIOGRAPHY. W. Shurden, "The Development of Baptist Associations in America, 1707-1814," *BHH* 4 (1969):31-39.

W. M. Patterson

Trott, Samuel (1704-c.1065). Outstanding leader of Old School Baptists. He was born in Walpole, New Hampshire, and baptized in a Congregational church. He became a Baptist and was ordained pastor of the Morristown Baptist Church, New Jersey, in 1812. Moving to Ohio in 1815, and then to Kentucky, he probably adopted antimission* views there. Returning to New Jersey in 1821, he held pastorates at Morristown, Lambertville and Hopewell before moving in 1830 to the Welsh Tract Baptist Church in Delaware. From 1833 until his death he was pastor of churches in Fairfax and Loudon counties, Virginia. His prominence among Old School Baptists (see Hardshell Baptists) is evident at the Black Rock (Maryland) convention, where he preached the opening sermon, chaired the committee that drafted the Black Rock Address and also the correspondence committee, and pronounced the benediction. An able writer and gifted preacher, he opposed the prevalent millennial optimism, Sunday schools, and mission and Bible societies by writing articles in *Signs of the Times* and elsewhere and by addressing Old School gatherings.

BIBLIOGRAPHY. B. C. Lambert, *The Rise of Anti-Mission Baptists* (1989); N. H. Maring, *Baptists in New Jersey* (1964).

N. H. Maring

Truett, George Washington (1867-1944). Baptist pastor and denominational leader. Born near Hayesville, North Carolina, he attended the Hayesville Academy from 1875 to 1885 and then taught in a one-room school. To earn funds to study law, in 1887 he opened a school in Hiawassee, Georgia, which in two years grew to 300 students and three teachers.

Converted in 1886 during revival services, Truett joined the Hayesville Baptist Church. In 1889 he moved with his family to Whitewright,

Texas, where he became active in the Baptist church and was ordained in 1890. Soon after, he was chosen financial agent of Baylor University* and in twenty-three months raised sufficient funds to rid the school of a $92,000 debt.

In 1893 he entered Baylor as a student, and in 1897 he received his B.A. While in college he served the East Waco Baptist Church, and upon his graduation he became pastor of the First Baptist Church, Dallas, where he remained until his death. During his forty-seven-year pastorate, membership increased from 715 to 7,804, with a total of 19,531 new members actually received and contributions in excess of $6 million.

Truett's ministry was distinguished by pulpit eloquence, pastoral effectiveness and outstanding leadership in his denomination. He served as president of the Southern Baptist Convention* for almost three years (1927-1929) and as president of the Baptist World Alliance* for five (1934-1939). He was active in founding the first Baptist hospital in Texas, was invited by President Woodrow Wilson to preach to American troops in Europe in 1918 and was elected in 1919 to lead in raising $75 million for denominational causes. On May 16, 1920, he preached his famous sermon "Baptists and Religious Liberty" to 15,000 people from the Capitol steps in Washington.

For fifty years Truett's ministry was woven into the life of Texas Baptists. Held in great esteem by all Baptists, he was viewed as an example of what a preacher and Southern Christian gentleman ought to be.

BIBLIOGRAPHY. *DAB* III; P. W. James, *George W. Truett: A Biography* (1939).

W. M. Patterson

Truett-McConnell College. An institution of higher education in Cleveland, north Georgia. Founded by the Georgia Baptist Convention in 1946 and opened for instruction in September 1947, this school is named for George W. Truett* and Fernando C. McConnell, prominent Southern Baptist clergymen. For most of its life it has been a junior college, although the achievement of senior college status was expected in 1993. It has been accredited by the Southern Association of Colleges and Schools since 1966. Its department of music is accredited by the National Association of Schools of Music. Presidents have included L. Clinton Cutts (1946-1951), Joe H. Miller (1951-1964), Warner E. Fusselle (1964-1972), Ronald E. Weitman (1972-1986) and H. M. Fulbright (1986-

1992). Beginning in 1973 the college has sponsored off-campus centers, which numbered thirteen in the academic year 1991-1992. Enrollment in the fall of 1991 included 478 students on campus and 1,158 in off-campus centers, with a full-time equivalency of 1,208.

BIBLIOGRAPHY. *ESB* 2:1430, 3:2027, 4:2525.

R. G. Gardner

Turner, Nat (1800-1831). Baptist preacher and slave insurrectionist. Born in Southampton, Virginia, on October 2, 1800, Turner was the slave of Benjamin Turner. A Methodist, Benjamin Turner encouraged his slaves to worship in his church along with whites. It was in this context that Nat Turner came to a knowledge of the faith and indicated that he had been called to preach. His parents taught him to read and write. A mystic, he spent long hours in meditation. Turner received signs and visions from heaven. He believed that he had been called by God as a prophet to liberate his people by the sword. So he planned an insurrection for August 21, 1831. Fifty-seven whites were killed, and Turner and sixty coconspirators were captured and returned to Jerusalem, the county seat. He made a full confession to Thomas A. Gray, and on November 11, 1831, he was hanged. According to William S. Drewry in *The Southampton Insurrection* (1900), Turner's body was delivered to physicians who skinned it and made grease of the flesh. In 1966 William Styron published a controversial historical novel, *The Confessions of Nat Turner* (1966), portraying Turner as a bloodthirsty sex fiend. But many African-Americans have seen him as a hero, and William J. Simmons* (*Men of Mark,* 1887) called Turner one of the greatest emancipators of the nineteenth century, "another John Brown."

BIBLIOGRAPHY. J. H. Clarke, ed., *William Styron's Nat Turner* (1986); G. S. Wilmore, *Black Religion and Black Radicalism* (1984).

L. W. Williams

Two-Seed-in-the-Spirit Predestinarian Baptists. Primitive Baptist* group founded by antimissions* leader Daniel Parker* and known for its doctrine of predestination. Parker taught that since the Fall persons are born with either the good seed of God or the bad seed of Satan, a doctrine he based on Genesis 3:15. Those with the good seed God prompts to repentance; those with the evil seed receive no such prompting.

This difference is present at birth and is beyond alteration.

A reading of Parker's *Views on the Two Seeds* (1826) and his *The Second Dose of Doctrine on the Two Seeds* (1826) corrects two common errors regarding the Two-Seed doctrine. The first is the assumption that the determinism of Parker's Two-Seed doctrine gave rise to his antimissions stance. Parker's antimissions views preceded his Two-Seed theory. Furthermore, Parker's opinions did not lead him to view missions* as useless; indeed, Parker supported missions done through itinerant preaching and church planting. Parker's objections were specifically to societal missions plans. The second erroneous assumption is that Parker championed an extreme double-predestinarian Calvinism.* In Parker's view, Two-Seed doctrine was an anti-Arminian* means of rejecting any teaching that God elected persons to damnation. Parker held that Christ died for the nonelect born of the evil seed and they were free to come to God for salvation. That they did not was a consequence of their free choice (unaided by godly prompting) and "not because they are the serpent's seed, or that God had reprobated them to destruction."

Two-Seed churches, found in Tennessee, Alabama, Kentucky, Indiana, Illinois and Texas, had no paid ministry and practiced the ordinance* of foot-washing.* Parker's Pilgrim Predestinarian Regular Baptist Church, which was constituted in Illinois and then moved to Texas in 1834, was perhaps the first non-Catholic church organized in Texas. Parker established nine churches in East Texas in his thirty-four years of wandering without a settled home.

Two-Seed churches are now near or in extinction. In 1970 there were no associations remaining, and only four churches with a total membership of about sixty-eight could be claimed.

See also PARKER, DANIEL; PRIMITIVE BAPTISTS.

BIBLIOGRAPHY. *ESB* 3:2028-29; O. M. Lee, "Daniel Parker's Doctrine of the Two Seeds" (Th.M. thesis, Southern Baptist Theological Seminary, 1962). W. L. Allen

U

Union Baptists. A small denomination, approximately 3,300 members strong, distributed over thirty-four churches in three associations: Union Baptist Association (thirteen fellowships in Allegheny County, North Carolina, and Grayson County, Virginia), Mountain Union Baptist Association (eleven fellowships in Cecil and Hartford counties, Maryland, Ashe and Avery counties, North Carolina, Chester County, Pennsylvania, and Grayson County, Virginia) and Original Mountain Union Baptist Association (ten fellowships in Ashe County, North Carolina, and Smyth County, Virginia). Doctrinally identical to many of the Regular Baptists* found in central Appalachia, these associations even employ the title Regular Baptist on the covers of their published annual session minutes, but not in their official names.

Union Baptists trace their distinctive origins to disputes that engulfed much of southern and central Appalachia before, during and immediately after the Civil War. Sympathy for the Northern cause split numerous Baptist churches in eastern Tennessee and northwestern North Carolina. In Ashe County, North Carolina, this dispute affected both Mountain Association and Senter Association—each Regular Baptist in origin, each with strong antimissions* and anti-secret-society positions, and each with a majority of members in the pro-South camp. The result was the frequent exclusion of individuals who joined the Union League, a secret order supporting Union causes. It was not until 1867, however, that these particular pro-Union Baptists came together to form Mountain Union Baptist Association. Almost 100 years later (1961) this organization then split over radio preaching, forming Mountain Union Baptists and Original Mountain Union Baptists. Senter later became Primitive,* and the Mountain Association ultimately splintered into Primitive, Missionary,* Regular, Separate,* and Southern* Baptist segments and offshoots.

See also REGULAR BAPTISTS.

BIBLIOGRAPHY. M. B. Bradley et al., *Churches and Church Membership in the United States, 1990* (1992); H. Dorgan, *Giving Glory to God in Appalachia: Worship Practices of Six Baptist Subdenominations* (1987); J. F. Fletcher, *A History of the Ashe County, North Carolina, and New River, Virginia, Baptist Associations* (1935).

H. Dorgan

Union Theological Seminary. Located in New York City, Union Theological Seminary was founded in 1836 by New School Presbyterians. Originally the New York Theological Seminary, the name Union was adopted in 1839 to reflect a general irenic spirit among New York Presbyterians of the era.

Union's early theology was determined by the interaction of Henry Boynton Smith and William G. T. Shedd. Smith strove for a mediating Christocentric system, while Shedd was an orthodox Calvinist.* In the late nineteenth century the seminary was also home for Phillip Schaff, the distinguished church historian.

A bitter chapter in Union's history erupted in the heresy trials of Charles A. Briggs from 1891 to 1893. Briggs, a professor of Hebrew, presented controversial views of the authority of the Bible, and a full-scale investigation of his teaching was launched in the New York Presbytery and later the General Assembly. Briggs lost the trial, but the seminary stood with him. Eventually Union lost its denominational relationship but became a champion of the freedom of Christian scholars.

Under the presidency of Henry Sloane Coffin, notable faculty appointments of Reinhold Niebuhr and Paul Tillich were made; Auburn Theological Seminary moved to the campus in 1939 and serves the continuing Presbyterian constituency.

A number of Baptists have been associated with Union over the years. Harry Emerson Fosdick* and Robert S. McCracken,* pastors at Riverside Church,* taught homiletics. Robert Handy and James Washington specialized in American religious thought beginning in the 1950s. Numerous Southern* and American* Baptist theological and collegiate educators have completed graduate degrees at Union/Columbia University.

BIBLIOGRAPHY. R. T. Handy, *A History of Union Theological Seminary in New York* (1987); G. R. Shriver, *American Religious Heretics* (1966).

W. H. Brackney

Union University. A four-year liberal arts school located in Jackson, Tennessee, and operated in cooperation with the Tennessee Baptist Convention. The school was founded in 1825 as the Jackson Male Academy and operated as such until the 1840s. When North Carolina ceded Tennessee to the U.S. government to become a new state, a provision was made for two colleges to be established, one of them in west Tennessee. In January 1844 the legislative charter gave the property rights of the Jackson Male Academy to the trustees of the new college, called West Tennessee College.

In 1875 the newly formed Tennessee Baptist Convention voted to receive the college at Jackson and to change the name to Southwestern Baptist University. The new school opened in 1874 with only a preparatory department, primary school and grammar school. When the school received a state charter in 1875, college classes were begun. Soon the new Baptist school was offering three bachelor's degrees and one professional degree (LL.B).

In 1907 the school's name was changed to Union University, and John William Conger served as its first president. In 1927 Union and another local college, Hall-Moody Junior College, were consolidated. The Union campus was in the downtown area and was confined by the city, so in 1968 the trustees voted to purchase a new campus site and move the campus to the north side of the city. Seven years later, in 1975, the school was moved eight miles to its new campus. On the new site the educational complex was designed to house all of the academic facilities under one roof.

BIBLIOGRAPHY. *ESB* 2:1435, 3:2029-30, 4:2527.

C. Blevins

United American Free Will Baptist Church. Predominantly African-American denomination.

The church was an outgrowth of the white Free Will Baptist* church of North Carolina, which has origins dating to the eighteenth century. The black group was organized in 1867, and the first edifice was built at Shady Grove. Several churches came together to form an annual meeting in 1887 and a general conference in 1901.

Consisting of district, quarterly, annual and general conferences, the United American Free Will Baptist Church (UAFWBC) mixes congregational polity and the general conference system. However, in relation to doctrine, the decisions of the conferences take precedence over those of the local churches. Basically, the group's Arminian* theology has been inherited from its white counterpart, but its presiding officer is called "senior bishop."

A multipurpose church headquarters has been recently constructed in Kinston, North Carolina. It includes a new Bible college, which opened on August 24, 1991. The church also publishes a newspaper, *The Free Will Baptist Advocate.*

There are approximately 100,000 members in 900 churches, which are primarily located in North Carolina, Florida, Georgia, Mississippi, Louisiana and Texas. The presiding senior bishop is J. E. Reddick, and close ties remain with white Free Will Baptists.

A group with a similar name, the United American Freewill Baptist Conference, was organized in Tallahassee, Florida, in 1968. Although information on this group is quite obscure, a brochure on file at the American Baptist Historical Society states that it traces its history to the Negro General Conference of Freewill Baptists (1898), that its headquarters is located in Lakeland, Florida, and that D. L. Bright became general bishop in 1976. Evidently this organization is a splinter from the earlier group.

BIBLIOGRAPHY. H. L. McBeth, *The Baptist Heritage* (1987); W. J. Payne, *Directory of African American Religious Bodies* (1991); H. A. Ploski and J. Williams, *The Negro Almanac* (1988).

L. H. Williams

United Baptists. A denomination that had its origin in the late eighteenth and early nineteenth century "uniting" of several Separate Baptist* and Regular Baptist* associations of Virginia and Kentucky. While compiling statistics for *Churches and Church Membership in the United States, 1990,* Clifford A. Grammich Jr. of the Glenmary Research Center identified 436 "United Baptist" fellowships, containing 54,248 members, concentrated primarily in Arkansas, Indiana, Kentucky, Missouri, Ohio, Tennessee and West Virginia, with outpost churches in Arizona, Florida, Idaho, Illinois, Michigan and Wisconsin.

Uniteds have no national organization, and theologically they are diverse, with one association (Union, in Arkansas and Idaho) corresponding with some Free Will Baptists,* another (Mount Zion, in Kentucky and Ohio) corresponding with an Old Regular* association, and a third (Cumberland River, in Kentucky and Ohio) corresponding with—but not a member of—the American Baptist* association. In atonement doctrine they vary from general atonement coupled with pure free will to a limited atonement with limited free will; and in gender codes, worship practices, church governance and degrees of insularity they tend to be less closed and traditional than are Appalachian Primitives* and Old Regulars. United Baptists, however, usually preserve such "old-time ways" as foot-washing,* natural water baptism, rhythmically chanted sermons (in Appalachia) and lined singing (particularly in Kentucky).

As the great western revivals swept the settled areas of the Blue Ridge and the Cumberland between the 1780s and 1803, they stimulated growth in Baptist numbers and created a spirit in which divergent groups could set aside doctrinal disputes that had divided them. For United Baptists the most significant of these unitings occurred in 1801 between the South Kentucky Association (Separates) and the Elkhorn Association (Regulars), a joining that not only created the United Baptist denomination but later spawned the Old Regular Baptists. The "Terms of Union Between the Elkhorn and South Kentucky, or Separate, Associations" included the following agreement: "that . . . preaching Christ tasted death for every man, shall be no bar to communion." This article allowed the general-atonement Separates to correspond with the more limited-atonement Regulars, and ultimately resulted in the present United Baptists' clustering more toward the "general" or "universal" end of the atonement doctrine spectrum.

See also OLD REGULAR BAPTISTS.

BIBLIOGRAPHY. M. B. Bradley et al., *Churches and Church Membership in the United States, 1990* (1992); L. T. Crismon, *Baptists in Kentucky, 1776-1976* (1975); H. Dorgan, *The Old Regular Baptists of Central Appalachia: Brothers and Sisters in*

Hope (1989); R. T. Semple, *History of the Baptists in Virginia* (1810).   H. Dorgan

University of Chicago, The Divinity School. An institution for theological education having Baptist roots. Midwestern Baptists in 1865 chartered the Baptist Union Theological Seminary* (also known as Morgan Park Seminary) near Chicago and in 1891 merged this with the new University of Chicago.

A Baptist Yale Semitic professor, William Rainey Harper,* joining with founder John D. Rockefeller, ensured that the Divinity School, the university's first professional school, would be well supported. While the university blended religious and nonreligious voices, the Divinity School, which granted and grants both professional and academic degrees, was ecumenical. Under Baptist deans Shailer Mathews* and Shirley Jackson Case* the faculty breathed a spirit of progressivism, confidence in science and reason, and faith in modernity, and even promoted a formal movement called Modernism.

Originally focusing on sociohistorical studies of the Bible under men like Case and Edgar Johnson Goodspeed,* by the 1920s the Divinity School came to concentrate on philosophical theology, again largely of a modernist sort. The school helped lead the antifundamentalist faction in denominational battles.

By midcentury a sort of "process theology," inspired by philosopher Alfred North Whitehead, came to dominate. Subsequently, thanks to efforts of Joachim Wach and Mircea Eliade, the school became a center for the study of the "history of religions." Chicago devotes itself not only to a small ministry program but also—and largely—to the education of teachers and researchers. After the Second Vatican Council in 1965 great numbers of Catholics came to be the largest single element. The close ties to Baptist churches were long gone, but the free spirit of the Baptist heritage remained with the school, whose endowment and board are still that of the Baptist Theological Union.

See also BAPTIST UNION THEOLOGICAL SEMINARY AT CHICAGO.

BIBLIOGRAPHY. L. E. Axel, *God or Man at Chicago: The Chicago School of Theology* (1975); T. W. Goodspeed, *William Rainey Harper* (1928); W. J. Hynes, *Shirley Jackson Case and the Chicago School* (1981); C. Peden, *The Chicago School* (1987).   M. E. Marty

University of Lewisburg. *See* BUCKNELL UNIVERSITY.

University of Mary Hardin-Baylor. Baptist General Convention of Texas educational institution. The University of Mary Hardin-Baylor (UMHB) began as the Female Department of Baylor University* in 1845 at Independence, Texas. The oldest college for women west of the Mississippi, UMHB was Texas Baptists' only women's school for more than 100 years. Horace Clark directed the Primary and Female Department of Baylor University and supervised the official separation from the university in 1866, when the department became Baylor Female College. In 1885 Baylor united with Waco University. With a pledge of $32,000 and land, Belton outbid other cities for the college.

The seventy-five-acre university continues to operate under the charter it received in 1845. The name changed to Mary Hardin-Baylor College in 1934 because of the gift of a $900,000 trust fund from the John G. and Mary Hardin family to Texas Baptist schools. The Belton school received 25 percent of the dividends from the money. With this financial base the school began to build and grow.

Mary Hardin-Baylor remained a female college until 1968, when the first male student graduated. It received university status in 1978. In the early 1990s President Jerry G. Baucum directed the university staff and faculty as they worked with more than 1,700 students. Almost 10 percent of the students are internationals, coming from thirty-eight different countries. Baucum administers an endowment of more than $12 million and an annual budget of almost $12 million.

See also BAYLOR UNIVERSITY.

BIBLIOGRAPHY. F. Brown, "Mary Hardin-Baylor College," *ESB* 2; E. James, *Forth from Her Portals* (1986); E. M. Townsend, *After Seventy-five Years* (1920). R. Beck

University of Mobile. Formerly Mobile College, a four-year Baptist college in Alabama. In 1956 the Mobile Baptist Association resolved to establish a junior college in Mobile under the charter of Howard College (now Samford University*). Instead, a four-year college was incorporated in 1960 and chartered in 1961. William K. Weaver Jr. was elected as the first president. The college began its first academic year on September 9, 1963, with the motto "The fear of the Lord is the beginning of wisdom." The University of Mobile is a coeducational, privately endowed, independent, residential undergraduate and graduate institution located on 765 acres twelve miles northwest of downtown Mobile. The university is one of three colleges and universities associated with the Alabama Baptist State Convention. The 1,700 students may pursue a bachelor of arts or bachelor of science degree in thirty-seven academic areas. Graduate degrees are offered in education, business administration, nursing and theology. The university is accredited by the Southern Association of Colleges and Schools, the National League of Nursing and the National Association of Schools of Music. Unique to the University of Mobile is the Dwight Harrigan Forest Resources Learning Center on 125 acres near the historic Chicasaboque Creek. On July 1, 1993, the college was renamed the University of Mobile, with a branch campus in Nicaragua.

BIBLIOGRAPHY. A. H. Reid, *Baptists in Alabama: Their Organization and Witness* (1967).

J. F. Loftis

University of Richmond. Oldest, largest institution of higher education related to the Baptist General Association of Virginia (BGAV). In 1830 BGAV leaders organized the Virginia Baptist Education Society, which, in 1832, opened Virginia Baptist Seminary north of Richmond and in 1834 relocated it two miles west of the state capital. In 1914 the institution moved to its present campus of 350 acres around a lake, now in West End Richmond. Though the society's original purpose was to educate Baptist ministers, by 1834 nonministerial students predominated, and the 1840 charter of Richmond College, successor to the seminary, even prohibited theological instruction until 1858.

Richmond College admitted women in 1898 and opened coordinate Westhampton College for women in 1914, though since 1976 the university (so named in 1920) has become essentially coeducational. Other divisions are the T. C. Williams School of Law (1870), the E. Claiborne Robins School of Business (1924 evening, 1949 day) and the first-of-a-kind undergraduate Jepson School of Leadership Studies (1990).

In 1969 E. C. Robins Sr. gave the university $50 million after a charter change rendered the school independent. The BGAV's board continues to nominate a portion of the university's trustees, who in 1992 were more than half Baptist.

The BGAV's annual appropriation in 1992-1993 was $340,000. The university awards fifty Baptist scholarships and supplies several specific services to the denomination. An endowed chaplaincy is the center of a broad program of religious and service activities. In 1992-1993, endowment was $340 million (forty-fifth in the United States), operating budget $82 million, and enrollment 2,900 full-time undergraduates, 530 full-time graduate and law students (mostly law), and 1,300 part-time students.

BIBLIOGRAPHY. R. E. Alley, *History of the University of Richmond, 1830-1971* (1977); W. H. Daniel, *History at the University of Richmond* (1991).

R. B. James

V

Vacation Bible Schools. While there is not general agreement on the validity of this history, it appears that among Baptists the Vacation Bible Schools program (VBS) had its genesis between 1898 and 1901 in New York City. The idea of a summer program for children was adopted on an ecumenical basis between 1905 and 1915 by the Interdenominational Association of Daily Vacation Bible Schools. As with many other benevolent agencies and programs of that era, the motivating concern was for idle children, idle churches and idle students. Underprivileged children were the chief target of a missionary spirit.

Northern Baptists (see American Baptist Churches in the USA) began promoting VBS in 1915 through the American Baptist Publication Society.* Southern Baptists* first gave printed attention to VBS materials published in 1925 by the Sunday School Board.*

The assessment of the play life of children led some leaders to think that children's summer hours needed more direction. It was a common conclusion among Baptists that the idleness of summer should not be missed as a spiritual opportunity. Throughout the decades of the twentieth century, Baptists have viewed the VBS as an agency of evangelism and outreach. Not only the children but also the children's families have been pursued with a Christian witness through this summer program. The VBS has served to demonstrate the educational advantages of short-term concentrated programs of Christian education which complement the educational advantages of long-term periodic programs of Christian education such as the Sunday school.

BIBLIOGRAPHY. V. Cully and K. B. Cully, eds., *Encyclopedia of Religious Education* (1990); M. J. Taylor, ed., *Religious Education: A Comprehensive Survey* (1960). W. B. Rogers Jr.

Valder, Hans (1813-1899). Hans Valder apparently was the first Norwegian Baptist pastor in the United States. Born in Norway, he was converted in 1841 and became a Baptist in 1842. Two years later he was ordained by the church in Ottawa, Illinois, to minister to the Norwegians in the area. In 1848 Valder gathered the First Norwegian Baptist Church in Leland, Illinois. In that same year the American Baptist Home Missionary Society* appointed Valder a missionary to his fellow Norwegians. The Leland work did not prosper, and the church does not appear to have attracted more than a handful of members. Valder apparently became discouraged. Between 1849 and 1853 he ended his ministry in Illinois and moved west. Finally setting in Minnesota, Valder became a successful business leader and served in the state legislature. His religious history during this period of his life is not clear. Apparently he became a unbeliever shortly after leaving his Illinois pastorate. Later he publicly supported the noted agnostic Robert Ingersoll in his crusade against the church. Valder's agnosticism may not have been permanent: it appears that in the 1890s he may have returned to the church and to faith in Christ. G. T. Miller

Vassar, Matthew (1792-1868). Baptist philanthropist and founder of Vassar College. Born at East Tuddingham, Norfolk, England, Vassar immigrated to Dutchess County, New York, in 1796 with his parents, James and Anne Vassar. After his father's brewery in Poughkeepsie was destroyed by fire in 1811, Vassar launched an independent brewing business which prospered. On March 7, 1813, he married Catherine Valentine.

In 1845 Vassar and his wife visited Europe. A visit to Guy's Hospital in London "first suggested the idea of devoting a portion of my estate to some charitable purpose." About this time he also took an interest in a girls' school operated by his niece, Lydia Booth. Booth later sold the school to Milo P. Jewett. The business transaction brought Jewett into contact with Vassar, and the plan of a college for women began to take shape. In 1861 Vassar provided an endowment of almost unprecedented size ($400,000 hand-delivered in a tin box to the trustees) for the first true liberal arts college for women in America. Vassar College's early board of trustees included Henry Ward Beecher and Samuel F. B. Morse.

Committed to an educational experience that was Christian but never sectarian, Vassar at least partially expressed his intentions in educating women in an address to the college trustees on February 23, 1864: "The strongest incentives to goodness and the most valuable religious tendencies, will be found to flow most of all, like an emanation, from the presence of gifted, cultivated Christian women." While addressing the trustees of the college on June 23, 1868, Matthew Vassar collapsed and died.

BIBLIOGRAPHY. *DAB* X; E. A. Haight, ed., *The Autobiography and Letters of Matthew Vassar* (1916).   M. D. Floding

Vedder, Henry Clay (1853-1935). Baptist historian. Raised in upper New York, Vedder graduated from the University of Rochester and the Rochester Theological Seminary.* He worked as a journalist in New York for eighteen years. In August 1894 he accepted a professorship of church history at Crozer Theological Seminary.* His numerous works include volumes on biblical studies, Baptist missions,* the German Reformation, Balthasar Hubmaier and Baptist history. It is the latter two fields for which he is best known. He was an early prototype of the historian who gives close attention to both the social dimensions of history and the theological elements. Baptist fundamentalists* tried unsuccessfully on more than one occasion to have him removed. After he retired from Crozer in 1926, he spent the rest of his years as a journalist. His works include *A Short History of the Baptists* (1891), *The Baptists* (1902), *Balthasar Hubmaier, the Leader of the Anabaptists* (1905) and *The Reformation in Germany* (1914).   H. W. Pipkin

Vermont Academy. Baptist educational institution in Saxton River, Vermont. The Second Great Awakening* in New England contributed to an interest in the founding of academies, colleges and seminaries. Despite their small size and poverty, Vermont Baptists participated in this excitement. Their early schools, however, were poorly planned and financed. In 1866 the Vermont Baptist Convention began planning a new academy. A committee of seven, chaired by T. H. Archibald, surveyed the Baptists of the state about the need and possible location of a classical school. The endowment for the school was to be $100,000, of which $20,000 was given by Charles L. Jones, $20,000 by Saxton River citizens and $30,000 by a canvass of Vermont Baptists. Levi K. Fuller was another important early contributor. The remaining funds were raised by subscription. The school opened in 1871. The increase in the number and quality of public high schools between 1880 and 1920 forced the Vermont Academy to become a private school devoted to preparing candidates for college. Like other such church-related academies in New England, Vermont Academy moved through a sequence of titles. First it described itself as Baptist; then as Christian; and finally as private. At present the academy has no formal connection with the Baptist denomination.
                    G. T. Miller

Vick, G. Beauchamp (1901-1975). Fundamentalist* Baptist pastor, educator and one of the founders of the Baptist Bible Fellowship.* The son of a Southern Baptist* preacher, Vick worked for the railroad in Fort Worth, Texas, where he met the flamboyant J. Frank Norris,* who hired him as the youth director at First Baptist Church.

From 1928 to 1936 Vick did evangelistic work with Wade House and Mordecai Ham, then became "general superintendent" of Temple Baptist Church in Detroit, which Norris pastored in addition to his church in Fort Worth. Vick was named copastor with Norris in 1948, then pastor in 1950, when he also became president of Norris's Bible Baptist Seminary* in Fort Worth. He rapidly reduced the seminary's debt, but he ran into conflict with Norris and his lieutenant Louis Entzminger* over who was in charge of the institution. When a dispute broke out in 1950 over which set of bylaws controlled seminary business, Norris tried to fire Vick without consulting the board of trustees. A number of the pastors in Norris's World Baptist Fellowship* supported Vick. When attempts at reconciliation failed, dissenters founded the Baptist Bible Fellowship* and started a new school, Baptist Bible College,* in Springfield, Missouri, with Vick as president. Vick continued his dual role as pastor of Temple Baptist Church and president of Baptist Bible College until his death in 1975, at which time the church claimed about 14,000 members and the college

2,400 students.

BIBLIOGRAPHY. B. V. Bartlett, *A History of Baptist Separatism* (1972); J. O. Combs, *Roots and Origins of Baptist Fundamentalism* (1984).

T. P. Weber

Virginia Intermont College. A college associated with the Baptist General Association of Virginia. The school was founded in 1884 as the Southwest Virginia Female Institute in Glade Springs, Virginia. Baptists J. R. Harrison and M. M. Morris helped to establish the institute on the model of Hollins College, another female institution in Virginia.

In 1891 the school was moved to Bristol, Virginia, where it came under control of certain members of the First Baptist Church. The name was changed to Virginia Institute. By 1912 it was known as Virginia Intermont College. The school maintained junior college status until 1972, when it became a four-year coeducational college. Among other programs, Virginia Intermont is known for its B.A. program in social work and its equestrian programs.

BIBLIOGRAPHY. *ESB* 2, 4.

B. J. Leonard

Voluntarism, Baptist Views of. Voluntarism is a key historic principle significantly developed among Baptist groups. It pertains to the doctrine of the church, its support and extracongregational relationships.

Various Anabaptist* and Separatist writers were among the first in modern Christian history to espouse the terminology of voluntarism. Peter Ridemann (1506-1556), founder of the Hutterite Brethren, described the church as gathered by the Holy Spirit and founded upon the free will of its members. Robert Browne (1550-1633), an English Separatist, wrote of the church as united with Christ and to each other by voluntary consent. Likewise, John Greenwood (d. 1593) suggested that no Christian should submit to the authority of a false church. Seventeenth-century Baptist writers drew heavily upon such theology.

Among early English Baptists, John Smyth* stressed that the visible church is a body of saints voluntarily joined together by covenant and obedience to God. Moreover, Smyth taught that church officers were to be elected by vote of the membership and that churches were to be supported by the voluntary offerings of members only. Both English General* and Particular* Baptists wrote confessions of faith* stressing the voluntary consent of membership and the freedom to associate in noncoercive relationships with other Christians.

In the United States, Baptists were characterized by organizational voluntarism. In the eighteenth century many strong congregations maintained tenuous relations with associations, notably First Baptist, Middleborough, Massachusetts, which Isaac Backus* served. When opportunities for mission* and benevolence emerged in the 1790s, American Congregationalists organized voluntary societies of individuals to meet the demands. At first Baptists hesitantly cooperated, then they withdrew, as in the New York Missionary Society founded in 1796. Choosing instead to create their own voluntary bodies, Baptists built a network of local, regional and national single-purpose voluntary associations between 1800 and 1850. Among the leading societies were those for foreign missions, domestic missions, education and moral reform. In the North the overall system of denominational organization was a conglomeration of loosely connected voluntary societies. Historians have suggested that this was the result of New England sectional autonomy, Jacksonian democracy and frontier individualism.

Canadian voluntarism evolved distinct from the Baptist experience in the United States. The term *voluntary,* in Canadian usage, applies to the position taken by Baptists and Methodists in the struggle against establishment education in the provinces of Nova Scotia and Upper Canada in the 1830s and 1850s, respectively. The Anglicans and Presbyterians both pressed their claims to public revenues to maintain parochial schools. The evangelical groups urged a voluntary system of education, meaning that religious schools should be supported by those who desired them. Robert A. Fyfe of the Canadian Literary Institute and Edmund A. Crawley of Horton Academy were the leading advocates of Canadian voluntarism in education.

In the twentieth century the voluntary tradition among Baptists has been manifested in doctrines like "soul liberty," separation of church and state, the autonomy of the local church, and the associational principle, by which Baptists believe that associations, conventions, unions and alliances beyond the congregation are purely voluntary and noncoercive.

BIBLIOGRAPHY. W. H. Brackney, *Voluntarism: The Dynamic Principle of the Free Churches*

(1922); T. T. Gibson, *Robert Alexander Fyfe: His Contemporaries and His Influence* (1988); R. T. Handy, *A Christian America: Protestant Hopes and Historical Realities* (1984); W. S. Hudson, *American Protestantism* (1972).

W. H. Brackney

Wake Forest University. The first institution of higher education founded by the Baptist State Convention of North Carolina. Chartered as Wake Forest Institute in 1833, Wake Forest opened its doors on February 3, 1834, as a manual labor school. There were sixteen students under the tutelage of principal Samuel Wait. The manual labor feature was dropped in 1838, and much of the farmland was sold to help pay debts. A new charter was issued in 1838 under the name Wake Forest College.

Wake Forest's fortunes rose and fell with the economy of the country. The economic crisis of 1837 pushed Wake Forest to the edge of bankruptcy. Under the presidency of Washington Manly Wingate, Wake's financial condition was stabilized, only to be shaken again by the Civil War. Wingate returned after the war and restored the college to sound financial foundation.

Wake Forest began to improve its academic programs with the presidency of Charles Elisha Taylor (1884-1905). Academic departments were added and two new schools begun: law in 1894 and medicine in 1902. Taylor's successor, William Louis Poteat,* is known for strengthening the sciences. He also gained notoriety for his defense of the evolution theory.

In 1941 the school of medicine moved to Winston-Salem, where it affiliated with the North Carolina Baptist Hospital and expanded its program to a four-year operation.

In the post-World War II years, with a grant from the Z. Smith Reynolds Foundation and several subsequent gifts from other Reynolds family members, the decision was made to move Wake Forest College from the village of Wake Forest to Winston-Salem. Groundbreaking was held on October 15, 1951, and the first classes on the new campus were held in the summer of 1956. Harold W. Tribble was the president at this time. In 1967 Wake Forest officially changed its name to Wake Forest University to reflect the growth and devel-opment of its professional schools and graduate programs.

A major change in Wake Forest's relationship with the Baptist State Convention of North Carolina occurred in 1979. At the convention an agreement was reached whereby Wake Forest would no longer be considered an institution of the convention and would no longer receive Cooperative Program funds from the convention. Designated gifts from individual churches would continue to be channeled through the convention.

Wake Forest enjoys a national reputation as one of the leading private liberal arts colleges in the United States. Presently offering the master's degree in nineteen departments and the Ph.D. in eight, Wake Forest had an endowment of $336 million in 1992, ranking it twenty-fourth in the nation in total endowment.

BIBLIOGRAPHY. *ESB* 2:1471-74, 3:2039, 4:2537-38; G. W. Paschal, *History of Wake Forest College,* 3 vols. (1935-1943).

G. Clayton

Walker, David (1785-1830). Abolitionist pamphleteer, critic of white Christianity and agent for the black *Freedom's Journal.* Though born free in North Carolina, Walker deeply empathized with those enslaved, and he toured the South observing their oppression. In 1827 Walker moved to Boston, opened a clothing store and became active in Baptist life. During 1829 to 1830 he authored three editions of the revolutionary document *Walker's Appeal, in Four Articles,* which condemned American slavery as the worst in history, called upon enslaved African-Americans to overthrow the system, using violence if necessary, and displayed contempt for slaveholding Christianity. Walker's *Appeal* caused shock and fear among slaveholders and disturbed some black and white antislavery spokespersons. In June 1830 Walker died mysteriously, perhaps the victim of poisoning.

BIBLIOGRAPHY. *DAB* X; H. A. Ploski and J. Williams, *The Negro Almanac* (1989); M. C. Sernett, *Afro-American Religious History* (1985); S. Stuckey, *Ideological Origins of Black Nationalism* (1972). S. D. Martin

Walker, William (1809-1875). Tune-book compiler and singing master. William Walker was born near Martin's Mills, near Cross Keys, South Carolina, on May 6, 1809. Largely self-taught, he was known as a composer and music teacher at an early age. His most famous tune collection was *The Southern Harmony and Musical Companion* (1835), published in four-shape notation. There is evidence that Walker worked with his brother-in-law Benjamin Franklin White on this compilation, but only his name appeared on the title page, thus causing a rift between the two. Later White moved to Georgia and compiled his own book, *The Sacred Harp* (1844), which subsequently became more widely known. In the mid-nineteenth century these two books were so popular that they were stocked in general stores along with flour, sugar and other staples.

For years Walker was proprietor of a bookstore in Spartanburg and a leader in Baptist circles. After publishing the smaller *Southern and Western Pocket Harmonist* (1856) using four shapes, he turned to the more "progressive" seven-shape system in his *Christian Harmony* (1867) and *Fruits and Flowers* (1873). Although there are numerous tunes attributed to Walker in these collections, he is considered mainly an arranger. He died in Spartanburg on September 24, 1875.

BIBLIOGRAPHY. H. L. Eskew, "The Life and Works of William Walker" (M.C.M. thesis, New Orleans Baptist Theological Seminary, 1960); *The New Grove Dictionary of American Music* (1986) 4:470. H. T. McElrath

Wallace, Oates Charles Symonils (1836-1941). Canadian Baptist* educator. O. S. C. Wallace was born in Nova Scotia and educated at Newton Theological Institution.* He served as pastor of the Bloor Street Baptist Church in Toronto, the church that was most attended by students and faculty members from McMaster University.* In 1885 Wallace became chancellor of McMaster, which had been founded by the Baptists of Ontario and Quebec to provide a college and central seminary for the denomination in Canada.

Unfortunately, the Baptist denomination was deeply divided between its rural and urban churches. Part of Wallace's ability as a leader was his capacity to speak to both sides. The chancellor supported a modern understanding of the university and expanded its scientific program. Yet Wallace also realized that Baptists wanted a school that would produce students with a generous Christian character. Wallace worked hard to establish a Christian atmosphere of piety and service that would be attractive to both rural and urban church people.

The Canadian phase of the liberal*-fundamentalist* battle began during Wallace's chancellorship. Wallace appointed George Cross, a liberal and a graduate of the University of Chicago, to the theological department. His next appointment to that school, Isaac George Matthews, was a McMaster graduate. Conservatives were concerned over the socially progressive articles that Matthews had written as editor of the *Western Baptist.* The result was a controversy in the denomination that outlasted Wallace's own administration. The case was not settled until 1910, when the Baptist Convention of Ontario and Quebec voted affirmatively on Wallace's orthodoxy.

In 1905 Wallace resigned as chancellor to return to congregational ministry. Wallace's *Life of Jesus* (1893), written for children, was a popular religious book, and his *What Baptists Believe* (1934) was popular with laypeople throughout North America. G. T. Miller

Waller, John (1741-1802). Baptist pastor in Virginia involved in struggle for religious liberty.* Born on December 23, 1741, in Spotsylvania County, Virginia, Waller early earned the nicknames "Swearing Jack" and "Devil's Adjutant." He served on the grand jury that indicted Lewis Craig* for preaching. But Waller was so impressed by Craig that he was baptized in 1767 after an eight-month spiritual quest. In Fredericksburg in 1768, Waller and Craig were in the first group of Baptists (ultimately there were thirty-four) jailed in Virginia for preaching without a license. In all, Waller's participation in the struggle for religious liberty in Virginia would lead him to spend 113 days in four jails.

Ordained June 20, 1770, Waller became pastor of Lower Spotsylvania (Waller's) Church (1770-1793). A declared Arminian* by August 1776, he became independent, but in 1787 he was reinstated in the Baptist Association. His successful evangelizing anticipated the later camp meeting style.

On November 7, 1993, Waller moved to Abbeville, South Carolina, where he continued as a pastor and church planter until he died on July 4, 1802.

BIBLIOGRAPHY. L. P. Little, *Imprisoned Preachers and Religious Liberty in Virginia* (1938); R. B. Semple, *History of the Rise and Progress of the Baptists in Virginia* (1810); J. B. Taylor, *Virginia Baptist Ministers,* vol. 1 (1859).

R. B. James

Washington, Booker Taliaferro (1856-1915). President of Tuskegee Institute, adviser to presidents and advocate of racial accommodation and self-help. Born enslaved in Virginia, Washington attended Hampton Institute under the principalship of a Northern white man, General Samuel C. Armstrong; he graduated in 1875 and spent 1878 to 1879 at Wayland Seminary in Washington, D.C. Offered years later the opportunity to head Tuskegee Institute in Alabama, Washington built the fledgling enterprise into a great success. He is perhaps best remembered for his racial accommodation policy, which received national attention from an 1895 address delivered in Atlanta and reigned until the founding of the National Association for the Advancement of Colored People (NAACP) prior to 1910. Accommodation counseled blacks to stress economics over political agitation, industrial rather than liberal arts education, and friendship with Southern whites rather than quests for "social equality." Such counsel made Washington a hero for many Northern and Southern whites, including U.S. presidents, but critics, such as the scholar and civil rights advocate W. E. B. DuBois, warned that Washington's program would hurt African-American civil rights.

Washington, nominally a Baptist, was rumored to hold perspectives closer to Unitarianism; he believed in rational, practical religion. He ignited controversy among blacks in 1890 with criticisms of Southern black ministers. Washington was highly acclaimed and perennially present in the assemblies of black denominations, though some aspects of accommodationism were not palatable. A prolific writer, Washington authored the autobiography *Up from Slavery* (1901) and *The Story of the Negro* (1990).

BIBLIOGRAPHY. *DAB* X; R. M. Franklin, *Liberating Visions* (1990); L. R. Harlan et al., *The Booker T. Washington Papers,* vol. 3 (1974); A. Meier, *Negro Thought in America, 1880-1915* (1963).

S. D. Martin

Watchman-Examiner, The. A Northern Baptist weekly periodical that was the product of a merger between *The Examiner,* a New York publication begun in 1823, and *The Watchman,* a Boston newspaper first published in 1819. At the time of its founding, *The Watchman-Examiner,* with editorial offices in New York and Boston, enjoyed the widest circulation of any Baptist periodical in the North. Its first editor was Curtis Lee Laws,* a conservative Baptist from Virginia who had been editor of *The Examiner.* Laws was committed to the restoration of traditional Baptist theology and used the paper to this end. This editorial policy proved useful to the formation and development of fundamentalism.* In a 1920 column Laws coined the term *fundamentalist* as a designation for believers "who still cling to the great fundamentals and who mean to do battle royal for the faith." During the 1930s, when fundamentalists retreated from the institutions and churches of mainline Protestantism into their own subculture, *The Watchman-Examiner* encouraged and nurtured Protestants who felt increasingly alienated from the wider culture.

Laws remained editor until 1938, when he was replaced by John W. Bradbury. The paper continued in its conservative orientation despite this change on the masthead. It informed conservative Baptists about religious matters inside and outside the denomination, gave practical guidance about the Christian life and kept a watchful eye on the schemes of liberal Protestantism. In the late 1960s *The Watchman-Examiner* could not overcome a number of financial obstacles. It ceased publication in 1970, and its subscription list was turned over to *Eternity* magazine, a non-denominational evangelical periodical published in Philadelphia.

BIBLIOGRAPHY. D. L. Russell, *"The Watchman-Examiner,"* in *Popular Religious Magazines of the United States,* ed. M. Fackler (1994).

D. G. Hart

Wayland, Francis (1796-1865). Baptist minister and educator. Born in New York City, the son of a Baptist preacher, Wayland graduated from Union College in 1813 and studied medicine until 1816. However, a religious experience altered the course of his preparation, and he entered the ministry. He enrolled in Andover Theological Seminary* (1816) but soon took a teaching position at Union College (1817), where he remained until 1821.

In 1821 he was called to the First Baptist Church of Boston, Massachusetts, where he served as pastor for five years and acquired a reputation as a man of energy, insight and multiple gifts. Although he was unimpressive in the pulpit, his two published sermons "The Moral Dignity of the Missionary Enterprise" (1823) and "The Duties of an American Citizen" (1825) were widely circulated and acclaimed.

In 1827 he began his tenure as the fourth president of Brown University,* Providence, Rhode Island, a position he held until 1855. Wayland brought to the office a forceful personality, a wide range of knowledge and a concern for educational excellence, as well as strong convictions about teaching methods, curricula and textbooks. His determination to initiate change led to a reorganization of the university in 1850, with an expansion of the curriculum to include courses in science, modern languages and economics, and a system of elective courses. He also increased endowment, added new buildings and broadened the school's influence.

Respected as an administrator, a teacher and an author, Wayland touched thousands of students with his innovative ideas, intellectual breadth and passion for analysis, combined with a personal interest in them. In addition to his educational achievements he was involved in a wide array of civic affairs, including public schools, hospital administration, prison reform and community libraries. He also participated actively in Baptist denominational life and was a vigorous advocate of missions.*

The diversity of his interests is evident in his publications, which included Elements of Moral Science (1835), Elements of Political Economy (1837), Thoughts on the Present Collegiate System in the United States (1842), Domestic Slavery Considered as a Scriptural Institution (1845), A Memoir of the Life and Labors of the Reverend Adoniram Judson (1853) and Notes on the Principles and Practices of Baptist Churches (1857). The latter volume argued for the absolute autonomy of local congregations. Wayland's administration at Brown has been referred to as the "golden age of the university."

BIBLIOGRAPHY. DAB X; DARB; W. Hudson, "Stumbling into Disorder," Foun 1 (1958); J. O. Murray, Francis Wayland (1891); NCAB 8; F. Wayland Jr. and H. L. Wayland, A Memoir of the Life and Labors of Francis Wayland, 2 vols. (1868).   W. M. Patterson

Wayland Baptist University. Baptist General Convention of Texas educational institution. Located on an eighty-acre campus in Plainview, Wayland Baptist University has an annual budget of more than $11.5 million and endowment of $10.5 million to support an enrollment of more than 2,000 students. The school was begun by West Texas Baptists after James Henry Wayland gave $10,000 and twenty-five acres for a school. In 1908 the Wayland Literary and Technical Institution received its charter. Two years later the school became Wayland Baptist College, with I. E. Gates as president.

Wayland became a four-year college in 1947 and a university in the 1980s. In the early 1990s President Wallace Davis directed the university, together with its extension centers in other communities. Wayland is best known for being the first privately operated college in the South to voluntarily admit blacks on the same basis as other students. This policy began in 1951.

BIBLIOGRAPHY. Baptist General Convention of Texas, Texas Baptist Annual, 1990; ESB 2:1480-81.   R. Beck

Weaver, Rufus Washington (1870-1947). Baptist minister and educator. Born in Greensboro, North Carolina, Weaver received the B.A. and M.A. degrees from Wake Forest College* and the Th.M. and Th.D. degrees from the Southern Baptist Theological Seminary.* Ordained in 1893, he held pastorates in several states prior to his election as president of Mercer University,* where he served from 1918 to 1927. Under his leadership the school flourished. Weaver later moved to Washington, D.C., where he was pastor of First Baptist Church from 1934 to 1936 and executive secretary of the District of Columbia Baptist Convention until 1943.

Weaver's deep concern for religious freedom is evident in his Christian Faith at the Nation's Capital (1936) and Champions of Religious Liberty (1946). He also played a major role in organizing the Baptist Joint Committee on Public Affairs,* an agency composed of the major Baptist denominations and established to monitor church-state issues in Washington.

W. M. Patterson

Webb, Mary (1779-1861). Founder of first American woman's missionary society, social activist and Baptist churchwoman. Born in Boston in 1779, Mary Webb suffered a childhood illness that left her a paraplegic. In 1798 she joined the Baptist church pastored by Thomas C. Baldwin, who urged her to become involved in the church. With seven Baptist and six Congregational friends, Mary formed the first woman's missionary society in America in 1800—the Boston Female Society for Missionary Purposes. She served as secretary-treasurer for fifty years. She also helped found the Female Cent Society (1803), the Corban Society (1811) to raise money to educate young ministers, the Fragment Society (1812) to provide necessities for needy children, the Children's Friend Society to supply day care for children of working mothers and the Penitent Females' Refuge to work with prostitutes.

BIBLIOGRAPHY H. I. McBeth, *Women in Baptist Life* (1979); R. A. Tucker, *Guardians of the Great Commission* (1988).

R. Beck

Western Baptist Convention. A short-lived organization (1833-1842) created by Baptists for the purpose of cooperative ministry in the area west of the Appalachians. As Baptists expanded west, it was recognized that a structure was needed to tend to the peculiar realities of Baptists in the western states. Ephraim Robins and *The Baptist Weekly Journal* of Cincinnati promoted the convening of a Baptist convention in the west. Such a meeting was held in Cincinnati in November 1833: "A General Meeting for the Promotion of the Cause of Christ, as Connected with the Interests of the Baptist Denomination in the Western States." Seventy-four representatives came from Cincinnati; twenty-seven from other places in the west; seven came from the east. The question of slavery was very much at issue in all relations between North and South at this time, although every effort was made to exclude the problem from plans for expansion and development. The major project of the convention was the Western Baptist Theological Institute.* An education society was also created, as well as the American Indian Mission Society with headquarters at Louisville, Kentucky. At a meeting of the convention in Louisville in 1841 it was decided to terminate the convention arrangement the following year.

BIBLIOGRAPHY. *ESB* 2:1484.

H. W. Pipkin

Western Baptist Theological Institute. A short-lived nineteenth-century theological seminary in Covington, Kentucky, operated by the Western Baptist Convention.* Churches in the central western states depended on New Center, Hamilton and later Rochester to educate their pastors. The Western Baptist Education Society was created by the Western Baptist Convention. Under the leadership of John Stevens, O. N. Sage and others, the convention bought land in Covington, Kentucky, and built a campus. A native of Vermont, R. E. Pattison, was president and professor of theology. The institute opened its doors in the fall of 1845. During the first three years of operation, twenty-six students were enrolled. Most of the students were from the Northern states, and the school was to a large degree dominated by Northerners.

Generally speaking, the institute was not well received by Southerners, who saw in it a seedbed of abolitionist agitation. The fact that the institute opened its doors in the year in which Northern and Southern Baptists* separated over the issue of slavery (*see* Abolition Movement; American Baptist Churches in the USA) militated against the successful development of the institute. The participation of institute professors in the American Baptist Missionary Union* in 1847 only served to demonstrate to Southerners the institute's identification with the Northern and hence antislavery side. Attempts to overcome the conflict were to no avail. The institute was sold in 1855, and the proceeds were distributed equally between Northern (Fairmount Theological Institute, Ohio) and Southern institutions (Georgetown College, Kentucky).

BIBLIOGRAPHY. M. Anderson, "The Western Baptist Theological Institute" (manuscript, Southern Baptist Theological Seminary, 1946); W. Ashmore, "The Blotting Out of the Old Time Western Baptist Theological Institute" (manuscript, Southern Baptist Theological Seminary, n.d.); W. C. James, "A History of the Western Baptist Theological Institute, Covington, Kentucky" (thesis, Southern Baptist Theological Seminary, 1905).

H. W. Pipkin

Western Conservative Baptist Seminary. A conservative evangelical seminary in Portland, Oregon, with historic ties to the Northern Baptist Convention (*see* American Baptist Churches in the USA) and, more recently, the Conservative Baptist* movement. In 1925 Walter B. Hinson, pastor of the East Side Baptist Church, organized the Portland Baptist Bible Institute. After Hinson's death in 1926 the church called John Marvin Dean, prominent Chicago pastor and founder of the Northern Baptist Theological Seminary* (1913). Dean moved quickly to turn the Bible institute into the Western Baptist Theological Seminary, which from its founding in 1927 used the facilities of East Side Baptist Church (now renamed Hinson Memorial Baptist Church). Dean left Portland in 1929. Subsequently William Milliken led the seminary until 1944, the same year the school moved to a new five-acre permanent site in Portland.

During the 1940s, after twenty years of opposing the Northern Baptist Convention's "inclusivist policy" that allowed liberals to be appointed as foreign missionaries, conservatives founded their own Conservative Baptist Foreign Mission Society. When the Northern Baptist Convention denied recognition to the new society, hundreds of conservative congregations withdrew to form the Conservative Baptist Association. Western Seminary sided with the new Conservative Baptist movement, which soon struggled with its own identity issues. In contrast to the Denver Conservative Baptist Theological Seminary (founded 1950), which moved in a "new evangelical" direction, Western maintained a more fundamentalist* ethos: it hired only dispensationalists and operated within the orbit of institutions like Dallas Theological Seminary, Grace Theological Seminary and Talbot School of Theology.

Western's greatest growth occurred in the long presidency of Earl Radmacher (1965-1990), during which the seminary opened satellite campuses in San Jose, California, and Phoenix, Arizona, where complete M.Div. and D.Min. programs were offered. During the 1980s the seminary also pioneered in the use of video instruction. Despite its Baptist beginnings, Western now attracts students from a variety of evangelical groups.

T. P. Weber

Wharton, Lucie (Lulie) Kimball Pollard (1871-1948). Author and denominational leader with the Southern Baptist* Woman's Missionary Union* (WMU). Born in Baltimore, Maryland, on December 9, 1871, Lulie Kimball Pollard was educated in Baltimore public schools and the Peabody Institute before attending Mary Baldwin College in Staunton, Virginia, for one year. WMU was a part of Lulie's life from childhood, since her mother, Susan, was the organization's first recording secretary and her father, James, helped draw

up the constitution. In 1893 Lulie married Henry Marvin Wharton, Baltimore evangelist, pastor, bookseller and publisher, who had been her pastor and had baptized her when she was nine. Wharton provided the space for the original headquarters of the WMU in Baltimore.

Henry Wharton's evangelistic enterprise took the family to Philadelphia for over ten years. Upon her return to Baltimore in 1910, Lulie Wharton organized the WMU's personal service department. A specific concern of this social action program was immigrants. Wharton kept herself and the WMU aware of the current needs of immigrants by traveling and participating in nationwide conferences. She was a member of the Southern Sociological Congress. In 1914 she changed the name of Southern Baptist social work institutions from "settlement house" to "good will center," in order to present a more positive image.

During World War I Wharton mobilized coordination between local church WMUs and Red Cross chapters to provide war relief. She served as assistant recording secretary for the WMU from 1913 to 1921, at which time she became recording secretary, a capacity in which she served until 1938. Wharton helped celebrate the fiftieth anniversary of the WMU in 1936 by writing the booklet *Ready Pens Proclaiming Missions* to tell the story of the publishing activities of Southern Baptist women during the fifty years of WMU. In 1938 her address on the early struggles of WMU, "As My Mother Knew Them," was published in the annual report, and her book *The Fruits of the Years* was the study book for the Week of Prayer for Home Missions. Wharton retired after twenty-five years of service to WMU in 1938 and died in Weems, Virginia, on July 30, 1948.

BIBLIOGRAPHY. C. Allen, *A Century to Celebrate: History of Woman's Missionary Union* (1987); C. Allen, *Laborers Together with God* (1987).

P. R. Pleasants

Whidden, Howard Primrose (1871-1952). Baptist minister, politician and educator. Born in Nova Scotia, Whidden was educated at Acadia University, McMaster University,* Newton Theological Seminary* and the University of Chicago. Whidden taught at both McMaster and Brandon colleges before entering the Baptist ministry, serving first in Canada and then in Dayton, Ohio. In 1912 he was appointed president of Brandon College, a small Baptist college in Brandon, Manitoba, a position he held until 1923. Strongly supportive of conscription and nonpartisan government during World War I, he was elected to the Canadian House of Commons as a Union candidate in 1917. He represented Brandon until 1921.

In 1923 he was appointed chancellor of McMaster University, a Baptist institution then located in Toronto. The move to Hamilton, Ontario, was accomplished in 1930 under Whidden's direction. Whidden and the university became deeply embroiled in the fundamentalist*-modernist controversy that racked the Ontario-Quebec Baptist Convention in the mid-1920s. After his retirement from McMaster in 1941, Whidden edited the *Canadian Baptist* for three years.

BIBLIOGRAPHY. C. M. Johnston, *McMaster University,* 2 vols. (1976); C. G. Stone and F. J. Garnett, *Brandon College: A History, 1899-1967* (1969).

B. M. Moody

White, Charlotte (early 19th century). First single woman to apply for appointment by the Triennial Convention.* In 1815 White, a widow who had long felt a call to missions, applied for appointment to India. Knowing that the board would be reluctant to send a single woman, she asked to go with Mr. and Mrs. George Hough, volunteering to manage a school or to work with the women. The committee appeared hesitant to send a single woman. Charlotte informed the committee that she had bought all of her own provisions and would have $300 left which she intended to give to the mission fund. The committee then decided to appoint her, and she sailed with the Houghs in December of that year. On the mission field White met and married Joshua Rowe, a single missionary from England. Together they worked with William Carey* and in the city of Digha. After Joshua Rowe's death, Charlotte White Rowe continued their work. The Triennial Convention later refunded her contribution. Her birth and death dates are difficult to establish.

BIBLIOGRAPHY. R. P. Beaver, *American Protestant Women in World Mission: A History of the First Feminist Movement in North America* (1980); H. L. McBeth, *Women in Baptist Life* (1979).

C. Blevins

Whitsitt, William Heth (1841-1911). President of Southern Baptist Theological Seminary* and professor of church history. Born near Nashville, Tennessee, Whitsitt graduated from Union University* in Jackson, Tennessee. In 1861 his life was interrupted by the Civil War, during which he served as a chaplain in the Confederate Army. After the war he continued his education at the University of Virginia (1866) and the Southern Baptist Theological Seminary (1866-1868), followed by two years of study at the Universities of Leipzig and Berlin.

In 1872 Whitsitt gave up his pastorate in Albany, Georgia, to become the professor of ecclesiastical history at Southern Baptist Theological Seminary in Greenville, South Carolina. In 1895 he succeeded John A. Broadus* as president of the seminary. By then the seminary had relocated (in 1877) to Louisville, Kentucky. Only four years after assuming the presidency, Whitsitt was forced to resign.

The Whitsitt controversy was sparked by the discovery that Whitsitt was the author of an unsigned encyclopedia article which stated that Baptists "invented" immersion in 1641. Whitsitt explained that he had used the word *invent* in the old English sense of "discover" or "uncover"—meaning that in 1641 the Baptists had restored the primitive practice of baptism by immersion.

Nevertheless, Landmarkers,* who believed that Baptists had existed in unbroken succession since the days of John the Baptist, found Whitsitt's arguments unacceptable. Whitsitt, on the other hand, committed to an objective approach to church history, demanded that Baptist claims be supported by documentation. The seminary trustees concluded that harmony could not be restored apart from replacing Whitsitt. In 1899 he resigned both the presidency and his professorship.

Shortly thereafter he became professor of philosophy in Richmond College (now University of Richmond*), Virginia, where he taught until his death in 1911. Whitsitt wrote on a number of historically related subjects, with books including *Position of the Baptists in the History of American Culture* (1872), *The History of the Rise of Infant Baptism* (1878), *A Question in Baptist History* (1896) and *The Origin of the Disciples of Christ* (1888).

BIBLIOGRAPHY. *DAB* X; *ESB* 2; T. Meigs, "The Whitsitt Controversy," *QR* 31 (1971); W. A. Mueller, *A History of Southern Baptist Theological Seminary* (1959). W. R. Estep

Wightman, Valentine (1681-1747). Pioneer Baptist minister in Connecticut and New York

City. Born in North Kingston, Rhode Island, Wightman was a "Six-Principle" Baptist* who rejected many Calvinistic* emphases of the Regular Baptists.* In 1705 he established a church at Groton, Connecticut, the earliest Baptist church in the state except for the fleeting appearance of a Seventh Day Baptist* group in the 1670s. In 1712 he began preaching in New York City, helping to form the earliest Baptist church there in 1714. This church did not survive, being supplanted in 1726 by a congregation of Regular Baptists. Wightman also formed a number of churches in Connecticut. An advocate of the then-controversial practice of singing in worship (see Hymnody, Baptist), he also conducted a number of public debates on baptism.* He married Susanna Holmes in 1703 and left descendants who followed him in the Baptist ministry.

BIBLIOGRAPHY. *AAP* 6; I. Backus, *A History of New England, with Particular Reference to the Denomination of Christians Called Baptists* (1777). H. L. McBeth

William Jewell College. Liberal arts college affiliated with the Missouri Baptist Convention. The college is located at Liberty, Missouri, northeast of Kansas City. Chartered and founded in 1849, William Jewell College was the first four-year men's college west of the Mississippi River. The college is named for William Jewell, a Columbia, Missouri, physician who provided the initial $10,000 endowment. Jewell Hall, completed in 1853, continues to be the main classroom building of the campus and is listed on the National Register of Historic Places. The college granted its first bachelor's degrees in 1855. Operation of the college was suspended during the Civil War, and on two occasions federal troops occupied Jewell Hall.

The college experienced significant growth and advancement during the presidencies of John Priest Greene (1892-1923) and Walter Pope Binns (1943-1962). Under the leadership of J. Gordon Kingsley, president of the college since 1980, William Jewell has gained national recognition. The college offers a variety of curricular approaches that include interdisciplinary courses, tutorial learning, study opportunities abroad and an annual fine arts series featuring international performing artists. Recent additions to the campus include a multifaceted sports complex, the renovation of the theater and fine arts building, and the expansion and modernization of the Marston

Science building. The college has 95 full-time faculty, 1,791 students and an endowment of $50 million.

BIBLIOGRAPHY. H. I. Hester, *Jewell Is Her Name* (1967). A. L. Pratt

Williams, Annie Laurie (1861-1932). Author and denominational leader with the Southern Baptist* Sunday School Board.* Annie Williams was born in Montgomery, Alabama, on December 13, 1861, and died in Birmingham, Alabama, on February 14, 1932. While serving as the superintendent of the primary department for the Southside Baptist Church in Birmingham, she began her career of influencing the quality of programming Southern Baptists offered for children. In 1909 the Sunday School Board employed her as the first person to oversee elementary work, which position she held until 1932. She was the author in 1918 of the first Southern Baptist training material for elementary departments, titled *Plans and Programs for Cradle Roll, Beginners and Primaries.* Throughout her career Williams emphasized the importance of location for implementing children's programs, as well as setting high standards for teachers, equipment and curriculum. Her influence crossed geographical and denominational boundaries as she traveled extensively, lecturing on the necessity of quality children's programming for the church. Through her writing in her area of expertise she opened the door for more women to be accepted as authors by the Southern Baptist Sunday School Board and Broadman Press.*

BIBLIOGRAPHY. E. W. Thompson, "Southern Baptist Women as Writers and Editors," *BHH* 22 (July 1987). P. R. Pleasants

Williams, George Washington (1849-1891). Pastor, soldier, journalist, lawyer, legislator and foreign service worker. Williams was born in Pennsylvania and joined the Union Army in 1862. After an illustrious career in the army, Williams attended Howard University in Washington, D.C., and graduated from Newton Theological Institute* in 1874. He pastored the historic Twelfth Street Baptist Church in Boston and made unsuccessful attempts to launch newspapers in Washington, D.C., and Cincinnati. He graduated from Cincinnati Law School, won a seat in the Ohio legislature in 1879, worked for the Internal Revenue Service, served as the American minister to Haiti and worked for the Belgians in the Congo

Free State. Williams authored two monumental works: *The History of the Negro Race from 1619 to 1880* (1883) and *A History of the Negro Troops in the War of the Rebellion* (1888).

BIBLIOGRAPHY. *DAB* X; J. H. Franklin, *George Washington Williams* (1985); H. A. Ploski and J. Williams, *The Negro Almanac* (1989).

S. D. Martin

Williams, Roger (1603-1683). Founder of the first Baptist church in North America and champion of religious liberty.* Born in London, probably in 1603, the son of a shopkeeper, Williams studied first at the Charterhouse and later at Pembroke College, Cambridge (B.A., 1627). An Anglican minister, he became chaplain to Sir William Masham in Otes, Essex County, where on December 15, 1629, he wedded Mary Barnard, the daughter of a Puritan clergyman.

Sometime during his Cambridge experience Williams apparently became a Puritan, and in 1630 he sailed with his wife from Bristol to Massachusetts, landing at Nantasket on February 5, 1631. On board ship, Williams, after an intensive study of the New Testament, concluded that in order to be truly biblical the Puritans in New England should explicitly separate from the Church of England. There followed a succession of clashes with the Massachusetts authorities as Williams criticized the Puritan establishment for a variety of practices, especially for expropriating Indian land without negotiations and for having the civil magistrates attempt to enforce the first four of the Ten Commandments. On October 9, 1635, the colonial General Court (legislature) banished him to England, but before he could be deported he fled with his family and a few companions to the uninhabited regions to the south, outside the limits of Massachusetts. In the summer of 1636 he founded there a settlement that he named Providence.

As leader of the new colony, Williams purchased land from the Narragansett Indians and distributed it for use, befriended the Indians and learned their language, and during the Pequot War (1637) served all New England as a negotiator to restore peace to the region. In Providence he adopted the principle that "God requireth not an uniformity of Religion" and saw to it that all individuals and religious bodies enjoyed what he called "soul liberty"—that is, religious freedom. In 1642, faced with internal tensions and the expansionist designs of Massachusetts and Connect-

icut, Williams sailed for England to procure a charter for the cluster of settlements in the Narragansett region. His London trip resulted in the acquisition from Parliament on March 14, 1644, of a charter uniting the several towns into the colony of Rhode Island, fixing its boundaries, guaranteeing its independence and, for the first time in American history, granting complete religious liberty to all of its inhabitants. While in London he also published three books, the most important of which was *The Bloudy Tenent of Persecution*, in which he expounded the premises that underlay his lifelong commitment to religious liberty.

Williams was again dispatched to London in November 1651 when internal enemies seemed about to split and perhaps destroy the colony. On this occasion (1651-1654) he not only saved the charter but also became a friend of John Milton and Oliver Cromwell; he also published three more volumes, one of which was a reply to John Cotton's response to his earlier work—this one was entitled *The Bloudy Tenent Yet More Bloudy.*

Upon his return Williams served as president (governor) of the colony (1654-1657), and during his tenure he welcomed the first Jews and Quakers to Rhode Island, even though he disagreed with their views. In 1672 he engaged three Quakers in a tumultuous public debate for four days; he published the report in Boston in 1676 under the title *George Fox Digg'd out of his Burrowes.* Williams was reduced to poverty when his trade was disrupted by the bloody King Philip's War (1675-1676), during which Williams, though well over seventy, served as a captain in the colonial militia and later as a peace negotiator. He died in Providence sometime between January 16 and March 15, 1683.

In 1639, shortly after settling Providence, Williams had become a Baptist, and during that year he joined with a dozen others in forming the first Baptist church on American soil. However, a few months later Williams withdrew from the Baptists and pronounced himself a Seeker, one who had not yet discovered "the true church" as constituted by Jesus Christ in the first century. He agreed with Baptist insistence on religious liberty and separation of church and state, but he could not accept the Baptist claim that their congregations constituted "the true church" that could be entered only through their "true baptism." For the remainder of his life Williams would be a religious loner, searching for a church that he could recognize as created in the image of the first apostles. In the end he clung tenaciously to his basic Calvinist* theology and to his belief in religious liberty and separation of church and state; he died an independent evangelical Christian without a denomination.

Williams's original influence was greatest among his near coreligionists, the Baptists. It was through the Baptists that Williams's thought and reputation were transmitted to the young nation for whom he became a folk hero in the nineteenth century. In many ways Williams's Rhode Island, with its stress on freedom, individualism and being a place "where no man should be molested for his conscience"—and not Puritan New England with its emphasis on order, community and the mission of a "city on a hill"—was the prototype of the future American republic.

See also FIRST BAPTIST CHURCH, PROVIDENCE, RHODE ISLAND.

BIBLIOGRAPHY. T. D. Bozeman, "Religious Liberty and the Problem of Order in Early Rhode Island," *NEQ* 45 (March 1971):44-64; S. H. Brocknuier, *Irrepressible Democrat: Roger Williams* (1940); M. Calamandrei, "Neglected Aspects of Roger Williams' Thought," *CH* 21 (1952):239-59; J. Garrett, *Roger Williams: Witness Beyond Christendom* (1970); W. C. Gilpin, *The Millenarian Piety of Roger Williams* (1979); P. Miller, *Roger Williams: His Contribution to the American Tradition* (1953); E. S. Morgan, *Roger Williams: The Church and the State* (1967); H. J. Schultz, "Roger Williams, Delinquent Saint: The Religious Odyssey of the Providence Prophet," *ABQ* 19 (April 1962):253-69; R. Williams, *The Complete Writings of Roger Williams,* 7 vols. (1963); O. E. Winslow, *Master Roger Williams* (1957).

R. D. Linder

Williams, William (1821-1877). One of the original four faculty members of the Southern Baptist Theological Seminary.* Born in Eatonton, Georgia, Williams received his education at the University of Georgia (B.A., 1840) and Harvard University Law School (LL.B., 1847). In 1851 he felt a call to preach and became a pastor in Auburn, Alabama. In 1856 he accepted a position as professor of theology at Mercer University,* then located in Penfield, Georgia. When the Southern Baptist Theological Seminary opened in 1859, Williams was invited to become professor of ecclesiastical history and church government and pastoral duties. In 1872 he assumed James P.

Boyce's chair of systematic theology when Boyce had to spend much time away from the campus raising funds. He served several terms as vice president of the Southern Baptist Convention.* After a lengthy bout with consumption, he died at Aiken, South Carolina, on February 20, 1877.

BIBLIOGRAPHY. *ESB* 2:1503.

E. G. Hinson

Williams, William R. (1804-1885). New York City pastor. Williams's father was a Welsh clergyman who came to America in 1795 and pastored Oliver Street Church for twenty-seven years. Williams first went into law, but in 1832 he became founding pastor of the Amity Street Baptist Church, which he pastored until his death. Francis Wayland,* president of Brown University,* preached the sermon at his ordination on December 17, 1832.

Williams was known for being well educated and was rated as the equal of Robert Hall as a rhetorician. During his term of service as president of the New York Baptist Union for Ministerial Education from 1850 to 1851, the Rochester Theological Seminary* was founded. His personal library was reputed to have 25,000 volumes. His writing was literate and erudite, and he exercised considerable influence. His works included *Miscellanies* (1850), *Religious Progress* (1850), *Lectures on the Lord's Prayer* (1851), *Lectures on Baptist History* (1871) and *Eras and Characters of History* (1882). His funeral sermon was preached by the president of the Northern Baptists on April 4, 1885, at the Madison Avenue Baptist Church, New York City.

BIBLIOGRAPHY. *DAB* X.

H. W. Pipkin

Williams College (Arkansas). Baptist College in Arkansas. In 1941 H. E. Williams, pastor of the First Baptist Church in Pocahontus, Arkansas, and G. E. Neely began Southern Baptist College in Pocahontus. Permission was granted by the War Assets Administration to use the Marine Air Facility at Walnut Ridge, Arkansas, and the school was moved there in 1946. The Rural Theological Seminary of the South was part of the curriculum in the 1950s, which also included printing, photography, woodcarving and auto mechanics.

The two-year college was accredited by the Arkansas State Department of Higher Education in 1947 and by the North Central Association of Colleges and Universities in 1963. In 1948 the Arkansas Baptist State Convention included the college in its budget, and in 1968 it assumed ownership.

In 1983 the school began to offer four-year programs in education and religion. The name of the school was changed to Williams Baptist College in 1990. Currently 600 full-time and 200 part-time students are enrolled, and there are 25 faculty members.

BIBLIOGRAPHY. Williams College, *Catalogue* (1991).　　　　　　　　　　　　J. T. Greer

Winchester, Elhanan (1751-1797). Colonial Baptist pastor. Elhanan Winchester was born in 1751 into a poor family in Brookline, Massachusetts. Although Winchester appears to have had talent with languages, he received little formal education. In 1770 he became a Baptist and was ordained. After several years of itinerant ministry, Winchester moved to Welch Neck, South Carolina, where he became the pastor of the Baptist church. During his Southern ministry, Winchester preached to the slaves and became committed to their eventual emancipation. At this time Winchester held to a rigid Calvinism* based on the writings of John Gill. In 1779, following a period of itinerant preaching, Winchester became the pastor of the First Baptist Church in Philadelphia.*

By this time Winchester had adopted his own version of universalism. Like many of his contemporaries, he was a convinced millenarian and believed that God would soon fulfill the prophecies in Revelation. Although much of Winchester's exposition was conventional, he extended biblical prophecy past the second judgment. After this last judgment, God would meld the world into the lake of fire. There wicked persons and angels would suffer for a prolonged period. The purpose of this period of torment was to bring all to repentance and perhaps to purify the earth of its pollution. Once all had turned from their sins, Christ would restore the renewed earth to the Father, who would then be all in all.

Once Winchester's congregation became aware of his changed views, a council was called. After a heated meeting, Winchester was dismissed. The congregation itself divided, with about 100 people leaving with the pastor to form the Society of Universalist Baptists. In 1787 Winchester went to England, where he published tracts against slavery. Winchester returned to America penniless in 1794 and ended his days as an itinerant preacher.

G. T. Miller

Wingate, Washington Manly (1828-1879). North Carolina Baptist minister and educator. Educated at Wake Forest College* (1849) and Furman* Theological Institute (1849-1851), he was awarded honorary doctorates by Columbian College* and the University of North Carolina. Ordained a Baptist minister, he served several North Carolina churches. In 1853 he became a professor at Wake Forest College, and after a term as interim president, he came to serve as president of that institution from 1854 to 1879. He was an evangelist in the Confederate Army, served as editor of the North Carolina Baptist paper, the *Biblical Recorder,* and was widely recognized for his skill as a preacher and administrator.

BIBLIOGRAPHY. *ESB* 2.

B. J. Leonard

Wingate College. A liberal college owned and operated by North Carolina Baptists, located in Wingate, North Carolina. Established in 1889 by the Union Baptist Association as Wingate School, it was operated jointly by the association and the local public-school system as a private preparatory school until 1917. At that time it came under the control of several local Baptist associations, and later it was taken over by the Baptist State Convention of North Carolina. In 1923 the school become a junior college. The school admitted its first junior class in 1977 and graduated its first four-year students in 1979.

BIBLIOGRAPHY. *ESB* 1, 4.

B. J. Leonard

Wingren, Eric (1843-1922). Publisher of *Nya Wecko Posten,* the most influential Swedish Baptist* periodical for almost four decades (1880-1918). Born in Stugun, Jamtland, Sweden, on December 17, 1843, he was immersed in the fall of 1861 after a dramatic conversion experience. He studied in Gustaf Palmquist's Bible school in 1863 and was a member of the first class of Betelseminariet in Stockholm (1866-1868). After twelve years in pastoral and evangelistic work in Sweden, he emigrated to America in 1880. Pastor, teacher in the Swedish seminary and publisher of *Evangelisk Tidskrift,* Wingren soon turned his entire energies to the latter, changing its name in 1885 to *Nya Wecko Posten (NWP).* Serving as pastor and theologian at large for more than a generation of Swedish Baptists, he published extensively, including at least ten books, thirteen "annuals," a hymnbook, Sunday-school papers and a large number of tracts, in addition to weekly editorials and articles in *NWP*. Failing health forced his retirement in 1918 after selling *NWP* to the General Conference. He died in Chicago on September 19, 1922.

BIBLIOGRAPHY. G. A. Hagstrom, "The Centenary of an Influential Editor," in *Ebenezer*, ed. C. G. Ericson and J. O. Backlund (1944); A. Olson, *A Centenary History As Related to the Baptist General Conference of America* (1952).

N. A. Magnuson

Woelfkin, Cornelius (1859-1928). Baptist pastor, educator and denominational servant. Born in New York, September 15, 1859, Woelfkin was the son of John Fredereick and Christiana Austermuhl Woelfkin. Ordained to the Baptist ministry in 1886, he served in the following pastorates: Bengell, New York, 1885-1887; Hackensack, New Jersey, 1887-1892; North Church, Jersey City, New Jersey, 1892-1894; Green Avenue, Brooklyn, New York, 1894-1895; and Park Avenue Baptist Church, New York, 1912-1926 (known prior to 1922 as the Fifth Avenue Baptist Church). Woelfkin was professor of homiletics at Rochester Theological Seminary* from 1906 to 1912, president of the American Baptist Foreign Missionary Society* in 1911 and Sanders Lecturer on Baptist History and Polity at Union Theological Seminary.* He married Lille S. Distler on May 3, 1882, and wrote *Chambers of the Soul* in 1899.

Woelfkin is remembered for a strategic move at the Northern Baptist Convention in Indianapolis in 1922. When fundamentalists* sought to impose the New Hampshire Confession of Faith* upon the denomination, Woelfkin presented a substitute motion proposing that the Northern Baptist Convention affirm that "the New Testament is the all-sufficient ground of our faith and practice, and we need no other statement." Woelfkin's motion carried by a vote of 1,264 to 637 and remains today the anticreedal, anticonfessional stance of the American Baptist Churches in the USA,* the present-day name of the Northern Baptist Convention.

When nearing retirement at Park Avenue Baptist Church, Woelfkin prepared the way for the coming of Harry Emerson Fosdick* as his successor. From Park Avenue, with Woelfkin's support, Fosdick landed his plans for the well-known Riverside Church.* The pulpit at Riverside bears the inscription "Given in memory of Cornelius Woelfkin, Pastor of the Park Avenue Baptist

Church, 1912-1926, whose wise and progressive leadership made this church possible." He died January 6, 1928.

BIBLIOGRAPHY. H. E. Fosdick, *The Living of These Days* (1956); R. G. Torbet, *A History of the Baptists* (1973); *Who Was Who in America* 1.

C. A. Russell

Woman's American Baptist Foreign Mission Society. An organization of American Baptist* women formed in 1913 for the purpose of supporting missions. The society was created when the Woman's Baptist Foreign Mission Society of the East (established April 3, 1871) and the Woman's Baptist Missionary Society of the West (established May 9, 1871) combined. The society worked in cooperation with the male-led American Baptist Missionary Union* to recruit and support missionaries, with the understanding that the union would determine the missionaries' placement and type of service. The missionaries sent by the women's society emphasized and excelled in teaching and nursing on the mission field; they were leaders in working ecumenically, starting orphanages and boarding schools, and giving an important place to work with women and children. In 1955 the society merged with the boards of managers and the staff of the American Baptist Foreign Mission Society.*

BIBLIOGRAPHY. L. A. Cattan and H. C. Schmitz, *American Baptist Missions: One Mark of Greatness* (1961).　　　　　　　　S. L. Still

Woman's American Baptist Home Mission Society. American Baptist* missions* organization for women. The Woman's American Baptist Home Mission Society was organized on November 14, 1877, by women of New England. The society's purpose was missions education which would result in support for evangelism on the mission field. By 1878 the women were organized nationally and supporting missions in significant ways. They sent missionaries, raised money, and provided used clothing and other supplies for mission work. They gained supplies as local church societies fulfilled "White Cross" quotas, which instructed the churches in what they needed to make or buy. The missionaries sent by the society worked with all groups (including African-Americans, Native Americans, immigrants and Spanish-Americans). Their motto was "Christ in Every Home." In 1909 the Free Baptist Women and the Women's Baptist Home Mission Society merged with the Woman's American Baptist Home Mission Society to form the Woman's Society.

BIBLIOGRAPHY. L. A. Cattan and H. C. Schmitz, *American Baptist Missions: One Mark of Greatness* (1961).　　　　　　　　　　　S. L. Still

Woman's Mission to Woman, Baltimore Branch. Woman's Mission to Woman (WMTW) denoted a movement dating from the interdenominational Woman's Union Missionary Society, organized in 1861 in New York City. The purpose was to send women missionaries to evangelize women, especially in Asia. In 1867 the movement went south to Baltimore. The Baltimore WMTW was led by Ann Jane Baker Graves, a Methodist, noted author and mother of Rosewell Graves, an early Southern Baptist* missionary in China. Graves built on women's foreign mission interest in Baltimore dating from the 1813 Female Missionary Society* of First Baptist Church.

In 1868 Graves became a Baptist and called the first general meeting of Southern Baptist women. In October 1871 Baptist women of Baltimore formed their own branch of Woman's Mission to Woman. They sought controversial recognition at the 1872 Southern Baptist Convention* (SBC) and gained cooperation from the SBC Foreign Mission Board in July 1872. Prompted by Baltimore, the board appointed two single women that year. By 1879 the Baltimore committee was fostering more than 200 women's groups throughout the South. In 1892 the group became the Woman's Baptist Foreign Missionary Society of Maryland.

These efforts led directly to the formation of the Woman's Missionary Union, Auxiliary to the Southern Baptist Convention,* in 1888.

See also WOMAN'S MISSIONARY UNION.

BIBLIOGRAPHY. C. B. Allen, *A Century to Celebrate* (1987).　　　　　　　　　　　C. B. Allen

Woman's Missionary Societies in Richmond. In the spring of 1813 a Female Missionary Society was formed in the First Baptist Church of Richmond, Virginia, for the support of foreign missions. This followed a call issued in 1812 by Mary Webb,* representing the Boston Female Society for Missionary Purposes. The Richmond women were then contacted by Luther Rice* in his call for organizing the first convention of Baptists in the United States, the Triennial Convention of 1814.

The First Baptist women were joined in 1817 by a Juvenile Cent Society, the first girls' missionary society in the South. In 1822 the women joined with those of Second Baptist Church of Richmond in support of missionary Ann Judson* in Burma. In 1872 these and three other Baptist churches formed the Woman's Missionary Society of Richmond for the purpose of guaranteeing the support of Edmonia Moon (sister of Charlotte Moon*), one of two women being appointed by the Southern Baptist* Foreign Mission Board for service in China, after a twenty-year ban on women appointees.

The Woman's Missionary Union of First Baptist, Richmond, published its 179th anniversary history in 1992. The citywide society led to the formation of the Woman's Missionary Union of Virginia.

BIBLIOGRAPHY. C. B. Allen, *A Century to Celebrate* (1987).　　　　　　　　　　　C. B. Allen

Woman's Missionary Union, Auxiliary to the Southern Baptist Convention. Baptist women's organization organized in Richmond, Virginia, 1888, as Woman's Mission Societies during the "century of women and missions." The present name was adopted in 1890, and commitment continued for the support of women missionaries, missionary education of the young and special offerings for home and foreign missions.* Within a few years every state in the convention had Woman's Missionary Unions (WMUs), and most churches had multiple age-level organizations. The peak enrollment was 1.5 million in 1964. Missions publications climbed rapidly, as did mission giving.

Eventually headquartered in Birmingham, Alabama, WMU for several decades furnished housing facilities for missionary children (Greenville, South Carolina, 1905) and for women desiring seminary training for the mission field (Louisville, Kentucky, 1907). The latter was first called the Woman's Missionary Union Training School,* became the Carver School of Missions and Social Work* in 1953, in 1958 transferred to Southern Baptist Convention control and in 1962 merged with the Southern Baptist Theological Seminary.* Support for the college education of missionary children was another successful undertaking. Missions publications were also a major focus.

Conceived by a small group of dedicated, well-educated women, the WMU attracted many educated and professional women by the 1930s, providing opportunities for leadership and education. Historical reports on the organization suggest that it has been on the forefront of social issues and minority needs, an encourager of summer Bible school programs, and promoter of women's rights, race relations and higher education for women and children. The executive director-treasurer in the early 1990s was Dellanna W. O'Brien.

BIBLIOGRAPHY. C. B. Allen, *A Century to Celebrate* (1987).   S. F. Anders

Woman's Missionary Union Training School (1907-1953). Southern Baptist* institution for training women in missions* and social work, Louisville, Kentucky. Operated by the Woman's Missionary Union (WMU), Auxiliary to the Southern Baptist Convention,* the WMU Training School offered a curriculum of biblical studies (in conjunction with nearby Southern Baptist Theological Seminary*), domestic science, music, public speaking and personal evangelism. In 1904 four women went to Louisville to sit in classes with male students of the seminary. Local missionary societies formed a board of managers to supervise the women and raise funds for a home. As more students arrived, the home grew into a school which was adopted by the WMU on 1907 after a long controversy involving opposition by Annie Armstrong,* who feared the school intended to train women to preach.

Maude R. McLure* served as the school's first principal, and in 1912 she established a settlement house that provided service to neighborhood persons, many of them immigrants. In 1917 "House Beautiful" was built to house the student body; about seventy boarding and twenty-five day students were enrolled at that time.

In 1926 the seminary moved to suburban Louisville, leaving the Training School downtown. For the next fifteen years there were no coeducational classes, and the seminary professors traveled downtown to teach the women. This arrangement lasted until 1941, when the Training School moved into a new building, adjacent to the seminary, and coed classes were resumed.

On May 12, 1952, the WMU voted to restructure the school, opening classes to men and revising the curriculum. At that time the name was changed to Carver School of Missions and Social Work* to honor William Owen Carver,* a member of the seminary faculty who had been a valuable adviser since the formation of the school and had taught missions classes for many years.

The school continued under the new name until 1963, when it merged with the Southern Baptist Theological Seminary.*

BIBLIOGRAPHY. C. B. Allen, *A Century to Celebrate* (1987).   T. L. Scales

Women's Commission of the Baptist General Conference. Baptist General Conference* commission. Created in 1932, the Women's Commission worked to unify General Conference women's groups. The seven-member commission tried to coordinate the work of the societies. But by 1940 the commission was nonfunctional, and ladies' aid societies in churches worked individually. The Board of Women's Work came into existence in 1944 to coordinate these groups and to emphasize missions. As the General Conference matured, the board changed its focus to women's ministry rather than missions.* In 1975 the board defined five areas of work: spiritual growth, evangelism, service, missions and hospitality.

The board underwent a change in the 1980s and became the Women's Ministry program. Having been directed for many years by Dorothy Dahlman, the program was headed in the early 1990s by Pamela Heim.

BIBLIOGRAPHY. J. O. Backlund, *Swedish Baptists in America* (1933); Baptist General Conference, *Annual 1991*.   R. Beck

Women's Department, Auxiliary to Baptist World Alliance. Beginning in the 1911 congress of the Baptist World Alliance (BWA), women sought their own organization for communication and cooperative effort. Worldwide women's assemblies were held in 1911, 1923, 1928, 1934, 1939 and 1947.

In 1947 Mrs. George R. Martin of Norfolk, Virginia, was designated by the BWA to organize a women's department. Funded by the Woman's Missionary Union of Virginia, she invited European women to London in 1948 to form the European branch. Martin next organized the North American Baptist Women's Union in 1951, with Marion Bates of Canada as president. Before Martin's tenure as president ended in 1960, the structure was complete, with branches also in Africa, Asia, Latin America and the Southwest Pacific.

The Baptist Women's Day of Prayer Around the World, held on the first Monday each November, is the group's main project. An offering on this day funds the continental and worldwide budgets. The Women's Department trains women leaders, issues publications, conducts continental and world assemblies, and fosters national organizations. In 1992 146 nationwide women's organizations in ninety-four countries reported to the BWA Women's Department, and the Women's Department was encouraging development of affiliates in twenty-four other countries.

A permanent office and staff are located in the BWA Headquarters, 6733 Curran Street, McLean, Virginia, U.S.A.

BIBLIOGRAPHY. C. B. Allen, *A Century to Celebrate* (1987).

C. B. Allen

Wood, Nathan Eusebius (1849-1937). Prominent Baptist pastor and educator. Born of New England stock in Forrestville, New York, the son of a Baptist minister and church planter, Wood did his undergraduate and theological work at the University of Chicago.* After his marriage to Alice Boise, Wood served for six years as head of the troubled Wayland Academy and subsequently pastored large churches in Chicago, Brooklyn and Boston. In 1899 he became professor of Christian theology at Newton Theological Institution,* where he published his theological opus, *The Person and Work of Jesus Christ* (1908). His health failing, Wood left Newton in 1908 and for a decade pastored First Church in Arlington, Massachusetts, where he earned a reputation for strong preaching: during part of this time he served as professor of theology and missions* at Gordon College, a position he held until 1933. Wood was active in the Foreign Mission Society and in initiatives that sought union or cooperation among different Baptist groups.

E. C. Nordbeck

World Baptist Fellowship. A fundamentalist* organization founded by J. Frank Norris,* the "Texas Tornado." Norris was a leader of Southern fundamentalists during the 1920s. He attacked various Southern Baptist* enterprises and institutions at the same time that he built up his own First Baptist Church of Fort Worth, Texas, into the largest Baptist church in the country.

Always the controversialist, Norris was tried and acquitted twice for arson and once for murder. His disruptive behavior in Southern Baptist circles eventually got him expelled from all local, state and national Southern Baptist activities. It did not take Norris long to find another base of operations. In 1933 he and others

founded the Premillennial Baptist Missionary Fellowship* (PBMF), which gathered militant, separatistic and premillennialist Baptists from Texas and throughout the South. By 1938 Norris brought charges against the fellowship's president, took charge of the PBMF himself, then renamed it the Fundamental Baptist Missionary Fellowship (FBMF).

In order to provide pastors for his organization, in 1939 Norris established the Fundamental Baptist Bible Institute at his First Baptist Church, then renamed it the Bible Baptist Seminary* in 1944. The seminary lacked academic standing, but nevertheless attracted a student body of 200-300 annually during the 1940s.

By the late 1940s many of the FBMF's younger leaders resented Norris's dictatorial style. In 1948 Norris named G. Beauchamp Vick* president of the Bible Baptist Seminary, promising to relinquish control to Vick and an independent board of trustees. But when Vick tried to exercise his presidential authority, Norris abruptly fired him without board knowledge or approval. When members of the FBMF objected to this departure from the seminary's bylaws, Norris produced a new set of bylaws placing him in complete control of the seminary. When attempts at reconciliation failed, in 1950 a number of pastors left Norris's FBMF and formed the Baptist Bible Fellowship.* Those who remained loyal to Norris renamed their organization the World Baptist Fellowship. Today the WBF has approximately 500,000 members in 550 member churches and another 800 supporting churches.

See also INDEPENDENT BAPTISTS; NORRIS, J. FRANK.

BIBLIOGRAPHY. *EAR* 1:373-74; G. Dollar, *A History of Fundamentalism in America* (1973).

T. P. Weber

World Conservative Baptist Mission. A fundamentalist* missionary agency that split from the Conservative Baptist Foreign Mission Society. In 1919 conservative forces in the Northern Baptist Convention (NBC; *see* American Baptist Chruches in the USA) organized the Fundamentalist Baptist Fellowship* to stop the spread of theological liberalism within Northern Baptist institutions. The fundamentalists were especially concerned about the "inclusive policy" of the American Baptist Foreign Mission Society* (ABFMS), which allowed for the appointment of missionaries with different theological viewpoints. When the ABFMS vowed to appoint only "suitable evangelical men and women," the fundamentalists were not satisfied, and for another twenty years they continued to agitate for a stricter policy.

In 1944 conservatives in the Fundamentalist Fellowship founded the Conservative Baptist Foreign Mission Society (CBFMS) but failed to get the NBC to recognize it as another approved convention agency. By 1947 a few hundred congregations formed the Conservative Baptist Association* (CBA). At first many CBA churches retained their membership in the NBC, though a growing militancy within the ranks soon ended dual affiliation.* During the 1950s more militant Conservative Baptists campaigned for a more separatistic style within the CBA, the CBFMS and the newly organized Conservative Baptist Home Mission Society. For example, the "hard-core," as they called themselves, insisted that all CBA agencies adopt an explicitly premillennial (and even pretribulational) doctrinal position. When the CBFMS resisted their attempts, in 1961 the hard-core withdrew their support and founded their own missionary society, the World Conservative Baptist Mission, to reflect their militant and dispensational approach. Few CBA churches changed allegiance.

BIBLIOGRAPHY. B. Shelley, *A History of Conservative Baptists* (1971).

T. P. Weber

World Council of Churches, Baptist Participation in.

The response of Baptists to the ecumenical* movement as embodied in the World Council of Churches has been ambivalent. In a sense William Carey,* the pioneer Baptist missionary in India, was an ecumenical forerunner, as he suggested that representatives of various Baptist missionary societies in India and other countries of Southeast Asia should meet to share fellowship and information and to coordinate their activities. The World Missionary Conference held at Edinburgh in 1910 may be viewed as a fruition of this vision. The modern ecumenical movement, which dates from this time, succeeded in organizing the World Council of Churches (WCC) in 1938.

Some Baptist denominational bodies were charter members of the WCC, while others have steadfastly refused to join. The British Baptist Union, the American Baptist Churches in the USA,* the National Baptist Convention of America and the National Baptist Convention, U.S.A., Inc. (*see* National Baptists), as well as Danish, Dutch, Hun-

garian and German Baptist unions, belong. The Southern Baptist Convention,* with over 15 million members, comprises the majority of the world's Baptists who do not affiliate officially with the World Council. This means that approximately a third of the Baptist constituency worldwide belongs to various Baptist unions and conventions that have no formal ties with the WCC.

Even those denominational bodies that do belong represent varying degrees of cooperation. For example, during the last quarter of the twentieth century, Dale Moody and E. Glenn Hinson, professors at the Southern Baptist Theological Seminary,* served as unofficial participant observers in the Faith and Order Commission. However, all Baptists entertain reservations about some attempts of the WCC to promote organizational union among various denominations. As the 1990 Baptist World Alliance* response to *Baptism, Eucharist and Ministry: Faith and Order Paper 111* ("Lima Report") indicates, Baptists have serious reservations about this approach to organic union, while insisting that they are committed to a spiritual unity with all those who acknowledge the lordship of Christ.

BIBLIOGRAPHY. W. R. Estep, *Baptists and Christian Unity* (1966); M. E. Marty, ed., *Where the Spirit Leads* (1980).

W. R. Estep

Worship, Baptist.

Distinctive Baptist worship is founded in radical freedom of the Spirit allied with heart religion, the centrality of scriptural authority, and congregational responsibility. These permanent features were established in the early 1600s by the originators of the modern Baptist movement, John Smyth's* English Separatist congregation. Smyth considered the Spirit's unhindered movement among free believers the foremost requirement for authentic worship, writing: "The worship of the New Testament properly so called is spiritual, proceeding originally from the heart." This free-form worship developed over against the rigid uniformity prescribed by the Anglican Church of Smyth's day. Required forms or materials for worship were rejected for fear their use would quench the Spirit. Even the Bible was laid aside during worship. After being read to prepare for worship, it was prohibited by Smyth "as a help before the eye." The basic elements in Smyth's Sunday worship services were preparation through Bible reading, three to five one-hour sermons, spontaneous prayers and psalm-singing, a collection for the poor, and a closing business session.

Though the freedom-based nature of Baptist worship has resulted in many modifications, most early elements remain standard. Baptist services usually contain prayers, Scripture reading, congregational and/or choral singing, an offering, a sermon, and an opportunity for public expression of personal spiritual decisions.

The sermon, though not a particular style or type, is central to Baptist worship. Baptists have also made significant contributions to hymn-singing. Baptism* and the Lord's Supper* (or Communion)—called ordinances* rather than sacraments in order to deemphasize the objective mediation of grace and accent their nature as rites that Christ has commanded or ordained are essential though occasional observances. The accepted mode of baptism is immersion, and the subject a professing believer. Communion is understood by most Baptists as a commemoration. Baptist customs and traditions differ widely in regard to these. Ordained ministers normally perform these rites, but the congregational authority of Baptists allows any designated believer to do so. Some Baptist groups—Primitives,* Old Regulars*—practice foot-washing* as an additional ordinance or church observance.

While mostly maintaining the primary worship elements of its early heritage, Baptist worship has had a flexibility predicated on the subjective nature of individual liberty of conscience, resulting in great variety as it has adapted to diverse cultures. British Baptist worship became more structured and predictable as it differentiated itself from the rigid restrictions of prescribed forms and from the extreme subjectivity of the early Quakers. It is usually clearly organized, with a written order of service, composed sermons, hymns and prayers.

The British tradition was imported to America, where revivalism and the frontier experience tilted Baptist worship, especially in the Deep South and Southwest, toward simplicity, emotional expression and preaching for personal conversion. Some Baptist groups expressed worship through such symbol-observances as the testimony meeting, the right hand of Christian fellowship, the walking of the aisle and the mourner's bench. African American Baptist worship, begun in slavery times, has a spirit of passionate human freedom.

More recently Baptist worship has evolved many forms involving elaborate liturgy, charismatic spontaneity, evangelical enthusiasm and quiet nurture. In general, Baptist worship often stresses the personal and pietistic. Though always in danger of becoming captive to culture, Baptist worship worldwide continues to evolve new forms in accord with its traditional elements and its heritage of freedom.

BIBLIOGRAPHY. T. R. McKibbens Jr., "Our Baptist Heritage in Worship," *RE* 80 (Winter 1983); N. H. Maring and W. S. Hudson, *A Baptist Manual of Polity and Practice* (1991); *The New Westminster Dictionary of Liturgy and Worship*; S. F. Winward, *The Reformation of Our Worship* (1965).

W. L. Allen

Yates, Kyle Monroe (1895-1975). Seminary and university professor and pastor. Born in Apex, North Carolina, he received his education at Wake Forest College* (A.M., 1916; A.M., 1917), the Southern Baptist Theological Seminary* (Th.M., 1920; Th.D., 1922) and the University of Edinburgh (Ph.D., 1932). He served as pastor of several churches in North Carolina and Kentucky from 1917 to 1928, of Walnut Street Baptist Church in Louisville from 1942 to 1946 and of Second Baptist Church in Houston from 1946 to 1956. Yates was professor of Old Testament at Southern Seminary from 1922 until 1942 and distinguished professor at Baylor University* from 1946 until 1971. Yates was a prolific author; his books include *The Essentials of Biblical Hebrew* (1938) and numerous volumes of expository sermons. He also served on the translation committee for the Revised Standard Version of the Old Testament.

BIBLIOGRAPHY. *ESB* 4:2564.

E. G. Hinson

Yates, Matthew T. (1819-1888). Pioneer Southern Baptist* missionary to China. Born in North Carolina, Yates was converted at age seventeen and graduated from Wake Forest College.* In 1846 he married Eliza Moring and was appointed by the Foreign Mission Board of the Southern Baptist Convention for service in China. In 1847 Matthew and Eliza Yates arrived in Shanghai and established the Central China Mission. J. Lewis* and Henrietta* Shuck and Thomas Tobey and his wife soon joined them and founded the first Baptist church in Shanghai. By 1851 only the Yateses remained at the mission because of Mrs. Tobey's ill health and Henrietta Shuck's death. The Taiping Rebellion kept Yates from receiving financial support from the Foreign Mission Board, so he worked for years as a translator to keep the mission going. After decades of working essentially alone, Yates welcomed additional Southern Baptist missionaries in 1886. Yates survived revolution, cholera epidemics and many other illnesses, but finally succumbed to a stroke in Shanghai in March 1888.

BIBLIOGRAPHY. F. C. Bryan, *At the Gates* (1949); C. E. Taylor, *The Story of Yates the Missionary* (1898).

T. P. Weber